Hunters and Collectors

Studies in Australian History

Series editors:
Alan Gilbert, Patricia Grimshaw and Peter Spearritt

Hunters and Collectors

The Antiquarian Imagination in Australia

Tom Griffiths

CAMBRIDGE
UNIVERSITY PRESS

Published by the Press Syndicate of the University of Cambridge
The Pitt Building, Trumpington Street, Cambridge CB2 1RP, UK
40 West 20th Street, New York, NY 10011–4211, USA
10 Stamford Road, Oakleigh, Melbourne 3166, Australia

First published 1996
Reprinted 1996

Printed in Australia by Brown Prior Anderson

National Library of Australia cataloguing-in-publication data

Griffiths, Tom, 1957- .
Hunters and collectors : the antiquarian imagination in
Australia.
Bibliography.
Includes index.
1. Aborigines, Australian – Antiquities – Collectors and
collecting. 2. Aborigines, Australian – Historiography.
3. Antiquarians – Australia – Biography. 4. Collectors and
collecting – Australia. 5. Scientists – Australia –
Biography. 6. Australia – Historiography. I. Title.
(Series : Studies in Australian history (Cambridge, England)).

Library of Congress cataloguing-in-publication data

Griffiths, Tom, 1957–
Hunters and collectors : the antiquarian imagination in Australia
/ Tom Griffiths.
       p.   cm. – (Studies in Australian history)
Includes bibliographical references and index.
1. Australia – Antiquities – Collection and preservation.
2. Australian aborigines – Antiquities – Collectors and collecting.
3. Australia – Historiography. I. Title. II. Series.
DU196.G75   1966
994.01–dc20   95-24425

A catalogue record for this book is available from the British Library.

ISBN 0 521 48281 X Hardback
ISBN 0 521 48349 2 Paperback

For Libby, Kate and Billy

'These two strands—the love of the land we have invaded, and the guilt of the invasion—have become part of me. It is a haunted country.'

Judith Wright, 'The Broken Links' (1981),
in *Born of the Conquerors* (1991)

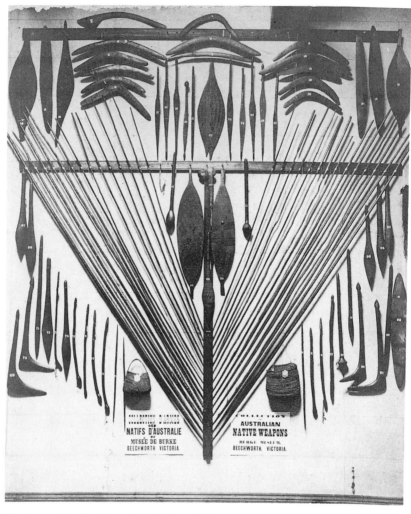

Hunting and collecting: this display of Aboriginal artefacts, most of them hunting implements collected by R. E. Johns in the 1860s, was sent as a Victorian contribution to the Paris Exhibition of 1878. *(Museum of Victoria)*

Contents

Illustrations

Maps

Acknowledgements

Four scholars in particular, all of them Australian, have challenged me through their work to undertake this study: Greg Dening, John Mulvaney, Bernard Smith and Graeme Davison. Greg Dening encourages historians to be ethnographers of themselves and of their society; he opens our eyes to the history-making all around us, and urges us to reflect upon the systematic, disciplinary knowledge that shapes our conversations as scholars. If the book as a whole is one response to Dening, then its three sections represent my unravelling of some of the ideas of Mulvaney, Smith and Davison. Each has sought to shape the public uses of history in Australia: Mulvaney as a commissioner of the Australian Heritage Commission, Australia's delegate to the UNESCO Committee on World Heritage, a defender of the Franklin River and outspoken advocate for the humanities; Smith as an art critic, author of *The Antipodean Manifesto* (1959), and a stirrer of the white Australian conscience; and Davison as a pioneering teacher of public historians, chairperson of the Historic Buildings Council of Victoria and a councillor of the National Trust of Victoria, to name just a few of their roles.

I was very fortunate to complete this research as the Thomas Ramsay Science and Humanities Fellow at the Museum of Victoria. I am grateful to the members of the Science and Humanities Committee, in particular Rod Home, Jane Lennon and Jim Bowler, for their support and encouragement. I have also enjoyed, and benefited from, the friendship and intellectual stimulation of all the staff in the Aboriginal Studies Department of the Museum, especially Gaye Sculthorpe, Ron Vanderwal, Lindy Allen, Mira Lakic and Melanie Raberts.

The book has grown out of, and been enriched by, my work as a public historian, and I am grateful to my friends and colleagues at the State Library of Victoria, the Historic Places Section of the Department of Conservation and Natural Resources, and Monash University for their interest and encouragement. In particular, I thank John Arnold, Bain Attwood, Anita Brady, Graeme Davison, Christine Downer, Meredith Fletcher, Rosemary Johnston, Jane Lennon, Ailsa McLeary, Tony Marshall, Alan Platt, Dianne

Reilly and students in the Master of Arts in Public History program at Monash. A course entitled 'A Short History of the World', which I taught with Tony Dingle at Monash University in 1993, inspired by the work of David Christian, stimulated me to explore further readings in Darwinism and the history of science. Research suggestions and helpful comments on earlier versions of this work were also received from Richard Aitken, Linda Barraclough, Tim Bonyhady, Ian Britain, Michael Cathcart, Greg Dening, Marie Fels, Paul Fox, Richard Gillespie, Sam Goldberg, David Goodman, John Hirst, Ken Inglis, David Lowenthal, Stuart Macintyre, Chris McConville, Donna Merwick, Patrick Morgan, John Mulvaney, Peter Read, George Seddon, Barry Smith and Bernard Smith. Others who assisted me with particular references and interviews are acknowledged in the notes. I am also grateful for the able assistance of staff at Cambridge University Press, in particular Phillipa McGuinness, Jane Farago and Carla Taines, and for the support of the series editors, especially Pat Grimshaw.

I am grateful to the Helen Schutt Trust for financial assistance towards the publication of this book, and to Ken Walker for his administrative support on behalf of the Museum of Victoria.

I would like to thank the staff of the archives of the following institutions: the National Library of Australia, Australian Institute for Aboriginal and Torres Strait Islander Studies, National Museum of Australia, Australian Dictionary of Biography (ANU), State Library of New South Wales, Mortlock Library of South Australia, South Australian Museum, Battye Library of Western Australia, John Oxley Library of Queensland, Araluen Arts Centre in Alice Springs, State Library of Victoria, Museum of Victoria, Royal Historical Society of Victoria, University of Melbourne Archives, Australian Science Archives Project, Public Record Office (Victoria), Department of Conservation and Natural Resources (Victoria), National Herbarium, Land Conservation Council of Victoria, Burke Museum (Beechworth), Warrnambool Public Library, Ballarat Public Library and the Centre for Gippsland Studies.

Earlier versions of some of these chapters were published in *Australian Cultural History, Australian Historical Studies,* the *Victorian Historical Journal, Dangerous Liaisons: Essays in Honour of Greg Dening* (edited by Donna Merwick), *A Heritage Handbook* (edited by Graeme Davison and Chris McConville), and *The Humanities and the Australian Environment* (edited by D. J. Mulvaney).

I enjoyed talking about these ideas with my parents, Kay and Ray Griffiths, who read drafts and constantly encouraged me. Libby Robin supported this work from its beginnings, read everything, and enriched it with her insight and constructive criticism. Kate and Billy Griffiths made the whole project a lot more fun, and asked some challenging questions.

Tom Griffiths

Introduction

'Human beings are history-makers', writes historian and anthropologist, Greg Dening. 'Of all the systems that are expressions of who a people are, the sharpest and clearest is their historical consciousness.'[1] This book has grown out of that conviction. In Dening's words, it makes history of people making history, because that is where they reveal themselves. It explores historical consciousness and environmental sensibilities in European Australia. Many of the book's concerns are suggested by contemporary debates about the perception and use of the Australian past: about the rights of indigenous peoples to land and history, the repatriation of artefacts by museums, the politics of conservation and environmental management, changing European sensibilities towards Australia and its original inhabitants, and the emergence of new popular, academic and bureaucratic forms of history-making. The book contributes to a growing interest in the roots of Australian historical consciousness.

History can take many forms. It can be constructed at the dinner table, over the back fence, in parliament, in the streets, and not just in the tutorial room, or at the scholar's desk. It can be represented through museums, historical societies, universities, books, films, recordings, monuments, re-enactments, commemorations, conversations, collections, and historic sites and places. History is the fruit of both popular and learned understandings, both amateur and professional socialisation.

This study aims to rediscover some of the Australian traditions of amateur historiography that professionals have, until recently, felt the need to ignore or disdain. In the twentieth century, professional historians turned their backs on the amateurs, that informal army of history enthusiasts whose knowledge of the past often grew from scientific curiosity or from intimacy with a place or community, and who drew upon a range of documentary, oral and environmental sources. Such attachment to locale was often disparaged by the new professionals as 'parochial', and such a mixture of authorities was dismissed as 'promiscuous'. This was 'the antiquarian imagination', a historical sensibility particularly attuned to the material evidence of the past, and possessing a powerful sense of place.

The word 'antiquarian' is here used a little mischievously, for it has generally become a term of contempt. In 1874, the German philosopher Friedrich Nietzsche, writing in a country where history was busy defining itself as a professional discipline, described the mind of the antiquarian:

> He is careful to preserve what survives from ancient days . . . All that is small and limited, mouldy and obsolete, gains a worth and inviolability of its own from the conservative and reverent soil of the antiquary migrating into it, and building a secret nest there. The history of his town becomes the history of himself;[2]

This is the enduring image of the antiquarian, as narrow, nostalgic and eccentric, preserving the relics of the past for their own sake. The antiquarian, writes Graeme Davison, possesses 'the particularising mind of the collector, the preservationist, the restorer. Antiquarian history seeks, not to transcend the past, but to preserve it, to re-enter it and, if necessary, to re-create it.'[3] The history of History has mostly ignored the 'mere antiquarians' and has focused on one particular institutional expression of historical curiosity, the university.[4] It is there, in the first academic history departments, that the foundations of Australian history are generally discerned. In recent decades, academic recognition of material culture studies, and oral, social, local and family histories, has opened the way for a rapprochement between amateur and professional, and a rediscovery of the material, archaeological side of our history.[5] Historians are beginning to turn again to a serious consideration of popular forms of history-making.[6] And, more recently, a 'public history' movement has explicitly addressed the relationship between trained historians and the popular past, trying to renew the dialogue between the academy and the community. Public history is itself an academic movement that comes from abroad and it, too, often aspires to be 'professional'. In this guise it sometimes appears to be another appropriation of an amateur field by the academy. It is important, therefore, to recognise the extent to which recent movements in popular history and heritage have drawn on earlier vigorous usages of the Australian past. It is time for an Australian history of public history.

The book explores the historical imagination of antiquarians, collectors, archaeologists, naturalists, journalists, urban progressives, historians and heritage managers. It is a cultural history that is alert to the metaphorical dimensions of science. It offers biographical sketches of forgotten but influential scientists and humanists, forgotten because they were 'amateurs', and influential because their commitment was to widely accessible forms of communication, such as exhibitions, collections, newspaper writings, popular books, monuments and the preservation of sites and places. They were collectors, conservers and interpreters of 'antiquities', a concept that embraced natural specimens as well as the artefacts of human culture, both Aboriginal and non-Aboriginal.[7]

Antiquities and the countryside traditionally occupied a common field of enquiry and aesthetics. Nature and history were inextricable categories: they provided puzzling objects for cabinets of curiosities, they both demanded scholarly story-telling, imaginative history-making. A wide-ranging and intensely personal interest in the past was made possible and urgent in the nineteenth century by new understandings of cultural and biological evolution. In many senses, however, these writers and collectors had their heyday in the early twentieth century, and their influence persisted to mid-century and into the politics of heritage today. Since the 1960s, new forms of antiquarianism have emerged in the upsurge of preservationism, the proliferation of museums and the popular pursuits of local and family history.

The antiquarian imagination in Australia preceded and paralleled the rise of professional archaeology and history, and deserves historical attention of its own. It has not been superseded by professional history but has proved remarkably resilient, even resurgent in our time. In its cultivation of field skills, attention to locale, undisciplined breadth, engagement with memory and 'sensuous enjoyment of material things', it represents a surprising source of invigoration for an academic history that has been isolated and constrained by professional specialisation and the supremacy of the word.[8] Because of these orientations, antiquarianism was also more exposed to the primary historical challenge of Australian settlement, the knowledge that the land had been—perhaps still was—someone else's.

In his 1980 Boyer Lectures entitled *The Spectre of Truganini*, Bernard Smith suggested that Australian culture is haunted by the dispossession and violence done to Aborigines. It is 'a nightmare to be thrust out of mind', writes Smith. 'Yet like the traumatic experiences of childhood it continues to haunt our dreams.'[9]

White writers for much of the nineteenth century often perceived the Australian bush as mournful and melancholic, an emotion commonly diagnosed as migrant nostalgia or literary romanticism. But Smith, in both his Boyer Lectures and a much earlier piece of work, has argued that the melancholic perception of Australian nature had more complex and indigenous sources.[10] Melancholy, he argues, was as much a product of fear and guilt as it was of homesickness and loneliness, a conflation of Aboriginal culture with the bush itself.[11] As dispossession proceeded, writers projected the pain and anxiety of colonial experience onto

Australian nature. Marcus Clarke's funereal, secret forests that 'seem to stifle in their black gorges a story of sullen despair' were, suggests Smith, a product of deep colonial processes of repression and projection.[12]

There was another source of melancholia described by Smith that was less a matter of conscience and more of environmental speculation, but the two were linked. It was shaped by the confrontation with the moral and historical puzzles of Australian primeval nature, which appeared to be a kind of fallen Nature, and by reflections about the environmental implications of convicts and Aborigines. These sources of melancholia, suggests Smith, were not chiefly aesthetic but 'moral, social and theological' and again arose not from distant longing or imported convention but from local experience of the land itself. Brooding, challenging questions confronted colonists: 'what had this land done to the savage; what would it do to the convicts; what role was it playing in the scheme of Creation; how could it be settled and what would it do to the settlers?'[13] This book offers a contemporary, scholarly response to the same moral and historical puzzles that Bernard Smith describes colonists encountering.

Smith's lectures responded to the burgeoning interest in Aboriginal studies that has characterised recent Australian scholarship and community debate, and themselves must have inspired more.[14] Since his lectures in 1980, as Smith himself has noted, the most significant development has been the emergence of black voices offering Aboriginal perspectives of dispossession, survival, and cultural creativity.[15] But Smith's central challenge is to those Australians who share his European ancestry: he urged attention to 'the effects of the continued existence and presence of the Aborigine in Australia upon the emergence and character of our own Australian culture'.[16] The challenge is not only to trace the image of the Aborigine in European art and ideas, a subject on which Smith and others have already done valuable work, but to study the environmental and historical imagination of white Australia in a cross-cultural context.[17] As Bain Attwood puts it, historians and anthropologists are increasingly turning from the objects to the subjects, from the collected to the collectors, as well as the points of engagement between them, 'thus revealing the historical processes of colonialism which were earlier suppressed'.[18]

In 1968, the anthropologist W. E. H. Stanner called the white Australian habit of denying the violence of the frontier 'the Great Australian Silence'.[19] The Great Australian Silence, I want to suggest, was often 'white noise': it sometimes consisted of an obscuring and overlaying din of history-making. But the denial was frequently unconscious, or only half-conscious, for it was part of a genuine attempt by white Australians to foster emotional possession of the land and was sometimes accompanied by respect for pre-existing Aboriginal associations. These historians, nature writers, antiquarians and urban progressives who influenced popular attitudes to nature and the past in the late nineteenth and early twentieth centuries tried to confront and overturn the melancholic strain of the local environmental and historical imagination. In doing so they had to construct a narrative of avoidance, one that curiously conflated a vision of pastoral peace and anticipation of war. Australians have often said that their nation was unusual in that it was not forged in civil war. This study draws out some of the ironies of that boast, and moves continually between the Australian frontier and the echoes of overseas war. It is, in one sense, an anatomy of the silence or 'white noise' generated by European settlement.

Two historical tensions, then, run throughout this work, one between Aboriginal and non-Aboriginal Australians and the other between amateurs and professionals. The changing shape of their relationships gives a structure and dynamic to a study that ranges over more than one hundred years. The professionalisation of disciplines and the ethic of social Darwinism were two international movements that cast their influence over the late nineteenth and early twentieth centuries, the period that lies at the heart of the book.[20] Both were products of the nineteenth-century formation of mass institutions and nation–states, the prevailing belief in progress, and the making of empires. The growing dichotomy between high and popular culture coincided in the first decades of the twentieth century with the height of social Darwinist influence in Australia, a circumstance that gave particular authority to the Great Australian Silence. Professional history defined itself as a science of the document and an evolutionary achievement of western culture at just the time that Australia itself formally became a nation. Aborigines, as a non-literate people, could have no 'history' and found no place in the national story.

But among 'amateurs', whose histories were prompted by field experiences and curiosity about objects and places, Aborigines could not be avoided. Settler Australians found their speculations about nature and the past were inextricable from a contemplation of Aboriginal culture. Historians and scientists, collectors and naturalists were constantly coming to terms with the hunters and gatherers who preceded them. The fact of prior Aboriginal occupation haunted their work and writings, as it does this study. Aboriginal voices occasionally emerge from this text to disturb or excite; the title of the book and some chapter headings hint at ambiguities and an overlay of meanings. Through their history-making, Europeans sought to take hold of the land emotionally and spiritually, and they could not help but deny, displace and sometimes accommodate Aboriginal perceptions of place. They were feeling their way towards the realisation that becoming Australian would, in some senses, mean becoming 'Aboriginal'.

This study ranges from the mid-nineteenth century to the present, and focuses on Victoria. Sometimes the Victorian context of people, places and institutions is quite distinctive, but the issues are offered as representative of Australian experience, particularly of southern, 'settled' Australia. The narrative occasionally makes excursions beyond the Victorian border and deals with people who were consciously seeking an 'Australian' antiquity.

Part one, entitled Collection, addresses the history of antiquarianism, archaeology and anthropology. It focuses on the culture and mentality of collection, and explores the changing role of museums. Part two (Possession) is concerned with environmental aesthetics, sensibilities and moralities, and with rituals and inscriptions of place. Australian frontiers, it suggests, are encircling and interior, and at times disturbingly intimate. The section begins by returning to Smith's analysis of melancholy and traces the cultivation of a happier, sunnier vision of the Australian landscape with all its ethical implications. Part three (Preservation) focuses on the institutionalisation of the past and the post-war enthusiasms for local and family history, museums, and the conservation of buildings and landscapes.

In a work that concerns itself a great deal with the phenomenon of collection, I here present a collection: a collective biography—a cluster of essays—in which people appear and reappear, sometimes as the central figures and at other times only in passing. Like a collector, I am interested not only in types, but also the casual propinquity of opposites. I have striven for an interlocking, overlapping narrative, so occasionally there is deliberate repetition of themes or detail. There is, I hope, a thematic resonance throughout. Biography allows me to display the personal complexity and ambivalence that undermines cultural expectations; *collective* biography enables me to reach beyond the individuals towards social habits and cultural metaphors. I have been determined, too, to draw upon a whole range of sources—oral, documentary, environmental—and in this way to be as 'promiscuous' as the antiquarians I have been studying.

PART ONE
Collection

CHAPTER ONE

Hunting Culture

In the two hundred years following the European invasion of Australia, the known age of the Earth increased from about 6,000 years to 4.6 billion. 'The discovery of this *terra nova*', writes historian Stephen J. Pyne, 'had an intellectual impact as powerful as that of the geographic discoveries of the Renaissance.'[1] What was its impact in Australia? Australia was a part of both these New Worlds, one of nature and one of the past. It was a recently 'discovered' continent and an apparently ancient one at that. To explore Australian space was to plumb global time.

To European eyes, Australia had relic forms of nature and a primitive people. It was a land of living fossils, a continental museum where the past was made present in nature, a 'palaeontological penal colony'.[2] It was in Australia in 1836, on the day he saw a live platypus for the first time, that Charles Darwin mused on the possibility of two Creators.[3] His later writing would draw on Australian examples and generate scientific ideas and social visions of special relevance to colonial experience.

This chapter draws attention to the imperial and cross-cultural context of the natural history tradition in Australia. What concepts of time and humanity inspired the work of colonial collectors and antiquarians? What role did Australia play in the empire of nature? What was the cultural history of hunting and collecting? Could one find history in this Aboriginal place? By briefly exploring such questions in a general way, the chapter sets the background to the more detailed studies that follow.

The abyss of time

In nineteenth-century Britain and Europe, geologists had opened up the 'dark abyss of time' and it cried out to be filled.[4] The known age of the earth increased a millionfold, the antiquity of humans was discovered, Darwin's theory of the transmutation of species linked humans and animals, and a hierarchical progression of cultural stages based on technological differences was sketched out for human races. In hindsight, these developments are gathered together and labelled 'the Darwinian revolution'. And some of the crystallisations were remarkably simultaneous: 1859 was the year of publication of Darwin's *Origin of Species*, and it was also a critical year in connecting archaeology and geology and accepting human antiquity.[5]

But these various changes were not necessarily causally linked or intellectually interdependent. There were clear relationships, of course. The Darwinian account of human origins, for instance, required a long human past. But it was possible to believe in an ancient earth but not ancient humanity. It was possible to believe in the antiquity of both without accepting the transmutation of species, as geologist Charles Lyell did for some time. It was possible to be a cultural evolutionist without being an enthusiastic Darwinian, like the influential philosopher Herbert Spencer.[6] It was possible for Darwin himself to succumb to the progressionist culture that his own theory undermined.

The discovery of an ancient age for the earth—and for humans—demanded a history. Archaeology, anthropology and natural history provoked nineteenth-century European society with a barrage of new information: dinosaurs and mammoths were dug up, ancient landforms were exposed and mapped, stone tools were found beside the fossils of extinct creatures, early human remains were exhumed, exotic peoples were encountered in distant lands.[7] How was this new information to be assimilated, and this enhanced vista of time to be measured, organised and understood?

The two dominant concepts of history in the nineteenth century were evolutionary theory and the idea of progress. They should have been in tension with one another. One eliminated purpose from nature, the other asserted a reassuring and predictable continuity. But, although they were formally contradictory, they came to be seen as synonymous. In the imperial context they merged into one powerful 'ethic of conquest', social Darwinism.[8] Social Darwinism justified the elimination or domination of indigenous societies as an inevitable natural process. It posited human history as a linear progression through a fixed sequence of stages from savagery to civilisation, a climb up a ladder that had European society on the top rung. It placed Aboriginal society on the lowest rung and labelled it a *biological* as well as cultural relic, a primitive human fossil society slipping into extinction.

But it was Herbert Spencer, not Darwin, who coined the term 'survival of the fittest'.[9] And Charles Darwin's theory of natural selection was radical in its vision of a totally contingent natural world, one ruled by chance and improbability rather than by a steady and progressive purpose or a predetermined set of stages. Not even Darwin was quite ready to embrace publicly that aspect of his theory. Such was the lure and comfort of the idea of progress that it overwhelmed and swallowed the radical potential of Darwinism. The transformation of species and the animal history of humanity could only be accepted if they were seen as purposeful. The full chaotic non-progressive implications of natural selection were not confronted until the twentieth century, and they are still being teased out.[10]

The idea of progress made a palatable story out of the discoveries of both new worlds—the underworld of the local past and the *terra nova* of the distant present. The ladder of social evolution made a reassuring temporal sequence out of present diversity.[11] It was a habit of the nineteenth century to compile chronologies, make narratives, construct genealogies. As W. E. H. Stanner put it, 'all thinking seemed to be at bottom a thinking about causes, origins, and development'.[12] History became a central paradigm for knowledge in the nineteenth century. The natural sciences strengthened as natural *history*, as observational, experiential and story-telling disciplines.[13] The present could be explained by a narrative of past events, and the past could be explained by an extrapolation backwards of the present (as with the uniformitarianism of geologists, for example).

European society became fascinated with the past: historical novels and cultural tourism became popular, museums were built, natural history was invigorated as a hobby and a science, architectural historicism prevailed and historical studies gained a new status.[14] In Germany, Leopold von Ranke conceived 'the most famous statement in all historiography' when he argued that history aimed to show 'what actually happened (*wie es eigentlich gewesen*)'.[15] Human history could be a scientific specimen, too. It could aspire to be as lifelike and as confident of the truth as the taxidermist's stuffed skin or the photographer's chemical image, those other nineteenth-century triumphs of representation.[16]

If history could be a science, then so could scientists write history. 'Evolutionary theory is first a form of imaginative history', writes the cultural historian Gillian Beer.[17] Perhaps social Darwinism is aptly named after all. In his book *Descent of Man* (1871), Darwin came to espouse the cultural evolutionist, hierarchical, progressionist implications of his theory, and gave the weight of his scientific authority to social visions. 'At some future period', he wrote, 'not very distant as measured by centuries, the civilised races of man will almost certainly exterminate, replace the savage races throughout the world.'[18] Social Darwinism confirmed a mid-nineteenth-century movement away from earlier humanitarian concerns about other races.[19]

But if social Darwinism provided a rationalisation for European imperialism, it also promoted deeply felt fears, particularly at the ends of empire. Evolution, by adding a biological dimension to history, extended the human lineage to a frightening extent. 'Many Victorian rejections of evolutionary ideas register a physical shudder', wrote Gillian Beer. 'In its early readers one of the lurking fears it conjured was miscegeny—the frog in the bed.' Darwin was in accord with his society to the extent that he was engaged in a search for origins, a genealogical enterprise of threatening proportions.[20] Cultural evolutionists became obsessed by the search for 'the missing link'. In an Australia with penal beginnings, *descent* had more immediate complications.[21]

Inheritance was one concern; environment was another. Australian colonists were haunted by the spectre of degeneration. There was an implicit danger in populating an ancient continent that seemed to be one vast museum of relics and fossils. Many popularisers of Darwin saw evolutionary theory as rationalising the free market, as emphasising an individual's *effort* to conquer environment. A stimulating environment drove organisms to advance themselves, a less stimulating one paralysed them or held them back.[22] The nature of Australia was impoverished and dangerous; it was fossilised, degenerative. It was vulnerable. Colonists believed that Aborigines had been stranded in time due to an insufficiently stimulating environment.

What message was there for Europeans in this, what ramifications for their relationship to the land? They were impelled to modify, import, destroy. Changing ecological relationships were an intrinsic part of colonialism.[23] The dangers of the strange, ancient environment could only be overcome by subverting the natural order, making it anew, acclimatising imported species, destroying indigenous nature, sponsoring aggressive biological imperialism. Inheritance and environment were Darwin's twin engines of change and they both resonated with special meaning in a convict society transplanted to the New World.

The empire of nature

Europeans had happened upon a continent of hunters; and they brought with them a hunting culture. But, for the colonists, these two forms of hunting symbolised the distance between their society and that of the Aborigines. Europeans perceived the indigenous culture as preoccupied with subsistence hunting, an activity that was seen as desperate and dependent. In the imperial culture, hunting was an elite sporting and intellectual pursuit, class-conscious and recreational: it was a quest for sport, science and trophies, a 'refined' hunting and gathering.[24] That transformation—from hunting to the Hunt, from dependence on nature to manipulation of it, from an essential economic function to an elite

The Bulletin

Registered at the General Post Office, Sydney, for Transmission by Post as a Newspaper.

Vol. 30.—No. 1518.   **THURSDAY, MARCH 18, 1909.**   Price 6d.

THE GRADUAL DEVELOPMENT OF BULL.

From John Bull to Aboriginal Bull: The *Bulletin*'s commentary on the social and environmental dangers of colonisation. The caption read: 'J. Bull has annexed another 15,000 square miles filled with niggers. (1) There was a white Bull once. (2) Then he became light brown, and bought a turban. (3) He grew still more brown, acquired a big sash and a curved sword. (4) His brownness increased, and he acquired petticoats and funny shoes. (5) Gradually he became so brown that he was practically black, and he undressed himself again and wore a loin-cloth. (6) And in the end he will annex so many niggers that he will be quite black, and the last scene will be an aboriginal Bull roasting his 'possum over a small fire.' (Bulletin *cover, 18 March 1909; used by permission)* social one—was seen by many nineteenth-century Europeans as a prerequisite of advanced culture.[25]

Palaeolithic or Neolithic, hunter or farmer: that was identified as the great watershed in human history, the great divide between savagery and civilisation.[26] The European invaders of Australia felt themselves to be on one side of that gulf and condemned Aborigines for being on the other. Aborigines, they observed, had failed to invent agriculture or farming, or to make permanent structures or visibly change the land. They had failed to sign history.[27] Europeans overlooked the evidence of Aboriginal firestick farming, their domestication of plants and impact on animals, their artistic and spiritual signatures, their emphasis on gathering as much as hunting, their seasonal housing and deep attachment to place, their relative affluence. These things were unobserved or unacknowledged by whites.[28]

But to list such oversights is still to apply the measures of the European. For the Aborigines, seasonality and impermanence were intentional, time was cyclical. The land was always original and its spirituality continually accessible. Signing history, it could be said, was not the purpose or desire of hunters; it might even be 'a principle, a metaphysic, that hunters reject'.[29] Nor was it their aim to separate the human and animal worlds, to distance themselves from nature by preserving or collecting. These were the obsessive preoccupations of the invaders.

In some ways, European pastoralists were more like the Aborigines than they knew. Livestock herding echoed aspects of kangaroo hunting. Pastoralism is, after all, a kind of domesticated hunting.[30] It is systematic predation, it supports a low number of people relative to the space it requires, it is nomadic within bounded territories, it grapples with a fringe environment that threatens to become desert, and it employs fire as a farming tool.[31]

The irony was that Europeans thought they had discovered a genuine wilderness, but found instead a 'park' unwittingly prepared for them. The trees were mature and well spaced, the grass was lush; one could walk or ride through these woodlands with ease. Some were suspicious of their 'luck'. This is how Charles Griffith described the plains west of Melbourne in 1845:

> That which from my first arrival has always struck me as the main characteristic of the country is, its remarkably civilised appearance. It is difficult . . . not to fancy that the hand of man had been engaged in combing and arranging the elements of natural beauty.[32]

And, of course, so it had. The grasslands and woodlands that Europeans found attractive had been sculpted by Aborigines who regularly fired the landscape to keep it open for hunting. The soil was enriched by thousands of years of their fires. This open landscape was not only primed for domesticated hunting, it was also perfect for the Hunt. Colonists described the land as like a '*gentleman's* park', and the term 'park' had its origins in twelfth-century Britain as a description of aristocratic reserves for hunting. Peter Cunningham, a naval surgeon and pastoralist on the Upper Hunter River (named after the governor!), wrote in the 1820s of the pleasure of riding through an open landscape: 'if a kangaroo or an emu should start up in your path, you enjoy a clear and animated view of the chase, until the dogs finally surround and seize upon their victim.'[33]

It was an open landscape in another sense. H. W. Wheelwright was one of many visitors to the Australian colonies who were attracted to 'the freedom of the bush, unshackled by the trammels of the British Game Laws'.[34] How many of Australia's convicts had been poachers at home?[35] Wheelwright was trained as a lawyer, came to the Victorian diggings in 1852 and, having no luck there, spent five years making his living by shooting birds in the Melbourne district. He and a friend roamed up and down the Mornington Peninsula and across to Westernport, never camping further than forty miles from Melbourne and their market. Wheelwright reflected that he had turned to 'the gun as a means of support', to a pursuit 'which had hitherto been only an amusement'. He recognised that his territory had only recently been the 'hunting-grounds' of the 'savage'. But it was 'game' that Wheelwright and his shooting mate were after and 'field sports' that they engaged in, and they did so with a firm sense of imported class grievance. 'The gun', wrote Wheelwright, 'had often brought both of us "to grief" in the Old World, so that we agreed that for once it should help us out in the New.'[36] In Australia, Wheelwright concluded, the shooter could enjoy a better day's sport than at home 'with no fear of a bullying gamekeeper before his eyes'.[37]

But European hunters found disappointments and deficiencies in Australian nature. 'I can tell of no hair-breadth escapes', wrote Wheelwright in his hunting memoir. 'Australia offers less attractions to the Gordon-Cumming school of sportsmen than any foreign country', he lamented.[38] Gordon Cumming hunted in southern Africa between 1843 and 1848 and gathered a large collection of animal trophies and African artefacts. He was an avid self-publicist and turned his African hunting feats into spectacular showmanship, including displaying his trophies at the 1851 Great Exhibition in the Crystal Palace.[39] 'Trophies' were prizes of the Hunt, mementoes of victory, the fruits of upper-class recreation; they represented the European conquest of exotic animals and humans. They became a popular type of interior decoration: they were the form in which 'the hunting cult and imperial power met on the walls of country houses'.[40] Heads were the most common trophies.

Compared with other reaches of empire, Australian fauna was too tame, and the Aborigines insufficiently war-like. Wild animals so underpinned the imperial adventure that Australian colonists set about importing them.[41] The acclimatisation societies that were strong in nineteenth-century Victoria were not just agents of nostalgia or economic diversification; they also championed the hunting culture. They set out to improve Australian nature, to stock it with real game that would provide genuine trophies. They were a dimension of a biological imperialism that accompanied and strengthened the expansion of Europe across the globe.[42]

Hunters were among the first conservationists; gamekeepers were selective preservers of nature. In Australia, the first protected species were imported ones: if 'the animals of the colony could not protect themselves, they were unfit to live in the country', was the belief of many colonists.[43] Game reserves were the antecedents of national parks. 'Even national parks themselves are a form of trophy', argues A. D. Graham, 'relics that are meant to perpetuate a likeness of what the hunter wants to see, despite his contrary impulse towards destruction.'[44] They were relics or 'monuments', and indeed, that was what they were called in early twentieth-century Australia.[45]

'Park' was also part of the language of dispossession, associated with English and Scottish enclosure of the eighteenth century.[46] Wildlife conservation separated human and animal living space and granted access to animals to an elite.[47] When game laws were introduced into Victoria in the 1860s, they were seen by many as an imported class evil of the mother country. The legislation, they protested, 'was not preserving game but keeping the people off a squatter's run'.[48] European efforts to preserve 'game', to conserve nature, were also often in opposition to the interests of the original human inhabitants.[49] Imperial conservation aided a restricted, recreational interaction with nature and promoted the imported Hunt over the dispossessed hunters.[50]

The study of natural history and the culture of hunting were closely aligned in the nineteenth century, and both were part of the imperial impulse. David Elliston Allen's engaging study, *The Naturalist in Britain: A Social History*, and Keith Thomas's *Man and the Natural World* both describe the increasing enthusiasm for natural history in the nineteenth century.[51] They analyse the study of natural history as a domain of cultural behaviour and draw strong links between it and British social fashions, technological developments, cultural sensitivities, aesthetics and class. Fern cases, butterfly cabinets, seaweed albums and shell collections were common adornments of the drawing rooms of affluent British families in this period. Collecting represented rational amusement,

'The Naturalists' Party' equipped with guns on an excursion of the Field Naturalists' Club of Victoria to the Bass Strait islands, early 1890s. *(Museum of Victoria)*

spiritual enlightenment and healthy recreation.[52] Gathering and possessing, classifying and cataloguing were appropriate middle-class pastimes. Collecting was respectable.

But the books by Allen and Thomas both have a domestic focus and underplay the global and racial dimensions of the pursuit of nature in the nineteenth century.[53] This was a period of widespread British imperial endeavour and also of intense scientific questioning prompted by encounters with exotic nature and humanity in distant lands. Both these influences—the imperial impulse and evolutionary science—greatly enlivened and broadened the concerns of naturalists in the nineteenth century and provide a context that makes the Australian experience historically central.

Museums flourished in this period the world over. They were extensions of the enthusiasm for collecting, classification and encyclopaedic knowledge.[54] They became institutional scrapbooks of nature and culture, presenting the newly conquered globe in microcosm. The middle classes had more leisure, wealth and education, and museums helped them use them. Museums were part of the ethic of progress; they celebrated it in their displays and furthered it by educating the populace about resources and technologies.[55] They enshrined the principle of learning by looking.[56] They were also the proving grounds of nationhood.

By the 1860s in the Australian colonies, there were collections open to the public in every capital city.[57] They were beachheads for international scientific enquiry and quickly became enmeshed in an imperial web of exchange and exhibition. The world exhibitions—such as London (1851, 1862), Paris (1854, 1867, 1878), Vienna (1873) and Philadelphia (1876)—were 'the nineteenth century's official visiting cards'.[58] 'They announced the arrival of new members among the society of nations', writes Graeme Davison; they were 'symbolic battlegrounds on which nations demonstrated their prowess and tested the strength of their rivals.'[59] Australian museums contested these battlegrounds by contributing materials, arranging colonial previews, and fostering home-grown world exhibitions in Sydney and Melbourne (1870, 1879, 1880, 1888).[60] They also participated, often vigorously, in the international network of artefact exchange. The first director of the National Museum of Victoria, Professor Frederick McCoy, was pre-eminent in his manipulation of these long-distance relationships and, by the mid-1860s, he had the most comprehensive collection in the colonies.[61]

Paul Fox has described the role that colonial museums and libraries played as storehouses and showcases of their hinterland, engaging with the continental interior as much as the empire.[62] The rhetoric surrounding the establishment of these institutions expounded on the contrast between nature and culture, between wilderness and civilisation. When Governor Henry Barkly opened the Melbourne Public Library in 1856, he recalled that the site of the library had once been a forest trodden only by the 'savage'.[63] When the German naturalist Hermann Beckler first visited the Melbourne Library in 1859 he informed his brother in Bavaria that 'at home one scarcely knew what civilization is' because 'you have never seen anything else'. Standing in a Melbourne cultural institution, Beckler *did* suddenly know what civilization was because he, too, recalled when 'natives may have camped on this very spot, . . . roasted their opossums in hot ashes, smoked their pipes and danced their corroboree'.[64]

In his book *The Empire of Nature*, John MacKenzie balances the studies by Allen and Thomas and places natural history in the context of empire by drawing on the literature of imperial hunting and the politics of the conservation of game (mainly in Africa). The urge to classify and order the world of nature went hand in hand with the organisation and domination of far-flung human societies: there was, in MacKenzie's words, 'a sweeping-up of exotic taxonomies, both human and zoo-logical'.[65] Classification meant collection, and collection meant killing. In Africa, hunters and soldiers like Robert Baden-Powell tended to elide their human and animal 'bags', and hunting metaphors were used to describe conflicts with Africans.[66] 'Stalking the African' was also sport, and Baden-Powell engaged in the 'chase for wild beasts of the human kind'.[67]

Collecting was a form of hunting. Wheelwright did both and especially wanted to discover a bird new to science.[68] Naturalists and antiquarians, whether they were in pursuit of nature or culture, were inspired by the thrill of the chase and the identification and possession of a new specimen. They compared 'bags' and jealously guarded their 'hunting grounds'. They wielded their cameras like guns and took 'shots'. A photograph was almost as good as a stuffed head, and an album of images was sometimes called a 'bag'.[69] In 1865, British archaeologist Churchill Babington compared the antiquary to the hunter:

> Like the naturalist, the antiquary must in the first place bring together a large number of facts and objects . . . The hunting out, the securing, and the amassing facts and objects of antiquity . . . are the field sports of the learned . . . Nimrod.[70]

The gathering of objects for study and display was seen as a refined and educated form of hunting, but it was no less imperial.

In some ways, the collectors mimicked the hunters whose artefacts many of them studied. They were themselves nomadic within defined and beloved territories; they talked of 'collecting grounds', 'stamping grounds' and 'beats'. They wrote of their 'hunting' and 'flinting', they boasted of 'pickings', of 'browsing over campsites', of 'bringing back quite a useful bag', of joyfully discovering 'virgin' sites. They moved alertly across the landscape seeking their prey. R. H. Croll wrote an article for the *Argus* in 1930 entitled 'Hunting the blackfellow' in which he described a collecting trip on the Birdsville Track that he undertook with Stan Mitchell. '[Mitchell] saw everything', he recalled. '[The plants and animals] were incidentals. His keen eye was all the time seeking other game. "Blackfellow!" he would call, the brakes would go on, and we would be out in a moment eager for the hunt.'[71] Croll was describing a hunt for artefacts not people, but the ambiguity was deliberate. There was more than an echo of the frontier in the language of collection.

Just as hunting was a prime stimulus to the making of artefacts, so was it to their collection. Evolutionary theory prompted new ethnological displays and perhaps the most influential British curator was a professional soldier, Lieutenant-General Pitt-Rivers. He was the first person to establish an archaeological and ethnological museum in Britain. He became an authority on rifles, then developed a more general interest in the technical progress of the design of firearms. His collection of guns came to include weapons from other cultures. This historical and cross-cultural 'series' demonstrated, he believed, a continuous, evolutionary development from the most primitive weapons to the most complex (those of his own culture and time).[72] Pitt-Rivers was interested in arrangement by form rather than geography and therefore in seeking 'missing links'. He was an ardent Darwinist and was entirely comfortable with the analogy between the evolution of species and the progress of human society. He compared the prehistorian to the palaeontologist, and extinct fauna to primitive humans. He condemned excessive state interference as meddling with 'the law of the survival of the fittest'.[73]

The boisterous use of hunting metaphors helped distinguish collecting, a 'manly' pursuit, from 'gathering' which—in hunter-gatherer societies—was a feminine task. The hunting and fighting artefacts of indigenous peoples were by far the most popular items for collectors' cabinets and trophies, whereas artefacts of women's subsistence activities and camp maintenance were rarely gathered. Also, few women's objects were made of wood and were less likely to survive in collections. European women *did* collect, and often balanced the material record. Mary Bundock in the Richmond River district of New South Wales, for example, collected rare examples of Aboriginal women's digging sticks and other domestic technology.[74] But men dominated the public conversations about collection and forged an understanding of it as a sort of muscular interior decoration, a manly domesticity.

Collecting had a strong domestic focus in its 'cabinet of curiosities'. It generated its own home-centred activities of maintenance, cataloguing, arranging and cleaning. The indoor work of a collector could easily be mistaken for dusting. R. E. Johns, an important Victorian collector, was depicted in *Australians 1888* as a happy and devoted family man ('a model middle class husband') who regularly assumed a share of domestic duties such as dusting and cleaning. Every Wednesday he 'cleaned out' the parlour and every Thursday dusted its furniture. But the parlour was where he kept his extensive ethnographic collection. He *was* devoted and he *did* do housework, but at least part of his dusting was of his specimens, cabinets and trophies, and he would have seen this work as his alone, and as the serious sport of a learned Nimrod.[75]

The popularisation of natural history in this period was inseparable from frontier experience, intimations of war, hunting prowess, evolutionary morals, social status and 'manly pursuits'.[76] Natural history became an outdoor school of character formation. Among its heroes and teachers were Baden-Powell in Britain, Theodore Roosevelt in America and Donald Macdonald in Australia.[77]

The order of things

Collecting has a history of its own. The age of European discovery and exploration in the sixteenth and seventeenth centuries saw the emergence of the private gentleman's 'cabinet of curiosities' as a showcase for the exotica of the New World. Francis Bacon wrote in 1594 of the essential apparatus required by a learned man. As well as a library, garden and laboratory, he needed

> a goodly, huge cabinet, wherein whatsoever the hand of man by exquisite art or engine has made rare in stuff, form or motion; whatsoever singularity, chance and the shuffle of things hath produced; whatsoever Nature has wrought in things that want life and may be kept; shall be sorted and included.[78]

The artefacts of nature and of history were displayed together. The private collection that came to form the basis of the Ashmolean Museum established in Oxford in 1683 included the dodo, the marine unicorn (or narwhal), the stirrups of Henry VIII, and 'Pohaton, King of Virginia's habit all embroidered with shells'. As Oliver Impey and Arthur Macgregor have commented in their *Origins of Museums*, 'those very traits of diversity and miscellaneity which serve in our eyes to impair the serious intent of these collections were essential elements in a programme whose aim was nothing less than universality'. There was an ambitious design behind the apparent 'shuffle of things'.[79]

The concept of 'antiquities' embraced the whole range of available material evidence, natural and cultural, oral and written.[80] Collectors combing their neighbourhoods drew few distinctions between an inscribed parchment, a shard of pottery, and a geological specimen. To the real antiquary, announced Sir John Simeon in 1859, 'every relic he picks up or secures, is pregnant with instruction, as bearing upon the history or the social life or habits of some past age'.[81] Joseph Levine, in his study of the early eighteenth-century British antiquarian, Dr John Woodward, has explored this quest for universality. He explains that Woodward

> thought (with most of his contemporaries) of a single historical past, God-created and accessible to both Revelation and reason, and he took upon himself the task of recovering, with his science and his history, the course that it had taken from the very beginning of time.[82]

Woodward lived at the beginning of a period when the search for antiquities reached a height of respectability in England, a status it maintained until halfway through the nineteenth century. It blossomed at a time when there were still clear limits to historical questioning. The Mosaic chronology was accepted, and antiquarians were filling in the gaps left in an established story.[83]

By the mid-nineteenth century, the antiquity of human existence and the transformation of species were issues of intense debate, and dumb relics were raising deeply disturbing questions about the origin and duration of human life. Antiquarians could not collect without engaging in debates over religion, science and history. And we cannot understand their lives or their collections without being aware of that ferment of ideas and, indeed, of all that has happened since in the social sciences. It was a time when 'cabinets of curiosities' were giving way to the scientific museum based on classificatory principles, and archaeology and anthropology were emerging as distinct disciplines from within anti-quarian studies. History, too, was seeking a more distinct professional status and began defining a science of the document.

When the British hunter of natural curiosities, Alfred Russell Wallace, was collecting in the Malay Archipelago in the 1850s, he found he could not give a convincing explanation to the Aru Islanders of why he collected shells, insects, birds and animals. He was 'set down as a conjurer and was unable to repel the charge'.[84] The transformation from conjurer to scientist is one possible version of the modern history of collecting, one further tale of western triumph. It is an account of science prevailing over magic, of the emergence of sophisticated systems of classification and specialisation from the undiscriminating jumble of collectors' cabinets. The collector's object ceases to be just another curio and becomes, instead, a piece of evidence fully integrated in a western vision of natural and cultural development.[85]

But modern museums, in their pretence of reality, retain an enduring magic. Taxidermy—the art of preparing and mounting animal skins in a lifelike manner—soon became part of the illusion: its products were deceptively real, its mechanics skilfully hidden. But, behind the scenes,

The street theatre of taxidermy: In 1899, following the death of Professor Frederick McCoy, the National Museum of Victoria was moved from the University of Melbourne, back to its central city site. *(Museum of Victoria)*

the hunter and the taxidermist had laboured discerningly, selecting the right beast while alive, restoring the appearance of vitality once dead.[86] Taxidermy was a major scientific art of the period, one that came to dominate museum displays for the next century. Taxidermists' shop windows were an early form of competition to the public museum.[87] The goal of lifelike representation—achieved by dissection, analysis and reconstruction—was something that taxidermists shared with nine-teenth-century German historians such as Barthold Niebuhr and Leopold von Ranke, who were advocating a science of history. Both were attempting to reinvigorate the dead skin of the past so that it could represent, even make a monument of, ephemeral reality.[88]

Melbourne's Frederick McCoy found taxidermy a useful ally in his stage-management of the local Darwinian debate. He was an outspoken anti-Darwinian. His zoological gallery displayed animals from six 'centres of creation' (echoing the American Louis Agassiz's approach) and denied the diversity and divergence of Darwinian evolution. Natural selection threatened to upset his careful taxonomies.[89] In 1865 he was the first to import gorillas, faithfully revived by the taxidermist, into Australia. The gorilla had a powerful hold on the European imagination: it was the ultimate quarry, the natural self.[90] Just two decades earlier, the gorilla had been regarded in the ˉvest as a mythical creature, no more real than the bunyip. Its bones were first studied by whites in 1847 and it was first killed by a white hunter and explorer, Frenchman Paul du Chaillu, in 1855. Du Chaillu's exhibition of twenty stuffed specimens in London in 1861 caused a sensation.[91] McCoy brought some of du Chaillu's trophies to Melbourne just four years later for his own piece of theatre. He wrote to the *Argus*:

> I have now placed in the National Museum a male gorilla . . . our group of male, female, and young, is almost the perfection of taxidermy, as far as the preparation goes . . . it is well for the inhabitants of a country so remote, under ordinary circumstances, from the chance of seeing actual specimens of this the greatest and most man-like of the anthropomorphous apes, to see how infinitely remote the creature is from humanity, and how monstrously the writers have exaggerated the points of resemblance . . . [92]

'Seeing actual specimens' was McCoy's corrective strategy, but he made sure that the gorillas were presented in a way that emphasised their 'remoteness' from humanity. His museum provided visual access to the expanding empire of nature, a window onto worlds.[93]

Taxidermy was cousin to taxonomy. It was nature made true to type, faithful to the hunter's experience, and loyal—above all—to the eye. 'Taxidermy', writes historian Donna Haraway, 'became the art most suited to the epistemological and aesthetic stance of realism.'[94] She argues, as does Bernard Smith in describing the European exploration of the South Pacific, that artistic realism and biological science were partners in the founding of the civic order of nature.[95] Both taxidermy and biology depend fundamentally upon vision as the discriminating sense; they were both part of that privileging of sight that Michel Foucault has discerned as a feature of the scientific natural history museum.[96]

In *The Order of Things*, Foucault identifies a rift in the archaeology of natural history in the seventeenth century. For Foucault, the contrast between the Renaissance and the Classical scientific ages was one between the theatre and the catalogue, the cabinet of curiosities and the classification table, between pure 'show' and sober scrutiny—a scrutiny that, in the management of humans, came to entail surveillance and discipline.[97] In the modern museum, the 'observing gaze' became the prime instrument of classification, a new way of connecting things, and as McCoy reminds us, not altogether without show. The shuffle of things became ideologically ordered.[98]

The invention of the camera represented the culmination of this western quest for visibility and lifelike representation. Anthropology and photography were both invented in the mid-nineteenth century, and formed a powerful partnership. Like taxidermy, both violated their subject, were scientific *and* historic, and constituted acts of collection that presupposed and transcended death. That is the nature (and culture) of collection. It appropriates and propitiates.[99] It is a form of ventriloquism that imposes and demands distance.

Collections suppress their own historical, economic and political processes of production.[100] Their sleight of hand is to allude to a relation between things that in social practice often have no relation.[101] Anthropologist James Clifford has wondered about the social and psychological strategies of collection in the west, and urges a critical history of collecting. 'A history of anthropology and modern art', he writes, 'needs to see in collecting both a form of Western subjectivity and a changing set of powerful institutional practices.'[102] Collecting is a 'crucial process of Western identity formation', 'an exercise in how to make the world one's own, to gather things around oneself tastefully, appropriately'. Collecting also assumes a certain notion of time; collectors are driven by urgency, by the need to collect 'before it is too late'—and we need to ask 'too late for what?' Their work is suffused with a sense of salvage, objects are rescued from out of time itself. Therefore, argues Clifford, 'collecting presupposes a story'.[103] And the stories not only give meaning to the objects; they also ensnare the collectors.

People without history

Anthropology and European Australia were born of the same colonial moment and derived legitimacy and identity from each other. The definition of anthropology as a discipline relied heavily on Australian raw material. Bernard Smith has commented on the irony that a surge of overseas scientific interest in Australian Aborigines in the late nineteenth century coincided with a wave of popular denial of their presence at home. The two movements—scientific and popular, international and local—fed off one another. Anthropology was the study of 'primitive' peoples, of people without history.[104] Europeans had a history and were continually *making* it, whereas 'primitive' peoples were the timeless subjects of a different form of analysis, anthropology. From its beginnings, then, anthropology defined itself against history. Anthropology's precursor, known as 'ethnology', was more historical in approach, for it aimed to tell the global story of the unity or diversity of the human species; it was concerned with a history of particularities across space. Anthropology became scientific partly by shedding this historical vision and embracing the regularity of the cultural evolutionary ladder, which offered general laws across time, synchrony rather than history.[105]

The differentiation between history and anthropology was, then, a consequence of colonialism and ethnocentrism.[106] But it was also part of the proliferation of disciplines of knowledge, a process that has characterised the modern state. Like anthropology, professional history was bound up with the global triumph of the west. It was a product of the making of empires, nations and mass institutions. History became scientific by being accurate and factual, by championing a discriminating infatuation with 'the primary source'.[107] Hunting for documents became the historian's identifying ritual. The arrival of the new vision of history was heralded by the utterance of several time-treasured aphorisms: Ranke's statement that history aimed 'to show only what actually happened', J. B. Bury's that history is 'simply a science, no less and no more', and Edward Freeman's that 'I wish no one to read me instead of my authorities.' No wonder that the first professional historians were archivists, nineteenth-century managers of the document.[108] Just as anthropology defined itself against history, so did history define itself—in the period of Australia's absorption of its frontier—as exclusive of the non-literate.

Europeans, in their negotiations with Aborigines, were not hunting culture, but nature. Aborigines, it was commonly perceived, had no history. They had not been in Australia long, and they had changed little while here.[109] They were caught in the fatal thrall of nature's continental museum. History was a neolithic invention. Instead of history Aborigines had myths, the mark of the primitive. For Europeans, time was the essence of history, but for Aborigines it was place that was historical. But even that attachment was denied them. They were dispossessed both physically and intellectually, for they were branded nomadic as well as timeless. The real nomads came from abroad, and brought their placeless, imperial history with them.[110]

Could Australia—this anthropological laboratory, this profoundly Aboriginal place—have a *history*? History was part of what put western culture at the top of the social evolutionary ladder; it was one of the gifts of civilisation and one of the tools of invasion. The substitution of history for myth was one of the triumphs of European civilisation, and it spiritually paved the way for the occupation of the New World.[111] Exporting history was one way of making it, and Europeans came to historicise the wilderness.[112]

But it was not wilderness, despite the efforts of the invaders. Anthropology in Australia was driven by the expectation of Aboriginal extinction, by the urgency of preserving the records of a dying race. The Tasmanians were confidently declared extinct, the only possible

'Group [of] Half-caste Islanders': Naturalists visiting the Bass Strait islands at the turn of the century took an interest in the 'strange community' of mutton-birders descended from Tasmanian Aborigines and European whalers and sealers. Donald Macdonald considered them 'a race in themselves, distinct from any other' (Argus, *13 August 1904*), and James Barrett, upon meeting the islanders in 1909, was moved to reflect that 'The treatment of the aborigines in Australia is not wholly creditable to the Australian people. We seem to have assumed that they must become extinct . . . ' (Argus *article reproduced in his* The Twin Ideals, *London, H. K. Lewis & Co., 1918, vol. 2, pp. 135-6)*

alternative to being timeless. The reality of Aboriginal survival, however, confronted anthropology with history. 'More than a few "extinct" peoples', writes James Clifford, 'have returned to haunt the Western historical imagination.'[113] Their re-emergence exploded the unifying empire of nature into hundreds of fragments of history.

CHAPTER TWO

Victorian Skulduggery

On the moonlit night of 9 February 1865, Reynell Eveleigh Johns, clerk of petty sessions at Moonambel in central Victoria, added to his collection of skulls. Finishing his day in court, he and two friends rode into the night for thirty miles to the fringe of the Wimmera. Johns recorded the night's activities in his diary with an unusual sense of drama:

> . . . after a short search we found the aboriginal graves we came to open and at once set to work with pick and shovel by the bright moonlight. The graves were on top of a sort of down, from which the plains sloped away on both sides, their surface of white grass studded with black groves of she-oak. It was a weird-looking scene, and the group at work at the graves was equally wild. The first we uncovered was 'Barney' but he was not the one we sought. However we took his skull, which was a good one, and then opened another grave where we found the skeleton we wanted—that of 'Peeler', an ex-native policeman. We took his skull which was better than Barney's and closed both graves.[1]

Their digging was finished a little before dawn, and Johns returned to do a heavy afternoon's work in court. A week later he had 'scrubbed up the blackfellow's skulls . . . until they looked quite clean and nice'. He noted with satisfaction that they were 'very good specimens', and then labelled and arranged them in his 'museum'.[2]

Did R. E. Johns sit uncomfortably in his courtroom on the afternoon after his grave-robbing raid? I don't think so. Although Johns' extended diary entry reveals his excitement and sense of triumph at securing such 'prizes', as he called them, this was not a clandestine raid. It took place at night because Johns worked during the day. His diary, which like all diaries was half-conscious of an audience, records the adventure in detail, almost with literary flamboyance. Indeed, that uncharacteristic theatricality is perhaps the only clue that Johns sensed the edge of respectability. It was a carefully planned collection exercise. Johns was a connoisseur of skulls. He was not after just *any* Aboriginal skull: possibly he had learned of this one while it was attached to a living specimen. His diary reveals the extent of his planning. A month before

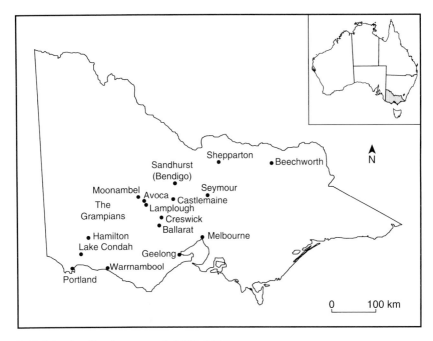

R. E. Johns' collecting ground, 1852-1910

the expedition he noted that 'Mackenzie tells me he has found the grave of Peeler, the aborigine whose skeleton I want, and will help me plunder it.'[3] Johns had either met or heard of 'Peeler', identified him as a collection target, used his contacts to trace him, rode through the night to secure him, and gave over his sitting room to display him. Interested citizens of Moonambel then had the opportunity to admire him. What was Johns' purpose in promoting this process? What made a 'good' skull? This chapter aims to restore a social and intellectual context to his collecting.

The collector

R. E. Johns was thirty years old when he initiated his piece of skulduggery. He had arrived in Adelaide from Devon in June 1849 with his mother, Caroline, his brother Louis, and his sisters Alethe, Lydia, Laura and Ilfra. Their emigration was prompted by the death in 1847 of his father, the Reverend John Johns, a Presbyterian pastor and minister to the poor. R. E. Johns was related, through his mother, to the Reynell family, who had emigrated ten years previously, and it was his influential uncle, Alfred Reynell, who set up Johns' career as a public servant. His

The collector: Reynell Eveleigh Johns (1834–1910) (*Museum of Victoria*)

first government appointments were briefly in Adelaide in 1850, and then in the gold offices at Castlemaine, Sandhurst and Avoca from 1852 to 1855. He had been lured to Victoria by the gold rushes, and returned to gold-digging in the Sandhurst area in 1855 and was appointed assistant clerk of petty sessions at Lamplough (near Avoca) in February 1860. From that time until his retirement in 1903 (he worked as a police magistrate

from 1888), he was in government employment, and served in Moonambel, Avoca, Geelong, Fitzroy, Shepparton, Seymour, Hamilton, Maryborough and Ballarat.[4]

The time that R. E. Johns spent on the central Victorian goldfields in
the late 1850s and 1860s was a formative period, not only for his career
in the courts, but also for his interest in science, nature and
anthropology. Financial stringencies meant that he walked everywhere,
often with a gun in his hand and a book in his pocket, covering the
distances between Lamplough, Moonambel, Landsborough, Avoca,
Maryborough and Carisbrook at a brisk four miles an hour. Since his
arrival in Adelaide at the age of fourteen, he had been a collector of
birds, insects, snakes, rocks and plants, and he continued to have ample
opportunities to add to his 'curiosities'. Some of them occasionally got
away. Aged sixteen, he tried to keep a possum as a pet but it 'bolted
through the window the first night'.[5] Once he achieved job security, his
life settled into a routine of court work, walking, collecting and reading.
He began to keep a scrapbook in which he pasted news-cuttings of
interest and transcribed passages from books. His diary-keeping became
more disciplined, and his entries more closely written. And in Lamplough
and Moonambel, the places of his first permanent appointments, he
found people who shared his interests.

The rush to Lamplough began in late November 1859 and drew a
population of 12,000 in a matter of weeks.[6] The local police court sat
for the first time on 27 January 1860 and, within a month, Johns had
been appointed there as assistant clerk. A year later, Johns' work took
him to the new rush at nearby Mountain Creek, later known as
Moonambel. Among his new friends were Robert Hurlock Jenkyns, a
chemist and druggist who was appointed deputy registrar of Births and
Deaths at Lamplough, William Selwyn Morris, an Avoca doctor and
antiquarian with whom Johns conversed 'on matters scientific and
historical'[7] and Bernhard Smith, a sculptor, painter and police magistrate
(in Stawell) who had an interest in astronomy. But the most influential
was Alvara Lofthouse Slater (1823-70), a doctor who had come to
Lamplough from Ararat, and who was a keen student of natural science.
He had gathered a collection of insects that was regarded by
contemporaries as world-class, and his rooms were a place where
'intelligent people of all sects and creeds met on a common ground, and
there could converse as freely as if at their own homes'. Slater, it was
recalled, 'was as much at home if entering into the arguments respecting
the origin of species or the immortality of the soul as he was in
manufacturing toys to amuse young children'.[8]

Frequent evening discussions and occasional daytime excursions with
Slater gave Johns' collecting new impetus and direction : 'I am collecting
the latter [insects] for Dr Slater'; 'spent a very long evening at Slater's,

in receiving a chemical lecture, which I enjoyed much'; 'Sewed up Slater's list of Australian birds for binding, and copied a good many of the names into my catalogue.'[9] As the local doctor, Slater also gave Johns access to, and some training in, various forms of medical curiosity:

> [Slater] has given me a specimen of a human foetus. I hope I shall succeed in making a neat preparation of it. . . .
>   [Slater] had procured me another foetus, but it proved too much macerated to be worth preserving. I am likely at this rate to be the guardian and 'preserver' of all the untimely-born bastards of the district.[10]

The unborn as well as the departed were prey to his eclectic scientific curiosity.

He and Slater spent much time in the early 1860s trying to catch possums and wallabies with foetus *in utero*. There was a popular belief that marsupials were born on the teat, a supposed miracle of spontaneous conception typical of perverse antipodean nature. Although scientists had been aware since 1833 that the young of the kangaroo developed within the uterus rather than on the nipple in the pouch, there was (until 1964) uncertainty about how the infant kangaroo actually got to the pouch, whether assisted by the parent or—as is the case—unaided. Investigation of the reproductive systems of marsupials enabled Slater and Johns to rehearse the challenge that their science offered to bush folklore.[11]

Johns participated in the politics of reproduction in another way. He learnt taxidermy from Slater, a craft that enabled him to reconstitute reality from dead matter. Johns in turn offered informal classes to other interested residents of his district.[12] He practised revolver shooting, went on 'sporting' excursions with the gun, and then painstakingly revived his specimens.[13] Johns collected products of that other narrative tool that privileges (and imitates) the eye: photography.[14] He also bought a telescope and a microscope.

Johns rapidly acquired the role of custodian of all things curious, bizarre, unmentionable or merely interesting: 'I had a singular kid [young goat], born without eyes, nostrils or proper mouth, given to me this morning & preserved the head in spirits'. He dined on 'native companion' [the brolga] and then studied the 'singular formation' of its breastbone.[15] The discovery of new species was one of his aims. In 1862 he proudly counted 96 in his collection of stuffed birds. The search for something new led him to correspond with Professor Frederick McCoy of the National Museum of Victoria. The professor's identification of some unusual bones as just those of a dog prompted Johns to confide to his diary: 'Alas! for my hopes of bringing into notice an animal hitherto

The Challicum bunyip: A sketch of the figure of a 'bunyip' cut by Aborigines in the turf near Ararat, Victoria. *(R. E. Johns' Scrapbook no. 1, Museum of Victoria)*

unknown'.[16] In his quest for novelties, Johns was echoing the hopes of every cabinet collector.

People in the Avoca district, as well as correspondents in other colonies, frequently directed specimens his way: 'Walker gave me a live rock wallaby, which I killed for skinning'; 'Rec'd a long letter from Jones, with specimens of native plants and two pair of formidable wild boars' tusks'; 'Received ... a letter & carved Chinese bamboo cap from Jenkyns'. In August 1865, he opened yet another series of packages to find not only 'a beautiful skull of a Tasmanian aborigine', but also 'a superb South Sea chief's club, skins of native tiger and tiger-cat, crab's claws of wondrous size, specimens of tree-fern wood, skulls of wombat & native devil, and other wonders'. The help he was given by family, friends and those he called 'my collectors' left him grateful and amazed: 'How it comes to pass that all I know thus strive to serve me I cannot think ....'. Of his close friend, May Gatenby, he wrote: 'The sweet girl must have ransacked the whole country side to add to my museum'.[17]

Johns collected stories as well as objects. One of the subjects that he pursued was the bunyip, a mythical creature of Australian waterholes. Johns collected testimony about it, both Aboriginal and European: 'They generally describe it as a huge creature 16 or 18 feet long, with a head something like a horse's', he wrote in a short, unpublished paper in 1867.[18] It was 'an animal of gigantic size and ferocious nature' that was 'said to devour human beings whenever he can seize them'.[19] In 1856, Johns first heard of a figure of a large animal that was cut in the turf on the banks of a creek near Ararat in Victoria. Aborigines, he was told, were still in the habit of visiting the place each year in order to trace and clear the outline afresh. They asserted that the figure 'had been traced around the dead carcase of a bunyip either killed or found dead there (I have heard both stories) by some of their tribe long ago'. The tracing was about eleven paces long and four paces across at its widest point.[20]

In collecting bunyip stories and speculating on their origins, Johns was probing Aboriginal antiquity. He dismissed the 'bold theorists' who supposed that the bunyip might be a survivor of the plesiosaurus, a genus of extinct marine reptiles. It might, he thought, be a freshwater seal. Had there been other large animals in Australia, and could Aborigines have known them?[21] Sir Richard Owen, the outstanding British interpreter of the fossil vertebrates of Australasia, had mistakenly described an elephant fossil from Australia.[22] Johns chased the rumour down, just as he chased the bunyip, and noted in his scrapbook in 1886 that there were no such remains of elephant, mammoth or other *pachyderm* here. In hunting the bunyip, Johns was on the heels of *Diprotodon* and other gigantic extinct marsupials, for Aboriginal monster legends may have had their origin in knowledge of giant fossil bones and in hunting the animals themselves. When shown the remains of extinct marsupials, Aborigines often identified them as the bunyip, and their legends about the creatures led to fossil discoveries.[23]

Johns' curiosity was wide-ranging. He collected anything old, unfamiliar or marginal. It is no wonder, then, that he was drawn to the material culture of Aborigines and that his chief fame became as a collector of ethnographic objects. By 1868, he had gathered an impressive collection of almost one hundred Aboriginal artefacts. They came to constitute one of the most significant collections of the material culture of south-eastern Australian Aborigines (Kooris). They were mainly well-used wooden hunting implements: boomerangs, throwing sticks, clubs, shields and spear-throwers. Occasionally Johns practised using them, just as he did his revolver.[24] When he took them into his sitting room, often mounting them in trophies on his wall, they ceased to be local in meaning and became jigsaw pieces in a global intrigue.

The ethnologist

In the evenings after work in court, Johns often sat down with his scrapbooks. They were magnificent ledgers, demanding of a table. They were infused with the excitement of the new world, of human and natural variety, of mysteries, speculations and explanations. They were pot-pourris of science, magic and superstition, clippings and notes from his wide reading of local and English newspapers. His eye was attracted by accounts of earthquakes, eclipses and shooting stars, reports of large gold nuggets, monster snakes, enormous earthworms, giant sea serpents and tall trees, tales of classical antiquity, archaeological treasures and intriguing fossils. He carefully preserved newspaper articles about 'the last Tasmanians', collected accounts of extinct creatures such as the New Zealand moa or Mauritian dodo, and wondered about the bunyip. He followed with interest any stories of theatrical magic or exhibitionist trickery, water divining or spiritualism, cannibalism and sacrifice, Stonehenge and Druids, pygmies and giants, mummies and pyramids. He called the wooden inkstand he made himself 'Stonehenge', as it was 'so Druidical'.[25] He speculated upon universal folkways and the ancient symbolism of such phenomena as the cross, the circle and the week. He read keenly about Egyptian and Roman civilisation and noted contemporary discoveries of their antiquities. He gathered mythology and folklore from the world over, and sensed that he could contribute to it from his own colonial outpost. His scrapbooks are like the sideshows of a fair—they abound in the grotesque, exotic, shamanistic. Each seems a diversion, but together they represent the heart of the enterprise. They were part of a serious quest. They mirrored and complemented his sitting room cabinets in their indiscriminate diversity. They constituted his own multi-volume anthropological compendium, a raw *Golden Bough*, a sort of folkloric bible.[26]

The goldfields on which Johns mined and worked were thick with gossip and legend. Gold-digging was, after all, a sort of archaeology. On first seeing the diggings at Castlemaine in 1852, Johns confided to his diary that 'the place looks like a vast graveyard'.[27] This community of incidental archaeologists gave Johns access to both New Worlds of which Australia was a part: the earthy depths of strata and time, and a mobile populace of international gossip and learning. The latest from California was shouted from the neighbouring tent. An American who called at Johns' tent told him that at home he had found 'a straight tusk' seventy feet down in Californian wash-dirt, and the two men spoke of other American oddities and antiquities unearthed by miners.[28] Johns pasted into his scrapbook the reports of bizarre underground finds, both local and from abroad. In late March 1855, Johns learned of an important local find, 'the most remarkable discovery yet made in the goldfields relative to the ancient levels', as his ethnological friend S. D. S. Huyghue described it. It was a carved wooden head in a saturated and carbonised state, found at a depth of 60 feet 6 inches in a mining hole at Creswick. Huyghue, who sketched it for Johns and the local press, speculated that

A page from Johns' scrapbook: Johns followed with interest the discovery of the gorilla and sketched it in his scrapbook in 1859. *(R. E. Johns' Scrapbook no. 1, Museum of Victoria)*

'The type of this head ... is not that of the present aborigines and suggests the existence of a different race at the period when some incipient Phideas cut it out of a knot or root.'[29]

This intimation of a local classical past preceding or congruent with the Aboriginal presence was common in Australia, as it was with

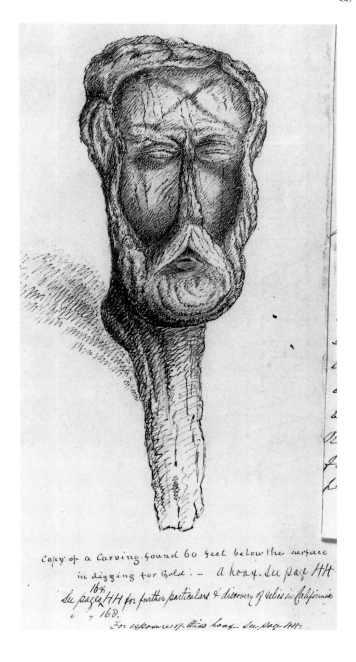

Copy of a Carving found 60 feet below the surface in digging for Gold. — a hoax. See page 144

See page 144 for further particulars & discovery of relics in California

+ 168.

For exposure of this hoax. See page 144.

A hoax: S. D. S. Huyghue's sketch of a carved wooden head found in a mining hole on the Creswick goldfields in 1855. *(R. E. Johns' Scrapbook no. 1, Museum of Victoria)*

American Indians. In 1860, another colonist found in a garden in Newstead a 'rudely carved piece of sculpture . . . apparently of considerable antiquity'. It was reported that it represented the head of an Aborigine and was covered by 'something resembling the Grecian helmet'.[30] Although Johns followed these discoveries with great interest, he was sceptical. In the case of the Creswick find, he noted that he was later told it was 'an elaborate hoax', carved out of a piece of fossil wood from the shaft by a miner. Johns, in true courtroom style, knew who the perpetrator was, explained the good credentials of his own informant, and considered the case closed.[31] Ethnologists grew wary of hoaxes and forgeries.[32] Popular awareness of the currents of scientific curiosity must have been sufficient to justify the efforts that tricksters put into these pretences of antiquity, these precursors of Piltdown.

Profound and sometimes disturbing questions channelled Johns' curiosity and compilations. What was the relationship between humans and animals, and between different peoples across the globe? Was human diversity racial or environmental? Where did the Australian Aborigines fit in the global human story? How long had they been here? Were there people in Australia before them? His scrapbooks and his collection are his attempts to answer these questions, or at least to accumulate evidence about them. He was fascinated by missing links and monsters, reports of human children reared by animals, and the brutal characteristics of people.[33] He followed the gorilla discoveries in Africa with interest and when McCoy acquired some of Paul du Chaillu's giant taxidermic specimens, Johns carefully cut the museum director's letter out of the *Argus* and pasted it into his scrapbook.[34] He collected rites and customs from around the world, from New World peoples and European gipsies and peasant cultures. Johns was seduced by the vision of a new, universal, comparative science of custom that was emerging in the mid-nineteenth century.

In the early decades of the nineteenth century in Britain, the biblical tradition of anthropological thought had been in the ascendancy. The Christian view of human origins generated a number of dominating and influential assumptions—that all humanity was descended from Adam and Eve and was therefore unified and equal, that humans had appeared recently on earth, that human diversity around the newly conquered globe was due to the degeneration since Creation of non-Christian savage peoples, and that humans and animals were distinct and unrelated. 'Ethnology' was the term used to describe scientific interest in these matters; it was the study of the linguistic, physical and cultural characteristics of dark-skinned, non-European, 'uncivilised' peoples.[35] Its central concern was to document the original unity of the human species, and to explain diversity through diffusionary and historical models.[36] The most influential British ethnologist of this period was James Cowle Prichard who wrote *Researches into the physical history of mankind* (first published 1813). Prichard's work focused on language and culture (the distinctiveness of humans), explained human differences through environmental influences (rather than innate biological ones), and was firmly committed to the idea of human unity (monogenism).

By the middle of the nineteenth century, the monogenist, ethnographic, diffusionist, environmentalist tradition represented by Prichard was under attack.[37] The influence of racialism on scientific enquiry strengthened. The change in scientific outlook can be characterised as a shift from 'monogenism' to 'polygenism', from a belief that humanity was one species descended from a single pair, to a view that humanity consisted of several separate 'types' or species with independent histories and different moral, intellectual and biological capacities.[38] It was a change from a view of humans as primarily social beings, distinct from the natural world, to a view of them as primarily biological beings embedded in nature.[39] The result was that, by the 1850s, European and British scientists were moving towards a 'scientific racism', a classification of the peoples of the world into fixed and distinct racial types. 'By 1850,' writes historian Nancy Stepan, 'racial science was far less universalistic, egalitarian and humanistic in its outlook than it had been in 1800.'[40]

Among antiquaries, interest was turning to different kinds of relics. In the series of notebooks kept between 1845 and 1860 by Joseph Bernard Davis, one of the early British craniologists, there was a transition from traditional antiquarian interests (noting local folklore, visiting churches and cemeteries, rubbing brasses) to those of digging barrows and collecting skulls.[41] In 1865 he published *Crania Britannica*, a study of ancient British skulls, and in 1874 produced an analysis of Tasmanian crania modelled on the work of American polygenist Samuel George Morton.[42] Scientists and antiquarians increasingly worked with a fixed, typological conception of race and became preoccupied with quantification and measurement, especially of the skull. It was an arithmetic of arrogance. No matter what method they used, the scientists found what they were looking for: a physical index to their own racial superiority.[43] 'By the end of the nineteenth century,' writes Nancy Stepan, 'the skull had become the arbiter of all things racial . . . to be a race scientist meant to a large extent to be a measurer, a student of the skull, and to dwell in museums.'[44] It is not surprising, then, that the collecting activities of the well-read R. E. Johns in distant Australia were reflecting a similar drift of interests by the early 1860s.

He was not alone in his quest, although he was often a lonely man. As well as his dispersed network of collectors, Johns cultivated a range of contacts who shared his interests in ethnology and Aboriginal culture. He was an avid correspondent and poured much of his energy into his letters, few of which survive.[45] In addition to his correspondence with McCoy at the National Museum of Victoria, Johns wrote to Alfred Howitt, the magistrate and pioneer Australian anthropologist, and to Robert Brough Smyth, the Victorian secretary of mines who compiled *The Aborigines of Victoria* in 1878. He read James Dawson's *Australian Aborigines* (1881) and may have known of the ethnographic collection that Dawson established in the Camperdown Museum in Victoria's western district. Johns knew of E. M. Curr's *The Australian Race* (1886-7) and the ethnological exhibitions of the Victorian collector H. E. Pain. In the 1890s he met Joseph Archibald, father of the editor of the *Bulletin* who was also curator of the Warrnambool Museum and an enthusiast for Aboriginal antiquity. Johns donated some material to his museum.[46] He also had dealings with the manager of the Lake Condah Mission for Aborigines, the Reverend J. H. Stähle, and met or corresponded with local historians and naturalists of Victoria's western district.

Johns' correspondence with fellow ethnologists illustrates his interests and methods of pursuing them. In 1872-3 he corresponded with the surveyor and ethnologist P. L. S. Chauncy and the bureaucrat Robert Brough Smyth about 'stone circles' in Victoria. Their interest was prompted by the publication in the popular English journal, *Chambers' Miscellany*, of illustrations of large stone circles up to one hundred feet in diameter, said to be found on Victoria's western plains. The Aborigines, it was reported, had no traditions respecting these 'megalithic monuments' and denied all knowledge of their origin. There was even, suggestively, a subdivision of the Mount Elephant squatting run named 'Stonehenge'. The reference was incorporated in the popular book, *Pre-Historic Times* (1865), written by the British archaeologist, Sir John Lubbock. The report raised two issues of concern to ethnologists: what were the technological capacities of the Australian Aborigines, and had they been preceded in Australia by another race? In the same period, American archaeologists interpreted the great earthworks they found as beyond the cultural capacity of American Indians and therefore the product of an earlier, imaginary race of 'Moundbuilders'.[47]

Johns wrote to the editor of *Chambers' Miscellany*, identified the source of information—the western district settler, Francis Ormond—and then set about running the rumour to ground. He wrote seeking the opinion of 'the all-accomplished Secretary of Mines', Brough Smyth, whom he did not like and whose reply he found 'eminently unsatisfactory'. Brough Smyth was dismissive: 'I need not say that these piles were not raised by the hand of man.' He considered them natural piles of volcanic stones. Johns then wrote to Mr D'Elboux, contract surveyor for the Mount Elephant district 'requesting him, if he knows or can hear of any such structures, to survey and send me plans of one or two, if he can do so for 5 [pounds]'. He also wrote to Chauncy, district surveyor of the Ballarat district, who then wrote to James Manifold, a pastoralist near Mount Elephant. Manifold believed that the likely objects of interest had been the smaller half-circles of stones that had once formed Aboriginal shelters on the volcanic plains. Johns received the letter via Chauncy, and promptly sent a copy to the editor of *Chambers' Miscellany*, asking that its contents be communicated to Sir John Lubbock. Johns was concerned that Lubbock's classic text, which he greatly admired, 'should be defaced by no statement so erroneous as one making any Australian aborigine capable of conceiving the necessity for, or erection of, a temple or monument of any description'. Although Johns had orchestrated the whole affair, it was Lubbock, Chauncy, Brough Smyth, and later A. S. Kenyon and Dermot Casey who published the findings, all without reference to Johns. This was the way Johns worked, indirectly but effectively through a matrix of informants and collectors.[48]

In 1887, Johns struck up a friendship by letter with Thomas Worsnop, Adelaide town clerk, amateur ethnologist and author of a history of Adelaide.[49] Worsnop wrote *The Prehistoric Arts, Manufactures, Works, Weapons, etc., of the Aborigines of Australia*, which was published in 1897, the year before his death. Worsnop began his book by explaining that the antiquities of prehistoric humanity in Europe, Asia, Africa and America had been fully investigated, but 'with respect to Australia, . . . it has been considered until lately that she has no antiquities'. He believed that the artistic productions of the Australian Aborigines compared very favourably with the illustrations in books such as Sir John Lubbock's *Pre-Historic Times* and *Origins of Civilisation*. Johns helped Worsnop with information for his book (and was generously acknowledged) and the two met in Adelaide in 1890. Worsnop had heard of cave paintings in Victoria Valley in the Grampians and asked Johns to describe them for him and to collect any traditions concerning them.[50]

Johns' closest ethnological friend was Samuel Douglas Smith Huyghue (1815–91), who arrived in Australia from Canada in 1852 and became a clerk in the Office of Mines at Ballarat the following year. From this vantage point, Huyghue had an intimate view of one of the colony's formative events, the Eureka uprising of December 1854. He sent Johns an eye-witness account of the rebellion.[51] Huyghue is also known for his goldfield water-colours, and for his illustrations to Withers' *History of Ballarat*.[52] He and Johns probably met on the diggings or through the public service, and were drawn together by a shared interest in ethnology. In Canada, Huyghue had developed a strong concern for

Indian affairs, wrote novels and articles about their culture and deplored the impact of the European on their traditions. He shared much of his knowledge with Johns, and several notes and papers of his—on the 'Archaeology of North America', on the traditions of 'The Wampum', and on the Tamils and 'Hindoos' of India—survive in Johns' papers. The parallels with the Australian Aborigines must have struck Huyghue, and perhaps he helped turn Johns' mind to the urgency of the historical moment they were living in.[53]

Johns foreshadowed many of the issues on which following generations of Victorian ethnologists would exercise their minds—stone circles, eel traps at Lake Condah, the cave art of the Grampians, the relationship between mainland and Tasmanian Aborigines, the existence of earlier races, and evidence of antiquity.[54] But he wrote little down about Aborigines himself. He was concerned with them in the abstract, in the world picture. Johns was trying to piece together a global history of humanity and to discover Australia's place within it. His compilation of customs was part of that transformation of travel literature into scientific text that marked the nineteenth century and typified ethnology.[55]

Johns' amateur studies exhibited a confluence of categories we are now careful to separate: science and superstition, anthropology and folklore, history and antiquarianism. He was meticulous in his notetaking and cross-checking, he annotated his scrapbooks with later identifications of hoaxes, he occasionally conducted experiments, and his reading was earnest and scholarly. But he retained his promiscuity of interest, his indiscriminate curiosity for things rare, exotic, old or magical, and his heavy reliance on hearsay evidence, surprising in a court employee. His work parallels the interests of British folklorists of the same period. They collected customs like any other relics of remote antiquity and read them as clues to a pre-Christian, pagan or Aryan inheritance; they examined the formal attributes of traditions and beliefs and compared them across immense gulfs of culture and time, creating the same juxtapositions as in Johns' scrapbooks. Their work later fell into academic disrepute in Britain, and the emerging 'scientific' discipline of anthropology distanced itself from it.[56]

British folklorists collected at home across a gulf of class condescension. Johns collected in the Antipodes across cultures, or as he would have put it, races. Both worked within a tradition that disdained the native informant and preferred to work with mute 'relics' and 'survivals' that could be analysed for their formal properties. Johns shared the folklorists' fascination with antiquity and exotica, and looked for Australian versions of it. Britain's Stonehenge shadowed his search for Aboriginal stone circles, Egyptian civilisation inspired his interest in an Aboriginal 'mummy', and mammoths were evoked by local discoveries of large fossil bones.[57] As a colonial collector, he had as his province a rather unknown chapter of the established story. This presented a double challenge. He had not only to assimilate the new with the old, but— collecting intensely in the 1860s—he was finding that the old no longer looked so familiar.

The reader

Johns read assiduously and earnestly, taking notes, cross-referencing, corresponding about books, discussing them with friends, and recording titles in his diary. He was elaborately literate. His family in England had had literary connections, with the Hazlitts and with Lady Byron, and his father published three volumes of poetry and wrote hymns.[58] A career in the courts further refined his natural orderliness and accentuated the literariness of his everyday life. For Johns, life was lived to be written down. His marathon of diary-keeping over fifty-five years was testimony to that. His handwriting was tiny, compact, discrete. Words—like objects—were to be collected, arranged and preserved. As evidence of thought or action, they were as good as objects; Johns preferred both to experience. Local objects and imported words challenged one another through his reading. Among the authors whom he studied in the 1860s and 1870s were the great scientists of the century, the travellers, naturalists, ethnologists and anatomists who generated international debate on nature, race and humanity. It was under the influence of this debate that the scientific world turned an urgent and interested eye on Australia and its Aborigines.

Archaeologist and historian John Mulvaney, in a series of writings, has shown how scholarly interest in the Australian Aborigines grew dramatic- ally under the influence of evolutionary ideas.[59] He has particularly drawn attention to the passage in Lyell's *Antiquity of Man* (1863) where T. H. Huxley compared prehistoric skulls recently unearthed in Europe with those of contemporary Australian Aborigines, whom Huxley regarded as 'probably as pure and homogenous in blood, customs, and language, as any race of savages in existence'.[60] Mulvaney has described how, during the twenty years following Huxley's influential study, accu- rate descriptions were published of over 150 Aboriginal crania and skeletons.[61]

This new scientific enthusiasm arose from the perception of 'modern savages' as a type of early humanity. Australia's Aborigines were regarded as the most primitive (and therefore best) examples. The constraints of Mosaic chronology had earlier demanded other explanations, such as human regression, for the existence of these apparently 'primitive' civilisations. But, under the impact of evolutionary thinking and a greatly increased time perspective, people like the Australian Aborigines became regarded as relics, survivals from a lost past, keys to the history of humanity. In *Prehistoric Times* (1865), a book admired by R. E. Johns, Sir John Lubbock summarised the new developments in anthropology and archaeology for a wide audience. Like Lyell, he surveyed the emerging evidence for human antiquity, but also devoted several chapters to a study of living 'primitive' people.[62] He concluded that 'the Van Diemener and the South American are to the antiquary what the opossum and the sloth are to the geologist.'[63]

Scientists writing in the emerging physical anthropological tradition were those most influencing Johns. Robert Chambers' popular evolutionary treatise, *Vestiges of the Natural History of Creation* (published anonymously in 1844), introduced a biological dimension to evolutionary thinking and provided a naturalistic narrative of the progression of species to higher and higher forms. Johns first read *Vestiges* in August 1861 and exclaimed 'I admire it very very much.'[64] He re-read it in April 1865 and again considered it a 'splendid work'.[65] He was familiar, too, with some of the writings of the French comparative anatomist and naturalist, Georges Cuvier (1769-1832) whose science tended towards a polygenetic view of human racial differences by conceiving of physically determined biological types.[66] Johns also read Louis Agassiz (1807-73), a disciple of Cuvier who became America's dominant theorist of polygeny.[67]

In 1850 Robert Knox published *The Races of Men: A philosophical enquiry into the influences of race over the destinies of nations* (London 1850). Johns read it in 1871. Knox argued hereditarian racial doctrine in an extreme form. He had studied medicine in Edinburgh and worked as an army surgeon at Waterloo and in South Africa, where he had dissected the bodies of fallen blacks.[68] In Paris Knox studied comparative anatomy under Georges Cuvier and in 1828 was implicated in the Burke and Hare case where murdered bodies were used for dissection. Certain human races were, Knox argued, 'entitled to the name of species'. He argued that 'race is everything in human history'.[69]

Phrenology, the popular science of headshapes, also encouraged a physical formulation of race in mid-century. Phrenologists believed that the shape of the skull reflected the structure of the brain; they claimed that they could read heads for personality traits and moral and intellectual capacities. Phrenology was a serious science that influenced the views of evolutionists like Robert Chambers, Herbert Spencer and Alfred Russell Wallace. It was the subject of frequent lectures in the mechanics institutes of Australia, and the phrenological journals discussed many issues central to colonial experience: racial extinction, miscegenation, the careful selection of marriage partners, acclimatisation.[70] Johns flirted with phrenology. Of a mesmeric and phrenological lecture he heard in 1868, he wrote: 'I tried to be influenced but could not be.'[71]

On the eve of the publication of Darwin's *Origin of Species* (1859), racial science in Britain was moving towards biological determinism and a polygenist view of human origins. Darwin's theory of natural selection strengthened the first trend and challenged the second. It ensured that biology became a powerful source of metaphors for human affairs, but—with its theory of common descent—it supported monogenism. A historian of British anthropology, George Stocking, has described how Darwin's comprehensive evolutionism resolved many of the tensions between polygenists and monogenists by affirming human unity, yet relegating the savage to ape status. Darwinism could be at once monogenist and racist.[72] Evolutionary theory provided a new, scientific language and a host of fresh metaphors with which to express old prejudices. The resilience of mid-nineteenth-century 'scientific racism' in the face of the Darwinian revolution was striking, and the curious synthesis of polygenism and evolutionism has attracted scholarly attention.[73] The result was the transformation of ethnology into anthropology. Social evolutionism was established as an alternative to the ethnological paradigm. Johns was caught—at times uneasily—in that transition.

Johns drew together his own synthesis, and Darwin's theories were not at the centre of it. It was difficult in the nineteenth century to be a Darwinist without being a social evolutionist, but it was possible to be the reverse.[74] Questions of human antiquity and questions of human evolution, which the twentieth century came to view as intimately connected, were then coincident and separable.[75] Johns embraced the first revolution—the discovery of geological and human antiquity and the strengthening of cultural evolutionism—but he retained strong reservations about Darwinism. The authors that excited him were Robert Chambers, Charles Lyell and John Lubbock. Johns read Charles Lyell's *Antiquity of Man* (1863) only two years after its publication in England. It took him just four evenings and he was 'delighted with the temperate and truly philosophical spirit of the work'.[76] He did not need to accept Darwin's theory of natural selection to be enthusiastic about Chambers' vague and progressive evolutionism, Lyell's depth of time, or Lubbock's ladder of social development. Peter Bowler has remarked that it was once common for historians of anthropology to invoke the publication of Darwin's *Origin* as the key stimulus in the emergence of cultural evolutionism. But Bowler, together with writers such as George Stocking and John Burrow, has drawn attention to 'the peripheral nature of

Darwin's theory'. '*Cultural* evolutionism', emphasises Bowler, 'would almost certainly have become popular whether or not the theory of natural selection had appeared.'[77] The clearest evidence for this, he suggests, is the non-Darwinian character of the cultural evolutionists' model, which proposed a uniform ladder of progress rather than a branching tree of infinite possibilities.

Darwin's other challenge was to religious orthodoxy. In 1864, after talking to a friend, Mrs Alley, Johns concluded that religion was 'all rot—hers, at least'.[78] In May 1865 he 'had a long discussion with Melville on the geology of the Book of Genesis'. In 1872, he took his sisters, Laura and Ilfra, to hear Bishop Perry lecture on the Bible, 'and a very weak affair the said lecture was'.[79] But local parsons were favoured discussion partners and in the 1890s he was still having 'hot arguments' with ardent advocates of evolution.[80] In 1891 he recorded: 'I finished Siggers' book on "Science and the Bible", which I find as unsatisfactory as other efforts to reconcile the two, and very unworthy of its clever author.' Siggers' book argued that natural selection could not explain the higher mental faculties that separated humans from animals and invoked 'the Great First Cause Himself'.[81]

Among the remnants of his often intense correspondence with Huyghue is a short paper by Johns entitled 'Concerning Religion' and dated 1879. In it, Johns elegantly and boldly expressed a number of his beliefs. Of the Bible he wrote:

> . . . while admitting it to be, as a whole, the most interesting literary monument of antiquity & the most perfect collection of religious writings, we possess; and to contain more sound practical wisdom and knowledge of mankind, and, in the New Testament, a higher and purer code of morality, than any other book I have read or heard of, I find it to include so many contradictions, so many abominations, and so many (as I believe) downright falsehoods in its historical statements, that I cannot possibly believe it to be [the miraculously revealed word of God].

But he felt the need for another qualification: 'I am not a Darwinian, believing that that great naturalist and reasoner has attempted to prove too much, and has quite failed in establishing his theory'.[82]

His testimony gives us some insight into the intellectual excitement and anguish of his preceding two decades and of the content of his evening discussions with Slater and others. It reminds us, too, of the urgency of his reading. Johns called himself a deist, and believed in a future existence. He did not believe in miracles, and was prepared to see the Bible as a flawed 'monument of antiquity'. He had read Renan's *Life of Jesus* (1863) and was sceptical about the supernatural.[83] He nevertheless argued against 'dreary materialism' and came to follow spiritualism, which allowed for the existence of an other world that was open to experimental curiosity.[84] He shunned the church for twenty-three years until two weeks after his marriage to Alice Humphreys in April 1873. Johns felt himself caught between science and the Bible, and perhaps between rationalism and love. He would have seen himself as a partisan of science against religious orthodoxy, just as he keenly branded the hoaxes of popular folklore. But he was not a Darwinian. Johns rejected the Bible, and he rejected Darwin. It may have been relevant that both were monogenist.

In contemplating a history of races, he and other colonists were guessing their own future—the future of *their* race—in an ancient continent populated by 'savages'. Although embracing the new lengthened chronology established by geologists and naturalists, Johns rejected evolutionary theory as a total explanation of the origins of human life. Yet his collection work, through his unique 'museum', was to serve the overseas thirst for evolutionary wares.

The showman

It was perhaps the community support for his collecting that made Johns think of his sitting room of curiosities as a museum. He first refers to it by that name in his diary in 1862. But during 1861 he clearly begins to think of it as an organised collection, with labels, series, 'trophies' of native weapons hanging on the wall, a case of stuffed birds, a wardrobe of quadruped skins, and a catalogue. Johns began to 'play the showman' to visitors, some of whom came specially to see his museum. Miss Winspear examined his collection with great attention, the Fletcher family were amused by it until past sunset, and 'Carr came out, accompanied by the Avoca parson, Mr Bertram . . . They both came to see my museum, as did Sutherland and his brother in-law, Mr McCallum, so I had a good houseful.' Later in 1865 he recorded that 'The ladies all came in the evening & stayed until dusk rummaging my museum which they seemed to appreciate & admire.' In the following year he was able to claim with pride that his museum had 'become one of the attractions of Moonambel'. It had become a community resource, created and used by a widening circle of people. This process was to continue, and reached a culmination that Johns probably never imagined.[85]

In 1868, R. E. Johns decided to offer his museum to the Avoca Shire Council. 'I am tired of it, as of most other things', he wrote. 'It takes up much of my time, and I want to be as little encumbered as possible, and able to wander without much expense. I am restless.'[86] He had suffered several emotional blows in the preceding days, the most serious of which was a disappointment in love. His impulse to free himself of his past, and of the gathered past of others, began his museum's journey to other audiences.

Johns moved quickly. He offered to donate his museum to the shire on the condition that they provide accommodation for it. The editor of the *Avoca Mail and Pyrenees District Advertiser* acclaimed the proposal. Describing Mr Johns as 'a most assiduous collector of native and foreign curiosities', the paper explained that as 'the nucleus of a much larger collection in the future, this donation will prove invaluable ... To a Mechanics' Institute, a museum would be a most appropriate adjunct.'[87] The Avoca Shire Council considered the offer on 12 March 1868. Although they recognised Mr Johns' generosity, they believed that 'the museum would be to the Council like the white elephant of the King of Siam'.[88] The editor of the *Avoca Mail* was up in arms:

> We live in strange times undoubtedly, and it is not altogether a rash speculation to entertain that the sudden changes of our Australian atmosphere have an effect upon the human brain, especially the concrete brain of public bodies. Our readers will scarcely believe their eyes in reading the report of the meeting of the Shire Council on Thursday last, when they find that the particularly handsome offer of Mr Johns of Moonambel, to present his interesting and valuable museum to the Council as an exhibition for the amusement and instruction of the public of Avoca was REFUSED! Expressions of thanks for such generosity were of course given, but the offer was refused on the ground we suppose of ignorance in the appreciation of such a generous gift ... Very few up-country towns, if any, in this colony can offer such an attraction as Mr Johns' museum would afford, and we of Avoca would at all times be prompt of taking visitors to what would be about the only public curiosity, or rather nest of curiosities in the place. We are not so rich in objects of veritable interest as to throw away such a chance as this, and if the people of Avoca are alive to what is beneficial to the advancement of the town and district, they will not permit such a golden opportunity to slip away from them without an independent effort to secure the kindly profferred gift.[89]

Adding to the ire of the Avoca editor was the knowledge that the same museum was the subject of solicitations from the Ballaarat East Public Library. This institution, formed in 1862, was soon to move into a new building, the foundation stone of which was laid in January 1867. Its report for that year heralded the intention to 'set apart a portion of the new building for a mining and mineralogical museum, and also for the preservation of relics connected with the early history of the colony'. Already promised to them was 'a large and unique collection of native weapons and implements' from Andrew Porteous, protector of Aborigines at Carngham, and they were seeking further material. The library probably learnt of Johns' distinguished collection from his friend S. D. S. Huyghue, who was still living in Ballarat.[90]

But Johns had other plans. Several years earlier, his close friend Slater had moved from Moonambel to an appointment as resident surgeon at the Ovens District Hospital in Beechworth. They had remained in contact by letter and through occasional return visits from Slater, and Johns continued to collect insects for his medical friend. Three days after the Avoca Shire Council's decision, he wrote to Slater, asking him to offer his collection for sale to the Beechworth Burke Museum. Their response was prompt: they would buy the collection, and voted £25 for its purchase. 'It is but about a tenth of its value, but Slater says they can afford no more', Johns noted in his diary. 'Well, I'm satisfied, for I know he'll take care of it, and that's what I think most of . . . ' By the middle of May 1868, he had packaged up his museum and sent it off. 'Then I fell to work to clean & tidy my long-disordered room, & made it look pretty neat again, though very empty.'[91]

But two days later he joyfully received 'a beautiful preparation in spirits of four young thylacine in the mother's pouch', and two weeks later met an old acquaintance 'who says he is collecting native weapons & implements for me'.[92] Johns had established a momentum of preservation and collection which he could not stop. He had now opened communication with formal museums—with McCoy in Melbourne, and with Slater at the Burke—and he continually forwarded items to them. In January 1870 he visited Beechworth to sit at Slater's deathbed, and took the opportunity to visit the museum 'where I saw my old curiosities, much added to and pretty well arranged'.[93] In the 1880s, another friend from Lamplough and Moonambel days, R. H. Jenkyns, became curator of the Burke Museum, and so Johns' link with the institution was further strengthened, and his donations continued to flow into it. In 1876, Johns' collection of Aboriginal artefacts was given special attention, and was 'artistically arranged to now form an attractive feature of the Museum'.[94] In September of the following year, several commissioners for the colonial contribution to the Paris International Exhibition of 1878 visited Beechworth in search of potential exhibits. They were clearly impressed by this renovated display for, on their return to Melbourne, they wrote seeking loan of the collection for the Paris Exhibition. The Burke Museum sensibly demanded a £200 guarantee, and Johns, too, was contacted. 'I am exceedingly glad', he wrote, '. . . it will doubtless be extremely interesting to ethnologists.'[95]

The Paris Exhibition of 1867 had introduced a new section of exhibits entitled 'The history of labour', which displayed the history of the arts and crafts of humanity from prehistoric times to the eighteenth century.

The nineteenth century, symbolically separate from this evolutionary display, was represented by the ultimate artefact, the machine.[96] Johns' collection, placed at the very beginning of such a progression at the 1878 exhibition, proclaimed to the world the primitive nature of Australia's relic savages.

The ventriloquist

Ventriloquism is the art of throwing one's voice, of speaking through things, of manipulating intimacy with the inanimate. I can only guess that this was R. E. Johns' social habit. My portrait of him as a collector is constructed, appropriately enough, from his collection. Although the documentation seems rich, it is all of his own making; the sources are relentlessly primary.[97] There are few glimpses of him through the eyes of others, for R. E. Johns kept to himself and was easily overlooked. He was, as his obituary in the *Hamilton Spectator* put it, of a 'quiet, retiring disposition'.[98] He was not a public man, and was rarely revelatory in private—even those painstaking personal records, even fifty-five years of a diary, are mostly formal and cryptic. He became more famous for his collection—for his collected residue of others' lives—than for his own life.[99]

Gathering and possessing, classifying and cataloguing were essentials of Johns' life, central to his identity. They were appropriate middle-class pastimes, entirely fitting for a clerk of courts who later became a police magistrate with a wife, children and a servant.[100] The compatibility of collecting and domesticity was clear in Johns' enthusiasm for acquiring interesting furniture.[101] Cabinets of curiosities could be decorative as well as distracting, and whatnots displaying bric-à-brac were part of the crowded fashion of Victorian interiors. Collecting, then, could be supremely social and worldly. Johns 'played the showman', at first to his neighbours and then to the world, partly because it was his chief means of being social.

Johns was not really a showman at all. That term had a pre-scientific echo about it, conjuring up a world of illusion and entertainment that nineteenth-century collectors and museums were escaping from.[102] Anyway, 'show' was not part of Johns' personality. He was a reserved, private and vulnerable individual. His bachelorhood had been long and, at times, unhappy. He considered his own behaviour usually 'very stupid' when women were present and he found himself socially awkward: 'I can't dance, sing, or "talk pretty"'.[103] His museum, his diary and his reading were a discipline and a solace, perhaps also an escape. He had been separated from his mother and sisters since 1852, his mother died in Hobart in 1861, and his sisters came to live with him in Avoca in 1869. His devotion to family was strong and enduring, but for long frustrated.

R. E. Johns (aged 38) and Alice Humphreys (aged 17) on their wedding day in 1873. *(Museum of Victoria)*

For the second half of his life, he shared his tidy home with Alice Humphreys, whom he married in April 1873. Her father was 'an old hunter' who lived at Landsborough. Alice was born in 1856 when Johns was still gold-digging; she was seventeen when they married and almost twenty-two years his junior. He worried about that.[104] She promised herself 'infinite amusement from the perusal of . . . [his] diary'.[105] She would have discovered there, if he had not already told her by letter, that he had harboured an earlier love for Patty Woolley, who married his friend George Griffin in 1869.[106] It was this romantic disappointment that made Johns want to rid himself of his collection in 1868, a decision so sudden and self-punishing that we are alerted to the emotional foil played by his museum. It is equally revealing that he could not stop himself collecting, and that a museum sprouted wherever he went. Separation from his collection was a disorienting experience. In preparation for his marriage to Alice in 1873, he renovated his house, which caused great disruption to his collection. Several months after the wedding, he recorded with relief in his diary: 'Now I've a museum once more, & am myself again.'[107]

Collecting was his life, but it also distanced him from life. He mediated his own society and personal relations through his museum. How, then, did he relate to the people whose material culture he collected? Did R. E. Johns know any Aborigines? Possibly not. Recently, some historians have argued persuasively that the Australian colonial frontier was more intimate and personal than we have allowed, that there was as much sharing and accommodation between black and white cultures as there was confrontation and violence.[108] I think they are right. But where was the frontier, and how was it constituted? Johns, by any definition, was well behind it. He inhabited 'Australia Felix', Victoria's western district, a landscape where European pastoralism became most conspicuously triumphant. By the time Johns arrived in the Avoca area, many of the *Djadja wurrung* people had gone, their land swallowed by sheep and cattle runs. The memory of them was sustained only by a yarning postman, an artefact found in a paddock or propped on a mantelpiece, and a visible presence of a hundred or so people on the fringes of town.[109] Johns' friend, William Templeton, was the resident mining warden at Avoca and reported to the Parliamentary Select Committee on Aborigines of 1858 that their main support was through begging, prostitution and occasional employment in stripping bark. Templeton noted that there were few children among them, so that their extinction 'ere long must be expected'.[110]

Occasionally the settlers were given a glimpse of Aboriginal history-making. In May 1860, while Johns was in Lamplough, there was what the local paper described as 'an extraordinary exhibition' given by Aborigines. Decorated with white chalk and red paint, the Aborigines performed a corroboree in five acts in front of an unusually large audience at the Theatre Royal. In one scene, two of them killed a third and buried him under one of the trapdoors of the stage, whereupon he then appeared all smothered with white chalk out of another trapdoor and was supposed to have 'jumped up white fellow'.[111] Although the paper condemned the exhibition as 'altogether very reprehensible', it was undoubtedly a popular performance and the Aborigines gained some power by it. When booked to appear at Back Creek, ten miles away, they refused to walk there and demanded paid passages in Cobb's coach or the provision of a special conveyance.[112]

The 'jumped up white fellow' story was a common Aboriginal explanation for the presence of white people in their country. Just as whites viewed Aborigines as the dawn of humanity, so Aborigines saw Europeans as resurrected ancestors, both groups explaining the other through history.[113] A paler skin was the Aboriginal experience of birth; so whites appeared to be dead Aborigines reincarnated, risen from the grave. They were the ghosts of black people returning home to a land they could not imagine leaving. But for Johns, it was the Aborigines who were the ghosts.

The social context of Johns' collection work was totally European. He was, if you like, a receiver of 'stolen' goods, an accessory after the fact. Even 'Peeler' was probably notorious by hearsay. Johns was an ethnologist, not an ethnographer. In this sense he contrasts strongly with people like Alfred Howitt, Baldwin Spencer, Edward Curr and James and Isabella Dawson, who knew the Aborigines as people, and spent as much time observing and talking to them as they did collecting and recording.[114]

From his diaries, it is possible to see how he gathered his distinguished collection: 'Louis [his brother, then in Melbourne] has sent me a splendid set of native weapons from Aunt Mary', 'Received my box of native weapons from Tasmania', 'I then wrote to Walter, telling him how to pack and send me the spears &c.', 'Barker gave me a native stone tomahawk','[Dr Morris] gave me a fine native shield' and, the following year, 'a splendid specimen of aboriginal basket-work', 'John Rostron visited me in the afternoon & promised me some native weapons', 'Walker brought me a fine lot of native weapons this morning'.[115] He rarely encountered or learnt of their context of use. Once he was given a shield that (he was told) had been used by King Billy of Ballarat, a man identified in that area as 'the last of the tribe'.[116] Johns was so distant from the act of dispossession that he was rarely confronted by the implications of his collecting. But in his use of terms such as 'trophies', 'prizes', 'ransack' and 'plunder'—and in his theatre of midnight digging—we can discern some conscious imperialism.

Overseas anthropological theorists such as Sir James Frazer, E. B. Tylor and Lewis Henry Morgan were to spin strong literary webs that bound them to Australian field-workers such as Alfred Howitt, Lorimer Fison, Baldwin Spencer and Frank Gillen. Their manipulation of the fact-gatherers, the power of the field-workers' testimony in giving strength to arid theories, the mutual dependence of these distant allies, are all strikingly documented.[117] Sir James Frazer, who never sighted a savage, built his life's work on their intimate doings, and could do so only because of the power of the pen. So, in a nineteenth century geared more to learning by looking, what of the power of the object? The great exhibitions of the nineteenth century, international showcases of culture and progress, had a powerful mass appeal, and exerted an intangible but strong intellectual influence. E. B. Tylor, who won for anthropology the status of a science, wrote in the preface to H. Ling Roth's *Aborigines of Tasmania* (1890) of the seminal influence of the 1862 London exhibition on the development of his evolutionary theories.[118] Seeing a Tasmanian artefact must have been as important a moment for him as was Frazer's receipt of freshly written testimonies from central Australia.

R. E. Johns' collection therefore played a role in this international interplay of fact and theory which cast Aborigines as evolutionary survivals, the world's most primitive beings. It was, perhaps, a powerful role, for the typological arrangement of nineteenth-century exhibitions and museums ensured that Aboriginal artefacts were at the beginning of any linear sequence. Armchair theorists were only too ready to disregard the original context of these chunks of culture. The irony is that Johns, the field-worker, one of the major collectors of Aboriginal organic material culture in south-east Australia, knew the Aborigines no better.

When we get close to the 'frontier'—and Johns was not very close—we find it evaporating either into intimacy or distance.[119] Collection was often an act of distancing. But history and the hierarchy of sources value its products as those of intimacy. When we focus on R. E. Johns in his sitting room in central Victoria in the 1860s, even there we find our collector caught in an abstract international intrigue about people no one knew. The second-hand nature of his collection may have given his objects an illusion of cultural purity and his work the certainty and simplicity of salvage. This is frontier archivism; his objects came to him wrapped and parcelled. Perhaps Johns, even at the point of 'contact', handled them with the same sense of reverence and distance that we now accord his collected objects in museums. His excavation of Peeler may have been the closest he got to his 'prehistoric' people.[120]

CHAPTER THREE

The Stone Age

'The stone age' was the term most used to characterise Aboriginal culture in the first half of the twentieth century. It was a powerful metaphor of primitiveness. It conveyed the image of a static culture, one that was unmalleable, set, impermeable, discrete, inorganic. It confounded the culture with its most enduring artefacts, stone tools. Collection therefore defined—and confined—the indigenous culture, for by the early twentieth century stone artefacts were the most widespread landscape mementoes of Aboriginal presence in south-eastern Australia. This circumstance highlights the importance of R. E. Johns' early collection of wooden implements. It was only later in the century, when organic artefacts were less in currency, that Johns turned to the collection of stone implements, the scouring of middens, and the building of a special cabinet for his flints.[1]

In the early nineteenth century, Scandinavian antiquarians, driven by nationalism, conducted excavations of ancient barrows and middens and proposed a 'three-age system' of prehistory to explain their findings. The early inhabitants of northern Europe, they suggested, had successively used stone, bronze and iron tools. By the mid-nineteenth century, the three-age system was accepted as a valid pattern for the whole of Europe.[2] 'The stone age' was the most primitive phase. But it was not monolithic. The stone age of the Scandinavian archaeologists was based on discoveries of *polished* stone implements, and soon an earlier and much longer period of more primitive *chipped* tool manufacture was identified. The British archaeologist John Lubbock called them the Palaeolithic (chipped) and the Neolithic (polished) periods—the Old and New Stone ages. Soon a progressive sequence of tool-making cultures was invented, each phase named after characteristic sites and tracing human development from primitive stone hand-axes to carefully worked and mounted tools.[3]

In some parts of the world, about nine thousand years ago, there was a clear transition from Palaeolithic to Neolithic, from chipped or flaked tools to ground-edge chopping tools. The transition in tools accompanied broader economic and social changes, from hunting to animal husbandry and from food-gathering to farming.[4] In Australia, the categories were not so clear. There was a gradual change from large, heavy stone tools to lighter, smaller ones, and from general purpose tools to more specialised ones.[5] But 'Palaeolithic' choppers were still in use when Europeans arrived, and some 'Neolithic' implements were apparently ancient. Australia was later to provide the oldest evidence in the world for the edge-ground technique.[6] For the collectors, 'Palaeolithic' people using edge-ground axes in a non-agricultural context was another example of antipodean reversal. In 1878, Robert Brough Smyth was one of the earliest ethnologists to state that these European categories were misleading when applied to Aboriginal Australia. But the periods nevertheless remained influential until the mid-twentieth century.[7]

Aborigines did not use only stone tools; in fact the dominant raw materials of Aboriginal technology were perishable organic substances, such as wood, bone, teeth, reeds and shells.[8] John Mulvaney has commented on the irony that, for a people labelled 'stone age', Aborigines living in Victoria in recent millennia seem to have become particularly neglectful of stone industry and devoted their tool-making energies to other materials.[9] Perversely, though, it was European Victorians who led the collecting mania for stone. Their side of the country was one of the areas of Australia most completely settled by Europeans, rapidly impoverished of organic Aboriginal presence; only the stone residue endured, it seemed, and it was for many decades more discussed than were the surviving people. 'The stone age' was a phrase commonly used to label Aboriginal culture, but it could more appropriately describe this early twentieth-century period of artefact collecting by Europeans. Collecting stone artefacts was a peculiarly strong pastime in Victoria, and defensively so. Towards the end of the period of this collection work—by the mid-twentieth century—white attitudes to Aborigines were changing. Expectations of extinction were confronted by the reality of survival, and evidence was mounting of the antiquity of Aboriginal occupation. Stone tool collectors often resisted that transition, a stance that influenced their relationship with the emerging discipline of archaeology. The discovery of Aboriginal antiquity was both reluctant and intuitive in the period before radiocarbon dating rapidly deepened human time in Australia. Before turning to 'the stone age' of collection, I will survey some of the scientific debates about Aboriginal antiquity in the nineteenth and early twentieth centuries.

Intimations of antiquity

'It is easy to forget', writes archaeologist Donald Grayson, 'that the antiquity of people on earth had to be discovered.' Yet that discovery

Prospecting a midden. *(S. F. Mann Album, Museum of Victoria)*

took place only a century ago. Grayson, in his study of *The Establishment of Human Antiquity*, has argued that the discovery of stone tools in ancient geological settings was critical to this revolution in thinking in Britain and Europe. First of all, around 1700, stone tools began to be recognised as such, separated off from the puzzles known generally as 'fossils'. Then, as the industrial revolution gathered pace, a growing group of surveyors, prospectors and engineers mined and mapped geological strata.[10] Geology became a historical science, and geologists mapped and measured time. William Smith, an engineer and canal-builder in England, and Georges Cuvier in France generated stratigraphic maps of bands of rocks that represented distinct eras in the Earth's history (Cambrian, Silurian, Devonian, etc.)[11]. But did humans have a geological history? Did archaeology and geology intersect?

It was geologists and palaeontologists who began to discover human antiquity, through a reading of the fossil record. By the early 1800s it was realised that different groups of strata contained different and characteristic assemblages of fossils, and that the fossil content of strata therefore allowed links to be made between strata in different places on the earth.[12] So an ordered, global sequence was established, but the age of strata remained purely relative until time markers could be identified. The fossilised bones of extinct animals found in the superficial strata became those markers. They came to represent a pre-biblical, pre-human era, the time of the last geological upheaval.

Georges Cuvier established the reality of animal extinction. Previously thought of as an affront to the Creator, extinction became accepted around 1800 because Cuvier used, as examples, animals so large that their rediscovery on the hoof was unlikely.[13] The signal species—ground sloth, woolly mammoth, woolly rhinoceros, mastodon—became, in the first half of the nineteenth century, symbols of a pre-human antiquity. Their remains were found with the gravels and clays of Pleistocene glacial action, deposits that were interpreted as *diluvium* or 'Drift', the product of catastrophic flood action (biblical or otherwise). The discovery, about 1860, of stone tools associated with the bones of these extinct animals, firmly established human antiquity.

The scientific discovery of human antiquity in Australia has been even more recent, occurring within the last few decades. It awaited the twin revolutions of professional archaeology and radiocarbon dating, both of which emerged in local practice in the 1950s.[14] But there were earlier intimations of antiquity, and the patterns of local enquiry echoed the European revolution. Geologists and palaeontologists again made the initial speculations and discoveries, their work perhaps even more important in Australia because the typical cultural clues were absent. There were no shards of pottery, no tools of different metals, no buildings or 'monuments' that Europeans recognised, and no domesticated plants or animals other than the dingo. The question continually asked by the natural historians was: 'Did humans have a geological history in Australia?' They, too, searched for time markers in the strata, and worried about extinction. Could artefacts be found by digging? If Aborigines were 'primitive', were they also ancient? Had large animals become extinct as in Europe, and if so, had they once been contemporary with Aborigines? Did people watch the volcanoes blow? What were the local clues to antiquity?

Australia was soon characterised by European scientists as a place of refuge for creatures that could no longer survive elsewhere. When Nicholas Baudin's French expedition (1800-04) returned with the clam *Trigonia*, which had been dredged off King Island, Jean Baptiste Lamarck was struck by its resemblance to forms he knew only as fossils.[15] But this continental museum of the imagined European past had its own secrets. There were fossils within 'fossils'.

In 1830, Major Thomas Mitchell and George Rankin discovered the first Australian fossil vertebrates in the Wellington Caves of New South Wales. Rankin lowered himself into the cave by means of a rope which he unknowingly attached to a projecting giant bone.[16] Sir Richard Owen, the British comparative anatomist, identified the remains as the fossils of gigantic marsupials, *Nototherium* and *Diprotodon*. In the following century, local palaeontologists and geologists—J. W. Gregory and

T. S. Hall in Melbourne, E. C. Stirling, Ralph Tate and H. Y. L. Brown in
Adelaide, and Gerard Krefft and Robert Etheridge in Sydney—were
prominent among those who made further collections of vertebrate
fossils, including entire skeletons found on the dry surface of South
Australia's Lake Callabonna in the early 1890s.[17] These natural scientists
became the experts on local human antiquity because the bones of their
trade were Australia's signal species, the geological markers of antiquity.
The discovery of human relics with such bones would have established
ancient Aboriginal occupation. But the evidence of positive association
was elusive. Krefft claimed to have found the fractured crown of a human
molar tooth with the Wellington Cave fossil bones, but the association
was dubious. Much later, it was shown that the tooth was that of an
animal.[18]

A further proof of antiquity would be to find human relics in stratified
beds with or below volcanic rocks. After all, Aboriginal legends spoke
of fiery mountains. Some finds were lightly dismissed: an Aboriginal
canoe said to have been found under basalts near Dargo, and possible
signs of Aboriginal camp-fires under lava flows in a Collingwood quarry.
But an intriguing case that was carefully considered was one that
brought together volcanics and extinct fossils, and became known as
'The Buninyong Bone'. This was a cut fragment of bone found by
Ballarat miners in the 1890s in a bed of silt under basalt. The bone was
a fragment of rib of a giant marsupial, *Nototherium mitchelli*. It was
roughly fractured, flattened in two places by abrasion, and at one end
was a long, sharp straight cut in the bone that many considered must
have been made by a human implement. The geological evidence was
conclusive: the setting was volcanic. The palaeontological identification
was also sure. But the artefact was ambiguous. Baldwin Spencer,
A. S. Kenyon and T. S. Hall discredited it, Alfred Howitt was sceptical.
J. W. Gregory followed Kenyon's reading of the artefact, and concluded
that it was not typical of Aboriginal workmanship. Several years later,
in 1911, Spencer experimented with fossil jaws of a leopard-sized
carnivorous marsupial, *Thylacoleo carnifex*, and concluded that cuts
like that on the Buninyong Bone could have been made by the teeth
of such an animal.[19]

Australian strata yielded other puzzling objects, even images of classical
antiquity such as those scrutinised by R. E. Johns in his gold-digging
days.[20] Other relics were fossicked from the goldfields. At Ballarat, a stone
basalt axe, grooved where it was once mounted on a handle, 'was
unearthed during the process of gold-prospecting twenty-two inches
below the surface, in a place which evidently had never before been
disturbed'.[21] Intriguing finds were given names—'The Pejark Marsh
Bones', 'The Buchan Bone', 'The Bodalla Tomahawk', 'The Colongulac

Bone'—and their possible human associations were discussed in the scientific journals.[22]

In 1926, Donald Macdonald, nature writer with the *Argus*, was sent a number of fossil bones of two species of giant kangaroo by J. E. Lockie of Puralka in south-west Victoria. His opposite number and friend at the *Herald*, Charles Barrett, visited the site and reported on the finding of 'The Puralka Flint' and other stone implements in apparent association with the bones. Barrett enthused about the possibility of 'a race of Australian cave men that existed centuries before the Pyramids were built'. Barrett handled the implement and was impressed by 'the glaze of antiquity'.[23]

One of the most celebrated and debated finds of the 1890s was dug out of a limestone quarry at Warrnambool. On 5 December 1890, men quarrying slabs for the Warrnambool Town Hall found a sheet of stone fifty feet below the surface which was thought to bear the impression left by two human beings who had once sat side by side at the foot of an ancient sand dune. On the face of the slab were two broad, smooth impressions made by the buttocks of a man and a woman, their gender identified precisely. There was also a slab with some footprints, but this was 'built into the walls of the Town Hall'. The curator of the Warrnambool Museum was Joseph Archibald, R. E. Johns' acquaintance (they met soon after the quarry discovery) and a keen collector and antiquarian. Archibald believed that the imprints strongly suggested the presence of people in Victoria when Tasmania was linked to the main-land.

Joseph Patrick Archibald exemplified Australian antiquarianism and the way its earnest delvings into a mythical past incorporated Aboriginal as well as local European origins. Born in 1823 in Ireland, Archibald gained some education at a Mechanics Institute in Cambridge that gave him a life-long devotion to literature and learning, and to the creation of public institutions that would foster them. He went to work as a draughtsman, and at the age of nineteen joined London's metropolitan police. Ten years later he was appointed second-in-charge of a detach-ment of fifty-five London police selected to serve on the Victorian gold-fields. He arrived in Melbourne in 1853. Archibald was a devout Catholic and possessed, in the estimation of historian Sylvia Lawson, 'an unblinking seriousness', a 'faith in effort' and a 'naive and trusting devo-tion to "knowledge"—or more properly to information'.[24] He knew many of England's historic places and showed his children stereoscopic views of them. His son, Jules François Archibald, grew up to become founding editor of the *Bulletin*. His daughter Lucy recalled that her father 'was intensely interested in the new land', and she remembered his 'picturesque stories' of 'Aboriginals in a Wild State', the gold escort, escapes from bushrangers, 'Chinatown in Castlemaine', the Cobb and Co. coaches, shipwrecks, and tales of Tower Hill (an extinct, flooded volcano near Warrnambool) and of its water 'getting quite Hot'. 'Then there was the story of the Spanish ship on the coast', she added. Joseph Archibald was an enthusiast for the Mahogany Ship, a relic hidden in Warrnambool's coastal dunes that some (including Archibald) considered a lost sixteenth-century Portuguese caravel, and others believed to be a whaler's punt. In the limestone slab he felt sure that he had another local lien on antiquity.[25]

Archibald's museum in Warrnambool did not (as was later claimed) hold a piece of wood from that ship, but there *was* something from many other wrecks—from the *Childers*, the *Loch Ard*, J. P. Fawkner's *Enterprise*, and the *Schomberg*, for instance. Archibald established the museum almost single-handed, although the idea was first suggested to him in 1873 by Henry Laurie, a Warrnambool journalist who was later appointed foundation professor of philosophy at the University of Melbourne.[26] The museum became, for a while, a focus for a lively and literate group of townspeople, but 'it was always a grief and disappointment to my father', wrote Lucy Archibald in the 1930s, 'to find that the town folk on the whole took so little interest in what he tried to do'. They did, however, bring him all sorts of historic memorabilia. As well as items salvaged from wrecks along that treacherous coast, the museum boasted a fine collection of Aboriginal weapons and implements, and a range of memorabilia associated with the Henty family, the first white pastoralists in the district. This included a Henty piano, the springs of Edward Henty's dog cart—claimed to be 'the first vehicle made in Victoria'—and 'one of Henty's Harpoons found in a whale'. The museum also possessed letters associated with John Batman, Ludwig Leichhardt and Robert O'Hara Burke, a pistol that belonged to Major Mitchell's exploring party, early coins, an old wooden plough, and pre-industrial agricultural implements from 'the world before the Flood' (as Archibald put it) such as a distaff and spindle for spinning and a quern, a handmill for grinding corn. Archibald took satisfaction from the fact that 'in this, the newest of all the countries in the world, we should be joining hands with remotest antiquity by means of these primitive implements'.[27] Warrnambool was indeed a place with an aura of history about it, for even the houses were made of local stone 'in which footprints of men and birds were found'.

Archibald was proud that his museum was salvaging the past. The quarrymen regularly noticed intriguing patterns in the stone. 'Many of us have told gentlemen of these things', they complained, 'but have been laughed at, and do not like it.' Archibald suffered the same fate. He regretted that the nature of the imprints in the 1890 limestone slab undermined serious consideration of their significance. The fact that the ancient couple had evidently sat very close together, he explained, 'seems to have great weight with certain frivolous young visitors to our Museum, who profess to derive comfort from the reflection that "that sort of thing" has the sanction of remote antiquity'. More senior commentators, who would have preferred a head to a bottom any day, argued the archaeological specificity of buttocks or drew attention to the inordinate size of the footprint built into the town hall. J. W. Gregory thought the print too large and uniform to be that of a naked foot, and concluded:

> If this slab be evidence that aboriginal man lived in Warrnambool at the time that the lower beds of the Warrnambool sandstone were laid down, I think it is also evidence that those people wore a modern type of boot. In that case Professor Spencer's view that the Australian aborigines show no signs of degeneration will have to be seriously reconsidered.[28]

One wit linked Archibald's two obsessions when he suggested that the prehistoric bottoms imprinted in the limestone were those of the skipper of the Mahogany Ship and his wife.[29]

By the early twentieth century, the strengthening scientific opinion was that, although Aborigines were primitive, they were probably without antiquity. But there was genuine uncertainty and a frustrating lack of evidence. Brough Smyth, writing in 1878, found it 'startling and perplexing' that no evidence of antiquity could be found, and he was impressed by the ubiquity of Aboriginal material culture.[30] Even by 1904, when J. W. Gregory reviewed the evidence for human antiquity in Victoria and decided that Aborigines were recent arrivals (perhaps only 300 years earlier), he believed that his conclusion went against prevailing opinion. He stated that there seemed to be a general belief in Victoria— which he had himself subscribed to on his arrival—that Aboriginal people had witnessed the last of the volcanic eruptions, and recorded them in their legends. Gregory, once he 'considered the evidence critically', abandoned that view. He dismissed much of the evidence discussed above, argued that artefacts found in coastal middens were all superficial, and that stone axe quarries at Mt William near Lancefield were 'all small and shallow, and no great amount of stone has been removed from them'. The Sydney geologist, Robert Etheridge, came to the same conclusion in 1890 (and reviewed some of the same evidence) when he argued that there were no geological traces of humanity in Australia.[31]

For both Etheridge and Gregory, the most persuasive evidence to the contrary was presented by one of the most debated issues in Australian anthropology and archaeology: 'the problem of the Tasmanians'. The physical and technological differences between Tasmanian and mainland Aborigines had prompted endless speculation among scientists, collectors and ethnologists. The 'Tasmanian problem' captivated scientists because it brought together the the two vital issues of race and antiquity. Did the Tasmanians come from Africa, southern India, southeast Asia or from the Pacific?[32] Had they once lived on the Australasian mainland, perhaps long enough ago for them to cross to Tasmania on an exposed land bridge? In 1898, Alfred Howitt had argued to the Australian Association for the Advancement of Science Conference that people crossed to Tasmania before the formation of Bass Strait.[33] Etheridge and Gregory found this the strongest intimation of antiquity but finally dismissed it for lack of evidence.

The negative conclusions of Brough Smyth, Etheridge and Gregory dampened expectations of Aboriginal antiquity in the early twentieth century.[34] The three found the Victorian data particularly persuasive because no other colony had been so thoroughly dug over by 'sharp-sighted miners'. 'In no country in the world have the gravels been searched so thoroughly . . . as in Victoria', concluded Brough Smyth, the former secretary of mines.[35] Yet they had found nothing that was convincing. The arguments of Brough Smyth, Etheridge and Gregory revealed frustration with existing lines of enquiry. Aboriginal legends appeared to be misleading, underground evidence had not been forthcoming or was unreliable, ancient Tasmanian migration from the mainland was mere speculation and the search for a link between humans and megafauna had been fruitless.

Since the context of found objects had proven so difficult to interpret, attention turned in the early twentieth century to the objects themselves, particularly those that offered clues partly independent of context. Collecting skulls of any age, particularly of Tasmanians, had long been a scientific obsession. Collecting skulls challenged the boundaries between science and crime, between the museum and the magistrate. Race and antiquity (combined in that notion of 'primitiveness') distinguished collection from culpability, but the ambiguity was exciting, as R. E. Johns—magistrate with a museum—knew. In the 1920s or 1930s, when the Melbourne *Herald* nature writer, Charles Barrett, was fossicking at Henley Beach in South Australia, he found an Aboriginal skull—'a beauty, with full complement of teeth in the upper jaw'. 'The problem was', he wrote, 'to get back to Adelaide with my prize without being arrested for "creating a disturbance".' 'Imagine', he mused, 'a quiet-looking grey haired man, seated in a tram car with a human skull upon his knees! It simply isn't done in South Australia!' He hid it in his coat, bought some brown paper at the nearest tea room, wrapped it up, put it in a band-box, and took it back to Melbourne where it found its place 'in a glass-case in a scientific institution'.[36]

In the first few decades of the century, reported finds of *ancient* skulls attracted debate. Skulls were eloquent relics. Antiquity, it was believed, could be read by an analysis of a skull's 'prehistoric' or 'primitive' characteristics, for example, a low flat receding forehead, a uniformly thick skull, or ridges above the eye. 'Primitive' skulls, it was expected, would be older than 'modern' ones, and so the hunt for primitive features shadowed the more difficult search for antiquity.

The interest in Australian fossil skulls at this time must have been influenced by the finding of the fabricated Piltdown skull and other fragments in England from 1912. The Piltdown gravel pits in Sussex were secretly seeded with fragments from a modern human cranium and an orangutan's jaw, and the resulting assemblage of 'Piltdown Man' was hailed as an ancient and primitive missing link. Much scholarly speculation has been devoted to the identification of the forger (the hoax was not discovered until 1953), but the more interesting questions are about why the intellectual climate was ripe for a hoax, and why so many eminent scientists readily embraced such a forgery. It was a compelling find for those palaeoanthropologists who wanted to unearth an early form of humanity in which the brain was more highly developed than other parts of the body. In the early twentieth century it was becoming popular to interpret human prehistory as a series of racial conquests in which higher forms of humanity had successively conquered inferior predecessors. An ancient fossil with a modern brain found on English soil therefore had nationalist implications. Piltdown Man may have been a product of international rivalry over antiquity, as it enabled England to have an ancient relic comparable with those of Europe. It also offered a racist comparison with the archaic Asian finds of the same ancient period.[37] Australia's link with Piltdown was not merely in timing. One of the most enthusiastic promoters of the English relic was the Australian-born anatomist Grafton Elliot Smith, who also became a participant in investigations into Australian fossil skulls.[38] In Australia, though, racism and antiquity were more ambiguous ideological partners.

The first ancient Australian skull was found near Talgai in southern Queensland in 1886 but was kept for almost thirty years in a station homestead before coming to scientific attention just two years after Piltdown. It was thought to be that of a fifteen-year-old boy, and geologist Sir Edgeworth David and anatomist J. T. Wilson laid it before the British Association when it met in Sydney in 1914. Finding the skull's exact original location took scientists years of grappling with the vagaries of local memory, but it was said to lie 'in the same condition as the fossil bones of extinct kinds of marsupial animals'.[39] In any case, it was large and thick boned, what archaeologists now call 'robust' as opposed to the 'gracile' or lightly built form of modern humans. Edgeworth David, who was convinced of Aboriginal antiquity from other evidence, inferred the 'strong probability' that it dated from the Pleistocene and 'proves that in Australia man attained to geological antiquity'.[40] David compared it with the controversial Piltdown finds. Grafton Elliot Smith was also lecturing in Sydney that same night, and he too mentioned Talgai.[41]

In November 1925, another archaic, robust skull of great size was unearthed at Kow Swamp near Cohuna on the Murray River by a contractor who was digging an irrigation channel. Professor Colin MacKenzie, a comparative anatomist who the year before had established the National Museum of Australian Zoology in the new capital of Canberra, claimed that the Cohuna skull was older than all known human remains, including the Piltdown skull. In words that echoed Joseph Archibald thirty-five years before, MacKenzie explained that when the skull was moved to his Canberra museum, it would become 'the oldest skull specimen in the world in the newest city'.[42] There was considerable scientific debate about it. Elliot Smith was again a commentator and considered that the oldest human remains in Australia were probably no more than 4,000 to 5,000 years old.[43] The geologist D. J. Mahony thought the skull primitive, but not Aboriginal, and he diagnosed the red loam in which it had been embedded as geologically recent. Other scientists, such as Professor Joseph Shellshear of the Department of Anatomy at the University of Sydney, visited Cohuna and found it impossible to confirm the circumstances of collection. Draper Campbell, a stone collector and dental expert, suspected that MacKenzie's reconstruction of the skull's missing teeth was affected by his desire for 'something really simian looking'.[44]

In September 1929, a skull of more dubious provenance was found in a dilly bag alongside the body of an Aboriginal woman who had recently died under a mulga bush in the Jervois Ranges in central Australia. Again, Sir Colin MacKenzie claimed that the skull was ancient and significant.[45] Frederic Wood Jones, professor of anatomy at the University of Melbourne, dismissed MacKenzie's statement as 'ridiculous' and liable to 'render Australian science suspect by physical anthropologists in other lands'.[46] In 1933, R. H. Croll visited the Jervois Ranges and met Tom Hanlon, on whose station James O'Neill was said to have found the skull. Hanlon, too, was sceptical and was possibly confused between the owner of the dilly bag and the skull in her possession:

> O'Neill came here and asked if there were any skulls about. I told him of this one lying in the paddock. I was astounded to hear later that it was a million

years old! . . . I knew the gin whose skull it was: she has two strapping sons here now, Archie and Jack.[47]

As with the Talgai and Cohuna skulls, scientists found it as difficult to interpret the sludge of reminiscence surrounding collection as it was to decode the earthy sediments of deposition.

The Jervois skull of doubtful provenance and antiquity received much more publicity than another event in 1929, one which was well documented and represented a watershed in Australian archaeology. In 1929, an archaeological dig at Devon Downs rockshelter on the banks of the Murray River in South Australia demonstrated the existence of an Australian stratified site of some antiquity. Norman Tindale and Herbert Hale both of the South Australian Museum excavated to a depth of twenty feet and identified evidence of cultural and environmental change. In a detailed excavation report published in 1930, they documented their analysis of stone and bone artefacts and postulated three major cultural phases of Aboriginal occupation.[48] The importance of their work was to indicate that environmental change had occurred and that technological change could be related to chronological phases. Few understood the significance of this dig and the Victorian collectors long ignored or disparaged the insights it offered.[49]

In 1936, the International Commission for the Study of Fossil Man (which reported to the International Geological Congress) requested reviews of evidence of human antiquity from several Australian states. The sub-commission for Victoria, consisting of D. J. Mahony, B. Baragwanath, Frederic Wood Jones and A. S. Kenyon, submitted a twelve-page analysis of artefacts, bones and skulls and concluded that 'it must be regarded as reasonably certain that man has not a geological history in Victoria'.[50] Just four years later, following another chance find, the scientific community would reverse that conclusion.[51] But the 1936 review of evidence was conducted within a particular culture of collection, and was implicitly defensive of it. The dominant antiquarian enthusiasm in early twentieth-century Victoria was the surface collection of Aboriginal stone tools, objects that offered not an index of antiquity but, instead, one of primitiveness.

A Victorian stone circle

In the first half of this century, the donations of stone tool collectors literally filled the National Museum of Victoria. During the second world war, truckloads of stone artefacts were removed to an outside store to clear museum space.[52] That is where they mostly still are today, stranded in a warehouse in boxes layered with dust. There are probably over 100,000 individual stone artefacts and most of them were collected this century. Some of them are labelled 'Unregistered, No locality known'. Many, though, are identified with approximate place of origin. These artefacts constitute a much underused and almost forgotten part of the south-eastern Australian archaeological record. Archaeologists who conduct field surveys today rarely consult these collections, perhaps do not even know they exist. Yet surely we cannot interpret what remains in the field without discovering what has been so recently removed.

These boxes of artefacts are, of course, very difficult sources to use, hard to access and often ambiguous in meaning and provenance. But researchers such as Mira Lakic and Louis Warren have shown that it can be done: it *is* possible to read the stones for some understanding of artefact distribution patterns at the time of collection.[53] But to do so researchers have also had to enter, to some extent, the mind of the collector, for it is the collector who stands between them and an understanding of the earlier field record.

There is another way in which these dusty boxes of artefacts are a valuable source. Their most thorough form of labelling links them to the name of their collector. Although there is vagueness about the dispersed places of origin of individual artefacts, there is precision about the person who gathered them together. In their sheer volume and disarray, these boxes of stone artefacts represent an orgy of collection that must interest us.

Who were the collectors of these stone artefacts? They were people such as A. S. Kenyon, Stan Mitchell, D. J. Mahony, T. D. Campbell, H. R. Balfour, S. F. Mann, and R. H. Croll. They were engineers, metallurgists, geologists, farmers, doctors and educationalists. They were 'amateurs' in the sense that they were not formally trained in anthropology or archaeology and found their chief employment in other fields. Even Baldwin Spencer, who inspired many of these collectors, was an amateur in this sense—his academic training was in biology and not the anthropology for which he became famous. His followers hardened their amateur status into a banner of distinction—they were suspicious of 'armchair theorists', as they called them, and advocated the value of field-work over any other sort of research. This intellectual stance led them to prefer local over imported interpretive frameworks, and what they called 'common sense' over more abstract reflective speculations. The contest, though, was not simply between theorists and practical collectors, but between different types of theory and technique.

Baldwin Spencer's life and work exerted a powerful influence over a generation of Victorian collectors. Spencer (1860–1929) was educated in Manchester and Oxford and took up the foundation chair of biology at the University of Melbourne in 1887. He established biological teaching and research on evolutionary principles and initiated a similar intellectual revolution at the National Museum of Victoria when he succeeded Frederick McCoy as the director in 1899. It was into his hands, in 1914, that the five large scrapbooks of R. E. Johns were delivered, a collection that Spencer considered 'the most valuable and unique of its kind that [the Museum] had ever received'.[54] For Spencer, those scrapbooks must have encapsulated some of the global variety and speculation that had excited his own fledgling scientific interests.

While in Oxford, Spencer and Henry Balfour assisted the anthropologist E. B. Tylor in transferring Lieutenant-General Pitt-Rivers' ethnographic collection from London to its Oxford museum, thereby absorbing the principles of typological classification of artefacts. Spencer's anthropological interests were revived when, as biologist on the Horn Scientific Expedition to central Australia in 1894, he met Frank Gillen, the Alice Springs postmaster and amateur collector of Aboriginal lore. The two collaborated in pioneering anthropological studies of central Australian Aborigines, in particular publishing *The Native Tribes of Central Australia* (1899) and *The Northern Tribes of Central Australia* (1904). Spencer's biological training and evolutionary principles shaped his perspectives of Aborigines as 'creatures, often crude and quaint, that have elsewhere passed away and given place to higher forms'. The Aborigine was to be compared with the marsupials, for both were products of biological polygenesis and had developed in entirely isolated ways, never beyond a primitive stage.[55]

Spencer was an energetic cultural and scientific leader in Victorian society, and a popular writer and lecturer. He was, at different times, president of the Royal Society of Victoria, the Field Naturalists' Club of Victoria, and the Victorian Football League, as well as a connoisseur and collector of Australian impressionist art. His Australia-wide political and intellectual influence has been superbly described by D. J. Mulvaney and J. H. Calaby in their biography of Spencer, *'So much that is new'*. Here Spencer's influence is traced mostly through the work of his disciples.

The circle of Spencer's heirs—we might call it a stone circle—is best represented in the work and attitudes of two men, A. S. Kenyon and S. R. Mitchell. They both took care to construct an intellectual lineage that linked them to Baldwin Spencer. Spencer's views were endorsed and propagated by Kenyon, and Kenyon's words were faithfully echoed by Stan Mitchell—he 'played Boswell to Kenyon's Johnson'.[56] The working and collecting lives of these three men dominated interpretation in this field in Victoria for over sixty years, from the late nineteenth to the mid-twentieth century. Their loyalty to one another entrenched and perpetuated views that were abandoned elsewhere.

Alfred Stephen Kenyon (1867-1943). *(From a painting by Graham Thorley, reproduced in the* Victorian Historical Magazine, *vol. 18, no. 72)*

Alfred Stephen Kenyon (1867-1943) knew rural Victoria personally and intimately, especially its north-western quarter. Born at Homebush, near Avoca, Kenyon briefly became a near neighbour of R. E. Johns when, in 1869, his family shifted to Avoca. Kenyon's father was a storekeeper and moved with his business to Ararat and, over the following six years, established general stores at Beaufort, Buangor, Stawell and Horsham. Young Alfred then had a taste of farming life when his father worked land at Bulgana, near one of the tributaries of the Wimmera River. The boy mustered stock and mended fences 'with a copy of Euclid in his shirt'. Drought forced the Kenyons to Melbourne in 1881, and Alfred was educated at St Stephen's Grammar School in Richmond and then at the University of Melbourne where he studied engineering and science. He did not complete his degree, and in 1888 joined the newly formed Department of Victorian Water Supply as a draughtsman.[57] Over the next few decades, Kenyon's mission as a public service engineer was to make marginal lands arable, and he became associated particularly with the opening up of Victoria's final frontier, the Mallee. Kenyon's responsibilities in the Mallee began late in the century and intensified in 1906 when he was appointed engineer of agriculture in the Department of Agriculture. In that role, he planned and administered the opening up of the northern and western Mallee, superintending irrigation and water supply activities for farmers, boring for water, the construction of silos and large-scale clearing and cultivation. In 1915 he celebrated his part in frontier history by publishing his first major work, *The Story of the Mallee*. He recommended the development of Red Cliffs, the extension of Merbein, and the establishment of the Robinvale Irrigation District, all of which drew on the waters of the Murray. In other parts of Victoria, he reclaimed land that was too wet for farming by supervising large drainage works at Koo-Wee-Rup and Cardinia in western Gippsland. His department was transferred in 1910 to the State Rivers and Water Supply Commission and, late in his career, in 1932, Kenyon was appointed a commissioner.

Kenyon's peripatetic job gave him ample opportunity for yarning and fossicking, two essential strategies of the collector. Like William Smith, the English canal-builder who (a century earlier) became fascinated by the stratigraphy exposed by his engineering, Kenyon found that his management of water and his excavations for channels and dams enabled him to probe remote corners and depths of his state. His colleagues at the Water Commission celebrated him (and others) in verse:

> We have a picnic Engineer, we call him A.S.K.
> He's roaming in the Mallee when he shouldn't be away.
> He runs a pre-historic car that's had a better day—
>   May his soul go marching on.[58]

His car was 'pre-historic' by association with the 'road metal' he was continually picking up and bringing home for the museum. It was his job—and his hobby—to talk to station-owners, managers and stockmen, and they told him of historical relics, skulls, bones and stone artefacts—in fact anything 'new' they had found.[59]

Kenyon would have done more than listen, for he was an acknowledged know-all. He loved letting people know when they were wrong on matters of fact. His favourite phrase was 'I say, So-and-so, you're wrong about such-and-such, you know.' His precision and dogmatism bullied a school of followers. When Kenyon chastised the Sydney collector C. C. Towle about his stone tool theories, Towle confessed his 'heresy' and only half in humour, urged: 'Please be merciful to me, a sinner.' Towle promised Kenyon that he would endeavour 'to keep on the straight and narrow path of lithic orthodoxy'.[60]

Although the habit of correction lost him friends, Kenyon's energy, breadth of knowledge and strength of opinion established him as an authority on matters Aboriginal and historical: 'there was never an historical nut that he could not crack', praised one contemporary.[61] In 1895 he married Alexandrine Aurelie Leontine Augustine Delepine from Jersey and they had one daughter, Justine, who wrote *The Aboriginal Word Book*.[62] Kenyon spoke French, read German, and was an active member of the Australasian Institute of Mining Engineers, the Royal Society of Victoria, the Field Naturalists' Club of Victoria and the Historical Society of Victoria.

In 1938, in his retirement, Kenyon became Keeper of Antiquities when a new Department of Antiquities was established at the National Museum of Victoria. Egypt, as a fount of civilisation, had always had a powerful fascination for colonials, and in the 1850s and 1860s the Public Library of Victoria rapidly became rich in Egyptian bibliographical resources through the energies of Redmond Barry and the librarian Augustus Tulk.[63] In the twentieth century, between the wars, there were great achievements in field archaeology in the Middle East, most notably the discovery of Tutankhamen's tomb in 1922. Under Kenyon as keeper of antiquities, the old records room in the National Museum of Victoria, which 'in itself was extremely sepulchral in effect', was turned into a Mummy Room and displayed the mummy of Tjeby which the museum acquired in 1925.[64] At about the same time, in 1939, the South Australian Museum was reorganising its Egyptian room through the efforts of Norman Tindale and Herbert Hale. There was satisfaction, as one Egyptologist put it in 1899, in linking 'the region of earliest civilisations to that of the latest' and Aboriginal artefacts were often exchanged for Egyptian antiquities.[65] Grafton Elliot Smith, an advocate of diffusionism—the belief that all world civilisation emanated from a centre—enthusiastically compared Australian and Egyptian material culture.[66] But Kenyon, despite his interest in Egypt, rejected Old World comparisons when it came to the study of Australia's own antiquities. He was elucidating cultural hierarchies, not parallels. He and Spencer distinguished between ancient civilisations and 'primitive' cultures, one requiring a humanistic approach and the other the scientific technique of taxonomy.[67]

Kenyon's interest in ethnology was quickened by his participation in that great ethnological debate of his time: the origin of the Tasmanians. In 1898, Kenyon read Alfred Howitt's paper in which he argued the strong likelihood of a mainland origin for the Tasmanians. Kenyon was convinced by Howitt, and turned from 'a merely desultory collector of stone and other implements' into 'a regular searcher for evidence' in Victoria of a former Tasmanian presence. It was at this time that Kenyon corresponded with R. E. Johns, possibly about this issue.[68] After discussions with Howitt, Kenyon decided to concentrate his search on the south-eastern Australian coastline, from Twofold Bay in southern New South Wales to Victor Harbour in South Australia. He was looking for ancient stone relics of a particular kind—of recognisable Tasmanian type—but he was also in search of antiquity, a depth of time and artefact that might predate the flooding of Bass Strait.[69] In 1899, Alfred Howitt wrote to E. B. Tylor of Kenyon's work, explaining that he had found Victorian artefacts that 'completely parallel' Tasmanian stone tools. Howitt continued: 'I introduced him to Spencer the other day who hopes to be able to secure a series from him for the National Museum.'[70]

This meeting may have been decisive. Kenyon, perhaps partly due to Spencer's influence, decided that even if the parallel typologies were there, the requisite antiquity was not. He later claimed that during more than a decade of scouring the coast, and then subsequent searching on inland excursions, he found no signs of antiquity. 'You will see therefore', Kenyon wrote in 1925 to Professor Sir Edgeworth David (who disagreed with him), 'that setting out on a quest for positive evidence, I gradually accumulated such a mass of negative evidence that I cannot believe the Tasmanian was ever here.'[71] Kenyon's views hardened against possible antiquity. Aborigines, he came to believe, had not arrived in south-east Australia until the last thousand years or so, perhaps only the last few hundred.[72] When, in the 1920s he collaborated with Charles Barrett on two publications about Aborigines, Kenyon found 'our romantic Charlie' and his intimations of antiquity a bit exasperating: 'Re Barrett, if you know him well you will know also that he is not capable of restraint. A romanticist of the purest order, a born phrase-maker & a journalist by profession, what can you expect.'[73]

Kenyon's views on Aboriginal culture and antiquity were echoed by Stan Mitchell (1881–1963) who began his serious study of stone implements in 1921 through the influence of Spencer and Kenyon himself.[74] Fourteen years younger than Kenyon, he dedicated his major work, *Stone-Age Craftsmen* (1949) to him. Mitchell was a mineralogist who became interested in Aboriginal artefacts when he found one on a geological excursion.[75] Like Kenyon, experience in the field stimulated and sustained his study, and, as for most amateur collectors, remained his chief qualification. 'Never was there a keener collector than Mitchell', wrote R. H. Croll.[76] He amassed one of the biggest private artefact collections in Australia and filled his Frankston home with his treasures: 'every drawer, every wall, every corner'.[77] A special building at his home eventually housed his museum.

Mitchell's father, James, was a bookseller and librarian from Scotland who settled in Victoria in 1854. Financial difficulties in the 1890s made it impossible for James Mitchell to continue his bookshop and stationery business in Collingwood and so, late in that decade, when young Stan was sixteen (and while Kenyon was sifting coastal sands in search of a Tasmanian connection), father and son went prospecting on the Dargo High Plains in Victoria's Alps. They stayed for a year, occasionally seeing cattlemen, possum hunters and other prospectors. The Mitchells lived in a large bush hut where Stan had intensive lessons in geology (his father was a keen mineralogist) and studied algebra with the aid of slate slabs from the river bed. The two sat by the fire at night, James writing letters and Stan reading mining and geology.[78]

After his time at Dargo, James Mitchell was appointed Australian representative to the Foote Mineral Company of America and soon began buying and collecting minerals for them. He helped the National Museum of Victoria to purchase several specimens from the dealer, and himself donated items to the museum collections. Meanwhile, Stan studied geology at the School of Mines at Melbourne Technical College while working full time with the Victorian Smelting and Metallurgical Works. He then established a mineralogy business in Abbotsford and travelled widely overseas with his work in the 1920s, which enabled him to visit museums in America and Canada. He gathered a very large personal collection of mineral specimens that was donated to the CSIRO. When, in 1931, Stan Mitchell was appointed honorary mineralogist to the National Museum of Victoria, he was building on a family tradition.[79]

What meanings did Kenyon, Mitchell and their fellow collectors find in the stones? By the early twentieth century, Aboriginal material culture was adopting new forms in response to a growing tourist market. Many collectors—in search of 'traditional' or pre-European Aboriginal artefacts— dismissed 'tourist art' as debased and felt that abandoned stone implements offered indisputable access to the 'prehistoric' past. The survival of the stones was apparently casual and accidental, so they could be 'discovered' and harvested for free, without Aboriginal mediation.

Stone artefacts were attractive because they were durable, discrete, countable; they were portable and collectable, fitted in a hand or a pocket, and could easily, even discretely, be shown off. Boasting and rivalry were endemic to collecting. 'MM [Mike Mudie] is just too fabulous as a collector', wrote the South Australian T. D. Campbell to Stan Mitchell. 'He's got all us experienced folk beaten to a frazzle.'[80] They boasted of their finds in terms of numbers of artefacts, or weight or volume. John Mulvaney recalled that 'some collectors who hailed Kenyon as mentor, indulged in extremes of rivalry and secrecy in their field forays'. Sometimes archaeological sites were disclosed only after they were exhaustively collected over, and some collectors disposed of unwanted finds down a disused mine shaft.[81] Geology was closely related to typology, and prospecting was akin to collecting. One western district collector ascribed his fossicking fervour to his inheritance of 'gold fever' from his migrant grandparents.[82] The excitement of the hunt often overwhelmed reflection: 'The trouble about all this collecting business is to settle down with the results', sighed Draper Campbell.[83]

A good collector was someone who left very little for followers to find. They spoke in terms of numbers of discrete pieces collected; the relationships between artefacts and between them and their sites were not as important as sheer volume ('loads and loads of stuff') or weight ('1 ton 6 hundred weight of specimens') or range and rarity of tool types, or priority of collection.[84] 'I was probably the first to collect on Hood's Drift', boasted Mitchell.[85] For all the interest in stone tool typology, there is a sense in which it is all just undifferentiated 'stuff', to use Kenyon's term.

The collectors made a distinction, more apparent to themselves than to others, between systematic collection and vandalism. They could boast about their own haul in the same breath as they condemned 'vandals'. C. C. Towle wrote to Mitchell in 1933, telling him of his Christmas collecting: 'I was out for 2½ days and returned home with 6 ground axes, 3 beautiful "choppers", about 200 points, nearly 100 eloueras, and so on. And I collected all this from an area that is supposed to be worked out.' He then finished the letter with a tirade against 'axe-mad collectors': 'They ignore everything except ground axes, and they have no regard for the genuine investigator. They will destroy a whole midden in order to find a ground axe or two.'[86] One Portland collector boasted to Mitchell in 1961 of his two-week 'hunting trip' to outback New South Wales: 'In all we sent home 13 Banana crates full weighing 2 Hundred weight to the case ... A most successful trip. We covered 2100 miles in the two weeks away.'[87] Mitchell was critical of this 'ethnologists picnic', as he called it, not because of the removal of material but because the stones were to be sold rather than placed in a collection or museum.[88] He and

Custodians of the stones: Stone tool collecting was primarily a masculine
activity, often self-consciously so. But some women also collected
Aboriginal stone artefacts and many assisted their husbands or curated
the homestead collection. Mrs F. Mitselburg (above), at her home east of
Broken Hill, shows her late husband's collection to Alfred Kenyon in
1917, and Aubrey Officer (below) presents her own assemblage.
(Museum of Victoria)
Charles Barrett believed that women were generally sceptical, even
mischievously careless, of this sort of collection: 'Wives of collectors may
wonder, if their tastes are not ethnological, why their husbands set such
store upon bits of flint and great hollowed flakes of sandstone! One has
heard a splendid stone hammer described as "road-metal". We almost
winced to see, at a lonely farmhouse, grinding mills put to common use,
as foot-scrapers!' *(Herald, 9 April 1929)*

Kenyon strongly resisted efforts to legislate against the collection of Aboriginal artefacts.

In 1937, Professor Joseph Shellshear, honorary archaeologist at the Australian Museum in Sydney, wrote 'An Appeal for the Preservation of Prehistoric Remains in Australia' in which he condemned the collector. Apart from 'sheer vandalism', wrote Shellshear, 'the cause of the destruction of prehistoric material in New South Wales is the collecting of implements'. He asked: 'Why do men collect these relics of ancient man?' His answer was that even where it was not for personal financial gain and was for the intrinsic interest of the objects, there was still a problem: 'the collectors have had their interest mainly centred on the implements, and subsequently have missed the more interesting cultural aspects'. Shellshear and Frederick McCarthy of the Australian Museum urged the need for education and legislation. 'The official interest in the preservation of the fauna and flora of this country gives hope that attention will be paid to the preservation of aboriginal material', wrote Shellshear.[89]

Mitchell was worried by this lobbying in the 1930s for protective legislation, yet he was at the same time presiding over a newly formed Council for the Preservation of National Monuments.[90] Even at the end of his life, Mitchell resisted efforts to legislatively curtail the freedom of private collectors, arguing to W. E. H. Stanner in 1962 that: 'Had this [proposed legislation] been in operation in the past much valuable material would have been lost to science.'[91] Towle criticised 'the true-blue "scientists" at the [Australian] Museum' and warned Mitchell:

> Please do not deceive yourself. The actions of Kenyon, yourself and a few others at the [Association for the Advancement of Science] Congress have caused you to be condemned to the deepest pit of fire for the rest of your natural life.[92]

The Victorians helped delay protective legislation in all states until the 1960s and 1970s.

Apart from the pleasures and perils of collection, what of the stones themselves? Could antiquity be ascertained from them? Many of the collectors began with this question but found the stones confusing and inscrutable. Their increasingly dogmatic rejection of Aboriginal antiquity was, in part, out of frustration. They could identify no clear sequence of technology. And patination—estimating the age of stone implements from their surface weathering—was found to be unreliable. Frederick McCarthy tried in 1940 to draw some tentative conclusions from it, but Mitchell showed that a well-developed patina could occasionally be achieved in a comparatively short period.[93] He concluded that patination required an understanding of the rate of weathering for different kinds of stone, and dating thereby reverted to a geological problem.

Typology was itself an artefact of the collector. Its main purpose in this period was to order, display and compare the products of their scouring. Collectors easily became fascinated by the formal relationships between objects in their cabinets rather than the cultural relationships between artefacts and the people who made them. Kenyon and Mitchell went further and interpreted the stones as evidence against 'culture'. To them, the objects were more interesting as stones than as artefacts. They were more natural than cultural. Many of the collectors came to ethnology through geology, and it was to geology that they returned to explain the diversity of Aboriginal stone artefacts. For Kenyon and Mitchell, typology was an extension of geology and they propagated geological determinism as the chief interpretive vision.[94]

Kenyon's conviction that Aborigines had been here for only a short period influenced his reading of their stone tools. He did not expect to find evidence of cultural change over such a brief period of occupation. He expected that implements would be found only on the surface of the ground, and that they would all be recent. Their form, he warned, reflected only the type of stone available and would tell the collector little about the mind of their maker, for 'the blackfellow used anything anywhere and any how'.[95] Kenyon's explanation of the variety of stone tools gave no role to cultural factors or individual creativity. 'Any local "culture" (the word is used reluctantly) can be shown to be due to local causes', wrote Kenyon together with D. J. Mahony and S. F. Mann in 1924.[96] He disparaged the Aboriginal 'stage of culture' as 'equivalent to that of a schoolboy of 10 to 12'.[97] His historical vision, then, was of a homogeneous Australian Aborigine, recently arrived, who had experienced no cultural change and whose material culture lacked invention.[98] The stone circle was closed.

Mitchell subscribed to the Spencer and Kenyon materialist school of stone culture and believed that different artefact types merely reflected local environmental factors. Comparative or distributional studies of artefacts were therefore pointless. Mitchell was not all that interested in the shape of the implement. He was convinced that all forms of implements were made and used from the beginning of Aboriginal arrival in Victoria, an event he dated no more than a few thousand years before, perhaps overlapping with the volcanic period. No change over time had occurred, so stratigraphy was also pointless.

Kenyon and Mitchell, and those within their circle of influence, were therefore surface collectors; they gathered artefacts from the ground and rarely dug for them. They resisted the deepening of their science in both time and space. They scoured the land but did not penetrate it. They relied on their culture's environmental intrusions—erosion, rabbits, grazing and ploughing—to sufficiently disturb the soil for their purpose. They did not dig because they felt certain there was nothing to find. Although they considered the Aborigines 'primitive', they believed their occupation of Australia was relatively recent. Furthermore, Aborigines were considered nomadic and without patterned or prolonged attachment to place. Collecting, explained Mitchell, was confined to the surface 'as is natural with relics of a truly nomadic people'.[99] They believed that the Aboriginal preference for sandy camping sites made stratigraphic investigations pointless, and that Australia's unusual extremes of weather had churned up the ordered layers of residue. Aborigines were afraid of caves, Mitchell believed, and so these rich cultural sites were rarely investigated. Above all, Aboriginal culture was considered to be static, so overwhelmed by inertia that it would become extinct.

This was Spencer's legacy. But whereas Spencer's ideas were shaped in dialogue with European theorists, Kenyon and his circle turned their backs on them. '[B]eware of the Jabberwock', Kenyon advised C. C. Towle in 1929, 'that is the man who writes on the old stone age and sich like piffle and for Gid's sake [*sic*] don't call anything Mousterian or Azilian.'[100] He was referring to the European stages of stone age culture sketched out in the nineteenth century. Kenyon believed that European and American social theories and classification systems were no help to the student of Aboriginal culture and, in fact, inhibited genuine, local insights. Kenyon warned against 'the evil influence of the European archaeologist' and condemned locals who relied on them as 'copyists'.[101] Mitchell recalled that 'Kenyon always impressed upon me the danger of conventionalism in following too closely what he termed *arm-chair theorists*, particularly in regard to stone cultures and to base my ideas on practical field work and commonsense.'[102] Robert Brough Smyth had, a generation earlier, initiated Australian suspicions of European model-builders when he questioned the applicability of John Lubbock's evolutionary theories.[103] Kenyon's isolationism went further with its nationalistic overtones. It was also a refinement of a general suspicion he held of theorists of any kind, local or imported. Field-work— *collection*—alone entitled one to speak. Towle recognised that for Kenyon there was a 'right kind of orthodoxy, [one] originating from experience, and not from the comfortable armchair by the fireside'.[104]

Kenyon's rejection of theory was partly a defence of field science (and of the amateur) against the rising power of the academy, and also a response to attacks on private collecting. It was partly nationalistic in its dismissal of imported categories and its championing of the potential of home-grown originality. But it was also a defence of a particular man and a certain sort of theory—Baldwin Spencer and cultural evolutionism, a partnership that had pioneered Australian anthropology. Kenyon was defending Spencer's vision against new developments in anthropology and archaeology overseas. In America, the first decades of the century saw the growing influence of the teaching of German-born and trained anthropologist, Franz Boas. Boasian anthropology espoused cultural relativism rather than evolutionary hierarchies, and emphasised diffusion over independent invention as a mechanism of cultural change.[105] This new theoretical stance was part of what Kenyon was rejecting when he emphasised cultural isolation, independent development and unilinear evolutionism. By then invoking geological determinism, Kenyon stifled any recognition of cultural creativity that an 'independent development' hypothesis may have spawned. His arguments isolated Aborigines from all possible sources of change: antiquity, waves of migration, diffusion and innate creativity.

In America, archaeologists influenced by Boas began to pay more attention to cultural change in 'prehistoric' times, and to use stratigraphic techniques to delineate sequences.[106] In Australia, similar developments were under way and they were disdained and ignored by the Victorian stone circle. Hale and Tindale's Devon Downs excavation of 1929 had used stratigraphy to document cultural and environmental change, and in 1936 at Lapstone Creek, Frederick McCarthy of the Australian Museum in Sydney demonstrated past cultural change by the excavation of a stratified series of different stone tool types.[107]

Why were these breakthroughs ignored? Nothing demonstrates the conservatism of the stone tool collectors as well as the efforts they put into marginalising or discrediting the findings of Devon Downs. The surface collectors had developed a strong prejudice against excavation, and a related scepticism about antiquity. As late as 1958, Mitchell rejected stratification as a useful technique in Australia.[108] For several decades, some Victorian artefact collectors considered that Tindale's excavation sites on the Lower Murray were unique in their stratigraphy and that similar sites could not be expected elsewhere.[109]

A suspicion of theory, personal animosity and interstate rivalry also played a part in the neglect of Devon Downs. The suggestion of cultural sequences smacked heavily of theory, and Tindale's ambitious speculation on meagre evidence attracted criticism even from supporters. There was also considerable personal animosity expressed towards Tindale in the 'stone gossip', as the collectors called their correspondence. 'Tinny' and his theories were made fun of: 'NBT is churning out an awful lot of what seems to be rubbishy stuff', 'perhaps he doesn't know what he's doing', wrote Draper Campbell to Mitchell.[110] When

Mitchell visited Adelaide in 1958 he did not see Tindale because, he explained to Charles Mountford, he 'was away thinking up some more Theories'.[111] Tindale was further isolated by his feud with a potential ally, Frederick McCarthy, who had also pioneered stratigraphy and culture sequences and whom Mitchell called, with a sectarian overlay, 'the ethnological pope of NSW'.[112] This comment was indicative of the politics of interstate rivalry, a debilitating influence in early archaeology. Different and competing schools of stone typology developed in various states, a circumstance that further isolated the Victorians from developments over the border.[113]

Suspicion of Devon Downs was part of a general resistance to historical thinking. Change over time—*history*—was an explanatory tool rejected by most of the stone tool collectors as it was by the new professional anthropologists.[114] Anthropology was institutionalised as an academic discipline in Australia in the mid-1920s and it took the form of a practical, present-oriented science that could serve government administration and cultural understanding. The uses of history were rejected by the Sydney professors of anthropology, A. Radcliffe-Brown and A. P. Elkin. There was a sense of urgency about investigating 'traditional' Aboriginal culture while it remained, and researchers therefore made trips to central and northern Australia to see Aborigines who had relatively little contact with whites.[115] Even members of the Victorian stone circle journeyed to the centre, and detailed social investigations were undertaken by systematic field-workers such as Phyllis Kaberry, Lloyd Warner, Donald Thomson and Ted Strehlow.[116] Annual expeditions organised between the wars by Adelaide's Board for Anthropological Research conducted physical anthropological studies, measuring Aboriginal mental and physical capacities with every imaginable technique.[117] Could Aborigines, for instance, feel pain? Anthropological research continued to dominate over archaeological investigations and over history. The two studies that could have drawn attention to Aboriginal adaptability—prehistoric archaeology and a history of culture contact—were overwhelmed by an anthropology devoted to discovering the 'essential Aborigine' locked in a disappearing present.[118]

Kenyon and others accepted this vision of anthropology. It did not share their fascination with stone artefacts, but it did not undermine it either. The Sydney collector, Towle, confessed to Kenyon that he found the Sydney environment less conducive than Victoria: 'Those connected with anthropology at Sydney University seem to be indifferent to the subject of stone culture ... [and] cannot discriminate between a flake and a piece of road metal.'[119] A. P. Elkin and his 'faction' ('the Elkin group of go-getters') were regarded with suspicion by the Victorians.[120] But both groups—anthropologists and stone tool collectors—were fascinated by 'the stone age' and its accessibility in Australia, and both made a sharp distinction between distant 'traditional' Aborigines, among whom one did field-work, and local 'half-castes' who were stranded from their past.

In the apparent absence of living, traditional Aborigines, then, research focused on the remains of dead, local ones. In Victoria, where the Koori people had been 'collected' onto missions and removed from the landscape, artefacts were scooped up by the truckload and most of the measuring was done on dead bodies as burial grounds were systematically plundered. Under the patronage of Sir Colin MacKenzie, George Murray Black, an engineer (taught by McCoy), farmer and hobby collector, dug up Aboriginal skeletons from burial mounds along the Murray River for over twenty years from 1929 to 1951. Black was a keen stone tool collector. In 1939 he wrote to D. J. Mahony, director of the National Museum of Victoria, about the lakes north of Wentworth as a stone collection area, recommending 'a large truck' for the purpose. He sent cases of skulls to the museum by train. He learnt of the whereabouts of burial places from old settlers and workmen, or from rabbiters who happened upon them in their digging, and he knew of more than he had time to excavate. Nor did he have time to investigate the antiquity of the remains he gathered, and he rarely dug below six feet. The age of the bones, it was later determined, ranged from recent to 14,000 years. For Black, though, anatomy rather than antiquity was the subject.[121]

'The Murray Black Collection', its name unintentionally memorialising both collector and subjects, consisted of over 1,600 skeletons that went to MacKenzie's Institute of Anatomy in Canberra (as his Museum of Australian Zoology was renamed) and to the University of Melbourne.[122] Skeletal material that was unsuitable for measurement was discarded in the field, and the bones that were sent to Canberra or Melbourne were checked, washed, catalogued and numbered.[123] Silverfish ate many of the labels.[124] Black arranged for the National Museum of Victoria to provide him with a written request 'to obtain *aboriginal specimens*, stone implements & other things, just in case the police or other busy bodies make a fuss'.[125] Were any of the 'busy bodies' relatives of the dead bodies? Black was indeed wary of the 'Mission half castes and abos' and plotted his 'poaching' expeditions to avoid them, 'as I don't wish to fall foul of the mission crowd who have a bad reputation locally'.[126] His collecting was based on the assumption that such people no longer existed or cared, but his scheming belied it.

The stone tool collectors disdained Aboriginal informants. Their collection work assumed extinction, often of the people, and certainly of their useful knowledge. '[W]e are not much better off', wrote Kenyon in 1911, 'than the British Archaeologist delving amongst the barrows and mounds of his native isle.'[127] That was the way they wanted it to be; that was their model for collecting. R. H. Croll enthused that Australia had the one considerable body of stone age people that survived, and then added: 'but—and it is an amazing thing—we have to guess at the meaning of much that we pick up'. The stone tool collectors were self-made detectives totally stranded from living testimony. Mitchell's work, it was reported, had 'at last made sense of the jumble of oddly shaped "worked" stones that collectors have accumulated since the blacks themselves disappeared'. Collecting called for ingenuity, for 'a major piece of detective work' and the need to 'discover from the stones themselves'.[128] Their science was built upon an invention of cultural discontinuity, upon the severance even of Aboriginal memory. It was symbolic that, in Victoria, the Anthropological Society met in an anatomy school.

The Anthropological Society of Victoria was formed in the year of the state's centenary celebrations. The coincidence was deliberate, for it was intended as a public display of conscience at a time of anticipated international attention. An Anthropological Society of Australia had existed under the leadership of a Sydney paediatrician and eugenist, Alan Carroll, from 1896 until his death in 1913, and had published a journal entitled *The Science of Man*.[129] Anthropological societies were formed in a number of states in the 1920s and 1930s, and efforts had been made in Victoria to formally encourage amateur scientific curiosity in the field. A Prehistoric Club, which later became the Ethnological Section of the Field Naturalists' Club of Victoria, was formed in Kenyon's Heidelberg home in 1927 to encourage collection of stone implements for Australian rather than overseas museums. But it did not flourish because, as Kenyon put it, 'the few we had were all dilettanti or collectors counting their catch for the day or claiming a heavier fish than the other man'.[130] The Anthropological Society of Victoria formed in 1934 had a more scientific as well as political purpose. It aimed to promote the study of anthropology and also 'to advocate a national policy for the preservation of the aboriginal races'.

The society coalesced around the energies of Frederic Wood Jones, A. S. Kenyon, R. H. Croll, Dermot Casey, S. R. Mitchell and D. J. Mahony. Seventy people were enrolled as foundation members, and the first public meeting of the society, at which Kenyon lectured, attracted over one hundred. The society prided itself on 'developing a public opinion in favour of the aborigines and other primitive people' and 'made recommendations or voiced protests to the authorities when the rights of these people were in jeopardy'. The society fenced Aboriginal rock paintings in the Grampians and at Langi Ghiran, and encouraged municipal councils to use Aboriginal names for streets and local features. But their political concerns were mainly outside their own state, for in

Victoria and Tasmania 'the question has ceased to be a live one'. They urged Commonwealth responsibility for Aboriginal welfare and put their faith in the benefits of science in government, particularly the employment of 'men trained in the psychology of the primitive mind'.[131] In 1935 a resolution of the society was forwarded to the Australian Prime Minister urging the regulation of the entry of white people into parts of New Guinea due to 'the fact that in general native races face grave danger when brought into contact with Europeans of losing their primitive culture and becoming degenerate'.[132]

Andrew Markus, in his book *Governing Savages*, has argued that during the first decades of the twentieth century the expectation of inevitable Aboriginal extinction was, in some quarters, no mere passive observation but an active stimulus to public policy in Australia, even a 'rationale for actions designed to ensure that the Aborigines would indeed die out'.[133] Through their trips to the outback, collectors and anthropologists learned of the living conditions of 'tribal' Aborigines, and of the controlled governmental neglect to which they were subject, and this experience sharpened the political edge of the anthropological societies. They were mechanisms for sympathisers to offer practical welfare assistance as well as for scientists to foster wider public recognition that extinction was *not* inevitable.

The 1930s were a watershed in Australian public opinion about Aborigines in the sense that opposing ideas were brought in sharpest proximity and sometimes met at the divide. In some ways, racism was increasingly entrenched but it was also articulately challenged by Aboriginal activists, white humanitarians and anthropologists. Aborigines directly manipulated the white political processes, a spate of white humanitarian groups were formed, such as the Victorian Aboriginal Group (1929), the Aboriginal Fellowship Group (1932) and the Aborigines' Uplift Society (1937), and professional anthropologists such as A. P. Elkin tried to shrug off the intellectual framework of social Darwinism that had dominated for over half a century.[134] Aboriginal material culture began to be valued as 'primitive art'. And Aborigines, it was realised almost with a shock, had 'survived', or at least could 'be preserved' if proper action were taken by white Australians. Racism and sympathy met in this injunction to 'preserve' for it sustained the image of Aboriginal culture as delicate and vulnerable, passive and static, an object rather than a subject of history.[135]

But in another sense, the acceptance of Aboriginal survival was an acknowledgement of them as historical beings, and so opened the way for acceptance of the antiquity of their occupation. Extinction and lack of antiquity were related beliefs; they were both traits of a timeless people. White Australians abandoned them at about the same time. The discovery of Aboriginal antiquity, always deeply known by Aborigines themselves, was not just a product of radiocarbon, but awaited cultural as well as scientific insights by Europeans.

Kenyon and his daughter Justine were office-bearers in the Victorian Aboriginal Group as well as being active in the Anthropological Society. The Victorian Aboriginal Group was formed in 1930 as a study group in response to the findings of the Bleakley Report, a federal government enquiry that described the appalling living conditions of Aborigines in the Northern Territory.[136] Kenyon and R. H. Croll were leaders of the study group. Its members were white Australians who, living in Victoria, saw nothing ambiguous in calling themselves an 'Aboriginal Group'.[137] Their aim was to achieve better conditions for Aborigines and to arouse public opinion and influence government towards that end. After 1933, when the group developed from a study circle into a more formalised society with political and missionary aims, Kenyon and Croll rarely attended meetings and women became the primary organisers, in particular Amy Brown and Val Leeper. Although the group initially advocated inviolable Aboriginal reserves because they believed that Aborigines were dying out, they also urged the introduction of Christianity. They fought for the establishment of federal control of Aboriginal affairs, and encouraged the use of 'expert advisers' such as scientists and missionaries. By the end of the 1930s, they began to adopt a policy of assimilation rather than protection. They rarely consulted or attempted to make contact with Aborigines even when they had the opportunity, and those of their members who did work with Kooris, such as Helen Baillie, were regarded as eccentric and sometimes undermined. The group distanced itself from the 1938 Aboriginal 'Day of Mourning' and deplored the tone of the Aboriginal manifesto published in that year by the Aborigines' Progressive Association.[138]

The stone tool collectors participated in the politics of sympathy, but also sustained an ideology of oppression. Kenyon, although a blunt and dogmatic man, represented this political ambiguity. He propagated a circular, insular interpretation of Aboriginal material culture that denied cultural creativity, but he acknowledged their original ownership of the land and spoke of them as the first explorers of the continent.[139] He expected Aboriginal extinction and announced its reality in Victoria, but worked to preserve distant, 'tribal' survivors. Typology was confusing, antiquity was elusive, cultural change was impossible, theory was evil. Kenyon developed a view that 'without geological evidence, stone implements have led only to perplexity', yet he spent decades removing them from the soil.

What meanings, then, were in the stones? Perhaps they had more to do with white culture than with black, and more to do with place than with object? Perhaps Kenyon and Mitchell were using a science of the past—expressed in collection—to articulate a history and geography of possession? Certainly it is suggestive that, as the 1930s progressed and the stone circle became more isolated in its opinions, Kenyon turned increasingly to writing history and Mitchell to the commemoration of place.[140] The collectors began to regret the impoverishment of their collecting grounds. They came to unexpectedly share, perhaps, a sort of Aboriginal attachment to particular places, often the same type of places, and they experienced an echo of their sense of loss. 'One is getting hard put to find a good collecting spot now', lamented Dandenong antiquarian Fred Smith in the late 1950s. When Draper Campbell learned that a pine plantation now covered one of his favourite collecting areas at Hood's Drift, he was regretful but philosophical: 'Thus does stone age give way to timber age.' As a collector, he was surprised by the strong 'call' of place, at 'how one gets a sentimental leaning towards those odd quaint spots & one always feels a sort of nostalgic urge to think about going to see them again "some day"'.[141] But he knew that there would now be little left to give those places meaning, and that the meanings were elsewhere. In the tens of thousands of stone tools stored at the museum, the Victorian stone circle had built a monument to a timeless, extinct culture. The only history they had recognised—and this they helped generate with a pioneering fervour—was the history of European pastoral ascendancy.[142]

CHAPTER FOUR

The Nuclear Family

In the post-war years, a global sense of the human past emerged from the shadow of a nuclear future. If the 1950s saw the height of social propaganda about the domestic nuclear family, then so too was it the period of a scientific construction of a global nuclear family, one in which racial differences were undermined by the discovery of a long, shared human past. Australia joined the global nuclear family in those years through the scientific discovery of its own human antiquity. And it did so through the efforts of a 'family' of professional archaeologists that colonised Australia chiefly from Cambridge, and who embraced the scientific potential of a product of the nuclear age, radiocarbon dating. It is tempting to suggest that both nuclear families—global and domestic—have since been made vulnerable by the same processes that produced the rise of feminism and the re-emergence of Koori self-consciousness.

Donna Haraway, in her book *Primate Visions* (1989), has argued that late twentieth-century primatology may be seen as part of a complex survival literature in global, nuclear culture.[1] She analyses the way debates about gender, race and nature have been shadowed by post-war anxieties and hopes about nuclear civilisation. Haraway studies the 1950 and 1951 statements on race published by the United Nations Educational, Scientific and Cultural Organisation and argues that a notion of 'universal man' was propagated by UNESCO in the hope of identifying a scientific (rather than political) human unity. Among anthropologists, universal man became 'Man the Hunter, the guarantor of a future for nuclear man'. By reaching back to early, universally shared human attributes such as bipedalism and hunting, physical anthropologists of the 1950s and 1960s were undermining the racism that their disciplinary ancestors exactly a century before had scientifically entrenched, a racism that the constitution of UNESCO had identified as the source of the second world war. In its place they pioneered a biological humanism, a language of populations and processes rather than races and types. This vision culminated in the Man the Hunter Symposium of 1966, organised by Irven De Vore and Richard Lee, which recognised the geographic and biological expertise of hunter-gatherer groups and posed research problems on a global basis.[2] 'Hunter-gatherer societies' had replaced 'the stone age'. The problem was that man the hunter, although 'a natural global citizen', was also 'a natural neo-imperialist'.[3]

He was, with hindsight, also a natural sexist. As the title of the symposium made clear, an unintentional scientific sexism was part of the solution to scientific racism.[4] Masculinist strategies were identified as the means by which humans broke out from the trees into the open savannah and took on a world view. Becoming human meant wielding weapons, developing curiosity and aggression, and gaining new territory. In a word, that was 'hunting'. Hunting, it was argued, drove the evolution of 'man'. That enchanted link between humans and large animals (extinct fauna), which has fascinated archaeologists and anthropologists, reappears here in a different guise. The link was both a clue to antiquity and a key to humanity. Hunting was the universal, masculinist act of human procreation, 'founding at once the nuclear family and the family of man'. It was a vision of promise, but also of threat. Universal man, being a hunter, was poorly equipped for nuclear culture.[5]

The scientific production of universal human nature following the second world war could not have proceeded without that other off-shoot of the nuclear age—radiocarbon dating, an absolutism that freed relativism.

Radiocarbon revolution

'Crosbie Morrison says Mummy can't keep her secrets any more ... ATOMS CAN TELL THE TRUTH', screamed a headline in the Melbourne *Argus* beside a photograph of an Egyptian mummy in the National Museum of Victoria.[6] It was the mid-1950s and radiocarbon was about to work its magic in the humble environs of the museum and public library lunch room, said to be the least radioactive space on the premises. This was to be Australia's first radiocarbon laboratory, established in the state that had least suspected antiquity. The atomic age shadowed the future, but illuminated the past.[7]

In the late nineteenth century, leading physicists (especially Lord Kelvin) had placed limits on the age of the sun and the earth by applying the second law of thermodynamics on a planetary scale. They argued that the sun and the earth could not be more than 100 million years old on the grounds that these bodies were constantly losing heat and could only remain warm for a limited period. The period calculated by the physicists was not long enough for the gradualism of geologists and the evolution of biologists to work their wonders. But in the first years of the twentieth century, physicists discovered that matter itself evolves and

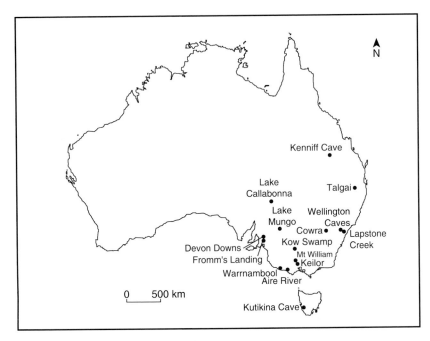

Archaeological sites mentioned in the text

generates an internal source of heat. Nuclear reactions enable the sun to burn for billions of years and radioactivity slows the loss of warmth of the earth's interior.[8]

Radioactive elements, by releasing energy as they decay, ensured antiquity and provided a way of measuring it. Radiometric dating of geological strata provided a chronology of the earth over billions of years. Radiocarbon 14 dating performed similar miracles with organic substances, although over a much shorter time-span. Every living thing contains carbon, and the radiometric clock starts when the living tissue— bone, wood, shell—dies. This absolute dating, a product of the atomic age, made it possible to piece together a chronology of the world's peoples, to reconstitute 'the family of man'. This was the post-war nuclear family writ large.

But even before radiocarbon, a local breakthrough in the search for antiquity had been made. Just four years after Victorians had reported to the International Commission for the Study of Fossil Man that 'it must be regarded as reasonably certain that man has not a geological history in Victoria', evidence of such a history was found.[9] The discovery of a fossil cranium at Keilor near Melbourne converted many of the doubters. Once again, the original setting of the relic was a matter for debate. In 1940, a quarry worker at Dry Creek on the Maribyrnong River, James White, felt his pick hit something hard, dug the object out of the soft river terrace silts and washed it in the creek. Debate about its age and exact geological context ensued for over a decade, some scientists believing that it was a burial only one hundred years old and others speculating an age of 150,000 years.[10] But D. J. Mahony and Frederic Wood Jones, who had dismissed all previous evidence of Pleistocene Aboriginal occupation, were convinced of 'the geological antiquity' of the Keilor find.[11]

It was Edmund Gill, curator of fossils at the National Museum of Victoria from 1948, who ingeniously pursued the challenge of dating the Keilor cranium by means of global sea level changes and who first systematically advocated the Australian application of radiocarbon dating. In the early 1950s he estimated the age of the Keilor cranium from geological evidence to be about 15,000 years, and radiocarbon dating later confirmed it to be about 13,000 years old.[12] Like McCoy and Spencer before him, Gill's career was shaped powerfully by his attitude to evolution; he combined spiritual convictions with scientific dedication. Born in New Zealand in 1908, he became director of Baptist Youth Work in Victoria but felt obliged to relinquish the position when church elders questioned him about his belief in the theory of evolution.[13] Sea level change and coastal extinctions were his particular interests, and he was convinced of the great antiquity of Aboriginal occupation. Gill's enthusiasm for dating ensured that Victorian evidence was among the earliest samples to be sent to America for dating, although the first results were unexciting. And it was Gill who transformed the museum and library lunch room into a local time machine. 'The Atom Bomb so fills the news that we seldom hear of the other results of radio-activity', regretted Gill.[14] By the mid-1950s, the radiocarbon revolution was ready to erupt and Pleistocene Australia was to be, perhaps, its most dramatic fall-out.

In the 'stone gossip' of the 1950s and early 1960s, collectors began to refer to 'the new man'.[15] His name was John Mulvaney, young, energetic and at the beginning of a career that would dramatically employ the potential of radiocarbon. He was also 'new' in the sense that he brought professional skills and perspectives to Australian archaeology. Although he was profoundly Australian in manner and outlook, to members of the stone circle paranoid about overseas influence he may initially have seemed to be 'the European', bringing Cambridge to the bush.[16] After completing a history honours degree and a Masters thesis on Roman Britain at the University of Melbourne, Mulvaney studied archaeology and anthropology at Cambridge under Grahame Clark and Glyn Daniel.

Mulvaney has referred to himself as one of 'the forerunners of a sizeable band of hunter-diggers which ventured into the Pacific world and which numbers Cambridge amongst its totemic centres'. He was part of what he called 'the Cambridge archaeological empire' which practised 'incipient, though benevolent imperialism'. 'What was intellectually satisfying to the [Cambridge] student', reflected Mulvaney, 'were the concepts of universality and interdependence in past human affairs.'[17] He was inspired by a world approach to prehistory, but unlike the expatriate Australian archaeologist Gordon Childe, Mulvaney was determined to apply his training in Australia: 'I hankered after the Iron Age but knew I must return to Stone.'[18]

Gordon Childe and Mulvaney met in Melbourne in 1957 and Childe examined artefacts from Mulvaney's first field excavation at Fromm's Landing on the Murray River near Devon Downs.[19] Childe was horrified by the dominance of stone typologists in Australian archaeology—it's 'all horribly boring unless you're a flint fan'. 'Mulvaney is the only man with first class techniques to tackle it seriously', he concluded.[20] Mulvaney was the beachhead of a new international science, and he would use the techniques of the nuclear age to decipher a 'stone age' land. Radiocarbon would illuminate what Mulvaney, in 1961, called 'the dark continent of prehistory'. One of his earliest publications was about 'A New Time Machine'.[21]

When Mulvaney returned to Australia (he was appointed a lecturer in the University of Melbourne History School in 1953 and in the late 1950s was elected secretary of the Victorian Anthropological Society), he found himself mixing with enthusiastic artefact gatherers, suspicious of theory, who competed for the best finds and jealously guarded their treasures. He was dismayed at their practice, yet was equally determined to work with them and learn from them. In Australia of the 1950s, the people with whom Mulvaney had to negotiate over access to sites and information were not the Aborigines, for there was 'not a dissident Aboriginal in sight', but the European collectors.[22] He had to come to terms with the ideology and practice of the stone circle, and with the legacy of Kenyon and Baldwin Spencer. Although he considered the work of the collectors to be 'antediluvian' and down 'the byways of antiquarianism and the haphazard fringes of lunacy', he treated their work seriously, and painstakingly sifted their often impressionistic accounts for insights into cultural change and typology.[23] His history and archaeology were interdependent, for in evaluating this legacy he also freed himself from it: he became a scholarly commentator on the Kenyon circle and a biographer of Spencer.[24]

Stan Mitchell took an interest in Mulvaney's digs, although the two clearly retained different opinions on the value of stratigraphy. In early 1960, Mulvaney invited Mitchell to join him on an excavation site at Aire River near Cape Otway. Mulvaney was venturing a stone tool analysis that invoked change over time, but Mitchell (just a year before his death) still preferred a static and spatial interpretation.[25] A stalwart companion on many of Mulvaney's digs was Dermot Casey, whose landrover, equipment, draughtsmanship and photography enhanced their pioneer excavations. Casey was a transitional figure, one of the earliest trained archaeologists in the field (he had worked with Sir Mortimer Wheeler in Britain), but a gentleman amateur in style who published little and mixed well with the cabinet collectors.[26] He helped found the Anthropological Society of Victoria and became its president in 1938, and was also president of the Royal Society of Victoria in 1947. Casey was honorary ethnologist to the National Museum of Victoria and donated all his finds to that institution. He may have helped Mulvaney bridge the rapidly widening gap between amateur and professional.

Dermot Casey, Norman Tindale, Fred McCarthy and Edmund Gill were the only people whom Mulvaney could recognise as Australian precursors of his own methodological rigour in excavation or analysis. All were affiliated with museums but none was a designated curator of archaeology.[27] Mulvaney, as 'the new man', was under pressure to arbitrate some of the existing archaeological disputes. He found himself mediating between Tindale and McCarthy, both of whom were venturing interpretations of culture change, but of a different and contradictory kind.[28] Mitchell and others extended a welcome to Mulvaney partly because they expected his work, particularly at Fromm's Landing ten miles downstream from Devon Downs, would 'probably blow sky-high Tindale's cultural succession'.[29] However Mulvaney, although critical of many aspects of Tindale's work, championed his stratigraphic approach and condemned the geological determinism that had for so long ignored Tindale's 1929 model of excavation.[30] Mulvaney lauded the Devon Downs excavation as 'the first systematic attempt, in Australia, to apply stratigraphic, rather than conjectural principles, to the uncovering of aboriginal prehistory'. He regarded 1929 as 'the year in which objective studies of aboriginal past and present reached maturity within Australia'.[31] Disciplinary maturity and objectivity were, he believed, the fruits of professionalism.

Mulvaney's archaeological career was directly coincidental with the radiocarbon revolution. It was a tool tailor-made for some professional magic. At school he had read Charles Long's *Stories of Australian Exploration* (1903), but the story that Mulvaney was to tell was of that forgotten discovery, exploration and colonisation of the continent by Aborigines. These were the opening words of his *The Prehistory of Australia* (1969): 'the discoverers, explorers and colonists of ... Australia, were its Aborigines'.[32] Even in 1952, when the only radiocarbon date for Australia was an age of just 500 years for one of

Gill's Warrnambool middens, Mulvaney believed that carbon 14 would usher in 'a completely new approach' to prehistoric social evolution, a move away from a static and passive picture of early human society towards a vision of it as dynamic and environmentally manipulative.[33] Radiocarbon and the discovery of ancient Australia have been so bound together that the technical limits of carbon 14 dating (about 40,000 years) are the current conservative limits of Australian antiquity.[34]

As a professional historian and archaeologist, trained in the careful sifting of evidence and the clear articulation of his methods, Mulvaney has characterised his influence as replacing conjecture with objective science.[35] His science was stratigraphy, and his perspective was global. His Cambridge training brought an emphasis on field-work, especially on digging and the identification of long stratigraphic sequences in different areas of the continent. Radiocarbon 14 ensured time depth as well as sequence and enabled different digs to be related by age. Antiquity and culture change, long subjects of debate, were conclusively established by Mulvaney and other archaeologists in the 1960s.

This was the decade of 'the deluge', 'the golden years' for Australian archaeology.[36] Many of the first archaeological appointments were made in universities, and professionals took up positions in state museums. The Institute of Aboriginal Studies (which later included Torres Strait Islanders in its title) was established at a conference in 1961 and by act in 1964. At Kenniff Cave in southern Queensland in 1962, Mulvaney dramatically confirmed the Pleistocene occupation of Australia with a minimal radiocarbon date of 13,000 years. Samples from a test dig at Kenniff Cave in 1960 had been sent overseas for analysis, and the results were finally heard over an expedition breakfast during a second dig in July 1962 when a telegram was picked up on the party's transceiver set. Mulvaney at first suspected a transmission error with an additional nought.[37] The 13,000 minimal age of human occupation in 1962 became 20,000 in 1965, over 30,000 by 1970 and had reached a probable 40,000 by 1980.[38]

Two discoveries at the end of the 1960s sharply confronted archae-ologists with a historical puzzle of global significance. Momentous finds are not always made in the field. Physical anthropologist Alan Thorne, while examining human skeletal collections in the National Museum of Victoria, came across a cardboard tray containing a heavily mineralised and partial skeleton of archaic or robust appearance. The only clue to its origins was a police stores department label with the address 'Superintendent of Police, Bendigo'. The museum's curator of anthropology, Alan West, dated the label, searched police records, and was able to discover that the skeleton was unearthed in May 1962 when Mr R. A. Andrews was deepening an irrigation channel on his property.[39] He and Thorne traced the exact burial site and even matched the partial museum skeleton with its remainder *in situ*. 'Well sleuthed fragments match' telegraphed Thorne to West after analysis of the bones in Canberra.[40] This burial and many others (some with grave goods) were on the shore of Kow Swamp on the Murray River near where the Cohuna skull had been found almost half a century before. Thorne at first expected the rugged and robust remains to be more than 20,000 years old, perhaps even up to 50,000. They were dated, though, at between 9,000 and 15,000 years in age, surprisingly contemporaneous with the gracile people represented by the Keilor skull. The Kow Swamp skeletons were the largest single population of the late Pleistocene epoch found in one locality anywhere in the world. Thorne found similarities between them and the *Homo erectus* fossils of ancient Java, and speculated on the early co-existence in Australia of two human groups who interbred. The skeletons were stored in the National Museum of Victoria.[41]

While Thorne was working on the Murray, the geomorphologist Jim Bowler was studying climate change in the Willandra Lakes in western New South Wales. On the impressive eroding dunes of the dry lakes, Bowler found ancient evidence of human occupation. In July 1968, as he stood over 'the first enigmatic bundle of burnt bones in a calcrete block on the ancient shorelines of Lake Mungo', he remembered the Keilor skull and the problems encountered in identifying its exact original setting. He therefore marked the spot with an iron peg and returned in March the following year with a team of archaeologists. The eroding fragments, later dated at 26,000 years in age and identified as the world's oldest cremation, were carefully packed in John Mulvaney's suitcase and returned to Canberra for analysis.[42] This and other finds at Lake Mungo identified a population of 'modern', gracile people who were living over 30,000 years ago, at a much earlier date than the apparently 'archaic' or robust Kow Swamp people.

The radiocarbon revolution, then, not only linked Australia to a world Pleistocene past, it also began to sketch out an intriguing human history and enabled archaeologists and anthropologists to offer a distinctive regional interpretation of hunter-gatherer society. Aboriginal culture, it emerged, was innovative as well as ancient; no longer could it be simply categorised as 'the stone age' of humanity, nor was it the quintessential hunter-gatherer society. Here were found the world's oldest cremation, perhaps the earliest human art, the first evidence of edge-ground axes, an early domesticated species in the dingo, millstones that predated agricultural revolutions elsewhere, and the most ancient evidence of modern humans.[43] As Tim Murray has observed, anthropologists like Bill Stanner and archaeologists like John Mulvaney introduced less reliance on the timeless universals of general anthropology and a more open attitude to the complexities of history.[44] The stone age was exploded away by evidence of antiquity and adaptation, and by new models of transformations from food collecting to horticultural societies. The mounds that James Dawson excavated in western Victoria in the late nineteenth century were, a century later, interpreted as evidence of intensification and social complexity. The stone circles that R. E. Johns and others dismissed in the 1870s as insubstantial and primitive became regarded in the 1980s as evidence of unusual and innovative sedentarism among hunter-gatherers.[45] The other factor that undermined stone age ideologies was the re-emergence of the people themselves, the assertion particularly since the early 1970s of a black national consciousness.

The Man the Hunter Symposium of 1966 took place on the brink of two cultural movements that would undermine both halves of the notion of 'universal man'. One was feminism which revealed the deeply gendered science behind the solution and responded with 'Woman the Gatherer'.[46] The other was the decline of the west, the fragmentation of the notion of universal culture and the assertion of post-colonial difference. In the words of James Clifford, the authority of the west 'to represent unified human history is now widely challenged and [its] very spatial identity is increasingly problematic'.[47] The post-war nuclear family has been sundered. The natives are re-inventing themselves in very particular ways.

Re-creation and reburial

White Australians experienced two mid-twentieth-century revelations: that Aborigines had an ancient history in this country, and that they had survived the European invasion.[48] John Mulvaney played a leading role in the transformation of 'prehistory' into 'history', and in the establishment of an awesome chronology for ancient Australia. Yet in the 1950s Mulvaney, living in Victoria, 'had never met an Aboriginal person'. 'I mean', he said, 'they just didn't "exist".'[49] In 1963 he travelled to the Northern Territory and had his first contact with Aboriginal Australians.[50] By the early 1970s he was urging fellow archaeologists that priority be given to 'Aboriginal-oriented research', by which he meant working with the people themselves.[51] Cultural politics changed with remarkable speed, and museums—those citadels of colonialism—became battlegrounds.

Aborigines had been expected to make their appearance in museums as objects of display and research, and rarely as audience, owners or curators. The realisation that they might be among 'the general public' led one major museum in the late 1960s to consider displaying a prominent notice to warn potential Aboriginal visitors that they might find exhibits disturbing should they enter the building.[52] Even by 1980 at the Museum of Victoria, according to one Aboriginal curator, 'there was little evidence of actual Aborigines about. If Aborigines did appear, first words were 'make sure the skull bay is locked" '.[53]

In the following decade museums increasingly turned their attentions from past objects to present people. In Victoria, Kooris were employed by the state museum as curators and trainees, Aboriginal 'keeping places' were established by Koori communities (the first at Shepparton in 1979), a representative Aboriginal committee was formed to advise the Council of the Museum of Victoria, a Koorie heritage trust was established, and the museum's Department of Anthropology became part of the Division of Human Studies and, in 1991, was renamed Indigenous Studies.[54] The Aboriginal Studies section of the Museum of Victoria put less emphasis on 'remote area' Aborigines and developed a strong orientation towards the Koori communities of its own state. The study of Aborigines resolutely crossed the great divide from science into the humanities.

The repatriation of the bones and other artefacts of indigenous people has begun. In the past decade, Australian museums and other institutions have returned for reburial by Koori communities the Crowther collection of Tasmania, the Murray Black collection and, in 1990, the Kow Swamp skeletons.[55] Although the futures of these collections were debated most intensely in the 1980s, there were clear signs of earlier challenge. In the early 1970s Kooris protested against the Kow Swamp excavations and the National Museum of Victoria was served with an injunction to halt archaeological work there, although this had already ceased. The Victorian chief secretary, John Rossiter, dismissed the Koori protesters as 'a small but vocal minority' and was concerned that archaeology in Victoria would be impeded or suppressed. In December 1973, David Anderson, a descendant of the 'Wamba Wamba people' on the Murray, rejected the assessment of the Aboriginal and Archaeological Relics Advisory Committee that the Kow Swamp find was not sacred, and explained that 'Aboriginal community groups have asked me to request that our historic cultural heritage, views and feelings be taken into consideration through consultation'.[56]

Ten years later, the director of the Aboriginal Legal Service of Fitzroy, Jim Berg, issued a supreme court writ against the National Museum of Victoria over its handling of Aboriginal relics and artefacts. The action was brought in 1984 by Berg when he learned, through the intervention of Aboriginal museum staff, that the museum was planning to send two skulls—the Keilor skull and a skull from Kow Swamp—for display in the American Museum of Natural History in New York. The skulls were to feature in an exhibition called 'Ancestors' which aimed to gather together from all over the world the 'hall-marks' of human evolution over 30 million years. Keilor and Kow Swamp would together pose the puzzle of two anatomically different human populations co-existing in Pleistocene Australia. Anthropologists were surprised that Kooris made no distinction between recent burials of known individuals and ancient fossil evidence. 'All skeletal material, therefore, is part of the Dreamtime', explained the museum anthropologist Ron Vanderwal to the Museum Council in 1984, 'and no difference is seen between what we see as the ancient past and the present.' The loan offer concerning the skulls was withdrawn and they remained in Victoria.[57] Jim Berg went on to establish the Koorie Heritage Trust, a private organisation now housed in the Museum of Victoria which has been spectacularly successful in raising funds to promote Koori culture, and which organised an exhibition entitled 'Koorie' that opened in the museum in 1988.[58]

In the early 1990s, the two great archaeological discoveries of the late 1960s were returned to their places of burial, but under very different circumstances. In late August 1990, the Museum of Victoria presented to the Echuca Aboriginal Cooperative the Kow Swamp collection of human remains and associated grave goods.[59] It is believed that they were reburied. On Saturday, 11 January 1992, the cremated remains of the young woman found by Jim Bowler at Lake Mungo were returned to the ancient shoreline and received by several hundred Aboriginal people, both locals and visitors, as well as scientists associated with the original find. The remains were placed in a specially made wooden box and stored in a large locked safe decorated with an Aboriginal painting in the visitor centre. Two keys are needed to open it, one held by archaeologists, and the other by Aboriginal people. Jim Bowler was involved in what he called 'a spiritual occasion', where he and other scientists publicly explained the circumstances of the find and Aboriginal elders formally welcomed the Mungo woman home.[60]

It was almost 130 years since R. E. Johns dug up Peeler from the edge of the Wimmera. Today, as reburials take the place of exhumations, the parallels between past and present are as strong as the differences. Peeler's people are claiming him back. Aboriginal bones in European museums are symbolic of oppression and dispossession. The liberation of these bones from European custody, their reverent return to the soil, is equally eloquent of modern Aboriginal self-determination and of the persistence of cultural ways and religious beliefs. Bones are powerful symbols and offer rich metaphors: archaeologists are accused of 'picking them over', Kooris are 'thrown a few' to keep them quiescent about land claims.

The return of Mungo Woman: Archaeologist Alan Thorne carried the Mungo woman's remains to a group of Aboriginal elders in a ceremony at Lake Mungo in 1992 (Age, 13 January 1992)

In a society where 'heritage' has been defined in material form as 'the things we want to keep' and where the historical context is one of invasion and dispossession, the modern reburial debate is frequently conducted in terms of 'who owns the past?'.[61] But Aboriginal custody is not the issue, for that is conceded, even championed, by most parties. Rather, the question is: does custody encompass the right to rebury remains of any age or provenance, irrespective of their archaeological significance? In other words, what sort of meanings are in the bones, and who has a right to them? The conversations at the graveside— whether it be for an exhumation or a reburial—are still about religion, science and history.

Archaeological evidence continues to play a major role in the struggle between evolutionists and creationists.[62] Now it is some Aborigines who are expressing the creationist view, who espouse polygenesis, who—it is suggested—have been influenced by the Christian biblical fundamentalism they got from the missions.[63] They claim a separate human origin within Australia, an antipodean genesis. In their need to create a distinctive Australian Aboriginal identity, they reject archaeological and anthropological arguments that Aborigines came from south-east Asia. They reject evolutionary theory, and are quick to point out that white people have not always believed in evolution.[64] The study of their bones may lead to contradictory readings of their history.

John Mulvaney resigned his position as honorary fellow of the Museum of Victoria in protest at the museum council's assent to what he regarded as a premature ministerial directive to return the Kow Swamp collection. He had argued for a 'keeping place' (similar to the Mungo solution) and believed that this option was still possible and would have future benefits to Aborigines as well as non-Aborigines. Mulvaney believed that the museum had failed to fulfil its educational obligations and to defend its investment in intellectual freedom. It had abetted another form of racial monopoly, and undermined the nuclear family. Mulvaney's vision of archaeology's 'essential humanism and universalism', his belief that 'prehistory knows no national boundaries', his influential advocacy of the notion of 'world heritage', were under attack from people who saw these as further instruments of imperialism.[65]

'Extinction Threatens Australian Anthropology' reported the American journal *Science* in July 1984.[66] Archaeologists and anthropologists from across the world wrote to Australia in protest at the proposed reburial of ancient Aboriginal bones.[67] Such actions, they claimed, threatened both the archaeological profession and world heritage. 'Reburying the material will certainly spell an end to the profession in Australia', warned one; 'reburial is equivalent to book burning', wrote another.[68] The recent centenary of Darwin's death (1982) kept nineteenth-century science at the forefront of their minds as they wrote.[69] Their letters were filled with the conviction that scientists of the second half of the twentieth century were very different to those of Darwin's era, and that 'modern research' contrasted with the 'misrepresentation and shameless treatment' of Aborigines in the past by 'so-called "scientists"'.[70] John Pfeiffer, author of *The Emergence of Man*, deplored the racism of the past and commented on the irony that reburial would affect work 'that has done much and promises to do much more to undo the racism of the past'.[71]

Two events, they felt, freed today's scientists from that past and from the burden of its guilt. One was professionalisation, which distinguished them from the amateurs or 'so-called "scientists"' of an earlier era. The other was the second world war. This awful rite of passage had, they believed, exposed the terrors of scientific racism and liberated them from it. C. S. Churcher of the University of Toronto wrote:

> I can understand the reaction of some human liberalists to the racial theories of the last century and part of this one, but I might remind them that we fought a World War to stop just such racist theories becoming established, and thus I do not consider that our generation has to shoulder the burden of guilt that the Victorians earned.[72]

Israeli scientists wrote with sympathy for the Aboriginal position: 'We Jews know well, alas, the results of such distortion of human values that reached a horrible climax with the murder of millions of our people by German and other nazis.' But they drew a firm distinction between 'legitimate scientific research' and the 'attempt of certain individuals, among them "scientists", to misuse science'. They agreed 'that wrong use of skeletal remains must be prevented' but urged that this should not preclude genuine science.[73] The amateur past of archaeology was not to be allowed to haunt 'real' scientists, particularly those who had suffered the purge of war and subsequently invested in the nuclear family. Reburial, warned the overseas scientists, would 'cut Australia off from the world community'—in both the ancient past and the scientific present.[74]

In the 1990s, with Kooris resurgent, there is a genuine contest between ways of knowing, between forms of history-making.[75] This is a conflict between white disciplinary science—centred on artefact and text—and black oral knowledge. What happens when 'the sacred' is made into 'heritage'? How do we measure the claims of Aboriginal views of the past against those of white professional history?

The two, of course, are interdependent. A consequence of dispossession is that the old culture often only survives to the extent that it has been appropriated and preserved by the new.[76] The archaeologists and collectors—like R. E. Johns—are both friend and foe to the indigenous people, both violators and mediators of their past.[77] In the past three decades, archaeological and historical research has been influential in changing public perceptions of Aboriginal culture, and an important tool used by Aborigines in their fight for political recognition and land rights. So the ways of knowing are not always in conflict. John Mulvaney has drawn attention to the fact that many Dreaming stories confirm the archaeological theories: they tell of beings coming from the sea, or of sacred sites now under water.[78]

European understandings of the past tend to draw boundaries between the past and the present. How far into antiquity, we ask, do modern Aborigines have a claim on human remains? How far into the future do Europeans carry the guilt of their forebears' exploitation? When did archaeology become an objective science and cease to be a cultural tool in the hands of the dispossessors? In brief, where does the past end and the present begin? Our obsession with material heritage—preservation as our principal means of appreciating the past—is a consequence of this disjunction.

Aboriginal views of the past place greater emphasis on continuity and re-creation and less on separation and preservation. Perhaps this cultural characteristic has been strengthened by modern political needs. Skeletal biologist Colin Pardoe has reported that some Kooris give more significance to a Cowra burial dated at no more than 150 years in age than they do to the famed Lake Mungo skeletons of 25–30,000 years in age. They valued the recent burial more highly because, they said, it 'showed the continuity of Aboriginal culture well into the late 1800s'.[79]

Let me finish by returning to Peeler, by putting some flesh on his bones. He was a native policeman. His name testifies to that, in its reference to Sir Robert Peel's Irish constabulary. We might be tempted to think of it as a derogatory nickname, and him as a dupe to the dominant culture. But the historian Marie Fels has made us think again about the role of the Victorian Native Police.[80] She has described how they used their new power and paraphernalia for their own individual and cultural ends. She argues that they moved easily across two worlds, doing the European job well, and making new and advantageous Aboriginal relationships where traditionally there had been no contact. In this sense, she suggests, the Native Police 'may be seen as an early stage in pan-Australian Aboriginal consciousness.'[81] Peeler was, then, very much a Koori. In death, he was used to represent a relic race. But in life, he may have been testimony to a creative, adaptive and resilient culture.

PART TWO
Possession

CHAPTER FIVE

Past Silences

D. H. Lawrence, in his novel *Kangaroo* (1923), wrote eloquently about the European sense of alienation from the Australian landscape:

> The strange, as it were, *invisible* beauty of Australia, which is undeniably there, but which seems to lurk just beyond the range of our white vision. You feel you can't *see*—as if your eyes hadn't the vision in them to correspond with the outside landscape. For the landscape is so unimpressive, like a face with little or no features, a dark face. It is so aboriginal, out of our ken, and it hangs back so aloof.[1]

This 'aboriginal' landscape, like its original owners, seemed without history. It seemed to resist or elude emotional possession. In 1867, the *Argus* art critic wrote of the 'complaint or regret often expressed in Australia' that 'the past owes nothing—as in other countries—to the present'.[2] His reference was to a landscape unable to tell a story, one apparently devoid of familiar human trace, and disturbingly free of the overlay of tradition.

In the late eighteenth century the contemplation of landscape had become a cultivated activity, one that involved recognising that stretches of land had associations and meanings that could be analysed as if part of an artistic composition.[3] Ancient monuments became valued because they gave a landscape form and structure as well as historical associations, and they provided places of contemplation and inspiration. Ruins romantically elided culture and nature and represented the gentle subsidence of one state into another. Classical ideals of monumentality came to underpin landscape beauty. In Australia, even those who were moved by the wonder of the land were disturbed by what it lacked. They were depressed by the historical and philosophical reflections prompted by the continent's absences and silences:

> An irresistible feeling of depression involuntarily succeeds to our admiration of the scene before us when we reflect on the fact that in all this vast wilderness there is not a single inhabitant; not the faintest trace of its occupation by man is apparent. No homesteads or roads, no enclosures or cultivation attest his presence . . . [4]

This was explorer James Calder's reaction in the 1840s to the alpine grandeur of south-west Tasmania.[5] Here was none of the dull monotony or flat barrenness that were the subjects of frequent criticisms of Australian landscape. But still there was a problem, one which Calder analysed:

> The country we describe is as yet without a history, without traditions, and indeed without association. Its past is a veritable blank, and we look back into it only to discover that it has nothing to reveal . . . There is no such thing as classical soil here . . . [6]

But there was another, haunting source of melancholy. In 1855, when Calder was walking from Hobart to the old convict station at Oyster Cove, he again recorded with admiration 'the varied and magnificent picture which lay before us'. Wonderful as the view was he could not savour it, for at Oyster Cove, among the dilapidated echoes of convictism, he came to visit a small group of Tasmanian Aborigines. Calder's delight in the land was again compromised:

> But if the view were a hundred times more prepossessing than it is, its attractions would be scarcely observed . . . when we know that within the walls of that desolate-looking shealing [hut] are all who remain of a once formidable people, whom a thirty years war with our countrymen have swept into captivity and their relatives to the grave.[7]

Classical soil there may not have been, but history there was, and it quickly estranged colonists from the land they wanted to possess.

The nature writer, Alec Chisholm, who grew up in the Victorian gold town of Maryborough at the turn of the century, spent much of his childhood roaming among the mining scars, ironbarks and wattles of the district's dry, open forests. Although he felt happy and free in the bush, sometimes 'the "brooding" of the trees became almost fearsome':

> This was the unhappy case, chiefly, when dusk enveloped the ridges and gullies on dull days in winter. The ironbarks now had shed their friendliness. They were, perhaps, revengeful phantoms of the black men who had once frequented these forests. Especially was I uneasy when passing a spot on a ridge-top in which white pipeclay contrasted with the sombre colour of the trees . . . [8]

Half a century earlier, the visiting writer William Howitt (Alfred Howitt's father) had reflected on the fantasies prompted by riding at night through the Black Forest near Mount Macedon. Among his imported reveries was a decidedly local one: he imagined that blackened stumps or fallen trees bleached to whiteness were 'like dark images of the natives, who have been pushed from their hereditary seats by the white man'.[9] These fantasies were echoes of frontier unease. The northern Victorian squatter, E. M. Curr, recalled how his decision to move into 'wild' country was resisted by his shepherds: 'On my men, all of them old hands, unoccupied country had a depressing effect, their ideas being that we should all be killed by the Blacks.'[10] From the very beginning, white Australians lived uneasily with the contradiction at the heart of their 'unoccupied country'.

In the Introduction I described how Bernard Smith has analysed Australian melancholy and diagnosed its historical and environmental causes. Fear and guilt arising from the violent occupation of Aboriginal land was one source, Smith argued, and moral speculations about primeval Australian nature another. In her autobiographical *My Australian Girlhood* (1902), novelist Rosa Praed tells of a conversation she had with an old shepherd:

> 'It's a queer country this Australia!', he said, 'I've wondered as I've been going along what was the beginning of it. Talk of its being new! Seems to me that it's as old as the world before Adam, and that it was just forgotten, when the Creator parcelled out man afresh, after the Flood . . . It's creepy like . . . As you walk on and on, there's a feeling comes over you that you've gone back to Genesis . . . for all you dig . . . there's no trace of man . . . no animals to speak of except kangaroos—and they're just monstrosities.'[11]

It was a common lament of Australian colonists that 'Australia lacked the human associations of a historic past; that it held man and nature in a timeless present'.[12] Settlers thought they had observed this temporal paralysis in Aboriginal culture, and some feared it held a threat for their own.

Smith has described the nineteenth-century tussle between the opposing perceptual conventions of melancholy (often associated with forests and desert) and of hope (sun and sheep).[13] He describes how, in the apparent absence of 'venerable remains of antiquity', the sunny, classical, pastoral vision came to offer an alluring parallel with the lands of antiquity. Woolly flocks and patrician pastures gave historical depth to the landscape and provided an escape from the melancholy glen and the stony desert. The 'phantoms' and 'shadows' could be chased away by the light.[14] From the 1890s until well into the twentieth century, sunshine and sheep pervaded the literary and artistic representations of Australia, eventually hardening into images of 'national heritage'. 'The rejection of the melancholy strain in our literature', warns Smith, 'led to a heartiness that was often shallow.'

Part two of this work explores that rejection, and the silences it created. Silence can take many forms: selective memory, a troubled conscience, a brazen rationalisation, denial, unconscious habit, the destruction of physical evidence or the erection of monuments.[15] These forms of history have often been overlooked because they were 'amateur', negative, unobserved, gossipy or genealogical. Aborigines and convicts were historical encumbrances to emotional possession of the continent by Europeans, and they represented the threatening influences of environment and heredity in colonial guise. This chapter explores the silences at the heart of 'empty, sunlit Australia', the lurking colonial shadows of bad blood and bad deeds.

The frontier

The euphemisms of the frontier, laconic and sharply edged, have entered the Australian language. Aborigines were 'civilised' or 'dispersed', white settlers boasted of the 'black crows' they had shot, the land itself received names—such as Murdering Creek and Slaughterhouse Gully—that more than hinted at violence.[16] These forms of language and description slip in and out of recognising the violence of the frontier. They reveal that many colonists accepted murder in their midst; but they reveal, too, their awareness that it could not be openly discussed. There were good reasons to be silent. Describing the organised shooting of Aborigines in Gippsland in the 1840s, F. J. Meyrick noted that 'these things are kept very secret as the penalty would certainly be hanging'.[17] In 1838 in New South Wales, seven white men had been executed by the government for the massacre of Aborigines at Myall Creek. The decision outraged squatters, who promptly condemned the government for hypocrisy and felt that they were now vulnerable on both sides of the frontier. Their slaughter of Aborigines did not cease; their habits of secrecy strengthened. Peter Gardner, in his study of the massacres of Aborigines in Gippsland, looks carefully at the diary of Pat Coady Buckley, the district's first squatter, and finds compelling evidence of censorship, partly contemporary, partly retrospective.[18] Even those who were appalled by what was happening found themselves forced into impotence and silence. Meyrick commented in 1846: 'If I could remedy these things I would speak loudly though it cost me all I am worth in the world, but as I cannot I will keep aloof and know nothing and say nothing.'[19]

There were indeed many troubled consciences on the frontier, people who were shocked by what others had done and fearful of what they might do themselves. Niel Black, a squatter in Victoria's western district, privately agonised over the murderous necessities of his new life, and carefully took up a run well within the frontier.[20] 'Rolf Boldrewood' (T. A. Browne), also a western district squatter in the 1840s, wrote of his experiences with an arch and sometimes bitter humour. With a mixture of confession and coyness, he played with his own past as if unsure of how much he could admit to his audience, or even to himself.[21] Those who had most to tell of the other side of the frontier found that they could not: the 'Wild White Man', William Buckley, became a powerful well of silence in early Port Phillip. George Arden commented that 'his extreme reserve renders it almost impossible to learn anything from him of his past life, or of his acquaintance with the aborigines'. Many regarded him as 'stupid', not just because he did not try to civilise the blacks during his long residence with them, but because he would not speak of the thirty years past.[22]

But it would be wrong to suggest that the realities of frontier life need to be divined from reluctant sources. The destruction of Aboriginal culture underpinned much colonial history-making. Social Darwinism was gaining currency about the time of the first rash of Australian centennial and jubilee celebrations, and most historical writings of this period reflect the belief that Aboriginal decline was inevitable and necessary. Although Darwinist theories allowed more open discussion of death on the frontier, the reasons and responsibilities for the death were further veiled. Alexander Sutherland, author of *The Origin and Growth of the Moral Instinct* (1898), was also a historian of Victoria. In 1888, he looked back and explained that the decline of the Aborigine was 'less a case of dying off than of failing to be born': 'mankind, as a race, cannot choose to act solely as moral beings. They are governed by animal laws which urge them blindly forward upon tracks they scarce can choose for themselves.'[23] Colonisation could be seen as a 'distinct step in human progress' involving the sacrifice 'of a few thousands of an inferior race.'[24] In 1907, J. S. Dunnett claimed that evolution was sending both Aborigines and native fauna 'hopelessly on towards the gulf of extinction.'[25]

This 'ethic of conquest', together with the imperial orientation of most colonial historians, structured historical narratives in a way that virtually banished the Aborigine.[26] Australia was frequently described as an unoccupied wasteland. 'Once upon a time,' began one 1939 potted history, 'there was a continent for the taking and no one cared to take it.'[27] This book's chapter titles betrayed the author's gentle contempt for a land without tradition. Chapter One, entitled 'Ancient History', recited the exploits of European explorers. Chapter Two, 'The Middle Ages', told of the early governors; and the next, 'The Renaissance', recalled Macquarie. The author played with the theory that 'Australia was formed by a meteor dropping from the sky. It was this impact, so the theory goes, which threw the earth's axis out of the perpendicular.'[28] The timeless land was, quite literally, out of this world.

The Aborigines capitulated, so many of these histories said. They faded away in the face of cosmic laws. Australia's 'pastures of peace' had been prepared for nothing other than the munch of sheep.[29] David Blair's *History of Australasia* (1878) argued that Australia offered a 'happy contrast' to the colonisation of the Americas and Africa, for 'no grander victory of Peace has this world ever witnessed than the acquisition of Australasia by the British nation'.[30] In the 1880s, Percy Russell described Australia as 'the only nation from the womb of Peace'.[31] The violence in their midst might never have happened. Henry Reynolds, writing of this period, has observed the dominant historical image used by colonists of 'drawing a curtain' over the past.[32] Darwinist theories did indeed draw a veil over the emotions; Sutherland wrote of the triumph of intellect over feeling.[33] Earlier historians had felt more able to speak of the brutality and familiarity of contact.[34] But the explanatory notions of social Darwinism made it difficult for colonists to recall the racial intimacy of the frontier, a world where white and black knew one another by name, borrowed traditions and skills, learnt and taught as well as fought. It was difficult to parade the evidence of Aboriginal tenacity, sophistication and land management, or to admit the depth of European fear as well as puzzlement. Many colonists knew all this and the sources show it, but it was not the job of historians to display it.

Silence, then, did not always take the forms of intentional or anguished suppression, or of philosophical resignation. It was very often an unconscious reflex, an unobserved accretion of silence. W. E. H. Stanner, a sensitive observer of Aboriginal culture and a champion of black rights, came to see these patterns of silence in his own past. In 1968, he turned back to the reports he had written on Aboriginal life in the Northern Territory thirty-six years earlier, and examined them for evidence of what he called 'forgetfulness'. He found that he had indeed unconsciously veiled the harsher realities of the life he had observed:

> Somehow, in them, I seem to have managed to draw a screen over at least the worst things of that frontier. There is no obvious sign of trying to put a good face on things; no indication of saving the eyes and ears of those to whom I was reporting; no palpable effort to write, as it were, for history; but on the other hand a very interesting absence of declamation.[35]

The reticence he noticed in his own habits of report-writing provided Stanner with particularly strong evidence of the workings of the Great Australian Silence.

Such patterns of thinking had evolved partly because colonists had no metaphors to help them describe the particular realities of this strange frontier. It was a frustration to many of them that the constant tension and sporadic conflict did not fit their image of a war, although they often used that term. Their experience was not of public violence against a respected foe, but more frequently a drama of betrayal, fear and disdain.[36] A proper war would have dignified their violence, brought it out in the open and allowed them the romance of heroes and campaigns. But the European discoverers of Australia had considered it to be *terra nullius*, a land whose inhabitants were in a state of nature, where the land was not cultivated or enclosed, and where there was no pre-existing state or legal system.[37] Australia was legally defined as a peacefully annexed colony rather than one that had been conquered; the Aborigines were British citizens and not recognised as a sovereign people.[38] John Batman's 1835 treaty with the Aborigines of Port Phillip was unusual in its symbolic recognition of prior ownership.[39]

Writers like Rolf Boldrewood tried to bring the theatrical glamour of overseas frontiers to the uneasy violence of their own. One of Boldrewood's fictional characters found what he wanted in the Maoris:

> In addition to such country for grass and roots as I never dreamt of it, to think of there being every probability of a war! A real war! It reminds me of the 'Last of the Mohicans', and all the joys of youth. We shall have 'Hawkeye', 'Uncas', and 'Chingachgook' turning up before we know where we are.[40]

It was Boldrewood, whose squatting run was on the lower Eumeralla in Victoria's western district, who made famous the sudden 1842 surge of conflict in his district called 'the Eumeralla War'.[41] H. G. Turner, in his history of Victoria, referred wistfully to 'the wars which our American cousins waged for two hundred years against the brave and crafty redskins', and to 'the storming by British troops of the native Pahs in New Zealand'. 'The early annals of Victoria', he lamented, 'embrace no pictures of campaigns.'[42]

The historian Jan Critchett, writing recently about the far western district of Victoria in the 1830s and 1840s, the setting and period of 'the Eumeralla War', explains that the frontier was local, shifting and inescapable. It was not a linear frontier, and the enemy was not on the other side of neutral ground; the disputed area was 'the very land each settler lived upon'. At the Winters' pastoral holding, Aborigines were encouraged to gather at the home station, but a large swivel gun was mounted ready for use. 'The "other side of the frontier"', argues Critchett, 'was just down the yard or as close as the bed shared with an Aboriginal woman.'[43] The violence on this 'frontier' was often domestic violence. Lieutenant-Governor La Trobe articulated the difference of this colonial frontier. In 1842, he wrote to the embattled settlers of the Port Fairy District of their difficult circumstances, reminding them that they lacked 'a well-defined frontier or neutral ground'. 'Here', he observed, 'there is not even such a line; the savage tribes are not only upon our borders, but intermingled with us in every part of this wide district.'[44]

The intermingling was due to the fact that Aborigines had a very different sense of land, social organisation and warfare.[45] They did not talk of 'land' but of their 'country', precise areas to which clans were attached. They did not want to leave their country even when Europeans took it from them. Many resisted or avoided the compulsory dislocations to mission stations. Jacky White, who was forced to move just a few miles to the Lake Condah Aboriginal Station, wrote to his former employer, Samuel Winter:

> if you will write to the government for us, and get us off here, I will do work for you and will never leave you . . . I always wish . . . to be in my country, where I was born . . . This country don't suit me I'm a stranger in this country I like to be in my country.[46]

The powerful attachment that Aboriginal people felt to particular parts of the country that they did not want to leave determined the 'inside' nature of their resistance to invaders. It also meant that land and property were rarely the sources of conflict in Aboriginal society. Violence was used for administering personal and social justice, and often in rivalry over women, and it seems that most Aboriginal attacks on Europeans were also for these reasons rather than over land itself. Nevertheless, Aboriginal violence of this kind sometimes significantly delayed the sustained occupation of land by Europeans.

The military flavour of Van Diemen's Land's 'Black War' was Australia's nearest equivalent to the colonial experience of other countries. It was the romance suggested by that event which first drew the newly arrived James Bonwick to the writing of colonial history.[47] And the popularity with settlers of that title, 'Black War', suggests that it enabled many to make sense of the frontier.[48] John West, in his *History of Tasmania* (1852), wryly commented on the 'curious mixture of martial ardour and civil pertinacity' that surrounded the organisation of the Black Line and its 'mimicry of war':

> Thus, like the warriors of the heroic age, they debated before they armed. . . . More busy civilians were anxious to the formality in incorporation, and the gradations of command. The townspeople were allowed their choice, between more active service and garrison duties. 'Gentlemen,' said an old

soldier, 'you may call yourselves marshals, generals, and colonels, but the duties assigned you are usually performed by a corporal's guard.'[49]

An earlier historian of this event, Henry Melville, observed that, '[d]uring the advance of the lines, the despatches received and sent equalled those forwarded by the allied armies during the last European war—in fact everything was carried on as if it were a great war in miniature.'[50] But the language and rituals of war, bestowed with great public enthusiasm on the Black Line and other colonial frontiers, soon became inappropriate as the detached resignation of the late nineteenth century took over.

Modern historians seeking to recognise the tenacity of Aboriginal resistance have had to be careful about using the notion of 'war'. 'Massacre history', as Bob Reece has argued, is white history. Aboriginal stories about Myall Creek tell of those blacks who escaped the violence, or of those who outwitted the whites.[51] Henry Reynolds has explicitly contrasted the forgotten Aboriginal dead with the revered fallen white warrior of Australia's overseas wars. 'All over the continent,' he argues, 'Aborigines bled as profusely and died as bravely as white soldiers in Australia's twentieth-century wars. . . . [But] do we make room for the Aboriginal dead on our memorials, cenotaphs, boards of honour and even in the pantheon of national heroes?'[52] It is a telling but problematic parallel. They are the words of a historian whose pioneering scholarship has employed the notion of a clearly defined frontier.[53]

Forms of commemoration, even where they have been sympathetic to the Aborigines or angry about their suffering, have served mostly to reinforce a sense of inevitability about what happened, and a misleading sharpness to the notion of frontier. History has memorialised those Aborigines who crossed 'the boundary' and accepted European terms, or those who, like Derrimut, 'betrayed' his people in 1835 by warning the vulnerable Port Phillip settlement of impending attack. And a rash of monuments commemorated the 'last of a tribe'. Like the funeral rituals lavished on the 'last Tasmanian Aborigines', these memorials represented a mixture of reverence, shame and comfort for Europeans.

Aboriginal elders were depicted as 'kings' and 'queens', emblematic of their race, and much was made of the loneliness of their deaths.[54] Newspapers wrote of 'the extinction of another native tribe' and recounted the statistics of population decline.[55] The 'last' local Aborigine was often given the status, through Christian burial, of an honorary white, almost as a symbol of the succession of races. When a memorial to the Aboriginal woman Agnes Edwards or 'Queen Aggie' was unveiled at Swan Hill in 1930, the local Victorian member of parliament, Frank Old, explained that the memorial would:

impress the rest of the aboriginals of the district of the fact that their race was thought of, and had its place in honor and historically would be remembered under such memorials by the white people's generations to follow after the aboriginal races and tribes had passed away, as the late Agnes Edwards, their queen, had done.[56]

Mr E. A. Gagen, president of the local branch of the Australian Natives Association which had erected the memorial, explained that since Australia 'at present is not rich in historical spots', the ANA was 'taking advantage of every opportunity that offers' to remedy the situation. He spoke of the Aborigines as a 'last remnant . . . giving way to higher civilisation'. The monument therefore designated a frontier, a clear divide between an Aboriginal past and a white Australian future. Agnes Edwards, however, had a much more pragmatic sense of the continuity and mutual accommodation of frontier life. When she was questioned about the loss of a fowl that was noticed after her visit to a nearby station, she replied: 'Ah well, Mr Laird, you binna taka my country, I taka your fowl.'[57]

These memorials probably entered local white consciousness as 'historic sites', monuments to white philanthropy, and as milestones of progress. They could be seen as visible evidence of the benevolence and sympathy of a people who had 'smoothed the dying pillow', and who had mourned the inevitable decline of another race.[58] They were like the photographs that became the cornerstone of many a local historical society collection. These featured the last of the local tribe—not an anonymous black but a personality with a name, Warrnambool's 'Wilmot' or 'Camperdown George', his dark skin cloaked in European cast-offs. Camped on the edge of town, named, adorned, and obviously much photographed, the apparent benign hopelessness of these people was a precursor of the monuments eventually erected to them.[59]

Sometimes, though, the memorials were raised in anger. James Dawson, an ardent fighter for the Aborigines of western Victoria, initiated in 1884 the erection of a memorial to the last of local clans in the Camperdown district.[60] Dawson was a farmer, collector, amateur taxidermist, and protector and friend of Aborigines. He came to Victoria from Scotland in 1840, bought a small property on the Yarra and then took up a cattle-run near Port Fairy in 1844. In 1866 he sold his station and leased land near Camperdown, where he remained until his death in 1900 aged 93. His western district ethnography, *Australian Aborigines*, was published in 1881. His only child, Isabella Park Dawson, was herself a champion of the Aborigines and became proficient in some Aboriginal languages.[61]

Wombeetch Puyuun or 'Camperdown George', known as 'the last of the local tribes', died in 1883 while Dawson was visiting Scotland and was buried in a boggy swamp outside the cemetery area assigned to white people. Dawson returned to Australia and, in anger and grief, transferred 'with [his] own hands' the remains of Wombeetch Puyuun to a central ornamental plot in the cemetery marked by a twenty-foot obelisk he commissioned. It bore engravings of a boomerang, club and message-stick and the dates 1840 and 1883 which, Dawson explained, signified the period of 'the extinction (extirpation would be a more appropriate term) of the local Aborigines'.[62] As well as an inscription honouring Wombeetch Puyuun, the obelisk carried the words: 'In Memory of the Aborigines of this district'.

Dawson demanded local contributions to his memorial fund, and embarrassed those who refused to be a part of it. He was not backward in unleashing his own memories of white violence and murder.[63] When the editor of the *Argus*, F. W. Haddon, refused to publish some of Dawson's frontier revelations, 'old Jimmy Dawson went for him with his umbrella'.[64] He sought donations from local landowners, 'all of the olden time', but received little support. In replies to his letters, local settlers of forty years revealed their unease about acknowledging dispossession. One wrote: 'I decline to assist in erecting a monument to a race of men we have robbed of their country.' Another rejected the very meaning that Dawson intended, saying that he failed to see the use of the obelisk, for it would 'point for all time to come to our treatment of this unfortunate race—the possessors of the soil we took from them'.[65]

Some early historians made similar challenges to their society, particularly before social Darwinism 'drew a curtain' across the frontier in the late nineteenth century. John West, G. W. Rusden, and James Bonwick, for example, did not shrink from describing the violence of the frontier. Bonwick was explicit in his exposure of white as well as black 'out rages'. He accused the early white settlers of 'a demoniacal propensity to torture the defenceless, and an insatiable lust, that heeded not the most pitiable appeals, nor halted in the execution of the most diabolical acts of cruelty, to obtain its brutal gratification'.[66] In the contemporary press, Bonwick was charged with 'having unjustly censured the European settlers of Tasmania'.[67]

This sense of betrayal has been echoed in recent times as further memorials to frontier conflict have been unveiled and as the direction of new scholarship has unfolded. The historiographical revolution of the 1970s and 1980s has made its way onto monuments.[68] Some believe that there is nothing to be gained by recalling white brutality; others believe that history should be celebratory and a story of progress 'for a contrary view robs life of any meaning it discloses'.[69] In a series of speeches, Hugh Morgan of the Western Mining Corporation has protested at the dragging down of heroes and has divined a radical, destabilising purpose behind the new history.[70] There are others who see a self-indulgent display of guilt at the heart of this reorientation.[71] Some have been unsettled by the challenge to European legitimacy. I visited King Island in 1979, only days after the archaeologist Rhys Jones had, on new field evidence, suggested that Aborigines had once inhabited the island. This was contrary to popular belief, and was the first indication of possible pre-European occupation.[72] The announcement left a wake of confusion among those islanders whose traditions assured them that there, at least, was one portion of Australia where the whites were first.

Victoria's 150th anniversary in 1984-5 represented an official attempt to reorient the habits of commemoration. Batman and Fawkner, whose names were literally up in lights over the Yarra in 1934, took back row seats in 1984. Henty relatives were miffed at the decline of their ancestor's role on the historical stage.[73] The state historian, Bernard Barrett, wrote and spoke about 'Victoria's 40,000th Anniversary'.[74] 'Celebration' was out; 'commemoration'—seen as a more neutral word—was in.

The History and Heritage Committee of the 150th board erected almost fifty plaques throughout Victoria. It was their aim to redress the historical imbalance by directing attention to hitherto neglected aspects of Victoria's past. About one-third of the plaques commemorated Aborigines or interracial conflict. Views on wording and subject matter were canvassed by the committee, and one group to respond was the Royal Historical Society of Victoria, a body with a long and committed tradition of local scholarship. While supporting the aim of using the plaques to balance the historical record, the society was 'concerned that many of the proposed plaques may, in fact, cause further divisions in Victorian society than presently exist'. Specific comments suggested several word changes—the use of the word 'impact' rather than the phrase 'corrupting influences', 'many centuries' instead of 'time immemorial', 'occupation' instead of 'invasion'. The society was worried by the effect of the generalised references to 'shooting or abducting' and to the introduction of 'fatal diseases'. Referring to the plaques commemorating Aborigines of the late nineteenth and early twentieth centuries, the society questioned 'the description of the subjects of these plaques as "Aborigines"' and suggested that 'a term indicative of their mixed breeding might be appropriate'. The Great Australian Silence continued to work in quiet ways.[75]

An alarming response to the new scholarship was the whisper that in parts of Australia today historical records of frontier life are being destroyed out of wariness and fear. Perhaps they are pastoral diaries which have been culled or scribbled over, perhaps they are letters burnt, or log-books slipped into bins. The threat is seen to come from the new wave of history which, many people believe, seeks to cast a condemnatory shadow over white pioneers. Descendants of the frontier dwellers are acting to defend them from this new, probing searchlight into their past. This protective manipulation of family reputations—this particular version of silence—has its clearest parallel in Australian history in the treatment of our convict origins.

The birth-stain

Attitudes to Australia's convict past have shown patterns of suppression and silence similar to those about frontier life. There was the same playing with words, the same social games of daring and avoidance. The phrase 'Botany Bay' has furnished rich imagery; 'Van Diemen's land' similarly. 'Convict' became a forbidden word in polite conversation. Colonists, often seen to be quite careless of etiquette, observed it very carefully when it came to discussion of local origins. One did not ask about background or parentage. Perhaps it was a reflex of egalitarianism, a positive assertion of talent and potential above inheritance and class. But there were enough family trees with missing branches, enough altered dates of birth and sufficient coyness about origins, for observers to realise that there was something there to be forgotten. Social life, forever publicly edging around a silence, spent a great deal of effort in privately exploring it. 'Nowhere are all particulars and incidents of persons past lives more minutely and rigidly canvassed', observed one newcomer to Van Diemen's land in the 1840s.[76]

Tight lips, however, characterised public treatments of the past. Although 'pioneers' populated Victorian and South Australian civic commemorations from quite early times, the embarrassment of New South Wales' origins caused a delay in the use of the term there. Where Victorian pioneer and old colonist associations were apt to be boastful about who was the first, in New South Wales there were problems about remembering the earliest arrivals.[77] Histories skipped straight to the pastoral era, or convicts were represented as incidental.[78] In the 1920s, members of the Western Australian Historical Society suppressed some recently discovered letters to a convict because, they argued, their state 'was founded as a free colony by gentlefolk: the convicts came later and unwanted, and should not be associated with it'.[79] Historical records were culled, even by government order. James Bonwick, that indefatigable recorder who took upon himself vast transcriptions of early Australian documents, was alert to gaps in the record. A consternated Tasmanian government expressed worry about what he might find. Bonwick discovered 'the total absence of long periods of official matter', and he cited the popular explanation that 'when Governor Collins suddenly expired in his chair, in 1810, two armed marines were stationed outside at the room-door while certain gentlemen were busily engaged in the destruction of documents'. This was 'possibly for private reasons', Bonwick suggested helpfully.[80] And even he, in compiling his transcriptions, omitted the names of transportees, 'save where needful'.[81]

The destruction of the material evidence of convict days—not just to protect reputations but out of sheer horror and distaste—was a graphic illustration of just how unbearable colonists found the past. The chief justice of Tasmania campaigned at the turn of the century for the destruction of all convict relics because they were visible reminders of shame and of a tainted past.[82] Others destroyed unofficially and for different motives. Richard Flanagan, in his history of Tasmania's Gordon River country, tells two stories about the penal buildings on Sarah Island in Macquarie Harbour. Tourist brochures and local histories say that they were dismantled for want of building materials at nearby ports. Folklore, however, suggests that the hated buildings were blown up in the 1890s by locals who despised them as memorials to cruelty and servitude.[83] When fire ravaged the Port Arthur penal settlement in 1897, there was some doubt whether it was intentional, an accident, or simply divine vengeance; but there were few who did not welcome it as a purifier.[84] Like the pyres lit at Aboriginal massacre sites throughout Australia, the clean flame was seen to erase past iniquities.

In the latter part of the nineteenth century, scientific beliefs about race, blood and genetic inheritance gave the narrow, moral concerns of family history a role in the making of national history. The same Darwinism that comforted colonists about the destruction of the Aborigines created dark suggestions in their minds about the consequences of their own convict beginnings. Perhaps the birth-stain was no mere issue of morality, but an actual physical inheritance? As recently as 1973, Peter Bolger wrote a history of Hobart Town that set out to disprove the 'long persisting and irrational fear that there could be genetic weakness passed down through the generations from an early convict ancestor'.[85] Although the British had proven themselves the fittest race through their colonisation of the world's 'open spaces', the quality of Australia's particular stock was under a shadow. In addition there were worries about the effects of a tropical climate, and about the doubtful consequences of inhabiting a continent whose insects, animals and Aborigines were all seen to be of the lowest forms.[86] As, indeed, were the convicts.

James Bonwick wrote in 1858 of his attitude to 'old hands', a common euphemism for convicts. He described them as a race apart—instantly recognisable because of their different features, mannerisms and speech. 'They are', he said, 'allied to departing tribes. . . . They will no more advance with progressive civilization than the blanketed Aborigine. Like the men of the woods they are rapidly dying off. A new and another race are elbowing them off the stage.' Like the Aborigines, 'old hands' were seen by Bonwick as nomadic and child-like.[87] And with their decline as certain as that of the Aborigines, the 'old hand', like the 'last of a tribe', could be indulged and pitied. The forms of explanation which had isolated the Aborigine were turned also on the convict.

Political action sought to translate these private urges of expiation and banishment into publicly symbolic actions. John Hirst, in his *Convict Society and its Enemies* (1983), has argued strongly that the anti-transportation movement was partly of this nature, and that our image of the convict system has been shaped by those who sought to get rid of it.[88] For some colonists, the exaggerated legend of convict suffering and official oppression expressed, but also justified, their embarrassment and shame; it was also a means of bringing about the system's end; and it distanced something uncomfortably in their midst.[89] In their quest for a new beginning free of the convict taint, colonists turned away from the continuity of their history, and suppressed the sense of Australian identity that had grown up among currency lads and lasses of earlier times.[90] In the same way, the sharing between Aboriginal and European on the early frontier was denied by those later histories that were written to demonstrate imperial triumph and the impersonal progress of natural laws.[91]

Another form of neutralising the past was the constant yearning for sacrifice, for the cleansing experience of fire on a national scale. Ken Inglis has portrayed this extraordinary characteristic of Australian history and prophecy, this willing-on of a nation to a consummation in conflict.[92] Colonists wanted to be tested; they wanted absolute evidence of their genetic quality. This burden of proof was regularly placed on sporting competitions with Britain, which reflected what was described as 'an unfilial yearning on the part of young Australia to triumphantly thrash the mother country'. Victoria even overlooked colonial rivalries to rejoice in New South Wales' victories in cricket, shooting and racing, because they provided 'an emphatic refutation of the theory, that there is a tendency to decay among the descendants of the early colonists'.[93]

But the ultimate test, they believed, would come in military conflict. The sons of convicts were prominent in support of the 1885 Sudan contingent.[94] The first world war was acknowledged quite openly as a test of race. Paul Staal, an ex-consul-general for the Netherlands in

Sydney, wrote in 1936 about Australians' sensitivity to 'the stain . . . on [their] birth certificate'. He no longer considered these concerns to be important for, as he put it, 'during the Great War—that crucial test of character—the new nation proved to be second to none, when it came to defending the honour of the Empire.'[95] As C. E. W. Bean's histories showed, it was indeed 'character' as well as physical prowess that had been under test in the trials of conflict.

The irony in this view of history was that it depended on denying the violence of European occupation. The myth-makers characterised Australia's history as tranquil. Yet there was always an air of unease about this portrait of 'the Quiet Continent', and not just because of its shaky factual basis.[96] It was that peace did not constitute history. A nation allegedly settled without bloodshed was a continent without history. Their birth-stains made many colonists turn away from what brief past their society had, and it isolated them from the long pre-European past. They were therefore constantly looking forward, straining after conflict, trial, sacrifice—after a proper history of which people could be proud.[97] When miners shed blood in defence of liberty at Ballarat in 1854, digger spokesman J. D. Owens declared that it was a 'proud day for Victoria . . . the beginning of the history of the colony'.[98] When a New South Wales contingent was sent to the Sudan in 1885, Victorian Premier James Service echoed earlier rhetoric when he declared that the gesture had 'precipitated Australia in one short week from a geographical expression into a nation'.[99] When Australian soldiers died in battle at Gallipoli in 1915, a director of Education, Peter Board, announced that 'on 25th April history and Australian history were fused, and fused at a white heat'.[100] To have achieved history—and a form of history that could be properly commemorated—was at the same time to have shed the uncomfortable burdens of that other past.

From a western hilltop

In the mid-1880s, a journalist and writer, Donald Macdonald, climbed to the top of Mount Leura near Camperdown in Victoria's western district. He was an early practitioner of the nature essay in Australia, consciously applying the literary tradition of the British naturalist Richard Jefferies to the landscapes of his own country. His descriptions, like those of Charles Barrett who followed in his footsteps, sought to evoke the human as well as natural dimensions of the land. A persistent theme of these nature essayists was the search for a lost pastoral haven; their aspirations were spiritual as much as scientific. Macdonald's own perspective on the land was decidedly social. He had already established himself as a pioneering sports reporter, and he was one of the first to speak of 'test matches' in his coverage of cricket. Later he was sent by the *Argus* as the earliest of Australian war correspondents at the South African War. His life was to be involved in the myth-making experiences of an 'emerging nation'.[101]

From Mount Leura, he surveyed the western plains. It was a landscape now virtually cleared of Aborigines. A few years before, James Dawson's monument had been erected at the foot of the hill. The way was open for the imprint of the new European landscape traditions that Macdonald would help to create. Some of the new sense of freedom felt by late nineteenth-century Europeans in the bush came from the knowledge that the Aborigines had been removed from it. Only the Norfolk Island pine, in its grim reminder of convict days, marred the Victorian vista.[102]

As Macdonald surveyed the scene below him, it was the destruction of the Aboriginal people that came to his mind. He mourned their passing. Macdonald's forebears, like many on the pastoral frontier, had lived closely with them. His great-aunt had spoken only an Aboriginal language until she was five.[103] He did not hide the violence of the frontier. 'The reason we know so little about these aborigines', he wrote, 'is that instead of studying we shot them.' He remembered tales of the poisonings, 'the use of arsenic instead of salt for seasoning', their callous murder as if they had been wild dogs. By 1905, Macdonald had a smoother rationalisation for their disappearance. In a summary of Australian life for overseas travellers and prospective immigrants, Macdonald confronted the 'old world delusion' of 'the fear of being attacked by wild blacks'. 'In most of the States the native races are extinct', he reassured his readers. 'The Australian, unlike the African, could not stand civilisation.'[104] Macdonald's lyrical view of nature made him sensitive to the culture of the Aborigines, yet his writing was founded on concepts of race and empire which condemned them. Sitting on the hill, he reflected sensitively about the way the Aborigines had used the land and he conjured romantic images of their occupation of these plains.

Yet, as he looked, another vision arose. It was of the profound and triumphant peace of this land. These plains, he wrote, 'have been furrowed with a ploughshare only, and no roaring cannon shot has ever burst the glebe. The song that the rain sings here is "I come to wash away no stain upon your wasted lea".' 'May that hymn of peace never alter', he prayed. Yet he knew that when the time came for Australia's connection with this land to be consummated in blood, 'Australians will fight as valiantly and fall as worthily as ever the old-world soldiers did in defending home.' And Macdonald knew that, in this hour of need, it would be from 'out here in the West', where there is 'a patriotism born of Nature's grandeur', that the stoutest defenders would come.[105]

Macdonald's vision from the hilltop found nothing uncomfortable in bringing together these two strands of history-making: one which strangely suppressed the implications of Aboriginal destruction, and the other which, to exorcise a dubious past, was perversely straining after conflict and sacrifice of another kind.

CHAPTER SIX

'The Natural History of Melbourne'

In *The Natural History of Selborne*, Gilbert White constructed a detailed and intimate view of his local world which has fascinated readers for two centuries. Published in 1789, it was a collection of letters describing the wildlife, seasons and antiquities of White's secluded Hampshire parish. Its emotional empathy, and its dependence on years of field observation within a small familiar territory, made it unusual at a time when scientists were straining towards idealised classifications and divisions of the natural world. White's intimate focus allowed him to see the relationships between living creatures, and between a place and its inhabitants, humans included. His work has been described as 'the first book to link the worlds of nature and the village'.[1] Its emotional dimensions rarely diminished its scientific accuracy; indeed, they were the source of its originality.

Selborne became as much a symbol of sentiment as of science. As urban and industrial growth gathered momentum throughout the nineteenth century, the peaceful, cyclical world of the parson-naturalist seemed like a lost Arcadia. By 1850, James Russell Lowell, the American writer and ambassador to England, described White's book as 'the journal of Adam in Paradise'.[2] Later in the century, the American nature writer, John Burroughs, visited Selborne and found quintessential England, an 'island coziness and unity' where all is 'one neighbourhood'.[3] Reverence for Selborne expressed a powerful yearning for community, for 'the English way of life' which many felt was increasingly under threat.[4] White's work became the fourth most republished book in the English language, and his life was dressed in legend. As Richard Mabey has shown, the parson-naturalist was not altogether a naive and retiring country man, nor was his book quite the spontaneous and unconscious uttering some have suggested.[5] Selborne matured over several decades as a literary achievement, and many of the qualities which made it radical were deliberately refined. White's wanderings in the hollow lanes of Hampshire were not altogether isolated from the literary and scientific conversations of his time.

One of his many literary links, albeit a slim one, was with Joseph Banks, fellow of the Royal Society. When White unsuccessfully invited

him to visit Selborne in March 1768, Banks was on the eve of his voyage
to the Pacific in the *Endeavour* with Captain James Cook. White, a
specialist on migrant birds who always felt the tug of their autumn
departure, felt a similar awe at the distant exploits of Joseph Banks. It
was natural for a man who suffered from 'coach sickness' when travelling
between counties to admire the resolution and 'contempt of dangers' of
a circumnavigator of the globe.[6] As Banks strode around the shores of
Botany Bay excitedly recording new species, White patrolled his parish
noting the comforting recurrence of old.

The two naturalists can be seen to represent contrasting visions of
nature. Banks was beginning the sort of natural history description that
would dominate in Australia for the next century and that he, as an
indulgent patron of science, would help direct. It centred on the work
of the collector and was generated by a wide-eyed thirst for the exotic.
The frontier was vast, the tasks of cataloguing, dissection and description
seemed unending. It was a colonial science, looking to England for
direction and interpretation. Work in the field was to be unreflective and
dispassionate, a lens for distant eyes.

The Natural History of Selborne was frequently slipped into colonial
baggage, as a portable distillation of 'home'. The affectionate empathy,
the sense of place, and the human associations of Gilbert White's
form of description would take longer to develop in the European
vision of Australia. All the comforting motifs of intimacy, tradition and
familiarity seemed absent in a new and alien land. Australian writers
inspired by Selborne faced the challenge of finding, or creating, local
symbols of sentiment. Blackberries could be imported as easily as
books. But indigenous nature and landscapes required original and
intimate readings to reconcile the immigrant. Donald Macdonald
(1859?-1932) and Charles Barrett (1879-1959) were leaders in this
quest. These Australian nature writers have received little scholarly
attention. Their romanticism has made them marginal to the history of
science, and their practical, descriptive orientation has placed them
outside the study of literature and culture. Yet their commitment to
ephemeral, widely distributed forms of art—the newspaper column
and essay—ensured that they were to profoundly influence the popular
perception of local landscape. And their work, like White's, became
entwined in debates about the definition and defence of a national
way of life.

In this chapter, I first introduce Macdonald's distinctive voice, which
emerged in the 1880s, then look at Barrett's evocation of Selborne in his
discovery of local nature in the early 1900s, and at his role as a
populariser at a time of growing professionalism in science. The second
half of the chapter addresses the broader social message of the nature

writers: their experience of war, their part in providing a moral literature for 'boys', and their efforts to define a heritage of place.

Village and farm

Keilor—now swallowed by the city of Melbourne—was, in the second half of the nineteenth century, a distinct agricultural community of about six hundred inhabitants. It nestled in the Maribyrnong River gorge, amidst the lava plain that stretched south-east to the city. It was here that Donald Macdonald grew up in the 1860s and 1870s, and it was the rural charm of Keilor that featured in one of his early nature essays for the Melbourne *Argus*. 'Village and Farm' was first published in the early 1880s and it sets out many of the themes that Macdonald was later to explore.

'My village', he wrote, 'is set deep in a hollow of the plain.'[7] The hills around it seem 'like a barrier shutting it in from the rest of the world'. The nearby city could be viewed from the tableland above, the clouds of smoke, the masts of shipping—one could even feel the throb of its factories—but the valley below was protected and enclosed. 'It is a peaceful place.'

The village harbours 'strange colonial experiences'. Some of its inhabitants are the gold-diggers of thirty years before, and perhaps recall passing through this village when it lay across the newly forged path to Bendigo. Nature, now, is as cosmopolitan and imported as the villagers themselves. Introduced trees abound, the gum trees are thinned out, the emu has been replaced by the hare, kangaroos by rabbits, and swans by 'highly civilised geese'. It was a different world 'before the sparrows came'.

Macdonald describes the community's rhythms and rituals—the idle gossiping, the reverent hush that marks a death, the political centre that is the blacksmith's bench. And, of course, 'the village possesses a tragedy', a tale of murder and intrigue by the banks of the creek—a story suppressed but shared, the true measure of community. But it is the rhythms of rural labour which enfold village life: the 'periodical awakening at harvest time', the arrival of a migrant labour population, men who, like nature, work in predictable cycles. And there is cattle-branding time, when the grazing plains above the village are regularly fought over by local herdsmen and cattle dealers from the city.

It is in the wheat field that Macdonald finds 'an illustration in miniature of the birth, progress and destruction of a world every summer'. As the wheat is fostered by the hand of man, there grows up within it a half-independent natural world. Hares nibble the young blades of wheat and grow up and shelter in the crop, often just old enough to escape as reaping begins. Grubs and slugs enter the field from the river side, and frogs and mice follow. They, in turn, are sought by snakes. As the summer advances, the quail retreat from the burnt-out plains and come to the wheat until nesting season. Hawks 'soon discover that the field is a splendid hunting-ground'. The harvest violently carves up this brief-lived community, but it is also instrumental. Slow young hares are shredded by the cutting blades, and quail's eggs are exposed to predators. The mice are taken away with the sheaves and the kestrels follow them to the stack-yards where both live through the winter, the tiny natural hierarchy transported from field to store.

Macdonald portrays a world where nature and the village appear as one, both largely transported from another world yet quick to establish old-time rhythms, and utterly interdependent. It is a wholesome, peaceful, cyclical world. Although there are serious political discussions at the blacksmith's bench, '[t]he subtleties of lobby politics or corner complications that so interest the journalist, and are gossip for the city man, rarely penetrate to Arcadia'. The farmers, in spite of occasional seasonal hardships, are happy. And they are the strongest source of imperial fervour, of loyalty to distant England. The country, Macdonald suggests is a source of wisdom: 'Nature's better part is often hidden in remote corners, her gems in almost inaccessible places. The most beautiful heaths in Australia grow on steepest ridges of the Grampians. So about farms healthy sentiments cling, I think.' He welcomes 'suggestions of the old world'. He looks for the signs of settlement and use, pleased to observe where the raw edge of pioneering days has been softened: the ivy-clad homes, the old-fashioned gardens, the hedge of hawthorn that hides 'the ugliness of post and rail'. In new settlements, the necks of the cattle are blackened by constant friction with charcoal tree stumps; here 'they are spotless' and 'are as ornamental as deer in an English park'. Although Macdonald is not blind to the delights of indigenous nature, he is gladdened by the luxuriance of the blackberry and the spread of the blackbird, thrush and starling, these reminders of home.

Macdonald's rural idyll has a note of nostalgia and regret. He observes with concern that as traditions are established in this new land, they are quickly swept away:

Can anything be old in this new country? From an antiquary's point of view, perhaps not. But a life-time is a long time. No memories can be older, and it is memory that makes this little old-fashioned village the dearest in the land . . .

But these human associations are constantly undermined. Writing in the 1880s, he laments the assaults on the pastoral world. He observes that '[i]f there had been less gold in Australia, the love of the land would be more the traditional affection of the British yeoman for the soil than what it is.' He thinks fondly of 'those old settled districts, where homesteads carry the traditions of more than one generation'. He contrasts them not only with goldfields where '[t]o-day the prospector's wand is waved above a lonely gully; to-morrow it is peopled; in a week deserted', but also with the recently settled selection areas of Victoria, 'those mushroom towns of the north'. This spirit of change, he observes, has become almost a national trait. Even the sacred cycle of the wheat field has suffered three eras in Australia's brief history—the change from sickle, cradle and flail to the reaping machine still with its human train, to the complete stripper, reaper and binder. It has, Macdonald concludes, taken 'all the poetry out of field labour and harvest time'. The new traditions, once established, are quickly swept away, and the village seems again like the community of the wheat field, which is renewed every summer.

Nature notes and queries

Macdonald was only in his mid-twenties when he wrote with such mature nostalgia of his boyhood home. His family had strong links with Victoria's pastoral beginnings. His mother, Margaret Harris, had been born on an isolated station on Victoria's western plains, and his father, Daniel, had emigrated from Canada and, in the late 1830s, worked for the Learmonth brothers at Ercildoune, west of Ballarat. Donald's mother died in the early 1860s, and he and his younger brother Jim were sent to live with an aunt in the little town of Keilor. Here they spent their youth swimming and eel fishing in the pools of Deep Creek. After a short time as a local pupil-teacher, and a period as a country journalist with the *Corowa Free Press*, Macdonald joined the *Argus* in 1881.[8] He was a tall, strongly built man, full of vitality and a fine sportsman, and he brought to the city an unmistakable country manner. He was quickly recognised as a talented writer by his colleagues and was later acclaimed by one of his editors as 'the greatest find' the Melbourne press ever had.[9] His first innovation came when he reported a cricket match between New South Wales and Victoria at the Melbourne Cricket Ground. Macdonald went beyond the usual progressive account of play and offered evocative and reflective summaries of the day's heroes and highlights. His new style revolutionised cricket reporting.[10] His cricket columns under the pseudonym 'Observer' became famous, and for fifty years he reported 'Test' matches in England and Australia.

Cricket and country writing—both versions of the pastoral—were traditionally overlapping domains in English letters. It was in the early 1880s that Macdonald began publishing his nature reflections and sketches of country life in the *Argus* and its weekly counterpart, the *Australasian*. He was inspired by Richard Jefferies (1848–87), the English country writer whose brief and intense career was ending as Macdonald's began, and whose book, *The Gamekeeper at Home* (1878), had fallen into young Donald's hands.[11] '[T]hings grow old so soon in the fields' wrote Jefferies reassuringly of the new agriculture in England, and Macdonald also looked to nature to soften the raw edges of colonial society.[12] Both men were versatile journalists, living in the city and writing of the country of their youth. Macdonald soon earned the title of 'Australia's finest nature writer', and was often compared with Jefferies.

Others in Melbourne, such as John Stanley James ('The Vagabond'), Francis Myers ('Telemachus') and Baldwin Spencer and T. S. Hall ('Physicus'), also began writing on nature, the countryside and popular science at this time. Melbourne's rapid growth in the final decades of the century meant that the city-dweller's recreational interests in the countryside began to affect the interpretation of Australian nature. City people developed a periodic, and often nostalgic, relationship to the bush, and saw it as a place of solace and escape.[13] The Field Naturalists' Club of Victoria was formed in 1880, and its members were chiefly Melbourne office-workers whose excursions took them just beyond the city fringe. The *Bulletin* writers and the Heidelberg painters were mostly city-dwellers, and Melbourne's famous artists' camps were pitched at the end of newly built suburban railway lines.

But Macdonald's writing was not only for a city audience. At the beginning of the new century, he began a different sort of newspaper column, one which opened a fruitful dialogue with his country readers. His regular nature essays in the Saturday *Argus* drew such a flood of letters that a new feature, 'Nature Notes and Queries', was established. So popular did it become that a second column, 'Notes for Boys', was initiated, and Macdonald continued both until his death in 1932. The columns functioned like a club, and two-thirds of its 'members' were from country districts. Regional authorities contributed regularly, enthusiastic correspondents swapped addresses with each other, and vexed issues were debated over several months. Odd specimens, in various stages of decomposition, arrived on Macdonald's desk. One reader wrote from 'a mining tent', and another enquired if it was the bellbird's note that sounded like a hammer on the anvil. His correspondents were often seeking identification of their finds or sightings, but more frequently they reported the behaviour of the wildlife they observed, its relationship to humans, changes in their local environments, regional variations in names and habits, and the boundaries of their known flora, fauna, and climate. They were tentatively exploring the geographical perimeters of their knowledge.[14]

Macdonald's 'Notes' filled a need for popular literature on birds and nature, as the few available handbooks were expensive and unwieldy. But he was not just dispensing instruction, for he frequently requested it from his correspondents. He made it clear that their collective work could be scientifically significant, and sometimes he assigned particular problems of observation to his widely dispersed team. Field-work was what was needed, keen observation in the open air. Macdonald remembered his own education on the banks of Deep Creek, and his message was: 'Never accept any authority as conclusive. Try and find out for yourselves.' The frontiers of knowledge, he urged, could be advanced through a direct, watchful, sensuous engagement with nature. Such advice inspired many young naturalists. One of them was Charles Barrett.

The old bush hut

The Heidelberg artist camps at the end of the 1880s gave their name to an Australian school of impressionist painting. The informal pitching of a camp, and the easy blend of canvas and bark, expressed the painters' sympathy with the bush. Roberts, Streeton, Conder and others were soon heralded as the pioneers of a fresh, more naturalistic vision of the Australian landscape. Their early camps symbolised their commitment to painting *en plein air* and to capturing ephemeral moments of light and colour. And the camaraderie of the tents was a gesture of solidarity appropriate to a group of artists who were quick to articulate their status as a 'school'.[15]

Similar motives led three young nature-lovers to establish camp at a bush hut near Olinda Creek in the Dandenongs in the early 1900s. Their influence was far more modest but, like the Heidelberg painters, they were fugitives from the city, and they were inspired by examples from abroad. They also felt themselves to be pioneers.

Charles Barrett, Claude Kinane and Brooke Nicholls named their hut 'Walden'. But, as Barrett put it, 'Unlike our Master, we paid taxes, having no Emerson to pay them for us; and also, we welcomed visitors, which Thoreau seldom did.'[16] One frequent visitor to the Olinda Creek bush hut was Donald Macdonald. Charles Barrett first met Macdonald in the 1890s, and it was he who encouraged Barrett to write about nature, and made him feel that there was dignity and purpose in such a career.

Donald Macdonald (left) and 'The Woodlanders' at 'Walden', the old bush hut on Olinda Creek. *(Reproduced from Charles Barrett, Koonwarra, London, Oxford University Press, 1939)*

Barrett's first book, *From Range to Sea: A Bird-Lover's Ways* (1907) drew on his Olinda Creek experience as well as observations from another bush hut by the coast, near Macdonald's weekender at Black Rock. The book was dedicated to Donald Macdonald who, Barrett wrote, 'showed me the way'. Barrett's daughter recalled frequent visits in later years to 'Uncle Mac's' bush acre at Black Rock where, in the peace and warmth of a book-lined study, the two men would talk and reminisce.[17]

Their plan was to spend all their weekends and holidays there and to monitor carefully, in words and photos, the natural history of their neighbourhood. Barrett wrote in 1905 that '[w]e desired to experience that return to Nature of which so much has been written in recent years; to leave the din and dust of the great city, and dwell awhile in the forest among birds and flowers and trees.'[18] Like the Heidelberg painters, and many turn-of-the-century clubs, they gave themselves nicknames. Barrett was 'The Scribe', Kinane 'The Artist' (photographer) and Nicholls 'The Doctor' (he was a city dentist). As a group they called themselves 'The Woodlanders', thereby invoking another recorder of rural ways, Thomas Hardy.[19] Their hut, set in the midst of an old orchard near Olinda Creek and a pleasant walk from the Lilydale railway station, was a base for bird-watching, plant identification, photography, a daily notation of observations, and plenty of yarning and letter writing. Their escapade, although made intermittent by their city jobs, was given significance by their constant evocation of a tradition of nature writing and observation of which they felt a part.

Charles Barrett, as the Woodlanders' 'Scribe', wrote five articles about their adventure for the *New Idea* in 1905-6, as well as more specialist pieces for the *Victorian Naturalist* and the *Emu*. These were his first published pieces, and in his later writings 'The Bush Hut' was to become a central symbol of his beginnings as a naturalist. He was born at Hawthorn in 1879, the son of Thomas Barrett, a master builder who became a wealthy mayor of Hawthorn in the boom years of the 1880s.[20] Charles grew up in one of 'Marvellous Melbourne's' new commuter suburbs, within reach of the burgeoning city but with nature in his backyard. He remembered regular holidays in Tasmania, especially at Longford, where his father had grown up. But soon these were to stop. Thomas Barrett's finances suffered in the depression years of the early 1890s, at just the time when Charles was to embark on his secondary schooling. 'I had to renounce hopes of a brilliant career', he wrote, 'to forget the dreaming towers of Oxford . . . Hard times made a naturalist of me. There was no money for luxuries, or amusements that must be paid for. So I took to rambling in the paddocks near home . . .'[21]

The uncertainties of city speculation had robbed him of the formal scientific education after which he hankered. But the bush offered him a different education: his talent as a writer and his practical knowledge of the outdoors enabled him to carve out a career as a populariser of science. He joined the Melbourne *Herald* in 1906, a job he owed to Macdonald's influence, and wrote a nature column for thirty years. He also published over sixty books on Australian natural history, landscape, Aborigines and folklore. Like R. E. Johns, he collected stories of the bunyip.[22] He was assistant editor of *Emu*, the journal of the Royal Australian Ornithologists Union, from 1910 to 1916, and editor of the influential *Victorian Naturalist* from 1925 to 1940. He tried to straddle the diverging streams of amateur and professional science, but found himself increasingly identified as an 'amateur' at a time when the field sciences were becoming marginal. He, in turn, became critical of the 'armchair theorists' whose books exhibited 'too great an inflow of scientific theory'.[23] So the scientific world was twice denied him.

Barrett found his mentors from a different sphere. If Macdonald were his local inspiration, he drew also on models from overseas. The whole Olinda Creek scheme had been suggested by readings of Thoreau's *Walden* (1854) during long winter evenings in Melbourne. *Walden* and Izaak Walton's *The Compleat Angler* (1655) were Barrett's two favourite books. Once ensconced in their chosen valley in the Dandenongs, the three nature-lovers were quick to compare it with the 'hill, dale, woodland and water' of Gilbert White's parish of Selborne.[24] The parson-naturalist was frequently invoked in Barrett's writings, as was Richard Jefferies. Barrett wrote to the American nature writer, John Burroughs, encouraging him to visit Australia.[25] And, from the hut, he wrote also to the South American and English naturalist, W. H. Hudson, whose *Hampshire Days* and *A Naturalist in La Plata* Barrett had found captivating. To his delight, Hudson replied:

> . . . it is a rare thing to be written to from Australia . . . My only advice to you, and to any man, is that of Thoreau—'follow your own genius'. Go on finding or making opportunities as you seem to have been doing already, in having a 'Walden Hut', and probably in other ways . . . [26]

These names—Jefferies, Burroughs, Hudson and Thoreau—were among the best-selling writers of the late nineteenth century. Barrett treasured Hudson's letters—one of which, he noted, was dated from Selborne—and read them aloud to his companions beneath the bark shingles of their bush hut.

At this Australian 'Walden', the camera, like the pen, was wielded with a self-conscious, imitative air. While Barrett was treasuring letters written from Selborne, Claude Kinane was sending some of his snapshots across the seas to the pioneering British nature photographers, Cherry and Richard Kearton.[27] Their *British Birds' Nests*, published in 1895, was the first bird book illustrated with photographs all taken in the wild, and the Keartons' *With Nature and a Camera* had encouraged the 'Woodlanders' to try their bark hut venture. Local photographers such as J. W. Lindt and Nicholas Caire had, since 1880, been freed by the dry-plate process to venture into fern gullies and forests. But Kinane's intimate pictures of birds in their nests, published in the *New Idea* in 1905–6 and in *From Range to Sea* in 1907, were some of the earliest examples of such images to appear in Australia.[28]

Their message was that nature could be captured with camera and field-glass instead of with gun and trap. In 1907 Donald Macdonald wrote of the recent 'complete change in popular sentiment for Nature'—the change from hunting and collecting to watchful observation.[29] Barrett declared that 'the best work of the taxidermist bears but a faint resemblance to Nature'.[30] He believed that 'the only way to study bird-life is to dwell among the feathered folk themselves', and he contrasted this method with that of the 'cabinet naturalists', satisfied only with their trophies.[31] But 'enlarged cabinets' remained a measure of success and an emblem of class among many field

The new photographic vogue. *(Reproduced from A. H. Chisholm,* Mateship
with Birds, *Melbourne, Whitcombe & Tombs Ltd, 1922)*

naturalists well into the twentieth century, and the Royal Australasian
Ornithologists Union (RAOU), founded in 1901, did not restrict the
collection of bird skins and eggs among its members until the 1920s and
1930s.[32] On RAOU excursions, while the sun set, continuous gurgling
noises emanated from rows of tents as eggs of waterfowl were

'Egging at the Narrows': Members of the Australian Ornithologists Union collect mutton bird eggs at Phillip Island in 1902. *(A. J. Campbell, Album no. 2, Museum of Victoria)*

blown, and members would periodically emerge with buckets of yolk and water.[33] These egg-collectors, wrote Barrett, 'could see no good in "fooling around with a camera".'[34]

Because it carried a conservation message, the camera assumed a totemic significance. Naturalists have often displayed what David Elliston Allen has called 'a mild theatrical streak', expressed in prominent dress and technology—a characteristic of a marginal group seeking symbols of their identity.[35] The outdoors photographer, crouched by his tripod and 'shooting' at wildlife, became a popular photographic subject himself, and the Woodlanders featured him in their published articles. The extent to which the camera mimicked the gun at the same time as replacing it was illustrated by a French professor's 1881 design of a 'photographic gun' which looked like a rifle, had to be propped on a shoulder, and offered sights down a barrel.[36]

The gun had been, for many, the only intermediary with nature. It offered a way for early naturalists to get a long, close look at the objects of study, so its use was often sympathetic and scientific. In addition, it was the centrepiece of a noble sport, one with aristocratic traditions and a class-based view of the landscape. Game laws, introduced in Victoria in 1861, represented the first local attempt to protect wildlife. But imported game was the main subject of this preservation order and, even then, many believed that its major purpose was to facilitate the continuance of resented English practices, and to promote private property rather than public wildlife. It was to be a further thirty years before similar protection was granted to native species.[37]

For the nature writers there was the complication that, in revoking the rights of the sportsmen, they were constraining one of those English landscape traditions that they were so ardently seeking to transplant. It was one of many tensions which revealed that they were caught between science and society. Macdonald never fully relinquished the hunting culture, and regarded the hunter H. W. Wheelwright as Victoria's first field naturalist, comparing him to Gilbert White.[38] Most naturalists of this period began with a shanghai in their pocket, and talked lovingly of the 'prizes', 'spoils' and 'trophies' won from their 'collecting grounds'.[39] Barrett could still rejoice that the eggs of the brown hawk 'make beautiful objects in the cabinet'.[40] Then there was the moral dilemma of the cuckoo, that bare-faced pirate and instinctive murderer. The Wood-landers carefully recorded in world-famous photographs, the baby cuckoo, hours old, push its host chicks from the nest. But could such behaviour be natural? W. H. Hudson had considered cuckoos possessed of 'a devilish intelligence' and the Woodlanders repeatedly replaced the abused chicks in the nest, to no avail.[41] And what of introduced plants and animals which, they observed, were steadily displacing native flora and fauna? It was a process that had a provocative human parallel. The acclimatised sparrow, wrote Macdonald, was 'a type of the race—an energetic venturesome pioneer . . . He has the old colonists' habit, too, of not caring much whose nest he seizes provided he is strong enough to hold possession against the original owner.'[42] One day, while waiting at a suburban railway station, Macdonald observed a parable of nature:

> I counted between the metals [of the railway track] nearly a score of foreign plants and grasses . . . All these aliens, scorched every minute with the grimy breath of throbbing engines, were flourishing, with scarcely a native plant or blade of native grass amongst them. It was typical of Anglo-Saxon colonisation.[43]

There was not just nature to be found out there, but moral lessons too, and bush traditions that hovered about, and gave meaning to every tree and grub. This form of nature writing became increasingly isolated from the concerns of mainstream science. It was not just because of its sentimentalism; it was also defending the outdoor 'amateur'. In the 1870s and 1880s, more of Victoria's distinguished scientists had worked outside the university than within it.[44] But this balance was to change in the succeeding decades. The cross-fertilisation of professional and amateur, academic and enthusiast, which distinguished the early years of the Field Naturalists' Club of Victoria, declined.[45] C. Hartley Grattan has drawn attention to the 'bifurcation of the culture into intramural and extramural' that occurred in the years 1880 to 1930.[46] The teaching of the principles of evolutionary biology, which gained impetus with the arrival of new professors in Sydney and Melbourne at the end of the 1880s, helped take the initiative away from the amateurs, as did a general reaction against collecting, which had formed the central task of the early scientists. The nature writers were pioneers of this new relationship to the environment—that of observing rather than collecting—yet they were also advocates of a human vision of the land against the detached professionalism of the new scientist.

Fifty years after European settlement in Victoria, it was a transformed nature that Macdonald described—full of the welcome, transplanted reminders of England—and it was a civilised nature of fields, farms, orchards and gardens. Its various transformations were part of what made it dear to him. And when Macdonald ventured further afield—to the Gippsland or Otway forests, the Riverina plains or the wild south coast— he was alert for evidence of Aboriginal occupation, for a shepherd's tracks, the spar of a wreck, or wild food.[47] Macdonald's 'country chatter', as he called it, also humanised the birds and animals. A laughing jackass criss-crossing the Murray River was, in the 1880s, 'seemingly a colonist of strong federal inclinations', and the big coots that visited Melbourne's Botanic Gardens observed 'the fashionable and certainly rational practice of spending their summer in the country and their winter in town'. If birds were like people, then so could people be like birds. When pondering the 'thankless tillage' of Wimmera farmers, Macdonald wondered if their homesteads would one day be deserted 'like the eagle hawks' nests one sees in the dead gum trees'.[48] Macdonald later told Jean Galbraith, whose articles about her Gippsland garden he admired, that the key to nature writing was 'the human touch'.[49]

Macdonald confronted 'Marcus Clarke's fine fancies', his descriptions of Australian nature as weird and disturbing, and dismissed them as 'unreal'.[50] The absence of a visible 'human touch' in the Australian landscape had alienated early colonists. In 1822, Barron Field was appalled at how Australian nature seemed to defy 'all the dearest allegories of human life'. The dominant perennial leaf, he wrote, 'does not savour of humanity ... There is no flesh and blood in it: it is not of us, and is nothing to us.'[51] Macdonald and Barrett wanted to cultivate popular sentiment in the land and its inhabitants. Like the *Bulletin* writers, they were putting folklore into print and giving it wider currency and greater respectability. This balance of learning and teaching, of drawing on popular traditions and sometimes correcting them, was clearly illustrated by the 'Notes and Queries' columns managed by both men.

Australian children, like Mary Fullerton in Gippsland, were growing up lamenting: 'How well we knew the wildflowers of the bush; how little we knew their names.'[52] Names were important to those trying to foster familiarity and intimacy with the land, and in this quest the 'scientist' was often an enemy. Barrett wrote in 1907:

> The pity is that so few of our wild-flowers have popular names. We have no poets to praise or endear them to the people. And so the long, unlovely names of the scientist cling like a curse to some of the most delicately beautiful objects on earth.[53]

Many made fun not only of scientific Latin but also of the clumsy new descriptive names. 'Oriel' of the *Argus* composed an Australian 'love-song', ending with the following verse:

> That day our troth we plighted—blissful hour,
>   Beginning of a joy a whole life long!
> And while the whole world seemed to be in flower
>   The Chestnut-rumped Ground-Wren burst forth in song.[54]

Macdonald prefaced his 1887 collection of essays with a defence of popular names which, he believed, 'serve quite as well as scientific terms for identification, and are generally more expressive and appropriate'. Even the title of the book, *Gum Boughs and Wattle Bloom*, was a sort of manifesto bypassing the claims of the *Eucalyptus* and the *Acacia*.

As the nature writers drifted further from the concerns of the scientific world, they found more in common with those artists, writers and poets who were beginning to define a distinctive Australian tradition. They valued their personal links with Henry Lawson, 'Banjo' Paterson, C. E. W. Bean and C. J. Dennis. A highpoint of the confluence of interest between nature writing and Australianism was A. H. Chisholm's eloquently titled book, *Mateship with Birds* (1922). It was introduced by C. J. Dennis, author of *The Sentimental Bloke*, who approved of Chisholm's 'fraternal attitude and methods' in relating to 'our mates the birds'. Chisholm returned the compliment by prefacing some of Dennis's books and by becoming his biographer. The young Chisholm had been one of Macdonald's rural correspondents, and took up his 'Nature Notes and Queries' column after his death.[55] In *Mateship with Birds*, Chisholm drew parallels between the fighting, cheerful Australian magpie and the Australian soldier. Like the soldier, the magpie had a distinct disposition shaped by the land—freer, more spacious, more resolute, democratic— it was an 'essentially Australian bird'. With a typical interest in names,

'Lecture round the Camp-fire by Donald Macdonald of Ladysmith' at the General Camp of the Australian Ornithologists Union at Phillip Island, November 1902. *(A. J. Campbell, Album no. 2, Museum of Victoria)*

Chisholm discussed the merits of calling it the 'Anzac-Bird'.[56] He was echoing a common preoccupation of Macdonald's and Barrett's: their social message was shaped powerfully by that antithesis of nature—war.

The nature of war

The anticipation and commemoration of war was central to Macdonald's writing. He was an active reporter of defence issues, and was involved with the Victorian volunteer forces and the reforms of the militia system. In 1899 he was sent by the *Argus* as the first Australian war correspondent to South Africa. He became a participant in the siege of Ladysmith and later gathered his dispatches into a book called *How We Kept The Flag Flying*.[57] On his return to Australia, although emaciated by hunger and hardship, he embarked on an Australia-wide lecture tour about his experience. His book was dedicated to those Australians who took part in the South African campaign, 'with a full appreciation of the patriotism and pride of race which has made Australasia a fighting unit in the British Empire'. Later on, along with many other commentators, Macdonald announced the birth of the Anzac legend at Gallipoli and gloried in 'the bravery of Australian and New Zealand farmer boys'.[58]

It was on his return from the Boer War that his 'Nature Notes' and 'Notes for Boys' became institutions. Although nature study was regarded as suitable for girls as well as boys, and some of Macdonald's correspondents were women, it was to 'boys' that his advice was particularly addressed. It was not just to curb their egg collecting and shanghais. Graeme Davison has observed that the literary image of Australian youth changed during the second half of the nineteenth century from one of robust 'currency lads and lasses' to that of stunted city larrikins.[59] The 'boy problem', as this product of the fear of urban degeneracy was often called, was common to western urban societies at the beginning of the twentieth century. There was great concern about the effect of city life on human health and morals and the future of 'the race'. In Australia this compounded with existing anxieties about the convict inheritance and the genetic influence of tropical climes. These worries generated a powerful need for the young nation to prove the vitality of its stock. Macdonald was one of those commentators to first write of cricket matches with England as 'Tests'.[60] But the true test of the new, southern race was war. Macdonald's 'Notes for Boys' clearly pointed to this grander destiny:

> Later on, perhaps, there may be a word to say upon more serious things, so that all the boys of Australia may grow with one aspiration—the defence of their country—ever in their minds. This is the greatest, the grandest aspiration in all the world, the undying resolution that as long as we have life, and strength, and courage no harm shall come to Australia.[61]

The experience of war focused many of Macdonald's concerns—his imperial fervour, his prediction that pastoral life was an ideal preparation for battle, a consequent faith in rural civilisation, and a life-long effort to bring its virtues to a city populace. In pursuing this range of causes, Macdonald offers a striking anticipation of C. E. W. Bean, who, as a recorder of outback life, a war historian, and town-planning advocate, remains probably the clearest example of the congruence of bush advocacy, concern for defence, and urban planning.[62]

Charles Barrett also wrote about nature for 'boys', and often with an explicit orientation to war. He wrote later that he was 'as happy as Larry' when he enlisted, and his commitment continued well beyond his formal war service.[63] After the first world war, Barrett worked with C. E. W. Bean, at the picturesque homestead at Tuggeranong, as editor of AIF unit histories, and during the second world war he visited troops in northern Australia and New Guinea, lecturing on practical bush-lore.[64] His book, *In Australian Wilds: The Gleanings of a Naturalist* (1919), was promoted as the heart-felt product of a returned soldier, come to seek peace in his old bush haunts.[65] *Australia My Country*, published during that war, was designed as a pocket-size companion for soldiers abroad, '[w]ritten by one who returned from the last war with a deeper love than ever for his own country'.[66]

But Barrett's attitude to war was ambivalent. His daughter recalled that when the first world war broke out, 'he couldn't kill, he wasn't interested, couldn't do that. But he had to do his share.'[67] Barrett enlisted in June 1916 and joined the Camel Brigade Field Ambulance which left for Egypt in May 1917. His letters home to his young daughter featured 'Soldier Daddy' practising bush-lore abroad—sketches of Barrett with a bird perched on his chair, a frog on his desk, a cricket on his paper, adorn the pages.[68] He edited issues of the field ambulance's journals, *The Stretcher* and *Cacolet*, and the soldiers' monthly, the *Kia-ora Cooee*, and his pen can be discerned in the feature columns 'Nature Studies in Palestine' and 'From a Naturalist's Haversack'. Barrett strained to maintain the peaceful rhythms of nature observation even in the face of war. Paul Fussell, in his book *The Great War and Modern Memory*, has remarked that 'since war takes place outdoors and always within nature, its symbolic status is that of the ultimate anti-pastoral'.[69] Barrett's writing offered a refuge from war, a 'recourse to the pastoral', to use Fussell's term. His most overt parody of the nature essay was his account of life in the army camp at Royal Park, titled 'In Camp with the Dinkum Soldier: A Bird-Lover Studies Some New Varieties'. In this piece, written in April 1917, Barrett described the camp routines of 'a man from the mallee' and 'a big Gippslander' almost as if they were specimens of nature.[70] And, indeed, for Barrett as for Macdonald, it was these men's proximity to nature, their country origins, that made them martial.

On his return from the first world war, Barrett wrote a 'Boys' Page' for the *Herald* and edited the paper, *Pals*, for seven years. Subtitled 'An Australian Paper for Australian Boys', *Pals* was the official organ of the Victorian branch of the Australian Boy Scouts' Association. From the first issue in 1920, Barrett made his themes apparent. On its cover was a drawing of a magpie attacking a nest-robbing boy with the caption '*Not* Pals'. Inside was a special article on 'One of our Pals: Donald Macdonald as Boy and Man', written by Barrett.[71] Much like its British counterparts, this Australian 'boy's own' paper projected a sacred male camaraderie whose strength and ingenuity was tested in serialised adventures about the confrontation of races.[72] Similar themes underpinned the stories that Macdonald and Barrett wrote for children. The best known of these was Macdonald's *The Warrigals' Well* (1901, written with John F. Edgar), which told of two proud agents of the empire, their race for gold in central Australia, their fights with Aborigines, and their personal quest for manliness and honour.

Richard White has described the dominance at the turn of the century of the ethic of 'the Coming Man', a masculine, racist, anti-urban, anti-theoretical cluster of values which could be either radical or conservative in its political implications.[73] The writings of Rudyard Kipling were its prime literary expression, and Lieutenant-General Baden-Powell its leading practical exponent. Macdonald admired both these men. He had yearned to meet his 'literary idol', Kipling, on his Australian tour of 1891, and chance brought them together during a train journey to Adelaide.[74] Baden-Powell, the hero of Mafeking and the founder of the Boy Scouts, visited Australia in 1912 and exclaimed of Sydney's proximity to bush and sea: 'What a place for Scouting!' In the same year Macdonald published a brief portrait of the 'soldier and scout', together with a synopsis of the lectures Baden-Powell gave during his tour of Australia and New Zealand.[75] Macdonald's *The Bush Boy's Book*, published a few years after scouts were established in Australia, was the movement's ideal handbook. Macdonald aimed 'to bring together inside the covers of one book all the bushcraft that thousands of Australians had gathered in more than a hundred years'.[76] It included chapters on 'The Bush Boy's Camp', 'The Bushman's Kitchen', 'Out with the Gun', 'Trapping for Profit', 'Codes, Ciphers and Signals', 'Bush Surgery' and many others. In a final chapter on 'Health, Strength and Happiness', Macdonald reserved several pages for a warning against drink. (He was later to write privately of drink as the greatest evil facing the youth of the cities.[77]) He finished his book with a story about the siege of Ladysmith during the Boer War, and about the physical triumph of those schooled in exercise and fresh air.

Macdonald was one of the writers behind the short-lived Melbourne journal *Bohemia*, and Barrett romanced his tenuous links with the leading figures of the *Bulletin* school. They both inhabited the fringes of bohemian literary culture and shared its obsession with a masculine ethic. Marilyn Lake has written of 'the emergent men's press' of the 1890s and early 1900s (especially the *Bulletin* and *Bull-Ant*), and has argued that the period saw a contest between men and women for control of the national culture, a conflict which often entered the home.[78] The growth of the suburbs separated 'home' from 'work', and it became very much identified as the woman's precinct.[79] Along with newspaper 'Notes for Boys' came the 'Lady's Pages'. The dominant images of 'national character' were masculine ones, and they were of nomadic, unattached, rural lives. The wandering bush worker and later, the swagman, epitomised the independence and uncomplicated camaraderie which city bohemians tried to foster in their all-male clubs and cafés. For some bohemians, the family life to which they returned at the end of the night was a source of embarrassment or mockery.[80] Macdonald's wife and daughter were hardly mentioned in his writing.

Barrett wrote of his wife, son and daughter with affection and friendship, but also participated in the disparagement of women typical of his male literary contemporaries.[81] Women, though, could be reverenced—and confined—as 'mothers'. Alec Chisholm's *Mateship with Birds* was dedicated 'To the Mother at Home', and he included a photo of two boys sitting beneath a nesting 'Mother Robin'.

Nature writing, though, was not an unambiguously 'manly' pursuit. It was one of the prose forms most used by women, and writers such as Louisa Atkinson, Louisa Anne Meredith and Jean Galbraith gained a wide audience. Nature study was one of the few 'respectable' outdoor pursuits allowed women of the Victorian age. It had been a women's magazine, the *New Idea*, which published Macdonald's 'Glimpses of Nature' articles under the pseudonym 'Owen Otway', and which first gave Barrett a forum for his writings about the 'Bush Hut'.[82] The young Barrett felt insecure about his romanticism, but Macdonald 'showed him the way' partly by convincing him of the manly, even martial dimensions of their craft.

There were other, more personal reasons for their marginality in a masculinist culture. Both men were married to outstanding women who had their own public roles, and with whom they shared strong intellectual bonds. In 1883 Macdonald married Jessie Seward, an art and music student who later became one of Melbourne's earliest women journalists. Indeed, she contributed to one of the new 'Lady's Pages'. Jessie and Donald's daughter, Elaine, recalled the household tensions over their two careers, her father expecting a supportive, self-sacrificing wife, and her mother claiming her right to a career, as well as to the joys of walking and cycling.[83] Jessie Macdonald was one of the early members of the Austral Salon, a Melbourne women's club founded in 1891, and also helped establish the Women's Writers Club in the early 1900s. One of its first fund-raising speakers was Donald Macdonald, telling tales of the Boer War.[84] Barrett's wife, Helen, was also a naturalist, and conchology was her special interest. She and Charles travelled and collected together, especially after their children had grown up, and she became the first white woman to visit parts of Arnhem Land.[85] Perhaps the nature clubs, with which Macdonald was involved and which formed the basis of the Barretts' social life, allowed a more comfortable mixing of the sexes than did many other societies of the time.[86] Macdonald's and Barrett's social and domestic lives were in tension with their public custody of a sacred male inheritance. This disjunction was, perhaps, one source of their longing for the bush, the billy by the fire, and the privileged, outdoor yarning of men.

Boys, nature, race and war were powerfully bound together in the preaching of the nature writers. 'Boys', they emphasised, was an ageless

Women naturalists: The nature clubs offered a social setting where middle-class men and women could respectably enjoy one another's company in outdoor activities. Women are pictured painting and cooking at the 'Ladies' Tent' on a 1902 ornithologists' camp. *(A. J. Campbell, Album no. 2, Museum of Victoria)*

term, expressive of a sort of freedom and emotional irresponsibility which they hankered after for life. 'The open air' was contrasted, sometimes, not just with the city, but with the feminine shackles of home. 'War', a man's world, tested the virility of the 'race' and left a visible, masculine imprint on the Australian landscape. Memorials to the distant dead were erected in almost every Australian town, and they became the centre of rituals enhancing the separateness of men.[87]

Nationalist aesthetics

The nature writers shared much with those urban progressives who, in the early twentieth century, were securing emotional and educational resources for the growing cities. The progressives were inspired by vitalist thought which had gained great influence in European culture during this period. Vitalism drew on both romantic and scientific trad-itions. It expressed belief in the irrational, emotional and spiritual aspects of man, seeing them as the source of life and creativity. Yet it sought also to harness and direct these inner forces and to use them rationally in social planning. The nature writers' resolution of this dichotomy can be seen in their controlled lyricism, their studied casualness, their interpenetration of intellect and feeling—and in their balance of spiritual and practical wisdom.[88]

Prominent among the progressives was Sir James Barrett (1862-1945, no relation to Charles), a Melbourne ophthalmologist and a member of the National Parks Committee of the Town Planning Association of Victoria. His vitalist inspiration led to his energetic support for outdoor recreation, the provision of open space in cities, the creation of natural reserves, the protection of historic buildings, and the preservation of 'national monuments', a term embracing the survivals of a past age and also places of natural beauty and interest.[89]

In the first decade of the twentieth century, James Barrett and Frank Tate, then director of Education in Victoria, introduced Arbor Day, Bird Day, Wattle Day and Discovery Day into Victorian schools. These were days marking special dates and places, days for schooling in the open air. Trees were planted, Wattle Park visited, cairns unveiled, speeches given, and compositions written up afterwards. It did not escape the children that they were being offered a vision of society as well as of nature. 'On Bird Day', wrote one schoolgirl in her class essay, 'we had fine speeches given us by human beings.'[90] Nature study was promoted as part of a broader campaign to link together 'the life of the school and the life of outdoors'.[91] The Gould League of Bird Lovers (of which Macdonald was a councillor) encouraged youngsters to protect rather than destroy.

Macdonald and Barrett were active in this educational campaign. The 'Notes for Boys' column was the suggestion of teachers at a Portsea summer school. Macdonald's advocacy of bush nursing, which again aligned him with the progressives, was based on his desire to protect the self-sufficiency of rural and outdoor life.[92] Barrett, especially after Macdonald's death, reached a national, even international audience with his promotion of nature study. In the 1930s, he was the author of the immensely popular *Sun* Nature Books, a series which approached a circulation of a million. He became the host of many visiting overseas naturalists, whom he often took to see the lyrebirds and platypus of Sherbrooke, and he was a fellow of both the London and New York Zoological societies, the latter of which, in 1931, devoted an entire issue of its journal to Barrett's natural history of the kangaroo.[93] His books on Australian wildlife, history and folklore, and of his travels to different parts of the continent, strained for a national audience. His most intense decades of writing—those following the Great War—were a period of widespread celebration and rediscovery of the Australian countryside. The experience of war made many people recoil from urban industrialism, and it was after 1920 that the Heidelberg painters became most revered. David Elliston Allen has called the parallel British phenomenon 'a connoisseurship of the countryside'; it was also 'a

'Mateship with Mother Robin': Schoolboys on Bird Day in the early twentieth century. *(Reproduced from A. H. Chisholm,* Mateship with Birds, *Melbourne, Whitcombe & Tombs Ltd, 1922)*

revolution by rucksack', and the same exuberant, physical engagement with the bush marked the Australian version.[94] 'Hiking' became popular between the wars, although this new phenomenon and 'ugly verb' were often disdained by men who saw it as an invasion of the bush by women.[95] Australian art and writing romanticised the swagman, that

European nomad made more common by the depression years. In 1943 Barrett edited *The Swagman's Note-book*, an anthology of outback writing and bush yarns, and over 100,000 copies were published, mostly for the troops. Tramping with book and pipe, rejoicing in the open air, seeking out 'the oldest inhabitant' of passing villages, pottering around churchyard cemeteries: these were the common holiday pastimes of literary men, and they were the motifs of Barrett's popular travel books in the 1930s and 1940s.[96]

Antiquities and the countryside traditionally occupied a common field of enquiry and aesthetics: Gilbert White, it must be remembered, also surveyed Selborne's antiquities. In their enthusiasm to read the landscape for a human past, the nature writers shared much with antiquarians who, from the late nineteenth century, were beginning to value the tangible reminders of European Australia's beginnings. From about the time of the 1888 centenary, areas of inner Sydney and Melbourne were being valued for their historic and primitive atmosphere. Bernard Smith has called this emerging perception 'a tradition at once popular, antiquarian and somewhat sentimental'.[97] The artist and social critic, William Hardy Wilson, was one prominent exponent of it, his most notable work being his charming sketches of buildings and homesteads, published in *Old Colonial Architecture in New South Wales and Tasmania*.[98] He 'collected' his buildings between 1912 and 1922 and explained that his style owed its 'particular beauty' in part to 'the golden splendour of the Australian sunlight'.[99] This vision was new in its warmth of feeling towards the local human environment, and it was profoundly conservative in its nostalgia for an earlier, pastoral Australia. The nature writers shared the antiquarians' nationalistic ardour—and their anti-modernist aesthetic. This ideological stance influenced their definition of a physical Australian 'heritage', a term which, in the late nineteenth century, usually referred to that intangible body of folkways and political lore which gave legitimacy to emerging nation-states.[100] The nature writers, with their efforts to create landscape traditions, assisted the demarcation of the valued past in particular sites and things. By the early 1930s, Barrett's descriptions of wildflowers and birds' eggs were being acclaimed as defining a 'national heritage' which needed to be preserved.[101] By the 1940s, he was identifying a 'heritage of stone'.

Barrett's book, *Heritage of Stone*, was an early published argument for the preservation of buildings as 'national monuments'. It grew out of his love for Tasmania. Its sketches and descriptions, like Wilson's, were a tribute to Georgian architecture, depicting entrances, doorways and windows, and shop-fronts, as well as individual buildings. Barrett's foreword explained that Tasmania, richly endowed by Nature, 'owes also something to the works of Man in the early days of settlement'. When

New South Wales and Van Diemen's Land were first colonised, he said happily, 'the form of contemporary architecture in England was a particularly graceful one'. By contrast, Sydney's rapid growth obliterated its early past, and '[w]hen Victoria and the other younger States were colonised, the style of architecture had changed and become ugly.' But Tasmania was full of beauty: 'What a gift to the landscape artist are the barns . . .'[102]

The nature of Barrett's nationalist aesthetic is further revealed in his sensitivity to another 'heritage of stone'. Like most Australian children of his period, Barrett learnt nothing about Aborigines at school, and only began to gather some knowledge when he was in his twenties. His interest was quickened by the gift of a stone axe, and by hearing the anthropologist Baldwin Spencer lecture to Melbourne audiences about his trips to central Australia. It was Barrett's time in Egypt during the Great War that stimulated his passion for archaeology. Camped with his division in the Egyptian desert, he went on nighttime rambles, following animal tracks in the sand. He was moved by a landscape full of evidence of the ancient Egyptians, the Bible stories, the Crusades. He fossicked for 'old flints' and developed a liking for the art of ancient Egypt. Back home, this ardent opponent of the natural history collector found nothing wrong in gathering artefacts of the human native.[103]

In Australia between the wars, Barrett developed strong views on Aboriginal welfare. He argued against those who considered Aborigines a dying race, and condemned Australia's history of white cruelty. The 1920s and 1930s saw new questioning about Aboriginal affairs, and Barrett must be seen as an influential shaper of popular opinion in Victoria. He was the *Herald*'s reporter on Aboriginal issues, and did much to foster interest in their culture.[104] He was more sympathetic than most to the growing evidence of Aboriginal antiquity. He was excited by finds such as the Cohuna skull in 1925, and believed that archaeological excavation had an exciting future in Australia.[105] Above all, he developed a strong interest in Aboriginal art. He was involved with the pioneering 'Primitive Art' exhibition at the National Museum of Victoria in 1929. He published several books on Aborigines, and gave particular attention to their rock paintings and carvings. He argued that 'every relic of the Aboriginals is worth preserving; and the caves and shelters, where they painted and carved, should be guarded as national possessions'. Unusually, he called for an Aboriginal art gallery in each capital city. He found these 'cave galleries' romantic places where 'imagination is stirred'; he allowed them to have aesthetic as well as cultural meanings.[106]

Barrett was a leader of opinion in many of these sympathies and insights, but his Australianist fervour also helped entrench existing simplistic notions of Aboriginal culture. He was influenced by narrowly nationalist schools of thought, represented by two men with whom he collaborated in writings about the Aborigine. One was A. S. Kenyon, who rejected the relevance of European developments in field archaeology because he regarded the especially primitive and passive character of the Aborigine to be unique, like the marsupial.[107] The other influence on Barrett was R. H. Croll, a member of Melbourne's art establishment whose interest in Aborigines was closely related to his antipathy to modernist painting. Croll, a great admirer of Donald Macdonald, edited the correspondence between Arthur Streeton and Tom Roberts, and became a champion of the Heidelberg school and its vision of a pastoral Australia.[108] Like Kenyon, he rejected the modern European influences in order to espouse an isolated, and deeply conservative, Australianism. That particular national prescription—of 'flocks rather than factories' or, as Croll put it, of 'wool, wheat and poets'—had a strong undercurrent of elitism, racism, and anti-urbanism.[109]

Critic and author Flora Eldershaw later described the 'romantic vision' of the 'landscape writers' of the 1940s and early 1950s. Although Eldershaw was writing of authors such as George Farwell, Alan Marshall, Colin Simpson and Elyne Mitchell, her words apply equally well to Barrett, the bulk of whose work preceded theirs:

> They are wonder books, bringing to the reader the marvels and curiosities of a very old country, 'the cenotaphs of species dead elsewhere'; the riddle of the dark races and their customs that are often vestiges of something forgotten long ago; the skills of the bushman born of sheer necessity, the folklore and magics that grow up in the void; old wives' tales on a grand and perturbing scale. Another aspect of their appeal is that they usually have homeliness to recommend them, familiar incidents, oft-repeated family jokes.[110]

Eldershaw saw the 'landscape writers' as consciously returning to origins, strengthening the nomadic tradition in Australian writing, and renewing the literary scene from the same sources of folklore which gave birth to the short stories and ballads of the 1890s. But it was a genre, she hinted, which easily lapsed into unquestioning convention. Many of these writers were brought together by the national travel magazine, *Walkabout*, founded in 1934. This, together with the journal *Wild Life*, established in 1938 and edited by the naturalist Crosbie Morrison, projected that same homeliness and wonder about the Australian landscape and its secrets, a community of the earth. These magazines were also, particularly in war-time, defining a tangible heritage from which Australians could draw strength and identity.[111] In 1941, *Walkabout* published a full-page advertisement which featured a photograph of a pastoral scene elegantly framed as if it were a painting, a finished cultural artefact, and

OUR NATIONAL HERITAGE

FROM THE WILDERNESS our pioneering forefathers won security for our future. Today, in acres of robust crops, is the countless gold of growing grain — and vast green pasture lands are priceless emeralds of our rich inheritance. Thus, should all else fail, there would still be good earth to nourish to life a new prosperity. Then, as now, we would drink to the future in Foster's Lager — Australia's National Beverage. It is fitting that this should be so. In the skilful, golden-glowing brew and very mellow flavour of Foster's is all the nourishing goodness of the finest barley, hops and sugar cane our fertile land can grow.

Our National Heritage: A full-page war-time advertisement for Foster's Lager linked 'national heritage' to a landscape of pastoralism and pioneering. (Walkabout, *1 April 1941)*

captioned with the words 'OUR NATIONAL HERITAGE'. The text referred to 'our rich inheritance' won by 'our pioneering forefathers', a resource which would restore us 'should all else fail', and a landscape which, of course, provided the finest hops, barley and sugar cane for Foster's Lager.[112]

Just as Selborne was particularly beloved by the British public in times of war, so did Barrett's fame reach its height in the 1940s. The following review article from the *Bulletin* of that time spelt out the need which Barrett filled:

> It's impossible to read a book as pleasant as Robert Gibbings's *Coming Down the Wye* (Dent) without wishing that it was a book by an Australian author about an Australian river. Except for the steadily-mounting total of Charles Barrett's nature-studies and an occasional surprise such as Elyne Mitchell's *Australian Alps*, Gibbings's type of documentary writing—an evocation of the spirit of the earth, animated by descriptions of its birds, beasts, fishes and flowers and enriched by local history—is so rare in Australia that hardly the beginnings of a tradition have been established . . .
>
> Written by an Australian about some corner of the Australian earth, a book such as this would do infinitely more to reinforce the spirit of the nation than any angry pamphlets about the New Order, any journalistic slang-whangings about Malaya or any earnest radio talks about our virtues, our failings or our duties. Australia, in short, needs to be written up; not by propagandists, but by a dozen or a score of writers who love the land as simply and as wholeheartedly as Charles Barrett does or as Gibbings loves the waters of the Wye.[113]

A writer in the *Bulletin* concluded that there were 'two Charles Barretts'. One wrote attractively as a lover of nature, the other 'seems to be under the necessity of boiling a pot'.[114] Barrett resented having to write 'pot boilers', as he, too, called them.[115] The broader canvas, and the goal of an Australia-wide readership, made his nationalism more conscious, his geography less intimate, and his use of the literary conventions of wattle, swagmen and bush language more laboured. Like the aging Streeton, he was caught in the conventions he had helped to popularise. His early, fresh joy in the landscape, his energetic overthrow of the melancholy, became a false heartiness. He went on adventurously exploring new frontiers—in the 1950s, in his seventies, he visited and wrote about New Guinea, where his son was working. But he had become a source of amusement, too. His contemporaries joked that the old fellow would 'end up as dingo tucker' in his nostalgic quest for bush communion.[116] He must have felt the increasing hollowness of his later prose. As relief, he wrote stories of imagined villages where an old man lived alone, close to books and nature. Through these semi-fictional reveries, he tried to return to the intimate world of the bush hut.[117]

When Donald Macdonald died in 1932, there were many who expressed their sense of loss and called for some permanent memorial to him. 'Macdonald was of national importance', wrote Nettie Palmer:

'Even his fugitive notes would be found of permanent value.' R. H. Croll supported Palmer's suggestion that a volume of collected work should be published.[118] R. E. Williams was sure that 'his part in the formation of a nation's character are so entrenched in our home life and life afield that they must endure'. Charles Foster echoed this sentiment when he wrote that Macdonald 'seems a fitting foundation-stone on which to build Australian tradition'. Another *Argus* reader wrote more personally:

> Donald Macdonald was a later and greater Richard Jeffries [*sic*]. I well remember the pleasure it gave me, an unknown immigrant 30 years ago, to read his charming articles in '*The Argus*'. To find so delightful an interpreter of nature in a new country was a joyous experience, and it greatly helped to reconcile me to unfamiliar and sometimes distasteful surroundings.[119]

Macdonald and Barrett carved homes for the heart out of the 'wilderness'.

In 1908, Bernard O'Dowd reviewed Charles Barrett's first book, *From Range to Sea*, for the *Socialist*.[120] O'Dowd was a correspondent of Walt Whitman's, a poet of bush and city contrasts and, in the early 1890s, a disillusioned victim of urban commerce and disease. In his review of Barrett, he referred to the 'classical nature-study book of the English language', Gilbert White's *Natural History of Selborne*, and also to the work of Jefferies, Burroughs and Walton. But, 'great as these books are', O'Dowd was brave enough to suggest the recipe for an even finer Australian equivalent:

> I am convinced that a 'Natural History of Melbourne', which would dwarf its great exemplar, could be written with no more material (and with no need of any more native enthusiasm for the subject) than is now to be found in Charles Barrett's 'From Range to Sea' and Donald Macdonald's regular notes in the *Argus*.

CHAPTER SEVEN

Land Rites

The land itself could not be 'collected', but it could be inscribed ritually and commemoratively. If artists and nature writers began the sentimental and imaginative appropriation of the land, then urban progressives pursued it rationally through social and educational planning. In Australia, as in America in the inter-war years, there was a deep commitment to natural values and to asserting their influence in social and political life. Environmental consciousness blended with the advocacy of racial purity and the assertion of white 'native' traditions. Pastoralism emerged as a favoured form of possession, one supremely adapted to claiming the open spaces of Australia, but one that also offered a balance between nature and civilisation, between country and town. There was in this period an advocacy of both nature and nation.[1]

This chapter explores institutional efforts in the early twentieth century to identify, create or preserve hallowed ground, to define a local geography of the past. Monumental history—the forward-looking, practical use of the past as a source of moral inspiration and example— is 'the natural mode of historical consciousness in new lands', writes Graeme Davison.[2] This chapter focuses on the work of the National Monuments sub-committee of the Field Naturalists Club of Victoria in identifying valued places, features or tracts of land, the Victorian Historical Memorials Committee in marking the paths of explorers, and the efforts to memorialise overseas Australian soldiers that gave impetus and edge to the local commemoration of pioneers. Charles Long, Frank Tate, Charles Daley, Isaac Selby, R. H. Croll, A. S. Kenyon, Stan Mitchell and Sir James Barrett were significant in these campaigns. Their work, like that of the nature writers, was stimulated by the national experience of overseas war, and was accompanied by the promotion of pastoral history, politics and aesthetics. A. S. Kenyon became an authority on the pastoral occupation of Victoria and celebrated its landscapes, in art as well as history.

John Rickard, in his *Australia: A Cultural History* (1988), has described Australian culture in the half century before the second world war as characterised by 'powerful pressures to conform'. He argues it was a period 'for coming to terms with the Australian condition, and therefore a time for the articulation of rites, codes and customs, while at the same time adapting to the now more insistent intrusions of the modern world'.[3] The European rituals of place or 'land rites' described in this chapter were part of that process; they aimed to secure the land emotionally and spiritually for the settler society. They played out in space a larger cultural negotiation between the imported and the indigenous, between European intellectual 'modernism' and Australian environmental 'primitivism'. Australians feared a 'half-caste' culture. In Victoria, land rites were most overt during the early decades of the twentieth century, the very period when acknowledgement of the violence and illegitimacy of the European invasion of Australia was most strongly suppressed and denied, and the period when many Victorian Aboriginal reserves were revoked and Kooris were losing what few land *rights* they had.

In Victoria, Aboriginal reserves and stations were created in the wake of the establishment of the Central Board for the Protection of Aborigines in 1860. The six largest stations were at Lake Tyers, Ramahyuck, Hindmarsh, Lake Condah, Framlingham and Coranderrk. All people of Aboriginal descent were encouraged to move to the reserves. The site, use and naming of reserves was often subject to Aboriginal influence, but their size and tenure were prey to settler 'land hunger' and the politics of race. In 1886, the Aborigines Protection Law Amendment Act redefined Aboriginality to exclude people with some white ancestry. 'Half-castes', as they were called, were forced off the reserves and were expected to integrate with the European community, and to be 'bred white'. 'Full-bloods' were, by genetic definition, condemned to disappear. The population of the reserves dropped, with the desired effect on board expenditure, and land was returned to the crown as stations and supply depots closed. In 1917, the board tried to concentrate Kooris into one mission station at Lake Tyers, but many found ways to stay in their home country.[4]

Were the Aboriginal reserves a recognition of black land rights or manifestations of white paternalism? Was this land conceded or given? Did the reservations represent a rounding up of Aborigines, a final loss of agency and visibility, or were they assertions of Aboriginal autonomy and rights?[5] Henry Reynolds has argued that there were 'strong links in the international law of the eighteenth and nineteenth centuries between the recognition of native title and the creation of reserves'.[6] The word 'reservation', he reminds us, literally meant to keep something back, to retain in one's possession. American law recognised reservations as a 'right acknowledged' rather than a 'favour conferred'.[7] This was certainly the Aboriginal viewpoint. Aborigines used the reserve system as a way of seeking secure tenure to land, often by manipulating the environmental politics of settler society. But Australian governments failed to respect both title and tenure; from the beginning of settlement there was tension between the policies of the Colonial Office in Britain and the practice of the colonial officers in Australia. The reserves were islands of precarious native tenure increasingly under siege. Imperial concern for Aborigines was resented on the frontier, and reserves became regarded in the colonies as voluntary (and therefore legitimately capricious) forms of benevolence.[8] Emphasising the comparative primitiveness of Aborigines was a way of excepting them from the land rights of other indigenous peoples. The vestiges of land rights were under attack just as settler land rites gathered momentum.

National monuments

When Europeans ventured into landscapes that were barren of recognisable history and culture, they often turned to the natural environment rather than the uncertain human past for temporal depth. Australian colonists found that it was the disciplines of natural science rather than history that first offered them a meaningful, but sometimes disturbing, landscape narrative.[9] One way to evoke emotional depth from a landscape locked in the present was to exploit its mystery and inscrutability. In literary and artistic terms, the new land was often portrayed on a giant canvas, awesome and vast, threatening and melancholic. European romantic sensibilities found suggestions of antiquity in primeval nature, seeing pillars of rock as ancient abandoned castles, and hunched, wrinkled mountains like creatures of old.[10] Bereft of a familiar past, it was to sublime nature that colonists often turned to satisfy this yearning. Edward Snell, an engineer and artist recently arrived from England, reflected in 1850 on his impressions of South Australia: 'I miss the picture galleries, Statues, and fine buildings of England, there are no fine old churches, or cathedrals, no antiquities here, except the sea and the hills.'[11] In America even more than in Australia, natural features had invited comparisons to castles, cathedrals and ruins. Cultural anxiety in a new society meant that monumentalism was a nationalistic way of appreciating landscape.[12] By the 1860s many Americans had embraced the geological wonderlands of the west or the towering redwoods in place of ancient human monuments as symbols of national identity. Natural landscapes were listed for protection under the United States Antiquities Act of 1906. Giant redwoods that had stood long before the birth of Christ, wrote explorer Clarence King in 1864, were 'monuments of living antiquity'.[13]

Australian colonists, like their American cousins, valued tall and ancient trees as well as the sea and the hills as local antiquities. Marcus Clarke found that ancient eucalypts evoked 'thoughts of the vanished past which saw them bud and blossom'. They were, he wrote, 'fit emblems of the departed grandeur of the wilderness'.[14] The Victorian landscape photographer, Nicholas Caire, measured many outstanding specimens of the towering mountain ash in the late nineteenth century. He called them 'the oldest inhabitants in the land' and regarded them as a passing race. He gave them names: King Edward VII, Big Ben, Uncle Sam, and he photographed them for posterity lest future generations, bereft of giant trees, doubted that they had ever existed.[15] Professor T. G. B. Osborn, an Adelaide botanist writing in the *Argus* in 1921, reminded readers that the tall ash trees 'were old and venerable when Cook dropped anchor in Botany Bay', 'in full vigour' when Columbus discovered the Americas, and 'if my former colleague, Professor J. W. Gregory, now of Glasgow, is correct, they were alive before the human race had penetrated into Victoria'.[16]

Tourist interest in trees and rocks as monuments often preceded that of historic sites or buildings. Maldon and Beechworth, two Victorian towns that were designated 'historic' in the mid-twentieth century and eventually learned to boast of their buildings, first drew tourists' attention to their local rock formations.[17] Maldon's early twentieth-century *Descriptive Souvenir* featured forty-eight photographs, sixteen of which were named rock formations ('The Sphinx', 'The Witch's Head', 'The Mopoke'), and Beechworth's *Illustrated Guide* of 1892 devoted a third of its photos to rocks.[18] Residents of Hahndorf in South Australia defended their trees as 'historic' a few years before their now-famous buildings.[19] *Walkabout* magazine, which was influential in defining notions of national heritage, regularly featured tall trees and Australian rock formations (duly named). The naturalist Crosbie Morrison gave one of his 1943 radio talks about the fantasies of rocks, and their propensity to look like 'ancient ruins'.[20]

In Australia, a literary club jokingly included among its objectives the aim 'to establish a society for the erection of ancient ruins in Australia'.[21] From the late nineteenth century, people began to scour the fields and they found that some Australian ruins really did exist, such as deserted farmhouses and old windmills. 'Certainly', wrote Edgar Harris in 1922, 'our ruins are not so picturesque as those of the Old World.' And there was a further deficiency: 'They are less "permanent"'.[22] The newly defined Australian heritage was in disturbing flux. Ruins, it seemed, might be created in a generation, but 'permanent ruins' really were a misnomer.

In 1936, a Victorian Council for the Preservation of National Monuments was formed as a sub-committee of the Field Naturalists Club of Victoria. The use of the term 'monument' was significant. It implied something that was scenic, discrete, massive, discontinuous, *monumental*: something that visibly erupted from the landscape, or was imposed upon it. 'Monument' also implied a memorial purpose, as if it represented something that was disappearing, or had already been lost. Stan Mitchell, as the current president of the club, convened the foundation meeting at the National Herbarium on 12 September.[23] The gathering deplored the desecration of landmarks of historic and scenic value and requested that the Victorian parliament introduce legislation to preserve scenic attractions, historic buildings and relics, and natural objects of scientific interest.[24] The idea of 'national monuments' was to extend protection from areas or species in general to individual specimens or groups of specimens, and to inanimate objects as well. In this sense, it was the 'collection' of places, the connoisseurship of things *in situ*.[25] Japan and America were mentioned as models of good conservation practice. Mitchell, who travelled widely with his mineralogical business, had been especially impressed by the Japanese. 'In Japan', he said, 'one frequently sees old and venerated trees supported by poles or even concrete pillars, wistaria vines swathed in straw bindings, and roads diverted to preserve trees and shrubs.'[26] Among groups supporting the movement were the Australian Natives' Association, the Country Women's Association, the Royal Automobile Club, the Municipal Association, the Historical Society, the Town Planning Association, and many natural history bodies.[27]

The 'monuments' that the council felt warranted protection included canoe trees, roadside trees, rock formations, old camping grounds, and 'places of historical association'. There were stories of lamentable neglect and deliberate vandalism. A tree at Cooktown in Queensland that Captain Cook had tied his boat to had been ignored for many years until it was eventually burned. All that was left was a piece of its wood preserved at a local school. The 'Dig Tree' of Burke and Wills was 'slowly breaking up' and had not yet received a second inscription.[28] A portion of a tree inscribed by Major Mitchell near Hamilton had been earlier preserved as a 'monument'.[29] One of the tallest mountain ash trees, Furmston's Tree, was discovered in 1933 and visited by a civic delegation from Healesville. It became a popular site of pilgrimage for hikers, and was nominated as a national monument in 1945.[30] The council was concerned about vandalism—in the form of graffiti—at such places as the Sisters Rocks near Stawell. Mitchell said that the rocks appeared 'to be a suburban directory'.[31] When Mitchell joined a Royal Geographical Society of Queensland expedition to the Carnarvon Ranges, he was again disgusted by the vandalism he observed, by names scrawled on Aboriginal rock art in 'Mooleyamber Gorge'. 'It was as bad as autographing a picture in the National Gallery', he declared.[32] The former federal politician, King

O'Malley, asked what had become of the foundation stone of Parliament House, a piece of polished granite laid on Kurrajong Hill, Canberra, by the King during his visit to Australia as Prince of Wales in 1920. 'What kind of vandalism do you call the removal of that historic stone?' he asked.[33]

Tourism cultivated this concern for visible, visitable places, and provided economic justification for their defence. At the Carnarvon Ranges, Mitchell envisaged a tourist camp with an airport—the area, he believed, 'should appeal strongly to overseas visitors as a natural museum of the Australian aborigines—the sole surviving stone age people in the world'. He believed strongly in the tourist potential of Aboriginal landscapes and in the restoration of Aboriginal names so as to 'give the place a definite character of its own which would possibly be unique in the world'.[34]

Stan Mitchell was an appropriate promoter of monuments; stone culture was his specialty. But monuments were site-specific, and Mitchell was the great collector, a strong critic of proposed legislative action against artefact gatherers. How is it that he could now so actively espouse the aura of place? 'Monuments' represented a collector's view of place; they were discrete sites and individual specimens plotted on the map that offered a sort of typology of space. Mitchell deplored desecration, not collection. He defended even Aboriginal places chiefly as sites of European sentiment. Their camping grounds were his collecting grounds. Mitchell's major work, *Stone Age Craftsmen* (1949), became most valued as an annotated guide to Victoria's collection sites.

There was a close link between the campaign to conserve nature and the efforts to mark historic sites, as revealed by the mutual use of the term 'monument'. Baldwin Spencer, one of the defenders of the Wilson's Promontory National Park, was also chairman of the Victorian War Memorials Committee. He expressed strong concern over the export of native animals and the destruction of forests. 'Patriotism', he urged, 'calls upon Australians to treat their heritage in land and freshwater fauna as a special and peculiarly Australian possession.'[35] The natural and human landscape was seen to be a valuable emotional and educational resource, increasingly under threat. Nature had to be preserved and explained and the past needed to be secured and made visible. Only then could popular attachment to the soil be secured. In September 1937 the Geelong Town Planning Association arranged a gathering at Dog Rocks near Batesford to propose the area for a national park. The president of the association, Dr F. Moreton, said that it was important that people visit the spot, 'to create a desire for possession'.[36]

Nature study in schools aimed to encourage a positive view of the country and to overturn what was cast as an imported (and distorted) negative outlook. In 1911, the Victorian director of Education, Frank

Tate, like Donald Macdonald, identified Marcus Clarke for special criticism. Referring to Clarke's depiction of kookaburras with 'horrible peals of semi-human laughter', Tate wrote:

> But then Marcus Clarke was English-bred, and did not come to Australia till he was eighteen years old. It makes all the difference in our appreciation of bird or tree or flower to have known it as a boy . . .
>
> It is time that we Australians fought against the generally received opinion that the dominant note of our scenery is weird melancholy. This is the note sounded mainly by those who were bred elsewhere, who came to us with other associations and other traditions, and sojourned among us. It will not be the opinion of the native-born when they find appropriate speech.[37]

Most of those involved in 'the memorial movement' in Victoria in the early twentieth century were native born and they believed that local nature and history would provide the sources of 'appropriate speech'.

In 1925, Sir James Barrett edited a collection of essays entitled *Save Australia: A Plea for the Right Use of our Flora and Fauna*. It included Charles Long's essay on monuments. It was an early and passionate defence of Australian nature and history on a national canvas, paying particular attention to the destruction of forests and the rapacious fur trade.[38] Tim Bonyhady has described the 1920s and 1930s as 'a period when the language of popular debate about the environment was both more extreme and more nationalistic than at any time before or since'.[39] Alongside the cloying nationalism was a strong advocacy for utilitarian conservation. A. S. Kenyon opposed grazing in water catchments, and James Barrett enunciated the ideals of environmental stewardship. Bonyhady has shown how many of Streeton's later paintings, which became regarded as repetitive and conservative, were protests against the despoliation of forests, soil and water. These conservationists used the language of war, lamenting the 'massacre' and 'murder' of nature; they were defending and marshalling national resources. Fire, the greatest threat to the forests, was represented on one 1940s Forests Commission poster as a genie with an Asian face.[40] 'Defense of forests necessary as defense against invasion' was one of Streeton's cryptic jottings linking nature to nation.[41]

In search of classical soil

The Tasmanian explorer and surveyor James Calder had regretted the absence in Australia of 'classical soil', of the visible and ennobling evidence of history.[42] Colonists found that recalling the Australian past was full of pitfalls. Yet there were still some pockets of classical soil they could till.

It was to the footprints of explorers that many turned. These imprints recalled heroes of national stature who had been early on the scene but were largely free of the penal taint, and—despite occasional bloody brushes with the original inhabitants—it had rarely been their burden to defend the possessions they claimed. In 1822, members of the Philosophical Society of Australasia marked the spot at Botany Bay where they thought Cook and Banks had landed in 1770, their uncertainty of the exact spot a measure of the urgency of their task.[43] Judge Barron Field published a sonnet on the occasion:

Here fix the tablet. This must be the place
Where our Columbus of the South did land;
He saw the Indian village on that sand,
And on this rock first met the simple race
Of Australasia, who presum'd to face
With lance and spear his musquet. Close at hand
Is the clear stream, from which his vent'rous band
Refresh'd their ship; and thence a little space
Lies Sutherland, their shipmate; for the sound
Of Christian burial better did proclaim
Possession, than the flag, in England's name.
These were the commelinae Banks first found;
But where's the tree with the ship's wood-carv'd fame?
Fix then th'Ephesian brass. 'Tis classic ground.[44]

Planting a body was a more sacred appropriation of land than was planting a flag. These traces of English humanity on an alien soil needed a more permanent memorial than could be offered by 'wood-carv'd fame'.

Cook was a less ambiguous figure than Governor Phillip for a symbol of European beginnings and was popular for commemorations and statues. He came to so dominate reflection that, in 1888, many thought they were celebrating the centenary of Cook's landing. Even George Belcher, parliamentarian and Geelong pioneer, and a man full of a sense of history and occasion, wrote in his diary on 26 January of that year: '100 years ago today since Capt. Cook landed at Sydney and planted the British flag on the Australian Continent'.[45] Victoria also made its tenuous claim on the great navigator. After all, it was a part of the Victorian coast which had given Cook his first sighting of eastern Australia, and which he had named Point Hicks. Cook, by sighting the Victorian coast and then turning north, had 'missed his chance' according to A. S. Kenyon (who much preferred Flinders anyway).[46]

For the state's centenary, a cottage built by Cook's father in Great Ayton, Yorkshire, was transported to Melbourne's Fitzroy Gardens, and the space it left in the English village was marked by a great boulder from Cape Everard, the renamed Point Hicks. Russell Grimwade, who purchased the cottage and presented it to the Victorian government, had great faith in the historical eloquence of both cottage and boulder. The exchange of these chunks of nature and culture, labelled vandalism by a British newspaper, was meant to solemnise Victoria's link with this early English presence.[17]

Lieutenant Hicks sighted Victoria from Cook's *Endeavour* on 19 April 1770. In 1911, the Victorian Education Department declared that date 'Discovery Day'. Foundation Day or ANA Day—January 26—had disqualified itself by falling outside the school year, embalmed in summer somnolence. Would it, in any case, have had too many penal associations for a state proud that it had escaped, just, a convict beginning? So 19 April became a day for schoolchildren to reflect on the discoverers, and to be reminded that Australia was indeed a home, for it had a history as a home should have.[18] But this Victorian appropriation of Cook was foiled by the landing at Gallipoli in 1915. April 25 became a sacred day on the Australian calendar and gave history teachers quite enough to do that week. The rhythms of the school year were again lined up beside the annals of history and a new day was proclaimed: November 19 became 'Pioneers' Day', for it commemorated the date Edward Henty landed at Portland and became, as schoolchildren were told, Victoria's first permanent settler. What made Henty 'permanent' were his sheep and his plough, with which he transformed the land. His plough became an object of display, a relic, and the turf it first turned was marked by a monument. It was classic ground.

The early twentieth century saw an increase in official attempts to mark out Australia's past in place and time. In Victoria, a 'memorial movement' was led by Sir James Barrett, Charles Long, Frank Tate, and Alfred Kenyon and Charles Daley of the recently formed Historical Society of Victoria. Between about 1910 and the early 1930s, this Victorian Historical Memorials Committee initiated the erection of over one hundred cairns and plaques to explorers throughout the state.

In 1925 Charles Long published an essay entitled 'Monuments, Local Histories and Commemoration Days'. The three, he explained, must be closely related: 'The local history should be appealed to periodically to explain the reason for the erection of the monument, and the monument should be made the centre for commemoration services at regular intervals.'[49] He believed that monuments caused one to pause and reflect, encouraged a sense of history, and also had a broader, national value: 'by the feeling of close relationship to the past and the recognition of race kinship that they engender, they aid in cementing together that race, and urging it onward to fresh efforts . . . '[50] Long introduced these values to Victorian children through *The School Paper*, which he edited from 1896.[51] He was an ardent imperialist and an Australian nationalist and the author of books such as *Stories of Australian Exploration* (1903) and *British Worthies and Other Men of Might* (1912). He and Frank Tate regarded schools as 'laboratories of good citizenship' and Tate urged 'school power' as a contribution to national survival under 'the law of the survival of the fittest'.[52] *The School Paper* carried graphic descriptions of warfare, accounts of heroic exploits and reports of local military parades and activities. Monuments and local history could help the Australian child feel 'that history belongs not merely to distant countries and a long-dead past, but has been and is being made on the very spot where he dwells'.[53] Looking around him, Long was moved to ask: 'Can the worth as an Imperial asset of, say, the statue of Australia's first Governor in the Domain, Sydney, or of the statue of the martyred hero of Khartoum, in the neighbourhood of Parliament House, Melbourne, be overestimated?'[54]

The Victorian Historical Memorials Committee wanted to create an instructive landscape, one that would offer places of association, refuges of reflection, and material evidence of humanity. In a summary of their work published in 1944 by Charles Daley and Sir James Barrett, pre-European Australia was characterised as possessing 'no evidences whatever of bygone civilisation or of vanished empires such as distinguish the four continents'. There was, they regretted:

> a complete absence of 'storied urn or animated bust,' of 'column trophied for triumphal show,' as in Europe; or of 'temples, palaces and piles stupendous,' as in Africa, Asia, and even America—the mute but dignified memorials of vast changes and vicissitudes in the history of nations in remote ages.[55]

It was this deficiency that they sought to overcome. Their chosen heroes were Matthew Flinders, George Bass, Hume and Hovell, Angus McMillan, Paul Edmund de Strzelecki, Major Mitchell and Charles Sturt. A. H. Hansford plotted their journeys on the map of Victoria and where they intersected with more modern pathways, a cairn was built. The lonely cairn translated a mark on a map into a place. Together, they made a string of places, points along a journey. The Hume and Hovell memorials, said Kenyon, lay across Victoria 'like a scarf of honour'. Barrett compared these lines of cairns to the King's crosses in Great Britain, and Daley described them as 'concrete and tangible, yet symbolic and inspiring'. They were pillars of rough stones, their rugged and unrefined nature 'emblematic of the time and conditions' they commemorated. It was also explained that a cairn of individual stones was democratic in its meaning: 'they did honour to all pioneers, each stone being a record of some brave deed or act of sacrifice.'[56] They were makeshift obelisks, another classical image planted in Australian soil.[57]

The simple cairns were also cheap and easy to erect. This was a virtue for a scheme which depended on the enthusiasm of local committees along the explorer's route. The cairns varied little from one town to another, although one committee was commended for erecting the highest. The simpler they were, the more urgently they could be erected. Their primary role was to mark historic spots before they were forgotten; the cairn itself could be elaborated later if necessary. Inscriptions were to be very simple, for the aura of place said it all.

The unveiling of the explorers' cairns were occasions for speeches about country life, immigration and defence. Donald Macdonald, as an eloquent and popular advocate of the 'life of the open air', sometimes attended and joined the speakers by the memorial. The organisers themselves made their cairn-unveiling journeys a great celebration of the country, a conscious and joyous balance to their city lives as well as a 'pilgrimage' along the explorer's route. Decentralisation was encouraged, closer settlement urged. It was thought that the cairns helped humanise these distant regions, anchored local sentiment, and declared that the land had been won. Sometimes local Aboriginal identities were incorporated in the ceremony, generally those identified as 'the last of the tribe'. The cairns thus acquired a triumphal air in their linear march across the land they claimed.

Alfred Kenyon described one of the Memorials Committee's tours in Gippsland in 1927.[58] He was keen to point out that all members of the Victorian Historical Memorials Committee were native born and that most of the executive of the Victorian Historical Association were 'full born Australians'. The official tour group numbered thirteen and included Kenyon's daughter, Justine, whose marginal status was confirmed by her role as a 'chauffeur'. The party was led by Sir James Barrett and was accompanied by the Governor of Victoria, Lord Somers. They began the tour at Benambra 'where [Angus] McMillan on his second and successful attempt took off', and were there greeted by 'the few remaining pioneers' seated on their horses, together with schoolchildren, boy scouts and girl guides. The cairn unveiled by the Governor commemorated the early settlers and was situated 'quite fittingly in the schoolgrounds'. That night was spent at Bruthen at a shire banquet, 'the forerunner of many more' wrote Kenyon, licking his lips. At Yarram, the whole town had declared a holiday and awaited the vice-regal party in their thousands; at Korumburra, the officials enjoyed 'another luxurious repast' and a display of bullock driving 'with verbal accompaniments'.

Along the route, twenty-four cairns were unveiled, over ten thousand people assembled 'including a considerable proportion of children', and nearly one hundred speeches were made. Kenyon was impressed by the country people they met along the way and noted the duty they felt 'to hand on to their children the lands—made available for them by the discoverers, and to hand it down as a British possession'.[59] As if the symbolism was so far insufficient, the Bairnsdale cairn to Angus McMillan, 'the discoverer of Gippsland', was erected over the grave of an Aboriginal 'king', 'Bruden Munjee'.[60]

The first memorials in this series were unveiled in a landscape relatively barren of public monuments. Melbourne boasted statues of Burke and Wills, Redmond Barry, General Gordon, and a few others, and country towns had one or two erected to the discovery of gold, the 'last' Aborigine, or to soldiers who served in the Boer War. But throughout the 1920s, memorials to the Great War claimed their central places in almost every community. The Victorian Historical Memorials Committee gained impetus from this parallel movement. If the overseas defenders of this land were to be honoured, then so should the founders and discoverers of it. The comparison gave further solemnity to the explorers' cairns. Their victory, it was said, was 'bloodless', but it had been a sort of war nonetheless.[61]

While the cairns to their usurpers were erected, another cairn of stones was being built at the National Museum of Victoria. As described in chapter 3, collectors were removing the field evidence of Aboriginal occupation and piling up their tens of thousands of Aboriginal stone tools into a sort of central memorial cairn to 'the stone age'. While one set of cairns was inventing places for the European imagination, the other cairn was leaching the landscape of Aboriginal meaning, disassembling place.

Pioneers and soldiers

The echo of war gave impetus to another Victorian memorial initiative of this period. It was a campaign to save the Old Melbourne Cemetery site at the north of the city block and to erect Victoria's Great War memorial in its grounds. The threat to the site came from the rapidly developing Queen Victoria Market on its northern border. The cemetery, which dated from 1837, was superseded by the present Melbourne General Cemetery in the early 1850s, but continued to accept burials. In 1915 the crown land grant for the Old Cemetery was revoked, and plans began for the exhumation of bodies.[62] The Old Cemetery and Soldiers Memorial Union was formed to protect and develop the historic site, and its leader, Isaac Selby, wrote *The Old Pioneers' Memorial History of*

Melbourne (1924) as a passionate defence of the Old Cemetery. It was, he said, Melbourne's earliest memorial. Burke and Wills' statue was falsely proclaimed as the city's first public memorial, argued Selby, for it was preceded by twelve memorials erected by public subscription in the Old Cemetery. He called it 'the greatest historic cemetery in Australia'. Referring to Sydney's cemetery which was destroyed, he found 'no comparison between the ground given over partially to murderers, forgers and perjurers, and our own, where the anti-transportation men were buried'. Selby also noted that 'while we are one of the youngest capitals, Victoria is old; it was the first part of Australia seen by Cook'.[63]

The original name of his society demonstrated the dual nature of Selby's claim on the land—to save the pioneers and to build a new memorial to the soldiers. His rhetoric drew them powerfully together:

> Surely here is the spot on which to erect our national memorial to the heroic men who fell at the front, to bind up the older and newer history together, associating the story of the men who created our city with that of those who defended our Empire; then there would have been in the heart of Melbourne an Old and New Testament, sanctified and sealed by the ministry of the pioneers, and the sacrifice of immortal men and women who gave their lives for the liberty of the world. I propose to build here a tower of strength and a hall of fame, in a garden beautified by the flora of Victoria.[64]

The two sets of heroes were compared repeatedly. Both had died young. Many of the pioneers were themselves soldiers, 'Old Grenadiers, Napoleonic Heroes'. Perched on the edge of the southern sea over which many emigrants had sailed, the memorials in the Old Melbourne Cemetery must have initially seemed like those overseas war graves, tombs stranded from loved ones.[65] Richard Howitt called them, in 1843, 'foreign graves'.[66] There was the irony that at the same time as Australia was seeking assurances of the permanency of overseas war graves, Melbourne councillors were moving to rip up those in their backyard. Selby bitterly remarked that the permanency of an overseas cemetery was 'contingent, I presume, on the Frenchmen never wanting a vegetable market in that district'.[67]

Isaac Selby was a litigious character. Born in London in 1859, he emigrated with his parents to New Zealand, and later in Melbourne became known as an evangelist, a freethought lecturer (for a period), and a writer and speaker on historical topics.[68] In 1904, while on a lecture tour in the United States, he sought a divorce from his wife and conducted his own case before Judge Hebbard in a San Francisco court. The *Australasian* reported the proceedings: 'When the judge issued a decree in favour of his wife, Selby became enraged. He produced a

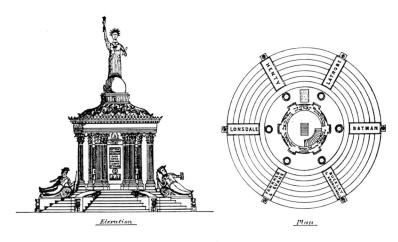

Elevation *Plan*

THE OLD PIONEERS' MEMORIAL
FLAGSTAFF GARDENS
Melbourne

Isaac Selby's design for an Old Pioneers' Memorial in the Flagstaff Gardens:
Liberty stands 'where the pioneer and the Anzac place it', surrounded by
eucalyptus leaves, Victorian laurel, the figures and names of pioneers, and
picture panels telling the history of Melbourne 'from the survey of Victoria by
Captain Cook' to the first world war. *(From Selby,* The Old Pioneers' Memorial
History of Melbourne, *Melbourne, The Old Pioneers' Memorial Fund, 1924)*

revolver, and fired at Judge Hebbard on his seat on the bench.' The shot,
fortunately, missed its mark.[69] Selby was sentenced to seven years
imprisonment for attempted murder and to a period in a lunatic asylum.
He claimed that he had been writing a book against bloodshed, and had
fired a shot only to test the strength of the American legal system.[70] When
Selby returned to Melbourne and took up the cause of the Old Cemetery,
he brought to his campaign a bitter zealousness which alienated some
of his supporters. The Historical Society of Victoria stood aside from
much of the debate about the Old Cemetery, and was criticised by him.[71]
Selby also failed to co-operate with a parallel organisation, the Old
Melbourne Cemetery Preservation League led by A. H. Padley, which
placed more emphasis on the religious significance of the cemetery. But
Selby's passion was informed by a detailed knowledge of early Melbourne
that makes his long and rambling book fascinating reading. One reviewer
called it 'Selby's gossip' and referred to him as 'a chatterbox grown-up
and full'.[72]

Selby distinguished his 'memorial' history from 'purely literary'
history.[73] His primary sources were monuments and the people who

visited them. He compared the cemetery memorials to coins and stone implements: they were 'our native curiosities', and 'a part of our archaeology', he wrote. By making this link with archaeology, Selby felt he was invoking the 'scientific spirit' which, he explained, had revolutionised history through the work of people such as Henry Thomas Buckle and Charles Darwin. His arguments were shaped by a clumsy positivism. Like the sociologist Auguste Comte who described three stages in the evolution of thought, Selby saw three stages in the history of Melbourne—Foundation, Separation and Federation. Just as evolution was supposed to condemn Aborigines to museums and graveyards, so did it disdain the thing which threatened Selby's cemetery—the centralised market: 'To the evolutionist the centralized retail market is a rudimentary organ of commercialism; it belongs to primitive conditions, and is seen to-day in New Guinea . . . It belongs to the age of barter and bargain.'[74] The material evidence of the past, Selby believed, was a privileged source, 'the faithful servant of the Historian': Monuments mark exact spots, and give exact dates and descriptions, and thus lead to true conclusions.[75]

He contrasted the stones in the cemetery, which he regarded as 'archaeological', with the 1914 statue of Captain Cook erected on the St Kilda foreshore which, while it kept Cook's name in the public mind, 'marks no historic spot'.[76] The spirit of place was powerful. Westgarth and Garryowen wrote their histories of Melbourne after wandering in the Old Cemetery. Selby himself used the social life of the graveside as an entrée into the private worlds of memory and family. With its community of tombs, many of them primitive red gum slabs, the cemetery alone could evoke the raw village intimacy of early Melbourne. The Mayor of Melbourne, Frank Stapley, apparently bewildered by Selby's ardent defence of the site, asked him if he viewed the ground as the Chinese did, and thought the land itself celestial.[77]

Selby replied that it was historical, not celestial. There were those who criticised him 'for using History as an argument'.[78] Although Selby fought, above all, to save the cemetery site, he was forced to negotiate various compromises which involved, first, a pioneers' corner on a remnant of the original site, and later, the removal of selected graves and monuments to the Flagstaff Gardens. In the design he put forward for the Flagstaff option, 'the Westminster Abbey of Victoria', two monuments were set apart—John Batman's and the unknown Anzac—and each was carefully provided with space for ceremonies around it.[79]

The obelisk above Batman's grave became the symbol of the fight for the Old Cemetery. For many years his burial site had been neglected and unmarked, and there was even doubt about exactly where it was. By 1880, to a colony beginning to take pride in its early history and confident now of Batman's status as the 'Founder of Melbourne', this oversight seemed a disgrace. Historian J. J. Shillinglaw led a campaign which, in 1882, resulted in the erection of a bluestone obelisk over what was thought to be Batman's last resting place.[80] But he was to have no rest. The Old Cemetery and Soldiers Memorial Union met frequently at Batman's grave and developed a tradition of marking 'The Birthday of Australia' with a service, lecture, and 'Foundation Celebrations' at his tomb.[81] Selby had observed with pleasure as children from the King Street State School had gathered at his monument in the Old Cemetery to learn of the beginnings of their city.[82] Would the obelisk have the same meaning elsewhere? If moved to the Flagstaff Gardens, it would at least stand where Melbourne's first burials had been. But the monument was moved to the banks of the Yarra, which Batman possibly did not sail up in June 1835, and his grave was transferred, ironically, to a cemetery named Fawkner.[83] His new tomb, an obelisk of Harcourt granite, was unveiled on Foundation Sunday, January 27, 1924, by his young great-great-grandson, Leslie Batman Weire. Selby reminded the gathering that it was Batman who 'gave civil freedom to Victoria, and saved it from the stain of penal contamination suffered by other colonies'.[84]

Convicts and war provided some of Selby's ammunition, they were the substance of his 'use of History as an argument'. But he was prepared to use other arguments as well, and called on the language of Sir James Barrett and Charles Long when he wrote: 'We are trying to realise the ideal, and give the country the culture of the city, and the city the health and ozone of the country, therefore we fight for the preservation of such open spaces as the Cemetery.'[85]

Charles Long occasionally presided over protest meetings about the fate of the cemetery. Selby respected his work and used many illustrations from *The School Paper* in his *Memorial History*. They agreed about the setting aside of commemoration days and ceremonial spaces to prompt reflection on the past.[86] The cemetery was a plot of country in the city, an open space lively with gossip, a piece of Melbourne turf with a village past.

A centennial pastorale

Melbourne was always going to be the place for a village, and that promise of its foundation was celebrated in 1934 and 1935. Melbourne's Centenary Celebrations were bracketed by two symbolic moments: the landing at Portland on 19 November 1834 by Edward Henty and John

Batman's diary entry for 8 June 1835 that stated: 'This will be the place for a village.'[87] The icons of imperialism were marshalled into the presence of Victorians for the occasion: His Royal Highness the Duke of Gloucester, third son of His Majesty King George V, arrived in October; Lord Baden-Powell, Chief Scout, lent his presence to the Boy Scout Jamboree held at Frankston in December and January, the largest to be organised outside Europe; the Poet Laureate John Masefield was invited and wrote a poem; Cook's cottage was reassembled in the Fitzroy Gardens; and Rudyard Kipling's ode in honour of centennial Melbourne was read at the dedication of Melbourne's new Shrine of Remembrance on 11 November. Military and imperial rhetoric was so prominent in proceedings that the second National All Australia Anti-War Congress was held in Melbourne in November 1934 as a provocative counterpoint.[88]

The progress of the state was expressed in rural metaphors of growth, fertility and plenty.[89] Kathleen Ussher, author of the celebratory centenary book entitled *Hail Victoria!*, described Victoria's history as a 'story of the Argonauts setting out in search of the Golden Fleece'.[90] The Duke of Gloucester even sheared six merino sheep, said to be descendants of John Macarthur's flocks.[91] The Centenary Art Exhibition, organised by Bob Croll, honoured the legacy of McCubbin, Streeton and Roberts and awarded its prize to Rex Battarbee. Melbourne's strengthened identity as a 'Garden City' was one of the enduring products of centenary image-making. Even Captain Cook's cottage was valued as much for its mid-city whiff of rural nostalgia, its village air, as for its dubious historical associations.

For descendants of the gold generation, the pastoral era of Victoria's beginnings was shrouded in an alluring and freeing mystery. Their own forebears escaped the moral ambiguities of that particular frontier. Many historians took to the stage during Victoria's centenary or wrote commemorative texts, but perhaps the most influential and persistent during this decade was A. S. Kenyon. After Baldwin Spencer's death (in July 1929), when the debate about Aboriginal antiquity took new directions, Kenyon stopped collecting stone artefacts and started, quite intensely, to write history. He was also a regular public speaker. Kenyon collaborated with A. H. Greig, Charles Daley and Charles Long to write *Victoria: The First Century* (1934), the official centenary history.

Kenyon was the leading writer of Victorian pastoral history and even today historians rely on the work that he did with R. V. Billis in documenting the squatting age. The 'greatest romance' in Australian history, reflected Kenyon:

> is the rise of the sheep breeder or pastoralist . . . the finest example of man's mastery over the opposing forces of nature, of his justification of his position at the head of the organic world, is . . . the breeding of fine wool.[92]

Kenyon quoted Adam Lindsay Gordon, that 'poet and horseman', to prove that 'the life of the pastoralist is the ideal one'. Possession, explained Kenyon, came naturally to squatters: 'Some were from the professions . . . all possessors of some means.'[93] Through an account of the pastoralist, Kenyon told the story of what he called 'the peopling of the continental spaces' or 'the filling up of Victoria's vacant corners'. Billis and Kenyon produced a much used map of squatting runs in Victoria which represented pastoral holdings as discrete, bounded territories (rather like Aboriginal tribal areas) that pieced together into a jigsaw claiming the whole of the state.[94] The map was exhaustive of space. Kenyon, who disparaged Aboriginal antiquity, was compiling his map of squatting runs at about the same time that Norman Tindale, the pioneer archaeologist, was mapping Aboriginal territories.[95]

Kenyon did not suppress the historical precedence of the Aborigines: 'gold was first discovered by the aborigines just as they were the original discoverers of Australia', he wrote.[96] He used words like 'dispossession' and 'occupation' but in a context that defused them. Australia's occupation by Europeans was simple, he claimed, because of 'the absence of any coloured race worthy of consideration'.[97] He described it as '[a]n occupation where the dispossessors and the possessors lay down in amity side by side like the lion and the lamb, with the usual result to the lamb'.[98]

Kenyon went out of his way to excuse the squatter of any violence towards Aborigines. 'The old-time mission station has more to answer for than the squatter's station', explained Kenyon.[99] His was a class history, of wealth versus labour. Any frontier violence, said Kenyon hedging his bets, was perpetrated by the lower classes and was unsanctioned and regrettable. He repeatedly scoffed at the tales of massacres and poisoned flour, while admitting that the rumours were widespread. In fact his continual slapping down of these stories reveals that a strong current of oral testimony of frontier violence did exist, and that Kenyon and others sought to control and suppress it. Massacre history has sometimes been depicted as a product of white academics in the 1970s and 1980s, but Kenyon provides evidence that it existed much earlier in a popular, oral form. Kenyon was not inhabiting a silence, he was creating it. He was confronting a cacophony of undisciplined voices. Noise there was, and he sought to overwhelm it. Kenyon's carefully constructed 'white noise' was in response to an unruly babble of whispers.

A. S. Kenyon's other work demonstrated the strong links between his collecting of artefacts and broader cultural and political debates in Australia. As a water engineer, he was involved in reclaiming marginal land for pastoral and agricultural use. He irrigated dry land and drained wet land, making the open spaces productive. In his many public talks he urged the development of northern Australia and advocated a white Australia. He spoke out against those who attempt 'to raise obstacles to settlement of new lands, to assert the impossibility of their successful utilisation for primary production & to decry the white man's ability to endure the inland climatic conditions'. Australia's pre-eminence, wrote Kenyon, was 'due to it having been white from its very foundation'.[100]

A country childhood

Many of the writers and reformers trying to bring the country to the city had made that migration themselves, or associated the bush with formative periods of their lives. If they had since seen 'their country' swallowed by the city, there was extra poignancy to their memories. Bringing the country to the city, then, was like bringing the past to the present; it was a historical as well as a visionary enterprise, a form of urban planning tinged with nostalgia.

Donald Macdonald cherished memories of Keilor, and Charles Barrett recalled the open paddocks of Hawthorn or harked back to the old bush hut at Olinda Creek. Alfred Kenyon had worked as a boy on his Wimmera farm, J. H. Leach (of *Australian Bird Book* fame) grew up in Creswick, and A. H. Chisholm wrote of the haunted forests of his upbringing in Maryborough. The peripatetic Stan Mitchell anchored his memories with accounts of *his* bush hut during Dargo days, and Charles Long, born at Wallan, later turned a historian's eye on the town of his first teaching appointment, Alexandra.[101] Charles Daley grew up in Bendigo and worked there as a head teacher, as well as at Maldon, Stawell, Geelong and Sale, before moving to the metropolis, and Frank Tate hailed from Castlemaine. They were mostly children of the gold generation, all born in the decade or two following the 1850s. Theirs were not the longings of immigrants for an abandoned rural inheritance in distant lands, but rather, strong personal attachments to beloved places in their own backyard.

There has been much debate about the origin of the Australian bush legend. Was it an artefact of nomadic rural experience propagated to a burgeoning urban populace, or was it the imaginings of alienated city writers and artists about terrain they hardly knew?[102] In both interpretations 'the bush' is seen as an amorphous territory, the spacious home of the itinerant worker or a wide, inviting horizon for the urban escapee. The only intimacy to be found in these open spaces, according to these interpretations, was shifting and social rather than locational. 'In a country urbanised before a landscape was colonised', argues art historian Ian Burn, 'a "geography" of the land continues to be shaped as

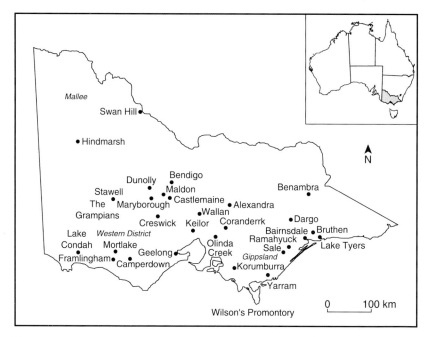

Victorian country towns and localities

much by imagination as by reality . . . *The bush* had a cultural meaning before *the landscape* acquired a specific form.'[103]

Less attention has been given, however, to the decades that followed the 1890s—partly because they are seen to be culturally conservative— and to the possible source of many country or bush 'imaginings' as nostalgia, the personal experience of contrast between country and city, and therefore about very particular places. Coming to the city was, for many of the descendants of Victoria's gold generation, a coming of age. For them, the country became associated with childhood innocence, earthiness, health, and community. This was not 'the bush' of the itinerant pastoral worker or of the dreaming city-dweller, but very particular sites of provincial upbringing, keenly remembered. Although these people became defined as 'urban', the country was as close and as personal as their own childhood.

Bob Croll waxed lyrical about his birthplace of Stawell, a former goldmining town near the Grampians in western Victoria. He was born there in 1869, and later confessed that he was one of those local boys who defaced the nearby Sisters Rocks with graffiti.[104] He came to Melbourne when he was appointed to the Victorian public service in 1886. Croll praised his country cohort of the late nineteenth century:

about fifty years ago [he wrote in the early 1940s] there was a freshening of this city of Melbourne by an influx of country boys. The day of appointment to the Public Service by patronage had gone and the lads of the villages were proving the mettle of their pastures by scoring in the new examinations which had been set.[105]

Croll spent much of his life celebrating the benevolence of these pastures. 'How few Australians would pass a full examination in things Australian!' he exclaimed in 1937. 'City knowledge—yes!—but (to paraphrase Kipling) what do they know of Australia who only the cities know!'[106] In another passage, he wrote:

If I could be Dictator of Australia I would insist that every child should be born in the country, and reside there for the first ten or twelve years of his life . . . It would build a fit nation, physically strong, intellectually bright. No more slum children.[107]

In his published memoir, *I Recall* (1939), he wrote that 'Stawell has a halo about it which grows more definite to me with the years of separation.'[108] 'The bush about the old town', he recalled, gave him his 'liking for nature in all its shapes'. He remembered bringing home a baby kookaburra in his pocket . . . [109]

When Croll first came to the city, he worked at the Melbourne Public Library, where he met Kipling during his Australian visit in 1891.[110] He remained in the Victorian public service until his retirement in 1934 as senior clerk of the Education Department and registrar of the Council of Public Education. The historian David Blair, who was also briefly R. E. Johns' local member of parliament, gave Croll early encouragement with his writing, assuring him he had 'quite the literary turn'.[111] One of Croll's most popular books, *The Open Road in Victoria* (1928), described walks in the Victorian countryside and went to a second edition within three weeks of printing.[112] He followed in 1930 with another book of walks entitled *Along the Track*, which was advertised as 'a fresh-air tonic'. He regularly invoked Baldwin Spencer and Donald Macdonald as mentors, sometimes following in their footsteps or echoing their prose. Croll had joined the Melbourne Amateur Walking and Touring Club about 1898 and claimed to have walked some three thousand miles in Victoria. He served a term as president of the Wallaby Club, a walking club for professional and university men, and therefore had his turn as custodian of the 'Anzac Stick', a tree root torn from a Gallipoli dugout that was made into the president's walking stick.[113] Croll was also a connoisseur of landscape painting and joined the Victorian

Robert Henderson Croll (1869–1947): This signed photograph is reproduced from Croll's *An Autobituary* (Melbourne, Bread and Cheese Club, 1946) which he published a year before his death.

Artists' Society in 1908 and was later elected a lay member of the council. He was a founding member of the Victorian Aboriginal Group and the Anthropological Society of Victoria, and became a supporter of Selby's Old Pioneers' Memorial Fund.[114] He was a keen collector of Aboriginal artefacts, and his son Robin helped Murray Black on one of his grave-robbing excursions.[115] Croll exemplified the self-satisfied conservatism of inter-war Melbourne establishment culture with its coalition of interests in landscape, Aborigines, painting, collecting artefacts, and country (or 'field') experience. The title of his books evoked *wide* horizons and the *open* road.

'There is nothing for it but to do our best to make the city realise there is a country vital to their existence', wrote Sir James Barrett to Croll in 1944.[116] The Field Naturalists Club of Victoria annually held 'Wild Nature Shows' in the Melbourne Town Hall, and visitors did not miss the contrastive meaning of 'wild', particularly when it was displayed in the city's civic centre. 'Mummy, this isn't Melbourne, how did we get here?', was one child's comment about the exhibition, recorded with satisfaction by organisers.[117] Children could go there to see Charles Barrett's pet possum, the Reverend George Cox's nature collections, portraits of Aborigines beside a model of the Piltdown skull, Stan Mitchell's stone implements, or they could watch Mitchell demonstrate Aboriginal fire-lighting techniques.

The Bread and Cheese Club, a Melbourne institution founded in June 1938 by J. K. Moir, provided a city base for celebrators of the country. The club, which was devoted to 'Mateship, Art and Letters', has been aptly described by John Arnold as 'the urban manifestation of the "Walkabout" school of Australian nationalism'.[118] It had gathered over two hundred members by 1943. Moir, a noted book collector, was the 'Knight Grand Cheese' (president) of the Club, and Bob Croll the 'Honourable Trencherman' (vice-president). Moir's house at 474 Bridge Road, Richmond, which was a disused hotel that he bought about 1944, became a Melbourne meeting place for lovers of Australiana and the outdoors.

John Kinmont Moir was the club's 'Oknirrabata' or Wise Old Man and he had his roots firmly in the pastoral Australia he was later to celebrate. He was born in November 1893 at Normanton in northern Queensland where his father managed a station.[119] When Moir was about ten, his family moved to Melbourne when his father became managing agent for a firm with large pastoral holdings, and seven years later Moir took to working as a jackeroo in New South Wales. From the 1920s he worked as an accountant in Melbourne. He became best known for his patronage of collectors and writers and for his outstanding personal collection of books, pamphlets, manuscripts and photographs which he donated to the Victorian State Library in the mid-1950s. Bill Harney, the Northern Territory writer, recalled his visits to Moir's house in a poem that evoked the collector's world of 'Plaque and picture and inscribed jug 'midst spears and an inscribed bell . . . Australia's past goes by me as I stand on a sacred floor'.[120] The librarian John Feely recalled 474 Bridge Road as 'a veritable Aladdin's Cave' with a 'museum of Australiana'. 'His camera was always with him', recalled Harry Hastings Pearce, 'and anything, object, building, place, monument, etc. was certain to be taken, even if it meant a special journey, or the going of miles out of one's way.'[121] Moir, this great inscriber and collector of inscriptions, was keen on erecting plaques and marking historic spots. He inaugurated the Adam Lindsay Gordon Wattle Movement (distributing seeds from the poet's grave for planting throughout the world), was patron of the Gordon Lovers' Society, a member of the Ballarat Gordon Cottage Memorial Committee, the Gould League of Bird Lovers, the Wattle League, a life member of the Lawson Society, and a councillor of the Royal Historical Society of Victoria.[122]

In the foundation year of the Bread and Cheese Club, Moir (with the support of the Field Naturalists Club of Victoria) instituted the Australian Natural History Medallion to recognise services to the description and study of local nature. Winners included Alec Chisholm, Charles Barrett, Crosbie Morrison and Stan Mitchell. The medallion was inscribed not with native flora or fauna, but with the portrait of an Aborigine sitting by a camp-fire at night. In the same year as the medallion was inaugurated, members of the Bread and Cheese Club organised a Melbourne exhibition of Albert Namatjira's paintings.[123] The club frequently used and promoted motifs of Aboriginal culture.

Aboriginal words and symbols increasingly became part of the 'appropriate speech' of the native born in the early twentieth century, and were used to define a white indigenous culture. When dealing with the black past, settler Australians experienced the tensions between conquest and inheritance. In 1904, the New South Wales governor was welcomed to the town of Singleton by a 'native arch', a display of local Aboriginal artefacts bridging the main street with the word 'Welcome' formed out of boomerangs. Just a few years before, the residents of Singleton had petitioned to have the local Aboriginal population removed from the town. This was the only public exhibition of an impressive collection of Aboriginal artefacts gathered since the 1890s by Alexander Morrison, a newspaper proprietor in Singleton. Many of the Aboriginal artefacts may have been made for him, or given to him, by Kooris at the nearby St Clair Mission.[124]

When Agnes Edwards, 'Queen Aggie, last of the Moolpas', died in Swan Hill in 1928, her obituarist wrote:

> We may think in white of the bush and love as whites the bushland. In degree
> of thinking and loving it will not be intenser than that in the blacks we may
> despise . . . There is a spirit in the bush that belongs to them more than to
> white people. It is that which has been inherited . . . [125]

A group of poets centred on Adelaide and calling themselves
'Jindyworobaks' was formed in the late 1930s and drew inspiration from
Aboriginal images and understandings of landscape. They rejected
'pseudo-Europeanism' and advocated 'environmental values'.[126] As early
as 1925, the artist Margaret Preston advocated the use of Aboriginal
decorative motifs in homes and public places and, in promoting an
'indigenous art of Australia', she hoped to rid herself 'of the mannerisms
of a country other than my own'.[127] Alfred Kenyon and Stan Mitchell,
who rejected European models in archaeology, both encouraged the use
of Aboriginal names for landscape features, and Justine Kenyon published
an Aboriginal word-list. Donald Macdonald gave his Jolimont home an
Aboriginal name, 'Woongara', which he hoped meant 'rest'.[128] Croll used
'Barak' as a pen-name and Kenyon often wrote under the pseudonym of
'Kulin', Barak being a prominent Wurundjeri elder and 'Kulin' the name
for Aboriginal people of the Port Phillip area. Croll and Alec Chisholm
were members of the Melbourne Savage Club, a 'bohemian' society that
playfully exploited and assumed the symbols of indigenous peoples.[129]
European use of the word 'native'—which in one context could be so
derogatory and in another so proud—was expressive of the appropriation of indigenous citizenship. Members of the Australian Natives' Association fostered a respectful sense of succession through their
sponsorship of monuments to the 'last of the tribe', and they were rarely
worried by any ambiguity about 'native'. But the Aborigines were, and
briefly formed a *Real* Australian Native Association.[130]

During these years the primary source of Aboriginal imagery and of
native lore became central Australia, an area of tenuous white settlement.
The grandest Australian pilgrimage—a land rite of continental size—
became the journey to the centre. In his sixties, Bob Croll discovered
central Australia, an experience that 'quickened' and politicised his
interest in Aboriginal culture. In the ten years from 1929, the year of
Baldwin Spencer's death, he made six journeys in Spencer's footsteps to
central Australia. Croll's own country in Victoria, the place of his
childhood, was occupied, secure and beloved, mapped by the walking
tracks that he helped to popularise. But what of the empty spaces at the
heart of the continent? For Croll, as for many others in the first half of
the twentieth century, the centre was a stretched, blank canvas waiting
to be inscribed. Croll visited central Australia in the company of both
artists and scientists and dabbled in two of the emerging forms of white

fascination with the centre, painting and psychology.[131] He was confronted by the antiquity of the land—and by its perilous future.

In the first decades of the twentieth century, these country-born urban progressives pursued their fascination with the inscription and ritual of place, with the invention of names, monuments, cairns and pilgrimages. They were drawing the land into their grasp with a net of meaning and ceremony, filling its spaces and defending its silences. They championed an indigenous culture, a *white* indigenous culture, that denied, displaced and sometimes accommodated Aboriginal traditions. They were feeling their way towards a conviction that being Australian would mean, in some senses, being Aboriginal. 'It's curious how persistent is that love of one's native heath', confessed Bob Croll soon before his death, 'I am a very aboriginal in that regard.'[132]

CHAPTER EIGHT

Journeys to the Centre

The relationship of Victorians to the centre and the north of the continent had been mediated for half a century by responses to the ill-fated Burke and Wills expedition of 1860–1. Memorials to the explorers were rapidly erected in Melbourne and country towns; these included statues, obelisks, clocktowers, fountains, mechanics' institutes and, of course, Beechworth's Burke Museum. The status of Burke and Wills as household names and Australian heroes, however, declined between the wars. The Boy Scouts, who had been active celebrants of Burke and Wills, abandoned their annual commemoration at Royal Park in 1914, and few new memorials or accounts of the expedition appeared for the next two decades. This was partly because the Anzacs had become the pre-eminent heroes in popular culture, and also because local explorers were increasingly the subjects of memorials. But it was also because, as the centre became more accessible and its perils less unknown, historians became more critical of Burke and Wills and judged the expedition an avoidable disaster.[1] After the Great War, outback isolation began to break down, and the Australian inland was perceived more as a frontier of settlement and less as a howling wilderness. When Baldwin Spencer and Frank Gillen embarked on their anthropological journey inland in 1901, they were hailed as a latter-day Burke and Wills team, another Victorian duo penetrating the heart of the continent.[2] But because of their own field-work and publications, and their legion of followers, the images of the inland that emerged in the ensuing decades were more complex and social than that of the lone explorer pitched against nature.

From the 1920s to the 1950s, there was a great surge of interest in the Australian outback and the Victorian antiquarian imagination ballooned northwards. Writers and artists journeyed to the centre and celebrated it for a largely urban audience.[3] There was an efflorescence of travel writing that grew directly out of the nature writing closer to home. Charles Barrett's career illustrates the continuity from the bush hut, which was the site of the evocation of intimate, local nature, to the exploration of distant frontiers. The railway arrived at Alice Springs in 1929, and by the early 1930s aeroplanes were landing at Hermannsburg Mission and Pioneer coaches were making regular stops there.[4] The

'Broken Hill–Wilcannia coach': A. S. Kenyon's Darling River collecting expedition, 1917. *(Museum of Victoria)*

magazine *Walkabout* was founded in the year of Victoria's centenary celebrations, and carried a mixture of travel writing, Aboriginal art and lore, and celebration of European heritage. It was later said of *Walkabout* that it 'as much as anything else, discovered outback Australia [for] the popular imagination'.[5] Burke and Wills returned to favour from the late 1930s, partly through the efforts of one of the writers who helped popularise the inland, Frank Clune. His book, *Dig: A Drama of Central Australia* (1937), offered a heroic and partly fictional account of the explorers and sold 60,000 copies in ten years.[6]

The experience of the first world war helped establish the primacy of the pastoral vision in Australian national imagery, but it also generated new sources of sacred and ancient landscapes. From 1914 thousands of Australian troops were stationed in Egypt, and the first contingent was housed in tents under the pyramids at Giza.[7] Diggers inscribed their names on the monuments of the Nile Valley or, like Charles Barrett, sifted the sands for antiquities.[8] Many fought in the Palestine and Syrian theatres or bunkered down in the parched terrain of Gallipoli. At home, in the ensuing decades, the red heart began to replace the golden summers, and these had earlier supplanted the sombre forests.[9] Hans Heysen visited the War Museum in Sydney three times to see George Lambert's Palestine landscapes, and he began to paint the arid inland, even waiting in good seasons for the green grass to burnish.[10] The Australian outback was monumental. Travellers commented on the classical middle-eastern imagery of the desert: 'One might liken Mt Conner to a walled, medieval city; or Mt Olga to a ruined temple or palace of a bygone Pharaoh', wrote Charles Mountford.[11] In his book *National Life and Landscapes*, the art historian Ian Burn has argued that, increasingly during the 1930s, 'an imagery of the outback—of a parched, harsh inland, the antithesis of pastoral prosperity—was being popularly accepted as another, more modern symbol of Australia'.[12]

'The outback', as Ann McGrath has observed, is a term that is intrinsically colonial, measuring space in terms of European settlement. Other names echoed this valoration: 'the back country', 'the outside track', 'our back yard'.[13] Yet, if these names suggested marginality, the idea of 'The Centre' strongly evoked the power and integrity of the interior, and also the sense of pilgrimage with which many made their visit. *The Red Centre*, the title of a book by zoologist H. H. Finlayson published in 1936, was even more organic with its image of a heart—the luminous, pulsing heart of Uluru.[14] For others, such as geologist J. W. Gregory, it was *The Dead Heart of Australia* (1906), silent and disturbing. Croll and others explicitly championed 'the red heart' over 'the dead heart'. Croll's own *Wide Horizons* (1937) captured the revelatory dimension that such a trip offered to urban Australians.

Visitors to the centre instantly became self-appointed experts. 'There is a temptation', confessed geologist C. T. Madigan in 1936, 'after a man's first visit to Central Australia or the Northern Territory, to set up as an authority.'[15] There were many issues on which they felt urged to pronounce: the 'problem' of the Aborigines, particularly of half-castes, the development of the north, life on the frontier, the protection of scenery and the future of tourism. They felt they were making history by going there. Anthropologist C. P. Mountford, who wrote the popular *Brown Men and Red Sand* (1950), had made an expedition to the centre that was described as 'one of many that has helped to make the history of Australia'.[16] History, it seemed, happened on frontiers, though that was where telling it could be most embarrassing.

The frontier was a site of pioneering experience, and even, in some neglected expanses, of apparent exploration. For adventurous and scientific Australians of the early twentieth century, two frontiers beckoned: the white ice and the red heart, the far south and the immediate north. The relationship between the Antarctic and the centre seems perverse, but was real in the career of many scientists of the period and genuine in the common offer of physical and intellectual challenge. Some, such as C. T. Madigan, Charles Laseron, Edgeworth David and Griffith Taylor, ventured in both directions.[17] Others, such as Baldwin Spencer and J. W. Gregory, went north after almost going south.[18] 'The heroic days of exploration are almost over', sighed Madigan at the beginning of *Central Australia* (1936). A few years later, in 1939, he traversed the Simpson Desert and lived to tell the tale in *Crossing the Dead Heart* in 1946.

Frank Foster, the government stock inspector at Tibooburra in outback New South Wales in the 1940s, collected local history. 'My garden won't grow anything', said Foster, indicating a bare expanse of sand beside his bungalow, 'so I've filled it with these . . . ' 'These' consisted of 'trophies' he had picked up around the district, or that people had brought into him. The garden and his nearby office, like R. E. Johns' sitting room eighty years before, constituted a museum of Aboriginal curios and craftsmanship, geological specimens and diprotodon bones.[19] The writer George Farwell described Foster as 'collecting the stone tablets of Australia's ancient history'. Farwell, when considering these 'white man's middens', wondered about the relics of value to be found even in Australia's short white man's history, and of the humour that 'history should turn commonplace objects into things of rare value'.[20] In the 1940s, he learned of the rusted remains of a camel saddle excavated from an outback cattle station, a relic of the tragedy of Burke and Wills.[21] Farwell wrote of ghost towns and jam tins, explorers' tracks and the rubble of miner's houses.

Central Australia was also the land of another culture. It was where 'tribal' Aborigines lived. *Walkabout* represented this dimension, too, in its name. Travelling to the centre was to travel differently. One 'went walkabout' in Australian culture to become liminal, to escape or to return to source. So travelling to the centre was a release and a pilgrimage, but it was also an exploration of Aboriginality, or at least of one's personal experience of it. For twentieth-century white Australians, it was often the first time they had met or recognised an Aborigine.[22] 'We had enjoyed an experience such as now falls to the lot of few whitemen', Baldwin Spencer recalled: 'We had actually seen, in their primitive state, entirely uncontaminated by civilisation, men and women living in the Stone Age.'[23] Travelling to the heart of the continent was a journey back through time. Bob Croll felt that, in journeying inland, he was 'moving in the fourth dimension'.[24] Anthropologist Charles Mountford, according to his publishers, believed: 'that the closer his [expedition] party came to the very heart of Australia the more primitive would be the aboriginal culture they found—a unique survival of the Stone Age. In this he was not disappointed.'[25] It was time-travel in another sense—back to the frontier, back to 'the old Australia [that] is passing'.[26] So it was suffused with 'a haunting nostalgia' and a 'melancholy' that many found appealing.[27] It was typical of antipodean inversion that Australia's frontier should be its interior.

Australian Aborigines and native fauna were mentioned in the one breath by scientists and conservationists of the 1920s, 1930s and 1940s: 'what will our govts ever do for abos or native animals?' wrote the exasperated naturalist David Fleay to R. H. Croll in 1946.[28] In the language of marsupial appreciation, Aborigines were described as 'one of the most lovable races of men'.[29] Aboriginal skills were recognised and often greatly admired, but they were the skills of clever animals. The Aborigine was portrayed as the supreme hunter: 'So close is he to the heart of Nature that he deceives Nature herself', wrote the journalist Ernestine Hill.[30] Ion Idriess, a best-selling author and promoter of the inland, frequently compared Aborigines to animals, to 'desert rats' or 'giant baboons'.[31] In museums the language of natural history continued to apply to Aborigines even into the 1950s when the National Museum of Victoria planned an exhibition on 'the life story of the Australian Aboriginal'.[32] H. H. Finlayson, a zoologist who did field-work in the centre in the summers of 1931–5, likened the white sympathy extended to Aborigines to that 'which might be lavished on the disappearing marsupials'.[33] He himself compared them, in some ways, to the 'predatory carnivores' he was studying.[34] The way to get to know them, he advised, was to use them as collectors and to help them with their hunting.[35] And he argued that the centre should become both national park and Aboriginal reserve, seeing no contradiction between them.[36]

Arthur Groom, author of *I Saw a Strange Land* (1950), arrived at the same conclusion. Between his two trips to the centre (one in the 1920s and the other in 1946), Groom believed that Aborigines had changed from dying remnant to surviving race. On his second trip he particularly noticed the children. He was interested in the tourist potential of Australia's heart, and his return trip was made to conduct a twin investigation into 'primitive wilderness' and 'nomadic natives'. He asserted, in the face of some local scepticism, an 'essential connecting link between protection of scenery and aboriginal welfare'.[37] 'I had come to a definite conclusion', wrote Groom, 'that the wilderness areas of Central Australia belong firstly to the natives, and to the white man only on sufferance.'[38] He used the terms 'wilderness', 'heritage', 'tourism' and 'education'. These were the future white uses of the centre, and they were futures predicated on the survival, therefore the *protection*, of Aborigines as well as the scenery. He was arguing the case for tourism, and a passive role for Aborigines within it. The danger was that tourism could be the collection mentality gone wild; it might be an orchestrated final frontier. Groom made fun of 'several dear old souls' newly arrived in Alice Springs from Adelaide, who wanted to know:

Where might one purchase aboriginal weapons? My husband is most *vitally* interested in the aboriginal question. He *already* has several boomerangs and spears from the Nullarbor Plain, and is *particularly* anxious to get a big collection before these unfortunate people are allowed to die out. I *do* hope the authorities *really* do something about it all.[39]

The future of 'our' Aborigines, as they were increasingly called, was as 'museum pieces ... in a heritage landscape'.[40] The possessive article signalled their assimilation into the national culture, and their growing role as a national emblem.[41]

In the 1920s and 1930s Aboriginal symbols became increasingly used in Australian art, design, advertising and popular culture. This was part of a general discovery of 'primitive art' by western artists in the early twentieth century. Vlaminck, Picasso and others began to draw artistic inspiration from trips to ethnographic museums. The transformation of the primitive into the modern, of anthropology into art, and of exotic curiosities into aesthetic objects, was partly due to the combined impact of Boasian cultural anthropology and Freudian psychology. 'The cultural' was also 'the personal', and even 'the other' could have a self. But the modernist appropriation of tribal productions as art, warns James Clifford, remained imperialist and was often just as timeless and as dismissive of contemporary invention as was the ethnographic vision. But it was 'not simply imperialist', he conceded, for it was imbued with 'strong critiques of colonialist, evolutionist assumptions'.[42]

The first major world exhibition of 'primitive art' (featuring works from Africa, Polynesia, Melanesia and North America) was held in Paris in 1919, but Australian Aboriginal art was not represented and Aborigines were described as 'totally ignorant of art'.[43] Europeans were long unwilling to credit Aborigines with the capacity for art. Their material culture was valued ethnographically, but rarely artistically. One of the few early exceptions was R. E. Johns' Adelaide correspondent, Thomas Worsnop, whose book *The Prehistoric Arts, Manufactures, Works, Weapons, etc. of the Aborigines of Australia* (1897) drew attention to unusual and innovative artistic productions as well as traditional ones.[44]

The first major exhibition of Aboriginal art in Australia was held in Melbourne in July 1929 at the National Museum of Victoria. It was organised by Charles Barrett, Alfred Kenyon, R. H. Croll, and D. J. Mahony. It included carved trees, shields, spears, ceremonial boards, some of Spencer's collection of bark paintings from northern Australia, and even representations of Aboriginal rock art that artist Percy Leason copied from a Grampians cave onto a large papier mache model.[45] George Aiston, a former police trooper and then storekeeper on the Birdsville

Aboriginal Art Exhibition, Melbourne, 1929: J. A. Kershaw, Director of the National Museum of Victoria, puts the finishing touches to the first major exhibition of Aboriginal art in Australia. *(Museum of Victoria)*

Jack Noorywauka and Stan Loycurrie demonstrate their skills outside the mia mia they built in the exhibition area. *(Museum of Victoria)*

Track, brought two Aranda men with him to Melbourne—Jack Noorywauka and Stan Loycurrie—who built a mia mia in the exhibition area, demonstrated tool-making and performed ceremonies. The anthropologist A. P. Elkin explained at the formal opening of the exhibition that part of its allure was the chance it offered to explore 'the psychic' as well as physical conditions of 'primitive man' and to discover 'the true motive underlying his art'.[46] Charles Barrett favourably compared the art of indigenous 'primitives' with that of imported modernists. The exhibition drew a crowd 'so large that it was almost impossible to move about'.[47]

In the following decades, the dominant source of Aboriginal images became the Aranda people of central Australia who had received the attentions of Spencer, Gillen and the Strehlows and who many white visitors were able to meet at the Hermannsburg Central Lutheran Mission west of Alice Springs. Aranda culture became representative of 'traditional' Aboriginal society.[48] A photograph of an Aranda man known as 'One-Pound Jimmy' in a hunting pose, first published in *Walkabout* in 1936 and subsequently in advertisements and on stamps, became a popular symbol of 'the unspoiled primitive native' despite the fact that 'Jimmy' had recently been dispossessed and was a refugee from the Coniston massacre of 1928.[49] Boomerangs, shields and didjeridus became widespread motifs and were even used (along with wool and wheat) to endorse Foster's Lager.[50] The Victorian arts and crafts movement began to incorporate elements of Aboriginal design, particularly through the efforts of Frances Derham, who visited Hermannsburg in May 1938.[51] The artist Jessie Traill, another visitor to Hermannsburg, held an exhibition in Melbourne in 1928 of central Australian landscapes, hailed as 'the first of its kind in Australia'. The Victorian artist and sculptor, William Ricketts, visited Hermannsburg in the mid-1930s and returned to populate the wet fern gullies of the Dandenongs near Melbourne with the clay faces and figures of a desert people.[52]

However, Hermannsburg became most famous for its Aranda water-colour painters, particularly Albert Namatjira. In 1934, Bob Croll accompanied the painters Rex Battarbee and John Gardner on their second trip to the centre. Battarbee was born in Warrnambool, Victoria, in 1893. His older sister, Florinda, who had trained with Walter Withers and taught art in Warrnambool, encouraged her youngest brother in his art.[53] Battarbee may have visited Joseph Archibald's museum, for he later became a keen collector of what he called 'Abo stones'. Around Warrnambool itself, he had little contact with Aborigines, although he did meet 'Wilmot', an Aboriginal elder known locally as 'the last of the tribe'.[54] Battarbee was wounded in France in the first world war and returned to painting partly as a therapy. By the late 1920s he was looking for new sources of artistic imagery and he made his first painting trip inland with his friend, the Melbourne commercial artist John Gardner, in 1928. In 1932, they visited Hermannsburg for the first time, where Rex left crayons at the mission school, the first art materials made available to the Aboriginal children.[55] Two years later, Croll, who had just retired from the Victorian public service, accompanied them on a return trip to the centre and to Hermannsburg. Croll admired and encouraged their artwork: 'Rex is solid; Jack is brilliant', he noted in his diary.[56] During that trip, Battarbee and Gardner exhibited their paintings of the inland in the Hermannsburg schoolroom. The Aranda people were intensely interested. Croll had already noticed the fascination of the Aranda with European images of their land, particularly their desire to place and name the landscapes. He was proud of the fact that he was made a member of the Aranda tribe ('an honorary member, thank goodness—have you ever seen an initiation ceremony?').[57]

It was on this trip that the Aranda artist, Albert Namatjira, struck up a friendship with Rex Battarbee. On seeing the paintings, Namatjira asserted 'I can do the same.'[58] Under the patronage of Lady Huntingfield and the Anthropological Society of Victoria, an exhibition of his water-colours was held in Melbourne in December 1938. Namatjira's life had tragic and heroic proportions. He moved between two worlds and was celebrated—and eventually condemned—for doing so. He became a symbol of the government's assimilation policy and was given the rights of citizenship generally denied to full-blood Aborigines. But in 1958 Namatjira was sent to gaol for six months' hard labour for supplying liquor to another full-blood, and he died shortly after his release. It was important to non-Aboriginal Australians that Namatjira was a full-blood, an 'unspoilt man of nature'.[59] His friendship with Battarbee was celebrated, and Namatjira was cast as the student.[60] Even Namatjira's art was both acclaimed and spurned as 'assimilation art', and its indigenous influences were for some time neglected. Bob Croll and Charles Barrett were among those who helped 'discover' and publicise his painting, and the cause of Aboriginal art no doubt benefited, but it was the learned nature of Namatjira's art that they emphasised, and his fine gums and clear skies represented, for them, the triumph of the Heysen/Streeton vision of Australia.[61] Because Croll had celebrated the Tom Roberts school of landscape painting, his association with Namatjira brought the Aboriginal painter within the fold of the pastoral tradition.[62] Yet Namatjira's art, like Heysen's, also signalled the emergence of new, outback images of Australian landscape, a world that Sidney Nolan and Russell Drysdale were soon to represent.

The apparently 'derivative' aspects of Namatjira's art, which Croll and others celebrated, meant that his work was coolly received by those sections of the art establishment who considered that his paintings were not 'primitive' enough. Those who promoted Namatjira, therefore, did so partly to challenge what Bernard Smith has called 'the primitivistic assumptions that lay at the heart of modernism', and to champion the pastoral traditions of nationalist painting against imported European fashion.[63] Croll, a critic of modernism who had his copy of Lionel Lindsay's *Addled Art* specially bound, became a key figure in the promotion of Namatjira. His appreciation of 'the primitive' was carefully distinguished from its latter-day exponents: 'the difference between to-day's pseudo-primitives and their prototypes, such as the Australian aborigines, being that the natives' work is based on observation, reason and belief. It never wantonly misleads.'[64] Charles Barrett, too, made it clear that he preferred the 'real' primitives, 'the Old Masters', as he called the ancient Aboriginal painters, whose work he considered 'far more significant than that of the Cubists, the Futurists, and other weird schools . . . '[65] The part which Croll and Barrett made Aboriginal art play in their anti-modernist politics—portraying it as guileless and unconscious—undermined their parallel efforts to give it a place in galleries.[66]

Philip Jones, in a penetrating study of Namatjira's cross-cultural 'travelling', has placed his painting in the context of the general desanctification of Aboriginal symbols in the 1930s.[67] The period of

Namatjira's rising fame was a period of severe decline in Aranda ceremonial life. Aranda men handed over many of their sacred objects to the anthropologist Ted Strehlow, apparently with ceremony and finality. Strehlow spoke later of 'a terrible silence' descending upon central Australia as ceremonies were performed for the last time. Jones argues that Namatjira participated in the general appropriation, desanctification, and incorporation of Aranda sacred objects and motifs in western-style art. His art contributed to rendering secret/sacred objects and ceremonies symbolically inert, to the disempowerment of his native world. But the power he sought was over other images. When, on seeing Battarbee and Gardner's work, he asserted 'I can do the same', he wanted, perhaps, to 'take control of the way in which his landscape, the Aranda landscape, was being depicted'. And, through his art, Namatjira made a counter-claim on the land, conveying an attachment that foreshadowed the political era of land rights.[68]

Space and race

In the first half of the twentieth century, nationalist anxieties and prophecies were played out in debates about environment, population and race, often on a backdrop of central and northern Australia. There, according to much of the rhetoric of visionaries, were the 'vast, empty spaces', the beckoning continental potential of Australia. 'Space' was an environmentally neutral word, a quantifiable national resource that was demonstrably underused. J. M. Powell has drawn attention to the popular habit in this period of superimposing European countries on maps of the Australian outback as a way of dramatising the wastage and potential of the land.[69] E. J. Brady, in his book *Australia Unlimited* (1918), argued that Australia had been undersold by artists and writers peddling a melancholy and gloomy vision of Australian land. The lack of a local history of war, claimed Brady, meant that the negative drama of the Australian elements had been overplayed.[70]

The geographer Griffith Taylor was one of the few who, by translating space into environment, challenged the ethic of development. He suffered popular and academic prejudice as a consequence. His introductory textbook on Australia was banned by Western Australian education authorities in 1921 because it emphasised the predominating influence of aridity.[71] In the same year, the Commonwealth superintendent of Immigration advised Australians travelling abroad to speak well of Australia: 'Such words as "drought" and "strike" and "rabbit" and "taxes" and "politics" should be thrown overboard as the vessels put out to sea.'[72]

The open spaces, it was continually argued, needed to be talked up; they needed to be developed and populated for two reasons. One was for defence of the nation, the other was for defence of race. 'Populate or perish!' was the cry. So few people inhabiting the vast lands closest to Asia was regarded as a precarious sort of possession, perhaps ominously reminiscent of the diffuse hunter-gatherer economy so recently supplanted. That knowledge of their own swift usurpation was haunting. In the words of Judith Brett: 'White Australia's continuing fear of invasion must be seen as a massive collective projection of the knowledge of white Australia's origins.'[73]

Were white people biologically equipped to populate the tropics in considerable numbers? Discussions about the future of the centre and north of the continent revived polygenist assumptions that the characteristics of races were so fixed that they could not adapt to new climates. But hereditary determinism seemed fatalistic in a society with convict origins.[74] In the nature-nurture debate, which progressives continually kept alive, Australians inclined more to environmental optimism than did Americans or the British. But the two sides of the equation—heredity and environment—combined to create fears of race degeneration in demanding environments. The themes of decay, reversion, atavism and decline lurked within much of the speculative literature about the centre and the north. George Farwell, in writing about the decline of outback towns, described how 'here in recently occupied Australia, the land is reclaiming its own again, returning to its primitive silences'.[75] The land, it seemed, was always ready to assert its Aboriginality.

Evolutionary rationalisations and prophecies, therefore, continued to have their uses on this northern frontier as they had in the south. Ion Idriess offered this view of the future of the north in 1946, in biblical cadences:

> And alas! The Stone Age man will fade away. And there will come mighty herds of cattle. And plains that for a thousand years have known only the call of the jabiru, the howl of the dingo, the cackle of wild fowl and the lonely passing of wild geese in the night will soon be green under cultivation. And where rose the smoke from the wild man's corroboree grounds will rise the smoke from many a homestead chimney. Aye, and from virile towns too. Time marches on—time waits for no man.[76]

Possession, cultivation, population and progress: this represented the march of time, the sanction of history. And not just any population would do. The towns that Idriess envisaged were *virile* towns, they were healthy, pure and white, towns equipped for the perpetuation of the race.

In the 1930s settler Australians realised that the Aboriginal population was increasing, particularly those they derisively called 'half-castes'. In

1901, the *Bulletin* had warned Australians about becoming 'a community of mongrels'.[77] By 1937 Bob Croll was quoting an observer who declared that 'the principal output of Central Australia, in live stock, was cattle, sheep, and half-castes'.[78] 'Half-castes', he wrote, 'are the Mahomet's coffin of ethnology'. Croll declared that Kipling's dictum that East can never meet West 'is unfortunately nonsense. They shouldn't meet but they do.'[79] Part of the politics of the admiration of 'full-bloods' in this period was a contrastive disparagement of half-castes. It was a common theme in outback literature, and indeed in broader policy debates of the early twentieth century, that 'traditional' Aborigines and white civilisation were incompatible, that Aborigines could not survive contact with modernity.[80] They required isolation and protection, as Arthur Groom had urged. But protection from what, and for whom? The fence had two sides. Aborigines should be accepted as 'brothers' in Christianity, Groom cautioned, 'but not as brothers and sisters-in-law'.[81] Give them the wilderness and retain white sanctity.

But white pioneers and Aboriginal women were continually messing up the genetic categories that anthropologists and politicians were trying to impose upon them.[82] 'Black velvet' was often regarded as one of the natural resources of the land, there to be used by any canny pioneer, especially in a part of the country where there were few white women.[83] But Aborigines and settlers also formed lasting relationships, and the white men living with black women were called 'combos'. Theirs was considered to be a sadly deflected virility. At the same time, the birthrates of non-Aboriginal Australians were in decline. This was the Anglo-Saxon nightmare of 'race suicide'. That champion of the baby health movement, Sir James Barrett, anticipated the Birth-Rate Royal Commissioners of 1903–4 when he argued in 1901 that the fault lay with the increased use of contraceptives and with 'female emancipation'.[84] Women were especially reprimanded for this failure in their duty to their race. Not only were they unavailable when the frontier men needed them, but those who lived in comfortable suburban settings were wilfully squandering the opportunities for procreation.

The eugenics movement, founded by Darwin's cousin, Francis Galton, warned that the quality of the white race would be diminished if the unfit outbred the fit, if the slum families reproduced at the expense of the middle classes, and if the expanding half-caste population threatened racial purity. Concern about half-castes was related to the concerns about slum children in early twentieth-century Australia. Both were regarded as 'unfit' by progressives who were keen to devise various forms of social engineering to increase 'national strength' and make society more 'efficient'.[85]

Both were also subjects of study for the emerging science of psychology. Sigmund Freud was another in a long line of European theorists who quarried data from Aboriginal Australia. For social progressives concerned about a growing population of 'mixed descent' and speculating upon the 'primitive' mind and genetic 'throwbacks', psychology seemed to be a reformist tool with the answers. Professor S. D. Porteous, a psychologist who was born and educated in Victoria, applied his expertise in the study of abnormality to the mentality of Aborigines. While at the University of Melbourne about 1917, Porteous did intelligence testing linking delinquent boys and Aboriginal children. In 1929 he returned from his post as professor of clinical psychology at the University of Hawaii to further his study of the Aboriginal mind. He conducted field-work in western and central Australia, testing Aboriginal skills and intellect.[86] At his side helping him conduct the tests was Bob Croll, enjoying his first trip to the centre.[87] Both Croll and Kenyon, writing in the 1930s, believed that a solution for the 'Aboriginal problem' required 'the employment of a scientist'.[88] Kenyon, who in 1933 journeyed to the centre to see the ultimate stone, was more specific: it must be a scientist 'trained in the psychology of the primitive mind'.[89]

Dr Cecil Cook, Chief Medical Officer and Chief Protector of Aborigines in the Northern Territory from 1927 to 1939, was one scientist with a policy. He believed in 'breeding out the colour' by inducing half-caste women to marry European men, a eugenist solution and also a typical progressivist one for it focused social control on women.[90] Cook envisaged that the half-caste women would thereby have legitimate, fair-skinned babies and the European men who were their partners would be prevented from cohabiting with Aboriginal women. The policy recognised the scarcity of white women in the north but virtually ignored the presence of half-caste men. The scientific and official notion of 'breeding out the colour' stands in rather dramatic contrast to the popular disapproval of miscegenation.[91]

Cook's policy of 'breeding out the colour', which was also enshrined in government advocacy of 'assimilation', contradicted popular sentiment and official action. The historian Peter Read has analysed the origins of the 'assimilation' policy in New South Wales, and has shown how it was really just a refinement and continuation of the older policy of 'dispersal'.[92] Read has described the traumatic effects of the policy of dispersal in the Wiradjuri country of New South Wales in the twentieth century. Europeans were fearful of Aboriginal community, of the threatening independence Aborigines gained by association with each other. 'Dispersal' therefore aimed to undermine black communities through the implementation of policies of disruption and dissociation, particularly the elimination of reserves. The techniques of dissociation included expulsion orders and the removal of children, as well as the enforcement of restrictive entrance requirements to thinly populated reserves so that they could soon be deemed 'uninhabited'. The aim of dispersal, and of reserve closure, was the extinction of Aboriginality, and it was a policy justified by the assertion that Aborigines were doomed anyway. Yet 'dispersal' was itself a response to the *increase* in the Aboriginal population. Those white humanitarians who, in the 1920s and 1930s, voiced outrage at events in the remote north such as the Coniston massacre and who extended sympathy and assistance to the Aborigines of the centre, were often ignorant and neglectful of the discrimination and 'mundane brutality' in their midst.[93]

The great Australian loneliness

Racial and environmental speculation, the silence and loneliness of the frontier, ambivalence over miscegeny, the spectre of violence and the rhetoric of development were all found in the popular writings of Ernestine Hill, whose work has been aptly described by Meaghan Morris as 'a compendium of imperial paranoia'.[94] Born in Rockhampton, Queensland, in 1899, Ernestine Hill was one of the writers who popularised outback and northern Australia, and was a frequent contributor to *Walkabout*. She claimed to have ghost-written Daisy Bates' *The Passing of the Aborigines* (1938), itself a powerful influence on popular opinion about Aborigines and the north. She also wrote uncritically of the Coniston massacre of 1928, a punitive raid by whites in which up to one hundred Aborigines were killed.[95] Hill's two major works were *The Great Australian Loneliness* (1937) and *The Territory* (1951). Meaghan Morris, in a perceptive analysis of Hill's writing, describes it as suffused by the theme of decay and inhabited by the dead and the dying, by phantoms, ghosts, corpses and skeletons.[96] Hill branded 'the Aborigine' as child-like for being 'frightened of his own shadow', but her own writing vividly documented the spectres that haunted the European imagination.[97]

Hill herself was described by Katharine Susannah Prichard as 'a strange, otherwhereish sort of creature'.[98] And, in northern Australia, Hill found a landscape of spirits:

> Empty sunlit Australia was peopled by these shadows and sprites. The old-time bushman, riding the track, travelled a haunted world and never knew it—faces in the rocks, a bunyip in every waterhole, a banshee in the cry of a crow, witches in the whirlwind, in every bush a leprechaun, in every cave a *Doppelgänger* or poltergeist hiding. Everywhere was the half-human of kindred Greek mythologies, the centaur, the satyr, the men with crocodile heads or with emu feet.
>
> There was a sermon in every conspicuous stone.[99]

She represented the travel writer as collector, for all the ways of life she described in the north—both black and white—were presented as being in jeopardy, dying out and vanishing.

Hill chided Aborigines for 'ceding [their] country', for 'selling [their] birth-right for a stick of tobacco and a quartpot of tea'.[100] She presented their dispossession almost as carelessness. The Aborigine, in Hill's terms, was 'doomed', left 'far behind in the race of the ages, marooned on an island continent of sunny climate'.[101] That sun was psychologically dangerous, an enervating influence on 'lazy Australia', so perhaps in populating her adopted land with shadows and ghosts, with dark clefts of local history, Hill was fortifying it. In calling the Aborigine 'a child of his environment', she was absolving him of responsibility but, at the same time, warning her own people.[102] In Australia, they inherited 'an environment of which we have no comprehension'.[103]

Over thousands of miles of outback travel, Hill treasured in her suitcase a split of wood about the length of her arm, a piece of Charles Sturt's boat in which he had intended to cross the Inland Sea. The boat had hung in a homestead for over sixty years, gradually whittled away by souvenir-hunters until, when Hill passed by, nothing was left but the keel. 'First keel of those strange waters', she mused, 'it was a geological joke, fifty million years too late.'[104]

Hill was a great advocate of development. 'Let us build reservoirs and towns', she urged.[105] Those spaces needed to be filled. She dedicated *The Great Australian Loneliness* 'to the men and women of the Australian outback, and to all who take up the white man's burden in the lonely places'. She made the contrast between the vast plains of silence and loneliness and the 'six, now alarmingly seven, big cities of premature birth', between '[s]mug, colour-conscious White Australia below the twentieth parallel, and black, white and brindle struggling together above it'. The underpopulated plains were 'an unknown land dreaming away its youth in melancholy, that cries with all its voices for the love and faith of men'.[106]

'Is there a throw-back to the Australian black?', she asked Dr Cecil Cook. And what of the Northern Territory's 'Living Tragedy', the half-castes? They could, she was assured, be easily 'eliminated' and 'submerged' by 'breeding them white', by giving them 'every opportunity to outgrow their heredity'.[107] But the fact that they existed at all, Hill insisted, was the fault of white women: 'If there is any blame for Australia's present half-caste problem, it lies at the self-contained flat door of the white woman of the overcrowded cities, for men are only human.'[108] But twentieth-century journeys to the centre, unlike that of Burke and Wills, were rarely one-way.

Ernestine Hill was preoccupied by the power of heredity and environment. She called these twin determinants those 'mighty marshalled forces . . . that make playthings of us all'.[109] Gregor Mendel and Sigmund Freud hover in the background of her prose like ghosts of the inland, offering genetics and psychology as clues to unravelling the future of Australia's races.[110] Under her pen, remote Australia re-emerges (or remains) in its guise of human scientific laboratory, the site of 'a vitally interesting ethnological experiment'.

Defence of the nation's purity—racial, cultural and artistic—'verged on the pathological', comments Stuart Macintyre of Australia between the wars.[111] On the giant canvas of the centre, the anxieties of urban, southern Australians were writ large.[112] There, confronted by an enduring Aboriginal presence, the impulses of collection and possession appeared more problematic, and 'preservation' became a problem of race.

PART THREE
Preservation

CHAPTER NINE

The Discipline of Memory

'Preservation', writes David Lowenthal, 'has become our principal mode of appreciating the past.'[1] Especially since the 1960s and 1970s, the preservation, restoration and interpretation of historic relics, buildings and landscapes has boomed across the western world. 'Only in this generation', continues Lowenthal, 'has saving the tangible past become a major global enterprise.'[2] 'Heritage' has come to mean 'the things we want to keep', as the Hope enquiry into the Australian National Estate put it in 1974.[3] It is now a word that refers particularly to the material legacy of the past, to things that are both tangible and fragile, things that need to be 'kept', 'saved' and 'preserved'.[4] So dominant has this notion of salvage become that Robert Hewison suggests that one definition of 'heritage' is 'something that is under threat'.[5]

Some commentators on the Australian scene have portrayed the fascination with heritage as a recent phenomenon, as primarily a product of 1970s nationalism.[6] And indeed, in the 1970s the Whitlam government initiated a series of important reforms including committees of enquiry into the National Estate (1974) and Museums and National Collections (1975). It also established the Australian Heritage Commission which maintains a Register of the National Estate and promotes awareness of places of natural and cultural significance. These initiatives mark the preservation movement of the last few decades as vigorous and distinctive.

But we must not underestimate the depth and continuity of the public, popular past. As explored in part two, nationalism and heritage were even more strongly linked at the beginning of this century, and 'heritage' had earlier meanings and forms. As Graeme Davison writes: 'What was new in the [heritage] movement of the 1960s and 70s was not its nationalistic focus, but its progressive redefinition from a spiritual to an essentially material concept.'[7] Formerly, 'heritage' was more concerned with ideals. It generally took its physical form in memorials and monuments, in signifiers that staked out terrain and provided podiums for speech-making. In the western world in the post-war period, 'heritage' became more self-referencing. It changed in meaning from the spiritual to the tangible, from a moral preoccupation with possession to a material fascination with preservation.

The preservation impulse had emerged and hardened over the preceding two centuries. In his book *The Past is a Foreign Country* (1985), David Lowenthal identifies a number of impulses to preservation that date from the late eighteenth and nineteenth centuries.[8] One was the sense of threat and loss brought by unparalleled social and environmental change: 'Nothing so quickens preservation sympathies as the fear of imminent extinction, whether of a building, a bird, or a folkway.'[9] The pace of change had become great, and the need for security more intense. Lowenthal suggests that another impulse to preservation was the gradually dawning belief that history was not structured by romance or destiny, but was an organic process subject to contingencies, each moment unrepeatable but linked in a traceable chain of causality.

The evolutionary, scientific vision of history was, I have argued in chapter 1, part of the turmoil of Darwin's legacy.[10] It led to a premium being placed on tangible monuments and relics, on original and authentic physical sources that could be conserved as evidence of unique past experience. This was history as tourism, where 'the past was a foreign country' and where native testimony—in some material form—was a priceless souvenir. And, indeed, this archaeological sense of the past as something that could be dug up or recovered as 'talismanic bits and pieces' did become closely allied with the growing needs of twentieth-century tourism.[11] 'Nature has become scenery; archives have replaced memory', argues Lowenthal.[12] In saving the past, he suggests, we are ironically distanced from it: 'Preservation, by contrast with memory, segregates a tangible past required to be unlike the present.' Preservers, like collectors, destroy as they salvage.[13] It is taxidermy on a massive scale.

Part three of this book addresses some of the Australian manifestations of the impulse to preserve. It studies the new interpreters of the popular past—in academia, the bureaucracy and the community—and the way that their views of history were affected by different pressures that emerged in twentieth-century Australia—professionalism, tourism and environmentalism. A recurrent issue in these chapters is the relationship between oral and literate culture, popular and learned traditions, amateur and professional, insider and outsider. I examine some of the collisions or transitions between these worlds. Aborigines and settlers were, of course, often distinguished in this way. But such tensions also existed within the historical consciousness of both cultures.

From the late nineteenth century, Australians began to 'institutionalise the past', as Stuart Macintyre has called it.[14] As well as collecting relics, colonists began to make, transcribe and preserve historical records; they began to marshall memory, to socialise and document it. Chris Healy has shown how 'history' was almost an absent category in colonial Australian museums, but that what was collected of local European historical interest consisted mainly of paper records rather than objects. Artefacts were mainly Aboriginal—they were specimen-like—whereas paper was the stuff of history. Documents were the defining substance of the scientific and literary historical imagination.[15]

This chapter focuses on the writing-down of memory and traces the social dimensions of historical consciousness particularly as it was expressed in the first historical societies. Professional history was founded on the distinction between oral and literate cultures, and between memory and history. Memory is fluid and personal, whereas history is a collective and public activity that requires verifiable sources and institutions for its transmission.[16] Memory is expected to be first-hand, whereas history is second-hand no matter how 'primary' the source. But memory is also social.[17] It is most suspicious to historians when it ceases to be personal and becomes communal, when it reaches back beyond a lifespan and becomes handed-down rather than actually lived. It then offers itself as history, but it is neither recollection nor research. 'When I was young my father always used to tell me stories', explained Vince Phelan, a custodian of the history of Dargo in the Victorian alps. When speaking of the past, Phelan's voice has been described as becoming 'flat and unhurried', his face 'impassive as the process of recollection begins'.[18] History is *the* discipline of memory—it specialises in hindsight. But it is also a craft that has a strange, oppositional relationship to memory and constantly exercises that discipline against it.

Seasons of memory

Is it possible to identify seasons of memory, periodic surges of wistful story-telling? Nostalgia, argues Christopher Lasch, is the ideological twin of progress—its flip-side—and it finds its purest literary expression in the convention of the pastoral.[19] Until the twentieth century, nostalgia was a medical term describing a condition of acute homesickness. Immigrants in a rapidly changing society must have suffered it doubly. In European Victoria, there have been periodic high seasons of memory, waves of nostalgia commencing in the 1850s, 1890s, 1930s and 1970s that were prompted by loss, depression or disruption.[20] Each of these waves of anguished searching for a past was characterised by popular yearnings for the intimate world of early colonial beginnings or for 'lost' rural places, and by anxieties about geographical and generational succession.

Early Port Phillip society was bereft of the elderly. Visitors commented on the youth of the colonists, and married or middle-aged men were as scarce as women.[21] E. M. Clowes, writing in 1911, wrote: 'It is interesting to remember that in those early days Victoria was a country with no old people.' She told the story of some Victorian children who had never seen an old man or woman, and who were terror-stricken when they first visited their grey and wrinkled Scottish grandmother.[22]

Just as Port Phillip's early pastoral society of the 1840s began to mature, it was engulfed by a new wave of immigration which obliterated what little sense of tradition may have become established, and which introduced a further influx of youth. The discovery of gold overwhelmed Victoria's pastoral origins and heralded a new beginning and a social revolution that dated its foundation from 1851. In March of that year, an Old Colonists' Festival Dinner had been organised by some of the founders of Port Phillip. They planned to make their reunion dinner an annual tradition. But, within two years their chairman, William Kerr, was lamenting that they felt 'strangers in a strange land', as newcomers swamped them.[23] The *Argus* interpreted their actions as a move by 'these hoary sages . . . to secure the reverence of the new race that now crowd our streets'.[24] Victoria's first major day of commemoration, Separation Day, inaugurated just a few days before the discovery of gold, died away quickly. It meant little to the bulk of the population who, in the pursuit of mineral wealth, were busy making their own history. In 1856 at Castlemaine, a town built with gold, Separation Day (1 July) was notable for its non-observance. After all, rationalised the *Mount Alexander Mail*, 'The Separation was an event anterior to the advent of the largest part of the existing population.'[25]

In May 1869, the theatrical entrepreneur and politician George Coppin called a public meeting to form the Old Colonists' Association of Victoria, with the primary concern of helping pioneers unable to provide for their old age. The association saw itself not only as a charity, but also as a historical society. It honoured those who had founded the colony 'without burdening it with the convict taint'. Members were encouraged to write down details of their lives and achievements in a Registration Book, and to donate any memorabilia of early settlement. 'Captain Lonsdale's notebook relating to original land sales in Melbourne' was one such item donated.[26] Societies such as this one—they called themselves Old Colonist or Old Pioneer Associations—defined membership according to dates of arrival or birth in the colony. Sometimes the honour could pass to male descendants. Their meetings encouraged communal reminiscing, and had an air of competition about them as pioneers vied for the earliest memory, the oldest residency or the most prestigious personal associations. Victorian definitions of 'the pioneer' initially restricted membership to the pre-gold era, but gradually accepted and eventually embraced the digger.[27]

The gold generation presided over Victoria's next bout of nostalgia. Alec Chisholm, who grew up in the declining gold town of Maryborough in central Victoria at the turn of the century, described a community 'living on memories—dreaming, perhaps, of events of the 1850s'.[28] These echoes of gold provided 'the scene of our inheritance in my boyhood', wrote Chisholm, and he 'gave seemly respect to our few remaining human relics of the throbbing fifties and sixties'.[29] He continued:

> we even boasted possession of veterans who had fought in Australia's own little rebellion of 1854, the Eureka Stockade. One in particular I remember. He strutted about the town with an odd mingling of dignity and geniality, and as he passed we boys nudged each other and whispered, 'That's old Bob—; he was on Eureka!'. None of us, as I recall, was at all clear then what 'Eureka' implied, but we had gathered from our elders that it was a famous victory of some kind, and we realised also that to be 'on' rather than 'at' Eureka set the seal to a man's fair fame.[30]

Tilly Aston, a blind writer and teacher who also grew up near Maryborough, wrote a book about *Old Timers* in 1938. She called them 'stranded adventurers', a 'driftwood population', 'left by the flood' as the tide of the gold-rushes receded. 'Their queer, unconventional ways were always a theme of interest with the rest of the community, who patronised them, or thought they did, nicknamed them, and were scandalised at their occasional peccadilloes.' In writing about them, Aston honoured them as 'the real history-builders of this Australia of ours' and, writing in the wake of economic depression, reminded her readers that 'our heritage is spiritual as well as material and cannot be assessed in acres and sterling'.[31]

As the immigrant miners aged in the 1880s and 1890s, and as they opened their newspapers to read the black-bordered obituaries of their contemporaries, they marvelled at the changes they had initiated and observed, and worried about what would be lost with their deaths. Their lifetimes coincided with an era of amazing material progress. They held in their heads memories of such change as they thought would never again be seen. The history that they spoke and wrote was a story of origins and a compilation of 'firsts' that revelled in the contrast between a recent but primitive past and a progressive present. In an essay entitled 'The Parochial Past', Graeme Davison identifies several broad styles of Australian local history writing.[32] 'Pioneer history' is the title he gives to these accounts of achievement within a lifespan in which personal memoir and national history were fused and research and recollection indistinguishable.[33]

But there was the problem of succession. Who would continue their good work? Who would appreciate the value of steady-going industry and long-term commitment, particularly in a boom colony of the 1880s where short-term speculation and thinking were rife? Old immigrants increasingly regretted the ignorance and waywardness of young 'natives'. The dialectic between these generations, argues Graeme Davison, supplied late nineteenth-century Melbourne with much of its social dynamic.[34] 'Patriarchal history' is the second style of local history writing that he describes. It was written by the sons and daughters of the pioneers; it sought to secure an inheritance rather than an appropriation. 'With the change from pioneer history to patriarchal history', writes Davison, 'there was a subtle change of style and vocabulary: from recollection to recording, from celebration to commemoration, from testimony to chronicle.'[35] This was the era and style that produced 'the memorial movement' of the early twentieth century, the nostalgia among urban progressives for their country childhoods, and the 'back-to' celebrations in declining country towns. 'It was thought that only decadent towns had the "comeback" movement', lamented one of the organisers of the 'Home To Horsham' festivities in 1929.[36] Patriarchal history tried to turn memories into monuments and strained to defend recently invented traditions from the continuing sweep of change. It is the nature of filial piety to be hedged with self-doubt. The first historical societies were one product of this intergenerational tension.

Institutionalising the past

The first historical societies had *preserving* and *recording* as their primary aims and they distanced themselves from the rambling reminiscing of old colonists' societies. And they were more in search of a national past than a local one. Many made 'Australia' part of their title and provided platforms for the anticipation or celebration of federation. In these ways they shared more than has been realised with the emerging professionals who later distanced themselves from them.

One of the earliest learned associations with a stated historical aim was the Royal Geographical Society of Australasia founded in 1883, with branches promptly established in New South Wales, Victoria, Queensland and South Australia. Anyone was qualified to be a member 'who is interested in the progress of Australia, and is activated by the patriotic desire of seeing the natural resources of this great country brought to light and developed, and the land become the home of happy and contented millions'. Alexander C. Macdonald, the inaugural honorary secretary of the Victorian branch, looked forward to 'the day when smiling homesteads, flocks and herds, towns and cities shall be in places that are now wildernesses; . . . the day when a man may proudly say, "I am an Australian"'.[37] Macdonald was born at Campbelltown in New South Wales in 1827 and had first overlanded to Port Phillip in 1847. He loved the bush, had learned some Aboriginal lore as a child, and made their languages his life-long study.[38] The Victorian branch of the society counted among its members the historian J. J. Shillinglaw, the photographer J. W. Lindt, and the botanist Ferdinand von Mueller, and later H. G. Turner and Charles Long. Mueller, like Bonwick, lamented that the feats of Australian explorers were being forgotten. The group was historical in orientation and included among its aims 'the collection and publication of Historical Records of Geographical Interest, and the memoirs of distinguished travellers, explorers, [and] geographers'. 'The work of the geographer', they reminded themselves, 'goes hand in hand with that of the pioneer.' It was to this body that Joseph Archibald spoke of his 'Ancient Wreck' and prehistoric limestone slab.[39] The Geographical Society later shared rooms with the Historical Society of Victoria and amalgamated with it in 1920.[40]

James Bonwick was elected an honorary member of the Geographical Society of Victoria in 1892. His life and work illustrate the impulse to preserve the Word, both written and oral. Born in England in 1817, Bonwick came to Hobart as a teacher in 1841, worked briefly in South Australia in the early 1850s and left for the Victorian goldfields in 1852. As a traveller, writer and educationalist, he steeped himself in oral tradition and became a local pioneer of oral history. Of his work, *The Last of the Tasmanians* (1870), he wrote:

> The difficulties of collecting materials for such a work must be considered. It was not a mere hunt through Blue Books. The forest depths, the sultry plain— the homes of peace, the dens of penal woe—have each brought something to the store. The laugh of the Bushman, the sigh of gentle womanhood, the grief at lost affection, the curse from some remembered wrong, have been the varied accompaniments of tales thus told.[41]

His mission was to write upon Australian subjects especially for Australian youth, and to cultivate in them a regard for local history.[42] He regretted the lack of respect for the history of Australian exploration. He published dozens of books, collected documents and believed that Australian children should have ready access to copies of original records.[43] So, while he devoted the first part of his life to gathering and writing down bush-lore, he spent his final decades in London immersed in archives, sitting in a 'draughty room of stone and iron' peering at documents under dim gaslight.[44] He was drawn to London as the fount of colonial history, as 'the best searching-ground for contemplating Colonial historians' because of its imperial monuments and early Australian associations, and he was determined to import at least some of those sources of inspiration.[45] Bonwick carried out research in London in the early 1880s for his *Twenty Years of Australia* (1882) and *Port Phillip Settlement* (1883), and then for the next twenty years worked for all Australian colonies except Western Australia in transcribing records. His transcripts provided the basis for *A History of New South Wales from the Records* (1889, 1894) and his 125,000 sheets of manuscript formed the basis of *Historical Records of New South Wales* (eight volumes, 1892–1901). This was the predecessor of *Historical Records of Australia*, which its editor called 'the birth-certificates of the nation'.[46]

In the mid-1880s, soon after the Geographical Society was formed, a group called the Historical Society of Australasia was established in Melbourne. At its first meeting in 1885, the president—the historian David Blair—declared its rather different charter. It aimed, he said, to be 'a select society, and could not in any sense of the word be called a popular one'. He went on to say that 'The study of history in its widest sense must be left to the select few—to the aristocracy of the intellect.' The society's aims were 'the cultivation and advancement of the study of History, and especially as it relates to Australasian colonies, and the collection of information for the compilation of a complete and accurate History of Australasia'. Blair wanted to lay the groundwork for 'a complete and authentic history of the British Empire in the South'. This was a very different vision of history, one which sought to distinguish itself from the practical, open membership of the Geographical Society and the popular, nostalgic feeling for history represented by the old colonist groups. It was a brief institutional expression of Melbourne's lively, nationalistic literary scene of the 1880s and the society lived and died within two years probably as a result of political and scholarly rivalries.[47] Blair certainly took the opportunity at its first meeting to denounce George William Rusden's recently published three-volume *History of Australia* (1883) as 'detestable', and to tell society members that it was their duty 'to endeavour to establish the truth'. Members included John S. Elkington, professor of history and political economy at the University of Melbourne, Thomas F. Bride, chief librarian of the Melbourne Public Library, A. C. Macdonald of the Geographical Society, the journalist and author James Smith, and Alexander Sutherland, headmaster of Carlton College and author (with his brother George) of the very popular school text, *History of Australia from 1606 to 1876*

(1877). Most of them had been born overseas and were members of Melbourne's rising professional elite. The society, with its self-conscious professionalism, intellectual exclusiveness, wariness of 'legend', stress on original sources, and commitment to a history of British expansion in Australia, anticipated the consolidation of 'scientific' Australian history in universities early in the new century.[48]

About ten years later in 1896, another grandly named historical society was formed in Victoria, this time in Ballarat. Called the Australian Historical Records Society, its members were old diggers wanting to preserve the stories and historical documents of the golden years. They interviewed old timers (many of whom had been '*on* Eureka', or had at least heard the musketry) and gathered diaries and written transcripts of reminiscences. At their first meeting, several members boasted of the relics they had hoarded. Mr J. Noble Wilson declared that he had an Aboriginal skull among his possessions. What was the reaction of the gathering when Dr Usher stood up and claimed to have in his collection 'the skull of an old pioneer'?[49]

The group aimed to 'gather together, reduce to writing and preserve by deposit in some suitable place a record of the more interesting incidents in the lives of the pioneers'. W. Coulthard, the recording secretary, conducted interviews. Of one with Charlotte Francis Drew, he wrote:

> On my journey out into the bush on the Buninyong Road to interview Mrs Drew, I naturally pictured in my mind, some aged feeble old lady, whom I felt to submit to cross examination would be unjust, but far from this being the case, I was met at her gate by a robust, stalwart woman . . . with rake in hand . . . busy in her extensive garden.[50]

Priority was given to documenting memory, to 'reducing it to writing'. A historian of Eureka, John Molony, has suggested that Eureka was not sung about in ballads because it was a legend that was quickly secured in print: 'it was made by, and became the possession of, those who had a stake in the land'.[51] Objects were gathered as well: in 1858 R. E. Johns added to his collection 'a trophy of the Ballarat riots—a pistol with which a policeman was killed'.[52]

But for many in Ballarat, Eureka remained a minor or equivocal symbol, and some of the tensions percolated through the proceedings of the society. Alfred William Crowe, who came to Ballarat in 1854, had been awakened by musketry on the December morning of the battle, ran to the top of Specimen Hill and watched the fighting through a heavy cloud of smoke. Although he admitted the arbitrary nature of the Victorian government of the time and the unfitness of its officials, he remained a strong advocate of the use of moral rather than physical force.[53] In Ballarat of the 1890s, the past seemed to confront him continually, and memories were prompted by weekly visits to his wife's grave, the sight of places where his children worked or played, and even by encounters with 'immense trees . . . a few standing remnants of the forest that once covered the earth'.[54] Through his membership of the society, his public reminiscing, his lectures on 'Early Days at Ballarat', his participation in commemorative activities, and even his diary-keeping, he continued to work through some of the passions and politics of Eureka. Writing to the paper in 1896 amidst festivities marking the fortieth anniversary of municipal government, Crowe reminded his fellow colonists that 'All the virtues under the sun were not found in those men, who in 1854 attempted to subvert the Government and establish a republic.'[55]

Partly because of Eureka—which became a symbolic battleground of political freedom—the society had a national vision; they were collecting information 'concerning Australia—not Ballarat or Victoria alone'. There was also no Australian city that was stronger for federation.[56] Shortly after the society was formed in early 1896, John Gavan Reilly of Creswick, describing himself as 'one of the first generation', wrote to the secretary seeking membership. He explained (at length) that he had 'endeavoured to keep the flame of patriotism burning in the hearts of my brother Australians' and that 'the hour has arrived wherein we should begin to collect and preserve the absorbingly exciting stories of a vanishing past, stories that can be told by the heroic hearts who shared in the struggles and triumphs of this glorious country'. The society's work, he hoped, would strengthen Ballarat's claim to become 'the Federal City of our island continent'.[57]

In 1897, the society decided to mark the grave of 'the last of the aborigines' in their district and sought the co-operation of the Australian Natives' Association. King Billy (also known as Frank) had died the year before and one of his artefacts had earlier found its way into R. E. Johns' collection. King Billy's breastplate was donated to the society soon after his death, as well as photos of King Billy and his hut. The Ballarat pioneers felt it was their duty to erect a monument in honour of 'the last ruler of the bush'.[58] In 1988, Ballarat Aborigines and their supporters chose the grave of King Billy for the site of their peaceful 'non-celebration' of the bicentennial Australia Day. Although some Kooris regarded the monument as an 'insult', it had become a place for them to affirm their survival.[59]

In 1901, the Australian Historical Society was established in Sydney. Although its formation was prompted by a concern for local history—by a keen sense of loss for the Old Sydney being swamped by the modern

Ballarat Kooris and supporters marked the bicentennial Australia Day in 1988 with a march to the grave of 'the last of the aborigines'. The grave was erected by the Australian Historical Records Society and the Australian Natives' Association in 1897. (Ballarat Courier)

city—the founders quickly ditched the suggested title of 'The Sydney Historical Society' and aimed to represent federal concerns and espouse national objectives. Like the other historical societies, one of its primary aims was to document the past, and its formation partly flowed from efforts made to house the historical collection of David Scott Mitchell, who became its first patron.[60] Because public discussion of Sydney's origins was still uneasy, the society's mission was to reclaim the past as a source of pride rather than shame. K. R. Cramp, president of the Australian Historical Society in the 1920s and 1930s, believed that through its programme of research and activities the society was 'doing public service in developing a purified and enlightened patriotism and stimulating a historical sense in the community'.[61] This purification mission was satirised by Miles Franklin and Dymphna Cusack in their novel, *Pioneers on Parade*, published the year after the 1938 sesquicentenary, in which a family's convict past was uncovered by the 'Purer History Society'.

In the wake of federation, state historical societies were established. The Victorian Historical Society was formed in 1909 (rejecting Sydney's invitation to become their Victorian branch), the Queensland Historical Society in 1913, the Western Australian Historical Society in 1926, and a brief-lived South Australian Historical Society in the same year (it was revived more successfully in 1974). They were a mixture of old families, professionals, the local professor of history, and some historical journalists and writers.[62] Sir Paul Hasluck remembered the first meeting of the Western Australian Historical Society in 1926:

> It was a cold winter night. In the cheerless room, lit by one bright unshaded electric globe hanging from the centre of the ceiling, the group of about twenty dignified ladies and gentlemen sat awkwardly on spindly chairs behind little wooden tables and kept their overcoats and furs on throughout the meeting.[63]

The monthly meetings, recalled Hasluck, were

> a social get-together . . . when much of the conversation was really a process of identifying each other and recalling how your cousin and my aunt used to do this or that, and his grandfather was the first person to take cattle from here to there, and someone else's uncle was standing on the beach when somebody's grandfather did something rather important.[64]

In spite of all the personal testimony and family intimacies, these early historical societies were still more notable for their national objectives and their cultivation of state-wide identities than for any evocation of, or affiliation to, particular places. Hasluck recalled that the Western Australian group felt a need for 'an assertion of our own identity as "sandgropers"'.[65] The societies shared an early emphasis on exploration, discovery and maritime subjects, and they advocated the priority of original documentation and the need for 'precision and accuracy' in historical research. The professors of history who were active in their foundation would not have felt out of place. The first historical societies were themselves nurturing, and sometimes imposing, a learned tradition—a discipline—on the social habits of memory.

The formation of the Victorian Historical Society

On 20 March 1909, an article by W. J. Hughston was published in the Melbourne *Argus*. It was titled 'Vanishing Records'. It consisted of a reported conversation which Hughston had some years earlier with a young and enthusiastic American student whom he had met while visiting the United States. The young American was studying the history of Australian land legislation and, on learning that Hughston came from Australia, he—as Hughston put it—'began to dig into me like an old document'. He particularly wanted to know about Victoria's pastoral period, the years before the discovery of gold. He was dismayed by how little the Australian could tell him of early Melbourne.

But 'it's not too late yet', urged the American student.

> There must be plenty of old pioneers yet living who have the whole history of that section in their heads right from the start . . . Write down everything you can hear . . . It's a kind of patriotic duty to preserve the records of the birth of a nation. It is a period that stands by itself forever—the first contact of the white race with the primal world.[66]

Hughston was profoundly moved by what the student had to say, particularly, one suspects, because it came from a foreigner, and a young one at that.

He finished his article in the *Argus* with a plea. Of Victoria's pastoral period, he said: 'For me that period was a remote and peaceful landscape, seen through a golden haze. It was the only period of true local colour that Victoria has had—an idyllic time, rudely broken by the din of the gold rush.' 'There must still be with us', pleaded Hughston,

> . . . many who remember Batman and the village streets of early Melbourne, and the old swamp behind Spencer street, and the quiet stream fringed with tea-tree which was the Yarra. . . . How interesting, too, would be a reunion of these old people. What old memories they would exchange.

The period of which Hughston spoke was seventy years ago, the span of a lifetime, then only just within the grasp of memory. That gave his article of 1909 a sense of urgency.

One of the readers of his article was Alfred Woolley Greig, aged thirty-six, who became chief clerk then registrar (1937-9) of the University of Melbourne. Sensing a common obsession, he promptly wrote to Hughston, offering clerical assistance in launching a historical society to do the work suggested. Hughston replied with the suggestion that they meet in the portico of the Public Library of Victoria. Following their discussion, they agreed to seek the advice of the notable collector, E. A. Petherick, whose treasures of Australiana were then temporarily housed in the Melbourne Exhibition Building. Together, they hatched the plan for a historical society. Their letters were subsequently pasted into the opening pages of the society's first correspondence scrapbook.[67]

Over the next few weeks, throughout April and early May 1909, Greig laid the groundwork for a successful inaugural meeting. He wrote to important and interested people, hoping to secure their statements of support and, more critically, their attendance at the meeting planned for 21 May. The Speaker of the Legislative Assembly, the Hon. Frank Madden, agreed to act as chairman, and the explorer and politician, Sir John Forrest, promised to address the meeting, as did Henry Gyles Turner. James Bonwick had died just three years earlier, but his grandson agreed to come as his representative. Donald Macdonald was solicited for an early lecture. Alfred Deakin, then embroiled in a dramatic bid for his third period as prime minister, regretted that he could not come for all of the first meeting, but expressed the hope that he could call in before it closed. He was soon enlisted as a member of the historical society's council. The poet, Bernard O'Dowd, wrote to Greig : 'Am in entire sympathy with aims—indeed, consider establishment of some such means of preserving the raw materials of our future noble historical tapestry a civic duty as Australians.' Greig extracted expressions of support from the defunct Australian Historical Records Society of Ballarat (which had its last meeting in 1906), the recently formed Australian Historical Society in Sydney, and the Australian Natives' Association. Links with the University of Melbourne were cemented from the beginning. Professor Harrison Moore, lecturer in law and history, was on the society's first council and, as adviser to the Victorian and federal governments on constitutional law, he brought disproportionate but highly esteemed expertise to shape the little constitution of the historical society. And Jessie Webb, lecturer in history, was one of the few women to be named in the early records of the society. She performed a fundamental role: the society's first council meetings were held in her rooms in the Block Arcade.[68]

On 21 May 1909, a large gathering in Furlong's Music Studio in the Royal Arcade moved that a body called the Historical Society of Victoria be formed. Mr Frank Madden, in the chair, reminisced extensively. He remembered coming up the Yarra in 1857. He remembered Cole's Wharf, the Cremorne Gardens, and the Survey Paddock. He scoffed at those who, in later years, had predicted that the cutting down of the Mallee would lead to Melbourne being overwhelmed with dust. It was a meeting which was well attended, well behaved and well reported. About 160 members were quickly enrolled. The society was launched, it seemed, without a hitch.[69]

Not quite. All of Greig's careful forethought and groundwork had not headed off a major catastrophe. In Melbourne's Athenaeum Hall just a few weeks later, an even better attended meeting launched a rival society. Entitled the Early Colonists' and Natives' Guild of Victoria, its meeting was chaired by the Victorian Premier, Mr John Murray, and it quickly claimed a membership of 490, three times that of the fledgling Historical Society of Victoria. Its stated aims were very similar: to collect the reminiscences of pioneers, and to gather the records of Victorian history before they were lost. But it had a different style.[70]

The Early Colonists' Guild began its meeting with selections from a pianola. The soft music drifted through the hall as old colonists filed in, meeting one another and chatting. The formal business began when the organiser, Mr A. H. Padley (who later became involved in the campaign to save the Old Melbourne Cemetery), read out a list of names from the early days. Who recalled them, he asked? There were murmurings of satisfaction and a warm sense of familiarity, for all the names were well known to the gathered company. 'Who, then, was the earliest colonist in the room?' asked Mr Padley. There was a buzz of excitement. 'I came here in 1839', said one. 'Why, I was here in 1837!' cried another. 'But I was here in 1834', claimed another.

A white-haired colonist then slowly mounted the platform. Shaking a forefinger to emphasise his words, the old gentleman spoke with great feeling: 'My name is Cowell', he said.

I arrived in Tasmania in 1828. (Applause) I remember seeing a great crowd on the wharf at Launceston on May 27, 1835. I saw Batman, Gellibrand and Fawkner, and I witnessed the departure of the first white men who went over to Port Phillip. My father said: 'Take off your hat, lad.'

The room erupted in applause.

The Premier, Mr Murray, moved that the guild be set up. But then a dissenting voice was raised. Alexander Macdonald, who just a week or two earlier was nominated to the first council of the Historical Society of Victoria, stood up. He explained that a similar society to the proposed guild already existed. There was not room for two societies, he said. And he observed that, actually, he was the oldest colonist present, beating Mr Cowell of Tasmania by four and a half months. The Premier, obviously badly briefed and annoyed at being caught in this uncomfortable position, said that competition between the two societies was most unfortunate. He had no choice but to move that the guild be established, and suggested that amalgamation be discussed.[71]

The unease and tension that emerged at that meeting continued throughout 1909.[72] The Historical Society of Victoria made membership open to all, and defined a systematic and scholarly programme of recording and preserving knowledge of Victoria's past. It aligned itself strongly with the professions—education and law particularly—and it set out to influence the way history was taught and practised. Ernest Scott urged the society to remain broad in its interests and to

enable attention to be given to the extent to which the course of Australian development has been affected by currents of opinion in Great Britain, by general British policy, and even by European politics in a very wide sense . . . This is a scarcely explored field.[73]

The society forged links with established historians and teachers of history and played a part in the emerging History Department at the University of Melbourne. It put a high value on memories and reminiscing—too high a value, thought Professor Harrison Moore—but it urged careful documentary research.[74] It aimed to be popular but serious.

By contrast, the Early Colonists' Guild made its membership narrow and hierarchical: those who had resided in the colony since before 1855 could be enrolled as 'pioneers', and those who dated back to before 1870 were accepted as 'members'. At their meetings, competitive reminiscing was encouraged—to the nostalgic tones of the pianola. Socially it was a lively group; intellectually it was less disciplined. It aimed to be popular by being exclusive. Some of the early descriptions of the Historical Society of Victoria were in implicit contrast to this rival group. The Historical Society of Victoria was described as 'not one of frills and feathers'. It was not, someone declared, just 'a society of greybeards'. The point was, and it was a telling one, that the society boasted from its inception that it counted young people among its members as well as old.[75] And the 'study of the aboriginal races of Victoria' was one of its stated objectives. The editor of the Beechworth newspaper wrote to Greig, telling him of R. E. Johns' artefacts in the Burke Museum, saying they were 'considered the finest collection of aboriginal weapons anywhere in the States'.[76]

The rivalry of the Early Colonists' Guild shadowed the first year of the Historical Society of Victoria. At its first annual general meeting, the Hon. Frank Madden, as president, explained that 'the society had not been as great a success as members had wished'. 'The cause was easy to see', he said, '—certain people tried to usurp the position of the society, or, in colloquial language, to "jump its claim".' But he noted with pleasure that 'those people' seemed to be disunited and quarrelling.[77] And, indeed, the first annual meeting of the rival guild, held just a few days before in July 1910, was reported in the *Age* as an 'Extraordinary Fiasco'. To the thirty elderly members who had come along, the chairman, Mr Padley, announced that the guild had a £50 debt. Following some heated questions, Padley declared that 'he had not come there to be heckled', and then began abusing the absent Premier, Mr Murray, for reneging on the promise of a government grant to the guild. Some members of the audience moved that the guild be 'put out of its misery' and, as business continued to be conducted, the members gradually filed out.[78]

Amateur and professional

Although academic historians have often spurned 'the collection mentality' and rambling reminiscing of the antiquarian, or distanced themselves from the environmental dilettantism or activism of the recent heritage movement, their own discipline became 'professional' on the back of the same impulse to preserve. Professional history was a product of preservation: it was a 'scientific history' that flourished on the reverence for records. 'It is the civil servants responsible for the classification of national records . . . who may lay claim to the title of the earliest of professional historians', argues Philippa Levine of Victorian England.[79] Emerging nations drew on the past and invented traditions to prove the continuity and coherence of their identitites.[80] The development of national identities and bureaucratic mass societies together with the growing fascination for primary sources promoted 'the ideology of the factual', an institutionalised, material-based science of the past.[81] 'Scientific history was seen to be different from romantic legend, sacred text, and political manipulation of the past because it demanded accuracy', writes Dening.[82] And accuracy (and accountability) demanded the repetitive scrutiny of evidence and therefore its reliable preservation.

Bernard Smith has argued that, over the past few centuries, there has been an increasing reification of morality and tradition, with the result that the writing of history becomes increasingly the history of sacred and timeless property. He observes that 'it is only through heritage that myth is provided with the acceptable scientific face that modern societies demand'.[83] Preserved things—heritage—have become the stuff of history, both observed and written. Property, ownership, display, access, preservation, documentation: this became the new language of the past. And university-trained historians became its priests.

The first academic historical journal in Australia, *Historical Studies: Australia and New Zealand*, was established in 1940, and the first PhD in history at an Australian university was awarded in 1947. The dramatic expansion of tertiary education after the second world war meant that the number of academic historians in Australia expanded from less than twenty to over 500 in the following thirty years.[84] John La Nauze, professor of History at the University of Melbourne, declared in 1959 that 'Australian history has become a "professional", or "academic", or "scholarly" subject'. Australian history had been redeemed by the universities and La Nauze, writing as 'one who saw the world before the flood', knew exactly whom it had been rescued from. 'Antiquarians', he wrote:

> still pursue their hobby, at once so interesting and so harmless. But an indiscriminate interest in relics and incidents simply because they are old or happened some time ago is no longer taken to be the same thing as an interest in history, except perhaps by the organisers of historical exhibitions.[85]

La Nauze's commentary, coming at the end of the 1950s, captures the confidence and arrogance of the new professionals. The word 'local' acquired pejorative overtones, and the term 'antiquarian' became derogatory. Historians developed a distinguishing science of the document and regarded the university cultures of Britain and Europe, rather than their own backyard, as the source of their discipline. Newly appointed professors traced their intellectual lineage back to Oxford and Cambridge and thereby to the influential German school of history.[86] For La Nauze and other academics, becoming 'professional' meant becoming international, institutional, urban, exclusive, detached and scientific. Above all, it meant a recognition of university standards and style.[87] And it wrote amateurs out of the history of History.

Australian history was often said to begin with the appointment of academic historians. The symbolic dawn may have been Manning Clark's journey from Melbourne to Canberra in 1949 to take up the first chair of Australian history. Or was it his opening lecture in a course of that name at the University of Melbourne in 1946, when he claimed to 'set out on a journey without maps'?[88] Or was it in 1927 when Professor Ernest Scott first lectured on Australian history? Or perhaps it was even earlier when Scott was appointed as professor of history at Melbourne in 1913. Or was it when George Arnold Wood arrived from England to take up the Sydney chair in 1891 and soon developed a strong commitment to the history of his adopted country?[89] These have been some of the possible beginnings identified by post-war academic Australian historians wanting to discern the origins of their discipline.[90]

Under the influence of nineteenth-century German scholarship, historians not only began to focus on textual sources, but also professionalised their preservation, cataloguing and publication. Although they were equally dependent on the preservation impulse and on means of 'institutionalising the past', the academics promoted a division of labour that consigned the tasks of collection, transcription and preservation to the amateur.[91] Yet they themselves, as exponents of 'scientific history', often eschewed concepts in favour of facts. They were often caught up together in the same enterprise, but wished not to admit it.

Ernest Scott, a foundation member of the Historical Society of Victoria before he was a professor, had been a journalist and parliamentary reporter. He was born in England in 1867 of 'one father & one mother, unless I am misinformed', and emigrated to Australia in 1892 where he was employed by the Melbourne *Herald*.[92] He had a 'ringside seat' at the rise of the Federation movement and its culmination: from 1897 to 1901 he worked as a Hansard reporter with the Victorian parliament, and then with the Commonwealth parliament until 1913.[93] His journalistic sketches of the Federal Convention in Adelaide in 1897 won wide recognition.[94] While a journalist he wrote authoritative books on early Australian exploration, on French voyages in Australian waters (1910), and biographies of the French explorer La Pérouse and Matthew Flinders (1912, 1914).[95] On the strength of this research, he was appointed to the chair of history at the University of Melbourne in 1913.

In a period when the writing of history in the western world was undergoing 'an exceptionally sharp change from history as *literature* to history as *science*', Scott was a transitional academic figure.[96] Although he was himself untrained in history, he became a great advocate of that training in others: he was critical of Frederick Watson's editing of *Historical Records of Australia* and believed 'a trained historian ought to be in charge of the work'.[97] He championed history as a distinctive intellectual discipline, with its own method, its own logic, its own way of answering questions. He consciously created a school of history.[98] He relentlessly sent his students to the original documents. 'His devotion to truth was a religion with him; and he followed his facts', recalled a student and later professor, Stephen Roberts.[99] 'Every fresh fact makes a difference', declared Scott.[100] Scott prided himself on burrowing beneath the conclusions of 'leading authorities' and subjecting original sources to his own 'narrow scrutiny'; he aimed to discover 'exactly what was done'.[101] The trained historian, he said, was a distinct being, a different person with a different mind.[102] But he argued that proper history required the qualities of both literary and scientific endeavour and he admired literary historians such as Macaulay and Carlyle. He specifically rejected the argument that scientific scholarship must be colourless and impartial; he argued, instead, for the chemistry of good faith and good training.[103]

In 1939, on the occasion of Scott's knighthood a few months before his death, Professor Keith Hancock told him: 'We remember that it was you who discovered Australian history for us.'[104] Stuart Macintyre has outlined the genealogy of academic Australian history, and has traced the 'lines of descent' from professors George Arnold Wood and Ernest Scott. He has described how Scott's history was part of an imperial endeavour, one concerned to legitimate and celebrate British possession of Australia.[105] This early articulation and preservation of a national past went on both inside and outside the academy and the emerging discipline of local historical knowledge was put to the service of the recently formed Australian nation-state. Scott played bridge weekly with Charles Barrett and Donald Macdonald, and Barrett said that he owed his interest in Australian history to him.[106] And, like Alfred Kenyon, Scott delighted in the game of finding and correcting facts, and although disturbed by the history of Aborigines, was dismissive of their culture.

He, too, was moved by the scientific romance of Australian exploration, land settlement, pastoralism, and the anticipation and celebration of distant war.[107] The opening sentence of Scott's *Short History of Australia*, published a year after Gallipoli in 1916, was: 'This Short History of Australia begins with a blank space on the map and ends with the record of a new name on the map, that of Anzac.'[108]

The untrained Scott perhaps had to be particularly careful to distance himself from an amateur past.[109] In this, also, he was little different to his fellow members of the Historical Society of Victoria who were struggling to distinguish themselves from reminiscing old colonists.

Public histories

The historian J. H. Plumb, in *The Death of the Past* (1969), drew a sharp distinction between 'the past' and 'history', one popular, the other scholarly. He considered them mutually exclusive and prophesied that critical historical method, in all its rationality, was destined to replace the primitive, pre-industrial sanction of the past. The rapidity of social change, he argued, had weakened the hold of the past.[110] Plumb's statement may have been the high-water mark of the belief that scientific or objective history—a truly professional product—would dispel the power of the popular past. It was an approach that allowed little room for the serious study of popular forms of history-making, many of which have boomed since Plumb's prophecy. In fact, when written in 1969, Plumb's words were already being overtaken. David Lowenthal considered Plumb's prophecy dubious: 'the cult of nostalgia, the yearning for roots, the demand for heritage, the passion for preservation show that the spell of the past remains potent'.[111]

Graeme Davison has responded to Plumb in a series of stimulating articles about the Australian popular past. Like Lowenthal, Davison is fascinated by the paradox that while history in schools and universities is in decline in the late twentieth century, it is blossoming in its popular forms. Through studies of local histories, family histories, school texts, monuments and museums, the heritage movement and professional history, Davison turns Plumb's thesis on its head and argues that ours 'is a society with a strong sense of the past, but with only a weak sense of history'.[112] Far from dying, Davison suggests, the appeal of the past may grow stronger as social change accelerates.

Since Plumb's prophecy, antiquarianism has been resurgent in new forms. There has been an exponential growth in historical societies, new museums have proliferated, the membership of the National Trust and family history associations boomed, and many buildings, historic sites and cultural landscapes were preserved, all examples of a growing public need for a visible, visitable, tangible, touchable past. Aspects of this recent shift in popular historical consciousness are studied in the following chapters.

The professional or academic engagement with this powerful new surge of the antiquarian imagination has been labelled 'public history'. Public history is an old pastime but a new discipline. It describes the renewed interest of trained historians in the popular past, both as a source of employment and a subject of study. It emerged as a distinct area of teaching and practice in the 1970s, and built on growing popular and academic enthusiasm for local and oral history. In Britain in the late 1960s, an explicitly political 'people's history' movement was established and the practices of local and oral history were central to its sense of difference. The movement, which became associated with Ruskin College, Oxford, and the *History Workshop Journal* (published from 1975), took pride in situating itself outside or on the fringes of institutions of higher education, and drew inspiration from working and trade union experience.[113] In Australia, professional historians moved into the amateur domain of local history from the 1950s and they rediscovered oral history in the 1960s and 1970s. With a sense of pioneering, they began to 'write down memory' and 'dig into people like old documents' just as members of late nineteenth-century historical societies had done, although with different purposes and technologies.

'Public history' was the term Americans gave in the mid-1970s to their more politically conservative version of these extra-academic enthusiasms. There, private corporations and government agencies were more frequently the allies of public historians, and the boundary-marking rituals of new professionals were quickly invented. Public history courses were established in America from 1976, a journal called *The Public Historian* was founded, professional associations formed, ethics discussed, contracts drafted and fees set. It is the American term that has been adapted for Australian usage, although Australian public history has drawn on both the American and British approaches and has a style of its own.[114]

Public history in Australia has been closely identified with the preservation movement. Historians were slow to become actively engaged in the research and defence of the material remains of the past, and public history represented the profession's attempts to make amends. As late as 1982, John Mulvaney rebuked Australian historians for playing 'little positive part in the National Trust movement, conservation issues or in the moves which produced the Hope Inquiry into the National Estate'. He regretted that their new interest in public history seemed to be motivated by 'economic necessity' rather than any 'moral or ethical need for them to take some public role'.[115] Architects, architectural historians and archaeologists were the most outspoken professional activists in the heritage field, partly because historians felt more at home with documents than buildings, but also because, as Graeme Davison puts it, they are 'more inclined to take a relativistic view of historical significance'.[116] But, as public history began to define itself in Australia in the 1980s, it was predominantly through heritage work and institutions rather than through public policy or business or community history.[117] The defining institutions for public historians in Australia, as for the first professional historians and record-keepers in nineteenth-century England, were government heritage agencies rather than the academies, corporations, trade unions or historical societies. It was there in government heritage bureaucracies that professionalism and antiquarianism coalesced in 'the public interest' and produced public history.

Public history is frequently identified as a response to 'a crisis of the profession'.[118] It offers itself as an antidote to 'scientific history', a reaction against the insularity and elitism of history as it developed in the post-war academies. In going 'public', historians often espouse the democratisation of historical practice, and the empowerment of 'the people'. But, in the enthusiasm to invent and defend their field of practice, public historians may undermine their own ideals. For public history can be distinctly 'private', representing another intrusion of the expert into the amateur realm, a further act of disciplining. Sometimes the term 'public history' is used narrowly to describe a new job market for historians, one that has fortuitously emerged as the expansion of universities slowed. Public history is increasingly the province of private consultants who are neither permanent bureaucrats nor tenured academics; that liminal status can be invigorating and creative, but it also necessitates professional advocacy and defence of its own. Consequently, American historian Ronald Grele has argued that public history can 'offer a definition of professionalism almost as narrow as that of the academy'.[119] The name 'public history' even seems to suggest that history originated in the universities and was only later made public.[120]

The dynamic of professionalisation, with its creation of a metropolitan elite, undermines localism and undervalues amateurism. The post-war intrusion of academics into the intimate world of local history, for example, illustrates some of the professional anxieties of public history. Local history was long seen as the parochial realm of the amateur and enthusiast, and as the quintessential domain of the antiquarian. It was there, as Nietzsche put it, that the antiquarian built 'a secret nest . . . The history of his town becomes the history of himself.'[121] In local history, one's social being is inextricable from one's history. But it is more than that: it is one's qualification to write at all. No wonder, then, that the first academic historians to venture into those intimate worlds risked both professional and social isolation. In 1953 Weston Bate, who had just completed a Master of Arts thesis on the history of the first twenty years of the Melbourne suburb of Brighton, felt caught between the local and academic worlds: 'Somehow,' he confided to another university trained local historian,

> I have exalted the standing of local history in my own mind to a level I can't possibly maintain. How can one enter all the multitudinous facets of local life with the authority one's training, or even a simple logical approach, suggests that one should have?[122]

In a climate where reviewers were reluctant to see even the best local histories as more than 'chronicle', Bate was concerned about how a thesis in local history would be received by academic examiners.[123] He soberly reflected that 'I don't think there has been any convincing local history published yet in Australia.'[124]

The writing of local history by outsiders seemed a contradiction in terms. University education in history, it was believed, would bring attention to the national dimensions of the local story, and a critical eye to historical sources, particularly to the use of centralised documentary records that were rarely local in either provenance or preservation. But it also questioned and sometimes dissipated the particularity, intimacy and pride that had sustained the genre. Only an outsider, an urban academic addressing an audience of non-locals, could apologetically call his history of a country town 'a strictly limited project, in no sense part of my mainstream activity'.[125] And locals could find themselves overlooked in their own town by these 'blow-ins'. 'As I wandered around the streets of Blackall', lamented Professor Malcolm Thomis, recalling his research into the history of the Queensland town in the 1970s, 'I encountered no disillusioned urban intellectuals to turn my footsteps in the right direction.'[126]

But public history's promise lies in its perennial professional anxiety, its in-between status, its capacity to draw on that local world as well as that of the urban intellectuals. It demands that historians recognise the power of memory and place. Oral history and local history, which study these phenomena, have been regarded with suspicion by the academy because they value experience as much as training, people as much as paper, and the parish as much as the nation. They challenge two of the founding orientations of 'scientific' history: national history and documentary science. And above all they suggest, as does public history, that historians take memory seriously, not as a frustrating filter to be discounted, but as a social reality to be engaged with.[127]

Although public history is frequently aligned with the preservation movement, its radical potential is to counter it. As Lowenthal has observed, preservation and memory can be opposites: one disconnects, segregates and makes foreign; the other enlivens, associates and (sometimes) makes familiar. The historian Michael Frisch suggests that public history is concerned with repairing the fracture between history and memory: 'We need projects that will involve people in exploring what it means to remember,' writes Frisch, 'and what to do with memories to make them active and alive, as opposed to mere objects of collection.'[128] The pianola of the Early Colonists' Guild beckons. Memory and history sustain and shape one another more than either admits; there has been a continual dialogue between popular and learned traditions of historiography. It is a virtue of public history that it examines and builds on that process, making historical consciousness—which historians perversely take for granted—of vital concern. And it urges historians to explore, rather than to discipline, memory.

CHAPTER TEN

Keeping Places

Aboriginal family and local history has proliferated in the same period that settler Australians have turned to histories of place and kin, and has been shaped by some of the same forces: the personal search for identity, attachment to locale, the growth of nationalism and tourism. But the Aboriginal antiquarian imagination has distinctive characteristics, even as it engages with European technologies and the adopted media of memory. Whereas the settler's loss is generally that of distant kin and country, Aborigines have been disinherited in their own land. Just as settler Australians invent traditions in a land they have only recently inhabited, so do Aborigines sustain, rediscover and create associations of place in a climate of political and social needs. Some of the characteristics of the new Aboriginal history—such as an embracing sense of family, an oral vernacular, and certain moral stances—are quite distinctive.[1] But others—such as a deep attention to place, respect for the ownership and lineage of knowledge, and the constant interplay between public and private, speaking and writing, memory and invention—are characteristics of white local history, too.

Because of their attention to particular places, local and colonial historians were always more alert to the Aboriginal past than were academic historians, who were overwhelmingly concerned with establishing their discipline through the writing of national history. Even as Aborigines were written out of national histories, they found a place in local histories—as individuals who lingered in local memory, namers of landscape features, or as makers of 'traditional' artefacts. The recent rediscovery of the Aboriginal past has as much to do with a new academic valuing of the local and the oral as it does with cross-cultural enlightenment. But it is also a product of Aboriginal cultural resurgence, and the appearance of new forms of history-making that are vitally concerned with place.

White locals

In 1975, the Pigott Report, *Museums in Australia*, described the proliferation of museums since the 1960s as 'primarily a grass-roots movement, one of the most unexpected and vigorous cultural movements in Australia in this century'.[2] In a regional survey of museums undertaken in 1975 for that committee, archivist Frank Strahan reported the results of what he called 'the new nationalism':

> a newly found respect and affection for Australian history, particularly local history, is the basic reason for the appearance of all but a couple of the museums surveyed ... Australians are aggressively (if rawly) aware of a separate identity, willing to take an unselfconscious look at themselves, and compulsively salvaging the old blacksmith's tools, bottles, bedsteads or bicycles as a historical backdrop, justifying their new image.[3]

One museum in Port Macquarie boasted a hot cross bun over a century old.[4] The poet Les Murray fondly saw these little local museums as examples of 'folk scholarship'; they 'jumble quaint old junk in with historically valuable relics ... country people are saying to their children, and to us, in effect, 'Here's how we lived, and how our forebears lived. Your origins are here.''[5] Strahan noted that, with only one exception, all twenty-four museums surveyed stated 'tourist attraction' as a primary aim. Tourism, he noted, 'breeds intense rivalry and threatens to usurp promotion of the new nationalism as the main aim of museums'.[6] What was new and unpredictable about the nationalism was its intensely local expression. Local history and family history both strengthened as popular pastimes and gained some acceptance as scholarly disciplines. One gave special emphasis to the influence of environment, the other to heredity, 'those mighty marshalled forces ... that make playthings of us all'.[7] Perhaps, in a local, familial setting, they could be tamed, or at least understood.

'Parochial', like 'antiquarian', has generally become a term of disdain. But the word had its origins in the notion of a 'parish', an area not just of administrative convenience, but one of intimate allegiances and loyalties. Gilbert White was a parish priest and, in the very first sentence of *The Natural History of Selborne*, proudly called his book a 'parochial history'.[8] As Les Murray has observed, when communities preserve their histories they are 'concerned not with patterns or ideologies, but with the living quiddity of each person, each being, each object ... there is no background or foreground, nor is anything either aggrandised or relegated'.[9]

Local history is indiscriminate about everything except place and loyalty. It is like collection, but an inversion of it, because place and affiliation become pre-eminent. Paul Carter has noted that local history 'is notably laconic. The most surprising facts are reported cheek-by-jowl.'[10] It was this propensity that Hal Porter affectionately parodied in his history of Bairnsdale, which offers a conscious cascade of indulgent juxtapositions.[11] These inexplicable non-sequiturs endow a place with 'a mythic inevitability', continues Carter. 'In local histories', he writes, 'the place serves much the same function as the plot in fiction: it is a means of unifying heterogeneous material, of lending it, rhetorically at least, a unique destiny.'[12] Local history offers 'a ritual of repetitions . . . a cult of places'.[13] It is a historical consciousness that is Aboriginal in emphasis. It is place that is historical, and time is translated into it.[14] Bob Croll recalled listening to a man, nearly sixty, who lived at Wonnangatta in the Victorian alps: 'his steady voice tells of what makes history to him—the big flood of such a year, the coming of the rabbit, the first appearance of St John's wort, and what not'.[15] The 'steady voice' is the impersonal voice of tradition singing the new songlines.

Local historical societies are a recent phenomenon in Australia. In the late nineteenth and early twentieth centuries, when historical societies were national or state-wide in purpose, local history was sustained in the schools. Schools were, after all, where books and writing intruded with most design upon the community of talk: 'Instead of oral instruction', cautioned one nineteenth-century inspector of schools, 'books must be used.'[16] It was often children who wrote down local history for the first time. 'So, watch out!' residents of one country town were recently warned: 'Somewhere below you, you might hear a little voice say "Excuse me, can you tell me when you were built and who settled you first?"'.[17] Historians of small communities later came to rely heavily and gratefully on the words that schoolchildren had recorded.[18] Local history exhibitions were organised through schools in Victoria in 1906 and again in 1922 to celebrate fifty years of compulsory education in Victoria. Regional school magazines were established in the early 1920s, and many of the contributions were historical and written by children.[19] The first sustained formation of country historical societies took place in the 1930s, and the first Australian genealogical societies were established at the same time.

The state historical societies encouraged the formation of local societies initially without much success. In Victoria, the Reverend George Cox established one at Yarram in 1911, and A. W. Greig commended him: 'Your patient building up of local history is far beyond anything I have come across in that line so far.' Greig regretted 'that there is only one of you. If you could be multiplied and set down in half a dozen different provincial centres what a harvest could be reaped—while yet there is time.'[20] By the 1930s, some country historical societies had been established in Australia, but it was not until the 1960s and 1970s that the numbers increased dramatically. In Victoria the number of historical societies increased tenfold from about 30 in the mid-1960s to over 300 in the 1990s, and comparable exponential growth took place in other states in the same years.[21]

'A historical landscape peopled with events, buildings and figures from the past and verified by historical fact was a triumph of possession', argues Philippa Levine of British antiquarians in the nineteenth century:

> Nostalgia provides an insufficient explanation for the popularity of organised antiquarian pursuits. It was rather an alternative cultural force of amazing vigour, an attachment to local identity motivated in many ways by the same sentiments as that civic pride which spurred on the town hall and sewer builders of the later nineteenth century.[22]

Historical societies in Australia a century later were engaged in the same assertion of provincial dignity and distinctiveness, the same realisation of place and identity through a reconstitution of the past.[23] 'We have a chance to build up an entire area from the historical angle', urged one local organiser, who was also sympathetic to Aboriginal claims to land in northern Australia.[24] The focus of these new groups was proudly, and sometimes narrowly, local. They resented the loss of historic documents to Melbourne archives: 'these records belong to the country, *us*, not Melbourne', fumed one historical society member. He warned his compatriots that urban professionals were 'stealing our heritage'.[25] 'Parochial patriotism and myopia', as one historical society organiser described it, has sapped purpose from some of the original state societies.[26] But competitiveness with the city, and with other localities, and a keen sense of their own territory, provided sources of energy and inspiration for these newer societies.

Local identity was often forged from collections of paper and things, and preservation could overwhelm education. The Goldfields Historical Society in central Victoria, formed in 1960, was torn between entertainment and scholarship, collection and research. Society meetings could include a few slides of wildflowers, a talk on the local diggings, some historical extracts from the local paper, 'a few magic tricks for the boys present', and a display of historic objects.[27] 'A museum is a good thing', wrote their energetic curator, John Alderson, ' . . . but it is not the study of history . . . As a body we have not done any research into any subject whatever.'[28] But the custodians won over the researchers and the society's primary purpose soon changed from 'the promotion of the study of history' to 'the preservation of articles relating to the early history of the area'.[29]

Some historical societies explicitly avoid the burdens of institutional collection. When I visited the Mortlake Historical Society in western Victoria in 1984, I asked the president if the society had a collection. 'No', was his reply, 'we keep material under our respective beds.' I was not sure if this was literally true or a sort of metaphor. He seriously extended it at a later stage. 'Material,' he explained, 'is safer under various people's beds than it is under one collective bed.' Even before arriving in town I had heard mutterings about the district's beds. 'They talk a lot about their beds down there', one former speaker warned me. In spite of all these cautions, it was still a surprise when the president invited me into his bedroom to cast my historian's eye under his four-poster. As the local doctor, he had an unusual bedside manner. 'Later on in Show and Tell', reported the society's secretary, 'our Medical President brought out his discoveries found while crawling around under Marg Harwood's bed.'[30]

Local history offered a genealogy of place. But for settler Australians, the search for historical identity—for roots rather than just an anchorage—led overseas and required a genealogy that transcends place. Their 'roots'—such a powerful metaphor of the land—were perversely to be found in another distant land. Family history, like local history, has long and often neglected antecedents in European Australia. Its recent manifestation as a popular hobby has kinship, of course, with the persistent colonial concerns over blood and breeding, genetics and race, that have already been described. Australia's earliest and largest organisation for family historians, the Society of Australian Genealogists, was founded in 1932 and began with forty-six members. Alfred Kenyon was one of its early subscribers. To commemorate the sesquicentenary of New South Wales, P. C. Mowle edited the *Genealogical History of Pioneer Families of Australia*, which was originally published in 1939 and achieved its fifth edition in 1978. Mowle emphasised the value of giving 'a permanent record' to the country's patriarchs and in demonstrating 'the close bonds of kinship which exist between the families in Australia and those of the Mother Country'.[31] '[F]amily hearsay', he explained, 'has been disregarded unless documentarily supported.'[32] Dr Harvey Sutton, prominent in the public health movement of this period, encouraged young boys and girls to discover their line of heredity: 'it is time all Australians realised that heredity is one of the paramount things from which a solid and courageous nation is developed'.[33] The Genealogical Society of Victoria was founded in 1941, the same year as the publication of Alexander Henderson's *Henderson's Australian Families: A Genealogical and Biographical*

Record.[34] Professor Ernest Scott, writing his foreword to Henderson with full awareness of the pastoral families who were both its primary subject and audience, posed the question: 'Is there any logic or good sense in being very particular about the ancestry of a bull, a ram, a horse or a dog, and being supercilious or indifferent about the ancestry of a human family . . . '?[35] Eugenics, occasionally a justification for family history in the 1930s, echoed in his words.[36]

By 1972, the membership of the Society of Australian Genealogists had climbed from its original 46 to 629, and then it boomed. By 1982, it had 7,500 members, and it peaked in 1987 at just under 10,000. It has since declined from its bicentennial high to about 8,500.[37] What are its attractions? Partly it is the thrill of the chase, the excitement of 'collecting ancestors' as one put it, and genealogists are quick to tell you that new technology (such as photocopying) has assisted the hunt.[38] But it is deeper than that. Graeme Davison has drawn attention to the claim that Australia, next to America, has the highest per capita population of genealogists in the western world: 'It is, above all, in modern, recently-founded, "non-traditional" societies that the search for ancestors is most vigorously pursued', he writes. It is a history, continues Davison, that affirms family relationships just when they are most under threat from mobility, divorce and intergenerational conflict.[39] For these reasons, it can be a dangerous activity in small communities. Schools that encourage family history for homework do so at their peril, warns one family historian: 'your father's not who you think he is'.[40] John Spurway, in a history of family history in Australia, has argued that 'the search for geographical identity—for "deep-rootedness"—has been fundamental to family history'—as it has been to local history.[41] Family reunions, which are the spur to many written histories, are a genealogical version of the 'back-to'.[42] Many older Australians, suggests Spurway, 'want to unravel all the fine detail of their attachment to the soil'.[43]

By 'older Australians', Spurway refers not just to the age of the hobbyists but to the 'Anglo-Celts' who, he finds, dominate the hobby of family history and who perhaps see it as a defence against the modern inroads of multiculturalism and Aboriginal land rights. The widespread embarrassment about convict origins has dramatically diminished since the 1960s, but some descendants of First Fleeters still feel that they are on the nose. 'You never hear a mention that the Bicentenary is about the landing of the First Fleet', observed one in 1987. 'Original Australian descendants are the most discriminated against people', declared another.[44] It is, they claim, no longer because of the convict taint, but because of official endorsement of a multicultural society. Convict descendants noticed that the many-nations Tall Ships—a universal symbol of migration—were chosen as the official totems of Australia's

Bicentenary celebrations ahead of the British First Fleet. And so Australia Day became a forum for jousting not only between blacks and whites, but also between defenders of Australia's British traditions and immigrants from other lands.[45]

Some use genealogy to strengthen white claims on the land. Les Murray describes the notion of 'particular, successive ancestors' as 'a purely white matter'. He argues that white Australians can and do possess the land imaginatively in very much the Aboriginal way, but that history is literally on their side rather than the Aborigines':

> We have recently been awed by the discovery that the Aboriginals have been here for thirty or forty thousand years, but I think that too much is often made of this. Forty thousand years are not very different from a few hundred, if your culture has not, through genealogy, developed a sense of the progression of time and thus made history possible.[46]

But Aborigines are among those who have used genealogy—and history—most desperately and imaginatively in order to progress their cause.

Black histories

In the last two decades, history written and spoken by Aborigines has intervened powerfully in public culture in Australia. When Bernard Smith delivered his Boyer Lectures in 1980, he observed a 'new sense of nationhood among Aborigines' and drew on a few well-known 'Black Voices'—Kath Walker, Kevin Gilbert, Jimmie Barker, Charles Perkins, Colin Johnson (Mudrooroo Narogin).[47] But he regretted that published work by Aboriginal writers was still scarce. By 1988, when he returned to that forum as one of a series of Bicentennial Boyer Lecturers, Smith found the situation 'totally different' and noted 'a major upsurge in Aboriginal cultural activity in film, in theatre, in poetry, music, the novel, and the visual arts'.[48] The practice of history, particularly local and family history, has been at the heart of this cultural resurgence, and of the making of Aboriginal identity. In the 1980s and 1990s, Aborigines have written autobiographies, recorded the memories and stories of their elders, used history in the making of land claims, sought the return of artefacts and bones, and rediscovered relatives from whom they were separated.[49]

These newer forms of Aboriginal history resemble aspects of historical practice in traditional society. Peter Sutton has described the resemblances and differences between urban Aboriginal history and traditional myth. A perception of history, he says, 'is now powerfully constitutive of urban Aboriginal identity', it is the past as the present as in the Dreaming: 'the Aboriginal person is likewise the historical Aborigine—not merely the survivor but the embodiment of the scarifying processes of conquest, dispossession, resettlement, missionisation and welfareism'. Both traditional approaches to the past and the newer forms of history, he observes, are highly local, focus on identities and events rather than processes and forces, and emphasise history as the property of particular people.[50]

This new Aboriginal history embraces the media of tape, video, camera and radiocarbon. Its language depicts 'culture' as both commodity and essence, both object and spirit. The word can specifically mean 'traditional culture', a possession that they can 'lose' or 'keep', a quantifiable resource that some have 'lost a lot of'. But in keeping culture, one's responsibility is to 'keep it strong', as if it is an intensified essence from which one renews and remakes the whole.[51] Preservation and creation come together in the rhetoric, not unlike the cosmology of the Dreaming whose creative forces are both ancient and ever-present, both historical and accessible. Although Kooris mostly seek to emphasise the continuities of tradition and identity, they do not deny the loss—or the invention. Their attitude to heritage is underpinned by acceptance of loss, whereas the settlers are transfixed by the dilemmas of preservation. 'White people', say the Yarralin of northern Australia, 'don't know what to remember and what to forget, what to let go of and what to preserve. They don't know how to link the past with the present; they fail to recognise their own stories.'[52]

For Aborigines, life in 'settled' Australia has been decidedly unsettled. They have been dispersed, concentrated, relocated, detached from their land and from one another, and continually kept moving. Their territories of nomadism have had to enlarge; they have survived by continuing to travel lightly in patterned ways. Albert Mullet is a descendant of the Gunai (Kurnai) and Gunditjmara peoples, his grandmother and grandfather from eastern and western Victoria respectively, and himself a product of geographical disruption. He recalled how his family moved back and forth across the state border to avoid welfare authorities who were trying to take Aboriginal children away from their parents. 'So a lot of us in that area of Gippsland become like "wetbacks"', he recalled, using a term that describes Mexicans who enter the USA illegally:

> they'd transport us over the border into New South Wales with our family over there for a month or two months or six weeks, and then they'd move us back again when the welfare got pretty severe over there. Now the way they used to do it—there was a bloke who used to have a fish run, and fish

truck, his name was Snowy Fountain, and he used to have the fish run from Moruya right through to Melbourne, picking up fish all the way down. So he had a policy with his drivers that any driver that didn't pick up an Aboriginal person that was on the road hitch-hiking, they would get the sack. So it was very convenient for our people's transport because a lot of our families are married in along the coast with Kooris up in that area, Eden, Wallaga Lake, all through that area ... So our families keep going just like the rainbow serpent all around the coast.[53]

The rainbow serpent, a supernatural maker of places, here becomes representative of the pathways of survival, the journeys that weave a community from the experience of dispossession and dispersal. Kooris learned to sustain a community across distances and to inscribe the land with routine patterns of mobility. 'Beats', 'lines' and 'runs' connected sympathetic households, family and region, country and city.[54]

Aborigines whose lives have been shattered by social dislocation and legislative intrusion have turned to new ways of rediscovering family associations and local identity. The organisation 'Link-Up' was formed in 1980 with the aim of reuniting Aborigines with the families from which they were taken.[55] A book called *Lookin for your mob: A guide to tracing Aboriginal family trees* (1990) introduces the methods of black genealogical research.[56] James Miller, author of an Aboriginal family history, urges fellow Kooris to trace their ancestry through the documents as well as the spoken stories: 'Most ... would have a family history just like mine—a story of triumph over oppression.'[57] Aboriginal genealogies collected from around Australia by the archaeologist Norman Tindale from 1928 to 1957 have become crucial keys to identity and kin for many Aborigines today. The South Australian Museum administers an Aboriginal Family History Project that researches and interprets these handwritten genealogies, which were originally gathered to investigate the 'half caste problem'.[58] 'Genealogies help them to make decisions on marriages for their children, help them to choose their partners; genealogies also help them to identify their land claims', explains Aboriginal researcher, Doreen Kartinyeri.[59]. What began as a research tool for scientific interest in human biology, and a political tool for turning Aborigines into landless whites, has become a crucial map of human affiliations, a forgotten family photo album, and a route back to land.

Genealogies are a foreign artefact adapted to Aboriginal purposes. Aboriginal notions of kinship have been communal and environmental rather than individual and linear, and in traditional society, genealogical memory was often suppressed.[60] 'The family' was frequently used against Aboriginal people, both scientifically and socially. Settler Australians, who equated culture and blood, were obsessed by the need to 'breed out the colour'. They calculated Aboriginal genetic inheritance in family fractions, calling them 'half-castes', 'quadroons' and 'octoroons'. The western nuclear family became an instrument of cultural suppression as tens of thousands of Aboriginal children were removed from their kin, taken into white homes, insulated from their upbringing and taught to disown their extended family ties. But locality and family have remained the anchors of Aboriginal identity, traditional ties which were often sharpened by loss.[61] Koori society 'emphasises allegiance', wrote the anthropologist Diane Barwick of Victorian Aborigines in the 1970s.[62] 'Which place do you come from?' and 'Which family is yours?' are the questions Kooris continue to ask of one another—and of themselves.

Family history worries away at the secret things, the skeletons in the cupboard—or the museum. Those exploring Aboriginal lives and lines of descent keep coming up against silences and discontinuities, strange partners of the Great Australian Silence. Some secrecy was traditional. Ray Yarry remembered how, in New England (NSW) in the 1930s, the location of bora rings was only vaguely indicated by elders, as a warning to the uninitiated: 'They used to just tell me like where they were but they wouldn't take me near it. It was a secret.'[63] Scraps of dialect, magical and spiritual beliefs, stories, traditions and ceremonies were also kept secret for fear of mockery from whites.[64] Some young Kooris turned away from their culture, saying to their elders: 'It is hard enough trying to learn the ways of the white people . . . without keeping up with the old ways.'[65] They giggled and felt ashamed of distinctive traditions: 'We're like white folks, now.'[66] For others, valued inheritances seemed just out of reach. George Dutton, an initiated leader in western New South Wales, wept when he heard a traditional song recounting names and places.[67] Gordon Williams spoke of the decline of initiations in far northern New South Wales: 'That was before my time, see. That law sort of faded out. If they'd have kept it up, I'd have been in it . . .'[68] Older people were sometimes reluctant to burden their children with the stigma of custom.

Sometimes family history is made harder by the fact that forebears abandoned allegiances and edged away from Aboriginal identity because it was a handicap in a racist society.[69] In *My Place* (1987), Sally Morgan tells how she rediscovered her Aboriginal heritage by exploring a suppressed family past.[70] But to rediscover that past and its evidence of avoidance can be to risk ignominy and ridicule from Aboriginal people who never ceded their identity. 'The act of passing [as white] is a horrendous crime in Aboriginal circles and places of knowing', writes Jackie Huggins. 'We vindictively remember those who have passed and (unlike whitefellas and largely those who study us) can never forget nor forgive these traitors . . . Instant coffee doesn't mix easily with pure spring water.'[71] A generation earlier, Kooris were more ready to accept that 'some *kuri* children will be lost, for the colour is a heavy burden . . . we don't blame the weak ones who want to pass'.[72] Some younger Aboriginal people find the profound lack of bitterness of their parents' generation both frustrating and amazing. Mabo-style land claims, with their lure of a route back to land through 'family history', will pressure some of the older people to remember what they want to forget. 'Passing' was a pretence of assimilationist Australia; if it were physically possible, then whites assumed it would be socially desirable. It meant one could scrape through the cultural exam. But those of Aboriginal descent now wonder if it was also, like 'passing' from life into death, a one-way trip.

Now, one is more likely to proclaim than to suppress one's Aboriginal identity.[73] Australians have departed from any genealogical criteria of racial identity, defining Aboriginality as belonging to those people who claim it and are accepted as such by the community in which they live.[74] Genealogical criteria, which were once used to define blacks who could pass as whites, may now be used against whites seeking to 'pass' as blacks. Among settler Australians there has emerged what one Aboriginal bureaucrat has called a 'trace-back-a-black' racket as a way of gaining access to federal government funds. The pressure of false claims of Aboriginality has forced some officials to go beyond the usual definition of Aboriginality. Genealogy, using family trees going back as far as 1815, has found a new bureaucratic use.[75]

Although the cultural identity and continent-wide political consciousness of Aborigines is acknowledged, they are still often denied a *local* history, particularly in southern Australia. '[A]ny claim for cultural continuity by Aborigines at a local level, is often met with shock and disbelief', observed archaeologist Sharon Sullivan in 1985.[76] And even the emphasis on 'continuity' can itself deny Aborigines a history. The land rights process in the Northern Territory since the passing of the 1976 Aboriginal Land Rights Act has focused on evidence of 'traditional ownership', a definition that emphasises anthropology over history. It is generally anthropologists and linguists who record and interpret the Aboriginal evidence, compiling genealogies, observing land use and ceremonies, mapping sites and dreaming tracks, joining bush food collecting expeditions, and gathering 'stories for country'.[77] The anthropologists need to show that timeless traditions continue to the present and that a traditional relationship with the land has survived disruption, even dispossession. In such a context, evidence of historical change may undermine the claim, particularly if Aborigines have adapted voluntarily to new circumstances. The historian is therefore expected to demonstrate the impact of European settlers, explain any Aboriginal dislocation, and dramatise Aboriginal passivity and European agency.[78] The dominance of the notion of sacred sites has also placed an emphasis on Aborigines as religious beings rather than economic ones, and therefore portrays them as natural opponents of 'development', and as anti-historical.[79] The traditional divide is perpetuated: anthropology deals with 'the other', whereas history is concerned with Europeans.

The Mabo judgement rewrote history as well as the law. It rejected the idea of Australia as *terra nullius*, recognised that native title existed in 1788, and made *history*, particularly post-contact history, the defining element of continuing Aboriginal relationships to land. The critical questions now are those of recent local history: has a connection with land been maintained, and has native title been extinguished? Continuity of possession or association is now more important than continuity of tradition.

In those parts of Australia where fewer Aborigines remain in possession of their land, heritage legislation has offered a means by which Aboriginal people can gain some recognition for their association with place, and some control over those places. Between 1965 and 1976, every Australian state enacted legislation aiming to preserve places of Aboriginal heritage. Aboriginal co-operation with European forms of site recording have sometimes led to better land rights results than the broader area claims generally pursued in remote Australia.[80] But fears often surround site recording. Older Aborigines sometimes considered it dangerous. National Parks archaeologist in New South Wales Howard Creamer observed that helping researchers to document the location and significance of certain sites had been held partly responsible for the deaths of old Aboriginal people.[81] European farmers fear being 'Mabo-ed', as they put it. 'We've found things', confesses one Queensland farmer uncomfortably. 'There would be things all over that no way are people going to show anyone. You'd have to be stark raving mad.'[82] One Victorian land-holder recently offered local Kooris the option of digging out and carting away the grinding stones embedded in his paddock. Kooris are re-establishing their custodianship of heritage sites. At the greenstone axe quarry at Mt William, for example, custodianship of the site over two hundred years has moved from the Woiwurrung to Lancefield residents and Victorian scientists (such as Kenyon and Mitchell), then to archaeologists and state-based heritage agencies. Now local Kooris are reasserting their control.[83] At Mootwingee (NSW) in 1929, Alfred Kenyon was accused (by whites) of removing valuable stone carvings for the collections of the National Museum of Victoria.[84] In 1984, a blockade of sites at Mootwingee was organised by the Western Regional Aboriginal Land Council which demanded the local employment of Aborigines, the revision of guidebooks to recognise that Kooris still exist, and the permanent closure of some sacred sites to visitors. The change in spelling to Mutawinttji now signals the change in management to tourists.[85] As prehistoric sites have become known to Kooris, some have been 'adopted' and reinterpreted, and occasionally sites have been created. Howard Creamer recorded that, in 1980,

> an Aboriginal elder, originally from another area, named an impressive granite rock outcrop near Tamworth 'Wave Rock', because of its resemblance to a wave; the site was recorded at his request because he believed that in the past it must have been an increase site for rain.[86]

Site-related Aboriginal myths were always a mixture of invention and memory, a sort of poetry.[87]

What is the route back to land for those indigenous Australians who have no personal attachment to country, for people like Graham Atkinson, born in Echuca in 1948, who 'find it hard to determine what areas my ancestors came from or possessed'?[88] 'Keeping places' is a term for Aboriginal museums that is both descriptive and wishful. It both describes a storehouse for objects and invokes possession of the land; it is persuasive of a local history. When John (Sandy) Atkinson adapted that phrase for use at an Aboriginal Keeping Place he helped establish in Shepparton (Victoria) in the 1970s, he was avoiding the word 'museum', which had so many negative meanings for Aboriginal people.[89] A 'keeper' was traditionally an elder who cared for his clan's sacred objects, and some of these places were established to hold locally any cultural material returned from state museums. The Shepparton Keeping Place, situated in one of R. E. Johns' collecting grounds, was the first of many keeping places that have been established in eastern Australia over the last two decades. Where Aborigines have been dispossessed and have less chance of reclaiming their land, objects can become almost as important as country, as the Museum of Victoria has discovered. Keeping places are a response to loss, artefacts of discontinuity despite their name. Few historic local artefacts survive. The keeping places can therefore sometimes appear as generalised memorials, emphasising the traditional past, using dioramas, underplaying regional diversity, displaying the material culture of a hunter-gatherer lifestyle, and failing to convey a view of contemporary Koori culture.[90] But keeping places and cultural centres are economic as well as cultural ventures.[91] They have been shaped by some of the same forces—nationalism and tourism—that brought the settlers' folk museums into being, and they can be just as homogeneous. The boomerang has joined the blacksmith's tools, bottles, bedsteads and bicycles as a heritage object, a universal commodity of past cultures. 'Come and see a forty thousand year old culture ... and take it back with you!' was the invitation issued by a poster designed by the Koorie Unit of the Victorian Tourism Commission.[92]

Where traditions have been abandoned or lost, people of Aboriginal descent have had to reconstruct them. 'You *build* Aboriginality, boy, or you got nothing', Grandfather Koori told Kevin Gilbert.[93] Much of what is now being incorporated as Aboriginal cultural knowledge in settled Australia is the result of historical research, acquired rather than inherited.[94] 'Most of our knowledge', says Robert Murray who grew up on the Cowra Mission in New South Wales, 'comes from books, or from the screen, or from what people tell us. Not from our own people.'[95] For many Aborigines, part of the attraction of family history is that it becomes local history, offering a route back to ancestral lands. When Ruby Langford read about Millie Boyd, an Aboriginal 'cleverwoman' from her own locality, the spiritual custodian and 'Keeper' of Nimbin Rock, she found that 'the hair was standing up on the back of my neck'. 'Here was information about a culture I had lost when I came to Sydney. Only it wasn't lost. There was a direct line from Uncle Ernie Ord ... '[96]

Margaret Somerville, in two collaborative books with Aboriginal people of New South Wales, has explored surviving Aboriginal links with place in settled Australia. In *Ingelba and the Five Black Matriarchs* (1990) and *The Sun Dancin'* (1994) she investigates Ingelba and Burrabeedee, Aboriginal communities that are now dispersed. The books document the return of Aboriginal descendants to the land of their elders, journeys that they make physically themselves, and emotionally through photos, stories, objects and writings. The research is both geographical and genealogical, the sources both oral and written, artefactual and environmental. Patsy Cohen, who inspired the book on Ingelba, was born in 1937 and was taken from her mother and made a state ward at the age of four. That is when her memory starts, there in the courthouse. Her two most significant memories, then, are of departure and return: when she was taken from her mother, and the moment, at the age of nine, when she discovered that she was Aboriginal. The place of that revelation was Ingelba.[97]

At Ingelba and Burrabeedee, the links with land were fought for, and sometimes documented by, women who 'straddled two eras of Aboriginal history': they were born before the areas were settled by whites and they lived to secure a power base in white society.[98] Descendants of these women are Somerville's collaborators, renewing the links with land today. Burrabeedee is a small parcel of land near the Warrumbungles that belongs to the local Aboriginal people. In the 1880s, an Aboriginal woman, Mary Jane Cain (1844-1929), started Burrabeedee Mission and claimed the land for her family. Like many Aborigines in this period, Cain asked for the land as an economic base, for farming, but also claimed her rights as an original owner, as 'the only native belong in to here'.[99] People came from all around the district when they heard 'she had made a reserve for the dark people'.[100] Kooris remained there until the 1950s when they were displaced by a second wave of dispossession generated by the government policy of assimilation.

Janet Robinson, a direct descendant of Mary Jane Cain, told Somerville apologetically: 'I don't know any blacky stories.' Robinson was two when she left the mission, and later cried when she went to school and realised she was black. 'The only thing I read about round Coonabarabran was *The Red Chief* book [by Ion Idriess, 1953]', she explained, 'and that's the only thing I ever read about Aborigine.'[101] Ion Idriess constructed the story of the 'Red Chief' from written notes of a tale told in the 1880s by an Aborigine named Bungaree, known as 'King of the Namoi River Tribe at Gunnedah' and also, as it happens, Patsy Cohen's grandfather. The 'Red Chief' lived perhaps two centuries before Bungaree and was buried beneath an intricately carved stump in Gunnedah opposite the Wesleyan parsonage. His bones were dug up by a Gunnedah doctor and collector, Edward Hayne, who was keen on skulls, and whose actions caused fear and some anguished story-telling. Hayne later sent the skeleton, and part of the carved stump, to the Australian Museum in Sydney. The Red Chief's story, like his skeleton, was archived, and became Janet Robinson's only image of a tribal past.[102]

A recurrent theme of these Aboriginal local histories is the tension and dialogue between written and oral sources, between 'the pencil' and 'the mouth' as Marie Dundas, one of Somerville's Koori collaborators, puts it.[103] Somerville is the scribe, while the Kooris are the talkers and rememberers. But it is Somerville who emphasises the importance of oral knowledge, whereas her informants especially value the written word. Somerville's priority was to record the authentic rhythms of Koori speech, to document this 'reclamation of babble'.[104] Patsy Cohen, by contrast, considered the discovery of a small published booklet of memoirs their 'greatest find'. She valued her own text as an object, 'an artefact to preserve'. Surrounded by loss, she turned to writing for permanence. Cohen hoped to record some bora rings at Ingelba; she wanted to have National Parks staff 'record it so that it would be looked after and kept', but 'Pop', an old man 'who held the knowledge', was deeply suspicious of this translation of his lore. So Cohen recorded them 'in an even more permanent way' through her text.[105]

Memories of their culture are preserved in another way by the women, through the collection of precious objects that remind them of previous owners. With the semi-nomadic lifestyle of Kooris, these collections are stored in trunks, where they can be locked away and easily transported. 'I remember my aunty, they all had trunks, and others in Kempsey', recalls Grace. 'They kept photos, papers and things their husbands or brothers made them and gifts, books.' Somerville was invited to observe the ritual of the trunk. Granny Morris's trunk is well known among Armidale Aboriginal people; 'many visit to view its contents and hear the stories'. The trunk contained over sixty items, each wrapped in a container or cloth: old pipes in a hand-sewn lizard skin pouch, small glass bottles with semi-precious stones from fossicking days, notebook, letters, flour bags. The ceremonious unfolding and story-telling reminded Somerville of the Aboriginal women she had lived with in the desert out of Papunya, who had stored and surveyed their sacred objects in the same way.[106]

The message of these histories is that places can be reclaimed through writing and talk, that continuity of occupation is not the only measure of possession. On Mumbulla Mountain near Bega on the New South Wales south coast, huge granite boulders make shapes and faces in the forest. This was a place of initiation for the Yuin people, where young males 'go up the Mountain as boys; they come back as men'. For several weeks they were led around the sacred places, performing ceremonies in the forest, at bora rings and waterfalls, and learning from their elders that 'The Law comes from the mountain.' Although the last known initiation ceremony may have occurred there about 1918, Mumbulla Mountain has once more become a place of significance and power to the Yuin people, many of whom today live north of the mountain at Wallaga Lake. 'Mumbulla Mountain is of vital importance to the culture and dignity of the 3,500 Aborigines living on the South coast today', explained Yuin elder Guboo Ted Thomas in 1980.[107]

In 1978-9, the Yuin people defended their mountain from woodchip logging on the basis that it was a sacred place. They remembered walking through the forest from Wallaga to Bega, supplementing their government rations with food from the bush and the sea while the old people taught them stories and songs and pointed out the sacred places in the hills. As a child, Guboo Ted Thomas remembers being told that one day he would be taken to the mountain to be initiated. But he never was, as the ceremonies fell into disuse. When, in 1978, the Forestry Commission logged to within 50 metres of a teaching place, Thomas 'went to see for himself'.

> It didn't take me long to find the sites. I had a fair idea of what to look for and where to look from what I had been told by the old people, and I could feel the spiritual power in these places when I got close to them.[108]

When the Yuin people publicly defended their spiritual home, their arguments were met with profound scepticism by government, the timber industry and the local white community. Jean Draper, the honorary secretary of the Truthful Reporting of Eden's Environment Society (TREES), questioned the descent of the Aboriginal campaigners. 'THE LINE HAS BEEN BROKEN', she declared. 'How many full-blooded Aborigines are left in the area today?' The New South Wales Minister for Conservation, Lin Gordon, said that there would need to be more evidence to justify the claim than just someone 'knocking two sticks together and chanting'. When politicians and timber industry officials toured the mountain, they saw no sacred sites. 'Rocks are rocks, mountains are mountains', declared the *Canberra Times*. A local white resident, who was quick to point out that his family association to the area dated back to 1845, considered the sites 'a figment of somebody's imagination', explaining that 'it's only in the last twelve months or so that I've heard any mention whatever of Aboriginal sacred sites'.[109] Guboo Ted Thomas wrote in exasperation to the state Premier:

> These are sacred matters which must be kept quiet. We do not talk about these things even among ourselves unless it is absolutely necessary. These are our laws that come to us from the mountain. We only talk . . . when we are forced to do so in order to protect our sacred places from ignorant white people to whom only the dollar is sacred. So you can see why these things never become public knowledge until early 1978. It is not a question of making up stories, it is a question of our sacred heritage which we are trying to protect and to build up once again.[110]

Logging was suspended while an archaeologist, Brian Egloff, investigated the claim. As well as the oral traditions of the Yuin, Egloff was able to draw on the handwritten testimony of the anthropologist Alfred Howitt who, in 1883, encouraged the organisation of a major regional initiation ceremony so that he could observe and describe it. Howitt's notes and sketch map in the Museum and State Library of Victoria reveal that in April 1883, between 130 and 150 people gathered at what was almost certainly Mumbulla Mountain for almost two weeks of ceremonies.[111] Just over one hundred years later, the New South Wales government acceded to the petition of the Yuin people and declared the mountain top an Aboriginal Place. It is now also on the Register of the National Estate. Further archaeological surveys in forest areas have since been supported by Aboriginal people and government.

'Mumbulla Mountain is like a church to the Aboriginal people in a spiritual way', explained Guboo Ted Thomas in 1980. He went further: 'we think it can be important to white Australians also'.[112] Here is an invitation to share pride in the long Aboriginal past, and a recognition, too, that settler Australians will form parallel—and not necessarily competing—emotional attachments to the land. Local history is promising ground for cultural convergence between black and white Australians, *convergence* being, as Les Murray and Bernard Smith have argued, 'a fact, a subtle process, not a proposed ethical programme'.[113] Near Mumbulla Mountain and very close to Wallaga Lake is Gulaga (Mt Dromedary). It is a mountain that features in the creation myths of the Yuin people, a place where a few of their ancestors crawled out of the water and survived a great flood. Mt Dromedary is now a landscape where Europeans have farmed and lived for several generations. At its base is the century-old Spring Hills homestead where Mal Dibden and his father have worked since 1948. Dibden feels a strong attachment to the farm, and to the working, social landscape of his childhood. But he is drawn also to the mountain that looms forever above his farm, particularly to its temperate rainforest where he finds a lonely, romantic spiritualism. He walks barefoot through the mountain forest, through the sassafras and tree-ferns; he echoes Guboo Ted Thomas when he says it is 'like walking in the best church in the world'.[114]

CHAPTER ELEVEN

'Progress through Preservation'

In an essay entitled 'On perceiving the Australian suburb' written in the mid-1970s, Bernard Smith described the late development in Australia of a historical vision of the built environment. Landscape painting, he argued, was the dominant artistic genre in colonial and early twentieth-century Australia, and it led to a vision of the 'mythical Australian' as a creature of nature 'who lies on the other side of history'. As a historical perception of the environment emerged, Australians began to accept the place of humans and their works in the landscape; they began to see towns, cities and suburbs as personal environments, as places of character and art. Smith described this as 'a mode of vision by which . . . the past is apprehended as a sensuous quality of things presently observed'. This popular historical perception, he suggested, 'as distinct from book history, often begins with an awakened respect for the fabric of old buildings'.[1]

Smith sketched out some of the origins of that perception in the 'gentler vision of architects and antiquaries' who, from the late nineteenth century, began sympathetically to discern the historical character of the Australian built environment. These were nature writers, antiquarians and historical society members, some of whom were discussed in part two, people like Charles Barrett and William Hardy Wilson who were feeling their way towards a 'heritage of stone'. As Smith recognised, theirs was a pastoral and patrician view of history, one of flocks and vineyards, barns and homesteads, of 'Georgian and Regency monuments'. It was this vision that was perpetuated in organised form in the National Trusts established after the second world war and which, in more recent years, has broadened its definition of 'the historic' to include, for example, workers' cottages and industrial buildings.[2] Smith puzzled over the sources of this historical perception and noted that 'it can arise with dramatic suddenness in a society and affect radical changes in the priorities given to popular values . . . things that were once seen as merely old and obsolescent are seen in a new light as human heritage'.[3]

This chapter addresses the growth of that historical perception of the built environment in post-war Australia and gives it a social and political context by focusing on negotiations over heritage in country towns. It was in country communities that the powerful post-war alliance between tourism and conservation of the built environment ('progress through preservation') was first tested. And it was there that the emerging heritage professionals sometimes encountered resistant, local historical visions. Heritage issues in country towns challenge the whole community. They raise fundamental questions about a town's economic viability, cultural independence, and image. They question accepted notions of progress. They often unearth latent anxieties about a town's future—and its past—and demand that they be addressed openly and urgently. The politics of a small community are intimate, inescapably personal and immediate. The councillor lives next door to the campaigner, and the disputed site is around the corner. Yet, paradoxically, local heritage debates often centre on the desirability of involving outside, impersonal forces. The city—as a model of modernity, a source of power and money, and arbiter of the historic—looms large in the country town's negotiation with its heritage.

The ethic of progress

In Australia the cities were first, and remain dominant. The towns were their outposts, initially with closer links to the city than to their own hinterlands. Towns began, perhaps, as staging-posts, at river crossings, on the sites of gold-rushes, or as rail-heads. They mediated the flow of people, goods and services between city and country, they catered for travellers as much as stayers. They were competitors for the services the city farmed out to them. They were dependent on distant powers and vulnerable to the chance of gold or seasons. They craved progress. Associations with that magic name were ubiquitous, and they measured their town's fortunes against others.[4]

Because of the country town's economic orientation to outsiders and passers-by, its appearance had to be both testimony to past progress and a hopeful lure for more. Founders of the gold towns, where the environment was transformed in a few years, expressed their wonder and boastfulness in their buildings. They took pride in turning a makeshift settlement into a statement of permanence, canvas into stone, wilderness into civilisation. The foundation stone of the town hall of Ballarat West (Victoria) was laid in 1860 by R. M. Serjeant, local member of parliament, in a landscape where eight years earlier he had been lost in the bush. The classical design of the town hall, chosen carefully by competition, gave historical depth and dignity to the instant society.[5]

The built environment is a legacy as much of anxiety and decline as it is of confidence and progress. The anguished reality of prolonged recession (the experience of many country towns from the turn of the century) preserved some of the nineteenth-century townscapes we treasure today. But decline also left its impact. In the 1920s at Maldon (Victoria), as at other goldfields in recession, houses were removed entirely to more prosperous towns. These vacant allotments were visible wounds in the town's honour, reminders of lost neighbours.[6]

Anxiety could also be expressed in the impulse to build, and to build monumentally. Michael Roper has argued that, in Bendigo (Victoria), the city's buildings, monuments and rituals began as celebrations of industrial progress, but in later years became monuments to past achievement and bulwarks against decline. The town's economic downturn from 1875 coincided with the period of greatest attention to the appearance of its buildings, parks and gardens. Such solid and ornate grandeur would itself, it was hoped, be the harbinger of prosperity.[7]

In the twentieth century, the car leached many small country towns of their independence, industries and population, and made them more vulnerable to the city, or to the larger towns in their region. Increased private mobility gave some towns new life as tourist resorts. The car also transformed the environment with symbols of the new age. Between 1955 and 1965 in Clare (South Australia), three new bulk petrol depots were opened, five new service stations built, a drive-in theatre established, a park turned into caravan sites, and the old bridges at either end of the town replaced with wider reinforced concrete ones.[8] Modernisation, which meant being like the city, became the measure of progress, the progress that many towns had lost.

Images of the past, of a European classical past, had once usefully bestowed a dimension of history and comparative progress to colonial towns which grew up overnight. By the mid-twentieth century, local vernacular elements of the past—above all, the verandah—were being destroyed in the name of progress.

On the verandah

The Australian author Hal Porter (1911–84) first observed the world from the security of a verandah in Bellair Street in Kensington, Melbourne. The verandah was a formative influence; it was to make him an observer for life. At the age of six, he moved with his family to Bairnsdale, a town on the river flats of East Gippsland, Victoria. He recalled his youth there in his autobiography, *The Watcher on the Cast-Iron Balcony* (1963), and wrote a rich and nostalgic history of his country community in *Bairnsdale: Portrait of an Australian Country Town* (1977).[9] In his history, Porter introduced Bairnsdale through the veil of its cast-iron balconies, now demolished. The 1920s, the years of his youth, the swansong of iron filigree, are the focus of the book. These were Bairnsdale's finest years, Porter opined, a time when it still had intimacy and charm together with mature trees and old buildings. What had happened, he wondered, as he looked at the denuded town of the 1970s? His history is both nostalgic evocation and bitter condemnation:

> It was one of the town's (the shire council's) unbelievably inartistic and comfort-destroying blunders to strip Main Street buildings and such late Victorian hotels as the Grand Terminus, the Main and the Albion of their wide verandahs and shady balconies, profusely trimmed with apparent tatting in cast-iron. What now irks the eye is what the eye knows was designed not to be seen—walls marred by closed-for-ever upstairs doors, and ill-balanced sash-windows . . . Aesthetically it is an innutritious town.[10]

Porter argued that 'tearing irreverently down is as much a clue to a town's nature as reverently putting up', and he was puzzled and chilled by the destructiveness of local government, particularly since the second world war. He wrote of Bairnsdale, but he saw it as a typical Australian country town: outwardly respectable, guided by petty ambitions, straining for modernisation, and turning vengefully on its verandahs.[11]

Verandahs quickly became one of the few characteristically Australian elements of the built environment. They were popular and sensible. They offered protection from the sun and rain, they touted for custom, and were bowers of social life and refuges from the street. The verandah is a powerful metaphor for Australian environmental sensibilities. It was a symbol of empire, an artefact of European colonial expansion. It echoed the awnings, tents and canvas towns of early Australian settlement, effectively memorialising transplanted European beginnings and representing a new start in a strange land. It provided a tentative, halfway step into the outside world, an area of negotiation and contemplation, curiosity and detachment. It offered a framed prospect such as Porter had enjoyed, a European version of the Aboriginal rock gallery. Architect Philip Drew sees the verandah as a touchstone of national identity: 'For Australians to stand on the verandah of their own house,' he writes, 'is to find themselves.'[12]

But as many Australian towns entered a period of decline or little growth in the early twentieth century, verandahs began to decay or look shabby. The first stirrings of public recognition of the historical dimension of the local landscape are to be found in negative feelings towards verandahs. Shabby or not, they were seen to be elements of the past, and were hated for it. Within a few decades they were treasured for the same reason. No one doubted that they were historic; what changed was the way country towns regarded visible history.

In Bendigo the revolution was so compressed it was comic. When, in 1960, the Bendigo City Council ordered the removal of all post-type verandahs during the next ten years, it was eleven years behind Bairnsdale and thirty years later than many councils across New South Wales. The *Bendigo Advertiser* expressed concern at this serious delay in modernising:

> Many towns throughout Australia have now abolished verandah posts . . . And the transformation in each case has been almost unbelievable. Travellers passing from one provincial centre to another cannot avoid making unflattering comparisons in the case of towns that have lagged behind.[13]

First impressions are crucial, argued the *Advertiser* editorial. 'A town can be immediately classified as bright and progressive, or frowsy and "dated", by a single glance.' Bendigo needed to look progressive, to impress outsiders in order to attract custom and investment. In arguing against verandahs, the *Advertiser* disparaged the feelings of residents 'who do not travel around much' and who found verandahs 'quite homely and satisfactory'. It condemned the verandah by comparing it to raw elements of the past: the fast-disappearing mullock heaps from the mines, a shanty town, the Wild West, even the posts were like prison bars (of convict days?). And the posts, it was said, were a hazard to that idol of the new age, the car. Councils came under pressure from road hauliers and bus operators who regarded verandahs as dangerous and inconvenient obstacles. Steel cantilever awnings, on the other hand, did not obstruct parking and 'give an instant impression of cleanliness and brightness, expansiveness, modernity and civic pride'.[14]

Mary Fry has studied the Bendigo Council's change of attitude. Within four years of the passing of the by-law, the case for preserving a couple of examples of verandahs and iron lace was gathering strength on the grounds of their potential as tourist attractions.[15] In 1967, the newly formed local branch of the National Trust successfully gained exemptions from the verandah by-law and, in 1970, citizen campaigns saved two hotel verandahs. The council doggedly stuck to its course in the face of many protests. But in 1979, the city engineer recommended repeal of the by-law, using the same arguments that had initially condemned the verandah: aesthetics, appeal to visitors, and issues of safety and shelter. The new factor was that a link was perceived between history and tourists, and this provided a formula by which the progress ethic could be negotiated. The only recorded car accident with a verandah in the period had involved a cantilever awning.

By 1986, observes Mary Fry, the council was so keen on verandahs that it sanctioned their addition even to buildings for which they were never intended. A new owner wishing to establish an antique business proposed that a verandah be added to a building designed without one in 1877. The National Trust and architectural advisers pointed out that the noted architect William Vahland had based his design on fifteenth-century Italian buildings, and had demarcated ground and first floors with a Greek key motif, a form of signature for the architect which would be obliterated by a verandah. The Bendigo Council overruled the objection on the basis that verandahs were typically Victorian and provided protection from sun and rain.

Many country towns, particularly in New South Wales, were denuded of their verandahs because they had ordered demolition earlier than Bendigo. Joe Glascott wrote in the *Sydney Morning Herald* of the 'great verandah hatred' which had swept through the state, leaving buildings like 'aged aunts in mini-skirts'.[16] The main street of Wagga Wagga (NSW) was ironically condemned to be viewed on tourist posters through the one remaining cast-iron balcony. Other towns, such as Forbes (NSW), Yass (NSW) and Ballarat saved some of theirs through tenacious citizen campaigns. In York (WA), the threat to verandahs from a council by-law in the late 1960s was the catalyst which prompted the development of its new role as a historic town.[17] At Maffra (Victoria), verandahs were the main issue in the council elections of 1976. A 'Save our Verandahs' committee was formed, meetings were held, a petition of over 1600 signatures was gathered, and the verandahs were preserved. For many it was the 'greatest thing to happen to council', as it had involved the community in decision-making like never before.[18]

Towns readily adjusted to the notion of tourism because they were used to showing their wares, used to being orientated to the needs of passers-by for economic gain. Many had fostered tourism to local beauty spots since the turn of the century. But, as some towns were to discover, the history tourist was a different species. This uneasy alliance between conservation and business, between history and progress, has been forged most conspicuously in the 'historic towns'.

'Historic towns'

In the 1940s, George Farwell wrote about 'Old Towns in a New Age'. These were the country towns, in the hills or on the outback plains, that were in decline. In them he found what Henry Lawson called a 'painful sense of listening', a straining to recover the senses and sounds of past grandeur. They were stranded, left silent, by the retreat of civilisation.

He was moved by them, by their air of former greatness, and their accidental preservation of a decaying, but poignant yesterday. He wrote of Tibooburra, Hill End, Wentworth, Wilcannia ... These remnants of the past, he asked, 'can we ever bring them back to life, or link them with the present?'[19]

Farwell was writing at the beginning of a great change in the perception of the built environment in Australia. The ensuing decades have seen many attempts to link these 'old towns' with the present without obliterating their character. They were called historic not because they were necessarily early or first, nor because of their uniformly outstanding buildings and landscape, but because fate preserved them while other towns changed. They were small enough to have retained their integrity, and to be preserved as total environments. National trusts, formed throughout Australia in the two decades following Farwell's questioning, had begun by preserving individual buildings. By the 1960s the trust was pioneering efforts to conserve whole living environments, at just the time that government was beginning to finance re-created historic villages.[20]

This 'preservationist history', as Davison has called it, was a further step in the benign process of the professional invasion of local history, for it was generally led by the adopted children of a locality whose 'love affair with its physical fabric' preceded their social integration.[21] It was informed by a generalised nostalgia and an appreciation of the pictur-esque, and its purpose was primarily the conservation of things rather than values. The visibility of this version of the past ensured its strong alliance with tourism.

In 1963 in Berrima (NSW), the state branch of the National Trust, together with the Department of Tourist Activities, the Royal Australian Historical Society, the Royal Australian Institute of Architects and local organisations, sponsored the formation of the Berrima Village Trust in an effort to save the town's special Georgian character. In 1964 in Richmond (Tasmania), the Royal Australian Institute of Architects called a meeting to consider the future of the town, which might soon be engulfed as a dormitory suburb of Hobart. A Richmond Preservation and Development Committee (later Trust) was formed. In 1966, the Victorian branch of the National Trust announced the classification of the former gold town of Maldon as a 'Notable Town', following an intensive survey by the School of Architecture at the University of Melbourne. In each case, although local residents were involved from the beginning, the initiative was taken by outsiders, primarily by architects from the city. Their message to the citizens of these declining towns was that there would be 'progress through preservation', and that the tourist lured by history would offer them a new economic future. But the preservation bodies in these towns, and in many other towns that followed their lead, quickly discovered that there were pitfalls in going public on heritage. And, although bodies like the National Trust were resentfully credited with much power, their ability to control what was happening was minimal.[22]

At Berrima, the trust watched helplessly as one of the town's central buildings, the Surveyor General Hotel, was unsympathetically altered in the years following its intervention. The Richmond Preservation and Development Trust, which included six local residents, played no more than an advisory role to council. Its power was limited severely by a lack of money, a council uninterested in history, and by the town's social climate which discouraged political activity. One of the aims of the group was to retain the Australian sprawl and low-density character of the town, and to resist attempts to turn Richmond into a neat, intimate 'English village'. The threat was seen to come not just from unsympathetic intrusions of the present, but also from false images of the past.[23]

The trust's publicity of Maldon's 'notable town' status attracted an instant surge of tourists, and local houses were bought by Melbourne people as weekenders. New buildings were erected and property values rose. The council planned to rip up the slate flagstones to make the streets safer for the town's new visitors, and businesses wanted new signs and coats of paint to attract custom. Bogus history was slapped onto the streetscape. The trust had inadvertently put under threat the very environment it wanted to preserve.[24]

But it had no power to preserve it.[25] Trust classification was an estimate of value, not a programme of legislative action. When the Maldon Shire Council was not prepared to fund the preparation of an urgently needed planning scheme, the trust encouraged the State Government Town and Country Planning Board to assume planning control over the town through the declaration of an Interim Development Order in 1970. This generated intense local opposition. Residents bridled at restrictions on their rights as property owners and, above all, resented direction from Melbourne.[26] In Beechworth (Victoria), similar battlelines were drawn. The trust had proceeded cautiously, winning some local support with its successful restoration of a powder magazine in 1966 and then, through a constructive partnership with the shire council, forged a joint plan for preservation of the whole town. But, by 1970, the impact of planning restrictions and the ogre of Melbourne dictatorship made Beechworth, like Maldon, a flashpoint. 'Why don't they [the trust] buy the complete town and ruin the value of their property, not the townspeople's', demanded one angry Beechworth resident.[27]

This was an option put, not quite in those terms, to Berrima residents. In 1967, the New South Wales government, under the National Parks and Wildlife Act, moved to acquire and proclaim Berrima as a 'historic site'. A public meeting was held on 4 April 1967 in the Berrima Court House. It was 'long, lively, loquacious, at times noisy, and even occasionally heated'.[28] A residents' committee was set up which, two months later, reported that although it favoured the acquisition of specific historic sites in Berrima by the government, it did not support proclamation of the whole town, and certainly not acquisition by resumption. Later that year, freehold land in and around Hill End (NSW), which George Farwell had found 'crumbling to pieces' but whose hotel bar of polished cedar had impressed him, was purchased by the government to be administered as a historic site.[29] Resentment about outside control still lingers among its tiny population. In 1988, above that cedar bar was a notice urging: '. . . Let's make the Heritage Council a thing of the past.'

Much of the early opposition from residents of historic towns grew out of frustration at the lack of guidelines offered when they did want to make changes to their homes or main street. Heritage managers frequently found themselves in the position of being negative. 'The National Trust won't let me' became a common refrain. The provision of guidelines for paint colours, signwriting, fences, and other features helped overcome frustration. In Maldon, the finalisation of the town plan in 1977 was accompanied by the publication of a detailed conservation study, the appointment of a part-time architectural adviser, and the establishment of a small revolving fund to provide low-interest loans to owners for restoration work.[30] These features made heritage management a positive and more predictable intrusion. This model has since been followed in other towns. There is still lively dissent, of course, particularly about signs and colours. Some think the approved dominance of cream, green and brown makes a town 'look like a bloody ice-cream'. In Beechworth in 1987 there was strident debate about bright signs, and: what exactly was the colour of the past? When defending a luminous Flag Inn sign, one councillor argued that 'the British Empire was built on red, white and blue and these colours were used one hundred years ago'.[31]

More fundamental was the age-old tension between city and country which heritage matters exacerbated. The initiative for preservation of whole towns came mostly from the city. It sometimes seemed that those who lived amidst the fruits of urban progress wanted the past somewhere, elsewhere, available to be visited. Locals felt that outsiders were dictating to them, shaping their environment for what other outsiders— tourists—were supposed to want to see. And there seemed little awareness of the less visible social impact of those demands.

Tourism was offered as the solution to these concerns, but residents of historic towns quickly developed scepticism about its value. Some, like Hahndorf (South Australia), had a history of difference. Established in 1839 by German Lutherans seeking religious freedom, it harboured different cultural and environmental practices from its beginnings. There were times, particularly during the first world war, when it denied those differences. But its history is full of debates about its independence and environment which presaged those consequent on its definition as 'historic'. Battles about its main street elms, first in 1913 and then in 1963, were a stimulus to the broader conservation campaign about the whole townscape.[32] Other historic towns had courted earlier sorts of tourists. Beechworth, situated among the hills of north-east Victoria, advertised itself as a sanatorium and beauty spot from the end of the nineteenth century. For others, such as York, a closed, agricultural community 100 kilometres from Perth, tourism of any kind was an entirely new phenomenon.[33] But for all historic towns the 'history tourist' was to be a novel experience.[34] They came to look at the town itself, to peer and snoop at people's frontyards. And they came, probably, just for a few hours. 'They come in with a clean shirt and a quid, and go out with both', was how one Beechworth resident put it.[35] This was a particularly stressful form of tourism, and of limited value to the local economy. Some towns, such as Braidwood (NSW) and Hahndorf, already have as many tourists as their environment and weekends can stand, and there is caution about encouraging more. Others, such as Hill End, now attract only half as many as they did ten years ago. The limits of tourism as a solve-all have been sighted. And many conservationists believe that false history now poses a bigger threat than does rampant development.[36]

Resident opposition in historic towns was often portrayed in terms of different visions of the town's future, or simply as a dispute between those who appreciated history and those who did not. But it also concerned a conflict of historical perspectives. The new, imported view of heritage made buildings the historical centrepiece. It introduced an aesthetic and a language which were impressive but foreign. For locals it represented a puzzling admiration for architecture above all else, and a strange faith that these buildings could somehow be articulate about the past. Locals had traditions of their own, generally centred on the pioneers, or stories of past grandeur. They treasured a history which was not visible. Those buildings they did regard as special were because of someone who lived there or something that happened there. The new concentration on buildings also tangled with the often intense rivalry between town and country sections of rural shires, a ready-made resentment about attention lavished on the town centre.[37] In the 1990s, heritage agencies have tried to accommodate these more personal, local meanings of places by formally assessing 'social value', a criterion which explicitly 'emphasises aspects of living cultures rather than dead fabric'.[38]

In many of these historic towns, the long, agonising decline which had preserved their streetscape had left raw memories. In Charters Towers (Queensland), writes Shirley Symes, the years following the first world war were 'a period of bitterness and rejection of traditional ideas, reminders of the past—older people wanted to forget the heartbreak and poverty that in some cases followed the closing down of the mines and the loss of jobs and opportunities'. When, in recent years, plans were first discussed regarding the restoration of the Stock Exchange, a familiar retort was 'Why? It only brings back sad and bitter memories to me.'[39] Often the first public buildings to be preserved in a town were the major commercial or government agencies rather than those informal buildings beloved by locals. As residents themselves became more involved in heritage decisions, and as historians joined architects in the conservation field, attention turned to different elements of the townscape.

In Beechworth, threatened demolition of a popular local grandstand drew a response of surprising vigour. The grandstand, which watches over Baarmutha Park, was built in 1897. By July 1986, decay had made it dangerous and the Beechworth Shire Council called for tenders for its demolition. There was immediate dismay among residents, calls for its preservation, and offers of action. The Save Our Grandstand Committee which was formed successfully applied to the Victorian National Estate Committee for a grant of $8,000 to make the grandstand safe. Local builders and craftspeople with experience in restoring nineteenth-century buildings volunteered their expertise and labour. Individuals and institutions gave money and supported fund-raising events with enthusiasm. Sporting and other groups suggested possible future uses for the grandstand. Residents surprised themselves—and the shire council—with the support they generated. The council was more used to championing the vision of 'the historic town' in the face of local apathy and resentment. Here was evidence of widening support for the 'progress through preservation' ethic. But it is clear, too, that the grandstand is for the locals, not the tourists. It has been a centre of informality and fun, and has been closer to the local heart than Beechworth's preserved government buildings which were often seen as official and alien. And the grandstand dates from other than the gold era, its gala days more within the memory of aging residents.[40]

Heritage debates in historic towns are changing, too, because many of the outsiders are no longer outside. They have come to stay, to open businesses catering for the tourists, or to enjoy the lifestyle of an attractive, historic country town. The battlelines have been internalised.

Higher property values are forcing out some of the long-established businesses and putting pressure on the older and poorer residents. In some of the old mining towns there are now new outsiders. The gold that created them threatens to destroy them, as miners return with their bulldozers and machinery. They claim modern mining to be a heritage, a traditional activity more continuous with the past than antique shops and paint-scraping. In all of the historic towns, the public use of history offered a new future in economically troubled times, and has largely preserved their physical character and special atmosphere. But behind the calm and peace of their historic aura, these towns have been experiencing their greatest social changes this century.

'Historic towns' were the frontier of the heritage movement in the 1960s and 1970s. They witnessed the new alliance of tourism and history, and they brought about the growing involvement of government in heritage controls. The legislative mechanisms pioneered in the historic towns are now being applied to other country communities, and it is perhaps there—in the towns that do not call themselves 'historic'—that the current challenges lie.

Modern battles

It is more common for a town to draw only a part of its identity from its history, and for its historic features to be isolated elements of a modern environment. A town may be in the grip of progress rather than just anxious about it, and signs of its early settlement may have been swamped. A town's most historic features may be visually unexceptional. Many of its unusual characteristics may be recent in origin and therefore seen to be less exotic. In places where few fine buildings were built, or have been allowed to survive, saving the remaining historic features is paradoxically harder. The arguments of tourism, historic integrity, age, or architectural merit may be less relevant. The less visible ties of social history may have to carry the defence. Concerned residents lead the campaigns against what they see to be unsympathetic local councils, and it is they who call on outside controls for assistance. This contrasts with the historic towns, where outside individuals and government, sometimes in partnership with the council, have felt the need to educate reluctant locals.

Much legislation in the 1970s and 1980s has aimed to put power and money at the disposal of locals. But councils continue to assert their right to determine their own priorities over and above any national duty to hold a building or landscape in trust. Although councils are more and more involved in commissioning conservation studies, they are often reluctant to implement them. Ballarat City Council severely whittled down the conservation study it commissioned in 1978, and the tabling of Bendigo's 1977 study made it a local election issue, and the new council opposed it.[41]

Goulburn (NSW), founded in 1828 and the second oldest inland city in Australia, was the subject of a heritage study in 1982, jointly funded by the Goulburn City Council and the Heritage Council of New South Wales. Bruce Pennay has described the local council's cool response to a report which recommended that 200 properties be preserved.[42] Some of the reasons for the council deferring implementation of the recommendations surfaced in a debate about 'Brackley', an imposing pair of town houses built near the end of the 1840s. These villas stood in the middle of land which had been acquired by council for a new civic centre. A commission of enquiry into the conflicting proposals for 'Brackley' heard historical evidence which related mostly to the building's social history—its various owners and occupants, the insight it offered into social mobility and the contribution of the town's lawyers, and its role as a document of broad patterns of settlement and development. The commissioner accepted its importance and recommended its retention, believing that the council's plans for a civic centre would not be greatly affected. But the Minister for Planning and Environment bowed to local pressure and did not place it under a permanent conservation order. The buildings were demolished with little local protest. Bruce Pennay concluded that although the commissioner decided that 'Brackley' was significant to the state, the local community decided that it was not significant to Goulburn.

Industrial heritage in country towns is a particularly political issue. Relatively few Australian towns are independent producers for a national or state-wide market. Where they do have that status it is generally because of an industry's long commitment to the district. So heritage and industry are likely to occupy the same ground. Warrnambool, Victoria's fifth largest city and the principal urban centre within its western district, boasts both Fletcher Jones and a Nestlé Company Milk Condensery. The first buildings erected at the Nestlé site were a group of residential cottages for the first officers of the company. Built in 1909, they were the earliest surviving example of on-site industrial housing in Victoria. They had been classified by the National Trust but were not on the Historic Buildings Register. In 1984, Nestlé successfully applied to the Warrnambool Council for a demolition permit for the cottages. The company planned to build a new access road to improve security. This was said to be part of a general restructuring which also involved the transfer of some functions to Nestlé's plant in Gympie, Queensland.[43]

The Warrnambool Council was anxious not to impede Nestlé in any way, for fear of causing it to leave the district. But some local residents severely criticised their council's decision. In the face of this opposition, Nestlé suspended demolition while the Historic Buildings Council heard evidence about whether the cottages should be added to the register and thus preserved. Nestlé stepped outside usual procedures by directly lobbying the Minister for Planning and Environment about registration. Ten months after the suspension of demolition, and following a personal visit to the site in February 1986, the Minister announced that he had accepted the HBC's recommendation that the cottages be registered.[44] Nestlé appealed to the Planning Appeals Board which considered the case a year later. At the hearing, although the company had earlier confirmed its commitment to the Dennington site, it now argued that preservation of the cottages could jeopardise development plans in Warrnambool. 'Cottages threaten regional economy', screamed the local paper.[45] There was less and less argument about history. The new Minister made a personal visit to the site. Then, in July 1987, following the recommendation of the Planning Appeals Board, he sanctioned demolition.[46]

It was testimony to the power of industry in the politics of the country. But the most interesting aspect of the case, perhaps, was the strength and nature of local feeling, particularly considering the cottages' isolation from Warrnambool. Reaction to the city council's decision was immediate and brought about an alliance of conservation and housing groups. These residents called on Nestlé to retain the cottages either for the company's use or as rental accommodation for the general community, which was suffering a severe housing shortage.[47] Here, conservation could assist disadvantaged groups rather than, as was more frequent, putting accommodation beyond their means. Others argued on the grounds of their historic significance and added that happy local memories were attached to the cottages by those who had grown up in them or near them.[48] A Nestlé Cottages Preservation Group was formed in April 1985 and quickly gathered 2000 signatures on a petition. Tourism was hardly an issue. The community defended them not as artefacts but as homes, future and past.

Since 1975, Warrnambool has had a historical park, Flagstaff Hill Maritime Village, but in the same period the town has lost much of its genuine streetscape. Of six historic buildings featured on the 1976 Flagstaff Hill calendar, only one survived intact five years later. The Warrnambool Urban Conservation Study, presented in 1983, met with some hostility and seemed to prompt several demolitions by owners trying to beat controls.[49] Where only pockets of the past remain, tourist arguments tend to align themselves with the creation of a concentrated, artificial past at the expense of the real historical environment. The contrast was highlighted in Warrnambool by a dispute which concerned Clovelly Flats, situated opposite the Flagstaff Village. The building was originally the Warrnambool Hotel, first built in 1847, but what survived dated from the 1850s. The trust classified the building in 1980, and an application to have it included on the Historic Buildings Register was made by a resident, Rod Duncan, in 1977.[50] Lack of response from the owner had delayed consideration of its listing. In March 1981, residents who noticed a bulldozer beside the building discovered that council had issued a demolition permit. The issue split the local historical groups and revealed their different perspectives. The local branch of the National Trust supported preservation of the flats. The historical society, however, condemned them. In a letter thereafter frequently cited, the historical society informed the Warrnambool Council that the building had been changed and added to over the years and was therefore not original, and that only the site was of historic importance. 'We would also like to add', continued the letter, 'that it is an ugly building in a prime position.'[51] However, a six-month Interim Preservation Order was promptly placed on the building by the Historic Buildings Preservation Council, and a hearing held in late April was followed by assurances of a quick decision. But further delays led to the building being partly demolished on the morning after the expiry of the six-month order. There had been a 'misunderstanding', as a last-minute three-month extension to the order had been issued.[52]

The Clovelly Flats dispute coincided with publicity of a substantial grant ($20,000) made by the Warrnambool City Council to the Flagstaff Hill Maritime Village opposite. In addition, the new owners of Clovelly, who supported demolition, had tendered for the building of a historic restaurant in Flagstaff, so although the links were close, the visions were far apart. Many residents drew attention to the irony that an authentic, original building was being demolished by the same council that was heavily investing in a re-creation across the road. The history that was shuffled into Flagstaff, some said, seemed to free the town of any further obligation to the past.[53]

These modern battles draw attention to the different patterns of heritage debate in towns where only fragments of the past survive. Residents often call for government intervention themselves, as a way of placing limits on their local council. However, the delay introduced by distant bureaucracy and state-level politics sometimes takes the initiative and momentum away from local campaigners, and swings sympathy the developers' way. The interests of business and conservation meet less frequently than they do in 'historic towns'. Tourism is a marginal and sometimes oppositional cause. Heritage is advocated more as a resource for the community itself than as a lure for outsiders. The case for conservation rests more on social history. The chance of demolition is greater.

Perhaps the last word should be left with the watcher on the cast-iron balcony. Hal Porter's Bairnsdale had never been blessed with architectural riches, but those few worth saving had fatally attracted the wrecker: 'there are few memorable buildings—the fingers of one hand would do', he wrote in 1977.[54] It was the same year that the town was experiencing a building boom. It was the fastest growing municipality in Victoria in the 5,000 to 10,000 population group.[55] The discovery of off-shore oil, the tourism of the nearby lakes, and the area's attraction as a place to retire ensured its post-war growth. One of the few remaining old buildings was Bower House, built overlooking the river in 1868, eight years after Bairnsdale's foundation. Hal Porter was concerned that it possessed 'the very qualities—a history, old trees, architectural charm—which invite doom in Bairnsdale'.[56] Ominously, it had a generous verandah. It was the town's oldest substantial pioneer house and was in the heart of Bairnsdale's original riverine setting. It had been the home of William Potter (ironmonger), a Church of England Girls' Hostel, and a private hospital run by one of Bairnsdale's notable women, Sister Alice Bull. Thousands of Bairnsdale's babies were born there. Later it became a guesthouse, and was renamed 'Riverview'. Its history was a rich interweaving of the town's public and domestic life. But by the late 1970s, the architectural charm credited it by Porter was dulled by neglect. It had been willed to the Church of England diocese in 1964 with the instruction that it be used as a girls' hostel out of respect for its history. The church had mostly left it vacant and had let it run down. It became a winter refuge for vagrants. By 1978 it was considered unsafe and became subject to a council demolition order. Church officials claimed regret and helplessness, but also condemned it as 'old, draughty and uncomfortable'.[57]

The flood of local offers of help called their bluff. Expert architectural, engineering and general assistance was volunteered. Local heritage groups offered to call a public meeting to help the church consider its options for the site. Plans were drawn to illustrate how a restored 'Riverview' could be the centre of a new church development. Many people testified to the urgent need for hostel accommodation in Bairnsdale. The Bairnsdale Council suspended and then revoked its demolition order.

It was considered no small triumph in a town which before and since has shown little regard for elements of the past. Heritage advocates in Bairnsdale and towns like it are easily isolated by an apathetic and wary community, an unsympathetic council, a conservative local paper, and

'Heritage Week in Bairnsdale, Sunday 21st March 1982': Cartoon by Bairnsdale artist Val Urquhart

the sheer momentum of destruction. 'I know, only too well, how difficult it is to save anything in Bairnsdale', wrote Hal Porter to 'Riverview' campaigner, Marion Le Cheminant. 'This destructive bent is very Australian—no nation on earth has been, since World War II, so swift and ruthless as Australia in getting rid of important buildings.' Porter was pleased to learn of the efforts to save 'Riverview'.[58] For him, it was 'a haunted house'. In *The Watcher on the Cast-Iron Balcony*, Porter described how he first visited it as a schoolboy to deliver to Deaconess Rodda the proceeds of the first theatrical production in which he had appeared. Eight years later, he stood in anguish in its front room, then a private hospital, watching his mother die.[59] 'Riverview' was powerfully entwined with Bairnsdale's social and literary life. It seemed, finally, that these arguments had won.

But the local enthusiasm forced the church to show its hand. It did not respond to offers of help and pursued demolition by its own initiative. It also went to the Supreme Court to free itself of the restrictive terms of the will under which it received the property. 'Riverview' was demolished on a Sunday at the beginning of Heritage Week, 1982.

CHAPTER TWELVE

History and Natural History

In Victoria in 1985, a parcel of public land called the Langwarrin Military Reserve was renamed the Langwarrin Flora and Fauna Reserve, and some of the signs of its early military occupation were removed or obscured. The reserve, one of Victoria's oldest military camps, was established almost one hundred years earlier in 1886 and, in the course of its use for military training and as the site of a prisoner-of-war camp and venereal diseases hospital, the land was extensively cleared and grazed. In 1948 the Langwarrin and District Progress Association proposed 'that this little Park of 20 acres should be left as a Memorial Reserve in honour of old soldiers', but the idea was never followed up. By 1975, this island of remnant and regenerating vegetation was being valued in a different way. An ecological survey of the reserve was commissioned by the Cranbourne Shire Council and, a decade later, the land emerged under its new name as a sanctuary for nature conservation. Some large pine trees, evidence of the original settlement, were removed.

The author of the ecological survey, Winty Calder, had become fascinated by the area's military history, which she saw as integral to its natural history, but her book about its past could not be launched in the newly declared reserve. Perhaps this was due to a lack of toilets or catering facilities. Or it may have been because, as one senior land manager put it, 'there's a very conscious policy not to acknowledge history'. Park administrators were 'quite terrified of the power of the pictorial evidence' that showed clear paddocks pegged out with military teepees. The history carried unwelcome and contradictory messages for a flora and fauna reserve: that this bushland had been 'disturbed', that much of the site of this 'original remnant of vegetation' had been previously cleared, and that abused bushland could regenerate so quickly.[1]

This abbreviated tale of Langwarrin raises a number of issues, both positive and disturbing, that will be addressed in this chapter. The story alerts us to the fruitful collaboration that can easily arise between the disciplines of ecology and history in environmental studies. At the same

Before and after: Langwarrin Military Reserve as it was in 1890 (top), when 40 hectares had been cleared for military activities, and (bottom) regenerating bushland on the site of the former venereal disease camp hospital in the same reserve in 1982, now called the Langwarrin Flora and Fauna Reserve. *(Top photo is from the Millet Collection, reproduced from W. Calder,* Australian Aldershot: Langwarrin Military Reserve Victoria 1886–1890, Jimaringle *Publications, 1987, and the bottom photo was taken by Jane Lennon, Historic Places Section, Department of Conservation and Natural Resources, Victoria)*

time, however, our attention is drawn to an apparent conflict between the movements to preserve natural and cultural heritage.

In chapter 1, I explored some of the correspondences between history and natural history. 'Natural history' was a descriptive study, essentially medieval in origin. It was as concerned to document the social and cultural contexts of living things as it was to record the physical qualities of the things themselves: 'the history of a living being was that being itself', writes Michel Foucault.[2] The cultural and literary dimension of 'natural history' was professionally marginalised in the late nineteenth century by the rise of laboratory-based biology and the development of biological specialties such as biogeography and ecology. Nature writers like Donald Macdonald and Charles Barrett felt their scientific marginality, and remained committed to an older tradition of natural history, one positively attuned to 'the human touch'. Their successors as popularisers of nature—the environmentalists of the 1970s, 1980s and 1990s—were more 'professional' in political style and more 'scientific' in intellectual inspiration, and they often found the signs of human intrusion disturbing and morally perplexing.[3]

The metamorphosis of Langwarrin is but one of many examples from Australia and abroad that illustrate the marginal and even oppositional status of history in the modern evaluation and interpretation of perceived natural landscapes. This conflict is not new, but it is more sharply defined today. It is a result of two developments, both of which have accelerated in Australia since the 1960s: the dominance of ecological criteria in the assessment of environmental values, and the broadening of our historical perception of landscape from isolated sites to whole cultural patterns. In Victoria and some other states it is translated into a daily management issue by having the responsibility for 'historic places' vested in departments primarily devoted to nature conservation, a case of bleeding sepia into green.

This chapter will try to tease out some of the tensions between these two views of landscape, as well as areas of common or overlapping purpose. Science, like history, has a tenacious public dimension that continually interacts with its academic definition.[4] Therefore, although the discipline of ecology is briefly examined here, it is the popular movements and institutions inspired by those scientific insights that will be primarily addressed—in particular, the wilderness movement and the culture of park management. It is argued that, although apparently biocentric in rationale, the modern wilderness movement presents a historical vision of landscape that is unacknowledged and problematic. The central role of history in environmental evaluation is therefore urged, not just in the identification of carefully circumscribed sites or buildings, or in the assessment of perceived natural landscapes and whole cultural patterns, but as a way of broadening conservation debates to address social and moral questions as much as scientific ones. As a way of suggesting complexities rather than generalised simplicities, two recent environmental debates are briefly studied: the 'battle for the Franklin' in south-west Tasmania, and 'the revolt of the mountain cattlemen' in Victoria's high country.

History and ecology

Ecological science stresses the relationships between all living things and their environment. One view is that it humanises the biota, bringing concepts from the social sciences to bear on our understanding of the natural sciences: notions of community, neighbourhood, inter-dependence, sense of place. It seems a science with which historians should feel at home. But as it first developed—and it was rather like early anthropology in this regard—it had an anti-historical bias.

The first generation of academic ecologists, led earlier this century by Frederic Clements in the United States, worked with a model of biotic communities that assumed they were born, grew and died much as individual animals and plants did. In other words, every biotic community was expected to reach a certain state of maturity or climax which was stable if left undisturbed. Often the source of disturbance was human. This definition left humans outside of nature, and nature outside of history. Historical change was an aberration rather than the norm. It left us with the idea that before humans, there existed a timeless wilderness in which biotic communities were either reaching or remaining in climax. Human presence muddied the clear waters that researchers wished to plumb.[5]

By the mid-twentieth century, ecology had abandoned the organism metaphor, the notion of climax, and worked with the less teleological concept of 'ecosystem'. That is, actual relationships between species, rather than some mystical superorganism, became the object of study. The muddiness of humanity, the effect of humans on other eco-systems, could become a research interest rather than an obstacle. And, through the work of palaeobotanists who are reconstructing ancient environments, ecologists are discovering more change than stasis in nature.[6]

The growing dominance of ecological principles in landscape evaluation has introduced a biocentric rather than anthropocentric focus to park management. The first conservationists had been champions of the 'wise use' of resources; then there developed a movement to preserve aesthetically pleasing or spiritually uplifting places. The ecological vision shifted the emphasis to non-human values: the protection of gene pools, the integrity of ecosystems, the preservation of biological diversity, the independent rights of animals and plants. These evolving priorities became reflected in the sorts of national parks that Australians set aside from late in the nineteenth century: 'wastelands' or areas of little perceived economic value; scenery of outstanding grandeur or places of urban recreation; and, most recently, areas of biological richness or rarity, regardless of their scenic appeal.[7] Commenting on this new biocentric rationale, historian Jim Davidson has described 'the almost philatelic concern of the National Parks Service [of Victoria] to complete its set of parks drawn from the 62 major habitat types to be found in the State'.[8]

The human became the intruder in the national park landscape or 'wilderness', as these areas were increasingly called. In the United States in 1963, a committee reviewing national parks policy about wild animals recommended the re-establishment of populations of predatory animals (wolves, bears and mountain lions). They had been eliminated by earlier national park visions in favour of game species such as deer, and their reintroduction placed the human visitor in potential peril. If the occasional back-packer was killed and eaten, it was the way of the wilderness.[9]

Some streams of the environmental movement, such as 'deep ecology', are earth-centred and misanthropic. The group most identified with this philosophy is the American 'Earth First!' movement, described as 'the cutting edge of environmental activism throughout the American West'.[10] Formed in 1980, and perhaps evolving from the isolationist, frontier ethic of America's far West, it advocates unconditional wilderness protection and expansion, and the active sabotage of intrusive industries. A co-founder of the movement, Dave Foreman, accuses 'social ecologists' of deliberately underestimating the intrinsic failings of all human societies and institutions. He regards the human race as 'a cancer' on the planet. In answer to the question, 'why concentrate our efforts on preserving wilderness areas?', Dave Foreman answers: 'So that there is something to come back after human beings, through whatever means, destroy their civilization.'[11]

These examples seem to suggest that ecology is a grim science, a 'subversive science', as some have called it.[12] Perhaps, with all its warnings and forebodings, ecology might be characterised as the antithesis of romanticism, as offering a vision of nature 'virtually without an aesthetic'.[13] Is it really unromantic, anti-human, and anti-historical?[14] It certainly seems so when it is explained that maintaining a wilderness involves 'protecting the area against the influence of man and . . . removing the past influence of man'.[15] But such a policy does not represent a conflict between ecology and history; rather, it is an expression of an alternative historical vision that is as much about humanity and aesthetics as it is about science.

Ideas of wilderness

Many of the persisting definitions of wilderness are sensory: they concern boundaries of sight, lengths of walks in one direction, and the maintenance of an authentic sense of human danger and isolation.

Wilderness, wrote the American forester Aldo Leopold in 1921, was 'a continuous stretch of country preserved in its natural state, open to lawful hunting and fishing, big enough to absorb a two weeks' pack trip, and kept devoid of roads, artificial trails, cottages, or other works of man'.[16] Early Australian definitions of wilderness echoed the American version: a wilderness was somewhere 'that one may be able to travel on foot in any direction for at least a full day without meeting a road or highway', wrote the New South Wales bushwalker and 'father of wilderness', Myles Dunphy.[17] A more recent definition, provided in 1982 by Bob Brown, then director of the Tasmanian Wilderness Society, described wilderness as 'a region of original Earth where one stands with the senses entirely steeped in Nature and free of the distractions of modern technology'.[18]

These are primarily negative definitions, seeing wilderness in terms of remoteness and absence. They suggest how we might come to see wilderness as capable of being 'restored' by removing 'incursions' and 'distractions'. In the Virgin Islands, all traces of seventeenth- and eighteenth-century cultivation were expunged from a new national park so as to restore a 'wilderness' landscape.[19] Modern wilderness photographers enact this vision in their choice of frame, omitting the eroded path that led them to their view.[20] And if the definitions are about the feel and look of a place, then 'wilderness' need not be actually ancient, pristine and timeless; it just needs to seem so. In 1987, the eastern coast of Victoria's Wilson's Promontory, an area with a history of sealing, logging, grazing, mining and settlement, was declared a zone of high wilderness quality.[21] In Britain, 'wilderness' has come to mean the domesticated and ecologically poor landscape of the moors. But, as Marion Shoard has explained, 'most moorlands are relatively recent landscapes, created at most 4000 years ago through the destruction of forest to provide wood, charcoal or sheep runs'. The moors rely on burning and grazing for their continued existence, but offer loneliness and a primeval appearance to visiting humans.[22]

At Tower Hill, in south-western Victoria, the reconstruction of a natural landscape has been painstaking and artful. In 1855, James Dawson of Kangatong station commissioned Eugene von Guerard to paint the dramatic landscape of Tower Hill, an extinct flooded volcano. It was a romantic view of the wilderness before the white man: a densely vegetated scene bathed in golden light and featuring, in the foreground, some Aboriginal observers. Dawson revisited Tower Hill in 1891 and was disgusted by what he saw, a landscape degraded by clearing, grazing, timber-getting, and the introduction of exotic plants and animals. When the hill was declared a State Game Reserve in 1961, the then Fisheries and Wildlife Division of the Victorian Ministry of Conservation commenced a restoration programme based on von Guerard's painting. The detail of the painting was such that a naturalist, J. Ros Garnet, could identify at least twelve plant species. The artist's vision was used as a template. In the eighteenth century, landscape gardeners such as Capability Brown created artificial wildernesses based on the paintings of Claude and Poussin. In Australia, scientists scrutinised von Guerard's brushstrokes and turned art into nature.[23]

Jane Lennon, a former manager of Historic Places on public land in Victoria, has observed that 'the park management culture tends to eradicate the memory and relics of past European uses in favour of an image of naturalness and primitiveness'.[24] It is no surprise, then, that most historic relics removed from national parks have no continuing ecological impact in themselves.[25] They are removed for cultural reasons. Sometimes it is merely innocent tidying up, or it is an expression of national park priorities and resource constraints, rather than any aversion to history. Often, however, it is a question of aesthetics. History on public land is generally the ugly bits. In the *Descriptive Report* on wilderness in Victoria completed by the Land Conservation Council in 1990, historic relics, like maintained structures, were regarded as negatives in the evaluation of 'aesthetic naturalness'.[26] A century ago, many of these same landscapes inspired 'irresistible feelings of depression' in the first European explorers because they lacked familiar signs of human occupation.[27] Colonists wanted to see homesteads, enclosures, cultivation; they divined ruined castles in craggy outcrops. Now we grub out the real ruins and 'restore' the wilderness.

But, although they seem to deny history, wilderness zones are a form of historic park. Roderick Nash, in *Wilderness and the American Mind*, has traced changing attitudes to tracts of 'wild' land, from the perception of them as 'worthless' to their identification as 'wonders'.[28] Nash, together with one of his students, Alfred Runte, has argued that scenic nationalism was the main motivation for the creation of national parks in the United States.[29] As I described in chapter 7, wilderness was appreciated as a source of national identity, a reservoir of images that were unique and awe-inspiring, and a match for Old World cultural grandeur. As there was no European equivalent to wilderness, it eased cultural anxiety in new countries. To match the past accomplishments of European civilisation, Americans turned to 'the agelessness of monumental scenery', to a 'green old age', as explorer and surveyor Clarence King put it in 1864. In the identification of 'earth monuments', America made a competitive claim to antiquity and, through its national parks system, established a 'national museum'. And this was not just a museum of 'original earth', but one which embraced European history and pioneer nostalgia. 'Public appreciation of wilderness increased steadily as the nation's pioneer past receded', writes Nash. Wallace Stegner, novelist and historian, worried in 1960 that museums and roadside pioneer villages were poor substitutes for real wilderness in giving Americans a reminder of their formative national experience of frontier pioneering.[30]

'Historic interest' and 'natural beauty' coalesced in the early conservation movement. There was a belief that historic and natural landscapes could be treated together, that heritage enhanced scenery. The National Trust for Places of Historic Interest and Natural Beauty was formed in England in 1895, and an American Scenic and Historic Preservation Society in 1914. Australia's first centralised special authority for managing a system of national parks and reserves was formed in Tasmania in 1915 and was called the Scenic Preservation Board. Myles Dunphy's National Parks and Primitive Areas Council, founded in 1932, was keen to retain historic tracks in declared areas.[31] Bushwalking boomed in the inter-war period, and part of the enjoyment was learning the history and meeting the old-time inhabitants of the back country.[32] Stan Mitchell's Council for the Preservation of National Monuments drew up a list of national monuments that included the Ada River forest, the tall and notable 'Furmston's Tree' near Healesville, the Mt William Aboriginal Stone Axe Quarry and the house of the pioneering Henty family at Merino.[33] The language of conservation was interchangeable: Bob Croll argued for the preservation of 'museums of unusual vegetation' and, in 1953, the *Age* newspaper welcomed the proposed Victorian national parks system as saving 'the best of our past'.[34] This combined purpose was expressed in the broad brief of the 1974 Committee of Inquiry into the National Estate and the consequent concerns of the Australian Heritage Commission established two years later.

The wilderness movement of the 1980s distinguished itself from these antecedents in advocating the stripping back of later layers of history in order to recover an earlier ideal time. This fashion for restoration was reminiscent of earlier phases of building conservation efforts, when significant architectural features of later periods were sacrificed to allow a building to display a false purity of Georgian or Victorian style. This practice is now discouraged by the Burra Charter of Australia ICOMOS which urges that 'the contributions of all periods to the place must be respected'.[35]

The American historical geographer J. B. Jackson has speculated on the religious dimensions of 'the current movement to preserve wilderness or natural areas as fragments of what we might call the original design of creation'. Restoration or rescue is the essential element in the process:

There has to be (in our new concept of history) an interim of death or rejection before there can be renewal and reform. The old order has to die before there can be a born-again landscape ... the landscape has to be plundered and stripped before we can restore the natural ecosystem ... a kind of historical, theatrical make-believe is becoming increasingly popular ... There is no reason to learn, no covenant to honor; we are charmed into a state of innocence and become part of the environment. History ceases to exist.[36]

Restoring and maintaining wilderness, even if it denies history, is a complex historical enterprise. These areas re-create landscapes that we believe existed at an earlier time. In Australia that time is, symbolically, 1788. Wilderness zones are the Sovereign Hills of the bush.[37] They are preserved, managed, restored. They attract tourists. They offer the feel of the past, commemorate and mourn what we have lost.

Aborigines and wilderness

The trick is that these are no primeval, non-human landscapes. As Thoreau put it in 1859, 'What we call wilderness is a civilization other than our own.'[38] In Australia, in Sylvia Hallam's words, the land 'was not as God made it. It was as the Aborigines made it.'[39] The wilderness idea is not just anthropocentric, it is Eurocentric. It preserves or restores landscapes as Europeans supposedly found them—and as Aborigines made them—and it calls them untouched, pristine. Aborigines are thereby rendered invisible as agents in the landscape. Is this *terra nullius* in another form? Aborigines again find themselves classified with nature. Only now it is done with reverence, for they are no longer Primitive Savages; they are Ecological Beings.

If some landscapes are to be returned to a pre-European state, then their management needs to mimic Aboriginal fire regimes. The history of fire, like the history of wilderness, slips continually between the realms of the natural and the cultural, from the study of an independent phenomenon to the analysis of an artefact. In America from the late 1960s, there was an interesting change of attitude to fire in wilderness areas. It was considered more important to introduce fire than it was to suppress or withhold it.[40] Australians have long used fire as a tool with which to fight fire, but from the 1970s, with a growing understanding of the Aboriginal practice of firestick farming, light regular burning of national park and wilderness landscapes acquired a new, historical significance. But Aboriginal fire regimes varied across the continent and

 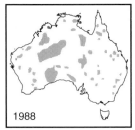 

'The Disappearance of Wilderness over the past 200 Years': This series of maps dramatically illustrates the depletion of wilderness. It also reveals the Eurocentric nature of the concept and postulates an Australia of 1788 that was, in a different sense, 'black'. *(Based on an illustration from* Wilderness News, September 1988)

the actual impact of Aboriginal burning is a matter of vigorous debate.[41] Managing or restoring a wilderness demanded an understanding of the local history of fire. In East Gippsland, recent archaeological and historical research has charged land managers with introducing intense and alien fire regimes to a forest with little fire history.[42] Are we restoring a historic landscape, or fashioning an entirely new one?

Some of our modern forests, which we may regard as wilderness, are European creations. They are no less valuable to preserve, but they present a different problem, and a different, even more fragile concentration of the past.[43] Les Murray, commenting upon Eric Rolls' history of the 'Pillaga Scrub', *A Million Wild Acres*, has put it this way:

> It was a paysage humanisé and moralisé which the Aborigines had maintained for untold centuries; the wilderness we now value and try to protect came with us, the invaders. It came in our heads, and it gradually rose out of the ground to meet us.[44]

Europeans created a literal wilderness with guns and smallpox and then, as a consequence of this displacement, an illusory wilderness of thickening forests.

Once we recognise the environmental interventions of hunter-gatherer societies, we also confront their conservationist credentials. Were the Aborigines and other indigenous peoples 'conservationists'? The enchanted archaeological link between humans and extinct fauna that drove the search for antiquity presents itself lately as a conservationists' conundrum. If the world-wide Pleistocene mass extinctions of large mammals were the result of original human colonisation, then what does it say of human nature, whether indigenous or industrial?[45] And what are the environmental sensibilities of contemporary Aborigines? In Australia in the late 1980s, H. C. Coombs and his colleagues assessed the land-use strategies and needs of Aborigines in the Kimberley, and discovered some attitudes that might disturb white environmentalists: cattle-raising had become culturally as well as economically important, feral animals were valued as food, and native fauna had commercial uses.[46] Although the Kimberley report concluded that Aborigines' 'concept of responsibility for the land has much in common with contemporary principles of sustainable development', the authors cautioned that Aboriginal culture in the Kimberley 'should not simply be *assumed* to be in a sustainable relationship with the environment'.[47]

Appreciation of Aboriginal manipulation of the environment is increasingly a factor in modern park management. But the old language and dismissive stereotypes still slip into the environmental handbooks. Terms such as 'untamed wilderness' appear in the first published draft of the *Kakadu National Park Management Plan* (1980).[48] The recent *Descriptive Report on Wilderness in Victoria* (1990) surveys the new scholarly insights that reveal the long and active engagement of Aborigines with a changing landscape, but concludes that '[b]efore the arrival of the Europeans, however, all of Australia was essentially unmodified.'[49] What can explain this slippage in wilderness rhetoric? First, environmentalists sometimes have an uneasy relationship with archaeologists. Secondly, where the past occupation of Aborigines draws attention to a history of massive landscape change, or where their present land rights claims threaten future landscape change, wilderness supporters have confronted political and philosophical difficulties. Both of these sources of uneasiness were evident in the battle to save the Franklin River in Tasmania's south-west in 1982–3.

Archaeologist Rhys Jones has postulated an intriguing human history of south-west Tasmania.[50] There, 20,000 years ago, the most southerly humans in the world hunted marsupials in an open tundra. The forest as we know it today was not there: it was confined to the sheltered river valleys. These people occupied the inland valleys until perhaps 12,000 years ago when, as the glacial period waned and the rainforests expanded, they and the animals they hunted abandoned the region. In quite recent times, just before the arrival of Europeans, Aborigines had begun to explore or colonise the south-west again. The archaeological evidence of this human history of the forest and tundra became critical in the protection of this World Heritage Area. According to former Prime Minister Malcolm Fraser, it may have been the most important factor of all in the saving of the Franklin.[51]

Three main groups opposed the plans of the Hydro Electricity Commission (HEC) to flood the Franklin. Those three groups—

Aborigines, archaeologists and environmentalists—formed an uneasy, shifting alliance. The tensions within that alliance may be more interesting and significant in the long term than the conflict all three groups had with the HEC. The sensitive relationship between archaeologists and Aborigines over the excavation of sites has been widely discussed, but the other two sides of the triangle have received less attention.[52]

Archaeologists working in the south-west found themselves and their discoveries marginalised by many supporters of the Wilderness Society. John Mulvaney has written that,

> as an archaeologist involved in the Gordon-Franklin dam debate, I initially found marked lack of interest in the Aboriginal prehistory cause from many environmental conservationists. The fact that humans occupied southwest Tasmania during ice age times, before the forests developed their impenetrability, perhaps ruined their idealistic concept of a timeless 'Wilderness'.[53]

Some environmentalists called the archaeologists 'mind merchants' and accused them of 'disturbing the forest' with invasive technology and science.[54]

There was, at times, 'open antagonism' between the Tasmanian Aboriginal Centre and the Wilderness Society. Some Tasmanian Aborigines were critical of what they saw to be the Wilderness Society's hypocrisy: that it was prepared to use the existence of early Aboriginal occupation of the south-west to support preservation of the Franklin, yet was reluctant to actively support land rights claims. '[T]he wilderness mob continually wanted to push us to the back, to quieten our struggle and keep conservation alone upfront', claimed Tasmanian Aborigine Jim Everett.[55]

Kutikina Cave became symbolically important to both of these debates. Rediscovered in 1977, it is a huge, deep limestone cavern and one of the richest archaeological sites in Australia. Its occupation has been carbon dated to 15–20,000 years ago. For the Hydro Electricity Commission, its timely discovery seemed trumped up. Even its first name, 'Fraser Cave', after the then Prime Minister, smacked of cynical politics. For Rhys Jones after eighteen years of searching, it was 'the site I have been looking for'.[56] For Tasmanian Aborigine Michael Mansell 'it was like coming home', 'the most important cultural thing that's ever happened to us'.[57] For Jim Everett it was a satisfying 'spanner in the works' for the environmentalists.[58] But, for one environmentalist at least, Bob Brown, 'the significance of the find left us speechless'. He was one of the party that revisited the cave with its modern discoverer Kevin Kiernan in 1979.

Brown had been searching for a reputed convict skeleton on Goodwin's Peak with the aim of putting recent history to the service of the wilderness cause. A lone skeleton would have been a powerful symbol of the awesome majesty of the south-west, good publicity for the campaign. But, instead, he happened upon far more ancient bones, those of ice age marsupials that Aborigines had hunted for food and cooked in a cave. These bones told not of an anguished death in an isolated wilderness, but of hearth and home in a populated landscape. It was not quite the history he had been looking for, but he embraced its message with awe.[59]

In the Victoria River country in northern Australia, one Aboriginal man, Daly Pulkara, speaks of land that has been cared for as 'quiet', and land that has been degraded by pastoralism as 'wild' country.[60] His 'wilderness' is European-made. Some wilderness supporters argue now that support for indigenous people must override fear of development, that 'the environment movement must drop its unconditional stance where the Aboriginal movement also has land rights claims'. The most anguished articles in *Wilderness News* in recent years have been on this subject.[61] The writers believe that this issue alone exposes and threatens an aspect of the movement they never before doubted: its morality. A former co-director of the Wilderness Society, Chris Harris, worried that a group 'so often seen as a bastion of morality . . . could be accused of hypocrisy and self-interest'.[62]

In 1991 the poet Judith Wright resigned as patron of the Wildlife Preservation Society of Queensland because of its failure to support Aboriginal land rights.[63] During the preceding decade, Wright was dismayed to find that her advocacy of both wilderness and Aboriginal land rights became, at times, politically contradictory. She called herself 'a member of an increasingly rare species—a person of European derivation whose childhood was spent almost in ignorance of city life'.[64] She was born in 1915 on a pastoral station near Armidale on the New England tableland of New South Wales. She remembered camping trips as a child to a favourite bit of bush on a high spur of the plateau, a special place for her, as it was for her father and grandmother before her. Her father was instrumental in having their camping ground proclaimed a national park. Nearby was Darkie Point, a jutting platform of the escarpment high above the valley. Young Judith Wright was puzzled by the name. Her father told her that, long ago, white settlers had driven the Aborigines over its cliffs, as reprisal for the spearing of their cattle. Remembering her childhood, Wright later wrote: 'Those two strands—the love of the land we have invaded, and the guilt of the invasion—have become part of me. It is a haunted country.'[65]

In the 1930s Wright briefly read anthropology under Professor

A. P. Elkin at the University of Sydney, but was alienated by the treatment of Aborigines as 'objects of study'.[66] Although her own roots were deep in frontier pastoralism, the prior occupants of the land were rarely mentioned by her family. In *The Generations of Men* (1955), Wright wrote affectionately and proudly of her family and presented a partly fictional narrative of her grandparents as pastoral pioneers. Shortly afterwards, she met Oodgeroo of the Noonuccal tribe (poet Kath Walker) and 'something of the reality of my family history began to dawn on me'. Twenty years later, in *The Cry for the Dead* (1981), Wright returned to that genre as a way of unravelling the implications of her political advocacy of land rights and conservation.[67] The dispossession and violence done to Aborigines became her theme. But there was also a sense that the land itself had been doubly dispossessed. Her forebears and the Aborigines had at least shared one thing—a love for that land— yet the descendants of neither now lived there.

In central Australia, at Uluru National Park, a CSIRO *Fauna Study* published in 1991 draws on both Aboriginal knowledge and European science in its description of vertebrate animals in the park.[68] The Anangu people were involved in field-work and their knowledge was given equal value to the fruits of scientific survey and analysis. The study gave formal recognition to the idea of an inhabited 'wilderness' and it creatively intertwined human and natural ecologies, science and tradition, history and natural history. The hunting and gathering rights of the Anangu within the park have also been negotiated and confirmed, even though their technology has changed.[69] A kangaroo hunt with guns, Toyotas, and a signature of blood on the T-shirt, remains an affirming cultural event for the Anangu, and sometimes a disturbing one for conservationists who make the journey to the centre.[70]

In 1991 the Wilderness Society undertook to include an article on Aboriginal land rights in each issue of its journal, and the Australian Conservation Foundation published an issue of *Habitat Australia* entitled 'Caring for Country, Aboriginal Perspectives on Conservation'.[71] The anguished self-examination of wilderness supporters in Australia reflects a wider alliance and sensitivity between environmentalists and indigenous people, as conservationists hear voices coming from the deserts and forests. 'We are the original conservationists', a Peruvian Indian leader recently told a conference of environmentalists in Peru. 'We are the true ecologists.'[72] It is their own argument, their own historical vision, thrown back in their faces.

European inhabitants

What of the other inhabitants of the wilderness, those Europeans who have worked there, whose lifestyles have been dependent upon it and who sometimes claim affinity and continuity with the Aborigines? Richard Flanagan, in his history of the Gordon River country in south-west Tasmania, has argued the case of the piners, those men who made a living from the forests by cutting Huon pine.[73] Flanagan castigates the modern conservation movement for ignoring the human history of the south-west, and for perpetuating a nineteenth-century romantic view of this wild area as uninhabited, unexplored, unappreciated. He laments that, in fostering this myth, conservationists have cut themselves off from their true antecedents, not only from the Aborigines, but from those Europeans who have lived and worked most intimately with the region. Flanagan throws out a powerful challenge to the conservation movement, but weakens his case by failing to extend to the environmentalists the same humanity and empathy he offers to the piners. Whereas the piners are given names and personalities, 'the modern conservation movement' is monolithic and anonymous, and the work of individual conservationists who have drawn inspiration from the history of that region and from the tales of the 'old timers' is not addressed. But the book's central argument remains an important and challenging one. Is the modern conservation movement the unique possessor of environmental sensibility? And how do we value the lifestyles, knowledge and artefacts of recent inhabitants of the wilderness against the sanctity of the land? These issues have recently been addressed in the debate over the future of Victoria's high plains, where mountain cattlemen have been taking their stock for summer grazing since the beginnings of European settlement.

Mountain cattlemen were among Victoria's earliest European explorers and farmers, penetrating to the high plains from the north in the 1830s. A century later, another form of transhumance began, that of scientists undertaking regular summer surveys of the impact of grazing on the alpine environment. Although initial scientific scrutiny was prompted by concern about water quality and soil erosion, ecological studies soon focused on the effect that grazing had on alpine plant communities. These studies provided the basis for opposition to the continued use of alpine grazing leases, and restrictions were first introduced in Victoria in 1945.[74]

Alpine vegetation evolved due to the former infrequency of fire and grazing. At high altitudes there were no browsing kangaroos or wallabies, and Aborigines probably did not burn 'the tops'. Europeans introduced accidental and deliberate sources of fire (to create a 'green pick') and their cattle initiated frequent and intense grazing by hoofed animals. Plants were defoliated, species variety reduced, mossbeds trampled and patches of ground laid bare. In a singularly provocative way, the cattle made meals of the wildflowers. As one ecologist put it, 'the showier flowers, particularly, are ice creams to cattle.'[75]

Beginning in the 1940s with the work of botanist Maisie Fawcett, scientists have conducted a fifty-year experiment in the Bogong High Plains. 'Exclosures' were built and maintained; these fenced out the cattle and created ungrazed control plots. The plots provided valuable successional data that could be compared with the compromised plant growth in neighbouring 'disturbed' areas. It emerged that cattle browsed selectively, exposed soil and constantly initiated the germination of shrubs. If left undisturbed, these shrubs would normally die and be replaced by grasses and herbs. But burning or grazing continually reverted the vegetation to this earlier shrub germination stage. Cattle interfered with and frustrated 'the snow grass climax'. Grazing, then, increases shrub growth in the long term. The elimination of grazing, although perhaps followed by short-term shrub growth, eventually leads back to (or, ecologically speaking, forward to) grassland.[76]

Cattlemen have defended their lifestyle with ecological arguments, and also with history. As well as claiming that 'alpine grazing reduces blazing', and that the grassland vegetation has reached equilibrium under existing grazing pressure, cattlemen have insisted that they represent a diminishing and valued cultural asset: a living link with Australia's pioneering past.[77] 'The Man from Snowy River' image is familiar, but one writer saw another, even grander association:

> Young men in caped coats and broadbrimmed hats tending their horses, . . .
> And suddenly I saw what they really were—the living ghosts of splendid
> young men who 70 years ago stood side by side, looking up the parapet of
> Gallipoli.[78]

The cattlemen claim affinity with the Aboriginal sense of place and use of fire, boast direct descent from the original pastoral families, and have sustained traditional techniques of stock management. Their scientific arguments have been thoroughly refuted or doubted, but their heritage arguments have rarely been addressed.

Although conservationists have often dismissed or ignored historical arguments, it is the ecologists themselves who have been conducting a massive historical enquiry. The roles seem reversed. Whereas the cattlemen's history speaks of continuity, stability and balance, a timeless ecological equilibrium which they claim extends back to the Aborigines, ecologists are trying to understand discontinuity and process. They are comparing today's grazed grasslands with what once existed and what one day might return. Their case rests on the results of an impressive historical experiment. They are trying to distinguish disturbance factors, to step outside the current cultural context. Maisie Fawcett's ecological work in the 1940s drew on the records of early exploration and

'Exclosures' on Victoria's High Plains: Botany students record vegetation in the Cope plot, January 1948 (above), and flowers inside the fence contrast with the grazed area outside, February 1949 (below). *(Soil Conservation Board, 'Bogong High Plains' file, Historic Places Section, Department of Conservation and Natural Resources, Victoria)*

settlement to piece together a century of environmental history. The plots, the 'exclosures', are part of this enquiry: they are primitive time machines. They are helping scientists to read backwards through time in order to see forwards ecologically.

Whether or not the cattlemen's declining lifestyle should be allowed to linger is one question. Another is whether this phase of alpine history should be memorialised at all. Historians and geographers have argued that these pastoral values, or some of them, should be represented in the mountain landscapes we save, and that a national park should in some cases maintain a historic grazed environment. In Victoria's alps, for instance, this is one possible future for the Wonnangatta Valley, an isolated and historic grazing property recently purchased by the Victorian government and added to the Alpine National Park. To those fighting for the elimination of exploitative land uses such as grazing, logging and mining from national parks, it is the ultimate indignity to envisage grazing as a park management tool. The issue was recently confronted with regard to the termination of the Gudgenby grazing lease in the Namadgi National Park in the Australian Capital Territory. John Mulvaney, speaking on behalf of the ACT Heritage Committee in 1988, advocated continuation of grazing at Gudgenby, which he described as 'an outstanding example of a mountain valley used historically for transhumance grazing, and later settled grazing'. He emphasised that this specific case did not imply support for grazing in national parks generally and that the committee would oppose the reintroduction of grazing or mining in a fragile wilderness ecosystem. Mulvaney urged the need 'to have regard to the intrinsic values that relate to given pieces of land'. The Gudgenby landscape, for instance, 'was not untouched wilderness when Europeans arrived, but was a manipulated system of open grassy woodland or open grass floored forest'. He went on to argue the specific historic, social and aesthetic values of the Gudgenby landscape as recognised by the Burra Charter and on the basis of what he called 'the deeply ingrained appreciation of rural cultural landscapes in the Australian psyche'.[79]

But, to environmentalists, the preservation of a 'living, working landscape' within a national park would set a worrying precedent. To some, even the preservation of the relics of such activities is compromising. Some nature conservationists argue that 'if you say you should retain the cattlemen's huts you are in effect saying that you approve of grazing'.[80] In recent decades, some huts in the Australian alps have been removed or destroyed by park officers, sometimes deliberately, sometimes with casual negligence.[81] The noted wilderness photographer David Tatnall, whose work has been very influential in the campaigns for national parks in East Gippsland and Victoria's Mallee, has recently taken a sustained photographic interest in the cattlemen's huts, State Electricity Commission (SEC) aqueducts and old timber tramways of Victoria's high country. 'I've noticed', he reflects, 'that since I've been talking a lot about the huts in particular and therefore about European history being significant, the Wilderness Society's attitude towards me has changed dramatically. . . . They want that [European history] obliterated.' Tatnall explains that

> I'm 100% behind the cattle coming off the high country, but I look at it as two issues: you take the cows away, the history's still there, and the history has to be put into perspective. . . . We can't change history by pulling a hut down.[82]

In work undertaken for the Historic Places Branch of the Victorian Department of Conservation and Environment, Linden Gillbank investigated the scientific discovery of the Victorian alps with a view to identifying important historic themes and sites.[83] She has told a story of scientific endeavour that complements the long history of grazing, and that has left historical evidence that is just as integral as are the vestiges of pastoralism to an appreciation of the alpine environment today. In poignant but sympathetic tension with the cattlemen's huts are those other sites of pilgrimage, the 'exclosures', the traditional and carefully maintained artefacts of the urban scientific community, now half a century in age.

Cultural landscapes

It is part of the 'green' aesthetic to separate, and sometimes eliminate, culture from nature, and 'wilderness' has become one of its simplest and most popular manifestations. Wilderness, to quote American historian Stephen J. Pyne, 'delighted in a stark juxtaposition of the wholly synthetic and the wholly natural; it preferred a pluralistic mosaic of distinct types to a melting pot of landscapes'.[84] Wilderness is 'an invention of civilised man', it has meaning only in contrast to civilisation.[85] In 1972, Michael McCloskey, director of the Sierra Club, a prominent American wilderness group, observed that wilderness preservation was already perceived by many environmentalists as 'parochial and old-fashioned . . . It looks suspiciously like a retreat to fantasy or withdrawal from the problems of the "real world"'.[86] So doubts have crept into the campaign itself. The rights of indigenous peoples have posed a moral dilemma. And older leaders of the movement—such as Bob Brown and Christine Milne in Tasmania—have distanced themselves from some of the efforts of younger members to eliminate historic relics from wilderness areas.[87]

Humanists, like many scientists, are trying to evolve concepts that transcend the boundaries between nature and culture, rejecting the pluralistic mosaic for the melting pot. History first found its way into land management considerations through the identification of discrete sites and buildings. The earliest historical reports for Victoria's Land Conservation Council in the 1970s were generally done by architects. They showed a preference for built structures, and emphasised visual over documentary criteria of significance. History on public land came to mean a place with an observable relic. This formula produced a strong bias towards mining sites and an unwillingness to recognise the cultural value of historical activities that persist to the present.[88] History became spatially and temporally isolated from the contemporary conservation debate.

Geographers, historians and landscape analysts have developed an imperial concept of 'cultural landscapes' partly in response to these deficiencies. The recent writings of Ken Taylor, Kevin Frawley and Jim Russell have outlined the historical origins of the concept and suggested some of its advantages and limitations for land management.[89] According to the Australian Heritage Commission, which has invited nominations under this new label, emergence of the concept represents a recognition 'that nominations of landscapes have been frequently couched in aesthetic or scenic terms; and historical documentation has in the past often been overlooked or, where provided, poorly linked to the physical evidence'.[90] Dispersed sites of individually lower importance may together form a pattern of significance. In this sense, the concept is a response to the tidying up mentality of the 'distinct types' management ethic. And it recognises the significance of persisting traditional land uses. Cultural systems, it seems to be saying, are as fluid and dynamic as ecosystems, and their continuity and balance just as important to protect. Like the ecologists' superorganisms, cultural landscapes are all embracing and somewhat mythical, both a stimulus and a frustration to research, and a nightmare to manage. Critics might question whether they are the 'melting pot' that produces a bland soup from individually exciting 'distinct types'. They represent more an approach than a geographical area. Their great advantage, and their welcome rationale, is that they cannot be easily separated from broader issues of land management. They are history's claim to have a say in the evaluation and appreciation of predominantly natural areas.

Historians, then, are doing what they do best: making light of others' sharp boundaries. The implications of their behaviour have been noted with concern. In 1988, the Australian National Parks Council carried a resolution to:

> increase the awareness of, and provide a united opposition to, the continuing campaign by organisations promoting cultural heritage issues to incorporate into National Parks activities incompatible with the conservation of natural values: in particular to counter the push to incorporate grazing and other forms of exploitative land uses in existing and future national parks under the heading preservation of cultural landscapes, and preservation of past traditional land uses.[91]

Wariness is understandable and sometimes warranted, for 'heritage' has become the banner under which groups threatened by nature conservation initiatives readily march. In 1990, when farmers in the Victorian Mallee rallied against new national park proposals in their region, they called themselves the Mallee Heritage Committee and carried banners reading 'People or Parks?'.[92] A timber industry submission to the Helsham Inquiry into Tasmania's Lemonthyme and Southern forests in 1987 made the following argument:

> There is a tendency to regard all forests as being part of the Natural Heritage. In fact most forests—and particularly the Lemonthyme forest where roading, mining and logging have taken place for a considerable time—comprise cultural heritage because they are 'the combined works of nature and of man' where forest operations and regeneration have clearly helped shape the existing forest . . . All forests are undergoing constant change and the change is and always has been substantially influenced by man over thousands of years, whether by the hunting and burning of the aborigines or the primitive logging of our early white settlers or the more sophisticated forest management of modern times . . . So it is then that we will serve our future generations best if we preserve our cultural heritage by permitting logging and reforestation in the Lemonthyme to continue rather than by attempting to create an artificial natural heritage by banning it.[93]

The use of such reasoning by grazing, mining and logging interests has led to scepticism about the use of historical or cultural arguments in environmental debate. Such arguments are frequently seen as opportunistic and self-serving, as if the discovery of Aboriginal environmental manipulation frees us from any further obligation to the land. Or they appear indiscriminate, as if they are saying that anything with a history (i.e., everything) is important. To research something, it seems, is to make it significant; alternatively the arguments seem romantic and nostalgic rather than rational and scientific. Critics believe that they pander to the emotions, distracting attention from the real issues. It was perhaps such prejudices that led the Helsham Inquiry to treat the archaeological evidence from the Tasmanian forests with ignorance and disdain.[94]

But, as British naturalist and historian Richard Mabey has argued persuasively, the solution to environmental conflict is to be found through the exploration of social and moral questions as much as scientific ones. Richard Mabey's commitment to nature conservation originated, as it does for most people, in a sense of personal loss—despair at changes in the landscape of his own county of Hertfordshire. His book, entitled *The Common Ground—A Place for Nature in Britain's Future?*, is an eloquent justification of the importance of the local and the personal in conservation debates.[95] On the surface, Mabey points out, the problems of conservation present themselves as practical ones—management ones or scientific ones. 'Yet underneath there are more fundamental and less easily resolved conflicts of values—about who can be said to "own" resources, about the relative importance of present livelihoods and past traditions—conflicts which involve deeply held personal beliefs and meanings.' To decide these conflicts, society turns to scientists, accountants and management consultants. Mabey criticises conservationists for concentrating less on exploring the richness and associations of the 'imponderables' than in trying to reduce them to 'ponderables'. Private and public meanings, he says, should not be excluded from the consideration of priorities just because they are unquantifiable.[96]

Many conservation challenges now lie outside the boundaries of national parks and wilderness zones, and some of the modern environmental threats (weeds, pollution, greenhouse effects) are disrespectful of lines on a map.[97] As the concerns of the natural and cultural heritage movements cross boundaries and geographically converge, so too might the groups learn to work together more closely. Richard Mabey's words of advice to nature conservationists are equally relevant to those concerned with cultural heritage. You can get too preoccupied with the exotic and the rare, he warns. In some cases, it is just as important that we maintain local associations or regional variety or national abundance. 'In some ways', writes Mabey, 'the local extinction may represent the greater overall loss, for here it is not just the species that is lost, but the day-to-day intimacy and associations, the neighbourliness . . .'[98] And here he is talking not about human artefacts but about bluebells and owls, species and ecosystems. He reminds us that conservation—whether of natural or cultural heritage—is legitimately about familiarity, personal values and meanings, local knowledge and associations. Historians and ecologists would agree that conservation is concerned ultimately with intimate relationships, human and non-human.[99] History—that stubbornly contextual and relativist craft—may be the tool that enables us to grope for a conservation ethic that is social as well as ecological.

Epilogue

At times the past forces itself shockingly upon the present, like an intrusion across a geological fault line. I remember in 1968, at the age of eleven, attending a meeting of the Hawthorn Junior Field Naturalists Club, an association formed in 1943 by Stan Mitchell. When it came to show-and-tell time and members produced exhibits of the past month's collecting, a boy aged precisely fourteen got up and showed us his birthday present. It was, he explained with some pride, an Aboriginal skull. It was a gift from his parents. He kept it in his bedroom. But for that evening it took its place on the display table between the rock specimens and beetles. At home that night, and for some time later, my family joked about it. What were we amused or scandalised by? That a human was a nature exhibit? That it was an Aboriginal skull that was so treated? That someone should live so intimately with it? That a boy should be given a human skull for his birthday?[1]

When I began this study I was myself a collector. I was employed as field officer for the State Library of Victoria, a job that involved the acquisition of historic manuscripts and pictures for the library's Australiana research collections. It was known as the 'cup of tea' job, for it took one into the lounge rooms of Victoria to discuss the future of family papers, and the likely public uses of quite personal pasts. That work exposed me to the politics of the past, to the dilemmas of collection, possession and preservation.

Perhaps I first thought of the subject of this research when, in 1986 while I was working for the library, I was told that the daughter of Charles Barrett was unsure what to do with her father's papers and photographs. I learnt then that Barrett was a journalist and nature writer who had died almost thirty years before. As well as letters and photos, his daughter showed me boxes that had not been opened since his death in 1959. In them were Aboriginal artefacts wrapped in newspaper; some of them were sacred objects that Barrett had collected on trips to central Australia. Even parcelled in a dusty box they were, I suspected, still full of power. Barrett's daughter asked that I take the artefacts to the Museum of Victoria where her father had donated material many years before. During the long drive back to Melbourne I felt increasingly conscious of

278

the boxes in the back of the station-wagon enclosing the secret/sacred objects. Whose were they? What meanings did they hold? What process had brought them here, a process that now implicated me? I thought of a scene at the end of *Raiders of the Lost Ark*, a film about the archaeologist-adventurer Indiana Jones, where the immensely powerful ark of the covenant is casually wheeled into the vaults of a state museum. Was I participating in the dispossession of a people and the disenchantment of the world? It was while driving the sacred stones across Victoria that I first thought of doing this research.

Now, at the close of it, I visit the museum and its new exhibition called *Keeping Culture Strong: Women's Work in Aboriginal Australia.*[2] As I enter the gallery, I hear bird calls, haunting music and Aboriginal voices. The exhibition seeks to balance the anthropological preoccupation with men in Aboriginal society, and it does so by portraying women at work, as food gatherers, artists, makers of clothes and utensils, organisers of ceremonies and custodians of community.[3] The cultural focus shifts from hunting to collecting. The introductory boards tell me:

> This exhibition celebrates the cultural heritage of Aboriginal women . . . Today Aboriginal people have successfully resisted pressures to totally assimilate to the wider community. Women are at the forefront of many community and cultural programs aimed at maintaining and reviving Aboriginal culture and identity.

Here I encounter some of the main themes of the exhibition: it is about the here and now, it is about continuity and survival. But not just passive survival; it is about resistance and re-creation. Today the silences are different. Kooris prefer the museum not to emphasise and isolate the ancient past or 'human evolution' because they still carry the weight of the nineteenth century and conjure images of 'the primitive'. And for legal and moral reasons, taking into account Aboriginal values and sensitivities, I was asked not to use any pictures of skulls in this work, however ancient, from whatever country.

Textures and colours in the exhibition are strong, the artefacts are beautiful: a dilly bag spills open showing its contents, a woman's tool kit; there are carved emu eggs and gorgeous decorative flowers made from bird feathers. There are grass and string baskets of a surprising variety of designs. There are makeshift dishes: the one that I look at with a mixture of horror and wonder is the car hub cap that has been hammered into a dinner dish. As I walk around, the thing that surprises me is just how many of these artefacts have been recently made and acquired. And I know who made them because there are names on the captions. These artefacts of beauty have mostly been made during and since the killing times; they are largely from the post-contact period. They proclaim not just survival but wilful, dignified, innovative adaptation.

There are some familiar photographs on the wall, blown up to huge size. I know some of these photos well, or think I do. They are photos from the missions, tourist postcards depicting the sad remnants of a 'dying race'. They are photos that make me, as a non-Aboriginal Australian, both curious and uneasy. But when I approach the photos and read the captions I get a shock: the black people are named, quite precisely, their relationships with one another explained, and perhaps my attention drawn to the craft work in their hands. The photo I thought was exploitative becomes instead affirmative, its sinister dimensions are cleverly, lightly undermined.

There are some grass baskets in a cabinet here, and there is a video running alongside. I crouch down and listen. The film introduces me to Connie Hart. She is shown walking among native grasses, fingering them, plucking them, twisting them. She is a basket-maker, and one of her grass baskets is on display. The caption says: 'Coiled basket by Connie Hart. Acquired in 1992 from maker, Portland Victoria'. The caption and the film give me some more information and I learn a little of Auntie Connie's story.

Connie Hart's mother, Frances Alberts, lived on Lake Condah Aboriginal Mission Station. It was established in 1867 in the stony rises between Hamilton and Portland. I know that R. E. Johns had dealings with the last manager there, the Reverend J. H. Stähle. Johns, to add to his collection, commissioned some craft work from Stähle, asked for some artefacts to be made by the Lake Condah Aborigines.[4] With a leap of faith, I suddenly realise that one of the baskets made for R. E. Johns may have been made by Connie Hart's mum, or she may have watched them being made. She was the Reverend Stähle's maid and housekeeper in the early 1900s. She was on the spot to be asked, one of a dwindling number remaining after the 1886 Aborigines Act dispersed the mission communities. As Connie grew up, she watched her mother select the grasses and make baskets. This is what Auntie Connie remembers:

No one taught me to make my baskets. I used to watch my mother do it and when she put her basket down and went outside, I'd pick it up and do some stitches. When I heard her coming back, I would shove it away real quick and run away. I was a great one for sitting amongst the old people because I knew I was learning something just by watching them. But if I asked a question they would say, 'Run away, Connie. Go and play with the rest of the kids.'

They didn't want us to learn. My mum told me that we were coming into the white people's way of living. So she wouldn't teach us. That is why we lost a lot of culture. But I tricked her. I watched her and I watched those old people and I sneaked a stitch or two.[5]

Connie did not make a basket herself until her mother died, over forty years later. She was, in a strange way, freed to rediscover her heritage. She remembered the stitch, she remembered the *puung'ort* grass, but she was 'frightened to do it'.[6] But she did do it, and she taught others to do it. In the exhibition, I found that Connie Hart taught Grace Cooper Sailor who taught Sharon Edwards, and their baskets are on display, too. You can see a modern lineage of revived craft there. Connie wanted to make an eel net, but no one seemed to remember how. So she came to the Museum of Victoria and she looked carefully—like no one else had looked before—at the one in the museum cabinet, the one collected by

Connie Hart beside the eel trap she made in the 1980s. *(Reproduced from Alick Jackomos and Derek Fowell,* Living Aboriginal History of Victoria: Stories in the Oral Tradition, *Cambridge and Melbourne, 1991)*

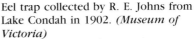

Eel trap collected by R. E. Johns from Lake Condah in 1902. *(Museum of Victoria)*

R. E. Johns from Lake Condah in 1902, and she went home and made one herself and it stood as tall as she did.[7] Did we expect—or even dare to hope—that museums might operate in this way?

With that thought in mind, I walk around the exhibition again, and I look more carefully at the captions. And there was something I should have noticed before. Here is a fish hook made from a small straight piece of bone, acquired in 1910 from the estate of R. E. Johns. There is a bone implement from a fibula of a grey kangaroo, acquired in 1927 from A. S. Kenyon. The magnificent possum skin cloak, made of eighty-three possum skins sewn with animal sinew, many with fine designs engraved upon them, is from the R. E. Johns collection. The forehead band made of string, the bark container from Ouyen, the grinding stones, all these are from the collection of A. S. Kenyon. They are displayed alongside the contemporary crafts and acquisitions, symbols of continuity, evidence of the continuing vitality of Aboriginal people. The European collectors would not recognise their collections here. Something fascinating had happened in the meantime.

I am intrigued by the way culture works, by the way it is 'kept strong'. Connie's craft survived because she 'tricked' her mum and her elders. They were trying to protect her from prejudice, from the brand of foreign skills, but she—as children often do—knew better. So, too, are the intentions and purposes of collectors undermined and subverted. R. E. Johns, who thought he was memorialising a dying race, whose collection went to Paris as proof of Aboriginal evolutionary doom, was at the same time unwittingly participating in, even encouraging, a process of local cultural renewal. Perhaps I am unfair, perhaps he was not unwitting.

Notes

INTRODUCTION

1 Greg Dening, 'Ethnography on my mind', in Bain Attwood (ed.), *Boundaries of the Past*, Melbourne, The History Institute, Victoria, 1990, pp. 16-17.
2 F. Nietzsche, *Thoughts Out Of Season*, Part 2, New York, Gordon Press, 1974, p. 24.
3 Graeme Davison, 'The Use and Abuse of Australian History', in Susan Janson and Stuart Macintyre (eds), *Making the Bicentenary*, special issue of *Australian Historical Studies*, vol. 23, no. 91, October 1988, pp. 55-76, at p. 67.
4 J. A. Moses (ed.), *Historical Disciplines and Culture in Australasia*, St Lucia, University of Queensland Press, 1978; Rob Pascoe, *The Manufacture of Australian History*, Melbourne, Oxford University Press, 1979; John Lechte, *Politics and the Writing of Australian History*, Melbourne, University of Melbourne Politics Department, 1979. But see the broader scope of Graeme Davison's writings on local, family and school histories, as well as on public history and heritage (referred to in chapter 9), and Stuart Macintyre's 'The Writing of Australian History', in D. H. Borchardt and Victor Crittenden (eds), *Australians: A Guide To Sources*, Sydney, Fairfax, Syme & Weldon Associates, 1987, pp. 1-29.
5 Bernard Smith, 'History and the collector', in his *The Death of the Artist as Hero: Essays in History and Culture*, Melbourne, Oxford University Press, 1988, pp. 95-100, writes of Australian intellectuals' distrust of 'the sensuous enjoyment of material things' and argues that 'the material, archaeological side of our history' awaits to be written.
6 See, for example, Richard Johnson *et al.* (eds), *Making Histories*, London, Hutchinson with the Centre for Contemporary Cultural Studies, University of Birmingham, 1982; David Lowenthal, *The Past is a Foreign Country*, Cambridge, Cambridge University Press, 1985; Philippa Levine, *The Amateur and the Professional: Antiquarians, Historians and Archaeologists in Victorian England 1838-1886*, Cambridge, Cambridge University Press, 1986; and Graeme Davison, 'The Use and Abuse of Australian History'.
7 Stuart Piggott has described the emergence in the seventeenth century of the student of antiquities 'as a type in the world of learning': *Ruins in a Landscape: Essays in Antiquarianism*, Edinburgh, Edinburgh University Press, 1976, and *Ancient Britons and the Antiquarian Imagination: Ideas from the Renaissance to the Regency*, London, Thames and Hudson, 1989.
8 Smith, 'History and the collector', pp. 97-8.

9 Bernard Smith, *The Spectre of Truganini*, Sydney, ABC Boyer Lectures, 1980, p. 17.

10 Smith's sustained treatment of the melancholic mode appears in his 'The Interpretation of Australian Nature during the nineteenth century', BA (Hons) thesis, English Department, University of Sydney, 1952. Aspects of his argument appear in his *Documents on Art and Taste in Australia: The Colonial Period, 1770–1914*, Melbourne, Oxford University Press, 1975, pp. 1–4, 30–33, 128–29.

11 Smith, *Spectre*, p. 21. In this later work, Smith is more forthright in identifying fear and guilt as a source of melancholy than in his earlier essay, where he nevertheless outlines the general argument. Another historian, Eric Rolls, has drawn attention to the *positive* responses to the land of many Europeans when they first experienced Australia. I think Rolls' observation is correct and not inconsistent with the development of a delayed literary and artistic sensibility that was still based on personal bush experience. See Eric Rolls, *From Forest to Sea: Australia's Changing Environment*, St Lucia, University of Queensland Press, 1993, p. 162.

12 Smith, *Spectre*. See also Marcus Clarke, 'The Buffalo Ranges, by Nicholas Chevalier', in Smith (ed.), *Documents in Art and Taste in Australia*, pp. 137–40; Smith's commentary is on p. 129.

13 Smith, 'Interpretation of Nature', p. 80.

14 For an analysis of the scholarship, see Bain Attwood, *The Making of the Aborigines*, Sydney, Allen & Unwin, 1989, chapter 6.

15 See his 1988 Boyer Lecture, one of a reflective bicentennial series by previous lecturers. Part of it was published in *Australian Society*, December 1988/ January 1989, pp. 43–4. Throughout this book I have used the term 'Aborigines' or, where I am referring to south-eastern Australian Aborigines in the post-contact period, 'Kooris'. 'Koories' is another, equally acceptable spelling. To describe non-Aboriginal Australians, I have used the terms 'colonists', 'settler Australians', 'whites' or 'Europeans'. The last two words are much less appropriate in post-war Australia, but they are apt and in usage for much of the period under study.

16 Smith, *Spectre*, p. 9.

17 See, for example, B. Smith, *European Vision and the South Pacific*, Oxford, Clarendon Press, 1960, and J. J. Healy, *Literature and the Aborigine in Australia, 1770–1975*, St Lucia, University of Queensland Press, 1978.

18 Bain Attwood, 'Introduction' to Attwood and John Arnold (eds), *Power, Knowledge and Aborigines*, Special edition of the *Journal of Australian Studies*, Bundoora, La Trobe University Press in association with the National Centre for Australian Studies, Monash University, 1992, p. xv.

19 W. E. H. Stanner, *After the Dreaming*, Sydney, 1969, p. 13.

20 C. Hartley Grattan wrote in 1974 of the need to look at the separation between the university and the broader community that was characteristic of the period from 1850 to 1930: 'Why were so many of the significant cultural workers of these decades based outside the universities in the public service, journalism, the church, or simply free-floating in a rather horrid bohemia?'

He went on to urge the study of 'the progress from history as an extra-mural possession to history as an academic preoccupation. Is it true that the transition began in 1927 when Sir [*sic*] Ernest Scott lectured on Australian History at the University of Melbourne?': 'Notes on Australian Cultural History', *Meanjin Quarterly*, vol. 33, no. 3, September 1974, pp. 232-42, see p. 238 and note 10, p. 242. See chapter 9.

1 HUNTING CULTURE

1 Stephen J. Pyne, *The Ice: A Journey to Antarctica*, Iowa City, University of Iowa Press, 1986, p. 249.

2 The penal colony quote is from Adrian Desmond, *Archetypes and Ancestors: Palaeontology in Victorian London, 1850-1875*, Chicago, University of Chicago Press, 1982, p. 104.

3 Adrian Desmond and James Moore, *Darwin*, London, Michael Joseph, 1991, p. 178. For comments on the Eurocentric notion that Australian nature was somehow deficient, see Stephen J. Gould, 'To Be a Platypus' and 'Bligh's Bounty', in *Bully for Brontosaurus*, London, Penguin, 1991, pp. 269-93, and George Seddon, 'Eurocentrism and Australian Science: Some Examples', *Search*, vol. 12, no. 12, December 1981-January 1982, pp. 446-50.

4 The phrase 'dark abyss of time' was coined by the eighteenth-century French naturalist and philosopher, Comte de Buffon (1707-88). See Peter Bowler, *The Invention of Progress: Victorians and their Past*, Oxford, Basil Blackwell, 1989, p. 131, footnote 1.

5 Donald K. Grayson, *The Establishment of Human Antiquity*, New York, Academic Press, 1983, Introduction; Bowler, *The Invention of Progress*, p. 76.

6 Or, indeed, like R. E. Johns. See chapter 2.

7 Pyne, *The Ice*, p. 252.

8 'Ethic of conquest' is Bernard Smith's term. See his *The Spectre of Truganini*, Sydney, Boyer Lectures, ABC, 1980. On social Darwinism in Britain and America see J. W. Burrow, *Evolution and Society*, London, Cambridge University Press, 1966, and Richard Hofstadter, *Social Darwinism in American Thought, 1860-1915*, Philadelphia, University of Philadelphia Press, 1945.

9 P. Bowler, 'The Invention of the Past', in L. M. Smith (ed.), *The Making of Britain: The Age of Revolution*, Hampshire and London, Macmillan, 1987, p. 169.

10 Bowler, *The Invention of Progress*, pp. 157-8; see Stephen J. Gould, *Wonderful Life: The Burgess Shale and the Nature of History*, London, Penguin, 1991, chapters I, IV and V.

11 Bowler, *The Invention of Progress*, chapter 5.

12 W. E. H. Stanner, *After the Dreaming*, Sydney, Boyer Lectures, ABC, 1969, p. 36.

13 Eugene Hargrove, *Foundations of Environmental Ethics*, Englewood Cliffs, NJ, Prentice-Hall, 1989, pp. 38-9. The older, essentially medieval sense of

the term 'natural history' was that of a descriptive (rather than story-telling) science.

14 On architectural historicism, see Charles Dellheim, *The Face of the Past: The Preservation of the Medieval Inheritance in Victorian England*, Cambridge, Cambridge University Press, 1984, p. 2.

15 Leonard Krieger ('the most famous statement') and Leopold von Ranke ('what actually happened') are both quoted in Stephen Bann, *The Clothing of Clio: A study of the representation of history in nineteenth-century Britain and France*, Cambridge, Cambridge University Press, 1984, p. 8.

16 Stephen Bann makes this interesting comparison between history and taxidermy in *The Clothing of Clio*, chapter 1. He also has an essay on photography (chapter 6). In 1892, Harold Frederic, in an article celebrating the fourth centenary of the European discovery of America, wrote: 'Within our own time history has ceased to be the thing that Hume and Washington Irving and Prescott and Lamartine understood it to be, and has become something as different as the chemistry of Pasteur is different from the fakir-formulas of Psalmanazar. Science has conquered even the making of human records.' *The Illustrated London News*, 26 November 1892, clipping in R. E. Johns, Scrapbook no. 4, Australian Manuscripts Collection, La Trobe Collection, State Library of Victoria.

17 Gillian Beer, *Darwin's Plots: Evolutionary Narrative in Darwin, George Eliot and Nineteenth Century Fiction*, London, Routledge & Kegan Paul, 1983, p. 8.

18 Charles Darwin, *The Descent of Man*, New York, Modern Library, n.d. (first published 1871), p. 521.

19 See chapter 2.

20 Beer, *Darwin's Plots*, pp. 9, 62.

21 See chapter 5.

22 Bowler, *The Invention of Progress*, pp. 157–8, also his 'Epilogue: Progress and Degeneration', pp. 192–201. For more on the discourses of degeneration, see Daniel Pick, *Faces of Degeneration: A European Disorder, c. 1848–c. 1918*, Cambridge, Cambridge University Press, 1989.

23 William Beinart, 'Review Article: Empire, Hunting and Ecological Change in Southern and Central Africa', *Past and Present*, no. 128, 1990, p. 173.

24 Beinart, 'Empire, Hunting and Ecological Change', p. 166. See also James Urry, 'Savage Sportsmen', in Ian and Tamsin Donaldson (eds), *Seeing the First Australians*, Sydney, George Allen & Unwin, 1985, pp. 51–67.

25 John M. MacKenzie, *The Empire of Nature: Hunting, Conservation and British Imperialism*, Manchester and New York, Manchester University Press, 1988, p. 164.

26 Here I have paraphrased Rhys Jones, 'The Neolithic, Palaeolithic and the Hunting Gardeners: Man and Land in the Antipodes', in R. P. Suggate and M. M. Cresswell (eds), *Quaternary Studies*, Wellington, Royal Society of New Zealand, Bulletin 13, p. 21.

27 For a stimulating meditation on the way hunter-gatherers related to nature, see Calvin Martin, *In the Spirit of the Earth: Rethinking History and Time*,

Baltimore and London, The Johns Hopkins University Press, 1992, p. 62.

28 This paragraph summarises a revolution in thinking about hunter-gatherer society in general and Aboriginal culture in particular that has occurred over the last few decades. For early expressions of these insights, see Marshall Sahlins, *Stone Age Economics*, London, Tavistock Publications, 1974, especially chapter 1: 'The Original Affluent Society'; D. J. Mulvaney, *The Prehistory of Australia*, Ringwood, Penguin, 1975 (first published 1969); and Geoffrey Blainey, *Triumph of the Nomads: A History of Ancient Australia*, Chippendale, NSW, Pan Macmillan, 1983 (first published 1975).

29 Martin, *In the Spirit of the Earth*, p. 62.

30 Paul Shepard, *Man in the landscape: A historic view of the esthetics of nature*, New York, Alfred A. Knopf, 1967, p. 50.

31 *Ibid.*, chapter 2. For a description of the way European graziers used fire in Australia, see Stephen J. Pyne, *Burning Bush: A Fire History of Australia*, Sydney, Allen & Unwin, 1991, chapter 12. See also Frederick Turner, *Beyond Geography: The Western Spirit Against the Wilderness*, Viking Press, New York, 1980, p. 24.

32 Charles Griffith, *The Present State and Prospects of the Port Phillip District of New South Wales*, Dublin, William Curry Jun. and Co., 1845, pp. 7-8.

33 Quoted in Paul Carter, *The Road to Botany Bay*, London, Faber & Faber, 1987, p. 241.

34 H. W. Wheelwright, *Bush Wanderings of a Naturalist, or Notes on the Field Sports and Fauna of Australia Felix*, London, Routledge, Warne & Routledge, 1861, p. ix.

35 There has been considerable debate about this issue. See, for example, L. L. Robson, *The Convict Settlers of Australia: An Enquiry into the Origin and Character of the Convicts Transported to New South Wales and Van Diemen's Land 1787-1852*, Melbourne, Melbourne University Press, 1965.

36 Wheelwright, *Bush Wanderings*, pp. viii-x.

37 *Ibid.*, p. xii.

38 *Ibid.*, p. xi.

39 MacKenzie, *The Empire of Nature*, pp. 28-9.

40 *Ibid.*, p. 30.

41 *Ibid.*, chapter 2.

42 On acclimatisation societies in Victoria see Linden Gillbank, 'The origins of the Acclimatisation Society of Victoria: practical science in the wake of the gold rush', *Historical Records of Australian Science*, vol. 6, no. 3, December 1986, pp. 359-74, although Gillbank puts less emphasis on the hunting culture; and for an exciting study of the impact of imported biota, see Alfred W. Crosby, *Ecological Imperialism: The Biological Expansion of Europe, 900-1900*, Cambridge, Cambridge University Press, 1986.

43 *Victorian Parliamentary Debates*, vol. 8, 1861-2, pp. 231-2, 415-6, quoted in F. I. Norman and A. D. Young, 'Short-sighted and doubly short-sighted are they . . . Game Laws of Victoria, 1858-1958', *Journal of Australian Studies*, no. 7, November 1980, p. 6.

44 A. D. Graham, *The Gardeners of Eden*, London, George Allen & Unwin, 1973, p. 156.
45 See chapter 7.
46 Paul Fox, 'Review of *The Road to Botany Bay*', *Transition*, no. 24, Autumn 1988, pp. 82-3; see also Don Watson, *Caledonia Australis: Scottish highlanders on the frontier of Australia*, Sydney, Collins, 1984.
47 MacKenzie, *Empire of Nature*, p. 201.
48 *Victorian Parliamentary Debates*, 1861-2, quoted in Norman and Young, 'Game Laws of Victoria', p. 6.
49 See chapter 11.
50 MacKenzie, *Empire of Nature*, p. 201; see also Terence Ranger, 'Whose Heritage? The Case of the Matobo National Park', *Journal of Southern African Studies*, vol. 15, no. 2, January 1989, pp. 217-49.
51 David Elliston Allen, *The Naturalist in Britain: A Social History*, London, Allen Lane, 1976; Keith Thomas, *Man and the Natural World: Changing Attitudes in England 1500-1800*, London, Allen Lane, 1983.
52 Lynn Barber, *The Heyday of Natural History, 1820-1870*, London, Jonathan Cape, 1980.
53 MacKenzie makes this point himself with reference to Thomas (*Empire of Nature*, pp. 26-7) and Allen (p. 36). For useful comments on the debate between MacKenzie and Thomas, see Beinart, 'Empire, Hunting and Ecological Change', pp. 173-5.
54 Sally Gregory Kohlstedt, 'Australian Museums of Natural History: Public Priorities and Scientific Initiatives in the Nineteenth Century', *Historical Records of Australian Science*, vol. 5, no. 4, 1983, p. 1.
55 S. Sheets-Pyenson, 'Cathedrals of Science: The development of colonial natural history museums during the late nineteenth century', *History of Science*, vol. xxv, 1986, pp. 279-300.
56 Graeme Davison, 'Exhibitions', *Australian Cultural History*, no. 2, 1982/3, p. 6.
57 There were also collections and displays in mechanics institutes, many of which were established in cities and towns from the 1830s and 1840s. See Ann Moyal, *'a bright and savage land': Scientists in colonial Australia*, Sydney, William Collins, 1986, chapter 5.
58 Werner Hofmann, *Art in the Nineteenth Century*, London, 1961, p. 165, quoted in Davison, 'Exhibitions', p. 5.
59 Davison, 'Exhibitions', p. 5.
60 For an account of how one collection travelled from central Victoria to the Paris Exhibition of 1878, see chapter 2.
61 Kohlstedt, 'Australian Museums of Natural History', p. 6. The botanist Baron Sir Ferdinand von Mueller provides another outstanding example of a Victorian scientist manipulating international networks of correspondence and exchange.
62 Paul Fox, 'Nineteenth century vision of the city of Melbourne', typescript of talk, 1988, kindly made available by the author.
63 Quoted in Paul Fox, 'The State Library of Victoria: Science and Civilisation', *Transition*, no. 26, Spring 1988, p. 20.

64 Hermann Beckler, 'A Visit to the Library in 1859', Manuscript translated and edited by Margery Ramsay and Walter Struve, *La Trobe Library Journal*, vol. 7, no. 25, April 1980, pp. 8-11. This manuscript is interpreted by Paul Fox in 'Nineteenth century vision'.

65 MacKenzie, *Empire of Nature*, p. 31.

66 *Ibid.*, p. 301.

67 Quoted in Beinart, 'Empire, Hunting and Ecological Change', p. 165.

68 Wheelwright, *Bush Wanderings*, p. 180.

69 R. O. Rosenhain to J. A. Kershaw, 14 April 1919: 'Both of us took our cameras & "shot" various views. Our "bag" we send you under separate cover ... ' (The 'bag' was a photo album by H. V. Mattingley and R. O. Rosenhain of Wilson's Promontory, 1918, and has the letter pasted inside the front cover.) Held in Aboriginal Studies, Museum of Victoria. See also Graham, *The Gardeners of Eden*, p. 156, and Susan Sontag, *On Photography*, Middlesex, England, Penguin, 1979.

70 Quoted in Philippa Levine, *The Amateur and the Professional: Antiquarians, Historians and Archaeologists in Victorian England 1838-1886*, Cambridge, Cambridge University Press, 1986, p. 91.

71 R. H. Croll, 'Hunting the blackfellow: Records in Stone and Bone', Argus, 26 Dec. 1930; later included in Croll, *Wide Horizons: Wanderings in Central Australia*, Sydney, Angus & Robertson, 1937, pp. 124-8.

72 Kenneth Hudson, *Museums of Influence*, Cambridge and New York, Cambridge University Press, 1987, p. 31.

73 General Pitt-Rivers, *An Address delivered at the opening of the Dorset County Museum, on Tuesday, January 7th, 1884*, Dorchester, James Foster, 1884 [republished by The Friary Press, Dorchester, 1984], p. 14.

74 Isabel McBryde, 'Miss Mary, Ethnography and the Inheritance of Concern: Mary Ellen Murray-Prior [née Bundock]', in Julie Marcus (ed.), *First in their Field: Women and Australian Anthropology*, Melbourne, Melbourne University Press, 1993, pp. 15-46.

75 G. Davison, J. McCarty and A. McLeary (eds), *Australians 1888*, Sydney, 1987, pp. 271, 312-15; Susan Janson comments on the special status of the parlour in 'R. E. Johns: Diary 1888', *Australia 1888*, Bulletin no. 13, November 1984, p. 90, but this dimension is not mentioned in the bicentennial volume.

76 MacKenzie, *Empire of Nature*, pp. 30, 41, 48, 50.

77 See chapter 6.

78 Francis Bacon, *Gesta Grayorum* (1594), quoted in Oliver Impey and Arthur Macgregor (eds), *The Origins of Museums: The cabinet of curiosities in sixteenth and seventeenth century Europe*, Oxford, Clarendon Press, 1985, p. 1.

79 Impey and Macgregor, *The Origins of Museums*, p. 1.

80 Richard Dorson, *The British Folklorists*, London, Routledge & Kegan Paul, 1968, pp. 2-3. See also Stuart Piggott, *Ruins in a Landscape: Essays in Antiquarianism*, Edinburgh, Edinburgh University Press, 1976.

81 Quoted in Philippa Levine, *Amateur and Professional*, p. 12.

82 Joseph Levine, *Dr Woodward's Shield: History, Science and Satire in Augustan England*, Berkeley, University of California Press, 1977, p. 3.

83 See Piggott, *Ruins in a Landscape*, chapter VI.

84 Quoted in George Stocking, *Victorian Anthropology*, New York, The Free Press, 1987, p. 99.

85 See James Clifford, *The Predicament of Culture: Twentieth Century Ethnography, Literature, and Art*, Cambridge, MA, Harvard University Press, 1988, p. 228; and David Goodman, 'Fear of Circuses: Founding of the National Museum of Victoria, *Continuum*, vol. 3, no. 1, 1990, pp. 19-20.

86 Donna Haraway analyses taxidermy in *Primate Visions: Gender, Race and Nature in the World of Modern Science*, London and New York, Verso, 1992, chapter 3.

87 Kohlstedt, 'Australian Museums of Natural History', p. 3.

88 See Bann, *The Clothing of Clio*, chapter 1.

89 F. B. Smith, 'Stalwarts of the Garrison: Some Irish Academics in Australia', *Australian Cultural History*, no. 6, 1987, p. 87; Kohlstedt, 'Australian Museums of Natural History', footnote 166.

90 Haraway, *Primate Visions*, p. 31.

91 Nancy Stepan, *The Idea of Race in Science: Great Britain 1800-1960*, London and Basingstoke, Macmillan Press, 1982, p. 16; Haraway, *Primate Visions*, pp. 31-2.

92 F. McCoy, 'Gorillas at the National Museum', *Argus*, 19 June 1865, clipping in R. E. Johns, Scrapbook no. 1, Aboriginal Studies, Museum of Victoria, p. 225.

93 McCoy's gorillas, and scientific controversy in Victoria at this time about the relationships between humans and animals, have attracted scholarly attention. See Barry W. Butcher, 'Gorilla warfare in Melbourne: Halford, Huxley and "Man's place in nature"', in R. W. Home (ed.), *Australian Science in the Making*, Cambridge, Cambridge University Press, 1988, pp. 153-69, and Colin Finney, *Paradise Revealed: Natural History in nineteenth century Australia*, Melbourne, Museum of Victoria, 1993, pp. 99-103. At the time of writing, the gorillas still occupied a corner of the museum's public display space, appropriately enough in McCoy Hall.

94 Haraway, *Primate Visions*, p. 38.

95 *Ibid.*, pp. 38-9; Bernard Smith, *European Vision and the South Pacific*, (second edition), Sydney, Harper and Row, 1985 (first edition, 1960).

96 Michel Foucault, *The Order of Things: An Archaeology of the Human Sciences*, London, Tavistock Publications, 1970, p. 129; see also David Goodman, 'Fear of Circuses', p. 20, and Carolyn Merchant, *Ecological Revolutions: nature, gender and science in New England*, Chapel Hill and London, University of North Carolina Press, 1989, pp. 20-1.

97 Foucault, *The Order of Things*, p. 129.

98 Goodman, 'Fear of Circuses', pp. 19-20.

99 Penelope Lively, *The Road to Lichfield*, 1977, quoted in David Lowenthal, *The Past is a Foreign Country*, Cambridge, Cambridge University Press,

1985, pp. 67-8. See Elizabeth Edwards (ed.), *Anthropology and Photography, 1860-1920*, New Haven and London, Yale University Press in association with The Royal Anthropological Institute, London, 1992.

100 Clifford, *Predicament of Culture*, p. 229.

101 Susan Stewart, *On Longing: Narratives of the Miniature, the Gigantic, the Souvenir, the Collection*, Johns Hopkins University Press, Baltimore, 1984, quoted in Clifford, *Predicament of Culture*, p. 220.

102 Clifford, *Predicament of Culture*, pp. 220-1.

103 *Ibid.*, pp. 218, 220, 231, 234, 236.

104 Eric Wolf has written a book called *Europe and the People Without History*, Berkeley, University of California Press, 1982, in which he studies the global interaction of cultures since 1492 and argues the need to overcome 'the boundaries between Western and non-Western history' (p. x).

105 Some of these issues are pursued in chapter 2. Greg Dening, *Islands and Beaches: Discourse on a Silent Land*, Carlton, Vic., Melbourne University Press, 1980, and 'A Poetic for Histories: Transformations that Present the Past', in Aletta Biersack (ed.), *Clio in Oceania*, Washington, Smithsonian Institution, 1990, pp. 347-80; Stocking, *Victorian Anthropology*, pp. 76-7.

106 Bruce Trigger, 'The Past as Power', in Isabel McBryde (ed.), *Who Owns the Past?*, Melbourne, Oxford University Press, 1985, p. 34.

107 Dening, 'A Poetic for Histories', pp. 352, 365-8.

108 Philippa Levine, *The Amateur and the Professional*, argues this of the British scene.

109 Walter Murdoch, introducing a history of Australia for schools in 1917, wrote: 'When people talk about "the history of Australia" they mean the history of the white people who have lived in Australia . . . the dark-skinned wandering tribes . . . have nothing that can be called a history . . . Change and progress are the stuff of which history is made: these blacks knew no change and made no progress, as far as we can tell.' *The Making of Australia: An Introductory History*, Melbourne [1917], quoted in Bain Attwood, 'Introduction' to Attwood and John Arnold (eds), *Power, Knowledge and the Aborigines*, special edition of the *Journal of Australian Studies*, Bundoora, Vic., La Trobe University Press in association with the National Centre for Australian Studies, Monash University, 1992, p. x.

110 For an interesting collection of essays on indigenous peoples and the discipline of history, see Calvin Martin (ed.), *The American Indian and the Problem of History*, New York, Oxford University Press, 1987.

111 Frederick Turner, *Beyond Geography*, p. xi.

112 Terence Ranger, 'Taking hold of the land: Holy places and pilgrimages in twentieth-century Zimbabwe', *Past and Present*, no. 117, November 1987, p. 159.

113 Clifford, *Predicament of Culture*, p. 16.

2   VICTORIAN SKULDUGGERY

1 Diary of R. E. Johns, 9 February 1865, La Trobe Collection, State Library of Victoria. Johns' diaries and papers cover the years 1855-1910. Other papers, letters, scrapbooks and artefacts are held by the Museum of Victoria (Aboriginal Studies section).

2 Johns, Diary, 17 and 20 February 1865.

3 Johns, Diary, 10 January 1865.

4 Brief notes on the Reverend John Johns in Johns Papers, State Library of Victoria, and details of R. E. Johns' public service appointments in his Papers at the Museum of Victoria.

5 Johns, Diary, 24 February 1851.

6 Denis Strangman, 'The Rush to Lamplough, near Avoca in Victoria, in 1859', working draft (66 pages), 1987, p. 7 (kindly supplied by the author). A shorter version of this paper has been published as 'A Forgotten Victorian Gold Rush: Lamplough, via Avoca, 1859-1860', *Victorian Historical Journal*, vol. 60, no. 1, March 1989, pp. 3-26.

7 Johns, Diary, 26 February 1860. According to Johns, Morris had written a local history of Wye in Kent, England, 'containing interesting notes on tumuli and ancient earthworks': Johns, Diary, 21 August 1875. I have not been able to locate this text.

8 Obituary of A. L. Slater, *The Ovens and Murray Advertiser*, 11 January 1870, and an unidentified obituary pasted into Johns' Diary, 11 January 1870. Charles Waterton, a famous British naturalist, was among those who praised Slater's collection.

9 Johns, Diary, 18 May 1861, 8 February 1863.

10 Johns, Diary, 26 February 1862.

11 e.g., Johns, Diary, 16 September 1861. For details of early studies of marsupials see Elizabeth Dalton Newland, 'Dr George Bennett: Sir Richard Owen's man in Australia?', Paper presented to the Nationalism and Internationalism in Science Conference, Melbourne, 22-26 May 1988, typescript, and Kathleen Dugan, 'The Zoological Exploration of the Australian Region', in Nathan Reingold and Marc Rothenberg (eds), *Scientific Colonialism, 1800-1930: A Cross Cultural Comparison*, Washington DC, Smithsonian Institution Press, 1987, pp. 79-100.

12 Johns, Diary, 28 June 1864.

13 e.g., Johns, Diary, 18 May 1861, 24 April 1864.

14 Two of Johns' photo albums of ethnographic subjects are held in the Museum of Victoria (Aboriginal Studies). See also Paul Fox, 'The Imperial Schema: Ethnography, Photography and Collecting', *Photofile*, Indian Summer Issue, 1989, pp. 10-17; also Johns, Diary, 26 June 1865.

15 Johns, Diary, 12 and 18 May 1864.

16 Johns, Diary, 2 March 1866. Six letters written by Johns to McCoy (10 February 1866, 20 January 1868, 13 March 1868, 10 May 1868, 8 June 1868, 8 February 1872) are held in the Museum of Victoria, Aboriginal Studies.

17 Johns, Diary, 18 September 1864, 11 August 1865.

18 Johns, 'The Bunyip and Mindai', 7 September 1867, Johns Papers, State Library of Victoria.

19 H. W. Wheelwright considered the bunyip a figment of the Aboriginal imagination, but had heard many a colonist swear they had stood face to face with it, and that they described it as 'like a polled cow, with carnivorous teeth', *Bush Wanderings of a Naturalist, or Notes on the Field Sports and Fauna of Australia Felix*, London, Routledge, Warne & Routledge, 1861, p. 55.

20 Notes by Johns and a sketch of the bunyip figure appear in his Scrapbook no. 1, Museum of Victoria, p. 243. See also Aldo Massola, 'The Challicum Bun-Yip', *Victorian Naturalist*, no. 74, October 1957, pp. 80-2.

21 Bones of extinct gigantic marsupials, such as nototherium and diprotodon, were found in Australia from 1830 and much scientific and philosophical speculation ensued about them.

22 Richard Owen, 'On the Discovery of the Remains of a Mastodontid Pachyderm in Australia', *Annual Magazine of Natural History*, no. 11, 1843, pp. 7-12.

23 P. Vickers-Rich, J. M. Monaghan, R. F. Baird and T. H. Rich, *Vertebrate Palaeontology of Australasia*, Lilydale, Vic., Pioneer Design Studio, 1991, p. 2. Johns' friend, the amateur ethnologist Thomas Worsnop (introduced later this chapter), concluded that bunyip legends were a 'relic' from the time 'when the Diprotodon roamed in the marshes of Central Australia, and when alligators or crocodiles inhabited the waters of all portions of the continent': *The Prehistoric Arts, Manufactures, Works, Weapons, etc., of the Aborigines of Australia*, Adelaide, C. E. Bristow Government Printer, 1897, p. 169.

24 Johns, Diary, 14 May 1862.

25 Johns, Diary, 18 May 1876.

26 Johns' five scrapbooks were donated to the National Museum of Victoria by his son Harold Johns in 1914, and are held in the Aboriginal Studies section. I refer to the scrapbooks as follows: no. 1 (small volume, new red binding, 1850s-1867); no. 2 (small volume, original binding, 1867-69); no. 3 (large volume, loose binding, 1869-80); no. 4 (large volume, original binding, 1882-95); no. 5 (large volume, new red binding, 1890-1901). The scrapbooks were indexed by Johns. The first few entries under 'A' in Scrapbook no. 4 provide a glimpse of the contents: Australian Aborigines, star-myths of, *1*; Abyssinian monkey torch-bearers, *1*; Arabs, Bedouin, *2, 32*; Aeneze Arabs, *2*; Arab women wear nose ring, *2*; Ainos aborigines of Japan, *3, 205, 439*; American Indian Messiah Montezuma, *4 [many entries on American Indians follow]*; Aztec empire in Mexico, duration of, *4*; Australian language & customs like Todas of India, *14*; Australian aborigines carry sacred stones, *15*; Archbishop, Siberian, *19*; etc.

27 Johns, Diary, 21 February 1852.

28 Johns, Scrapbook no. 1, p. 44.

29 A letter from Huyghue to Johns (with sketch), 29 March 1855, a printed notice of the find, and Johns' annotations are in Scrapbook no. 1, pp. 17

and 45. Although the original drawing in the scrapbook was by Huyghue, the printed copy was signed 'S.T.G.' [S. T. Gill]. The carved head was described and illustrated almost ninety years later by D. J. Mahony in 'The Problem of Antiquity of Man in Australia', *Memoirs of the National Museum of Victoria*, no. 13, 1943, pp. 7-56.

30 Scrapbook no. 1, p. 168.

31 Johns' annotation dated December 1863, Scrapbook no. 1, p. 45.

32 See, for example, C. W. De Vis, 'Remarks on a Fossil Implement and Bones of an Extinct Kangaroo', *Proceedings of the Royal Society of Victoria*, vol. xii, 1899, p. 85.

33 See, for example, his Diary, undated note 1854 and 19 August 1860.

34 Johns, Scrapbook no. 1, pp. 95, 110, 146 (for his sketch of a gorilla). See chapter 1.

35 George Stocking, *Victorian Anthropology*, New York, The Free Press, 1987, p. 47.

36 George Stocking, 'What's in a name? The Origins of the Royal Anthropological Institute (1837-71)', *Man*, vol. 6, no. 3, 1971, pp. 369-90.

37 Nancy Stepan, *The Idea of Race in Science: Great Britain 1800-1960*, London and Basingstoke, Macmillan Press, 1982, p. 44.

38 *Ibid.*, pp. 1-2.

39 *Ibid.*, p. 4.

40 *Ibid.*, p. 1.

41 Stocking, 'What's in a Name?', pp. 374-5.

42 J. B. Davis and J. Thurnam, *Crania Britannica: Delineations and descriptions of the skulls of the aboriginal and early inhabitants of the British Islands*, London, 1865, and Davis, *On the osteology and peculiarities of the Tasmanian, a race of man recently become extinct*, Haarlem, The Netherlands, 1874.

43 See Stephen J. Gould, *The Mismeasure of Man*, London, Penguin, 1981, especially chapter 2.

44 Stepan, *The Idea of Race in Science*, pp. xviii-xix.

45 Johns occasionally burnt them (e.g., Diary, 23 May 1869), and his son Harold destroyed many after his death.

46 Johns, Diary, 26 October 1890.

47 Bruce Trigger, 'The Past as Power', in Isabel McBryde (ed.), *Who Owns the Past?*, Melbourne, Oxford University Press, 1985, pp. 15-16.

48 Letters from Brough Smyth to Chauncy, Brough Smyth to Johns, and Johns to Chauncy, 1872-3, Chauncy Papers, Australian Manuscripts Collection, State Library of Victoria. Johns, Diary, 28 January, 22 February, 5 April, 10 April, 16 June 1873. For copies of letters from Peter Manifold to Chauncy, see also Johns' Scrapbook no. 2, p. 337. Chauncy and Brough Smyth published the findings in Philip Chauncy, 'Notes and Anecdotes of the Aborigines of Australia', in R. B. Smyth, *The Aborigines of Victoria* (2 vols), Melbourne, Government Printer, 1878, Volume 2, Appendix A, pp. 221-84, especially pp. 234-6; and Kenyon and Casey published articles about stone arrangements, especially one at Lake Wongan, in the *Victorian Naturalist*.

See A. S. Kenyon, 'Stone Structures of the Australian Aboriginal', *Victorian Naturalist*, vol. 47, September 1930, pp. 71-5 and D. A. Casey, 'An Aboriginal Ceremonial Ground at Lake Wongan near Streatham, Victoria', *Victorian Naturalist*, vol. 54, January 1938, pp. 130-3.

49 Thomas Worsnop, *History of the City of Adelaide, from the foundation of the province of South Australia in 1836, to the end of the municipal year 1877, with appendix and map*, Adelaide, J. Williams, 1878.

50 Worsnop to Johns, 12 October 1887, interleaved in Johns' Scrapbook no. 3, p. 179; Johns is acknowledged on pp. vi, 61, 70, 78, 99, 107, 109, 113 and 168 of Worsnop, *The Prehistoric Arts*. For an obituary of Worsnop (1818-98), see the *Adelaide Observer*, 29 January 1898, p. 16.

51 This survives in Johns Papers, State Library of Victoria.

52 William B. Withers, T*he History of Ballarat, from the first pastoral settlement to the present time: with plans, illustrations, and original documents*, Ballarat, Ballarat Star, 1870.

53 Gwendolyn Davies, Introduction to 'Eugene' [S. D. S. Huyghue], *Argimou: A Legend of the Micmac*, New Brunswick (Canada), Mt Allison University, 1978 (originally published 1842), pp. i-ix. Huyghue brought to Australia a small collection of North American Indian artefacts, now held by the Museum of Victoria.

54 On his investigations at Lake Condah, see his Diary, 28 December 1892, 9 January, 2 March, 14 April, 24 May 1893, and Scrapbook no. 5, p. 244; for his comparison of Tasmanian and Victorian implements see Johns to J. J. Arundel (of the Burke Museum, Beechworth), 8 October 1877, Aboriginal Studies, Museum of Victoria; and for his interest in cave art see Scrapbook no. 1, p. 241 and Scrapbook no. 5, p. 253.

55 Stepan, *The Idea of Race in Science*, p. xvii.

56 I have drawn on E. P. Thompson's sketch of this school in his *Folklore, Anthropology and Social History*, A Studies in Labour History Pamphlet, Brighton, John L. Noyce, 1979, pp. 5-6. See also Richard Dorson, *The British Folklorists*, London, Routledge & Kegan Paul, 1968.

57 Scrapbook no. 3, p. 382; Scrapbook no. 5, p. 42.

58 His sister, Ilfra, had Hazlitt as her middle name.

59 D. J. Mulvaney, 'The Australian Aborigines 1606-1929: Opinion and Fieldwork', *Historical Studies*, vol. 8, 1958, pp. 131-51, 297-314; 'Gum Leaves on the Golden Bough: Australia's Palaeolithic Survivals Discovered', in J. D. Evans, B. Cunliffe and C. Renfrew (eds), *Antiquity and Man*, London, Thames and Hudson, 1981, pp. 52-64; 'The Ascent of Aboriginal Man: Howitt as Anthropologist', in M. H. Walker, *Come Wind, Come Weather*, Carlton, Vic., Melbourne University Press, 1971, pp. 285-312. These are a selection from the wide range of Mulvaney's writings on this issue.

60 Charles Lyell, *The Antiquity of Man*, London, John Murray, 1863, p. 87.

61 Mulvaney, 'The Australian Aborigines', p. 301.

62 Peter Bowler, *The Invention of Progress: The Victorians and the Past*, Oxford, Basil Blackwell Ltd, 1989, p. 80.

63 Quoted in Mulvaney, 'The Australian Aborigines', p. 301.

64 Johns, Diary, 18 August 1861.

65 Johns, Diary, 30 April 1865.

66 Theoretically, however, Cuvier remained a monogenist.

67 Gould, *The Mismeasure of Man*, pp. 42–50.

68 Stocking, *Victorian Anthropology*, p. 64.

69 *Ibid.*, p. 64.

70 Stepan, *The Idea of Race in Science*, pp. 20, 25. See also David de Giustino, *Conquest of Mind: Phrenology and Victorian Social Thought*, London, Croom Helm, 1975.

71 Johns, Diary, 10 February 1868.

72 Stocking, *Victorian Anthropology*, pp. 67–9.

73 See especially Stepan, *The Idea of Race in Science*, and Stocking, *Victorian Anthropology*.

74 Stepan, *The Idea of Race in Science*, p. 77: 'the problem was how to be a Darwinist without being a social Darwinist?'

75 See chapter 1; also Donald K. Grayson, *The Establishment of Human Antiquity*, New York, Academic Press, 1983, p. 3.

76 Johns, Diary, 17 November 1865.

77 Bowler, *The Invention of Progress*, p. 34; J. W. Burrow, *Evolution and Society*, London, Cambridge University Press, 1966.

78 Johns, Diary, 31 March 1864.

79 Johns, Diary, 12 February 1872. Perry was probably canvassing similar issues to those he addressed in a Melbourne lecture in 1869 and published as *Science and the Bible*, Melbourne, 1869.

80 In this case the argument was with 'Wallace' at the Branxholme Manse at Hamilton, Johns, Diary, 21 June 1893.

81 Johns, Diary, 15 April 1891; 'Esegar' [W. S. C. Siggers], *The God and the Religion of Science and the Bible*, Melbourne, Melville, Mullen & Slade, 1890.

82 Johns, 'Concerning Religion', 1879, Johns Papers, State Library of Victoria.

83 Johns, Diary, 8 November 1873.

84 Johns read, for instance, Robert Dale Owens' *The Debatable Land Between This World and the Next*, London, Trubner & Co., 1874.

85 Johns, Diary, 27 March 1865, 13 November 1865, 20 January 1866.

86 Johns, Diary, 25 December 1867.

87 *The Avoca Mail and Pyrenees District Advertiser*, 8 February 1868.

88 Johns, of course, later gathered a scrapbook clipping all about this beast: 'The White Elephant of Siam', 1889, Scrapbook no. 5, p. 436.

89 *Avoca Mail and Pyrenees District Advertiser*, 14 March 1868. I am grateful to Helen Harris for this reference.

90 Ballaarat East Public Library, *Fourth Annual Report of the Committee of Management; also, Rules of the Ballaarat East Public Library*, Ballaarat, W. D. McKee, 1867, pp. 7–8.

91 Johns, Diary, 15 May 1868.

92 Johns, Diary, 17 May, 30 May 1868.

93 Johns, Diary, 5 January 1870.
94 Carol Cooper, 'The Beechworth Collection of Aboriginal Artefacts', BA (Hons) thesis, Department of Prehistory and Anthropology, Australian National University, 1975, p. 2.
95 Special General Committee Meeting, Monday 17 September 1877, Beechworth Athenaeum and Burke Museum Minute Book No. 4 (1873–83), Burke Museum, Beechworth, pp. 206–18, 308, 316–20. Johns to J. J. Arundel of the Burke Museum, 8 October 1877, Aboriginal Studies, Museum of Victoria.
96 Cooper, 'The Beechworth Collection', p. 14.
97 The diaries of R. E. Johns were not available to researchers until 1976 when they were located by a Canberra graduate in Prehistory, Carol Cooper, who tracked them down with a sustained curiosity and perseverance that Johns would have admired. Cooper described her quest and offered an introductory study of Johns in 'Reynell Eveleigh Johns: A Rediscovered Victorian', *La Trobe Library Journal*, 1977, pp. 90–6.
98 Obituary, *Hamilton Spectator*, 20 May 1910, p. 4.
99 But even in the Burke Museum, Beechworth, his name as a donor is not evident, except deep in the Minute Books which were often forgotten. When, in 1956, Aldo Massola, curator of Anthropology at the National Museum of Victoria, enquired after the donor of the Aboriginal artefacts in Beechworth, the honorary secretary of the 'Bourke [*sic*] Museum' replied that 'I could not say who . . . the "me" [on the labels] would be', W. Callaghan to the director of the National Museum of Victoria, 6 January 1956, 'Ethnology—Shire of Beechworth', National Museum of Victoria file, held in Aboriginal Studies.
100 He had two sons and three daughters: Harold, May, Nell, Arthur and Clare.
101 The will of R. E. Johns, dated 31 May 1905, Probate Office, Melbourne, mentions his 'pictures, books, furniture, curiosities, and other personal effects'. An inventory of furniture was later attached to it. (Information kindly supplied by Geoff Browne.)
102 P. T. Barnum, showman and museum-maker, represents the transition.
103 Johns, Diary, 3 October 1859, 3 December 1857.
104 Johns, Diary, 1 and 3 September 1872.
105 Johns, Diary, 1 and 3 September 1872, 26 December 1872.
106 Johns, Diary, 26 December 1872, 25 August 1872. Martha (Patty) Woolley married John George Griffin (1846–1923) at Portland in 1869. Griffin was an engineer and later became a mayor of Manly and Hurstville in Sydney.
107 Johns, Diary, 2 August 1873.
108 Marie Hansen Fels, *Good Men and True: The Aboriginal Police of the Port Phillip District, 1837–1853*, Carlton, Vic., Melbourne University Press, 1988; Bain Attwood, *The Making of the Aborigines*, Sydney, Allen & Unwin, 1989; and Jan Critchett, *A Distant Field of Murder*, Carlton, Vic., Melbourne University Press, 1990.
109 Johns records the testimony of 'John Martin, Post Office letter-carrier at Avoca' in Scrapbook no. 2, p. 365.

110 Quoted in Ian D. Clark, *Aboriginal Languages and Clans: An Historical Atlas of Western and Central Victoria, 1800-1900*, Monash Publications in Geography, no. 37, Department of Geography and Environmental Science, Melbourne, 1990, p. 147.

111 'Aboriginal Theatricals', *Mount Ararat and Pleasant Creek Advertiser*, 22 May 1860.

112 Denis Strangman, 'The Rush to Lamplough', p. 147.

113 Geoffrey Blainey makes this parallel in *A Land Half Won*, South Melbourne, Macmillan, 1980, p. 65.

114 Mulvaney, 'The Ascent of Aboriginal Man: Howitt as Anthropologist'; Mulvaney and J. H. Calaby, *'So Much That Is New': Baldwin Spencer 1860-1929, A Biography*, Carlton, Vic., Melbourne University Press, 1985; James Dawson, *Australian Aborigines* (first published 1881), facsimile edition introduced by Jan Critchett, Canberra, Australian Institute of Aboriginal Studies, 1981; Harley W. Foster, 'Edward Micklethwaite Curr (1820-1889)', in *Australian Dictionary of Biography*, vol. 3, p. 508.

115 Johns, Diary, 9 July 1862, 3 November 1862, 17 January 1863, 4 March 1863, 18 October 1863, 2 January 1864, 27 August 1864, 27 August 1865. Johns later commissioned some artefacts to be made by Aborigines at the Lake Condah mission: see chapter 12.

116 See chapter 9.

117 See especially Mulvaney, 'Gum Leaves on the Golden Bough' and 'The Ascent of Aboriginal Man'.

118 E. B. Tylor, Preface to H. Ling Roth *et al.*, *The Aborigines of Tasmania*, first edition, 1890, republished Hobart, Fullars Bookshop, 1968, p. v.

119 See chapter 5.

120 See chapter 4.

3   THE STONE AGE

1 R. E. Johns, Diary, Australian Manuscripts Collection, State Library of Victoria, 17 April 1893.

2 Peter Bowler, *The Invention of Progress: The Victorians and the Past*, Oxford, Basil Blackwell, 1989, p. 77.

3 *Ibid.*, pp. 82-4.

4 F. P. Dickson, *Australian Stone Hatchets: A Study in Design and Dynamics*, Sydney, Academic Press, 1981, p. 18.

5 Josephine Flood, *Archaeology of the Dreamtime: The story of prehistoric Australia and its people*, Sydney, Collins, 1989, p. 19.

6 Rhys Jones, 'The Neolithic, Palaeolithic and the Hunting Gardeners: Man and Land in the Antipodes', in R. P. Suggate and M. M. Cresswell (eds), *Quaternary Studies*, Wellington, Royal Society of New Zealand, Bulletin 13, 1975, p. 21.

7 Dickson, *Australian Stone Hatchets*, p. 19.

8 D. J. Mulvaney, 'The Stone Age in Australia', *Proceedings of the Prehistoric Society*, no. 4, New Series, vol. xxvii, 1961, pp. 58, 97, drawing on the observations of Brough Smyth and James Dawson.

9 Mulvaney, 'Stone Age', p. 97.

10 Donald K. Grayson, *The Establishment of Human Antiquity*, New York, Academic Press, 1983; see also Roy Porter, 'Gentlemen and Geology: The emergence of a scientific career, 1660-1920', *The Historical Journal*, vol. 21, no. 4, 1978, pp. 809-36.

11 Stephen J. Pyne, *The Ice: A Journey to Antarctica*, Iowa City, University of Iowa Press, 1986, p. 250.

12 Grayson, *Human Antiquity*, p. 25.

13 *Ibid.*, p. 46.

14 See chapter 4.

15 P. Vickers-Rich, J. M. Monaghan, R. F. Baird and T. H. Rich, *Vertebrate Palaeontology of Australasia*, Lilydale, Vic., Pioneer Design Studio, 1991, p. 3.

16 Thomas Mitchell, *Three Expeditions into the Interior of Eastern Australia With Descriptions of the Recently Explored Regions of Australia Felix, and the Present Colony of New South Wales*, London, T. & W. Boone, 1839, extract published in David Horton, *Recovering the Tracks: The Story of Australian Archaeology*, Canberra, Aboriginal Studies Press, 1991, pp. 26-9.

17 Vickers-Rich *et al.*, *Vertebrate Palaeontology*, chapter 1.

18 R. Etheridge, 'Has Man a Geological History in Australia?', *Proceedings of the Linnean Society of New South Wales*, second series, vol. v, 1890, pp. 262-5; D. Horton, 'Early thought on early man in Australia', *The Artefact*, 1981, pp. 63-4.

19 J. W. Gregory, 'The Antiquity of Man in Victoria', *Proceedings of the Royal Society of Victoria*, vol. 17, part 1, 1904, pp. 120-44; B. Spencer and R. H. Walcott, 'The Origin of Cuts on Bones of Australian Extinct Marsupials', *Proceedings of the Royal Society of Victoria*, vol. 24, part 1, 1911, pp. 92-123.

20 See chapter 2.

21 James Bonwick, *Daily Life and Origin of the Tasmanians*, 1870, p. 215, quoted in Etheridge, 'Has Man a Geological History in Australia?', pp. 261-2.

22 Spencer and Walcott, 'The Origin of Cuts'; C. W. De Vis, 'Remarks on a Fossil Implement and Bones of an Extinct Kangaroo', *Proceedings of the Royal Society of Victoria*, vol. xii, 1899, p. 85; Etheridge, 'Has Man a Geological History in Australia?'; Gregory, 'Antiquity of Man in Victoria'; D. J. Mahony, 'The Problem of Antiquity of Man in Australia', *Memoirs of the National Museum of Victoria*, no. 13, 1943, pp. 7-56; Edmund Gill, 'Geological evidence in Western Victoria relative to the antiquity of the Australian aborigines', *Memoirs of the National Museum of Victoria*, no. 18, 1953, pp. 25-92.

23 Charles Barrett, 'Prehistoric Victoria', *Herald*, 9 June 1926; 'The Puralka Flint', *Victorian Naturalist*, vol. xliii, February 1927, pp. 295-6; *On the*

Wallaby: Quest and Adventure in Many Lands, Melbourne, Robertson & Mullens Ltd, 1942, pp. 48-9.

24 Sylvia Lawson, *The Archibald Paradox: A Strange Case of Authorship*, Ringwood, Vic., Allen Lane, 1983, p. 3.

25 For biographical details of Joseph Patrick Archibald, see Lawson, *The Archibald Paradox*, pp. 1-6, and the Archibald Papers, Mitchell Library, Sydney.

26 Archibald greeted later suggestions that others had been involved with great annoyance and, as curator of the newspaper files, was in a position to annotate the historical record. Newspaper articles written in 1889 on the foundation of the Warrnambool art gallery and museum were annotated by Archibald: 'Cockman had no more to do with founding the Art Gallery than the man in the moon' and 'This is simple bunkum' were the tenor of his remarks. *Warrnambool Standard*, 1 April 1889, 3 April 1889, annotated originals held in the Warrnambool Public Library. Jan Critchett kindly drew my attention to these copies.

27 'The Museum—The Quern', *Warrnambool Standard*, 7 June 1892, clipping in J. P. Archibald, 'Warrnambool & District Newspaper Cuttings etc.', Mitchell Library, State Library of New South Wales. Other information about Archibald's museum has been gleaned from this book of cuttings as well as from J. P. Archibald, 'The Ancient Wreck at Warrnambool, 1890-95', Mitchell Library, and Lucy Archibald, 'Warrnambool, the scene of J. F. Archibald's early days', manuscript dated 21 May 1943, in the Archibald Papers (Aa 73/2), Mitchell Library, State Library of New South Wales. I have also drawn on a small collection of letters from Lucy Archibald to the Warrnambool Historical Society in the 1930s, held by the Warrnambool Public Library.

28 Gregory, 'Antiquity of Man in Victoria', pp. 132-3. The limestone slab remained on display in Warrnambool until 1951 when it was transferred to the National Museum of Victoria. In a local radio talk of 1947, the slab was compared to Tutankhamen's tomb which was discovered in 1922: Radio Talk [by E. D. Cooke?], 'Antiquity of Man' file, Warrnambool Public Library.

29 Unidentified newspaper clipping [1891] in J. P. Archibald, 'Warrnambool & District Newspaper Cuttings etc.', p. 4.

30 R. Brough Smyth, *The Aborigines of Victoria*, 2 volumes, Melbourne and London, Government Printer, 1878, vol. 1, p. 364.

31 Gregory, 'Antiquity of Man in Victoria', and Etheridge, 'Has Man a Geological History in Australia?'.

32 A useful summary of theories is provided by Geoffrey Blainey in *Triumph of the Nomads: A History of Ancient Australia*, revised edn, Macmillan, South Melbourne, 1982, chapter 3. For a study of speculation about Aboriginal origins generally, see D. J. Mulvaney, 'Fact, Fancy and Aboriginal Australian Ethnic Origins', *Mankind*, vol. 6, no. 7, June 1966, pp. 299-305. The American anthropologist A. L. Kroeber was critical of the Australian obsesssion with 'the problem of the Tasmanians': *American Journal of Physical Anthropology*, vol. 2, no. 3, September 1944, pp. 1-2.

33 Alfred Howitt, 'On the Origin of the Aborigines of Tasmania and Australia', *Australasian Association for the Advancement of Science*, vol. 7, 1898.

34 The Victorian geologist E. J. Dunn, speaking in 1916, shared their opinion: 'Of course, the one subject that is being discussed very keenly, and from two opposite points of view, is this: whether the Aborigines of Victoria have been here for a short or a very lengthy period. I think that they have not been here for long, notwithstanding those great heaps of ashes and shells.' *Victorian Geographical Journal*, vol. xxxii, part 1, 1916, p. 8.

35 Smyth, *The Aborigines of Victoria*, vol. 1, p. 364.

36 Charles Barrett, *On the Wallaby*, p. 51.

37 Frank Spencer, based on research by Ian Langham, *Piltdown: A Scientific Forgery*, London, Oxford and New York, Natural History Museum Publications and Oxford University Press, 1990; S. J. Gould, 'Piltdown Revisited', in *The Panda's Thumb*, Middlesex, England, Penguin, 1980, pp. 92–104; Bowler, *Invention of Progress*, pp. 189–91; and Roger Lewin, *Bones of Contention*, London, Penguin, 1987, pp. 60–2. For a personal account of Ian Langham's role in probing the Piltdown mystery, see Rosaleen Love, 'The Palace of the Soul', *Evolution Annie and other stories*, London, The Women's Press, 1993, pp. 83–93.

38 Michael J. Blunt, 'Sir Grafton Elliot Smith (1871-1937)', *Australian Dictionary of Biography*, vol. 11, pp. 645–6; D. J. Mulvaney, 'Blood from stones and bones: Aboriginal Australians and Australian Prehistory', *Search*, vol. 10, no. 6, June 1979.

39 'Antiquity of Australia', *Age*[?], 7 March 1925, clipping in unidentified [Kershaw?] Scrapbook, Museum of Victoria (Aboriginal Studies).

40 Mulvaney, 'Blood from stones and bones', p. 214. For Edgeworth David's argument for Aboriginal antiquity see his 'Geological Evidence of the Antiquity of Man in the Commonwealth, with special reference to the Tasmanian Aborigines' (1923), partly reproduced in Horton, *Recovering the Tracks*, pp. 123–37. For a description of 'robust' and 'gracile' forms, see Flood, *Archaeology of the Dreamtime*, chapter 4.

41 Mulvaney, 'Blood from stones and bones', p. 214.

42 'Prehistoric Man—The Cohuna Skull', *Age*, 21 April 1926, clipping in [Kershaw?] Scrapbook, Museum of Victoria. MacKenzie criticised those who considered Australia a young country and insisted that it was 'teeming with the history of past ages': 'The Aborigines of South Gippsland', in H. J. Malone, *A Short History of Central South Gippsland*, Buffalo, State School, 1932, p. 1. I owe this reference to Meredith Fletcher.

43 'Antiquity of Australia', *Age*[?], 7 March 1925, clipping in [Kershaw?] Scrapbook.

44 J. L. Shellshear to D. J. Mahony, 6 September 1942 and T. D. Campbell to D. J. Mahony, 20 August 1942, 'Ethnology—Antiquity of Man in Australia', National Museum of Victoria file, held in Aboriginal Studies.

45 'Jervois Skull—Is it Prehistoric?', *Argus*, 19 July 1931, clipping in [Kershaw ?] Scrapbook.

46 Undated clipping [1929], [Kershaw?] Scrapbook.

47 R. H. Croll, *Wide Horizons: Wanderings in Central Australia*, Sydney, Angus & Robertson, 1937, p. 74. Croll spelt the name as 'O'Neil'.

48 H. M. Hale and N. B. Tindale, 'Notes on some human remains in the Lower Murray Valley, South Australia', *Records of the South Australian Museum*, no. 4, 1930, pp. 145-218.

49 One who did recognise and publicise its importance was Charles Barrett. He called it 'the opening chapter of the Romance of Excavation in Australia': 'Ancient Man in Australia', *Herald*, 18 July 1930. For more on the reception of Devon Downs, see later this chapter.

50 A copy of the sub-commission's report is in 'Antiquity of Man', National Museum of Victoria file, held in Aboriginal Studies.

51 This was the discovery of the Keilor skull in 1940. See chapter 4.

52 D. J. Mulvaney, *Prehistory and Heritage: The Writings of John Mulvaney*, Canberra, Department of Prehistory, Australian National University, 1990, p. 149.

53 Mira Lilian Lakic, 'Grinding Away the Problem: An Investigation and Analysis of a sample of Aboriginal Grinding Stones collected from the Murray and Darling Rivers by AS. Kenyon', BA(Hons) thesis, Department of Archaeology, La Trobe University, 1988, and Louis Michael Warren, 'Collectors and Collections', BA(Hons) thesis, Department of Archaeology, La Trobe University, 1985. The difficulties that confront researchers are considerable. John Mulvaney recalls that in 1957 he attempted to study the provenance of stone hatchet heads in the museum and found some piled in a vast mound on the storeroom floor and others inaccessibly partitioned off in a part of the building assigned to the Department of Weights and Measures. Mulvaney, *Prehistory and Heritage*, p. 149.

54 Harold Johns' letter 'To the Inheritor . . . ', 1914, Johns Papers, State Library of Victoria.

55 D. J. Mulvaney and J. H. Calaby, *'So Much That Is New': Baldwin Spencer 1860-1929, A Biography*, Carlton, Vic., Melbourne University Press, 1985; Mulvaney, 'Classification and typology in Australia: The first 340 Years', in R. V. S. Wright (ed.), *Stone Tools as Cultural Markers: change, evolution and complexity*, Canberra, Australian Institute of Aboriginal Studies, 1977, p. 267.

56 Mulvaney and Calaby, *'So Much That is New'*, p. 251.

57 Biographical details have been gleaned from obituaries and notes in the Kenyon Papers, Australian Manuscripts Collection, State Library of Victoria, Box 1/1 (i)-(iv), and from Ronald McNicoll, 'Alfred Stephen Kenyon', in *Australian Dictionary of Biography*, vol. 9, pp. 572-3.

58 Poem entitled 'Water Commission', no author, undated, in Kenyon Papers, Box 1/1 (iii).

59 R. V. Billis, 'A Pastoral Historian Passes: Tribute to Mr Alfred Stephen Kenyon', *Australian*, 29 May 1943, clipping in Kenyon Papers, Box 1/1 (iv).

60 Towle to Kenyon, 25 March 1929 and 4 May 1929, Kenyon Papers, State Library, Box 13/1 (i).

61 *Herald*, 17 May 1943, clipping in Kenyon Papers, Box 1/1.

62 Justine Kenyon, *The Aboriginal Word Book*, 2nd edn, Melbourne, Lothian, 1951 (first published 1930). The blurb stated: 'If you want an aboriginal word for the name of your house, see that you get one with a meaning you can trust.'

63 Paul Fox, 'The State Library of Victoria: Science and Civilisation', *Transition*, no. 26, Spring 1988, pp. 14-26, and Robert S. Merrillees with the collaboration of Colin A. Hope and Graeme L. Pretty and a contribution by Piers Crocker, *Living with Egypt's Past in Australia*, Melbourne, Museum of Victoria, 1990.

64 Merrillees, *Living with Egypt's Past*, p. 14. The description of the room is Kenyon's.

65 Norman de Garis Davies, letter to the *Argus* on the arrival in Australia of the first antiquities from an excavation in the Nile Valley in 1899, quoted in Merrillees, *Living with Egypt's Past*, pp. 11-12. On exchanges, see Fox, 'The State Library of Victoria' and Merrillees, p. 12.

66 In 1914 Elliot Smith exhumed a Torres Strait mummy in the Macleay Museum, Sydney, and found technical similarities with ancient Egyptian practice: Merrillees, *Living with Egypt's Past*, p. 28.

67 D. J. Mulvaney, 'The proposed Gallery of Aboriginal Australia', in Robert Edwards and Jenny Stewart (eds), *Preserving Indigenous Cultures: A New Role for Museums*, Canberra, Australian Government Publishing Service, 1980, pp. 72-8, see p. 77.

68 R. E. Johns, Diary, 20 September 1898, mentions that he received a letter from Kenyon. Kenyon may have learnt of Johns' interests through references to him in Thomas Worsnop's *The Prehistoric Arts, Manufactures, Works, Weapons, etc., of the Aborigines of Australia*, Adelaide, C. E. Bristow Government Printer, 1897, a book with which Kenyon was familiar.

69 Kenyon to David, 8 January 1925, typescript copy, Box 36 'Miscellaneous (Kenyon & others)', Museum of Victoria, Aboriginal Studies storeroom.

70 Quoted in Mulvaney and Calaby, *'So Much That Is New'*, p. 251.

71 Kenyon to David, 8 January 1925.

72 Kenyon, 'Lecture on the Tasmanian Aboriginal', 30 August 1939, one of the National Museum of Victoria's 'Free Guide Lectures', typescript in Box 36 'Miscellaneous (Kenyon & others)', Folder 13.

73 Kenyon to C. C. Towle, 26 May 1930, Kenyon Papers. For more on Barrett, see chapter 6.

74 Stan Mitchell to W. E. H. Stanner, 16 February 1962, Mitchell Papers, Australian Institute of Aboriginal and Torres Strait Islander Studies (AIATSIS).

75 'Stanley Robert Mitchell', obituary, *Proceedings of the Royal Society of Victoria*, vol. 77, part 2, 1964, pp. 618-19.

76 Croll, *Wide Horizons*, p. 124.

77 Newspaper cutting, 'Peninsula Portraits No. 14: Mr S. R. Mitchell', 1 August 1957, in Mitchell Papers.

78 Copy of letter from James Mitchell to a friend, 31 August 1896,

S. R. Mitchell's undated notes on Dargo days, and newspaper clipping: 'A Man with an Interesting Job', by Esme Johnston, *The New Idea*, 14 March 1941, Mitchell Papers.

79 Julie Carter, 'S. R. Mitchell and Archaeology in Victoria', MA thesis, University of Melbourne, 1980, p. 92.

80 T. D. Campbell to Mitchell, 12 June [1960?], Mitchell Papers.

81 Mulvaney, 'Classification and typology in Australia', p. 268.

82 S. T. Scott to Mitchell, 12 September 1951, Mitchell Papers.

83 Campbell to Mitchell 19 February 1950, Mitchell Papers.

84 C. F. Kurtze to Mitchell, 3 July 1961, Mitchell Papers.

85 Mitchell to Campbell, 30 May 1962, Mitchell Papers.

86 Towle to Mitchell, 30 December 1933, Mitchell Papers.

87 C. F. Kurtze to Mitchell, 3 July 1961, Mitchell Papers.

88 Mitchell to Kurtze, 7 July 1961; Mitchell to Helen Wurm, Curator of Anthropology at the Australian Institute of Anatomy, 11 July 1961, Mitchell Papers.

89 Joseph Shellshear, 'An Appeal for the Preservation of Prehistoric Remains in Australia', *The Australian Museum Magazine*, 20 Feb. 1937, pp. 169–75; F. D. McCarthy, 'Aboriginal Relics and their Preservation', *Mankind*, vol. 2, 1938, pp. 120–6. Shellshear praised Hale and Tindale's work at Devon Downs: 'the scientific work is admirable . . . it is deplorable that this valuable site was not at once protected from the vandalism of private collectors' (p. 173).

90 The council was formed in 1936. Mitchell writes about both issues in a letter to Towle with no sense of contradiction: Mitchell to Towle, 17 August 1936, Mitchell Papers. For some elucidation of this apparent contradiction and for more details on Mitchell's advocacy for 'National Monuments', see chapter 7.

91 Mitchell to W. E. H. Stanner, 16 February 1962, Mitchell Papers.

92 Towle to Mitchell, 17 July 1937, Mitchell Papers.

93 Mulvaney, 'The Stone Age of Australia', p. 72; Mitchell, 'Patination', *Mankind*, vol. 3, no. 10, February 1947.

94 'Geological determinism' is Mulvaney's phrase; Frederick McCarthy called them the 'materialist school'.

95 Kenyon to Professor Wood Jones, 21 February 1922[?], Baldwin Spencer Papers, Box 22, Aboriginal Studies storeroom, Museum of Victoria.

96 Kenyon, D. J. Mahony and S. F. Mann, 'Evidence of Outside Culture Inoculations', undated typescript, Kenyon Papers, State Library, Box 9/2 (ii). This was published in *Australasian Association for the Advancement of Science*, no. 17, 1924, pp. 464–7.

97 Kenyon, untitled and undated paper, Kenyon Papers, State Library, Box 9/1 (xv).

98 See, for example, Kenyon, Mahony and Mann, 'Evidence of Outside Culture Inoculations'.

99 Mitchell to Dr J. C. Trevor, n.d., Mitchell Papers.

100 Kenyon to C. C. Towle, 12 March 1929, Kenyon Papers, State Library, Box 13/1 (i).

101 Kenyon, D. J. Mahony and S. F. Mann, 'Austral-Tasmanic Connexion', undated typescript of paper presented to AAAS Conference, Adelaide, Kenyon Papers, State Library, Box 9/2 (i).

102 Copy of letter from Mitchell, 1952, Mitchell Papers.

103 The best summary of the changing concerns of Australian stone tool typology is D. J. Mulvaney, 'Classification and typology in Australia'.

104 Towle to Kenyon, 25 March 1929, Kenyon Papers, State Library, Box 13/1 (i).

105 Bruce Trigger, 'The Past as Power: Anthropology and the North American Indian', in Isabel McBryde (ed.), *Who Owns the Past?*, Melbourne, Oxford University Press, 1985, pp. 21–2.

106 *Ibid.*, p. 22.

107 F. D. McCarthy, 'The Lapstone Creek excavation: two culture periods revealed in eastern New South Wales', *Records of the Australian Museum*, no. 22, 1948, pp. 1–34. Analysis and publication were delayed due to the war.

108 Carter, 'S. R. Mitchell', p. 150.

109 Mulvaney was told this 'by more than one influential artefact collector', 'Australian Archaeology 1929–1964: Problems and Policies', *Australian Journal of Science*, vol. 27, no. 2, August 1964, p. 40.

110 Campbell to Mitchell 19 June 1958, 12 June [1960?], Mitchell Papers.

111 Mitchell to C. P. Mountford, 9 January 1959, Mitchell Papers.

112 Mitchell to Campbell, 20 August 1961, Mitchell Papers.

113 Mulvaney, 'Classification and typology in Australia'.

114 The notion of time disturbed prevailing views of typology among the collectors. In a discussion of the term 'typologist', Campbell wrote to Mitchell: 'if as I imagine, a typologist is one concerned with the correct description of the morphology of implements and their systematic classification, then I very much feel like one and wish there were a lot more. If you mean—the so called chronological sequence and "cultural" sequence of implements then that is an aspect I am prepared to leave to some of the so called experts and authorities about the place.' Campbell to Mitchell, 22 October 1962, Mitchell Papers.

115 See chapter 8, 'Journeys to the Centre'.

116 Gillian Cowlishaw, 'Studying Aborigines: Changing Canons in Anthropology and History', in Bain Attwood and John Arnold (eds), *Power, Knowledge and Aborigines*, special edition of the *Journal of Australian Studies*, Bundoora, Vic., La Trobe University Press in association with the National Centre for Australian Studies, Monash University, 1992, p. 25.

117 P. G. Jones, 'South Australian Anthropological History: The Board for Anthropological Research and its early expeditions', *Records of the South Australian Museum*, vol. 20, May 1987, pp. 71–92.

118 Tim Murray, 'Aboriginal (Pre)History and Australian Archaeology': The Discourse of Australian Prehistoric Archaeology', in Attwood and Arnold (eds), *Power, Knowledge and Aborigines*, p. 17.

119 Towle to Kenyon, 15 May 1930, Kenyon Papers.

120 Mitchell to C. P. Mountford 9 January 1959, Mitchell Papers.

121 G. M. Black to D. J. Mahony, 18 June 1934, 20 October 1934, 12 October 1939, in 'Ethnology—Black, G. M.', National Museum of Victoria file, Aboriginal Studies; S. Sunderland and L. J. Ray, 'A Note on the Murray Black Collection of Australian Aboriginal Skeletons' [paper read 12 September 1957], *Proceedings of the Royal Society of Victoria*, vol. 71, part 1, Melbourne, February 1959, pp. 45-8; D. J. Mulvaney, 'Reflections on the Murray Black Collection', *Australian Natural History*, vol. 23, no. 1, winter 1989, pp. 66-73.

122 The skeletons of about half a dozen individuals collected by Black came to the National Museum of Victoria, but most of his donations to the Museum consisted of grindstones and other artefacts: Register of Acquisitions, National Museum of Victoria.

123 Sunderland and Ray, 'A Note on the Murray Black Collection'.

124 Gib Wettenhall, 'The Murray Black collection goes home', *Australian Society*, December 1988/January 1989, pp. 17-19; my notes from Jim Bowler, 'Lake Mungo, Newtonian conflict and Aboriginal mythology', a talk given as part of the Dean's Lecture Series, Faculty of Science, University of Melbourne, 22 September 1992.

125 Black to Mahony, 18 June 1934 and 12 October 1939, in 'Ethnology—Black, G. M.' file.

126 G. Murray Black to Sir Colin MacKenzie, Friday 18 October [no year given], National Museum of Australia Collection. Gaye Sculthorpe drew my attention to this letter, and showed me her transcript of it.

127 Kenyon, 'The camping places of the aboriginals of South Eastern Australia', paper read to the Historical Society of Victoria, 1911, Kenyon Papers, State Library, Box 9/3 (vi).

128 Undated *Argus* clipping, Mitchell Papers.

129 D. J. Mulvaney, 'Australasian Anthropology and ANZAAS: "Strictly Scientific and Critical"', in Roy MacLeod (ed.), *The Commonwealth of Science: ANZAAS and the Scientific Enterprise in Australasia, 1888-1988*, Melbourne, Oxford University Press, 1988, pp. 202-3. He describes the journal as containing 'useful facts and idiotic theories'.

130 Kenyon to Towle, 1930 [no month], Kenyon Papers, Box 13/1 (i).

131 A. S. Kenyon, 'Black and White Culture Contacts on the Australian Continent', undated typescript, Kenyon Papers, Box 9/1 (iii), and Evidence given by Kenyon to the Royal Commission on the Constitution of the Commonwealth, 24 October 1927, typescript, Box 9/1 (xvi); see also Croll, *Wide Horizons*, p. 158.

132 S. R. Mitchell, 'The Anthropological Society of Victoria', unpublished typescript (tenth anniversary reflection), 13 September 1944, Mitchell Papers.

133 Andrew Markus, *Governing Savages*, Sydney, Allen & Unwin, 1990, p. viii.

134 *Ibid.*, pp. viii-ix, 149, 158.

135 Cowlishaw, 'Studying Aborigines', p. 25.

136 J. W. Bleakley (Chief Protector of Aborigines, Queensland), 'The Aboriginals and Half-Castes of Central Australia and North Australia', *Commonwealth Parliamentary Paper*, no. 21, 1929.

137 Pro-Aboriginal groups in other states were more careful: the Association for the Protection of Native Races in New South Wales, the Aborigines' Friends Association in South Australia, and the Australian Aborigines' Amelioration Association in Western Australia.

138 Amy Brown Papers, Australian Manuscripts Collection, State Library of Victoria; The Victorian Aboriginal Group, *Annual Report*, Melbourne, 1935; Patricia Matthews, '"Uplifting our Aboriginal People": The Victorian Aboriginal Group, 1930-1971', BA(Hons) thesis, Monash University, 1985.

139 For example, 'Discovery of Australia', undated lecture, manuscript, Kenyon Papers, Box 2/2 (viii).

140 See chapter 7.

141 F. C. Smith to Mitchell, several undated letters [late 1950s], and Campbell to Mitchell, 14 February 1950, Mitchell Papers.

142 See chapter 7.

4   THE NUCLEAR FAMILY

1 Donna Haraway, *Primate Visions: Gender, Race and Nature in the World of Modern Science*, London and New York, originally published 1989, Verso, 1992, p. 3.

2 R. B. Lee and I. De Vore (eds), *Man the Hunter*, Chicago, Aldine, 1968.

3 Haraway, *Primate Visions*, pp. 187, 216.

4 *Ibid.*, p. 201. She points out that the symposium repeatedly undermined its title by paying attention to gathering, p. 216.

5 *Ibid.*, pp. 216, 226.

6 Undated clipping [mid-1950s] in the Mitchell Papers, AIATSIS: The article called carbon dating 'one of the less frightening developments of this atomic age'.

7 Some records and equipment associated with this laboratory are held at 'Scienceworks', the Spotswood campus of the Museum of Victoria.

8 Nigel Calder, *Timescale: An Atlas of the Fourth Dimension*, London, Chatto & Windus, 1983, pp. 14-41; Timothy Ferris, *Coming of Age in the Milky Way*, London, Vintage, 1988, chapter 13.

9 See chapter 3.

10 Edmund Gill, 'Story of Keilor Cranium', television talk, 4 May 1959, manuscript in Gill Papers, Museum of Victoria (blue box labelled 'E. D. Gill, Articles and Lectures', held in Aboriginal Studies). See also Edmund Gill, 'Some aspects of prehistory in Victoria', *Victorian Historical Magazine*, vol. 40, no. 4, November 1969, p. 175.

11 D. J. Mahony, in his 'The Problem of Antiquity of Man in Victoria', *Memoirs of the National Museum of Victoria*, no. 13, 1943, pp. 7-56, stated that

the Pleistocene age of the Keilor find 'seems irrefutable' (p. 23). In preparing this article, Mahony established a National Museum of Victoria file of correspondence and reviews entitled 'Ethnology—Antiquity of Man in Australia', now held in Aboriginal Studies. Wood Jones' acceptance of geological antiquity was published in *Nature*, 19 February 1944, but he defended his earlier view that Tasmania was not necessarily peopled from the mainland.

12 See Josephine Flood, *Archaeology of the Dreamtime: The story of prehistoric Australia and its people*, Sydney, Collins, 1989, pp. 57-8; Jim Bowler, 'Edmund Dwen Gill (1908-1986)', *Australian Archaeology*, no. 24, June 1987, pp. 48-52.

13 Jim Bowler, 'Edmund Dwen Gill', has drawn attention to 'one of the residing paradoxes of the Museum' that while its first director, McCoy, tried to discredit Darwin, the next, Spencer, took evolution to the extremes of cultural determinism, and then Gill, a deputy director from 1963 to 1973, was opposed by his church for accepting Darwin as consistent with his religion.

14 Gill, 'Measuring Age by Radiocarbon', undated manuscript in Gill Papers, Museum of Victoria.

15 See, for example, Mitchell to C. P. Mountford, 9 January 1959, Mitchell Papers.

16 T. Murray and J. P. White, 'Cambridge in the Bush?', *World Archaeology*, vol. 13, no. 2, 1981, pp. 255-63.

17 D. J. Mulvaney, 'Prehistory from Antipodean Perspectives', in John Coles (ed.), *Contributions to Prehistory offered to Grahame Clark: Proceedings of the Prehistoric Society*, vol. xxxvii, part II, December 1971, p. 228.

18 Mulvaney, 'Archaeological Retrospect 9', *Antiquity*, vol. lx, 1986, p. 98.

19 Mulvaney, 'Australia before the Europeans', *Bulletin No. 15*, Institute of Archaeology, London, 1978, p. 36.

20 G. Childe to O. G. S. Crawford, 6 August 1957, quoted in Tim Murray, 'Aboriginal (Pre)History and Australian Archaeology', in Bain Attwood and John Arnold (eds), *Power, Knowledge and the Aborigines*, special edition of the *Journal of Australian Studies*, Bundoora, Vic., La Trobe University Press in association with the National Centre for Australian Studies, Monash University, 1992, p. 4.

21 For 'dark continent' see Mulvaney, 'The Stone Age of Australia', *Proceedings of the Prehistoric Society*, no. 4, New Series, vol. xxvii, 1961, p. 56. His article, 'A New Time Machine' was first published in *Twentieth Century*, vol. viii, Spring 1952, pp. 16-23, and reappears in his *Prehistory and Heritage: The Writings of John Mulvaney*, pp. 11-15.

22 Mulvaney, 'Archaeological Retrospect', p. 99.

23 For 'antediluvian' and 'fringes of lunacy', see Mulvaney, 'Prehistory from Antipodean Perspectives', pp. 229 and 240, and for an evaluation of the collectors see Mulvaney, 'The Stone Age of Australia'.

24 A number of Mulvaney's writings on the Kenyon school of 'materialists' are referred to in chapter 3, and have been gathered together in *Prehistory and Heritage*, especially section 3.

25 Julie Carter, 'S. R. Mitchell and the study of archaeology in Victoria', *The Artefact*, vol. 3, no. 1, 1978, p. 10.

26 D. J. Mulvaney, 'Obituary: D. A. Casey, M.C., F.S.A.', *The Artefact*, vol. 2, no. 4, 1977, pp. 225–7. Casey's most notable overview of his discipline was presented in 1938: 'The present state of our knowledge of the archaeology of Australia', *Proceedings of the Third Congress of Prehistorians of the Far East*, Singapore, January 1938, pp. 22–9. His papers are held by the Australian Institute for Aboriginal and Torres Strait Islander Studies.

27 Mulvaney, 'Australia before the Europeans', p. 37.

28 'Cavemen come to blows' was one newspaper headline of 1962 describing the rival claims and field-work of McCarthy and Tindale. See D. J. Mulvaney, *Frederick David McCarthy and Norman Barnett Tindale: Citation for Honorary Degrees*, Canberra, Australian National University, 1980.

29 Mitchell to L. Black, 10 January 1959, Mitchell Papers, AIATSIS.

30 See D. J. Mulvaney, 'Australian Archaeology 1929–1964: Problems and Policies', *Australian Journal of Science*, vol. 27, no. 2, August 1964, pp. 39–44.

31 D. J. Mulvaney, 'The Australian Aborigines 1606–1929: Opinion and Fieldwork, Part II', *Historical Studies*, vol. 8, 1958, p. 314. Mulvaney's estimate of the significance of Devon Downs has been challenged by David Horton who, while acknowledging its importance, argues that Devon Downs was preceded by a number of systematic and scientific excavations: Horton, 'Early Thought on Early Man in Australia', *The Artefact*, vol. 6, 1981, pp. 53–69 and *Recovering the Tracks: The Story of Australian Archaeology*, Canberra, Aboriginal Studies Press, 1991, p. 153. Mulvaney's criticisms of Tindale's culture sequences can be found in his 'The Stone Age of Australia'. In 1980 he jointly nominated the two rivals for doctorates at the Australian National University, and in 1993 published a tribute to McCarthy's work: Mulvaney, 'Sesqui-centenary to Bicentenary: Reflections on a museologist', *Records of the Australian Museum*, Supplement 17, 1993, pp. 17–24.

32 D. J. Mulvaney, *The Prehistory of Australia*, Ringwood, Vic., Penguin, 1975 (first published 1969).

33 Mulvaney, 'A New Time Machine', p. 14.

34 Older dates for Aboriginal occupation have recently been obtained through thermoluminescent dating (50–60,000 years), and by arguing that increases in soil charcoal levels indicate human-initiated burning (100–120,000 years).

35 Mulvaney, 'Prehistory from Antipodean Perspectives', p. 229.

36 Mulvaney, 'Archaeological Retrospect', p. 100.

37 John Mulvaney and Bernie Joyce, 'Archaeological and Geomorphological Investigations on Mt Moffat Station, Queensland, Australia', *Proceedings of the Prehistoric Society*, vol. 31, 1965, pp. 147–212. Kenniff Cave was also important for its wide range of stone tools and Mulvaney was able to establish an influential model of culture sequence. Kenniff Cave eventually produced evidence of occupation through 19,000 years.

38 Mulvaney, 'Archaeological Retrospect', p. 102.

39 A. L. West, 'Aboriginal Man at Kow Swamp, Northern Victoria: The Problem

of Locating the Burial Site of the KS1 Skeleton', *The Artefact*, vol. 2, no. 1, March 1977, pp. 19–30.

40 *Ibid.*, p. 26.

41 This account draws on the following sources: Kow Swamp file, Museum of Victoria (Aboriginal Studies); *Age*, 23 August 1969, *Australian*, 23 August 1969 (clippings in Kow Swamp file); Alan Thorne and Phil Macumber, 'Discoveries of Late Pleistocene Man at Kow Swamp, Australia', *Nature*, no. 238, 1972; Flood, *Archaeology of the Dreamtime*, chapters 4 and 5.

42 Bowler, 'Edmund Dwen Gill', p. 50; Jim Bowler, Rhys Jones, Harry Allen and Alan Thorne, 'Pleistocene Human Remains from Australia', *World Archaeology*, vol. 2, 1970.

43 D. J. Mulvaney, *Discovering Man's Place in Nature*, Sydney, Sydney University Press for the Australian Academy of the Humanities, 1971, p. 10; Eric Wilmott, *Australia: The Last Experiment*, 1986 ABC Boyer Lectures, Sydney, ABC, 1987.

44 Murray, 'Aboriginal (Pre)History and Australian Archaeology', p. 16.

45 Harry Lourandos, 'Aboriginal spatial organisation and population: southwestern Victoria reconsidered', *Archaeology and Physical Anthropology in Oceania*, vol. 12, no. 3, 1977, pp. 202–25; Elizabeth Williams, 'Complex hunter-gatherers: a view from Australia', *Antiquity*, vol. 61, 1987, pp. 310–21.

46 For example, Frances Dahlberg (ed.), *Woman the Gatherer*, New Haven and London, Yale University Press, 1981.

47 James Clifford, *The Predicament of Culture: Twentieth Century Ethnography, Literature, and Art*, Cambridge, MA, Harvard University Press, 1988, p. 13.

48 See chapter 3.

49 Bain Attwood, 'Writing the Aboriginal Past: An Interview with John Mulvaney', *Overland*, no. 114, May 1989, p. 8.

50 Mulvaney, 'Archaeological Retrospect', p. 101.

51 Mulvaney, 'Prehistory from Antipodean perspectives', p. 245.

52 John Mulvaney, 'Museums, Anthropologists and Indigenous Peoples', *Bulletin of the Conference of Museum Anthropologists '89*, no. 23, April 1990, p. 1.

53 Gaye Sculthorpe, 'What has Aboriginalisation meant at the Museum of Victoria?', *Bulletin of the Conference of Museum Anthropologists*, no. 22, April 1989, pp. 17–24.

54 Gaye Sculthorpe, 'Aborigines and Anthropology in the Museum', Paper presented to the Australian Anthropological Society Conference, Melbourne, 29 September–1 October, 1993 (manuscript kindly made available by the author).

55 See 'Aboriginals want skulls returned', *Hobart Mercury*, 5 March 1982; Gib Wettenhall, 'The Murray Black collection goes home', *Australian Society*, December 1988/January 1989, pp. 17–19, and D. J. Mulvaney, 'Past regained, future lost: the Kow Swamp Pleistocene burials', *Antiquity*, vol. 65, no. 246, March 1991, pp. 12–21.

56 The Advisory Committee was established in the wake of the Archaeological and Aboriginal Relics Preservation Act passed by the Victorian Parliament in June 1972. Although it protected archaeological sites and portable relics, the Act did not recognise the possibility that there may be sites of traditional significance to living Aborigines and contained no expectation that Koori communities would be consulted about sites or relics. The Act did not exist at the time of Thorne's excavations. See P. J. F. Coutts, 'Management of the Aboriginal Cultural Heritage in Victoria', in Ministry for Conservation, *'No Future without the Past': Victoria Heritage Plan Conference Discussion Papers*, Melbourne, Ministry for Conservation, September 1981, pp. 1–2, 24. David Anderson's letter to the Advisory Committee, 3 December 1973, quotes an extract of John Rossiter's letter of 23 August 1973, and can be found in the Kow Swamp file, Museum of Victoria.

57 'Administration—General—Legal Action by Mr J Berg', Museum of Victoria file, held in Aboriginal Studies. The file includes the internal memo by Ron Vanderwal, Curator, Department of Anthropology, 10 April 1984, entitled 'Background to the Proposed Loan of the Keilor and Kow Swamp Crania to the American Museum of Natural History'.

58 Sculthorpe, 'Aborigines and Anthropology in the Museum'.

59 Mulvaney, 'Past regained, future lost: the Kow Swamp Pleistocene burials', *Antiquity*, vol. 65, no. 246, March 1991, p. 12.

60 'Mungo woman back with her people', *Feedback*, publication of the Aboriginal and Torres Strait Islander Liaison Officers of the Australian Heritage Commission, vol. 1, no. 3, April 1992, pp. 6–7; discussion with Jim Bowler, 12 October 1993. The preferred resting place of the Mungo woman is still under dispute among some of the Bagundji people: 'From Spirit to Spirit', documentary film screened on SBS television, 28 October 1993.

61 R. Hope, *Report of the National Estate*, Australian Government Publishing Service, Canberra, 1974, defined heritage as 'the things we want to keep'. Isabel McBryde edited an important collection entitled *Who Owns the Past?*, Oxford University Press, Melbourne, 1985. Aspects of the reburial debate can be followed in S. Webb, 'Reburying Australian Skeletons', *Antiquity*, no. 61, 1987, pp. 292–6; Robert Layton (ed.), *Conflict in the Archaeology of Living Traditions*, London, Unwin Hyman, 1989; *Bulletin of the Conference of Museum Anthropologists* '89, no. 23, April 1990; and D. J. Mulvaney, 'Past regained, future lost'.

62 Bruce Trigger, 'Alternative Archaeologies: Nationalist, Colonialist, Imperialist', *Man*, vol. 19, 1984, pp. 355–70.

63 Mulvaney, 'Past regained, future lost', p. 19.

64 Howard Creamer, 'Aboriginal perceptions of the past: the implications for cultural resource management in Australia', in P. Gathercole and D. Lowenthal (eds), *The Politics of the Past*, London, Unwin Hyman, 1990, p. 132.

65 Mulvaney, 'Past regained, future lost', and 'Archaeological Retrospect', pp. 104, 107; R. Langford, 'Our heritage—your playground', *Australian Archaeology*, no. 16, 1983, pp. 1–6. Mulvaney was appointed a commissioner

of the new Australian Heritage Commission in 1976 and was the Australian delegate to the UNESCO Committee on World Heritage in Paris in 1977. He was also a prominent activist in defence of the world heritage area of Tasmania's south-west in the early 1980s: see chapter 11, and his 'An archaeological treasure trove may drown' (1983) and 'Towards a national consciousness' (1983), both republished in *Prehistory and Heritage*, pp. 307-11.

66 Roger Lewin, 'Extinction Threatens Australian Anthropology', *Science*, vol. 225, 27 July 1984, pp. 393-4.

67 In July and August 1984, scientists wrote to Alan Thorne and to Victorian and federal parliamentarians about the Murray Black collection. Thorne appended copies of these to a letter he sent to Robert Edwards, director of the Museum of Victoria, 17 February 1986, Museum of Victoria files (Aboriginal Studies). The letters of protest came from Belgium, Canada, France, Great Britain, Israel, Italy, the Netherlands, the People's Republic of China, South Africa, the USA and West Germany.

68 Joe Zias, Curator, Department of Antiquities and Museums, Jerusalem, Israel, to Evan Walker, Minister for Planning and Environment, 26 August 1984, and Henry M. McHenry, Professor of Anthropology, University of California, Davis, USA, to Alan Thorne, 10 July 1984, copies in Thorne to Edwards.

69 Antonio Ascenzi, Eugenia Segre Naldini and Aldo G. Segre, professors at the Instituto Italiano di Paleontologia Umana, Rome, to Alan Thorne and the Australian Embassy in Rome, 27 July 1984, copy in Thorne to Edwards: 'In the years of the centenary of Darwin's death, it sounds a dark return to obscurantism'.

70 Bernard Wood, Professor of Anatomy, Middlesex Hospital Medical School, London, to B. Chamberlain, Opposition Spokesman for Planning and Environment, 9 August 1984, copy in Thorne to Edwards.

71 John Pfeiffer, California, USA, to Alan Thorne, 20 July 1984, copy in Thorne to Edwards.

72 C. S. Churcher, Department of Zoology, University of Toronto, Canada, to Thorne, 24 August 1984, copy in Thorne to Edwards.

73 Professor M. S. Goldstein, Professor B. Arensburg, Dr E. Kobyliansky and Dr Y. Rak of the Department of Anatomy and Anthropology in the Faculty of Medicine at Tel Aviv University, Israel, to Thorne, 24 July 1984, copy in Thorne to Edwards.

74 Professor A. Leguebe, head of the subdepartment of Anthropology and Prehistory at the Institut Royal des Sciences Naturelles de Belgique, Bruxelles, Belgium, to Thorne, 21 August 1984, copy in Thorne to Edwards.

75 See Deborah Bird Rose, 'Remembrance', *Aboriginal History*, vol. 13, part 2, 1989, pp. 135-48; Chris Healy, '"We know your mob now": histories and their cultures', *Meanjin*, vol. 49, no. 3, Spring 1990, pp. 512-23.

76 Greg Dening, *Islands and Beaches: Discourse on a silent land, Marquesas 1774-1880*, Carlton, Vic., Melbourne University Press, 1980, chapter 8: 'Dispossessed'.

77 See Epilogue.

78 Mulvaney, 'Past regained, future lost', p. 19.

79 Colin Pardoe, 'Sharing the Past: Aboriginal influence on archaeological practice, a case study from New South Wales', *Aboriginal History*, vol. 14, no. 2, 1990, pp. 208–23, see p. 209.

80 Marie Hansen Fels, *Good Men and True: The Aboriginal Police of the Port Phillip District, 1837–1853*, Carlton, Vic., Melbourne University Press, 1988.

81 *Ibid.*, p. 6.

5 PAST SILENCES

1 D. H. Lawrence, *Kangaroo*, Middlesex, England, Penguin, 1986 (first published 1923), p. 87.

2 Quoted in Jocelyn Gray, 'A New Vision: Louis Buvelot's Press in the 1870s' in Ann Galbally and Margaret Plant (ed.), *Studies in Australian Art*, Department of Fine Arts, University of Melbourne, 1978, pp. 15–26.

3 John Barrell, *The Idea of Landscape and the Sense of Place, 1730–1840: An Approach to the Poetry of John Clare*, Cambridge, Cambridge University Press, 1972, p. 5.

4 Quoted in Richard Flanagan, *A Terrible Beauty: History of the Gordon River Country*, Richmond, Vic., Greenhouse, 1985, p. 66.

5 The relationship between ideas of wilderness and Aboriginal occupation (in south-west Tasmania and elsewhere) are explored in chapter 11.

6 Quoted in Flanagan, *A Terrible Beauty*, p. 67.

7 Quoted in Cassandra Pybus, *Community of Thieves*, Port Melbourne, William Heinemann Australia, 1991, p. 5.

8 Alec H. Chisholm, *The Joy of the Earth*, Sydney and London, Collins, 1969, p. 64.

9 Quoted in Paul Carter, *The Road to Botany Bay*, London, Faber & Faber Ltd, 1987, p. 266.

10 Quoted in *ibid.*, p. 147.

11 Quoted in Bernard Smith, 'The Interpretation of Australian Nature during the nineteenth century', BA(Hons) thesis, English Department, University of Sydney, 1952, p. 58.

12 Bernard Smith, *Documents on Art and Taste in Australia: The Colonial Period, 1770–1914*, Melbourne, Oxford University Press, 1975, p. 129. Here Smith is referring particularly to Barron Field, William Woolls and Marcus Clarke.

13 The extent to which these perceptions were overlapping and competing is revealed by the fact that some of Marcus Clarke's most memorable evocations of melancholy were in response to a painting by Buvelot, an artist often identified as a pioneer of the 'sunny' vision. See Marcus Clarke, 'Waterpool at Coleraine', in Smith, *Documents in Art and Taste*, pp. 133–6. For a close study of Clarke's writings on Buvelot and Chevalier, see L. T. Hergenhan, 'Marcus Clarke and the Australian Landscape', *Quadrant*, no. 60, vol. 13, no. 4, July–August 1969, pp. 31–41. On Buvelot see Jocelyn Gray, 'A New Vision: Louis Buvelot's Press in the 1870s'.

14 Mrs Aeneas Gunn, author of *We of the Never Never* (1908), an account of life on a Northern Territory station, referred to Aborigines as 'shadows'.

15 Several writers have explored this theme, and I have drawn particularly on Bernard Smith, *The Spectre of Truganini*, ABC Boyer Lectures, Sydney, ABC Radio, 1980; W. E. H. Stanner, *After the Dreaming*, ABC Boyer Lectures for 1968, Sydney, ABC Radio, 1969, and '"The history of indifference thus begins"', *Aboriginal History*, vol. 1, 1977, pp. 3-26; Don Watson, *Caledonia Australis: Scottish Highlanders on the Frontier of Australia*, Sydney, Collins, 1984, and 'The War on Australia's Frontier', *Meanjin*, vol. 41, 1982, pp. 138-46; and Henry Reynolds, 'Violence, the Aboriginals, and the Australian Historian', *Meanjin*, vol. 31, 1972, pp. 471-7, and 'Progress, Morality and the Dispossession of the Aborigines', *Meanjin*, vol. 33, 1974, pp. 306-11. See also Michael Ignatieff, 'Soviet War Memorials', *History Workshop*, no. 17, Spring 1984, pp. 157-63, which briefly explores the 'rituals of forgetting', and Greg Dening, *Islands and Beaches: Discourse on a Silent Land, Marquesas 1774-1880*, Carlton, Vic., Melbourne University Press, 1980.

16 Rolf Boldrewood, in his *Old Melbourne Memories* (ed. C. E. Sayers), Melbourne, 1969, pp. 145-6, defines 'civilised' as 'i.e., shot a few of the more troublesome individuals'. James Bonwick, in his *The Last of the Tasmanians*, London, 1869, p. 58, tells of the 'black crows'; and Don Watson, 'The War on Australia's Frontier', and Peter Gardner, 'Massacres of Aboriginals in Gippsland 1840-1850', *Historian*, vol. 27, October 1975, pp. 19-24 also refer to some of the vividly named landscapes. Alan Jennings, a local historian of Ballangeich in Victoria's western district, recounted the violent origin of local names such as 'Dead Man's Flat' and 'Ghost Gully': 'Notes on the History of Ballangeich and district' [c. 1980], Australian Manuscripts Collection, State Library of Victoria.

17 F. J. Meyrick, *Life in the Bush*, London, 1939, p. 136.

18 Gardner, 'Massacres of Aboriginals', p. 21.

19 Meyrick, *Life in the Bush*, p. 137.

20 M. F. Christie, *Aborigines in Colonial Victoria, 1835-86*, Sydney, Sydney University Press, 1979, p. 40.

21 Boldrewood's conscience is perceptively analysed by J. J. Healy in his *Literature and the Aborigine in Australia 1770-1975*, St Lucia, University of Queensland Press, 1978, pp. 51-60.

22 James Bonwick, *The Wild White Man and the Blacks of Victoria* (2nd edn), Melbourne, 1863, p. 1.

23 Alexander Sutherland, *Victoria and its Metropolis*, Melbourne, Today's Heritage, 1977 (first published 1888), vol. 1, p. 29.

24 *Ibid.*

25 Quoted in Reynolds, 'Progress, Morality and the Dispossession of the Aborigines', p. 308.

26 The quoted phrase is from Bernard Smith, *Spectre of Truganini*, p. 15. The imperial orientation of colonial historians is discussed in Jill Roe,

'Historiography in Melbourne in the Eighteen Seventies and Eighties', *Australian Literary Studies*, vol. 4, 1969-70, pp. 130-38.

27 Paul Staal, *A Foreigner Looks at Australia*, London, 1936, p. 11. Staal had worked in Sydney as a consul-general for the Netherlands.

28 *Ibid.*, p. 20.

29 The persistence of this image is demonstrated by the title of a recent history of Mortlake, in Victoria's western district: *Pastures of Peace: A Tapestry of Mortlake Shire*, Mortlake, 1985. The local historians who compiled the book devoted considerable time and effort to the telling of the story of local Aboriginal people, but found no contradiction in the book's title.

30 Quoted in Reynolds, 'Violence, the Aboriginals, and the Australian Historian', p. 471.

31 Quoted in Stanner, '"The history of indifference thus begins"', p. 23.

32 Reynolds, 'Violence, the Aboriginals, and the Australian Historian', p. 472.

33 Sutherland, *Victoria and its Metropolis*, vol. 1, p. 29.

34 John West and James Bonwick, writing in the 1850s and 1860s, are examples of this earlier phase.

35 Stanner, *After the Dreaming*, p. 13. Another Australian anthropologist of this period, A. P. Elkin, recalled reaching the age of 27 in 'complete darkness' about the Aborigines, and remembered writing an honours thesis about Australia the 'virgin continent' waiting for the 'peaceful conquest' by the British: Tigger Wise, *The Self-Made Anthropologist: A Life of A. P. Elkin*, Sydney, George Allen & Unwin, 1985, p. 28.

36 David Denholm describes the fear and tension of the frontier in *The Colonial Australians*, Ringwood, Vic., Penguin, 1979, chapter 3: 'Men Bearing Arms'.

37 Alan Frost, 'New South Wales as *terra nullius:* the British denial of Aboriginal land rights', *Historical Studies*, vol. 19, no. 77, 1981, pp. 513-23.

38 Richard Broome has shown that this definition was occasionally manipulated according to convenience, and that Aborigines could be considered 'a nation at enmity with her Majesty's subjects' when control or revenge was desired. See his chapter, 'The Struggle for Australia: Aboriginal-European warfare 1770-1930' in Michael McKernan and Margaret Brown (eds), *Australia: Two Centuries of War and Peace*, Canberra, Australian War Memorial in association with Allen & Unwin, 1988. On the tensions between the British and colonial governments about native title, see Henry Reynolds, *The Law of the Land*, [2nd edn], Ringwood, Vic., Penguin, 1992.

39 For Reynolds' analysis of the political context of Batman's treaty, see *The Law of the Land*, pp. 125-8.

40 Rolf Boldrewood, *War to the Knife* (1899), quoted in Healy, *Literature and the Aborigine in Australia*, p. 60.

41 Boldrewood, *Old Melbourne Memories*, chapter VI ('The Eumeralla War').

42 Henry Gyles Turner, *A history of the colony of Victoria* (first published 1904), Melbourne, Heritage Publications, 1973, vol. 1, p. 216. Alexander Sutherland also pursued this theme: 'Of ordinary history we have none. Battles, sieges and rebellions; the deaths of kings and the changes of

dynasties; the dungeon, the axe, and the martyr's stake . . . But in exchange we have those triumphs of peace . . . ' (*Victoria and its Metropolis*, p. 30).

43 Jan Critchett, *A 'distant field of murder': Western district frontiers 1834-1848*, Carlton, Vic., Melbourne University Press, 1990, p. 23. The Winters' swivel gun is mentioned on p. 137.

44 Quoted in *ibid*, p. 23.

45 In the following paragraph, I am drawing particularly on Jan Critchett's analysis of Victoria's western district, *A 'distant field of murder'*, chapters 3 and 6.

46 Quoted in *ibid.*, p. 41.

47 James Bonwick, *The Writing of Colonial History*, Sydney, 1895, p. 4.

48 John West, *The History of Tasmania*, Launceston, 1852, facsimile edition, 1966, vol. II, p. 54.

49 *Ibid.*, pp. 48-9.

50 Henry Melville, *The History of Van Diemen's land from the year 1824 to 1835 inclusive* (ed. George Mackaness), Sydney, 1965 (first published 1835), pp. 96-7.

51 Bob Reece, 'Aboriginal Community History: A Cautionary Tale', unpublished paper delivered to the AHA Conference, Sydney, 26 August 1982. For an evaluation of the moral simplicities of massacre history, and a review of a recent version of it, see Peter Read, 'Unearthing the past is not enough' [Review of Roger Milliss, *Waterloo Creek* (1992)], *Island*, issue no. 52, Spring 1992, pp. 49-53.

52 Henry Reynolds, *The Other Side of the Frontier*, Ringwood, Vic., Penguin, 1982, pp. 199-200. Richard Broome, in 'The Struggle for Australia', also discusses the applicability of the notion of war to frontier conflict.

53 Reynolds, *The Other Side of the Frontier*, and *Frontier: Aborigines, Settlers and Land*, Sydney, Allen & Unwin, 1987. But in a more recent work, *With the White People*, Ringwood, Vic., Penguin, 1990, Reynolds has studied cross-cultural collaboration on a less easily defined 'frontier'.

54 'No sound of mourning moans from muffled bell,
       No solemn cannon booms a dead king's knell'
These were the opening lines of a poem entitled 'King Billy of Ballarat' published in the *Ballarat Star*, 3 October 1896. For more on King Billy, see chapter 9.

55 For example, *Ballarat Star*, 24 September 1896. For some further newspaper accounts of the deaths of 'the last of the tribe', see *Ballarat Star*, 23 September 1896, 28 September 1896, 30 September 1896; *Geelong Advertiser*, 12 November 1885, 14 November 1885, 10 August 1912, 12 August 1912; *Town and Country Journal*, 7 August 1886.

56 *Swan Hill Guardian*, 22 September 1930.

57 Jan Penney, 'Queen Aggie: The Last of Her Tribe', in Marilyn Lake and Farley Kelly (eds), *Double Time: Women in Victoria—150 Years*, Ringwood, Vic., Penguin, 1984, pp. 97-103, see p. 101.

58 One such monument erected by James Dawson in anger at settler violence

and neglect (see below) was pictured and described in Alexander Sutherland's *Victoria and its Metropolis*, p. 30, as a 'tribute' to an 'ill-fated race' destined to disappear.

59 Margaret Maynard and Helen Topliss describe the late nineteenth-century artistic 'projections of melancholy' in their essays in Ian and Tamsin Donaldson, (eds), *Seeing the First Australians*, Sydney, George Allen & Unwin, 1985.

60 For information on Dawson and his monument I have drawn on the following: James Dawson, Scrapbook (microfilm copy), La Trobe Collection, State Library of Victoria; *Town and Country Journal*, 7 August 1886; *Australasian Sketcher*, 7 April 1886; *Camperdown Chronicle*, 15 November 1884, 23 November 1887, 21 April 1900, 24 April 1900; *Argus*, 9 September 1876; *Geelong Advertiser*, 8 December 1979. See also Jan Critchett, 'Introduction' to facsimile edition of James Dawson, *Australian Aborigines* (first published 1881), Canberra, Australian Institute of Aboriginal Studies, 1981, and Henry Reynolds, *Frontier*, pp. 163-4.

61 Isabella Park Dawson, 'The Language of the Aborigines', *The Australasian*, 19 March 1870.

62 *Town and Country Journal*, 7 August 1886.

63 James Dawson, Scrapbook (microfilm copy), pp. 147, 156, 164-5; Peter Corris, 'James Dawson (1806-1900)', in *Australian Dictionary of Biography*, vol. 4. pp. 35-6. The Camperdown monument and several other such memorials are pictured in Aldo Massola, *Journey to Aboriginal Victoria*, Adelaide, Rigby, 1969.

64 L. Boyer to A. G. Stephens, 6 June 1903, quoted in Peter Corris, *Aborigines and Europeans in Western Victoria*, Canberra, Australian Institute of Aboriginal Studies, 1968, p. 18.

65 *Town and Country Journal*, 7 August 1886; *Australasian Sketcher*, 7 April 1886.

66 James Bonwick, *The Last of the Tasmanians*, chapter 3: 'Cruelties to the Blacks'.

67 E. E. Pescott, *James Bonwick, A Writer of School Books and Histories, with a bibliography of his writings*, Melbourne, 1939, p. 26.

68 See Chilla Bulbeck, *The Stone Laurel: Race, Gender and Class in Australian Memorials*, Cultural Policy Studies: Occasional Paper No. 5, Brisbane, Griffith University, 1988, and 'Aborigines, memorials and the history of the frontier', *Australian Historical Studies*, vol. 24, no. 96, April 1991, pp. 168-78; also Duncan Graham, 'The whole truth or monument to error', *Age*, 26 November 1988, and Bruce Scates, 'A Monument to Murder: Celebrating the Conquest of Aboriginal Australia', in Lenore Layman and Tom Stannage (eds), *Celebrations in Western Australian History (volume 10 of Studies in Western Australian History)*, Nedlands, University of Western Australia, 1989, pp. 21-31.

69 F. T. Macartney, 'Literature and the Aboriginals', in his *Australian Literary Essays*, Sydney, 1957, pp. 112-13.

70 An edited version of his 1985 Australia Day address, in which he defended the reputation of Governor Arthur Phillip, was published as 'A day to remember realities of history', *Age*, 28 January 1985, p. 11.

71 Francis West, 'Multi-cultural Wisdom for the Intellectual Trendies', *Age*, 27 September, 1980. Reactions, in 1964, to a proposed Myall Creek memorial are quoted in R. H. W. Reece, 'The Aborigines in Australian Historiography', in John Moses (ed.), *Historical Disciplines and Culture in Australasia*, St Lucia, University of Queensland Press, 1979, p. 262.

72 'Find May Change Island's History', *Age*, 1 February 1979. The new evidence—including 'stone choppers and pebble tools'—was discovered by chance during a weekend visit to the island.

73 'No glory for first settlers: Latter day Hentys Settle for a Picnic', *Age*, 8 November 1984.

74 Bernard Barrett, 'Victoria's 40,000th Anniversary', *Agora*, vol. 29, 1984, pp. 21–3.

75 Letter from the RHSV Research and Information Committee to the History and Heritage Committee, 10 October, 1984, Royal Historical Society of Victoria files. The wording on a number of plaques was altered as a result of this and other submissions.

76 L. A. Meredith, *Nine Years in Van Diemen's Land*, London, 1852, vol. 1, p. 36, quoted in Henry Reynolds, '"That Hated Stain": The Aftermath of Transportation in Tasmania', *Historical Studies*, vol. 14, 1969, p. 26; K. S. Inglis, *The Australian Colonists: An exploration of social history, 1788–1870*, Carlton, Vic., Melbourne University Press, 1974, pp. 13–15.

77 J. B. Hirst, 'The Pioneer Legend', *Historical Studies*, vol. 18, 1978, pp. 316–37.

78 K. S. Inglis, *The Rehearsal: Australians at War in the Sudan, 1885*, Adelaide, Rigby, 1985, p. 153.

79 Alexandra Hasluck, *Unwilling Emigrants*, 1959, p. xiii, quoted in Stuart Macintyre, 'The writing of Australian history', in D. H. Borchardt and Victor Crittenden, *Australians: A Guide to Australian History Sources*, Sydney, Fairfax, Syme & Weldon, 1987, p. 18.

80 Bonwick, *The Writing of Colonial History*, p. 11.

81 James Bonwick, *An Octogenarian's Reminiscences*, London, 1903, p. 239, quoted in Macintyre, 'The writing of Australian history', p. 17.

82 Kay Daniels, 'Cults of Nature, Cults of History', *Island*, issue 16, Spring 1983, p. 3.

83 Richard Flanagan, *A Terrible Beauty*, p. 74.

84 Reynolds, '"That Hated Stain"', p. 23.

85 Peter Bolger, *Hobart Town*, Canberra, ANU Press, 1973, p. vii.

86 Douglas Cole, '"The Crimson Thread of Kinship": Ethnic Ideas in Australia, 1870–1914', *Historical Studies*, vol. 14, 1971, pp. 511–25.

87 James Bonwick, *Western Victoria; its Geography, Geology, and Social Condition. The Narrative of an Educational Tour in 1857*, Geelong, Thomas Brown, 1858, pp. 103–4.

88 J. B. Hirst, *Convict Society and its Enemies*, Sydney, George Allen & Unwin, 1983.

89 Brian Elliott, *Marcus Clarke*, Oxford, Clarendon Press, 1958, p. 149.

90 Hirst, *Convict Society*, pp. 193-5, 213, 216.

91 James Urry, '"Savage Sportsmen"', in Ian and Tamsin Donaldson (eds), *Seeing the First Australians*, pp. 51-67, suggests an early intimacy between Aborigines and Europeans before the expansion of the frontier.

92 Inglis, *The Australian Colonists, The Rehearsal*, and 'The Anzac Tradition', *Meanjin*, vol. 24, 1965, pp. 25-44.

93 Quoted in W. F. Mandle, 'Games People Played: Cricket and Football in England and Victoria in the late Nineteenth Century', *Historical Studies*, vol. 15, 1973, pp. 511-35.

94 Inglis, *The Rehearsal*, pp. 83-5, 153.

95 Staal, *A Foreigner Looks at Australia*, pp. 25-6.

96 *Australia: The Quiet Continent* was the title of a history written by Douglas Pike (London, Cambridge University Press, 1970; first edition 1962).

97 In D. H. Lawrence's *Kangaroo* (1923), with which this chapter began, the visiting Englishman, Somers, opined: 'It always seems to me that somebody will have to water Australia with their blood before it's a real man's country. The soil, the very plants seem to be waiting for it' (p. 88).

98 Quoted in Geoffrey Serle, *The Golden Age*, Carlton, Vic., Melbourne University Press, 1968, p. 170.

99 Inglis, *The Rehearsal*, p. 27.

100 Peter Board, 'History and Australian History', address given at the Annual Meeting of the Australian Historical Society, 22 February 1916, *Australian Historical Society Journal and Proceedings*, III, 1915-17, p. 293.

101 Donald Macdonald, 'From a Western Hill-Top', in *Gum Boughs and Wattle Bloom, gathered on Australian Hills and Plains*, London, Cassell & Co., 1887, pp. 36-48; Hugh Anderson, 'Donald Alaster Macdonald (1859?-1932)', in *Australian Dictionary of Biography*, vol. 10, p. 249.

102 Macdonald comments on the Norfolk Island pine and its associations in his essay on 'A Melbourne Garden' in *Gum Boughs*, p. 59.

103 Elaine Whittle, 'Journalists' Child', Manuscripts Collection, Royal Historical Society of Victoria, pp. 4-5.

104 Macdonald, 'Australia To-Day: An Introductory Appreciation', *Australia To-Day*, 15 December 1905, p. 15.

105 Macdonald, *Gum Boughs*, pp. 39, 41, 43.

6 'THE NATURAL HISTORY OF MELBOURNE'

1 Richard Mabey, *Gilbert White: A Biography of the Author of 'The Natural History of Selborne'*, London, Century Hutchinson Ltd, 1986, p. 2.

2 *Ibid.*

3 Cited in Donald Worster, *Nature's Economy: A History of Ecological Ideas*, Cambridge, Cambridge University Press, 1985, p. 15.

4 See Martin J. Wiener, *English Culture and the Decline of the Industrial Spirit, 1850-1980*, Cambridge, Cambridge University Press, 1982, pp. 41-80.

5 Mabey, *Gilbert White*, pp. 8, 10 and throughout.

6 *Ibid.*, pp. 47, 112-13.

7 All quotations in this section are from Donald Macdonald, 'Village and Farm', in his collection of essays, *Gum Boughs and Wattle Bloom, Gathered on Australian Hills and Plains*, London, Cassell & Co., 1887, pp. 132-58.

8 Biographical details were gleaned from the following sources: Elaine Whittle (Macdonald), 'Journalists' Child', unpublished manuscript, written c. 1944, Box 53/1, Royal Historical Society of Victoria Archive (kindly brought to my attention by Patricia Barton); 'Men who made the *Argus* and the *Australasian*' and 'Historical Records of the *Argus* and the *Australasian*', MS 10727, Australian Manuscripts Collection, State Library of Victoria; *Labor Call*, 30 August 1923; obituaries and tributes in the *Argus*, 24, 26 November 1932, the *Age*, 24 November 1932, the *Sydney Morning Herald*, 3 December 1932, and *Newspaper News*, 1 December 1932; and Hugh Anderson, 'Donald Alaster Macdonald (1859?-1932)', in *Australian Dictionary of Biography*, vol. 10, p. 249.

9 The editor, David Watterston, was quoted in R. H. Croll, *I Recall: Collections and Recollections*, Melbourne, Robertson and Mullens, 1939, p. 121.

10 E. S. Cunningham, 'Donald Macdonald: An Appreciation', *Newspaper News*, 1 December 1932.

11 Charles Barrett, 'One Of Our Pals: Donald Macdonald as Boy and Man', *Pals*, 28 August 1920, p. 22.

12 Richard Jefferies, *The Life of the Fields*, London, Chatto & Windus, 1912 (first published 1884), p. 114.

13 See Bernard Smith, 'The Interpretation of Australian Nature during the Nineteenth Century', BA(Hons) thesis, University of Sydney, 1952 (kindly lent by the author). The Melbourne office-workers who dominated the Field Naturalists' Club of Victoria (formed in 1880) have been studied by Michael Evans in 'Taking to the Bush: Australian Landscape as a Condition of Practice for the Field Naturalists' Club of Victoria, 1880-1900', BA(Hons) thesis, University of Melbourne, 1982.

14 A column by Macdonald called 'Nature Lovers' Letters' first appeared in the *Argus* on 8 October 1904 and became 'Nature Notes and Queries' from 25 November 1904. His 'Notes for Boys' column began on 23 February 1909.

15 Margaret Plant has written about the imagery of tents in 'Visual Victoria: Waterfalls, Tents and Meat Pies', in A. G. L. Shaw (ed.), *Victoria's Heritage*, Sydney, Allen & Unwin, 1986, pp. 109-43.

16 Charles Barrett, *Koonwarra: A Naturalist's Adventures in Australia*, London, Oxford University Press, 1939, p. 35.

17 Interview with Mrs Beatrice Campbell (née Barrett), 1 May 1986.

18 'The Woodlanders' [Charles Barrett], 'Our Bush Hut on Olinda', Parts 1-5, *The New Idea: A Woman's Home Journal for Australasia*, October, November, December 1905, January, February 1906. The quote is from the issue of 6 October 1905, p. 354.

19 Thomas Hardy's novel, *The Woodlanders*, was published in 1887.

20 Biographical details about Barrett were gathered from his own published writings, many of which are reminiscent, and from the following sources:

Charles Barrett Papers, Australian Manuscripts Collection, State Library of Victoria; *Herald House News*, July 1939, p. 7, and August 1939, p. 3; *Herald*, 20 January 1959, p. 3; F. S. Colliver, 'Charles Leslie Barrett . . . ', *Victorian Naturalist*, vol. 76, 1959-60; Obituary by C. E. Bryant, *The Emu*, vol. 59, part 3, August 1959, pp. 226-7; and A. H. Chisholm, 'Charles Leslie Barrett (1879-1959)', in *Australian Dictionary of Biography*, vol. 7, p. 185.

21 Charles Barrett, *Australia My Country*, Melbourne, Oxford University Press, 1941, p. 69. Barrett's reference to 'the dreaming towers of Oxford' suggests another of Thomas Hardy's novels, *Jude The Obscure* (1896).

22 Charles Barrett, *The Bunyip and Other Mythical Monsters and Legends*, Melbourne, Reed & Harris [c. 1946].

23 For examples of this thinking, see Charles Barrett, 'The Blackfellow in Books' in Barrett (ed.), *Across the Years: The Lure of Early Australian Books*, Melbourne, N. H. Seward Pty Ltd, 1948, pp. 99-110, and his chapter entitled 'Hodman of Science' in his *On the Wallaby: Quest and Adventure in Many Lands*, Melbourne, Robertson & Mullens, 1942, pp. 20-35.

24 'The Woodlanders' [Charles Barrett], 'Our Bush Hut on Olinda', *New Idea*, 6 October 1905, p. 355.

25 Barrett, *Australia My Country*, p. 35.

26 Cited in Barrett, *Koonwarra*, p. 34.

27 *Ibid.*, p. 37.

28 For a brief history of Australian bird photography, see Peter Slater, *Masterpieces of Australian Bird Photography*, Adelaide, Rigby, 1980, pp. 36-47.

29 Preface to Charles Barrett, *From Range to Sea: A Bird Lover's Ways*, Melbourne, T. C. Lothian, 1907.

30 Barrett, *From Range to Sea*, p. 34.

31 *Ibid.*, pp. 21, 25, 34.

32 The first restrictions on egg collecting during RAOU camps were enforced in 1923, and it was finally prohibited in 1933: D. L. Serventy, 'A Historical Background of Ornithology with special reference to Australia', *The Emu*, vol. 72, part 2, April 1972, p. 48.

33 *Ibid.*

34 Barrett, *Koonwarra*, p. 36.

35 David Elliston Allen, *The Naturalist in Britain: A Social History*, London, Allen Lane, 1976, pp. 152-3.

36 *Ibid.*, p. 233 and plate 10.

37 F. I. Norman and A. D. Young, ' "Short-Sighted and Doubly Short-Sighted are They . . . ": Game Laws of Victoria, 1858-1958', *Journal of Australian Studies*, no. 7, November 1980, pp. 2-24.

38 See chapter 1 for an introduction to Wheelwright. Wheelwright himself knew and liked *Selborne*: H. W. Wheelwright, *Bush Wanderings of a Naturalist, or Notes on the Field Sports and Fauna of Australia Felix*, London, Routledge, Warne & Routledge, 1861, p. 177.

39 When Chisholm attended a meeting of the Bird Observers Club in the early 1900s, he 'began by confessing that [his] early interest in birds was

accompanied by a shanghai'. Macdonald, who was presiding, 'put [him] at ease immediately. "Don't worry, lad", he laughed, "that's the way we all began!"'. Alec Chisholm, *The Joy of the Earth*, Sydney, Collins, 1969, p. 162.

40 Barrett, *From Range to Sea*, p. 31.

41 Hudson is quoted in P. Morton, *The Vital Science: Biology and the Literary Imagination, 1860-1900*, London, George Allen & Unwin, 1984, pp. 70-5; 'The Woodlanders', *New Idea*, 6 January 1906, pp. 666-70.

42 Macdonald, *Gum Boughs*, p. 185. The sparrow's popular name, 'spriggy', memorialised a member of the Acclimatisation Society of Victoria, George Sprigg, who was credited with the first release of sparrows near Melbourne: Chisholm, *Joy of the Earth*, p. 103.

43 Macdonald, *Gum Boughs*, pp. 214-15

44 D. J. Mulvaney and J. H. Calaby, *'So Much That Is New': Baldwin Spencer 1860-1929, A Biography*, Carlton, Vic., Melbourne University Press, 1985, p. 94.

45 *Victorian Naturalist*, special historical issues, vol. 97, no. 3, 1980, and vol. 101, no. 1, 1984.

46 C. Hartley Grattan, 'Notes on Australian Cultural History', *Meanjin*, vol. 33, 1974, p. 238.

47 Macdonald, for instance, considered coastal middens 'worthy the attention of an Australian antiquarian', *Gum Boughs*, p. 255.

48 Macdonald, *Gum Boughs*, pp. 34, 68, 91.

49 Macdonald to Jean Galbraith, 14 January 1932, in Jean Galbraith Papers, Australian Manuscripts Collection, State Library of Victoria.

50 Macdonald, *Gum Boughs*, p. 160.

51 Barron Field, *Geographical Memoirs on New South Wales*, 1825, extract reproduced in Bernard Smith, *Documents on Art and Taste in Australia: The Colonial Period, 1788-1914*, Melbourne, Oxford University Press, 1975, pp. 34-8, see p. 36.

52 Mary Fullerton, *Bark House Days*, Carlton, Vic., Melbourne University Press, 1964 (1st edn. 1921), p. 65. Louisa Atkinson had written in the 1860s of the need for popular names for native flowers. A selection of her writings for the *Sydney Morning Herald* of the 1860s has been republished as *A Voice from the Country*, (introduced by Victor Crittenden), Canberra, Mulini Press, 1978, see p. 5.

53 Barrett, *From Range to Sea*, p. 18.

54 Quoted in Chisholm, *Joy of the Earth*, p. 167.

55 Between August 1918 and October 1922, Chisholm conducted a widely read weekly natural history column in the Brisbane *Daily Mail* and, from 1922 to 1927, a similar column in the Sydney *Daily Telegraph*. He was also inspired by Macdonald's example to form a Boys' Field Club in Sydney. Crosbie Morrison shared some of the writing of Macdonald's 'Nature Notes and Queries' column from the late 1920s and continued it for a short time after his death until Chisholm took over in 1933. When Chisholm became editor of the *Argus* in 1937, Morrison resumed the column. *Argus*, 9 July 1937, 3 July 1954.

56 A. H. Chisholm, *Mateship with Birds*, Melbourne, Whitcombe & Tombs, 1922, pp. 4, 155–64. I am grateful to Michael Evans for drawing my attention to this book, and for his stimulating talk on the 'Victorian Scientific Community' to the University of Melbourne Department of History in September 1985.

57 Donald Macdonald, *How We Kept the Flag Flying: The Siege of Ladysmith through Australian Eyes*, London, Ward, Lock and Co, 1900.

58 Macdonald, 'Anzacs at War: Three Phases', *Australia To-Day 1917*, 11 November 1916, p. 75. Macdonald is quoting 'an envious German critic'.

59 Graeme Davison, 'The City-Bred Child and Urban Reform in Melbourne 1900–1940', in Peter Williams (ed.), *Social Process and the City*, Sydney, George Allen & Unwin, 1983, pp. 143–74.

60 Notes in *ADB* file on Macdonald, *Australian Dictionary of Biography* office, Research School of Social Sciences, Australian National University, Canberra.

61 *Argus*, 23 February 1909.

62 K. S. Inglis, *C. E. W. Bean: Australian Historian*, John Murtagh Macrossan Lecture, St Lucia, University of Queensland Press, 1970. Davison, 'The City-Bred Child and Urban Reform', shows how Bean was developing his ideas from early in the century.

63 Barrett, *On the Wallaby*, p. 60.

64 Barrett, *Koonwarra*, pp. 72–3; Chisholm, 'Charles Leslie Barrett'.

65 Advertising brochure in Barrett Papers.

66 Review in the *Times Literary Supplement* (n.d.), clipping, Barrett Papers.

67 Interview with Mrs Campbell.

68 Barrett Papers.

69 Paul Fussell, *The Great War and Modern Memory*, London, Oxford University Press, 1975, pp. 231, 235.

70 *Everylady's Journal* [formerly the *New Idea*], 6 April 1917, pp. 202–3.

71 *Pals*, 28 August 1920.

72 See George Orwell's essay, 'Boys' Weeklies' (1939), and Frank Richards' reply, both published in Sonia Orwell and Ian Angus (eds), *The Collected Essays, Journalism and Letters of George Orwell*, vol. 1, Harmondsworth, Middlesex, Penguin, 1970, pp. 505–40.

73 Richard White, *Inventing Australia: Images and Identity 1688–1980*, Sydney, George Allen & Unwin, 1981, pp. 77–85, 101–4, 125–30.

74 Whittle, 'Journalists' Child', p. 211.

75 Macdonald, *Baden-Powell, Soldier and Scout; also a Synopsis of his Lectures during the Tour of Australia and New Zealand*, Melbourne, 1912.

76 Donald Macdonald, *The Bush Boy's Book*, Sydney, Cornstalk Publishing Company, 1928 (3rd edn; 1st edn, 1911), preface.

77 Macdonald to Jean Galbraith, 12 February 1932, Galbraith Papers.

78 Marilyn Lake, 'The Politics of Respectability: Identifying the Masculinist Context', *Historical Studies*, vol. 22, 1986, pp. 116–31.

79 Graeme Davison, *The Rise and Fall of Marvellous Melbourne*, Carlton, Vic., Melbourne University Press, 1978, pp. 138–40.

80 Sarah Stephen, 'Marriage and the Family in Bohemian Melbourne 1890-1914', *Australia 1888 Bulletin*, no. 9, 1982, pp. 20-8.

81 See, for example, Barrett, *On the Wallaby*, pp. 78, 116, and *Wanderer's Rest*, London, Cassell & Co., 1946, p. 55.

82 The 'Glimpses of Nature' series immediately preceded that of 'The Woodlanders'.

83 Whittle, 'Journalists' Child'.

84 A. A. Wheeler, 'Women's Clubs', in F. Fraser and N. Palmer (eds), *Centenary Gift Book*, Melbourne, Robertson & Mullens for the Women's Centenary Council, 1934, pp. 138-9. I owe this reference to Elizabeth Morrison.

85 'Life among the Aborigines: Mrs C Barrett Samples Native Food in NT', *Herald*, 8 January 1940.

86 In 1903, the FNCV took its members on the club's first official excursion to Mt Buffalo. Railway staff, when checking the compartments reserved for field naturalists, were surprised to find that half the party of 22 were women. Women were excluded from both Melbourne walking clubs of this period. See Linden Gillbank, 'How the Alps Started to Lose Their Grasslands', draft report for the Historic Places Section, Department of Conservation and Environment, Victoria, 1989.

87 K. S. Inglis, 'Men, Women, and War Memorials: Anzac Australia', *Daedalus*, vol. 116, 1987, pp. 35-59.

88 For this summary I have drawn on Donald Worster, *Nature's Economy: A History of Ecological Ideas*, Cambridge, Cambridge University Press, 1985 (first edition 1977), esp. pp. 17-21, and Michael Roe, *Nine Australian Progressives: Vitalism in Bourgeois Social Thought 1890-1960*, St Lucia, University of Queensland Press, 1984.

89 Roe, *Nine Australian Progressives*, pp. 57-88.

90 Quoted in Chisholm, *Mateship with Bird*s, p. 82.

91 Frank Tate, 'Education in Australia', *Australia To-Day*, 1 November 1910, p. 103.

92 Macdonald, 'Bush Nursing', in *Australian Bush Nursing Scheme*, Melbourne, Atlas Press, 1910.

93 'Kangaroos and Their Kin: Australia's National Animals in the Wilds and Captivity', *Bulletin: New York Zoological Society*, vol. 34, 1931.

94 Allen, *The Naturalist in Britain*, pp. 227, 247.

95 See, for example, Croll, *I Recall*, p. 84.

96 Two examples of this tradition are William Freame, *An Amateur Tramp: Rambles with Pen and Camera*, Parramatta, n.d., and Edgar C. Harris, *A Spring Walk: Windsor to Bulli*, Sydney, privately published, 1922 (brought to my attention by Bernard Smith).

97 Bernard Smith, 'On Perceiving the Australian Suburb', in his *The Antipodean Manifesto*, Melbourne, Oxford University Press, 1975, p. 90.

98 William Hardy Wilson, *Old Colonial Architecture in New South Wales and Tasmania*, Sydney, published by the author at Union House, 1924.

99 *Ibid.*, pp. 2-6.

100 On these issues, see Graeme Davison, 'The meanings of "heritage"', in Davison and Chris McConville (eds), *A Heritage Handbook*, Sydney, Allen & Unwin, 1991, pp. 1-13; and Smith, 'On Perceiving the Australian Suburb', pp. 91-4.

101 J. McRae (then director of Education, Victoria), foreword to Barrett, *Gems of the Bush* (the fifth *Sun* Nature Book), Melbourne, n.d. [c. 1934].

102 Charles Barrett, *Heritage of Stone* (illustrated by Chas H. Crampton), 2nd edn, Melbourne, Lothian, 1949, (1st edn 1945), pp. 7-8.

103 Barrett, *On the Wallaby*, pp. 73, 85, 88, 148, 190ff.

104 Barrett's clippings file in the *Herald* office is testimony to his persistent coverage (from the late 1920s) of Aboriginal affairs, particularly archaeology. Some of his opinions were brought together in Charles Barrett, *Blackfellows: the Story of Australia's Native Race*, London, Cassell & Co., 1942.

105 Barrett, *On the Wallaby*, pp. 48-51; Barrett, 'Ancient Man in Australia: Problems for Prehistorians', *Herald*, 9 December 1937.

106 Barrett and A. S. Kenyon, *Australian Aboriginal Art*, Melbourne, Brown Prior Anderson for the Trustees of the Museum of Victoria, 1947 (first published 1929), p. 12; Barrett and A. S. Kenyon, *Blackfellows of Australia*, Melbourne, n.d., p. 35; Barrett, chapter on 'Aboriginal Art and Artists', in *Blackfellows*.

107 See chapter 3.

108 Croll, *I Recall*; Mulvaney and Calaby, '*So Much That Is New*', p. 358.

109 Croll, *I Recall*, p. 63. J. S. MacDonald's famous praise of Streeton ('we can yet be the elect of the world, the last of the pastoralists, the thoroughbred Aryans in all their nobility') is quoted in Geoffrey Serle, 'James Stuart MacDonald (1878-1952)', *Australian Dictionary of Biography*, vol. 10, pp. 251-2.

110 Flora Eldershaw, 'The Landscape Writers', *Meanjin*, vol. 11, 1952, p. 219.

111 Libby Robin, 'Visions of Nature: Wild Life 1938-1954', *Victorian Naturalist*, vol. 102, 1985, pp. 153-61.

112 *Walkabout*, 1 April 1941, p. 49.

113 *Bulletin*, 5 May 1943.

114 *Herald* clippings file, under 'Barrett', n.d.

115 Interview with Mrs Campbell.

116 David Fleay to R. H. Croll, 24 April 1946, Croll Papers, Australian Manuscripts Collection, State Library of Victoria. Crosbie Morrison, on hearing of Barrett's latest elderly exploit, told Croll: 'I'm getting his obituary ready. Silly old ass!' (letter, 25 March 1946, Croll Papers).

117 Macdonald, *From a Bush Hut*, Melbourne, 1942, and *Wanderer's Rest*.

118 Their letters were published in the *Argus*, 29, 30 November 1932. They also pursued the issue in private correspondence (see Croll Papers), and lent their support to Elaine Whittle's publication of a collection of her late father's essays, *The Brooks of Morning: Nature and Reflective Essays*, Sydney, Angus & Robertson, 1933. 'I always wished I knew that man', Palmer confided to Mrs Croll: Palmer to Mrs R. H. Croll, 29 July 1932, Croll Papers.

119 *Argus*, 26 November 1932, p. 22; 2 December 1932, p. 7.
120 'Wood-Wind and Wattle Breath', *Socialist*, 11 January 1908.

7 LAND RITES

1 In order to draw out American and Australian parallels, I have here paraphrased Roderick Nash's analysis of American thought in the inter-war period in his *The Nervous Generation: American Thought, 1917-1930*, Chicago, Rand McNally College Publishing Company, 1970, pp. 77-90.
2 Graeme Davison, 'The Use and Abuse of Australian History', *Australian Historical Studies*, vol. 23, no. 91, October 1988, p. 56.
3 John Rickard, *Australia: A Cultural History*, Melbourne, Longman Cheshire, 1988, p. 192.
4 Diane E. Barwick, 'A Little More Than Kin: Regional affiliation and group identity among Aboriginal migrants in Melbourne', PhD thesis, Department of Anthropology and Sociology, Australian National University, 1963; Bain Attwood, *The Making of the Aborigines*, Sydney, Allen & Unwin, 1989.
5 Heather Goodall addresses these questions in 'Land in Our Own Country: The Aboriginal Land Rights Movement in South-Eastern Australia, 1860 to 1914', *Aboriginal History*, vol. 14, part 1, 1990, pp. 1-24.
6 Henry Reynolds, *The Law of the Land*, 2nd edn, Ringwood, Penguin, 1992, p. 139.
7 *Ibid.*, p. 140.
8 *Ibid.*, chapter VI.
9 This was a theme explored in part one. Terence Ranger also makes this point about the English in Africa in 'Taking hold of the land: Holy places and pilgrimages in twentieth century Zimbabwe', *Past and Present*, no. 117, November 1987, p. 158. On the 'informed regard for extraordinary stone formations' that developed in the eighteenth century, see Barbara Maria Stafford, *Voyage into Substance: Art, Science, Nature, and the Illustrated Travel Account, 1760-1840*, Cambridge, MA, and London, MIT Press, 1984, chapter 2: 'The Natural Masterpiece'.
10 David Lowenthal observed this also of Americans. See his 'The Place of the Past in the American Landscape', in David Lowenthal and Martyn J. Bowden (eds), *Geographies of the Mind*, New York, Oxford University Press, 1976, pp. 102-4.
11 Tom Griffiths, with assistance from Alan Platt (eds), *The Life and Adventures of Edward Snell*, Sydney, Angus & Robertson and The Library Council of Victoria, 1988, p. 79.
12 Alfred Runte, *National Parks: The American Experience*, Lincoln and London, University of Nebraska Press, 2nd edn, 1987, pp. xvi-xvii.
13 Quoted in Runte, *National Parks*, pp. 21-2; see also p. 71.
14 Marcus Clarke, 'Waterpool near Coleraine' (1874), in Bernard Smith (ed.), *Documents on Art and Taste in Australia*, Melbourne, Oxford University Press, 1975, pp. 133-6.

15 Nicholas Caire, 'Notes on the giant trees of Victoria', *The Victorian Naturalist*, vol. 21, no. 9, January 1905, pp. 122-8. For more about the natural and cultural history of these tall trees, the mountain ash, see Tom Griffiths, *Secrets of the forest: Discovering history in Melbourne's Ash Range*, Sydney, Allen & Unwin, 1992, especially chapter 1 and p. 143.

16 'Our Tallest Tree: A Challenge from California', by Prof Osborne [*sic*], *Argus*, 30 July 1921, clipping in [Kershaw?] Scrapbook, Museum of Victoria. For Gregory's views, see chapter 3.

17 For an analysis of the historic town movement, see chapter 10. Michael Sharland's early celebration of Tasmania's built heritage was entitled *Stones of a Century* (1952).

18 *Descriptive Souvenir of Past and Present Picturesque Maldon*, Maldon, The Tarrangower Times, no date. The other photos included three memorials, eleven flowers, and a selection of mines, civic features and streetscapes. Beechworth Progress Association, *Illustrated Guide to Beechworth and Vicinity*, Beechworth, James Ingram and Son, 1892.

19 See chapter 10.

20 Crosbie Morrison, 'Cloud picture and rock castles', Wild Life Talk No. 6, recorded 22 July 1943, Morrison Papers, Australian Science Archives Project, University of Melbourne.

21 Richard White, *Inventing Australia*, Sydney, George Allen & Unwin, 1981, pp. 94-5. It was the Dawn and Dusk Club.

22 Edgar C. Harris, *A Spring Walk: Windsor to Bulli*, Sydney, privately printed, 1922, pp. 19-20.

23 G. N. Hyam, a former president of the club, was also very active in the formation and promotion of the council.

24 *Argus* report of the meeting, 13 September 1936, clipping in Mitchell Papers.

25 G. N. Hyam, 'National Monuments', *Victorian Naturalist*, vol. liii, no. 5, 5 September 1936, pp. 81-3.

26 *Herald*, 10 January 1931, clipping in Mitchell Papers.

27 'Our Monuments', newspaper clipping, n.d., Mitchell Papers.

28 'National Monuments in Australia should be preserved—says scientist', unidentified clipping from a Queensland newspaper, Mitchell Papers; 'Historic Australian Tree', *Argus*, 13 April, 1928.

29 Anon., *Major Mitchell's Memorial Tree Presented to Town of Hamilton by Messrs Murray, of 'Brie Brie', Glenthompson*, Hamilton, Hamilton Spectator, 1909.

30 Sally Symonds, *Healesville: History in the Hills*, Lilydale, Vic., Pioneer Design Studio Pty Ltd, 1982, p. 106.

31 *Ararat Advertiser*, 12 July 1930.

32 Newspaper clipping, n.d., Mitchell Papers.

33 Newspaper clipping, n.d., Mitchell Papers.

34 'Tourist Camp in Carnarvons Suggested', newspaper clipping, n.d., Mitchell Papers.

35 *Herald*, 17 February 1921 ('Save Our Fauna').

36 'Project Supported—Park at Dog Rocks—Public Interest Aroused', 6 September 1937, unidentified newspaper clipping, Mitchell Papers.

37 Frank Tate, 'Introduction' to J. A. Leach, *An Australian Bird Book: A Pocket Book for Field Use*, Melbourne, Whitcombe & Tombs, 1911, pp. 1-6, see p. 3.

38 James Barrett (ed.), *Save Australia: A Plea for the Right Use of our Flora and Fauna*, Melbourne, Macmillan & Co., 1925.

39 Tim Bonyhady, 'A Different Streeton', *Art Monthly Australia*, no. 61, July 1993, pp. 8-12, see p. 9.

40 The poster is reproduced in Griffiths, *Secrets of the Forest*, p. 54.

41 Bonyhady, 'A Different Streeton', p. 11. The spelling is Streeton's.

42 See chapter 5.

43 Ken Inglis, *The Australian Colonists: An exploration of social history, 1788-1870*, Carlton, Vic., Melbourne University Press, 1974, pp. 239-40.

44 Barron Field, *First Fruits of Australian Poetry*, 2nd edn, 1823, p. 17 (reprinted by Barn on the Hill, 1941).

45 Quoted in Graeme Davison, 'Centennial Celebrations', first chapter of Graeme Davison, John McCarty, and Ailsa McLeary (eds), *Australians 1888*, Sydney, Fairfax, Syme & Weldon, 1987, p. 20.

46 A. S. Kenyon, 'Melbourne', manuscript of talk dated 8 February 1941, Kenyon Papers, State Library of Victoria, Box 2 (2) (xxxii).

47 Clipping from the *Herald* (n.d.), 'Capt. Cook's Cottage—Reply to British Criticism—"Not Vandals"', in Isaac Selby, Scrapbook, held in Selby Papers, University of Melbourne Archives. The British weekly was *The Children's Newspaper*.

48 See the speeches at the unveiling of a memorial to Mitchell at Mount Arapiles in 1913, *Horsham Times*, 2 May 1913, p. 6.

49 Charles Long's essay was published in James Barrett (ed.), *Save Australia*, pp. 25-34.

50 *Ibid.*, p. 27.

51 *The School Paper* was inspired by *Children's Hour*, a South Australian publication for schoolchildren that began in 1890. *The School Paper* had a circulation of about 150,000 a month by 1906, and special editions were being used in Tasmania and Western Australia. See Margaret Mary Sheehan, 'Duty and Self-Sacrifice in War: The Principles of "Good Citizenship" in the Victorian *School Paper* before 1914', BA(Hons) thesis, Monash University, 1987, p. 2.

52 Tate (1909) quoted in Sheehan, 'Duty and Self-Sacrifice', p. 5. The New South Wales director of Education, Peter Board, spoke a similar language. In the same year, 1909, he envisaged schools as 'the nurseries of the nation's morality' and its 'training grounds for national defence'. See S. G. Firth, 'Social Values in the NSW Primary School, 1880-1914: An analysis of school texts', in R. J. W. Selleck (ed.), *Melbourne Studies in Education 1970*, Carlton, Vic., Melbourne University Press, 1970, pp. 123-59, especially p. 125.

53 Charles Long, 'Local Chronicles', *Victorian Historical Magazine*, vol. 1, no. 2, April 1911, pp. 33–5. See also J. Alex Allan, 'The Late Mr C. R. Long', *Victorian Historical Magazine*, vol. xxi, no. 1, March 1945, pp. 47–8.

54 'Monuments, Local Histories and Commemoration Days', in Barrett, *Save Australia*, p. 27. For reflections on the function of 'monumental history', see Davison, 'The Use and Abuse of Australian History', pp. 55–76.

55 Charles Daley and J. W. Barrett, *Victorian Historical Association: Victorian Historical Memorials to Explorers and Discoverers*, Victorian Historical Association, Melbourne, 1944, p. 5.

56 These and following observations are drawn from newspaper reports of unveiling ceremonies in the *Geelong Advertiser* 20 April 1912; *Horsham Times* 2 May 1913; *Argus* 9 November 1925; *Sunraysia Daily* (Mildura) 14 January 1930; and the *Swan Hill Guardian* 13 January 1930. See also Charles Long's series of articles on 'Memorials to Victorian Explorers and Pioneers', Parts I–IV, in the *Victorian Historical Magazine*, vols IV, VII and IX (1915–1923), and Charles Daley's 'Commemoration of the Centenary of the Hume and Hovell Expedition', 'Unveiling of Memorials to the Explorers of Gippsland', and 'The Sturt Centenary', in the *Victorian Historical Magazine*, vols X, XI and XIV (1925-1931).

57 On 'the monumentality of Pharaonic architecture', see Robert S. Merrillees, with the collaboration of Colin A. Hope, Graeme L. Pretty and Piers Crocker, *Living with Egypt's Past in Australia*, Melbourne, Museum of Victoria, 1990, p. 58.

58 A. S. Kenyon, [Pioneers of Port Phillip], Address to the Rotary Club, Wednesday 11 May 1927, Kenyon Papers, Box 3/1 (vii)(f). Quotations in the following paragraph are from this manuscript.

59 *Ibid.* This sentence has a pencil line through it in Kenyon's handwritten manuscript.

60 The burial site had been successfully defended from development in 1867 by the anthropologist Alfred Howitt. Bairnsdale-born writer and conservative Hal Porter called the erection of the cairn sixty years later 'a provocative piece of symbolism for those who deal in symbols, and, while still wishing to live in Australia themselves, agitate for Australia to be given back to blackfellows' descendants': Hal Porter, *Bairnsdale: Portrait of an Australian Country Town*, Sydney, John Ferguson, 1977, p. 270. For more about Porter and Bairnsdale, see chapter 10.

61 A. H. Padley, *The Old Melbourne Cemetery*, Melbourne, Old Melbourne Cemetery Preservation League, c. 1920, p. 5. Further examples of the comparison between pioneer and soldier memorials can be found in 'The Genesis of Gippsland' by P. J. C. Wallace, *The Leader*, 6 March 1920, and 'Angus M'Millan Honored', *Gippsland Mercury*, 7 December 1923, both of which are cuttings in the scrapbook of the Rev. George Cox, Australian Manuscripts Collection, La Trobe Collection, State Library of Victoria.

62 Marjorie Morgan, *The Old Melbourne Cemetery 1837-1932*, Oakleigh, Australian Institute of Genealogical Studies Inc., 1982, pp. xiii–xv.

63 Isaac Selby, *The Old Pioneers' Memorial History of Melbourne*, Melbourne, The Old Pioneers' Memorial Fund, 1924, pp. 12, 13, 40, 368, 372.

64 *Ibid.*, pp. 15-16.

65 *Ibid.*, pp. 399-400.

66 Richard Howitt, *Impressions of Australia Felix*, London, Longman, Brown, Green & Longmans, 1845, p. 119.

67 Selby, *Memorial History*, pp. 18, 285, 289, 290.

68 These details are gleaned from his Papers in the University of Melbourne Archives.

69 'Judge Shot At', *Australasian*, 3 December 1904, p. 1350.

70 Draft letter to the *San Francisco Chronicle* (n.d.) in a scrapbook among Selby Papers.

71 *Memorial History*, pp. 303, 333.

72 *Bulletin* (n.d.), Scrapbook, Selby Papers.

73 Selby's reply to a review of his book, *Argus*, 18 August 1924, cutting in his Scrapbook, Selby Papers.

74 Selby, *Memorial History*, p. 126.

75 *Ibid.*, p. 367.

76 *Ibid.*, p. 304; *Argus*, 8 December 1914.

77 Selby, *Memorial History*, p. 424.

78 Selby's annotations on a letter from A. H. Padley to the *Herald*, 21 November 1918, in his Old Cemetery Notebook No. 1, Selby Papers.

79 Selby, *Memorial History*, p. 404 (map).

80 'A Memorial to John Batman' (handbill) and scrapbook of that title in the Papers of J. J. Shillinglaw, Box 57, La Trobe Collection, State Library of Victoria.

81 Handbills in the Selby Papers.

82 Selby, *Memorial History*, p. 12.

83 In his book, *John Batman and the Aborigines*, Malmsbury, Vic., Kibble Books, 1987, Alastair Campbell argues that Batman was not one of the party that rowed up the Yarra in June 1835.

84 'Batman's New Tomb', *Age*, 28 January 1924.

85 Selby, *Memorial History*, p. 134.

86 *Ibid.*, pp. 181, 200.

87 John Arnold and Julian Ross, *1934. A Year in the Life of Victoria*, Exhibition Catalogue, Melbourne, State Library of Victoria, 1984, p. 8.

88 For this summary of Centenary events I have drawn on *ibid.*, also Vikki Plant, '"The Garden City of a Garden State": Melbourne in the 1934 Centennial Celebrations', in Graeme Davison and Andrew May (eds), *Melbourne Centre Stage: The Corporation of Melbourne 1842-1992*, special issue of the *Victorian Historical Journal*, vol. 63, nos 2 & 3, October 1992, pp. 86-100.

89 See Plant, "The Garden City".

90 Quoted in *ibid.*, p. 92.

91 *Ibid.*, p. 92.

92 A. S. Kenyon, 'The Importance of Australian History', Historical talks for 3AR, No. 1, n.d., Kenyon Papers, Box 2/2 (xxx).

93 A. S. Kenyon, 'The Pastoral Pioneers of Port Phillip', Address to the Dickens Fellowship, 6 November 1930, Kenyon Papers, Box 3/1 (vii) (b).

94 R. V. Billis and A. S. Kenyon, *Pastoral Pioneers of Port Phillip*, Melbourne, 1932. Paul Carter, in *The Road to Botany Bay*, London, Faber & Faber, 1988, p. 167, comments on the artificiality of this map.

95 N. B. Tindale, *Aboriginal Tribes of Australia*, Canberra, Australian National University Press, 1974.

96 A. S. Kenyon, 'The Discovery of Gold', Lecture, Kenyon Papers, Box 2/2 (ix).

97 Kenyon, 'The Importance of Australian History'.

98 Kenyon, 'The Pastoral Pioneers of Port Phillip', Address to the Dickens Fellowship.

99 Kenyon, Draft letter to the editor of the *Age* entitled 'Treatment of the Aboriginals', 25 March 1930, Kenyon Papers, Box 13/1 (i).

100 Kenyon, 'The Importance of Australian History'.

101 Charles R. Long, 'A History of Alexandra, Parts 1 & 2', *Victorian Historical Magazine*, vol. 17, no. 2, November 1938, pp. 52-63, and vol. 17, no. 5, October 1939, pp. 167-82.

102 Russel Ward, *The Australian Legend*, Melbourne, Oxford University Press, 1966 (first published 1958), and Graeme Davison, 'Sydney and the Bush: an Urban Context for the Australian Legend', *Historical Studies*, vol. 18, no. 71, October 1978, pp. 191-209.

103 Ian Burn, *National Life and Landscapes: Australian Painting 1900-1940*, Sydney and London, Bay Books, 1990, p. 8 [italics original].

104 R. H. Croll, 'Before I Forget', unpublished typescript intended as a sequel to *I Recall*, Croll Papers, Box 1213/2.

105 'Introduction' to 'Before I Forget', Croll Papers, Box 1214/2. For an interesting and more recent commentary on this same phenomenon and the managerial advantages of a country education, see George Seddon, 'Managing a Resources Boom or In Praise of Country Boys', in Stephen Murray-Smith (ed.), *Melbourne Studies in Education 1982*, Carlton, Vic., Melbourne University Press, 1983, pp. 42-8.

106 Croll, *Wide Horizons*, Sydney, Angus & Robertson, 1937, p. 86.

107 Croll, 'Before I Forget', chapter 5, Croll Papers, Box 1213/3.

108 R. H. Croll, *I Recall: Collections and Recollections*, Melbourne, Robertson & Mullens, 1939, p. 13.

109 'Before I Forget', Croll Papers, Box 1213/2.

110 Crosbie Morrison, Wild Life Radio Talk no. 223, 1947, Morrison Papers, Australian Science Archives Project (ASAP).

111 Lilian Blair, daughter of David Blair, to Croll, April 1891, Box 1201/1 (b), Croll Papers. Johns regarded David Blair as a 'blackguard': Diary, Australian Manuscripts Collection, State Library of Victoria, 7 February 1868.

112 Croll, *I Recall*, p. 55.

113 Croll, 'Before I Forget', Croll Papers.

114 Croll, *I Recall*, p. 102; Selby to Croll, 11 January 1946, Croll Papers. For further biographical details see Croll's *An Autobituary*, Melbourne, Bread and Cheese Club, 1946, and Geoffrey Serle, 'Robert Henderson Croll, 1869-1947', *Australian Dictionary of Biography*, vol. 8.

115 Croll was sent boomerangs by the Gippsland missionary John Bulmer: Bulmer to Croll, 28 May 1902, box 1201/2(b). Part of Croll's collection is now in the Museum of Victoria.

116 Sir James Barrett to Croll, 14 March 1944, Croll Papers, Box 1200/4(b).

117 'The Wild Nature Exhibition', unidentified author, n.d. [probably 1940s], Kenyon Papers, Box 4/(xli).

118 John Arnold, 'An Extraordinary Man: John Kinmont Moir', *La Trobe Library Journal*, vol. 12, nos 47 and 48, 1991, pp. 100-6, see p. 101. I have drawn on Arnold for many of the biographical details that follow.

119 *Ibid.*

120 Bill Harney, 'To J. K. at 474', quoted in Arnold, 'An Extraordinary Man', p. 101.

121 Quoted in Arnold, 'An Extraordinary Man', p. 103.

122 Recollections of James Preston, quoted in Arnold, 'An Extraordinary Man', p. 103.

123 See chapter 8.

124 Morrison also collected Tasmanian convict relics, uniforms, guns, stamps, books and postcards. As a journalist who travelled extensively in the Hunter Valley, he had plenty of opportunities for collection. See Richard Mulvaney, 'From Curio to Curation: The Morrison Collection of Aboriginal wooden artefacts', Bachelor of Letters thesis, Department of Prehistory and Anthropology, Australian National University, 1983.

125 *Swan Hill Guardian*, 22 November 1928.

126 Geoffrey Serle, *From Deserts the Prophets Come: The Creative Spirit in Australia 1788-1972*, Melbourne, Heinemann, 1973, pp. 132-3.

127 Quoted in Philip Jones, 'Perceptions of Aboriginal Art: A History', in Peter Sutton (ed.), *Dreamings: The Art of Aboriginal Australia*, Ringwood, Vic., Viking, 1988, p. 168.

128 Elaine Whittle, 'Journalists' Child', Royal Historical Society of Victoria Archives, p. 62.

129 The Melbourne Savage Club was formed in 1894 on the model of the Savage Club of London. See David M. Dow, *Melbourne Savages: A History of the First Fifty Years of the Melbourne Savage Club*, Melbourne, The Melbourne Savage Club, 1947.

130 Andrew Markus, 'William Cooper and the 1937 Petition to the King', *Aboriginal History*, vol. 7, part 1, 1983, pp. 46-60, see p. 47. In 1877, some ANA members in Ballarat thought 'native' a little 'foreign-sounding': Marian Aveling, 'A History of the Australian Natives' Association, 1871-1900', PhD thesis, Monash University, 1970, p. 30.

131 On separate trips, Croll accompanied the psychologist Stanley Porteous and the artist Rex Battarbee. See chapter 8.

132 Croll, 'Before I Forget', Box 1214/2.

8   JOURNEYS TO THE CENTRE

1 Tim Bonyhady, *Burke and Wills: From Melbourne to Myth*, Sydney, David Ell Press Pty Ltd, 1991, chapters 16-19.

2 D. J. Mulvaney and J. H. Calaby, '*So Much That Is New': Baldwin Spencer 1860-1929, A Biography*, Carlton, Vic., Melbourne University Press, 1985, p. 201; see also pp. 284-86.

3 See Garry Disher, '"Before the age of hurry-up . . . "': Australian landscape writing 1925-1950', MA thesis, Monash University, 1978.

4 Jane Hardy, 'Visitors to Hermannsburg: An essay on cross-cultural learning', in Jane Hardy, J. V. S. Megaw and M. Ruth Megaw (eds), *The Heritage of Namatjira: The Watercolourists of Central Australia*, Port Melbourne, Vic., William Heinemann, 1992, pp. 137-75, see p. 138.

5 A. T. Bolton (ed.), *Walkabout's Australia: An anthology of articles and photographs from Walkabout magazine*, Sydney, Ure Smith, 1968, preface.

6 Bonyhady, *Melbourne to Myth*, pp. 294-6.

7 Richard White, 'Sun, sand and syphilis: Australian soldiers and the Orient, Egypt 1914', *Australian Cultural History*, no. 9, 1990, pp. 49-64, see p. 52.

8 Robert S. Merrillees with the collaboration of Colin A. Hope and Graeme L. Pretty and a contribution by Piers Crocker, *Living with Egypt's Past in Australia*, Melbourne, Museum of Victoria, 1990, p. 30.

9 D. J. Mulvaney, 'Environmental Issues', in Susan Bambrick (ed.), *The Cambridge Encyclopedia of Australia*, Cambridge, Cambridge University Press, 1994, pp. 43-51, esp. p. 45.

10 Ian Burn, *National Life and Landscapes: Australian Painting 1900-1940*, Sydney and London, Bay Books, 1990, pp. 191-2. The capital city war memorials also had similarities with ancient Egyptian temples, see Merrillees, *Living with Egypt's Past*, pp. 33-4.

11 Charles P. Mountford, *Brown Men and Red Sand: Journeyings in Wild Australia*, Sydney, Angus & Robertson, 1962 edition (first published 1950), p. 91.

12 Burn, *National Life and Landscapes*, p. 192.

13 Ann McGrath, 'Travels to a distant past: the mythology of the outback', *Australian Cultural History*, no. 10, 1991, pp. 113-24. *The Outside Track* was the title of one of George Farwell's collections of writings about the Australian interior (Carlton, Vic., Melbourne University Press, 1951), and Henry Hall wrote *Our Back Yard: How to make Northern Australia an asset instead of a liability*, Sydney, Angus & Robertson, 1938.

14 McGrath, 'Travels to a distant past', p. 115.

15 C. T. Madigan, *Central Australia*, London, Oxford University Press, 1936, p. 3.

16 J. B. Cleland (Chairman, Board of Anthropological Research, University of Adelaide), 'Foreword' to Mountford, *Brown Men and Red Sand*, p. 12.

17 See J. M. Powell on Griffith Taylor in *An historical geography of modern Australia: The restive fringe*, Cambridge, Cambridge University Press, 1988, chapter 5: 'Science and the frontier'.

18 On Gregory, see David Branagan and Elaine Lim, 'J. W. Gregory, Traveller in the Dead Heart', *Historical Records of Australian Science*, vol. 6, no. 1, 1984, pp. 71-84.

19 George Farwell, *Traveller's Tracks*, Carlton, Vic., Melbourne University Press, 1949, pp. 100-1.
20 *Ibid.*, pp. 9, 15.
21 *Ibid.*, p. 10.
22 This was John Mulvaney's experience as late as the 1960s. See chapter 4.
23 Sir Baldwin Spencer, *Wanderings in Wild Australia*, London, Macmillan, 1928, vol. 1, p. 183.
24 R. H. Croll, *Wide Horizons*, Sydney, Angus & Robertson, 1937, p. 129.
25 Fly-leaf of C. P. Mountford, *Brown Men and Red Sand*. Mountford repeats this expectation himself on p. 17.
26 H. H. Finlayson, *The Red Centre: Man and Beast in the Heart of Australia*, Sydney, Angus & Robertson, 1935, p. 16.
27 *Ibid.*, pp. 16, 26.
28 Fleay to Croll, 24 April 1946, Croll Papers, Box 1202/3 (d).
29 Cleland, 'Foreword' to Mountford, *Brown Men and Red Sand*, p. 12.
30 Ernestine Hill, *The Great Australian Loneliness*, Melbourne, Robertson & Mullens Ltd, 1952 [first published in Australia in 1940], p. 172.
31 Quoted in Andrew Marcus, *Governing Savages*, Sydney, Allen & Unwin, 1990, p. 45.
32 R. T. M. Pescott, Director, to J. Williams, Head Teacher, State School, Lake Tyers, 18 May 1956, in Museum of Victoria file entitled 'Ethnology—Lake Tyers Aboriginal Reserve', Aboriginal Studies. Part of the Coranderrk Aboriginal Mission Station in Victoria, which was closed after 1917, became a Fauna Reserve (now the Healesville Sanctuary) under the direction of Sir Colin MacKenzie.
33 Finlayson, *The Red Centre*, start of chapter IX.
34 *Ibid.*, start of chapter VII.
35 *Ibid*, p. 78.
36 *Ibid.*, p. 20. See chapter 11.
37 Arthur Groom, *I Saw A Strange Land: Journeys in Central Australia*, Angus & Robertson, Sydney, 1950, pp. 14-15.
38 *Ibid.*, p. 203.
39 *Ibid.*, p. 76 [emphasis original].
40 McGrath, 'Travels to a distant past', p. 121.
41 Jeremy Beckett, 'The past in the present; the present in the past: constructing a national Aboriginality', in Beckett (ed.), *Past and Present: The Construction of Aboriginality*, Canberra, Aboriginal Studies Press, 1988, pp. 205-6.
42 James Clifford, 'Histories of the Tribal and the Modern', chapter 9 of *The Predicament of Culture: Twentieth Century Ethnography, Literature, and Art*, Cambridge, MA, Harvard University Press, 1988, pp. 190ff. See also Philip Jones, 'Perceptions of Aboriginal Art: A History', in Peter Sutton (ed.), *Dreamings: The Art of Aboriginal Australia*, Ringwood, Vic., Viking, 1988, p. 163.
43 Jones, 'Perceptions of Aboriginal Art', p. 165.
44 See chapter 2.

45 *Argus*, 4 July 1929, *Herald*, 2 July 1929.

46 Paul Fox, 'Memory, the Museum and the Postcolonial World', *Meanjin*, 2/ 1992, Winter, pp. 308-18, see p. 314.

47 *Herald*, 10 July 1929.

48 Paul Fox makes this point in 'Memory, the Museum and the Postcolonial World', p. 313.

49 M. E. McGuire, 'Whiteman's Walkabout', *Meanjin*, 3/1993, Spring, pp. 517-25.

50 See the series of advertisements published in the magazine *Decoration and Glass* in 1945-8. Richard Aitken kindly brought these to my attention.

51 Jonathan Parsons, 'Aboriginal motifs in design: Frances Derham and the Arts and Crafts Society of Victoria', in Tom Griffiths (ed.), *Koori History: Sources of Aboriginal Studies in the State Library of Victoria*, special issue of the *La Trobe Library Journal*, vol. 11, no. 43, Autumn 1989, pp. 41-2.

52 For a perceptive review of Ricketts' sanctuary of sculpture, see George Seddon, '*Cuddlepie* and other Surrogates', *Westerly*, no. 2, June 1988, pp. 143-55.

53 Gayle Griffiths (curator), *Rex Battarbee 1893-1993*, exhibition at the Araluen Arts Centre, Alice Springs, November 1993.

54 Jane Hardy, 'Visitors to Hermannsburg: An essay on cross-cultural learning' in Hardy, Megaw and Megaw (eds), *The Heritage of Namatjira*, p. 145, and Jane Hardy, 'Reginald Ernest Battarbee ("Rex") 1893-1973', in *Australian Dictionary of Biography*, vol. 13, pp. 133-4.

55 Griffiths, *Rex Battarbee*.

56 Croll, diary of trip inland, 1934, Croll Papers.

57 'Before I Forget', Box 1213/2, Croll Papers. It was Aranda practice to assign a kinship status to visitors.

58 On 15 November 1993, a cairn was unveiled on the site of Battarbee's 'artists' camp' near Hermannsburg to commemorate the centenary of his birth. It included an inscription in Aranda naming the families of distinguished Aboriginal artists who formed the Hermannsburg school. Local people value the memory that it was Albert who approached Battarbee. Visit to the site and discussion, 25 November 1993.

59 Groom, *Strange Land*, p. 54.

60 In 1970 Warner Brothers was reported to be planning a film entitled *Battarbee on Namatjira*. Residents of Warrnambool, Battarbee's birthplace, were informed that Peter Finch would take the role of Battarbee and 'an American negro' would play the role of Namatjira. *Warrnambool Standard*, 20 January 1970, news-cutting in Press Cuttings File, 'Ethnology', Aboriginal Studies, Museum of Victoria. I do not know if the film was made.

61 See, for example, R. H. Croll, 'Albert Namatjira: An Arunta Artist', *Victorian Naturalist*, vol. 55, January 1939, pp. 160-2, and Charles Barrett, 'Albert of Hermannsburg and His Art', *Herald*, 23 July 1938.

62 Croll wrote the Foreword to the Bread and Cheese Club's publication on Namatjira, written by Charles Mountford: *The Art of Albert Namatjira*, Melbourne, Bread and Cheese Club, 1944.

63 Bernard Smith, *Noel Counihan: Artist and Revolutionary*, Melbourne, Oxford University Press, 1993, p. 324.

64 R. H. Croll, 'The Australian Aboriginal as Artist', in Charles Barrett and R. H. Croll, *Art of the Australian Aboriginal*, Melbourne, Bread and Cheese Club, 1943, pp. 13-14.

65 Charles Barrett, *On the Wallaby: Quest and Adventure in Many Lands*, Melbourne, Robertson & Mullens, 1942, p. 196.

66 See chapter 6.

67 Philip Jones, 'Namatjira: Traveller between two worlds', in Hardy, Megaw and Megaw (eds), *The Heritage of Namatjira*, pp. 97-136.

68 *Ibid.*, p. 113; Burn, *National Life and Landscapes*, p. 196.

69 J. M. Powell, *Griffith Taylor and 'Australia Unlimited'*, The John Murtagh Macrossan Memorial Lecture, University of Queensland, 13 May 1992, St Lucia, University of Queensland Press, 1993, p. 13. Croll, in his public talks, spoke about the size of Australia in similar terms. See notes of his talk to Grimwade House schoolchildren on 14 August 1941, Box 1220/1, Croll Papers.

70 Powell, *Griffith Taylor*, pp. 9-11.

71 *Ibid.*, p. 25.

72 Quoted in Jenny Keating, *The drought walked through: A history of water shortage in Victoria*, Melbourne, Department of Water Resources Victoria, 1992, pp. 6-7.

73 Judith Brett, *Robert Menzies' Forgotten People*, Sydney, Macmillan, 1992, p. 273.

74 C. L. Bacchi, 'The Nature-Nurture Debate in Australia, 1900-1914', *Historical Studies*, vol. 19, no. 75, October 1980, pp. 199-212, see pp. 199-200.

75 George Farwell, *Traveller's Tracks*, p. 10.

76 Ion Idriess, *In Crocodile Land: Wandering in Wild Australia*, Sydney, Angus & Robertson, 1946, p. 237.

77 Quoted in Richard Broome, *Aboriginal Australians: Black Response to White Dominance, 1788-1980*, Sydney, George Allen & Unwin, 1982, p. 93.

78 Croll, *Wide Horizons*, p. 144.

79 R. H. Croll, 'Hopeless! A Note on the Half-caste Problem', *Stead's Review*, 1 November 1929, p. 4.

80 See Andrew Markus, *Governing Savages*, Allen & Unwin, Sydney, 1990.

81 Groom, *Strange Land*, p. 194.

82 Gillian Cowlishaw, *Black, white or brindle: Race in rural Australia*, Cambridge, Cambridge University Press, 1988, pp. 3-4.

83 Ann McGrath, *'Born in the Cattle': Aborigines in Cattle Country*, Sydney, Allen & Unwin, 1987, chapter 4, esp. pp. 73-4.

84 Quoted in Bacchi, 'The Nature-Nurture Debate', p. 202.

85 Tony Austin, 'Cecil Cook, Scientific Thought and "Half Castes" in the Northern Territory 1927-1939', *Aboriginal History*, vol. 14, part 1, 1990, pp. 104-122.

86 Markus, *Governing Savages*, p. 40.
87 Austin, 'Cecil Cook, Scientific Thought', p. 110; Croll, *Wide Horizons*, p. 103; *Argus*, 23 May 1929.
88 Croll, *Wide Horizons*, p. 158; Kenyon, 'Black and White Culture Contacts on the Australian Continent', undated typescript, Kenyon Papers, Box 9/1 (iii). The Victorian Aboriginal Group, of which they were members, advocated a similar solution. See chapter 3.
89 Kenyon, 'Black and White Culture Contacts'.
90 Austin, 'Cecil Cook, Scientific Thought'.
91 Cowlishaw, *Black, white or brindle*, p. 97.
92 Peter Read, '"A rape of the soul so profound": some reflections on the dispersal policy in New South Wales', *Aboriginal History*, vol. 7, part 1, 1983, pp. 23-33, and '"Breaking up these camps entirely": the dispersal policy in Wiradjuri country 1909-1929', *Aboriginal History*, vol. 8, part 1, 1984, pp. 45-55.
93 Read, '"A rape of the soul so profound"', pp. 23-4.
94 Meaghan Morris, 'Panorama: The Live, The Dead and the Living', in Paul Foss (ed.), *Island in the Stream: Myths of Place in Australian Culture*, Leichhardt, NSW, Pluto Press, 1988, pp. 160-87.
95 Markus, *Governing Savages*, p. 47.
96 Morris, 'Panorama', p. 172.
97 Ernestine Hill, *The Great Australian Loneliness*, p. 178.
98 K. S. Prichard to Miles Franklin, 11 December 1947, in Carole Ferrier (ed.), *As Good as a Yarn with You: Letters between Miles Franklin, K. S. Prichard, Jean Devanny, Marjorie Barnard, Flora Eldershaw and Eleanor Dark*, Cambridge, Cambridge University Press, 1992, p. 181.
99 Ernestine Hill, *The Territory*, Melbourne, Robertson & Mullens, p. 349.
100 Hill, *The Great Australian Loneliness*, pp. 172-3.
101 *Ibid.*, pp. 171, 180.
102 *Ibid.*, p. 171.
103 *Ibid.*, p. 178.
104 Hill, *The Territory*, pp. 61-2.
105 *Ibid.*, p. 412.
106 Hill, *The Great Australian Loneliness*, p. 340.
107 *Ibid.*, pp. 226, 224-6, 229.
108 *Ibid.*, p. 230.
109 *Ibid.*, p. 227.
110 *Ibid.*, pp. 175, 224, 227, 232.
111 Stuart Macintyre, *The Oxford History of Australia: The Succeeding Age, 1901-1942*, Melbourne, Oxford University Press, first published 1986, paperback edition 1993, p. 227.
112 Julie Marcus has analysed the ways in which central Australia, particularly Uluru, continues to be a 'sacred centre of a rapidly developing settler cosmology': 'The Journey Out To The Centre: The Cultural Appropriation

of Ayers Rock', in Anna Rutherford (ed.), *Aboriginal Culture Today*, Sydney, Dangaroo Press, 1988, pp. 254–74.

9 THE DISCIPLINE OF MEMORY

1 David Lowenthal, *The Past is a Foreign Country*, Cambridge, Cambridge University Press, 1985, p. xxiv.

2 *Ibid.*, p. 385. For a recent appraisal of Australian and American urban historic preservation initiatives, see Alan Mayne, 'City as Artifact: Heritage Preservation in Comparative Perspective', *Journal of Policy History*, vol. 5, no. 1, 1993, pp. 153–88.

3 R. Hope, *Report on the National Estate*, Canberra, Australian Government Publishing Service, 1974.

4 Graeme Davison, 'The meanings of "heritage"', in Graeme Davison and Chris McConville (eds), *A Heritage Handbook*, Sydney, Allen & Unwin, 1991, pp. 1–13. See also Michael Bommes and Patrick Wright, '"Charms of residence": the public and the past', in Richard Johnson *et al.* (eds), *Making Histories*, London, Hutchinson and the Centre for Contemporary Cultural Studies, University of Birmingham, 1982, p. 269, for comments on the new 'sense of the past as a concrete presence', and the consequent identification of heritage with property rather than with knowledge and culture.

5 Robert Hewison, *The Heritage Industry: Britain in a Climate of Decline*, London, Methuen, 1987, p. 137.

6 For example, see Tony Bennett, *Out of Which Past? Critical reflections on Australian Museum and Heritage Policy*, Brisbane, Institute for Cultural Policy Studies, Griffith University, 1988.

7 Graeme Davison, 'The meanings of "heritage"', p. 7.

8 Lowenthal, *The Past is a Foreign Country*, pp. 391–5.

9 *Ibid.*, p. 399.

10 For an American study of this shift from theological towards naturalistic world views, and 'the precarious character of American historicism', see Dorothy Ross, 'Historical Consciousness in Nineteenth-Century America', *American Historical Review*, no. 89, 1984, pp. 909–28.

11 Bommes and Wright, '"Charms of Residence"', p. 294. See Chapter 10.

12 David Lowenthal, 'Heritage—and its Interpreters', *Heritage Australia*, Winter 1986, pp. 42–5, at p. 42.

13 Lowenthal, *The Past is a Foreign Country*, pp. 405, 410.

14 Stuart Macintyre, 'The writing of Australian history', in D. H. Borchardt and Victor Crittenden (eds), *Australians: A Guide to Australian History Sources*, Sydney, Fairfax, Syme & Weldon, 1987, pp. 16–19.

15 Chris Healy, 'Histories and Collecting: Museums, Objects and Memories', in Kate Darian-Smith and Paula Hamilton (eds), *Memory and History in Twentieth-Century Australia*, Melbourne, Oxford University Press, 1994, pp. 40–2.

16 Lowenthal, *The Past is a Foreign Country*, pp. 213, 249.

17 Popular Memory Group, 'Popular memory: theory, politics, memory', and Bommes and Wright, ' "Charms of residence" '. See also David Thelen (ed.), *Memory and American History*, Bloomington and Indianapolis, Indiana University Press, 1989.

18 James Cowan and Colin Beard, *The Mountain Men*, Reed, 1982, pp. 173-4.

19 Christopher Lasch, *The True and Only Heaven: Progress and its Critics*, New York and London, W. W. Norton & Co, 1991, p. 83.

20 There are some correspondences here with waves of enthusiasm for family history in America: the 1870s, 1930s and 1970s and 1980s. See R. M. Taylor, 'Summoning the Wandering Tribes: Genealogy and Family Reunions in American History', *Journal of Social History*, vol. 16, no. 2, 1982, pp. 21-38.

21 William Westgarth, *Personal Recollections of Early Melbourne and Victoria*, Melbourne and Sydney, George Robertson & Co., 1888, p. 109; Paul de Serville, *Port Phillip Gentlemen*, Melbourne, Oxford University Press, 1980, p. 37.

22 E. M. Clowes, *On the Wallaby through Victoria*, London, William Heinemann, 1911, pp. 7-8.

23 Quoted in Frances O'Neill, *Picturesque Charity: The Old Colonists' Homes, North Fitzroy*, Clayton Victoria, Monash Publications in History: No. 9, Department of History, Monash University, 1991, p. 3.

24 Quoted in *ibid.*, p. 3.

25 *Mount Alexander Mail*, 4 July 1856.

26 O'Neill, *Picturesque Charity*, p. 7.

27 John Hirst, 'The Pioneer Legend', *Historical Studies*, vol. 18, no. 71, 1978, pp. 316-37; Tom Griffiths, *Beechworth: An Australian Country Town and its Past*, Richmond, Vic., Greenhouse, 1987, pp. 57-72.

28 Alec H. Chisholm, *The Joy of the Earth*, Sydney and London, Collins, 1969, p. 60.

29 *Ibid.*, pp. 60-1.

30 Alec Chisholm, Introduction to Tilly Aston, *Old Timers: Sketches and Word Pictures of the Old Pioneers*, Melbourne and Sydney, Lothian Publishing Company Ltd, 1938, pp. 9-10.

31 Aston, *Old Timers*, pp. 13-15.

32 Graeme Davison, 'The Parochial Past: Changing Uses of Australian Local History', in Paul Ashton (ed.), *The Future of the Past? Australian History After the Bicentenary*, Nowra, Proceedings of the Royal Australian Historical Society Annual Conference with Affiliated Societies, 1989, pp. 5-19.

33 Extravagant examples of this fusion are Sir Henry Parkes, *Fifty Years in the Making of Australian History* (1892) and Sir Henry Ayers, *Pioneer Difficulties in Founding South Australia* (1891). On the character and influence of Australian attitudes to pioneers, see J. B. Hirst, 'The Pioneer Legend'.

34 Graeme Davison, *The Rise and Fall of Marvellous Melbourne*, Carlton, Vic., Melbourne University Press, 1979, pp. 2-4, 130-32.

35 Davison, 'The Parochial Past', p. 9.

36 *Horsham Times*, 22 October 1929, p. 5.

37 A. C. Macdonald, J. H. Maiden and T. H. Myring (eds), *Special Volume of the Proceedings of the Geographical Society of Australasia*, Sydney, Thomas Richards, Government Printer, 1885, pp. vi, 4-5, 121-131, 149-152.

38 'Obituary: The late Alexander Cameron Macdonald' (1827-1917), *Victorian Geographical Journal*, vol. xxxiii, part II, pp. 96-9.

39 *Transactions of the Royal Geographical Society of Australasia*, Melbourne, vol. ix, 1891; vol. x, March 1893, p. 8; vol. xi, June 1894, pp. 22-5.

40 For a brief account of the society, see John D. Adams, 'Frontiers of History and Geography', *RHSV Journal*, vol. 51, no. 1, March 1986, pp. 17-27.

41 James Bonwick, *The Last of the Tasmanians; or, The Black War of Van Diemen's Land*, London, 1869, Preface.

42 James Bonwick, *Western Victoria; its Geography, Geology, and Social Condition. The Narrative of an Educational Tour in 1857*, Geelong, 1858, Preface.

43 Brian Fletcher, *The 1888 Centenary Celebrations and New Developments in the Writing of Australian History*, Sydney, The University of Sydney, 1988, pp. 6-7.

44 Bonwick to Barton, 1888, quoted in Fletcher, *1888*, p. 7.

45 James Bonwick, *The Writing of Colonial History*, Sydney, 1895, p. 11.

46 Macintyre, 'The Writing of Australian History', p. 17; Alan Roberts, 'The Development of Australian Oral History, 1798-1984', *Oral History Association of Australia Journal*, no. 7, 1985, pp. 3-22. For biographical information on Bonwick, I have also drawn upon Guy Featherstone, 'Life and Times of James Bonwick', MA thesis, University of Melbourne, 1968, and 'James Bonwick (1817-1906)', in *Australian Dictionary of Biography*, vol. 3, pp. 190-2.

47 On Melbourne historiography of this period see Jill Roe, 'Historiography in Melbourne in the Eighteen Seventies and Eighties', *Australian Literary Studies*, vol. 4, 1969-70, pp. 130-8.

48 *Argus*, 9 May 1885, p. 10; R. T. Litton (ed.), *Transactions of the Historical Society of Australasia*, vol. 1, Melbourne and London, 1891. For an analysis of the membership, see Peter Biskup, 'The Historical Society of Australasia, 1885-6', *Canberra Historical Journal*, New Series no. 23, March 1989, pp. 16-23.

49 *Ballarat Star*, 25 January 1896.

50 Charlotte Francis Drew, Papers collected by the AHRS, 1896-1906, Ballarat Library.

51 John Molony, *Eureka*, Ringwood, Vic., Viking, 1984, p. 212.

52 R. E. Johns, Diary, 21 January 1858, Johns Papers, Australian Manuscripts Collection, La Trobe Collection, State Library of Victoria.

53 James Oddie (ed.), *Peter Lalor and the History of the Stockade*, Ballarat, the author in association with the historical 50th anniversary of the Eureka Stockade, 1904, pp. 37, 44-5.

54 Alfred William Crowe, Diary, 1 January 1896, Australian Manuscripts Collection, La Trobe Collection, State Library of Victoria.

55 *Ballarat Courier*, 16 January 1896. The letter is signed 'An Old Identity of the Early Fifties', but Crowe identifies himself as the author in his diary, 16 January 1896: 'Letter of mine in Courier giving reasons why I disapprove of the celebration to-morrow of the 40th year of municipal government.'

56 Weston Bate, *Lucky City: The First Generation at Ballarat, 1851-1901*, Carlton, Vic., Melbourne University Press, 1978, p. 266.

57 John Gavan Reilly, Papers collected by the AHRS, 1896-1906, Ballarat Library. Peter Mansfield has transcribed this letter and provides other details of the society in 'The Australian Historical Record Society 1896-1906', *Ballarat Historian*, vol. 1, no. 6, September 1982, pp. 23-31, and vol. 3, no. 2, September 1986.

58 *Ballarat Star*, 23, 24, 25, 28, 30 September 1896, 3 October 1896.

59 This was a meaning missed by the newspaper sub-editor: 'Marchers remember last Aborigine', *Ballarat Courier*, 27 January 1988.

60 K. R. Cramp, 'The Australian Historical Society—The Story of its Foundation', *Journal and Proceedings of the Australian Historical Society*, vol. iv, part 1, 1917, pp. 1-14.

61 Quoted in Gail Griffith, 'The Historical View from the Royal Australian Historical Society', in the Local History Coordination Project, *Locating Australia's Past*, Sydney, University of New South Wales Press, 1988, p. 9.

62 Macintyre, 'The writing of Australian history', pp. 18-19.

63 Sir Paul Hasluck (1977) quoted in Diane Foster, 'Grass Roots History in the West', in Alan Roberts (ed.), *Grass Roots History*, Canberra, Federation of Australian Historical Societies, 1991, pp. 36-44, see p. 37.

64 Paul Hasluck, *Mucking About: An Autobiography*, Carlton, Vic. Melbourne University Press, 1977, p. 143.

65 Quoted in Foster, 'Grass Roots History in the West', p. 37.

66 W. J. Hughston, 'Vanishing Records', *Argus*, 20 March 1909.

67 Hughston to Greig, 2 April, 15 April 1909, Records of Historical Society of Victoria, Correspondence File, Box 35/10 (a), Royal Historical Society of Victoria Archive. See also A. W. Greig, 'The Origin of the Historical Society of Victoria', *Victorian Historical Magazine*, vol. x, no. 2, November 1924, pp. 33-4.

68 Letters of 1909 in Correspondence File, Box 35/10 (a), Royal Historical Society of Victoria Archives.

69 *Age*, 22 May 1909, in Scrapbook of newspaper cuttings on the early years of the Victorian Historical Society, no. 1490, file entitled 'RHSV-Congresses', RHSV Archive.

70 Unidentified news-cutting, 11 June 1909, in Scrapbook of news-cuttings, RHSV Archive.

71 *Ibid.*

72 See typed memorandum by the Victorian Historical Society, 15 June 1909, concerning its relations with the rival group, in Correspondence File, Box 35/10 (a).

73 Ernest Scott to Greig, 1 July 1909, Correspondence File.

74 W. Harrison Moore to A. W. Greig, 29 May 1909, Correspondence File. Commenting on the society's Constitution and Objects, Moore wrote: 'too much prominence [is given] to personal history, & might carry us too far in a direction which is not very profitable. Reminiscences, as historical sources, are notoriously untrustworthy.'

75 Typed memorandum, 15 June 1909: '[The Victorian Historical Association is] an association moreover, not merely of old colonists, but comprising a large proportion of the younger generation of Victorians, who are willing to undertake the collection and classification of the historical records of the State, a work for which in some cases they possess special qualifications'.

76 Benjamin Eagleton, Editor of the *Ovens and Murray Advertiser*, to Greig, 24 September 1909, Correspondence File.

77 *Argus*, 26 July 1910, in Scrapbook of news-cuttings.

78 'Early Colonists' Guild—First Annual Meeting—Extraordinary Fiasco', *Age*, 23 July 1910, in Scrapbook of news-cuttings.

79 Philippa Levine, *The Amateur and the Professional: Antiquarians, Historians and Archaeologists in Victorian England 1838–1886*, Cambridge, Cambridge University Press, 1986, p. 2.

80 Eric Hobsbawm and Terence Ranger (eds), *The Invention of Tradition*, Cambridge, Cambridge University Press, 1983.

81 Greg Dening, 'A Poetic for Histories: Transformations that Present the Past', in Aletta Biersack (ed.), *Clio in Oceania*, Washington, Smithsonian Institution, 1990, pp. 347–80, see p. 352.

82 *Ibid.*, p. 367.

83 Bernard Smith, 'Art Objects and Historical Usage', in Isabel McBryde (ed.), *Who Owns the Past?*, Melbourne, Oxford University Press, 1985, pp. 74–85, see p. 83.

84 Macintyre, 'The writing of Australian history', p. 22.

85 John La Nauze, 'The Study of Australian History, 1929–1959', *Historical Studies*, vol. 9, no. 33, November 1959, pp. 1–11, see p. 3.

86 Stuart Macintyre, *History, the University and the Nation*, The Trevor Reese Memorial Lecture 1992, London, Sir Robert Menzies Centre for Australian Studies, 1992, pp. 4–8.

87 La Nauze, 'The Study of Australian History', p. 3.

88 Manning Clark, *The Quest for Grace*, Ringwood, Vic., Viking, 1990, p. 159: 'The historical map of Australia was almost a blank: I must set out on a journey without maps.'

89 R. M. Crawford, *'A Bit of a Rebel': The Life and Work of George Arnold Wood*, Sydney, Sydney University Press, 1975.

90 Stuart Macintyre sets out some of these imagined beginnings in his *History, the University and the Nation*, and he provides a much deeper local history in 'The writing of Australian history', pp. 1–29. The following three books on Australian historiography focus solely on post-war academic culture: J. A. Moses (ed.), *Historical Disciplines and Culture in Australasia*, St Lucia, Queensland University Press, 1978; Rob Pascoe, *The Manufacture of Australian History*, Melbourne, Oxford University Press, 1979; John Lechte,

Politics and the Writing of Australian History, Melbourne, University of
Melbourne Politics Department, 1979.

91 A. C. V. Melbourne told members of the Historical Society of Queensland
that their role was to collect records that the trained historian could then
interpret (1915), and Stephen Roberts told members of the Royal Australian
Historical Society that the majority of the work published in their journal
'tended to be in the nature of spadework' (1942): Macintyre, *History, the
University and the Nation*, pp. 17-18.

92 Scott was illegitimate. The quote is from Scott's flippant answers to a formal,
printed circular from *Who's Who*, in which he listed his address as 'Pleasant
at times', Scott Papers, 703/3/61, National Library of Australia.

93 'A historian passes ... ', *Bulletin*, 13 December 1939, in Scott Papers,
703/6/25.

94 'Historian's Career From Journalism to University', *Sun-News Pictorial*, 7
December 1939, in Scott Papers, 703/6/20.

95 Ernest Scott, *Terre Napoléon: A History of French Exploration and Projects
in Australia*, London, Methuen, 1910; *Life of Lapérouse*, Sydney, Angus &
Robertson, 1912; *The Life of Captain Matthew Flinders*, Sydney, Angus &
Robertson, 1914.

96 T. W. Heyck, *The Transformation of Intellectual Life in Victorian England*,
London and Canberra, Croom Helm, 1982, p. 122. Macintyre describes Scott
as a 'transitional' figure in his *Knowing and Possessing: Ernest Scott's
Circumnavigation of Australian History*, An inaugural lecture, Melbourne,
University of Melbourne, 1991, pp. 14-16.

97 Watson had medical degrees while Scott had no formal university training.
See Ann Mitchell, 'Dr Frederick Watson and *Historical Records of Australia*',
Historical Studies, vol. 20, no. 79, October 1982, pp. 171-97, see p. 196.

98 Scott, 'Why we teach history', Scott Papers, 703/7/519-534. See Kathleen
Fitzpatrick, 'Ernest Scott and the Melbourne School of History', *Melbourne
Historical Journal*, no. 7, (1968), pp. 1-10.

99 S. H. Roberts, 'An appreciation of Scott', *Australian Journal of Science*,
vol. 2, no. 3, 21 December 1939.

100 Ernest Scott, 'The Interpretation of History', lecture, Scott Papers,
703/7/509-18.

101 See the Preface to his *Terre Napoléon: A History of French Explorations
and Projects in Australia*, [2nd edn], London, Methuen & Co, 1911,
pp. v-viii.

102 Scott, 'The Historical Point of View', Scott Papers, 703/7/317-28.

103 *Ibid.*

104 Keith Hancock to Professor Sir Ernest Scott, 8 July 1939, Scott Papers,
National Library of Australia.

105 Macintyre, *History, the University and the Nation*, and *Knowing and
Possessing*. See also Macintyre, *A History for a Nation: Ernest Scott and the
Making of Australian History*, Melbourne, Melbourne University Press,
1994.

106 Charles Barrett, *Isle of Mountains: Roaming Through Tasmania*, London,

Cassell & Co., 1944, pp. 213–14, and *On the Wallaby*, p. 52. Barrett hoped there would someday be a memorial to Scott.

107 For an analysis of this alliance of science and romance, see Macintyre, *History, the Nation and the University*, pp. 10–12.

108 Ernest Scott, *A Short History of Australia*, Melbourne, Oxford University Press, fourth edition, 1920, p. v.

109 R. M. Crawford, in his biography of the Sydney professor of History George Arnold Wood notes the 'gentle irony' that the Oxford-trained Wood 'was far less the "professional" or new model historian than his Melbourne colleague who had attended no university': Crawford, *'A Bit of a Rebel': The Life and Work of George Arnold Wood*, Sydney, Sydney University Press, 1975, p. 359.

110 J. H. Plumb, *The Death of the Past*, London, 1969.

111 Lowenthal, *The Past is a Foreign Country*, pp. 411–12.

112 Graeme Davison, 'A Sense of Place', in Bain Attwood (ed.), *Boundaries of the Past*, Melbourne, The History Institute, Victoria, 1990, pp. 28–35, see p. 28. See also Davison, 'What Happened to History', *Historical Studies*, vol. 20, no. 79, October 1982, pp. 292–301; 'Learning History: Reflections on some Australian School Textbooks', *Australian Historical Association Bulletin*, no. 53, December 1987, pp. 2–8; 'The Use and Abuse of Australian History', *Australian Historical Studies*, vol. 23, no. 91, October 1988, pp. 55–76; 'The Parochial Past: Changing Uses of Australian Local History', pp. 5–19; *A Heritage Handbook* (edited with Chris McConville); 'The Broken Lineage of Australian Family History', in Donna Merwick (ed.), *Dangerous Liaisons: Essays in Honour of Greg Dening*, Melbourne, Melbourne University, History Monograph Series, No. 19, 1994.

113 Raphael Samuel, 'People's History', in Samuel (ed.), *People's History and Socialist Theory*, London, Routledge & Kegan Paul, 1981, pp. xiv–xxxix.

114 In this and subsequent paragraphs, I have drawn on Graeme Davison, 'Paradigms of Public History', in John Rickard and Peter Spearritt (eds), *Packaging the Past? Public Histories*, special issue of *Australian Historical Studies*, vol. 24, no. 96, April 1991, Melbourne, Melbourne University Press, 1991, pp. 4–15.

115 D. J. Mulvaney, Letter to the Editor, *Australian Historical Association Bulletin*, vol. 4, no. 30, March 1982.

116 Graeme Davison, 'Marrying History with the Future: The Rialto Story', *Victorian Historical Journal*, vol. 58, no. 1, March 1987, pp. 6–19, at p. 18.

117 However, a stream of policy-oriented public history could be followed through the writings and careers of historians such as Geoffrey Blainey, Noel Butlin, Hugh Stretton and Don Watson.

118 For example, Stuart Macintyre, 'The writing of Australian history', p. 27, and John Rickard, 'Introduction' to Rickard and Spearritt (eds), *Packaging the Past?*, pp. 1–3.

119 Ronald J. Grele, 'Whose Public? Whose History? What is the Goal of a Public Historian?', *The Public Historian*, vol. 3, no. 1, Winter 1981, pp. 40–8.

120 Davison, 'A Sense of Place', p. 31.

121 F. Nietzsche, *Thoughts Out Of Season*, Part 2, New York, Gordon Press, 1974, p. 24.

122 Weston Bate to Yvonne Palmer (who was then writing *Track of the Years: The Story of St Arnaud*, Carlton, Vic., Melbourne University Press, 1955), 15 March 1953, Palmer Papers, State Library of Victoria.

123 Bate, in the preface to his Brighton history, referred to his 'early fears that a local history might not impress my examiners': Bate, *A History of Brighton*, Carlton, Vic., Melbourne University Press, 1962. On the perception of local history as chronicle, see Ian Mair, 'The upsurge in Australian writing—Australian history and politics', *Age*, 9 December 1955, p. 18.

124 Bate to Yvonne Palmer, 11 January 1953, Palmer Papers.

125 Malcolm I. Thomis, 'Self-Perceptions of a Small Country Town: Blackall', *Australian Cultural History*, no. 4, 1985, pp. 24-33, see p. 24.

126 *Ibid.*, p. 24.

127 For a recent collection of Australian writings that take this approach, see Kate Darian-Smith and Paula Hamilton (eds), *Memory and History in Twentieth Century*, Melbourne, Oxford University Press, 1994.

128 Michael H. Frisch, 'The Memory of History', *Radical History Review*, no. 25, 1981, p. 22.

10 KEEPING PLACES

1 Diane E. Barwick, 'Writing Aboriginal History: Comments on a Book and its Reviewers', *Canberra Anthropology*, vol. 4, no. 2, October 1981, pp. 74-86.

2 *Museums in Australia*, Report of the Committee of Inquiry on Museums and National Collections including the Report of the Planning Committee on the Gallery of Aboriginal Australia, Canberra, Australian Government Publishing Service, 1975, paragraph 4.27.

3 Frank Strahan, 'Consultant's Summary Report of a Survey of Museums in the Albury-Wodonga region, and of two museum projects in Gippsland, presented to the *Committee of Inquiry on Museums and National Collections*', 26 June 1975, kindly made available by the author.

4 Les Murray, 'The Lore of High Places', in his *The Peasant Mandarin: Prose Pieces*, St Lucia, University of Queensland Press, 1978, pp. 45-50, see p. 45.

5 *Ibid.*

6 Strahan, 'Consultant's Summary Report'.

7 Ernestine Hill, *The Great Australian Loneliness*, Melbourne, Robertson & Mullens Ltd, 1952, p. 227 (see chapter 8).

8 Richard Mabey writes of the notion of parish in Gilbert White's work in *In a Green Shade: Essays on Landscape 1970-1983*, London, Hutchinson, 1983, p. 116. See Gilbert White, *The Natural History of Selborne*, London, J. M. Dent & Sons, 1906 (first published 1789), p. 3.

9 Les Murray, 'In a Working Forest', in Roger Macdonald (ed.), *Gone Bush*, Sydney, Bantam Books, 1990, pp. 29-47, see p. 47.

10 Paul Carter, 'Non Sequiturs', *Overland*, no. 109, December 1987, pp. 67-9, see p. 69.

11 Hal Porter, *Bairnsdale: Portrait of an Australian Country Town*, London, Sydney, John Ferguson, 1977. See chapter 11.

12 Paul Carter, *Living in a New Country: History, Travelling and Language*, London and Boston, Faber & Faber, 1992, p. 123.

13 Paul Carter, *The Road to Botany Bay*, London, Faber & Faber, 1987, p. xxi.

14 Peter Read has begun to explore the attachment that non-Aboriginal Australians feel to place: see his 'The look of the rocks and the grass and the hills: A rural life site on the south coast of NSW', *Voices*, vol. II, no. 2, Winter 1992, pp. 37-48, and 'Our lost drowned town in the valley: Perceptions of the inundation of Adaminaby 1956-1957', *Public History Review*, vol. 1, 1992, pp. 160-74.

15 R. H. Croll, 'Lonely Places', *Argus*, 17 May 1913.

16 Quoted in Yvonne Palmer, *Track of the Years*, Carlton Vic., Melbourne University Press, 1955, p. 190.

17 *Mortlake and District Historical Society Newsletter*, vol. 1, no. 6, October 1980, no. 7, November 1980, no. 9, February 1981; vol. 2, no. 3, September 1981.

18 In 1977 Alan French, historian of Wooragee near Beechworth, honoured the work of Colin Gray, aged 11, whose two school essays written a lifetime before were, he said, 'a true and unique record of our early history': Alan French, 'The Cheese Wring', *North-Eastern Historical Society*, vol. 17, no. 2, April-May 1977. Historians of St Arnaud came to rely on two ANA Prize essays written by schoolchildren in 1889: Palmer, *Track of the Years*, p. 8, footnote 12.

19 The Jubilee Exhibition of 1922 resulted in all state schools being invited to contribute histories of their districts and schools, and these now form a valuable collection. From Jumbuk in Gippsland came an unusual contribution, a 'History of the Local Blacks': State School Histories, MS 3528, Australian Manuscripts Collection, La Trobe Collection, State Library of Victoria. This was drawn to my attention by Meredith Fletcher. See her article: 'School Histories at the La Trobe Library', *Gippsland Heritage Journal*, no. 8, June 1990, pp. 52-3. Also in the early 1920s, a series of school magazines were produced: *The Gap* (Omeo and later Bairnsdale), *Echoes* (Sale Inspectorate Districts), *The Valley* (Warragul Inspectorate), *Forest, Lake and Plain* (Colac), *One and All* (Beechworth), *The Ark* (Ararat), *The Reef* (Stawell), *The Yarra Coo-ee* (Richmond), *The Link* (Warrnambool) and *The Rural Schools Magazine* (Terang). They contained accounts of local and natural history, pioneers, illustrations, and contributions from pupils, teachers and community members. See Meredith Fletcher, 'Early Gippsland School Magazines', *Gippsland Heritage Journal*, no. 7, December 1989, pp. 44-6. See also Charles Long, 'Local Chronicles', *Victorian Historical Magazine*, vol. 1, no. 2, April 1911, pp. 33-5.

20 A. W. Greig to Cox, 18 October 1913, in Cox's Notes, Australian Manuscripts Collection, State Library of Victoria.

21 In Victoria the number of historical societies affiliated to the Royal Historical Society of Victoria jumped from about 30 in 1967 to 72 in 1979 and over 200 by 1990. The total number in the state, including unaffiliated historical societies, is now over 300. In South Australia, the number of historical societies increased from 4 in 1950 to 9 in 1969 to almost 60 in 1989. And in New South Wales, the number of historical societies affiliated to the Royal Australian Historical Society grew from 1 in 1934 to 16 in 1950, 31 in 1960, 134 in 1970, 203 in 1980 and 255 in 1988: J. A. Bilszta, 'Analysis of the Historical Society Movement in Victoria', Report to the Royal Historical Society of Victoria, typescript, February 1985, RHSV files; discussion with Judith Bilszta, 8 August 1990; *Tenth Annual Report of the History Trust of South Australia for the Year Ended 30 June 1990*, Adelaide, History Trust, 1990, p. 8; table of affiliated societies in Gail Griffith, 'The Historical View from the Royal Australian Historical Society', in the Local History Cordination Project, *Locating Australia's Past*, Sydney, University of New South Wales Press, 1988, p. 12.

22 Philippa Levine, *The Amateur and the Professional: Antiquarians, Historians and Archaeologists in Victorian England, 1838-1886*, Cambridge, Cambridge University Press, 1986, p. 61.

23 Levine uses these terms of the groups she studies: *The Amateur and the Professional*, p. 61.

24 *Tailings*, no. 3, May 1963. John Alderson was editor of this newsletter of the Goldfields Historical Society based in Dunolly in Victoria. As well as writing several local histories he recorded his reflections on Aboriginal sovereignty and land rights, noting their profound relationship to land and arguing that 'our Government has not and does not recognise the Aborigines as part of the Australian community': *Subjection-Sovereignty? Implications of the Yirrkala Land Case*, Maryborough, Clanalder Press, 1972, p. 7.

25 *Tailings*, no. 2, April 1963.

26 Alan Roberts, 'The Future of Historical Societies', in Roberts (ed.), *Grass Roots History*, Canberra, Federation of Australian Historical Societies, 1991, p. 70.

27 *Tailings*, no. 2, April 1963.

28 John J. Alderson, 'Why do we have an Historical Society?', *Tailings*, no. 7, September 1963. Alderson was prompted by this experience to produce *A Handbook for Historical Societies*, Havelock, Clanalder Press, 1967.

29 Compare *Tailings*, no. 7, September 1963 and no. 11, November 1966.

30 *Mortlake and District Historical Society Newsletter*, vol. 2, no. 9, May 1982.

31 Mowle is quoted in Graeme Davison, 'The Broken Lineage of Australian Family History' in Donna Merwick (ed.), *Dangerous Liaisons: Essays in Honour of Greg Dening*, Melbourne, Melbourne University History Monograph Series, no. 19, 1994.

32 Quoted in John Spurway, 'The Growth of Family History in Australia', *Push*, no. 27, 1989, p. 72.

33 Kenyon Papers, Box 2/2 (ix).

34 Spurway, 'Family History', p. 71.

35 Quoted in typescript review of Henderson by A. S. Kenyon, Kenyon Papers, Box 2/2 (ix).

36 Davison, in 'Broken Lineage', draws attention to the scientific uses of genealogy in this period.

37 Spurway, 'Family History', pp. 54–5.

38 Davison, in 'Broken Lineage', quotes one enthusiast of the 1930s as remarking: 'Collecting stamps, seals, badges and such like hobbies are not to be compared with collecting ancestors.'

39 Davison goes on, however to explore the 'radical possibilities of family history', its potential to disturb as well as to console. See 'Broken Lineage'.

40 Interview with Linda Barraclough, 20 April 1993.

41 Spurway, 'Family History', p. 61.

42 Davison makes this comparison. The family tree computer software for Windows is called *Reunion*.

43 Spurway, 'Family History', p. 103.

44 'First Fleet families rally to the cause', *Times on Sunday*, 11 October 1987, p. 26.

45 Ken Inglis explored these tensions in a talk on ABC's Radio Helicon on Australia Day 1987, published in *Overland*, no. 106, March 1987, as '1788–1988: Visions of Australian History'.

46 Les Murray, 'The Human-Hair Thread', *Meanjin*, 4/1977, pp. 550–71, see pp. 567, 569.

47 Bernard Smith, *The Spectre of Truganini*, Sydney, ABC (Boyer Lectures), 1980, pp. 35–43.

48 Bob Hawke *et al.*, *Post Scripts: 1988 Boyer Lectures*, Sydney, ABC, 1989, p. 67.

49 Bain Attwood, 'The Paradox of Australian Aboriginal History', *Thesis Eleven*, no. 38, 1994, pp. 118–37.

50 Peter Sutton, 'Myth as history, history as myth', in Ian Keen (ed.), *Being Black: Aboriginal cultures in 'settled' Australia*, Canberra, Aboriginal Studies Press, 1988, pp. 251–68, esp. pp. 261, 265.

51 For example, Ruby Langford, *Don't Take Your Love To Town*, Melbourne, Penguin, 1988, pp. 261–2 ('people who carried the culture and kept it strong'). These generalisations are based on talking to Kooris and listening to tapes held at the Koori Oral History Unit, State Library of Victoria.

52 D. B. Rose, 'Hidden Histories', *Island*, no. 51, Winter 1992, pp. 14–19, at p. 16.

53 Albert Mullet, 'Living as a Koori in Victoria', A talk recorded in 1988 by the Koori Oral History Program, State Library of Victoria, published in Tom Griffiths (ed.), *Koori History: Sources for Aboriginal Studies in the State Library of Victoria, La Trobe Library Journal*, vol. 11, no. 43, Autumn 1989, pp. 3–4.

54 Tim Rowse, *After Mabo: Interpreting Indigenous Traditions*, Carlton, Vic., Melbourne University Press, 1993, pp. 93–4.

55 Coral Edwards and Peter Read (eds), *The Lost Children: Thirteen Australians taken from their Aboriginal families tell of the struggle to find their natural parents*, Sydney, Doubleday, 1989, p. xviii.

56 Diane Smith and Boronia Halstead, *Lookin for your mob*, Canberra, Aboriginal Studies Press, 1990.

57 James Miller, *Koori: A Will To Win*, London, Angus & Robertson, 1985, Appendix 1: 'How Kooris Can Trace Their Ancestry', p. 228.

58 'Policy Statement Concerning Access to Aboriginal Genealogies Recorded by Norman Tindale and Held by the South Australian Museum', 21 February 1992. I am grateful to Neva Wilson of the South Australian Museum for sending me information about the Aboriginal Family History Project.

59 Doreen Kartinyeri, Neva Grzybowicz and Barry Craig, 'The Aboriginal Family History Project at the South Australian Museum', *Bulletin of the Conference of Museum Anthropologists '89*, no. 23, April 1990, Canberra, University of Canberra, 1990, pp. 12-18, at p. 12; Discussion of Tindale genealogies at the Dharnya Centre, Barmah Forest (Victoria), 22 November 1988, recorded by the Koori Oral History Program, State Library of Victoria.

60 Sutton, 'Myth as history', p. 261.

61 Kartinyeri, *et al.*, 'Aboriginal Family History Project', p. 12.

62 Diane Barwick, 'The Aborigines of Victoria' in Ian Keen (ed.), *Being Black: Aboriginal cultures in 'settled' Australia*, Canberra, Aboriginal Studies Press, 1988, p. 27.

63 Alison Moore (ed.), *Three of a Kind: A History of Niangala, Weabonga and Ingelba*, Niangala, Niangala & District Historical Society Book Committee, 1991, p. 7.

64 Diane E. Barwick, 'A Little More Than Kin: Regional affiliation and group identity among Aboriginal migrants in Melbourne', PhD thesis, Department of Anthropology and Sociology, Australian National University, 1963, p. 325.

65 Peter Read, *A Hundred Years War: The Wiradjuri People and the State*, Canberra, Australian National University Press, 1988, p. 131.

66 Quoted in Gillian Cowlishaw, *Black, white or brindle: Race in rural Australia*, Cambridge, Cambridge University Press, 1988, p. 88.

67 *Ibid.*, p. 87.

68 Howard Creamer, 'Aboriginality in New South Wales: beyond the image of cultureless outcasts', in Jeremy Beckett (ed.), *Past and Present: The Construction of Aboriginality*, Canberra, Aboriginal Studies Press, 1988, pp. 45-62, at p. 51.

69 Peter Read, *A Hundred Years War*, pp. 131-2.

70 Sally Morgan, *My Place*, Fremantle, Fremantle Arts Centre Press, 1987. For two readings of Morgan's book, see Bain Attwood, 'Portrait of an Aboriginal as an artist: Sally Morgan and the construction of Aboriginality', *Australian Historical Studies*, vol. 25, no. 99, October 1992, pp. 302-18, and Tim Rowse, *After Mabo: Interpreting Indigenous Traditions*, Carlton Vic., Melbourne University Press, 1993, pp. 101-3.

71 Jackie Huggins, 'Always Was Always Will Be', *Australian Historical Studies*, vol. 25, no. 100, April 1993, pp. 459-64. Huggins was responding to Attwood's analysis of Morgan's *My Place*.

72 Barwick, 'A Little More Than Kin', p. 356.

73 Sutton, 'Myth as History', p. 258.

74 David Lowenthal, *Antipodean and Other Museums*, London, Sir Robert Menzies Centre for Australian Studies (Working Paper no. 66), 1991, p. 5.

75 Andrew Darby, 'Would-be blacks trying to cash in', *Age*, 14 January 1994.

76 Sharon Sullivan, 'The Custodianship of Aboriginal Sites in Southeastern Australia', in Isabel McBryde (ed.), *Who Owns the Past?*, Melbourne, Oxford University Press, 1985, pp. 139-57, at p. 144.

77 Ann McGrath, ' "Stories for country": oral history and Aboriginal land claims', *Oral History Association of Australia Journal*, no. 9, 1987, pp. 34-46, and 'History and Land Claims', in D. Kirby (ed.), *Law and History*, Melbourne, 1987, vol. 3.

78 McGrath, 'History and Land Claims'.

79 Jeremy Beckett, 'The past in the present; the present in the past: constructing a national Aboriginality', in Beckett (ed.), *Past and Present*, p. 207.

80 Jane M. Jacobs, 'The construction of identity', in Beckett (ed.), *Past and Present*, pp. 31-44.

81 Howard Creamer, 'Aboriginal perceptions of the past: the implications for cultural resource management in Australia', in P. Gathercole and D. Lowenthal (eds), *The Politics of the Past*, London, Unwin Hyman, 1990, p. 134.

82 Anna King Murdoch, 'A woman's long memories call upon a darker past', *Age*, 13 September 1993.

83 Isabel McBryde, ' "Dream the Impossible Dream"? Shared heritage, shared values, or shared understanding of disparate values?', *Historic Environment* (forthcoming), Papers from the 1993 Australia ICOMOS Conference.

84 *Barrier Miner*, 23 November 1929.

85 Creamer, 'Aboriginal perceptions', p. 136.

86 Creamer, 'Aboriginality in New South Wales', p. 56.

87 Sutton, 'Myth as history', p. 253; Kim Benterrak, Stephen Muecke and Paddy Roe, *Reading the Country: Introduction to Nomadology*, Fremantle, Fremantle Arts Centre Press, 1984, p. 14.

88 Kevin Gilbert, *Living Black: Blacks Talk to Kevin Gilbert*, Melbourne, Allen Lane, 1977, p. 156.

89 Interview with John (Sandy) Atkinson, 13 December 1994.

90 Julie Finlayson, *Australian Aborigines and Cultural Tourism: Case Studies of Aboriginal Involvement in the Tourist Industry*, Wollongong, The Centre for Multicultural Studies, University of Wollongong (Working Paper no. 15), 1991, pp. 70-2.

91 Official opening of the Echuca Aboriginal Keeping Place, 15 December 1988, Recording of proceedings, Koori Oral History Program, State Library of Victoria.

92 Finlayson, *Australian Aborigines*, p. 71.

93 Gilbert, *Living Black*, p. 304.

94 Creamer, 'Aboriginality in New South Wales'.
95 Quoted in Peter Read (ed.), *Down There with Me on the Cowra Mission: An Oral History of Erambie Aboriginal Reserve, Cowra, New South Wales*, Sydney, Pergamon, 1984, p. 15.
96 Langford, *Don't Take Your Love to Town*, pp. 259-60.
97 Patsy Cohen and Margaret Somerville, *Ingelba and the Five Black Matriarchs*, Sydney, Allen & Unwin, 1990, pp. x, 1.
98 Margaret Somerville, Marie Dundas, May Mead, Janet Robinson and Maureen Sulter, *The Sun Dancin': People and Place in Coonabarabran*, Canberra, Aboriginal Studies Press, 1994, pp. 65-6.
99 Somerville, *et al., The Sun Dancin'*, pp. 73-8; Joy Pickette and Mervyn Campbell, *Coonabarabran as it was in the beginning*, Dubbo, Macquarie Publications, 1981, p. 122; Heather Goodall, 'Land in Our Own Country: The Aboriginal Land Rights Movement in South-Eastern Australia, 1860 to 1914', *Aboriginal History*, vol. 14, part 1, 1990, pp. 1-24, at p. 8.
100 Somerville, *et al., The Sun Dancin'*, p. 77.
101 *Ibid.*, pp. 5, 121-2.
102 Ion Idriess, *The Red Chief*, Sydney and London, Angus & Robertson, 1953, Author's preface and Appendix.
103 Somerville, *et al., The Sun Dancin'*, p. 10.
104 *Ibid.*, p. 195.
105 Somerville and Cohen, *Ingelba*, pp. xv, 51.
106 *Ibid.*, pp. 145-6.
107 In this and the following paragraphs I have drawn on D. J. Mulvaney, *Encounters in Place: Outsiders and Aboriginal Australians, 1606-1985*, St Lucia, University of Queensland Press, 1989, pp. 220-24; Brian J. Egloff, *Mumbulla Mountain: An Anthropological and Archaeological Investigation*, Sydney, NSW National Parks and Wildlife Service, 1979; Denis Byrne, *The Mountains Call Me Back*, Sydney, NSW Ministry of Aboriginal Affairs and National Parks and Wildlife Service, 1984; and Guboo Ted Thomas, *Mumbulla-Spiritual-Contact*, Canberra, Australian National University, 1980; and tape of Guboo Ted Thomas, undated, recorded by the Koori Oral History Program, State Library of Victoria.
108 Quoted in Kenneth Maddock, *Your Land is Our Land: Aboriginal Land Rights*, Ringwood, Vic., Penguin, 1983, p. 147.
109 These reactions are reproduced in Byrne, *The Mountains Call Me Back*, pp. 25-6.
110 Quoted in Egloff, *Mumbulla Mountain*, p. 13.
111 Mulvaney, *Encounters in Place*, pp. 220-224.
112 Thomas, *Mumbulla-Spiritual-Contact*.
113 This is a combination of quotes from Les Murray and Bernard Smith, two prominent advocates of 'cultural convergence'. See Les Murray, 'The Human Hair Thread', *Meanjin*, vol. 36, no. 4, December 1977, pp. 550-71, and Bernard Smith, 'On Cultural Convergence', in Smith, *The Death of the Artist as Hero: Essays in History and Culture*, Melbourne, Oxford University Press, 1988, pp. 289-302, esp. p. 291.

114 Peter Read, 'The look of the rocks and the grass and the hills', p. 46; and Deborah Bird Rose, 'Breathing and seeing country', *The Olive Pink Society Bulletin*, vol. 4, no. 1, December 1992, pp. 22–7.

11 'PROGRESS THROUGH PRESERVATION'

1 B. Smith, 'On perceiving the Australian suburb', in George Seddon and Mari Davis (eds), *Man and Nature in Australia: Towards an Ecological Vision*, Canberra, Australian Government Publishing Service, 1976, pp. 289–304.
2 Graeme Davison, 'A brief history of the Australian heritage movement', in G. Davison and C. McConville (eds), *A Heritage Handbook*, Sydney, Allen & Unwin, 1991, pp. 14–27.
3 Smith, 'On perceiving the Australian suburb', p. 295.
4 For a brief, general survey of the development and characteristics of Australian settlement, see Max Neutze, 'City, country, town: Australian peculiarities', *Australian Cultural History*, no. 4, 1985, pp. 7–23. David Saunders' essay on 'Man and the Past' in Amos Rapoport (ed.), *Australia as Human Setting*, Sydney, Angus & Robertson, 1972, has some reflections on country town thinking.
5 Paul Fox, 'A Colonial City of Ideas', *Victorian Historical Journal*, vol. 58, nos 3 and 4, 1987, pp. 14–32.
6 Interviews with Maldon residents, March 1982.
7 Michael Roper, 'Inventing Traditions in Goldfields Society: Public Rituals and Townbuilding in Sandhurst, 1867–1885', MA thesis, Monash University, 1986.
8 Robert J. Noye, *Clare: A District History*, Coromandel Valley, Lynton Publications Pty Ltd, 1975, p. 85.
9 Hal Porter, *The Watcher on the Cast-Iron Balcony*, London, Faber & Faber, 1963, and *Bairnsdale: Portrait of an Australian country town*, Sydney, John Ferguson, 1977.
10 Porter, *Bairnsdale*, pp. 120–1.
11 *Ibid.*, p. 224. See also Porter's 'South Gippsland and its Towns', *Australian Letters*, vol. 6, nos 3 and 4, September 1964, pp. 22–50, and Patrick Morgan, 'Hal Porter's Bairnsdale', *Quadrant*, October 1977, pp. 76–9.
12 Philip Drew, *Veranda: Embracing Place*, Sydney, Angus & Robertson, 1992, front cover. Drew uses the spelling 'veranda'. In this paragraph, I have drawn on his exploration of the metaphor of the verandah; see pp. 40–2, 69, 99.
13 'A Brighter Bendigo—In 8 Years?' [Editorial], *Bendigo Advertiser*, 16 June 1961.
14 *Ibid.*
15 Mary Fry, 'Street Verandahs in Bendigo: Some aspects regarding the change of attitudes towards the street verandahs between 1940 and 1986', BA (Humanities) Research Project, Bendigo CAE, 1986.
16 *Sydney Morning Herald*, 4 January 1969.
17 'Verandahs in country towns', *Architecture in Australia*, April 1969; Margaret Pitt Morison and John White (eds), *Western Towns and Buildings*, Perth, University of Western Australia Press, 1979, pp. 235–7.

18 *Maffra Spectator*, 15 September 1976, see also 16 June, 4 August, 1 September 1976. Discussion in July 1988 with Flo Pearce of Boisdale (Shire of Maffra), a local historian who stood for council on the verandah issue in 1976.

19 George Farwell, 'Old Towns in a New Age', in *Traveller's Tracks*, Carlton, Vic., Melbourne University Press, 1949, pp. 9-15. See also his *The Outside Track*, Carlton, Vic., Melbourne University Press, 1951.

20 The following two collections of seminar papers on urban conservation provide an introduction to issues in historic towns: *Preservation of Urban Landscapes in Australia*, Dept of Adult Education, ANU, Canberra, and Australian Council of National Trusts, Sydney, 1968, and *Urban Conservation at the Local Level*, National Trust of Australia (Victoria), Melbourne, 1981.

21 Graeme Davison, 'The Parochial Past: Changing Uses of Australian Local History' in Paul Ashton (ed.), *The Future of the Past? Australian History After the Bicentenary*, Nowra, Proceedings of the Royal Australian Historical Society Annual Conference with Affiliated Societies, 1989, pp. 5-19. For a detailed study of preservationist history in one country town, see Tom Griffiths, *Beechworth: An Australian Country Town and its Past*, Richmond, Vic., Greenhouse, 1987.

22 James Jervis, *A History of the Berrima District, 1798-1973*, Berrima, Genealogical Publications of Australia on behalf of the Berrima County Council, 1962 [revised edition 1973]; 'Report of the National Trust (NSW) Branch' and Barry H. McNeill, 'Richmond: A Progress Report on Town Conservation', in *Preservation of Urban Landscapes*, pp. 45-50, 79-83; Miles Lewis and G. H. (Mick) Morton, *The Essential Maldon*, Richmond, Vic., Greenhouse, 1983.

23 McNeill, 'Richmond'.

24 Miles Lewis, 'Victoria's First "Notable Town"', *Trust*, February 1966, pp. 1-4 and Lewis and Morton, *The Essential Maldon*, pp. 136-40; Grant Blackman and John Larkin, *Maldon—Australia's First Notable Town*, Sydney, Hodder and Stoughton, 1978.

25 The public generally believed otherwise: *South Australian National Trust Newsletter*, no. 2, July 1962.

26 Bill Logan, *An Evaluation of the Conservation Planning Process in Victoria*, Melbourne, Footscray Institute of Technology, 1983, p. 50.

27 *Ovens and Murray Advertiser*, 12 November 1970; Tom Griffiths, *Beechworth*, pp. 95-104.

28 Jervis, *Berrima*, p. 194.

29 Farwell, *Traveller's Tracks*, p. 12.

30 Lewis and Morton, *The Essential Maldon*, pp. 139-40.

31 *Ovens and Murray Advertiser*, 8, 15, 22 July 1987.

32 For an account of the battle of the elms, see *Adelaide Advertiser*, 19 November 1963. See also Reg Butler, *Cork Elms and Controversy at Hahndorf*, Hahndorf, Hahndorf Branch of the National Trust of South Australia, 1985; Derek Whitelock (ed.), *Hahndorf: Past, Present and Future*,

Papers given at a University of Adelaide Seminar at Hahndorf on 16 October 1976, Adelaide, University of Adelaide, 1976.

33 Discussion with E. B. and C. Donegan, July 1988; Ian Grant, *Preservation and Restoration of Nineteenth Century Buildings: Australia*, London, UNESCO, 1972, p. 34.

34 See Councillor H. T. Ellsmore's 'Foreword' to Jervis, *Berrima*.

35 Griffiths, *Beechworth*, pp. 75-94, quote on p. 86.

36 Lewis and Morton, *The Essential Maldon*, pp. 138-9.

37 Griffiths, *Beechworth*, pp. 93-104.

38 Sandy Blair, 'Introduction', in Blair (ed.), *People's Places: Identifying and Assessing Social Value for Communities*, Canberra, Australian Heritage Commission, 1994, p. 1. See also Chris Johnston, *What is Social Value? A discussion paper*, Canberra, Australian Heritage Commission, 1992.

39 Shirley Symes, 'Charters Towers', *Australia ICOMOS Newsletter*, vol. 1, no. 3, Spring 1978.

40 'Save Our Grandstand Committee', submission to council and letters of support, 1987; information supplied by Meg Marshall, a member of the committee; letter from Marshall to the author, 13 January 1988; interviews with Beechworth residents, 1988.

41 Bill Logan, *An Evaluation of the Conservation Planning Process*, provides useful case studies of local government involvement in conservation planning. See also Ray Tonkin, 'A Role for Local Government in Urban Conservation?', Master of Urban Planning Minor Thesis, University of Melbourne, 1983; W. Jacobs, *Ballarat: A Guide to the buildings and areas, 1851-1940*, Ballarat, Jacobs, Lewis, Vines Architects in association with the City of Ballarat, 1981; Lawrie Wilson and Associates, *Bendigo Urban Area Conservation Study*, Melbourne, 1977.

42 Bruce Pennay, 'Deciding on a heritage in Goulburn', *Historic Environment*, vol. 5, no. 4, 1986, pp. 15-23.

43 My account of the Nestlé dispute in this and following paragraphs has been compiled from the files of the *Warrnambool Standard* for 1984-87. I am grateful to Marie Johnstone of the Warrnambool Public Library for her assistance.

44 *Warrnambool Standard*, 21 February 1986. The minister was Mr Evan Walker.

45 *Ibid.*, 19 February 1987.

46 *Ibid.*, 22 July 1987. The new minister was Mr Jim Kennan.

47 For example, see 'Cottages should be rented', *Warrnambool Standard*, 15 April 1985, and 'Group to fight cottage demolition', 29 April 1985.

48 'Demolition rocks Goanna', *Warrnambool Standard*, 22 April 1985.

49 Andrew Ward, Auty Wilson & Herriot Pty Ltd, *Warrnambool Urban Conservation Study*, Warrnambool, 1983; Logan, *An Evaluation of the Conservation Planning Process*, p. 126.

50 *Warrnambool Standard*, 7 March 1981.

51 Enid Suggett, Honorary Secretary, Warrnambool Historical Society, to the Warrnambool City Councillors, 17 March 1981, copy in Warrnambool Public

Library; 'Clovelly "Not Worth Saving"—Historical Society', *Warrnambool Standard*, 18 March 1981.

52 *Age*, 8 September 1981.

53 Letters to the editor, *Warrnambool Standard*, 11, 12, 13 March 1981.

54 Hal Porter, *Bairnsdale*, p. 120.

55 O. S. Green, *Sale: The Early Years—and Later*, Sale, Southern Newspapers, n.d. [1979?] p. 64.

56 Porter, *Bairnsdale*, p. 142.

57 *Bairnsdale Advertiser*, 7 September 1978, 7 December 1978, 4 January 1979, 23 August 1979 (letter from Hal Porter), 22 March 1982, 26 March 1982; *Gippsland Times*, 26 March 1982, *Age*, 30 March 1982; Marion Le Cheminant, File of correspondence and clippings on the 'Riverview' dispute, kindly made available to the author; Porter, *Bairnsdale*, pp. 142–3.

58 Letters from Porter to Le Cheminant, 19 January and 25 April 1979, in Le Cheminant, 'Riverview' file.

59 Hal Porter, *The Watcher on the Cast-Iron Balcony*, p. 1; see also Marion Le Cheminant, 'Hal Porter's Bairnsdale—Now', *Bairnsdale Advertiser*, 15 October 1979.

12 HISTORY AND NATURAL HISTORY

1 Winty Calder's main publications on the reserve are *Langwarrin Military Reserve: Ecological evaluation for the Shire of Cranbourne*, Melbourne, 1975; *Heroes and Gentlemen: Colonel Tom Price and the Victorian Mounted Rifles*, Melbourne, 1985; and *Australian Aldershot: Langwarrin Military Reserve, Victoria 1886–1980*, Melbourne, 1987. Telephone discussion with Winty Calder, September 1990; interview with Jane Lennon, 11 July 1990 (tape and transcript in the possession of the author).

2 Michel Foucault, *The Order of Things: An Archaeology of the Human Sciences*, London, Tavistock Publications, 1970, p. 129.

3 On the generational and political change that took place in the Australian conservation movement at the end of the 1960s, see Libby Robin, 'The Rise of Ecological Consciousness in Victoria: The Little Desert Dispute, its Context and Consequences', PhD thesis, University of Melbourne, 1993, and 'Of desert and watershed: The rise of ecological consciousness in Victoria, Australia', in Michael Shortland (ed.), *Science and Nature: Essays in the history of the environmental sciences*, Oxford, British Society for the History of Science, 1993, pp. 115–49.

4 Libby Robin has analysed aspects of the history of 'public science' in post-war Australia in 'The Rise of Ecological Consciousness in Victoria'.

5 In this and the following paragraph, I have drawn on William Cronon, *Changes in the Land: Indians, Colonists, and the Ecology of New England*, New York, Hill and Wang, 1983, pp. 10–12. See also Robert P. McIntosh, *The Background of Ecology: Concept and Theory*, Cambridge, Cambridge University Press, 1985, esp. chapter 1.

6 Donald Worster, 'Doing Environmental History', in Worster (ed.), *The Ends of the Earth: Perspectives on Modern Environmental History*, Cambridge, Cambridge University Press, 1988, pp. 294-8.

7 A useful review of the literature of conservation history in Australia is Kevin J. Frawley, 'The History of Conservation and the National Parks Concept in Australia: A State of Knowledge Review', in Kevin J. Frawley and Noel Semple (eds), *Australia's Ever Changing Forests: Proceedings of the First National Conference on Australian Forest History*, Campbell, Australian Defence Force Academy (Department of Geography and Oceanography), 1989, pp. 395-417.

8 Jim Davidson, 'Victoria', in *The Heritage of Australia: The Illustrated Register of the National Estate*, South Melbourne, Macmillan Co. and the Australian Heritage Commission, 1981, pp. 3-7.

9 Roderick Nash, *Wilderness and the American Mind*, 3rd edn (1st edn 1967), New Haven and London, Yale University Press, 1982, p. 328.

10 B. Tokar, 'Social Ecology, Deep Ecology and the Future of Green Political Thought', *The Ecologist*, vol. 18, nos 4 and 5, 1988, pp. 132-41, esp. 134.

11 *Ibid.*, pp. 134, 138; 'Forum: Only Man's Presence Can Save Nature', *Harper's Magazine*, April 1990, pp. 37-48 (report of a discussion between five environmentalists, James Lovelock, Dave Foreman, Robert D. Yaro, Daniel B. Botkin, Frederick Turner).

12 Oklahoma ecologist, Paul Sears in 1964, quoted in Donald Worster, *Nature's Economy: A History of Ecological Ideas*, Cambridge, Cambridge University Press, 1985, pp. 23, 58.

13 I have drawn here on some of the speculative phrases used by P. R. Hay in 'The Environmental Movement: Romanticism Reborn?', *Island*, vol. 29, Summer 1986/7, pp. 10-17, esp. 15.

14 Jim Russell describes some of the social and human implications of the Green vision in 'Challenging History: An Environmental Perspective', *Public History Review*, vol. 2, 1993, pp. 35-53.

15 J. G. Mosley, 'A History of the Wilderness Reserve Idea in Australia' [and minutes of discussion] in Mosley (ed.), *Australia's Wilderness: Conservation Progress and Plans*, Melbourne, 1978, pp. 27-33, 53.

16 Nash, *Wilderness*, p. 186. Under the influence of ecological thought, Leopold later expanded his definition to include science as well as recreation: Nash, *Wilderness*, p. 198. For a long-term history of the concept of wilderness, see Max Oelschlaeger, *The Idea of Wilderness: From Prehistory to the Age of Ecology*, New Haven and London, Yale University Press, 1991.

17 Patrick Thompson (ed.), *Myles Dunphy: Selected Writings*, Sydney, Ballagirin, 1986, p. 198. See also Patrick Thompson, 'Myles Dunphy, The Father of Australian Wilderness', in J. G. Mosley and J. Messer (eds), *Fighting for Wilderness*, Sydney and Melbourne, Fontana and the Australian Conservation Foundation, 1984, pp. 125-32.

18 Bob Brown, 'The Disappearing Wilderness', *Wilderness* (journal of the Wilderness Society), vol. 18, Dec. 1982, p. 7.

19 David Lowenthal, *The Past is a Foreign Country*, Cambridge, Cambridge University Press, 1985, p. 54. Other examples and some of the policy dilemmas are discussed in articles by S. S. Toothman and M. Webb in a special issue of *The Public Historian*, vol. 9, no. 2, Spring 1987, on 'The National Park Service and Historic Preservation'.

20 Interview with David Tatnall, 12 October 1990 (tape and transcript in the possession of the author). Tatnall distanced himself from this practice.

21 Jane Lennon, 'Timeless Wilderness? The Use of Historical Source Material in Understanding Environmental Change in Gippsland, Victoria', in Frawley and Semple (eds), *Australia's Ever Changing Forests*, pp. 419-40.

22 Marion Shoard, 'The lure of the moors', in John R. Gold and Jacquelin Burgess (eds), *Valued Environments*, London and Boston, George Allen & Unwin, 1982, pp. 55-73.

23 M. C. Downes, 'The History of Tower Hill to 1892', unpublished report for the Victorian Fisheries and Wildlife Division, Melbourne, 1961, pp. 32-4, 79; David Hansen, *Tower Hill and its Artists*, Warrnambool, Warrnambool Art Gallery, 1985.

24 Lennon, 'Timeless Wilderness?', p. 420.

25 There are, of course, exceptions to this generalisation. For example, artificial water holes in arid lands have an impact on the distribution of animal populations and some mountain huts are a favoured habitat of the rare mountain pygmy possum.

26 Land Conservation Council of Victoria, *Wilderness: Special Investigation Descriptive Report*, Melbourne, LCC, 1990, p. 116.

27 The phrase is that of explorer J. E. Calder writing of Tasmania in 1860 (and quoted at greater length in chapter 5), cited in Richard Flanagan, *A Terrible Beauty: History of the Gordon River Country*, Richmond, Vic., Greenhouse, 1985, p. 66.

28 Nash, *Wilderness*.

29 Alfred Runte, *National Parks: The American Experience*, 2nd edn, Lincoln and London, University of Nebraska Press 1979, republished 1987.

30 *Ibid.*, pp. 11, 22, 106; Nash, *Wilderness*, p. 261.

31 The 'Objects and Scope of Work' of Dunphy's Council can be found in Thompson, *Dunphy*, p. 171.

32 See chapter 6.

33 Sandra Bardwell, 'National Parks in Victoria, 1866-1956: "For all the people for all time"', PhD thesis, Monash University, 1974, pp. 448, 454.

34 R. H. Croll, Letter to S. R. Mitchell (Chairman, National Monuments Preservation Committee), 24 October 1936, Lands Department File 7/20—Box 187 ('Glenaladale—Historical and General'), Department of Conservation and Natural Resources; 'Preserving the Best of our Past', *Age* 27 July 1953, quoted in Bardwell, 'National Parks in Victoria', p. 559.

35 Australia ICOMOS (International Council On Monuments and Sites), *The Australia ICOMOS Charter for the Conservation of Places of Cultural Significance (The Burra Charter)*, Sydney, 1985, Article 16.

36 John Brinckerhoff Jackson, *The Necessity for Ruins, and Other Topics*, Amherst, University of Massachusetts Press, 1980, pp. 100-2.

37 'Sovereign Hill' is a re-created gold settlement in Ballarat, Victoria, that represents life in the 1850s.

38 Roderick Frazier Nash, *The Rights of Nature: A History of Environmental Ethics*, Leichhardt, NSW, Primavera Press, 1990 (first published, Wisconsin, University of Wisconsin Press, 1989), p. 37.

39 Sylvia Hallam, *Fire and Hearth: A Study of Aboriginal Usage and European Usurpation in Southeastern Australia*, Canberra, Australian Institute of Aboriginal Studies, 1979, p. vii.

40 Stephen J. Pyne, *Fire in America: A Cultural History of Wildland and Rural Fire*, Princeton, Princeton University Press, 1982, p. 16.

41 Rhys Jones, 'Fire-stick farming', *Australian Natural History*, vol. 16, 1969, pp. 224-8; David R. Horton, 'The burning question: Aborigines, fire and Australian ecosystems', *Mankind*, vol. 13, 1982, pp. 237-51.

42 Peter Gell and Iain Stuart, *Human Settlement History and Environmental Impact: The Delegate River Catchment, East Gippsland, Victoria*, Melbourne, Monash University Department of Geography and Environmental Science, 1989, pp. 67-9.

43 Eric Rolls, *A Million Wild Acres*, Melbourne, Nelson, 1981, p. 399.

44 Les Murray, 'Eric Rolls and the Golden Disobedience', in *Persistence in Folly*, Sydney 1984, pp. 149-67.

45 Jared Diamond, *The Rise and Fall of the Third Chimpanzee: How our animal heritage affects the way we live*, London, Vintage, 1991, especially part V.

46 Tim Rowse, *After Mabo: Interpreting Indigenous Traditions*, Carlton, Vic., Melbourne University Press, 1993, pp. 115-17. The report was entitled *Land of Promises* (1989).

47 I have here quoted Rowse's summary of the Kimberley report in *After Mabo*, p. 115.

48 Cited in Rhys Jones, 'Ordering the Landscape', in Ian and Tamsin Donaldson (eds), *Seeing the First Australians*, Sydney, George Allen & Unwin, 1985, p. 184.

49 LCC, *Wilderness: Descriptive Report*, p. 13.

50 Rhys Jones, 'The Extreme Climatic Place?', *Hemisphere*, vol. 26, 1981, pp. 54-9; 'Standing where they stood', *Hemisphere*, vol. 28, 1983, pp. 58-64; Rhys Jones, Don Ranson, Jim Allen and Kevin Kiernan, 'The Australian National University-Tasmanian National Parks and Wildlife Service Archaeological Expedition to the Franklin River, 1982: A Summary of Results', *Australian Archaeology*, vol. 16, 1983, pp. 57-70; B. Blain, R. Fullagar, D. Ranson, J. Allen, S. Harris, R. Jones, E. Stadler, R. Cosgrove and G. Middleton, 'The Australian National University-Tasmanian National Parks and Wildlife Service Archaeological Expedition to the Franklin and Gordon Rivers, 1983: A Summary of Results', *Australian Archaeology*, vol. 16, 1983, pp. 71-83; Rhys Jones, 'Ice-age hunters of the Tasmanian Wilderness', *Australian Geographic*, vol. 8, 1987, pp. 26-45.

51 R. Williams, 'Forum: Balmain Basket-weavers and the Volvo set *versus* Toorak tunnel vision', *Australian Natural History*, vol. 21, no. 7, 1984–5, pp. 286–8, quoted in Jim Allen, *The Politics of the Past*, Bundoora, La Trobe University Press, 1987, p. 9.

52 Jim Allen, 'Aborigines and archaeologists in Tasmania, 1983', *Australian Archaeology*, vol. 16, 1983, pp. 7–10; Sharon Sullivan, 'The Custodianship of Aboriginal Sites in Southeastern Australia', in Isabel McBryde (ed.), *Who Owns the Past?*, Carlton, Vic., Melbourne University Press, 1985, pp. 139–56.

53 D. J. Mulvaney, 'Reflections on the future of Past Cultural Landscapes', *Historic Environment*, vol. 7, no. 2, 1989, p. 2.

54 Allen, 'Aborigines and archaeologists', p. 9; telephone discussion with Jim Allen, 21 August 1990.

55 Chris Harris, 'Balance of Ethics: A Discussion', *Wilderness News*, vol. 8, no. 6, August 1987, p. 12; Jim Everett, 'Ecology, Politics and Aboriginal Heritage', *Ecopolitics II Conference Proceedings*, Hobart, Centre for Environmental Studies, University of Tasmania, 1987, p. 1.

56 James McQueen, *The Franklin: Not Just a River*, Ringwood, Vic., Penguin, 1983, p. 41.

57 *Ibid.*, p. 43.

58 Everett, 'Ecology, Politics and Aboriginal Heritage', p. 1.

59 Peter Dombrovskis and Bob Brown, *Wild Rivers*, Sandy Bay, Tasmania, 1983, p. 6; P. Thompson, *Bob Brown and the Franklin River*, Sydney, 1984, pp. 127–8; R. Green, *Battle for the Franklin*, Sydney and Melbourne, 1981, p. 96.

60 Deborah Bird Rose, 'Exploring an Aboriginal Land Ethic', *Meanjin*, 3/1988, pp. 378–87, see p. 386.

61 For example, Chris Harris, 'Balance of Ethics'; P. Sharp, 'Fear, disbelief and urgency in Kakadu', *Wilderness News*, no. 112, May 1990, pp. 11–12. See also J. Lark, 'Wilderness—Is it a Land Rights Issue?', *Chain Reaction*, no. 61, July 1990, pp. 29–32.

62 Harris, 'Balance of Ethics'; for an analysis of the moral dimensions of some Australian forest conservation campaigns, see Ian Watson, *Fighting over the Forests*, Sydney, Allen & Unwin, 1990, pp. 104–9.

63 Tim Bonyhady, *Places Worth Keeping: Conservationists, Politics and Law*, Sydney, Allen & Unwin, 1993, p. 135.

64 Judith Wright, 'The Broken Links' (1981), in *Born of the Conquerors*, Canberra, Aboriginal Studies Press, 1991, pp. 29–30.

65 *Ibid.*, p. 30.

66 Wright, *Born of the Conquerors*, p. xi.

67 *Ibid.*, p. x.

68 J. R. W. Reid, J. A. Kerle and S. R. Morton, *Uluru Fauna: The Distribution and Abundance of Vertebrate Fauna of Uluru (Ayers Rock–Mt Olga) National Park, Northern Territory*, Canberra, Australian National Parks and Wildlife Service, 1993, especially chapter 7 by L. Baker, S. Woenne-Green and the Mutitjulu Community.

69 Mutitjulu Community, *Sharing the Park: Anangu Initiatives in Ayers Rock Tourism*, Alice Springs, Institute for Aboriginal Development, 1991, p. 53.

70 Barry Hill, 'Travelling Towards the Other', *Overland*, no. 130, Autumn 1993, pp. 8-15.

71 *Habitat Australia*, June 1991.

72 A. Carothers, 'Defenders of the Forest', *Greenpeace*, vol. 15, no. 4, July/August 1990, p. 12.

73 Flanagan, *Terrible Beauty*. For a discussion of wilderness as World Heritage, see his 'Wilderness and History', *Public History Review*, vol. 1, 1992, pp. 103-17.

74 Linden Gillbank, 'How the Alps Started to Lose Their Grasslands', draft report for the Historic Places Section, Department of Conservation and Environment, Victoria, 1989. Aspects of this work have been published in Farley Kelly (ed.), *On the Edge of Discovery*, Melbourne, Text Publishing, 1993, pp. 133-54.

75 Dick Williams, 'The Impact of Grazing on Alpine Vegetation', Talk to the Royal Society of Victoria, 17 October 1990.

76 Gillbank, 'How the Alps Started to Lose their Grasslands'; Jenny Barnett, 'Alpine Grazing—The Research', *Parkwatch*, no. 154, September 1988, pp. 8-10. The campaign of the Victorian National Parks Association can be followed in its magazine, *Parkwatch*, and in Dick Johnson, *The Alps at the Crossroads*, Melbourne, VNPA, 1974.

77 The views of the cattlemen can be traced through their journal, *Voice of the Mountains*, and in B. Jameson, *Movement at the Station: The Revolt of the Mountain Cattlemen*, Sydney, 1987. A critical review of Jameson by Jenny Barnett can be found in *Parkwatch*, no. 149, June 1987, pp. 20-1. A detailed history of alpine grazing in Victoria is in Peter Cabena, 'Grazing the High Country', MA thesis, University of Melbourne, 1980.

78 J. Hepworth, 'The Dancing Valley of the Mountain Horsemen', appendix to Jameson, *Movement at the Station*, p. 137.

79 D. J. Mulvaney, 'Gudgenby: A cultural heritage asset', *NPA Bulletin*, vol. 25, no. 4, 1988, pp. 6-7. See also Kevin J. Frawley, 'The Gudgenby property and grazing in national parks', *NPA Bulletin*, vol. 25, no. 3, 1988, p. 4.

80 This argument was put to a photographer of the huts, David Tatnall. Interview, 12 October 1990.

81 For the story of Dibbins Hut, see David Tatnall, 'Dibbins Hut—heritage destroyed', *Parkwatch*, March 1988, p. 9; 'Listed for repair . . . demolished instead', *Australian*, 8 January 1990. See also Josephine Flood, 'Cultural resources of the Australian Alps', in Kevin J. Frawley (ed.), *Australia's Alpine Areas: Management for Conservation*, Canberra, 1986, pp. 12-24.

82 Tatnall, interview.

83 Gillbank, 'How the Alps Started to Lose Their Grasslands'. The Historic Places Section also commissioned reports on the alpine history of Aboriginal Contact and European Exploration (Peter Gardner), Water Utilisation (Ruth Lawrence), Grazing and Agriculture (Peter Cabena), Mining (Rob Christie), Recreation (Sue Hodges) and Forestry (Meredith Fletcher). Some of this work

was published in Babette Scougall (ed.), *Cultural Heritage of the Australian Alps: Proceedings of the 1991 Symposium*, Canberra, Australian Alps Liaison Committee, 1992.

84 Pyne, *Fire in America*, pp. 16-17.

85 Nash, *Wilderness*, p. 270.

86 Michael McCloskey, 'Wilderness Movement at the Crossroads, 1945-1970', *Pacific History Review*, vol. 41, 1972, p. 352.

87 Milne and Brown were commenting on Wilderness Society proposals to remove the modern signs of humans from south-west Tasmania, *Launceston Examiner*, 17 April 1990, pp. 1, 6; *Hobart Mercury*, 14 April 1990, pp. 1, 8; 'Erase signs of man, say greens', *Age*, 21 April 1990.

88 Peter Cabena, 'Submission to the LCC Statewide Assessment on Post Settlement History', unpublished report held in the Historic Places Section, Department of Conservation and Environment, Victoria. Part of this report was published by the LCC in its *Statewide Assessment of Public Land Use*, Melbourne, LCC, 1988, pp. 150-9.

89 Ken Taylor, 'Rural landscape protection—the need for a broader conservation base', *Heritage Australia*, Summer 1984, pp. 3-8, and 'Rural cultural landscapes', *Landscape Australia*, 1/1989, pp. 28-34; Kevin J. Frawley, '"Cultural Landscapes" and National Parks: Philosophical and Planning Issues', *Australian Parks and Recreation*, vol. 25, no. 3, Spring 1989, pp. 16-23, and 'Rural cultural landscapes: some unresolved issues', *Landscape Australia*, 1/1990, pp. 93-5; J. A. Russell, *Valuing Cultural Landscapes in the USA, Britain, and Australia*, Hobart, 1988, and 'The Genesis of Historic Landscape Conservation in Australia', *Landscape and Urban Planning*, vol. 17, 1989, pp. 305-12.

90 S. Blair and M. Truscott, 'Cultural landscapes—their scope and their recognition', *Historic Environment*, vol. 7, no. 2, 1989, p. 4. See also 'Cultural Landscapes', *Australian Heritage Commission Background Notes No. 34*, Canberra, AHC, 1987.

91 Quoted in Frawley, 'Cultural Landscapes' p. 16. Persuasive heritage arguments can be made for the preservation of landscapes of ecological disaster, such as the denuded hills of Queenstown, Tasmania. See Geoffrey Blainey, 'History of a Pummelled Landscape', in M. R. Banks and J. B. Kirkpatrick (eds), *Landscape and Man*, Hobart, 1977, p. 4.

92 *Age*, 7 May, 1990.

93 Gunns Kilndried Timber Industries, Submission to Commission of Inquiry into the Lemonthyme and Southern Forests, Launceston 1987 (submission by Brendan A. Lyons), pp. 7-8.

94 D. J. Mulvaney criticised the commission's 'travesty of cultural evidence' in a letter to the federal Minister for the Environment (dated 20 May 1988). It was published in *Wilderness News*, vol. 9, no. 5, July 1988, p. 18. See also *ANU Reporter*, vol. 19, no. 8, 10 June 1988.

95 Richard Mabey, *The Common Ground*, London, Hutchinson (in association with the Nature Conservancy Council), 1980, esp. chapter 1.

96 *Ibid.*, pp. 24–5.
97 This was a central theme of a talk given by Don Saunders, then director of the National Parks Service in Victoria, on 'Park Management Issues' (LCC seminar, Melbourne), 14 August 1990.
98 Mabey, *The Common Ground*, pp. 33–7.
99 Tokar, 'Social Ecology, Deep Ecology and the Future of Green Political Thought', p. 139.

EPILOGUE

1 Report of meeting and list of exhibits, 29 November 1968, *The Junior Naturalist*, Journal of the Hawthorn Junior Field Naturalists Club of Victoria, January 1969, p. 4.
2 Another reading of this exhibition, and of the nearby 'Koorie' exhibition at the Museum of Victoria, has been offered by Helen Verran in 'Othered Voices', *Arena Magazine*, February/March 1994, pp. 45–7.
3. Aboriginal Studies Department, *Women's Work: Aboriginal Women's Artefacts in the Museum of Victoria*, Melbourne, Museum of Victoria, 1992. The book was produced before the exhibition, which was opened later the same year. In what follows I have quoted occasionally from exhibition captions and texts, and I have drawn on discussions with staff in the Aboriginal Studies Department.
4. From 1893 onwards, Johns recorded many instances of commissioning, and often paying for, artefacts from the mission. He always dealt through Stähle, although on one occasion he 'paid the half-caste who brought them 7/-': Johns, Diary, Australian Manuscripts Collection, La Trobe Collection, State Library of Victoria, 28 April, 19 May, 29 May, 16 December, 23 December 1893, 5 January 1894, etc.
5. Alick Jackomos and Derek Fowell, *Living Aboriginal History of Victoria: Stories in the Oral Tradition*, Cambridge and Melbourne, Cambridge University Press and the Museum of Victoria Aboriginal Cultural Heritage Advisory Committee, 1991, p. 74. For biographical information about Connie Hart and her family I have also drawn on Merryl K. Robson, *Keeping the Culture Alive: an exhibition of Aboriginal fibrecraft featuring Connie Hart, an Elder of the Gunditjmara people with significant items on loan from the Museum of Victoria*, Hamilton, Aboriginal Keeping Place and Hamilton City Council, 1986.
6 Jackomos and Fowell, *Living Aboriginal History*.
7 Artefact X 16265, Museum of Victoria; Robson, *Keeping the Culture Alive*.

Bibliography

ARCHIVAL AND MUSEUM SOURCES

Administration—General—Legal Action by Mr J. Berg. National Museum of Victoria file, Aboriginal Studies.

Anon. 'Men who made the *Argus and the Australasian*' and 'Historical Records of the *Argus* and the *Australasian*', MS 10727, Australian Manuscripts Collection, State Library of Victoria.

Antiquity of Man. Warrnambool Public Library file.

Archibald, Joseph Patrick. Papers, Mitchell Library, Sydney.

Archibald, J. P. 'Warrnambool & District Newspaper Cuttings etc.', Mitchell Library, State Library of New South Wales.

——. 'The Ancient Wreck at Warrnambool, 1890-95', Mitchell Library, State Library of New South Wales.

Archibald, Lucy. 'Warrnambool, the scene of J. F. Archibald's early days', manuscript dated 21 May 1943, in the Archibald Papers (Aa 73/2), Mitchell Library, State Library of New South Wales.

——. Letters to the Warrnambool Historical Society in the 1930s, held by the Warrnambool Public Library.

Australian Dictionary of Biography. Research file on Donald Macdonald, Research School of Social Sciences, Australian National University, Canberra.

Australian Historical Records Society, Ballarat. Minutes of meetings and papers collected by the AHRS, 1896-1906, Ballarat Library.

Barrett, Charles. Papers, Australian Manuscripts Collection, State Library of Victoria.

——. Clippings file, *Herald* office, Melbourne.

Barrett, Sir James. Papers, University of Melbourne Archives.

Beechworth Athenaeum and Burke Museum. Minute Books, Burke Museum, Beechworth.

Beechworth residents. 'Save Our Grandstand Committee', submission to council and letters of support, 1987 [copy in possession of the author].

Bilszta, J. A. 'Analysis of the Historical Society Movement in Victoria', Report to the Royal Historical Society of Victoria, typescript, February 1985, RHSV files.

Brown, Amy. Papers (relating to the Victorian Aboriginal Group), Australian Manuscripts Collection, State Library of Victoria.

Cabena, Peter. 'Submission to the LCC Statewide Assessment on Post Settlement History', unpublished report held in the Historic Places Section, Department of Conservation and Natural Resources, Victoria.

Campbell, A. J. Photograph albums, Museum of Victoria (Aboriginal Studies storeroom).

Casey, Dermot. Papers, Australian Institute for Aboriginal and Torres Strait Islander Studies (AIATSIS).

Chauncy, P. L. S. Papers, Australian Manuscripts Collection, State Library of Victoria.

Cox, Rev. George. Notes (scrapbook), Australian Manuscripts Collection, La Trobe Collection, State Library of Victoria.

Croll, R. H. Papers, Australian Manuscripts Collection, State Library of Victoria. (I am grateful to Sue Hodges, field historian at the Library, for enabling me to gain access to these papers during the collection's move to a new building.)

——. Artefact collection, Museum of Victoria.

Crowe, Alfred William. Diaries, Australian Manuscripts Collection, La Trobe Collection, State Library of Victoria.

Dawson, James. Scrapbook (microfilm copy), La Trobe Collection, State Library of Victoria.

Downes, M. C. 'The History of Tower Hill to 1892', unpublished report for the Victorian Fisheries and Wildlife Division, Melbourne, 1961.

Education Department of Victoria. State School Histories, MS 3528, Australian Manuscripts Collection, La Trobe Collection, State Library of Victoria.

Ethnology—Antiquity of Man in Australia. National Museum of Victoria file, Aboriginal Studies.

Ethnology—Lake Tyers Aboriginal Reserve. Museum of Victoria file, Aboriginal Studies.

Ethnology—Black, G. M. National Museum of Victoria file, Aboriginal Studies.

Ethnology—Press Cuttings File. Aboriginal Studies, Museum of Victoria.

Fox, Paul. 'Nineteenth century vision of the city of Melbourne', typescript of talk, 1988, kindly made available by the author.

Galbraith, Jean. Papers, Australian Manuscripts Collection, State Library of Victoria.

Gill, Edmund Dwen. Papers, Museum of Victoria (blue box labelled 'E. D. Gill, Articles and Lectures', held in Aboriginal Studies).

Gunns Kilndried Timber Industries. Submission to Commission of Inquiry into the Lemonthyme and Southern Forests, Launceston 1987 (submission by Brendan A. Lyons).

Jennings, Alan. 'Notes on the History of Ballangeich and District' [c. 1980], Australian Manuscripts Collection, State Library of Victoria.

Johns, Reynell Eveleigh. Diary and papers (1855–1910), La Trobe Collection, State Library of Victoria.

——. Papers, letters, photo albums of ethnographic subjects, and scrapbooks, Museum of Victoria, Aboriginal Studies.

——. Artefact collection, Museum of Victoria.

——. Artefact collection, Burke Museum, Beechworth.

Kenyon, A. S. Papers, Australian Manuscripts Collection, State Library of Victoria.

——. Papers, Box 36 'Miscellaneous (Kenyon and others)', Museum of Victoria, Aboriginal Studies storeroom.

——. Artefact collection, Museum of Victoria.

Kow Swamp. National Museum of Victoria file, Aboriginal Studies.

Lands Department. File 7/20—Box 187 ('Glenaladale—Historical and General'), Victorian Department of Conservation and Natural Resources.

Le Cheminant, Marion. File of correspondence and clippings on the 'Riverview' dispute in Bairnsdale, kindly made available to the author.

Mitchell, Stanley Robert. Papers, Australian Institute for Aboriginal and Torres Strait Islander Studies (AIATSIS).

Morrison, P. Crosbie. Papers, Australian Science Archives Project (ASAP), Department of History and Philosophy of Science, University of Melbourne.

Mulvaney, D. J. 'Environmental Attitudes: The National Estate and the Conservation Ethic', manuscript kindly made available by the author.

Museum of Victoria Photograph Collection. Storeroom under the stairs, Aboriginal Studies.

National Museum of Victoria. Register of Acquisitions.

O'Meara, J. P. [?]. 'Diary of a tour to the country, 1889', Australian Manuscripts Collection, La Trobe Collection, State Library of Victoria.

Palmer, Yvonne. Papers, Australian Manuscripts Collection, State Library of Victoria.

Reece, Bob. 'Aboriginal Community History: A Cautionary Tale', unpublished paper delivered to the AHA Conference, Sydney, 26 August, 1982.

Royal Historical Society of Victoria. Records of Historical Society of Victoria, Correspondence File, Box 35/10 (a), Royal Historical Society of Victoria Archive.

——. Scrapbook of newspaper cuttings on the early years of the Victorian Historical Society, no. 1490, file entitled 'RHSV-Congresses', RHSV Archive.

Scott, Sir Ernest. Papers, National Library of Australia.

Selby, Isaac. Papers, University of Melbourne Archives.

Shillinglaw, J. J. Papers, Box 57, La Trobe Collection, State Library of Victoria.

Soil Conservation Board Photographs. 'Bogong High Plains' file, Historic Places Section, Department of Conservation and Natural Resources, Victoria.

South Australian Museum. 'Policy Statement Concerning Access to Aboriginal Genealogies Recorded by Norman Tindale and Held by the South Australian Museum', 21 February 1992. (A copy was kindly sent to me by Neva Wilson of the Museum.)

Spencer, Walter Baldwin. Papers, Box 22, Aboriginal Studies storeroom, Museum of Victoria.

Strahan, Frank. 'Consultant's Summary Report of a Survey of Museums in the Albury-Wodonga region, and of two museum projects in Gippsland, presented to the *Committee of Inquiry on Museums and National Collections*', 26 June 1975, kindly made available by the author.

Strangman, Denis. 'The Rush to Lamplough, near Avoca in Victoria, in 1859', working draft (66 pages), 1987 (kindly supplied by the author).

Suggett, Enid. Honorary Secretary, Warrnambool Historical Society, to the Warrnambool City Councillors, 17 March 1981, copy in Warrnambool Public Library.

Thorne, Alan. Letter to Robert Edwards, Director of the Museum of Victoria, 17 February 1986, Museum of Victoria files (Aboriginal Studies). Appended to the letter were copies of letters of protest about the reburial of the Murray Black collection, written in July and August 1984. The letters came from Belgium, Canada, France, Great Britain, Israel, Italy, the Netherlands, the People's Republic of China, South Africa, the USA and West Germany.

Whittle (Macdonald), Elaine. 'Journalists' Child', unpublished manuscript, written c. 1944, Box 53/1, Royal Historical Society of Victoria Archives.

INTERVIEWS, DISCUSSIONS AND INFORMAL COMMUNICATIONS

Allen, Jim. Telephone discussion about archaeological work in south-west Tasmania, 21 August 1990.

Barraclough, Linda. Interview about family and local history, and her experience of writing (with Minnie Higgins) *A Valley of Glens* (1986), 20 April 1993, and a field trip with Linda to the Upper Macalister Valley, 26–7 March 1993. (Tape of interview in the possession of the author.)

——. Letter to the author, April 1993.

Beechworth. Interviews with Beechworth residents about the campaign to save the Beechworth grandstand, 1988.

Bilszta, Judith. Discussion about the historical society movement, 8 August 1990.

Bowler, Jim. 'Lake Mungo, Newtonian conflict and Aboriginal mythology', a talk given as part of the Dean's Lecture Series, Faculty of Science, University of Melbourne, 22 September 1992.

——. Discussion on 12 October 1993 about recent developments in archaeology and museums.

Calder, Winty. Telephone discussion in September 1990 about the Langwarrin Flora and Fauna Reserve.

Campbell (née Barrett), Mrs Beatrice. Interview about her father, Charles Barrett, 1 May 1986.

Donegan, E. B. & C. Discussion about tourism in York, Western Australia, July 1988.

Hermannsburg, Central Australia. Visit to the site and discussion with residents about the heritage of Albert Namatjira, 25 November 1993.

Huggins, Jackie and Jane Jacobs, 'Kooramindanjie Place: The Memory of Violence', paper presented to the *Inventing Places* Conference, Department of Geography, Australian Defence Force Academy, 5 November 1993.

Lennon, Jane. Interview on 11 July 1990 about the history of historic places management in Victoria (see chapter 11). (Transcript in the possession of the informant and author, and tape held by the author.)

Maldon. Interviews with Maldon residents about their memories of life in the town, March 1982.

Marshall, Meg. Letter to the author about the 'Save the Grandstand Committee', Beechworth, 13 January 1988.

Palmer, Yvonne. Interview about her experience of writing *Track of the Years* (1955), 1984.

Pearce, Flo. Discussion in July 1988 about the campaign to save Maffra's verandahs, Boisdale (Victoria).

Saunders, Don. 'Park Management Issues', Land Conservation Council seminar, Melbourne, 14 August 1990.

Tatnall, David. Interview about his work as a landscape and nature photographer, 12 October 1990 (see chapter 11). (Tape and transcript in the possession of the author.)

Williams, Dick. 'The Impact of Grazing on Alpine Vegetation', talk to the Royal Society of Victoria, 17 October 1990.

PUBLISHED SOURCES AND THESES

Aboriginal Studies Department, Museum of Victoria. *Women's Work: Aboriginal Women's Artefacts in the Museum of Victoria*, Melbourne, Museum of Victoria, 1992.

Adams, John D. 'Frontiers of History and Geography', *RHSV Journal*, vol. 51, no. 1, March 1986, pp. 17-27.

Alderson, John J. *A Handbook for Historical Societies*, Havelock, Clanalder Press, 1967.

——. *Subjection-Sovereignty? Implications of the Yirrkala Land Case*, Maryborough, Clanalder Press, 1972.

Allan, J. Alex. 'The Late Mr C. R. Long', *Victorian Historical Magazine*, vol. xxi, no. 1, March 1945, pp. 47-8.

Allen, David Elliston. *The Naturalist in Britain: A Social History*, London, Allen Lane, 1976.

Allen, Jim. 'Aborigines and archaeologists in Tasmania, 1983', *Australian Archaeology*, vol. 16, 1983, pp. 7-10.

——. *The Politics of the Past*, Bundoora, La Trobe University Press, 1987.

Anderson, Hugh. 'Donald Alaster Macdonald (1859?-1932)', in Bede Nairn and Geoffrey Serle (eds), *Australian Dictionary of Biography*, vol. 10, Carlton, Vic., Melbourne University Press, 1986, p. 249.

Anon. *Major Mitchell's Memorial Tree Presented to Town of Hamilton by Messrs Murray, of 'Brie Brie', Glenthompson*, Hamilton, Hamilton Spectator, 1909.

Anon. 'Mungo woman back with her people', *Feedback*, publication of the Aboriginal and Torres Strait Islander Liaison Officers of the Australian Heritage Commission, vol. 1, no. 3, April 1992, pp. 6-7.

Arnold, John and Julian Ross. *1934. A Year in the Life of Victoria*, Exhibition catalogue, Melbourne, State Library of Victoria, 1984.

Arnold, John. 'An Extraordinary Man: John Kinmont Moir', *La Trobe Library Journal*, vol. 12, nos 47 and 48, 1991, pp. 100-6.

Aston, Tilly. *Old Timers: Sketches and Word Pictures of the Old Pioneers*, Melbourne and Sydney, Lothian Publishing Company Ltd, 1938.

Atkinson, Louisa. *A Voice from the Country* (introduced by Victor Crittenden), Canberra, Mulini Press, 1978.

Attwood, Bain (ed.). *Boundaries of the Past*, Melbourne, The History Institute, Victoria, 1990.

Attwood, Bain. 'Writing the Aboriginal Past: An Interview with John Mulvaney', *Overland*, no. 114, May 1989, p. 8.

——. *The Making of the Aborigines*, Sydney, Allen & Unwin, 1989.

——. 'Portrait of an Aboriginal as an artist: Sally Morgan and the construction of Aboriginality', *Australian Historical Studies*, vol. 25, no. 99, October 1992, pp. 302-18.

——. 'The Paradox of Australian Aboriginal History', *Thesis Eleven*, no. 38, 1994, pp. 118-37.

Attwood, Bain and John Arnold (eds). *Power, Knowledge and the Aborigines*, special edition of the Journal of Australian Studies, Bundoora, Vic., La Trobe University Press in association with the National Centre for Australian Studies, Monash University, 1992.

Austin, Tony 'Cecil Cook, Scientific Thought and "Half Castes" in the Northern Territory 1927-1939', *Aboriginal History*, vol. 14, part 1, 1990, pp. 104-22.

Australia ICOMOS (International Council On Monuments and Sites). *The Australia ICOMOS Charter for the Conservation of Places of Cultural Significance (The Burra Charter)*, Sydney, 1985.

Australian Heritage Commission. *The Heritage of Australia: The Illustrated Register of the National Estate*, South Melbourne, Macmillan Co. of Australia, 1981.

——. 'Cultural Landscapes', *Background Notes No. 34*, Canberra, AHC, 1987.

Aveling, Marian. 'A History of the Australian Natives' Association, 1871-1900', PhD thesis, Monash University, 1970.

Bacchi, C. L. 'The Nature-Nurture Debate in Australia, 1900-1914', *Historical Studies*, vol. 19, no. 75, October 1980, pp. 199-212.

Ballaarat East Public Library. *Fourth Annual Report of the Committee of Management; also, Rules of the Ballaarat East Public Library*, Ballaarat, W. D. McKee, 1867.

Bann, Stephen. *The Clothing of Clio: A study of the representation of history in nineteenth-century Britain and France*, Cambridge, Cambridge University Press, 1984.

Barber, Lynn. *The Heyday of Natural History, 1820-1870*, London, Jonathan Cape, 1980.

Bardwell, Sandra. 'National Parks in Victoria, 1866-1956: "For all the people for all time" ', PhD thesis, Monash University, 1974.

Barnett, Jenny. Critical review of B. Jameson *Movement at the Station: The Revolt of the Mountain Cattlemen* (1987), *Parkwatch*, no. 149, June 1987, pp. 20-1.

——. 'Alpine Grazing—The Research', *Parkwatch*, no. 154, September 1988, pp. 8-10.

Barraclough, Linda and Minnie Higgins. *A Valley of Glens: The People and Places of the Upper Macalister River*, Bairnsdale, Kapana Press, 1986.

Barraclough, Linda. 'John Paynter, alias 'Bogong Jack'', *Gippsland Heritage Journal*, no. 5, 1988, pp. 58-9.

Barrell, John. *The Idea of Landscape and the Sense of Place, 1730-1840: An Approach to the Poetry of John Clare*, Cambridge, Cambridge University Press, 1972.

Barrett, Bernard. 'Victoria's 40,000th Anniversary', *Agora*, vol. 29, 1984, pp. 21-3.

[Barrett, Charles], 'The Woodlanders'. 'Our Bush Hut on Olinda', parts 1-5, the *New Idea*, October 1905—February 1906.

Barrett, Charles. *From Range to Sea: A Bird Lover's Ways*, Melbourne, T. C. Lothian, 1907.

——. *Everylady's Journal* [formerly the *New Idea*], 6 April 1917, pp. 202–3.

——. 'One Of Our Pals: Donald Macdonald as Boy and Man', *Pals*, 28 August 1920, p. 22.

——. 'Prehistoric Victoria', *Herald*, 9 June 1926.

——. 'The Puralka Flint', *Victorian Naturalist*, vol. xliii, February 1927, pp. 295–6.

——. 'Kangaroos and Their Kin: Australia's National Animals in the Wilds and Captivity', *Bulletin: New York Zoological Society*, vol. 34, 1931.

——. *Gems of the Bush* (the fifth *Sun* Nature Book), Melbourne, n.d. [c. 1934].

——. 'Ancient Man in Australia: Problems for Prehistorians', *Herald*, 9 December 1937.

——. 'Albert of Hermannsburg And His Art', *Herald*, 23 July 1938.

——. *Koonwarra: A Naturalist's Adventures in Australia*, Oxford, Oxford University Press, 1939.

——. *Australia My Country*, Melbourne, Oxford University Press, 1941.

——. *From a Bush Hut*, London, Cassell & Co., 1942.

——. *On the Wallaby: Quest and Adventure in Many Lands*, Melbourne, Robertson & Mullens, 1942.

——. *Blackfellows: the Story of Australia's Native Race*, London, Cassell & Co., 1942.

——. *Isle of Mountains: Roaming Through Tasmania*, London, Cassell & Co., 1944.

——. *Heritage of Stone* (illustrated by Chas H. Crampton), 2nd edn, Melbourne, Lothian, 1949 (first edition 1945).

——. *Wanderer's Rest*, London, Cassell & Co., 1946.

——. *The Bunyip and Other Mythical Monsters and Legends*, Melbourne, Reed & Harris [c. 1946].

Barrett, Charles (ed.). *Across the Years: The Lure of Early Australian Books*, Melbourne, N. H. Seward Pty Ltd, 1948.

Barrett, Charles and R. H. Croll. *Art of the Australian Aboriginal*, Melbourne, Bread and Cheese Club, 1943.

Barrett, Charles and A. S. Kenyon. *Australian Aboriginal Art*, Melbourne, Brown Prior Anderson for the Trustees of the Museum of Victoria, 1947 (first published 1929).

——. *Blackfellows of Australia*, Melbourne, n.d.

Barrett, James. *The Twin Ideals*, London, H. K. Lewis & Co., 1918, 2 volumes.

Barrett, Sir James. *Save Australia: A Plea for the Right Use of our Flora and Fauna*, Melbourne, Macmillan and Co., 1925.

Barwick, Diane E. 'A Little More Than Kin: Regional affiliation and group identity among Aboriginal migrants in Melbourne', PhD thesis, Department of Anthropology and Sociology, Australian National University, 1963.

Barwick, Diane. 'Aborigines of Victoria', in Ian Keen (ed.), *Being Black: Aboriginal cultures in 'settled' Australia*, Canberra, Aboriginal Studies Press, 1988, pp. 27–32.

Bate, Weston. *A History of Brighton*, Carlton, Vic., Melbourne University Press, 1962.

——. *Lucky City: The First Generation at Ballarat, 1851-1901*, Carlton, Vic., Melbourne University Press, 1978.

Beckett, Jeremy (ed.). *Past and Present: The Construction of Aboriginality*, Canberra, Aboriginal Studies Press, 1988.

Beckler, Hermann. 'A Visit to the Library in 1859', Manuscript translated and edited by Margery Ramsay and Walter Struve, *La Trobe Library Journal*, vol. 7, no. 25, April 1980, pp. 8-11.

Beechworth Progress Association. *Illustrated Guide to Beechworth and Vicinity*, Beechworth, James Ingram and Son, 1892.

Beer, Gillian. *Darwin's Plots: Evolutionary Narrative in Darwin, George Eliot and Nineteenth Century Fiction*, London, Routledge & Kegan Paul, 1983.

Beinart, William. 'Review Article: Empire, Hunting and Ecological Change in Southern and Central Africa', *Past and Present*, no. 128, 1990, pp. 162-86.

Benjamin, Walter. 'The Storyteller: Reflections on the Works of Nikolai Leskov', in his *Illuminations* (ed. H. Arendt), 1968, pp. 83-110.

Bennett, Tony. *Out Of Which Past? Critical Reflections on Australian Museum and Heritage Policy*, Brisbane, Institute for Cultural Policy Studies, Griffith University, 1988.

Billis, R. V. 'A Pastoral Historian Passes: Tribute to Mr Alfred Stephen Kenyon', *Australian*, 29 May 1943.

Billis R. V. and A. S. Kenyon. *Pastoral Pioneers of Port Phillip*, Melbourne, 1932.

Biskup, Peter. 'The Historical Society of Australasia, 1885-6', *Canberra Historical Journal*, New Series no. 23, March 1989, pp. 16-23.

Blackman, Grant and John Larkin. *Maldon—Australia's First Notable Town*, Sydney, Hodder and Stoughton, 1978.

Blain, B., R. Fullagar, D. Ranson, J. Allen, S. Harris, R. Jones, E. Stadler, R. Cosgrove and G. Middleton. 'The Australian National University—Tasmanian National Parks and Wildlife Service Archaeological Expedition to the Franklin and Gordon Rivers, 1983: A Summary of Results', *Australian Archaeology*, vol. 16, 1983, pp. 71-83.

Blainey, Geoffrey. *Triumph of the Nomads: A History of Ancient Australia*, Chippendale (NSW), Pan Macmillan, 1983 (first published 1975).

——. 'History of a Pummelled Landscape', in M. R. Banks and J. B. Kirkpatrick (eds), *Landscape and Man*, Hobart, 1977.

——. *A Land Half Won*, South Melbourne, Macmillan, 1980.

Blair, S. and M. Truscott. 'Cultural landscapes—their scope and their recognition', *Historic Environment*, vol. 7, no. 2, 1989.

Blunt, Michael J. 'Sir Grafton Elliot Smith (1871-1937)', in G. Serle (ed.), *Australian Dictionary of Biography*, vol. 11, Carlton, Vic., Melbourne University Press, 1988, pp. 645-6.

Board, Peter. 'History and Australian History', address given at the Annual Meeting of the Australian Historical Society, 22 February, 1916, *Australian Historical Society Journal and Proceedings*, III, 1915-17.

Boldrewood, Rolf (ed. C. E. Sayers). *Old Melbourne Memories*, Melbourne, Heinemann, 1969.

Bolger, Peter. *Hobart Town*, Canberra, ANU Press, 1973.

Bolton, A. T. (ed.). *Walkabout's Australia: An anthology of articles and photographs from Walkabout magazine*, Sydney, Ure Smith, 1968.

Bommes, Michael and Patrick Wright. ' "Charms of residence": the public and the past', in Richard Johnson *et al.*, (eds), *Making Histories*, London, Hutchinson with the Centre for Contemporary Cultural Studies, University of Birmingham, 1982.

Bonwick, James. *Western Victoria; its Geography, Geology, and Social Condition. The Narrative of an Educational Tour in 1857*, Geelong, Thomas Brown, 1858.

——. *The Wild White Man and the Blacks of Victoria*, 2nd edn, Melbourne, 1963.

——. *The Last of the Tasmanians or the black war of Van Diemen's Land*, London, Sampson Low, Son and Marston, 1870.

——. *The Writing of Colonial History*, Sydney, 1895.

——. *An octogenarian's reminiscences*, London, 1903.

Bonyhady, Tim. *Burke and Wills: From Melbourne to Myth*, Sydney, David Ell Press Pty Ltd, 1991.

——. *Places Worth Keeping: Conservationists, Politics and Law*, Sydney, Allen & Unwin, 1993.

——. 'A Different Streeton', *Art Monthly Australia*, no. 61, July 1993, pp. 8-12.

Borchardt, D. H. and Victor Crittenden (eds). *Australians: A Guide to Australian History Sources*, Sydney, Fairfax, Syme & Weldon Associates, 1987.

Bowler, Jim, Rhys Jones, Harry Allen and Alan Thorne. 'Pleistocene Human Remains from Australia', *World Archaeology*, vol. 2, 1970, pp. 39-60.

Bowler, Jim. 'Edmund Dwen Gill (1908-1986)', *Australian Archaeology*, no. 24, June 1987, pp. 48-52.

Bowler, Peter. 'The Invention of the Past', in L. M. Smith (ed.), *The Making of Britain: The Age of Revolution*, Hampshire and London, Macmillan, 1987.

——. *The Invention of Progress: Victorians and their Past*, Oxford, Basil Blackwell, 1989.

Branagan, David and Elaine Lim. 'J. W. Gregory, Traveller in the Dead Heart', *Historical Records of Australian Science*, vol. 6, no. 1, 1984, pp. 71-84.

Brett, Judith. *Robert Menzies' Forgotten People*, Sydney, Macmillan, 1992.

Broome, Richard. *Aboriginal Australians: Black Response to White Dominance, 1788-1980*, Sydney, George Allen & Unwin, 1982.

——. 'The Struggle for Australia: Aboriginal-European Warfare 1770-1930' in Michael McKernan and Margaret Browne (eds), *Australia: Two Centuries of War and Peace*, Canberra, Australian War Memorial in association with Allen & Unwin, 1988.

Brown, Bob. 'The Disappearing Wilderness', *Wilderness* (journal of the Wilderness Society), vol. 18, Dec. 1982, p. 7.

Bulbeck, Chilla. *The Stone Laurel: Race, Gender and Class in Australian Memorials*, Cultural Policy Studies: Occasional Paper No. 5, Brisbane, Griffith University, 1988.

——. 'Aborigines, memorials and the history of the frontier', *Australian Historical Studies*, vol. 24, no. 96, April 1991, pp. 168-78.

Burn, Ian. *National Life and Landscapes: Australian Painting 1900-1940*, Sydney and London, Bay Books, 1990.

Burrow, J. W. *Evolution and Society*, London, Cambridge University Press, 1966.

Butcher, Barry W. 'Gorilla warfare in Melbourne: Halford, Huxley and 'Man's place in nature''', in R. W. Home (ed.), *Australian Science in the Making*, Cambridge, Cambridge University Press, 1988, pp. 153-69.

Butler, Reg. *Cork Elms and Controversy at Hahndorf*, Hahndorf, Hahndorf Branch of the National Trust of South Australia, 1985.

Cabena, Peter. 'Grazing the High Country', MA thesis, University of Melbourne, 1980.

Caire, Nicholas. 'Notes on the giant trees of Victoria', *The Victorian Naturalist*, vol. 21, no. 9, January 1905, pp. 122-8.

Calder, Nigel. *Timescale: An Atlas of the Fourth Dimension*, London, Chatto & Windus, 1983.

Calder, Winty. *Langwarrin Military Reserve: Ecological evaluation for the Shire of Cranbourne*, Melbourne, 1975.

——. *Heroes and Gentlemen: Colonel Tom Price and the Victorian Mounted Rifles*, Melbourne, Jimaringle Publications, 1985.

——. *Australian Aldershot: Langwarrin Military Reserve, Victoria 1886-1980*, Melbourne, Jimaringle Publications, 1987.

Campbell, Alastair. *John Batman and the Aborigines*, Malmsbury, Victoria, Kibble Books, 1987.

Carothers, A. 'Defenders of the Forest', *Greenpeace*, vol. 15, no. 4, July/August 1990, p. 12.

Carter, Julie. 'S. R. Mitchell and the Study of Archaeology in Victoria', *The Artefact*, vol. 3, no. 1, 1978, pp. 5-16.

——. 'S. R. Mitchell and Archaeology in Victoria', MA Thesis, University of Melbourne, 1980.

Carter, Paul. *The Road to Botany Bay*, London, Faber & Faber, 1987.

——. 'Non Sequiturs', *Overland*, no. 109, December 1987, pp. 67-9.

——. *Living in a New Country: History, Travelling and Language*, London and Boston, Faber & Faber, 1992.

Casey, D. A. 'The present state of our knowledge of the archaeology of Australia', *Proceedings of the Third Congress of Prehistorians of the Far East*, Singapore, January 1938, pp. 22-9.

Casey, D. A. 'An Aboriginal Ceremonial Ground at Lake Wongan near Streatham, Victoria', *Victorian Naturalist*, vol. 54, January 1938, pp. 130-3.

Chauncy, P. L. S. 'Notes and Anecdotes of the Aborigines of Australia', in R. B. Smyth, *The Aborigines of Victoria* (2 vols), Melbourne, Government Printer, 1878, volume 2, Appendix A, pp. 221-84.

Chisholm, A. H. *Mateship with Birds*, Melbourne, Whitcombe & Tombs, 1922.

——. *The Joy of the Earth*, Sydney and London, Collins, 1969.

——. 'Charles Leslie Barrett (1879-1959)', in Bede Nairn and Geoffrey Serle (eds), *Australian Dictionary of Biography*, vol. 7, Carlton, Vic., Melbourne University Press, 1979, p. 185.

Christie, M. F. *Aborigines in Colonial Victoria, 1835-86*, Sydney, Sydney University Press, 1979.

Clark, Eileen. 'Ecology or Heritage? A Question of Conservation', *Ecopolitics II Conference Proceedings*, Hobart, Centre for Environmental Studies, University of Tasmania, 1987, pp. 178-83.

Clark, Ian D. *Aboriginal Languages and Clans: An Historical Atlas of Western and Central Victoria, 1800-1900*, Monash Publications in Geography, no. 37, Department of Geography and Environmental Science, Melbourne, 1990.

Clark, Manning. *The Quest for Grace*, Ringwood, Vic., Viking, 1990.

Clarke, Marcus. 'Waterpool at Coleraine' and 'The Buffalo Ranges, by Nicholas Chevalier', in Bernard Smith (ed.), *Documents in Art and Taste in Australia: The Colonial Period, 1770-1914*, Melbourne, Oxford University Press, 1975, pp. 133-40.

Clifford, James. *The Predicament of Culture: Twentieth Century Ethnography, Literature, and Art*, Cambridge, MA, Harvard University Press, 1988.

Clowes, E. M. *On the Wallaby through Victoria*, London, William Heinemann, 1911.

Cohen, Patsy and Margaret Somerville. *Ingelba and the Five Black Matriarchs*, Sydney, Allen & Unwin, 1990.

Cole, Douglas. ' "The Crimson Thread of Kinship": Ethnic Ideas in Australia, 1870-1914', *Historical Studies*, no. 14, 1971, pp. 511-23.

Conference of Museum Anthropologists. *Bulletin '89*, no. 23, April 1990.

Cooper, Carol. 'The Beechworth Collection of Aboriginal Artefacts', BA(Hons) thesis, Department of Prehistory and Anthropology, Australian National University, 1975.

——. 'Reynell Eveleigh Johns: A Rediscovered Victorian', *La Trobe Library Journal*, 1977, pp. 90-6.

Corris, Peter. *Aborigines and Europeans in Western Victoria*, Canberra, Australian Institute of Aboriginal Studies, 1968.

——. 'James Dawson (1806-1900)', in Douglas Pike (ed.), *Australian Dictionary of Biography*, vol. 4, Carlton, Vic., Melbourne University Press, 1972, pp. 35-6.

Coutts, P. J. F. 'Management of the Aboriginal Cultural Heritage in Victoria', in Ministry for Conservation, *'No Future without the Past': Victoria Heritage Plan Conference Discussion Papers*, Melbourne, Ministry for Conservation, September 1981, pp. 1-31.

Cowan, James and Colin Beard. *The Mountain Men*, Reed, 1982, pp. 173-4.

Cowlishaw, Gillian. 'Studying Aborigines: Changing Canons in Anthropology and History', in Bain Attwood and John Arnold (eds), *Power, Knowledge and Aborigines*, special edition of the *Journal of Australian Studies*, Bundoora, Vic., La Trobe University Press in Association with the National Centre for Australian Studies, Monash University, 1992, pp. 20-31.

——. *Black, white or brindle: Race in rural Australia*, Cambridge, Cambridge University Press, 1988.

Cramp, K. R. 'The Australian Historical Society—The Story of its Foundation', *Journal and Proceedings of the Australian Historical Society*, vol. iv, part 1, 1917, pp. 1-14.

Crawford, R. M. *'A Bit of a Rebel': The Life and Work of George Arnold Wood*, Sydney, Sydney University Press, 1975.

Creamer, Howard. 'Aboriginal perceptions of the past: the implications for cultural resource management in Australia', in P. Gathercole and D. Lowenthal (eds), *The Politics of the Past*, London, Unwin Hyman, 1990.

Critchett, Jan. *A 'distant field of murder': Western district frontiers 1834-1848*, Carlton, Vic., Melbourne University Press, 1990.

Croll, R. H. 'Hopeless! A Note on the Half-caste Problem', *Stead's Review*, 1 November 1929, p. 4.

——. 'Hunting the blackfellow: Records in Stone and Bone', *Argus*, 26 Dec. 1930

——. *Wide Horizons: Wanderings in Central Australia*, Sydney, Angus & Robertson, 1937.

——. 'Albert Namatjira: An Arunta Artist', *Victorian Naturalist*, vol. 55, January 1939, pp. 160-2.

——. *I Recall: Collections and Recollections*, Melbourne, Robertson & Mullens Ltd, 1939.

——. *An Autobituary*, Melbourne, Bread and Cheese Club, 1946.

Cronon, William. *Changes in the Land: Indians, Colonists, and the Ecology of New England*, New York, Hill and Wang, 1983.

Crosby, Alfred W. *Ecological Imperialism: The Biological Expansion of Europe, 900-1900*, Cambridge, Cambridge University Press, 1986.

Cunningham, E. S. 'Donald Macdonald: An Appreciation', *Newspaper News*, 1 December 1932.

Dahlberg, Frances (ed.). *Woman the Gatherer*, New Haven and London, Yale University Press, 1981.

Daley, Charles and J. W. Barrett. *Victorian Historical Association: Victorian Historical Memorials to Explorers and Discoverers*, Victorian Historical Association, Melbourne, 1944.

Daley, Charles. 'Commemoration of the Centenary of the Hume and Hovell Expedition', 'Unveiling of Memorials to the Explorers of Gippsland', and 'The Sturt Centenary', in the *Victorian Historical Magazine*, vols X, XI and XIV (1925-1931).

Daniels, Kay. 'Cults of Nature, Cults of History', *Island*, issue 16, Spring 1983.

Darby, Andrew. 'Would-be blacks trying to cash in', *Age*, 14 January 1994.

Darwin, Charles. *The Descent of Man*, New York, Modern Library, n.d. (first published 1871).

Davidson, Jim. 'Victoria', in *The Heritage of Australia: The Illustrated Register of the National Estate*, South Melbourne, Macmillan Co. and the Australian Heritage Commission, 1981, pp. 3/1-3/9.

Davison, Graeme. *The Rise and Fall of Marvellous Melbourne*, Carlton, Vic., Melbourne University Press, 1978.

——. 'Sydney and the Bush: an Urban Context for the Australian Legend', *Historical Studies*, vol. 18, no. 71, October 1978, pp. 191-209.

——. 'What Happened to History', *Historical Studies*, vol. 20, no. 79, October 1982, pp. 292-301.

——. 'Exhibitions', *Australian Cultural History*, no. 2, 1982/3.

——. 'The City-Bred Child and Urban Reform in Melbourne 1900-1940', in Peter Williams (ed.), *Social Process and the City*, Sydney, George Allen & Unwin, 1983, pp. 143-74.

——. 'Centennial Celebrations', in Graeme Davison, John McCarty and Ailsa McLeary (eds), *Australians 1888*, Sydney, Fairfax Syme & Weldon Associates, 1987.

——. 'Learning History: Reflections on some Australian School Textbooks', *Australian Historical Association Bulletin*, no. 53, December 1987, pp. 2-8.

——. 'The Use and Abuse of Australian History', *Australian Historical Studies*, vol. 23, no. 91, October 1988, pp. 55-76.

——. 'The meanings of "heritage" ', in Graeme Davison and Chris McConville (eds), *A Heritage Handbook*, Sydney, Allen & Unwin, 1989, pp. 1-13.

——. 'The Parochial Past: Changing Uses of Australian Local History', in Paul Ashton (ed.), *The Future of the Past? Australian History After the Bicentenary*, Nowra, Proceedings of the Royal Australian Historical Society Annual Conference with Affiliated Societies, 1989, pp. 5-19.

——. 'A Sense of Place', in Bain Attwood (ed.), *Boundaries of the Past*, Melbourne, The History Institute, Victoria, 1990, pp. 28-35.

——. 'The Broken Lineage of Australian Family History', in Donna Merwick (ed.), *Dangerous Liaisons: Essays in Honour of Greg Dening*, Melbourne, Melbourne University Press History Monograph Series, no. 19, 1994.

Davison, Graeme, John McCarty and Ailsa McLeary (eds). *Australians 1888*, Sydney, Fairfax Syme & Weldon Associates, 1987.

Davison, Graeme and Chris McConville (eds). *A Heritage Handbook*, Sydney, Allen & Unwin, 1991.

Davison, Graeme and Andrew May (eds). *Melbourne Centre Stage: The Corporation of Melbourne 1842-1992*, special issue of the *Victorian Historical Journal*, vol. 63, nos 2 and 3, October 1992.

Dawson, Isabella Park. 'The Language of the Aborigines', *The Australasian*, 19 March 1870.

Dawson, James. *Australian Aborigines*, facsimile edition introduced by Jan Critchett (first published 1881), Canberra, Australian Institute of Aboriginal Studies, 1981.

de Giustino, David. *Conquest of Mind: Phrenology and Victorian Social Thought*, London, Croom Helm, 1975.

Dellheim, Charles. *The Face of the Past: The Preservation of the Medieval Inheritance in Victorian England*, Cambridge, Cambridge University Press, 1984.

Denholm, David. *The Colonial Australians*, Ringwood, Vic., Penguin, 1979.

Dening, Greg. *Islands and Beaches: Discourse on a Silent Land: Marquesas 1774-1880*, Carlton, Vic., Melbourne University Press, 1980.

——. 'A Poetic for Histories: Transformations that Present the Past', in Aletta Biersack (ed.), *Clio in Oceania*, Washington, Smithsonian Institution, 1990, pp. 347-80.

——. 'Ethnography on my mind', in Bain Attwood (ed.), *Boundaries of the Past*, Melbourne, The History Institute, Victoria, 1990, pp. 14-21.

Desmond, Adrian. *Archetypes and Ancestors: Palaeontology in Victorian London, 1850-1875*, Chicago, University of Chicago Press, 1982.

Desmond, Adrian and James Moore. *Darwin*, London, Michael Joseph, 1991.

De Vis, C. W. 'Remarks on a Fossil Implement and Bones of an Extinct Kangaroo', *Proceedings of the Royal Society of Victoria*, vol. 12, 1899.

Diamond, Jared. *The Rise and Fall of the Third Chimpanzee: How our animal heritage affects the way we live*, London, Vintage, 1991.

Dickson, F. P. *Australian Stone Hatchets: A Study in Design and Dynamics*, Sydney, Academic Press, 1981.

Disher, Garry. ' "Before the age of hurry-up . . . " ': Australian landscape writing 1925-1950', MA thesis, Monash University, 1978.

Dombrovskis, Peter and Bob Brown. *Wild Rivers*, Sandy Bay, Tasmania, 1983.

Donaldson, Ian and Tamsin (eds). *Seeing the First Australians*, Sydney, George Allen & Unwin, 1985.

Dorson, Richard. *The British Folklorists*, London, Routledge & Kegan Paul, 1968.

Dow, David M. *Melbourne Savages: A History of the First Fifty Years of the Melbourne Savage Club*, Melbourne, The Melbourne Savage Club, 1947.

Dugan, Kathleen. 'The Zoological Exploration of the Australian Region', in Nathan Reingold and Marc Rothenberg (eds), *Scientific Colonialism, 1800-1930: A Cross Cultural Comparison*, Washington, DC: Smithsonian Institution Press, 1987, pp. 79-100.

Dunn, E. J. 'Comments in Discussion', *Victorian Geographical Journal*, vol. xxxii, part 1, 1916, p. 8.

Edwards, Coral and Peter Read (eds). *The Lost Children: Thirteen Australians taken from their Aboriginal families tell of the struggle to find their natural parents*, Sydney, Doubleday, 1989.

Edwards, Elizabeth (ed.). *Anthropology and Photography, 1860-1920*, New Haven and London, Yale University Press in association with The Royal Anthropological Institute, London, 1992.

Edwards, Robert and Jenny Stewart (eds). *Preserving Indigenous Cultures: A New Role for Museums*, Canberra, Australian Government Publishing Service, 1980.

Eldershaw, Flora. 'The Landscape Writers', *Meanjin*, vol. 11, 1952, p. 219.

Elliott, Brian. *Marcus Clarke*, Oxford, Clarendon Press, 1958.

Etheridge, R. 'Has Man a Geological History in Australia?', *Proceedings of the Linnean Society of New South Wales*, second series, vol. v, 1890, pp. 262-5.

Evans, J. D., B. Cunliffe and C. Renfrew (eds). *Antiquity and Man*, London, Thames & Hudson, 1981, pp. 52-64.

Evans, Michael. 'Taking to the Bush: Australian Landscape as a Condition of Practice for the Field Naturalists' Club of Victoria, 1880-1900', BA(Hons) thesis, University of Melbourne, 1982.

Everett, Jim. 'Ecology, Politics and Aboriginal Heritage', *Ecopolitics II Conference Proceedings*, Hobart, Centre for Environmental Studies, University of Tasmania, 1987, pp. 1-2.

Farwell, George. *The Outside Track*, Carlton, Vic., Melbourne University Press, 1951.

——. *Traveller's Tracks*, Carlton, Vic., Melbourne University Press, 1949.

Featherstone, Guy. 'Life and Times of James Bonwick', MA thesis, University of Melbourne, 1968.

——. 'James Bonwick (1817-1906)', in Douglas Pike (ed.), *Australian Dictionary of Biography*, Carlton, Vic., Melbourne University Press, 1969, vol. 3, pp. 190-2.

Fels, Marie Hansen. *Good Men and True: The Aboriginal Police of the Port Phillip District, 1837-1853*, Carlton, Vic., Melbourne University Press, 1988.

Ferrier, Carole (ed.). *As Good as a Yarn with You: Letters between Miles Franklin, K. S. Prichard, Jean Devanny, Marjorie Barnard, Flora Eldershaw and Eleanor Dark*, Cambridge, Cambridge University Press, 1992.

Ferris, Timothy. *Coming of Age in the Milky Way*, London, Vintage, 1988.

Field, Barron. *First Fruits of Australian Poetry*, second edition, 1823 (reprinted by Barn on the Hill, 1941).

Field Naturalists Club of Victoria. *Victorian Naturalist*, special historical issues, vol. 97, no. 3, 1980, and vol. 101, no. 1, 1984.

Finlayson, H. H. *The Red Centre: Man and Beast in the Heart of Australia*, Sydney, Angus & Robertson, 1935.

Finney, Colin. *Paradise Revealed: Natural History in nineteenth century Australia*, Melbourne, Museum of Victoria, 1993.

Firth, S. G. 'Social Values in the NSW Primary School, 1880-1914: An analysis of school texts', in R. J. W. Selleck (ed.), *Melbourne Studies in Education 1970*, Carlton, Vic., Melbourne University Press, 1970, pp. 123-59.

Fitzpatrick, Kathleen. 'Ernest Scott and the Melbourne School of History', *Melbourne Historical Journal*, no. 7 (1968), pp. 1-10.

Flanagan, Richard. *A Terrible Beauty: History of the Gordon River Country*, Richmond, Vic., Greenhouse, 1985.

Fletcher, Brian. *The 1888 Centenary Celebrations and New Developments in the Writing of Australian History*, Sydney, University of Sydney, 1988.

Fletcher, Meredith. 'School Histories at the La Trobe Library', *Gippsland Heritage Journal*, no. 8, June 1990, pp. 52-3.

——. 'Early Gippsland School Magazines', *Gippsland Heritage Journal*, no. 7, December 1989, pp. 44-6.

Flood, Josephine. 'Cultural resources of the Australian Alps', in Kevin J. Frawley (ed.), *Australia's Alpine Areas: Management for Conservation*, Canberra 1986, pp. 12-24.

——. *Archaeology of the Dreamtime: The story of prehistoric Australia and its people*, Sydney, Collins, 1989.

Foss, Paul (ed.). *Island in the Stream: Myths of Place in Australian Culture*, Leichhardt, NSW, Pluto Press, 1988.

Foster, Diane. 'Grass Roots History in the West', in Alan Roberts (ed.), *Grass Roots History*, Canberra, Federation of Australian Historical Societies, 1991, pp. 36–44.

Foster, Harley W. 'Edward Micklethwaite Curr (1820–1889)', in Douglas Pike (ed.), *Australian Dictionary of Biography*, vol. 3, Carlton, Vic., Melbourne University Press, 1969, p. 508.

Foucault, Michel. *The Order of Things: An Archaeology of the Human Sciences*, London, Tavistock Publications, 1970 (French edition 1969).

Fox, Paul. 'A Colonial City of Ideas', *Victorian Historical Journal*, vol. 58, nos 3 and 4, 1987, pp. 14–32.

——. 'The State Library of Victoria: Science and Civilisation', *Transition*, no. 26, Spring 1988, pp. 14–26.

——. 'Review of *The Road to Botany Bay*', *Transition*, no. 24, Autumn 1988, pp. 82–3.

——. 'The Imperial Schema: Ethnography, Photography and Collecting', *Photofile*, Indian Summer Issue, 1989, pp. 10–17.

——. 'Memory, the Museum and the Postcolonial World', *Meanjin*, 2/1992, Winter, pp. 308–18.

Fraser, Frances and Nettie Palmer (eds). *Centenary Gift Book*, Melbourne, Robertson & Mullens for the Women's Centenary Council, 1934.

Frawley, Kevin J. (ed.). *Australia's Alpine Areas: Management for Conservation*, Canberra, 1986.

——. 'The Gudgenby property and grazing in national parks', *NPA Bulletin*, vol. 25, no. 3, 1988, p. 4.

——. ' "Cultural Landscapes" and National Parks: Philosophical and Planning Issues', *Australian Parks and Recreation*, vol. 25, no. 3, Spring 1989, pp. 16–23.

——. 'Rural cultural landscapes: some unresolved issues', *Landscape Australia*, 1/1990, pp. 93–95.

Frawley, Kevin J. and Noel Semple (eds). *Australia's Ever Changing Forests: Proceedings of the First National Conference on Australian Forest History*, Campbell, Australian Defence Force Academy (Department of Geography and Oceanography), 1989.

Freame, William. *An Amateur Tramp: Rambles with Pen and Camera*, Parramatta, n.d.

French, Alan. 'The Cheese Wring', *North-Eastern Historical Society*, vol. 17, no. 2, April–May 1977.

'From Spirit to Spirit'. Documentary film concerning Lake Mungo screened on SBS television, 28 October 1993.

Frost, Alan. 'New South Wales as *terra nullius*: the British denial of Aboriginal land rights', *Historical Studies*, vol. 19, 1981, pp. 513–23.

Fry, Mary. 'Street Verandahs in Bendigo: Some aspects regarding the change of attitudes towards the street verandahs between 1940 and 1986', BA (Humanities) Research Project, Bendigo CAE, 1986.

Fullerton, Mary. *Bark House Days*, Carlton, Vic., Melbourne University Press, 1964 (first edn 1921).

Fussell, Paul. *The Great War and Modern Memory*, London, Oxford University Press, 1975 (reprinted 1977).

Galbally, Ann and Margaret Plant (eds). *Studies in Australian Art*, Department of Fine Arts, University of Melbourne, 1978.

Gardner, Peter. 'Massacres of Aboriginals in Gippsland 1840-1850', *Historian*, vol. 27, October 1975, pp. 19-24.

Gathercole, P. and D. Lowenthal (eds). *The Politics of the Past*, London, Unwin Hyman, 1990.

Gell, Peter and Iain-Malcolm Stuart. *Human Settlement History and Environmental Impact: The Delegate River Catchment, East Gippsland, Victoria*, Clayton, Department of Geography and Environmental Science, Monash University, 1989.

Gilbert, Kevin. *Living Black: Blacks Talk to Kevin Gilbert*, Melbourne, Allen Lane, 1977.

Gill, Edmund. 'Geological evidence in Western Victoria relative to the antiquity of the Australian aborigines', *Memoirs of the National Museum of Victoria*, no. 18, 1953, pp. 25-92.

——. 'Some aspects of prehistory in Victoria', *Victorian Historical Magazine*, vol. 40, no. 4, November 1969, p. 175.

Gillbank, Linden. 'The origins of the Acclimatisation Society of Victoria: practical science in the wake of the gold rush', *Historical Records of Australian Science*, vol. 6, no. 3, December 1986, pp. 359-74.

——. 'How the Alps Started to Lose Their Grasslands', draft report for the Historic Places Section, Department of Conservation and Environment, Victoria, 1989.

Gold, John R. and Jacquelin Burgess (eds), *Valued Environments*, London and Boston, George Allen & Unwin, 1982.

Goodall, Heather. 'Land in Our Own Country: The Aboriginal Land Rights Movement in South-Eastern Australia, 1860 to 1914', *Aboriginal History*, vol. 14, part 1, 1990, pp. 1-24.

Goodman, David. 'Fear of Circuses: Founding of the National Museum of Victoria', *Continuum*, vol. 3, no. 1, 1990, pp. 19-20.

Gould, Stephen J. *The Panda's Thumb*, Middlesex, England, Penguin, 1980.

——. *The Mismeasure of Man*, London, Penguin, 1981.

——. *Wonderful Life: The Burgess Shale and the Nature of History*, London, Penguin, 1991.

——. *Bully for Brontosaurus*, London, Penguin, 1991.

Graham, A. D. *The Gardeners of Eden*, London, George Allen & Unwin, 1973.

Grant, Ian. *Preservation and Restoration of Nineteenth Century Buildings: Australia*, London, UNESCO, 1972, p. 34.

Grattan, C. Hartley. 'Notes on Australian Cultural History', *Meanjin*, vol. 33, 1974, p. 238.

Gray, Jocelyn. 'A New Vision: Louis Buvelot's Press in the 1870s' in Ann Galbally and Margaret Plant (eds), *Studies in Australian Art*, Department of Fine Arts, University of Melbourne, 1978, pp. 15-26.

Grayson, Donald K. *The Establishment of Human Antiquity*, New York, Academic Press, 1983.

Green, O. S. *Sale: The Early Years—and Later*, Sale, Southern Newspapers, n.d. [1979?].

Green, R. *Battle for the Franklin*, Sydney and Melbourne, 1981.

Gregory, J. W. 'The Antiquity of Man in Victoria', *Proceedings of the Royal Society of Victoria*, vol. 17, part 1, 1904, pp. 120-44.

Greig, A. W. 'The Origin of the Historical Society of Victoria', *Victorian Historical Magazine*, vol. x, no. 2, November 1924, pp. 33-4.

Griffith, Charles. *The Present State and Prospects of the Port Phillip District of New South Wales*, Dublin, William Curry Jun. and Co., 1845.

Griffith, Gail. 'The Historical View from the Royal Australian Historical Society', in the Local History Coordination Project, *Locating Australia's Past*, Sydney, University of New South Wales Press, 1988.

Griffiths, Gayle (curator). *Rex Battarbee 1893-1993*, exhibition at the Araluen Arts Centre, Alice Springs, November 1993.

Griffiths, Tom. 'The Debate about Oral History', *Melbourne Historical Journal*, vol. 13, 1981, pp. 16-21.

——. *Beechworth: An Australian Country Town and its Past*, Richmond, Vic., Greenhouse, 1987.

——. 'Past Silences: Aborigines and Convicts in our History-Making', *Australian Cultural History*, vol. 6, 1987, pp. 18-32.

——. 'In Search of Classical Soil: A Bicentennial Reflection', *Victorian Historical Journal*, vol. 59, nos. 3 and 4, November 1988, pp. 21-38.

——. ' "The Natural History of Melbourne": the culture of nature writing in Victoria 1880-1945', *Australian Historical Studies*, vol. 23, no. 93, October 1989, pp. 339-65.

——. 'Country Towns', in Graeme Davison and Chris McConville (eds), *A Heritage Handbook*, North Sydney, Allen & Unwin, 1991, pp. 142-60.

——. 'History and Natural History: Conservation Movements in Conflict?', in D. J. Mulvaney (ed.), *The Humanities and the Australian Environment* (proceedings of the 1990 Australian Academy of the Humanities conference), Canberra, Australian Academy of the Humanities, 1991, pp. 87-109.

——. *Secrets of the Forest: Discovering history in Melbourne's Ash Range*, Sydney, Allen & Unwin, 1992.

——. 'Victorian Skulduggery, Past and Present', in Donna Merwick (ed.), *Dangerous Liaisons: Essays in Honour of Greg Dening*, Melbourne, Melbourne University History Monograph Series, No. 19, 1994.

Griffiths, Tom (ed.). *Koori History: Sources of Aboriginal Studies in the State Library of Victoria*, special issue of the *La Trobe Library Journal*, vol. 11, no. 43, Autumn 1989.

Griffiths, Tom with assistance from Alan Platt (eds), *The Life and Adventures of Edward Snell*, Sydney, Angus & Robertson and The Library Council of Victoria, 1988.

Groom, Arthur. *I Saw A Strange Land: Journeys in Central Australia*, Angus & Robertson, Sydney, 1950.

Gunn, Mrs Aeneas. *We of the Never Never*, 1908.

Hale, H. M. and N. B. Tindale. 'Notes on some human remains in the Lower Murray Valley, South Australia', *Records of the South Australian Museum*, no. 4, 1930, pp. 145-218.

Hall, Henry. *Our Back Yard: How to make Northern Australia an asset instead of a liability*, Angus & Robertson, Sydney, 1938.

Hallam, Sylvia. *Fire and Hearth: A Study of Aboriginal Usage and European Usurpation in Southeastern Australia*, Canberra, Australian Institute of Aboriginal Studies, 1979.

Hansen, David. *Tower Hill and its Artists*, Warrnambool, Warrnambool Art Gallery, 1985.

Haraway, Donna. *Primate Visions: Gender, Race and Nature in the World of Modern Science*, London and New York, Verso, 1992.

Hardy, Jane. 'Reginald Ernest Battarbee ("Rex") (1893-1973)', in John Ritchie (ed.), *Australian Dictionary of Biography*, Carlton, Vic., Melbourne University Press, 1993, vol. 13, pp. 133-4.

——. 'Visitors to Hermannsburg: An essay on cross-cultural learning', in Jane Hardy, J. V. S. Megaw and M. Ruth Megaw (eds), *The Heritage of Namatjira: The Watercolourists of Central Australia*, Port Melbourne, William Heinemann, 1992, pp. 137-75.

Hardy, Jane, J. V. S. Megaw and M. Ruth Megaw (eds). *The Heritage of Namatjira: The Watercolourists of Central Australia*, Port Melbourne, William Heinemann, 1992.

Hargrove, Eugene. *Foundations of Environmental Ethics*, Englewood Cliffs, NJ, Prentice Hall, 1989.

Harris, Chris. 'Balance of Ethics: A Discussion', *Wilderness News*, vol. 8, no. 6, August 1987, p. 12.

Harris, Edgar C. *A Spring Walk: Windsor to Bulli*, Sydney, privately printed, 1922.

Hasluck, Paul. *Mucking About: An Autobiography*, Carlton, Vic., Melbourne University Press, 1977.

Hay, P. R. 'The Environmental Movement: Romanticism Reborn?', *Island*, vol. 29, Summer 1986/7, pp. 10-17.

Healy, Chris. ' "We know your mob now": histories and their cultures', *Meanjin*, vol. 49, no. 3, Spring 1990, pp. 512-23.

Healy, J. J. *Literature and the Aborigine in Australia 1770-1975*, St Lucia, University of Queensland Press, 1978.

Hergenhan, L. T. 'Marcus Clarke and the Australian Landscape', *Quadrant*, no. 60, vol. 13, no. 4, July-August 1969, pp. 31-41.

Hewison, Robert. *The Heritage Industry: Britain in a Climate of Decline*, London, Methuen, 1987.

Heyck, T. W. *The Transformation of Intellectual Life in Victorian England*, London and Canberra, Croom Helm, 1982.

Hill, Barry. 'Travelling Towards the Other', *Overland*, no. 130, Autumn 1993, pp. 8-15.

Hill, Ernestine. *The Great Australian Loneliness*, Melbourne, Robertson & Mullens Ltd, 1952 [first published in Australia in 1940].

——. *The Territory*, Melbourne, Robertson & Mullens Ltd, 1951.

Hirst, J. B. 'The Pioneer Legend', *Historical Studies*, vol. 18, no. 71, 1978, pp. 316-37.

——. *Convict Society and its Enemies*, Sydney, George Allen & Unwin, 1983.

History Trust of South Australia. *Tenth Annual Report of the History Trust of South Australia for the Year Ended 30 June 1990*, Adelaide, History Trust, 1990, p. 8.

Hobsbawm, Eric and Terence Ranger (eds). *The Invention of Tradition*, Cambridge, Cambridge University Press, 1983.

Hofstadter, Richard. *Social Darwinism in American Thought, 1860-1915*, Philadelphia, University of Philadelphia Press, 1945.

Home, R. W. (ed.). *Australian Science in the Making*, Cambridge, Cambridge University Press, 1988.

Hope, R. *Report on the National Estate*, Canberra, Australian Government Publishing Service, 1974.

Horton, David R. 'The burning question: Aborigines, fire and Australian ecosystems', *Mankind*, vol. 13, 1982, pp. 237-51.

Horton, D. 'Early thought on early man in Australia', *The Artefact*, 1981, pp. 63-4.

Horton, David. *Recovering the Tracks: The Story of Australian Archaeology*, Canberra, Aboriginal Studies Press, 1991.

Howitt, Alfred. 'On the Origin of the Aborigines of Tasmania and Australia', *Australasian Association for the Advancement of Science*, vol. 7, 1898.

Howitt, Richard. *Impressions of Australia Felix*, London, Longman, Brown, Green & Longmans, 1845.

Hudson, Kenneth. *Museums of Influence*, Cambridge and New York, Cambridge University Press, 1987.

Huggins, Jackie. 'Always Was Always Will Be', *Australian Historical Studies*, vol. 25, no. 100, April 1993, pp. 459-64.

Hughston, W. J. 'Vanishing Records', *Argus*, 20 March 1909.

Hyam, G. N. 'National Monuments', *Victorian Naturalist*, vol. liii, no. 5, 5 September 1936, pp. 81-3.

Idriess, Ion. *In Crocodile Land: Wandering in Wild Australia*, Sydney, Angus & Robertson, 1946.

——. *The Red Chief*, Sydney and London, Angus & Robertson, 1953.

Ignatieff, M. 'Soviet War Memorials', *History Workshop*, issue 17, Spring 1984.

Impey, Oliver and Arthur Macgregor (eds). *The Origins of Museums: The cabinet of curiosities in sixteenth and seventeenth century Europe*, Oxford, Clarendon Press, 1985.

Inglis, K. S. 'The Anzac Tradition', *Meanjin*, vol. 24, 1965, pp. 25-44.

——. *C. E. W. Bean: Australian Historian*, John Murtagh Macrossan Lecture, St Lucia, University of Queensland Press, 1970.

——. *The Australian Colonists: An exploration of social history, 1788-1870*, Carlton, Vic., Melbourne University Press, 1974.

——. *The Rehearsal: Australians at War in the Sudan, 1885*, Adelaide, Rigby, 1985.

——. 'Men, Women, and War Memorials: Anzac Australia', *Daedalus*, vol. 116, 1987, pp. 35-59.

——. '1788-1988: Visions of Australian History', *Overland*, no. 106, March 1987.

Jackomos, Alick and Derek Fowell. *Living Aboriginal History of Victoria: Stories in the Oral Tradition*, Cambridge and Melbourne, Cambridge University Press and the Museum of Victoria Aboriginal Cultural Heritage Advisory Committee, 1991.

Jackson, John Brinckerhoff. *The Necessity for Ruins, and Other Topics*, Amherst, University of Massachusetts Press, 1980.

Jacobs, W. *Ballarat: A Guide to the buildings and areas, 1851-1940*, Ballarat, Jacobs, Lewis, Vines Architects in association with the City of Ballarat, 1981.

Jameson, B. *Movement at the Station: The Revolt of the Mountain Cattlemen*, Sydney, 1987.

Janson, Susan. 'R. E. Johns: Diary 1888', *Australia 1888*, Bulletin no. 13, November 1984.

Jervis, James. *A History of the Berrima District, 1798-1973*, Berrima, Genealogical Publications of Australia on behalf of the Berrima County Council, 1962 [revised edition 1973].

Johns, R. E.—Obituary, *Hamilton Spectator*, 20 May 1910, p. 4.

Johnson, Dick. *The Alps at the Crossroads*, Melbourne, VNPA, 1974.

Johnson, Richard *et al.* (eds). *Making Histories*, London, Hutchinson with the Centre for Contemporary Cultural Studies, University of Birmingham, 1982.

Johnston, Esme. 'A Man with an Interesting Job', *The New Idea*, 14 March 1941.

Jones, Frederic Wood. *Nature*, 19 February 1944.

Jones, P. G. 'South Australian Anthropological History: The Board for Anthropological Research and its early expeditions', *Records of the South Australian Museum*, vol. 20, May 1987, pp. 71-92.

Jones, Philip. 'Perceptions of Aboriginal Art: A History', in Peter Sutton (ed.), *Dreamings: The Art of Aboriginal Australia*, Ringwood, Vic., Viking, 1988.

Jones, Philip. 'Namatjira: Traveller between two worlds', in Jane Hardy, J.V.S. Megaw and M. Ruth Megaw, *The Heritage of Namatjira: The Watercolourists of Central Australia*, Port Melbourne, William Heinemann, 1992, pp. 97-136.

Jones, Rhys. 'Fire-stick farming', *Australian Natural History*, vol. 16, 1969, pp. 224-8.

——. 'The Neolithic, Palaeolithic and the Hunting Gardeners: Man and Land in the Antipodes', in R. P. Suggate and M. M. Cresswell (eds), *Quaternary Studies*, Wellington, Royal Society of New Zealand, Bulletin 13, 1975, pp. 21-34.

——. 'The Extreme Climatic Place?', *Hemisphere*, vol. 26, 1981, pp. 54-9.

——. 'Standing where they stood', *Hemisphere*, vol. 28, 1983, pp. 58-64.

——. 'Ordering the Landscape', in Ian and Tamsin Donaldson (eds), *Seeing the First Australians*, Sydney, George Allen & Unwin, 1985.

——. 'Ice-age hunters of the Tasmanian Wilderness', *Australian Geographic*, vol. 8, 1987, pp. 26-45.

Jones, Rhys, Don Ranson, Jim Allen and Kevin Kiernan. 'The Australian National University-Tasmanian National Parks and Wildlife Service Archaeological

Expedition to the Franklin River, 1982: A Summary of Results', *Australian Archaeology*, vol. 16, 1983, pp. 57-70.

Keating, Jenny. *The drought walked through: A history of water shortage in Victoria*, Melbourne, Department of Water Resources Victoria, 1992.

Keen, Ian (ed.). *Being Black: Aboriginal cultures in 'settled' Australia*, Canberra, Aboriginal Studies Press, 1988.

Kelly, Farley (ed.). *On the Edge of Discovery*, Melbourne, Text Publishing, 1993.

Kenyon, A. S., D. J. Mahony and S. F. Mann. 'Evidence of Outside Culture Inoculations', *Australasian Association for the Advancement of Science*, no. 17, 1924, pp. 464-7.

Kenyon, A. S. 'Stone Structures of the Australian Aboriginal', *Victorian Naturalist*, vol. 47, September 1930, pp. 71-5.

Kenyon, Justine. *The Aboriginal Word Book*, 2nd edn, Melbourne, Lothian, 1951 (first published 1930).

Knox, Robert. *The Races of Men: A philosophical enquiry into the influences of race over the destinies of nations*, London, 1850.

Kohlstedt, Sally Gregory. 'Australian Museums of Natural History: Public Priorities and Scientific Initiatives in the Nineteenth Century', *Historical Records of Australian Science*, vol. 5, no. 4, 1983.

Lake, Marilyn. 'The Politics of Respectability: Identifying the Masculinist Context', *Historical Studies*, vol. 22, 1986, pp. 116-31.

Lake, Marilyn and Farley Kelly (eds). *Double Time: Women in Victoria—150 Years*, Ringwood, Vic., Penguin, 1984.

Lakic, Mira Lilian. 'Grinding Away the Problem: An Investigation and Analysis of a sample of Aboriginal Grinding Stones collected from the Murray and Darling Rivers by A. S. Kenyon', BA(Hons) thesis, Department of Archaeology, La Trobe University, 1988.

La Nauze, John. 'The Study of Australian History, 1929-1959', *Historical Studies*, November 1959, vol. 9, no. 33, pp. 1-11.

Land Conservation Council of Victoria. *Wilderness: Special Investigation Descriptive Report*, Melbourne, LCC, 1990.

Langford, R. 'Our heritage—your playground', *Australian Archaeology*, no. 16, 1983, pp. 1-6.

Langham, Ian. *Piltdown: A Scientific Forgery*, London, Oxford and New York, Natural History Museum Publications and Oxford University Press, 1990.

Lark, J. 'Wilderness—Is it a Land Rights Issue?', *Chain Reaction*, no. 61, July 1990, pp. 29-32.

Lasch, Christopher. *The True and Only Heaven: Progress and its Critics*, New York and London, W. W. Norton & Co., 1991.

Lawrence, D. H. *Kangaroo*, Middlesex, England, Penguin, 1986 (first published 1923).

Lawson, Sylvia. *The Archibald Paradox: A Strange Case of Authorship*, Ringwood, Vic., Allen Lane, 1983.

Layton, Robert (ed.). *Conflict in the Archaeology of Living Traditions*, London, Unwin Hyman, 1989.

Le Cheminant, Marion. 'Hal Porter's Bairnsdale—Now', *Bairnsdale Advertiser*, 15 October 1979.

Lechte, John. *Politics and the Writing of Australian History*, Melbourne, University of Melbourne Politics Department, 1979.

Lee, R. B. and I. De Vore (eds). *Man the Hunter*, Chicago, Aldine, 1968.

Lennon, Jane (ed.). *'No Future Without the Past': Victoria Heritage Plan Conference Discussion Papers*, Melbourne, Ministry for Conservation, 1981.

——. 'Timeless Wilderness? The Use of Historical Source Material in Understanding Environmental Change in Gippsland, Victoria', in Kevin J. Frawley and Noel Semple (eds), *Australia's Ever Changing Forests: Proceedings of the First National Conference on Australian Forest History*, Campbell, Australian Defence Force Academy (Department of Geography and Oceanography), 1989, pp. 419-440.

Levine, Joseph. *Dr Woodward's Shield: History, Science and Satire in Augustan England*, Berkeley, University of California Press, 1977.

Levine, Philippa. *The Amateur and the Professional: Antiquarians, Historians and Archaeologists in Victorian England 1838-1886*, Cambridge, Cambridge University Press, 1986.

Lewin, Roger. 'Extinction Threatens Australian Anthropology', *Science*, vol. 225, 27 July 1984, pp. 393-4.

——. *Bones of Contention*, London, Penguin, 1987.

Lewis, Miles. 'Victoria's First "Notable Town" ', *Trust*, February 1966, pp. 1-4.

Lewis, Miles and G. H. (Mick) Morton. *The Essential Maldon*, Richmond, Vic., Greenhouse, 1983.

Lively, Penelope. *The Road to Lichfield*, Middlesex, England, Penguin, 1977.

Local History Coordination Project. *Locating Australia's Past*, Sydney, University of New South Wales Press, 1988.

Logan, Bill. *An Evaluation of the Conservation Planning Process in Victoria*, Melbourne, Footscray Institute of Technology, 1983.

Long, Charles (ed.). *The School Paper*, Melbourne, Education Department of Victoria, 1896-1920s.

Long, Charles. 'Local Chronicles', *Victorian Historical Magazine*, vol. 1, no. 2, April 1911, pp. 33-5.

——. 'Memorials to Victorian Explorers and Pioneers', Parts I-IV, *Victorian Historical Magazine*, vols IV, VII and IX (1915-1923).

——. 'A History of Alexandra, Parts 1 & 2', *Victorian Historical Magazine*, vol. 17, no. 2, November 1938, pp. 52-63, and vol. 17, no. 5, October 1939, pp. 167-182.

——. 'Monuments, Local Histories and Commemoration Days', in Sir James Barrett (ed.), *Save Australia: A Plea for the Right Use of our Flora and Fauna*, Melbourne, Macmillan & Co., 1925, pp. 25-34.

Lourandos, Harry. 'Aboriginal spatial organisation and population: southwestern Victoria reconsidered', *Archaeology and Physical Anthropology in Oceania*, vol. 12, no. 3, 1977, pp. 202-25.

Love, Rosaleen. *Evolution Annie and other stories*, London, The Women's Press, 1993.

Lovelock, James, Dave Foreman, Robert D. Yaro, Daniel B. Botkin and Frederick Turner. 'Forum: Only Man's Presence Can Save Nature', *Harper's Magazine*, April 1990, pp. 37–48.

Lowenthal, David and Martyn J. Bowden (eds). *Geographies of the Mind*, New York, Oxford University Press, 1976.

Lowenthal, David. 'Australian Images: The Unique Present, The Mythical Past', in Peter Quartermaine (ed.), *Readings in Australian Arts*, Exeter, University of Exeter, 1978, pp. 84–93.

——. *The Past is a Foreign Country*, Cambridge, Cambridge University Press, 1985.

Lyell, Charles. *The Antiquity of Man*, London, John Murray, 1863.

Mabey, Richard. *The Common Ground*, London, Hutchinson (in association with the Nature Conservancy Council), 1980.

——. *In a Green Shade: Essays on Landscape 1970–1983*, London, Hutchinson, 1983.

——. *Gilbert White: A Biography of the Author of 'The Natural History of Selborne'*, London, Century Hutchinson Ltd, 1986.

Macartney, F. T. 'Literature and the Aboriginals', *Australian Literary Essays*, Sydney, Angus & Robertson, 1957.

McBryde, Isabel (ed.). *Who Owns the Past?*, Melbourne, Oxford University Press, 1985.

McBryde, Isabel. 'Miss Mary, Ethnography and the Inheritance of Concern: Mary Ellen Murray-Prior [née Bundock]', in Julie Marcus (ed.), *First in their Field: Women and Australian Anthropology*, Carlton, Vic., Melbourne University Press, 1993, pp. 15–46.

McCarthy, F. D. 'Aboriginal Relics and their Preservation', *Mankind*, vol. 2, 1938, pp. 120–6.

——. 'The Lapstone Creek excavation: two culture periods revealed in eastern New South Wales', *Records of the Australian Museum*, no. 22, 1948, pp. 1–34.

McCloskey, Michael. 'Wilderness Movement at the Crossroads, 1945–1970', *Pacific History Review*, vol. 41, 1972, pp. 346–61.

McCoy, F. 'Gorillas at the National Museum', *Argus*, 19 June 1865.

Macdonald, A. C., J. H. Maiden and T. H. Myring (eds). *Special Volume of the Proceedings of the Geographical Society of Australasia*, Sydney, Thomas Richards, Government Printer, 1885.

Macdonald, Donald. *Gum Boughs and Wattle Bloom, Gathered on Australian Hills and Plains*, London, Cassell & Co., 1887.

——. *How We Kept the Flag Flying: The Siege of Ladysmith through Australian Eyes*, London, Ward, Lock and Co., 1900.

——. 'Australia To-Day : An Introductory Appreciation', *Australia To-Day*, 15 December 1905, p. 15.

——. *Australian Bush Nursing Scheme*, Melbourne, Atlas Press, 1910.

——. *Baden-Powell, Soldier and Scout; also a Synopsis of his Lectures during the Tour of Australia and New Zealand*, Melbourne, 1912.

——. 'Anzacs at War: Three Phases', *Australia To-Day 1917*, 11 November 1916, p. 75.

——. *The Bush Boy's Book*, 3rd edn, Sydney, Cornstalk Publishing Company, 1928 (first edition 1911).

Macdonald, Donald (edited by Elaine Whittle). *The Brooks of Morning: Nature and Reflective Essays*, Sydney, Angus & Robertson, 1933.

McGrath, Ann. *'Born in the Cattle': Aborigines in Cattle Country*, Sydney, Allen & Unwin, 1987.

——. ' "Stories for country" ': oral history and Aboriginal land claims', *Oral History Association of Australia Journal*, no. 9, 1987, pp. 34-46.

——. History and Land Claims', in D. Kirby (ed.), *Law and History*, Melbourne, 1987, vol. 3.

——. 'Travels to a distant past: the mythology of the outback', *Australian Cultural History*, no. 10, 1991, pp. 113-24.

McGuire, M. E. 'Whiteman's Walkabout', *Meanjin*, 3/1993, Spring, pp. 517-25.

McIntosh, Robert P. *The Background of Ecology: Concept and Theory*, Cambridge, Cambridge University Press, 1985.

Macintyre, Stuart. *The Oxford History of Australia: The Succeeding Age, 1901-1942*, Melbourne, Oxford University Press, first published 1986, paperback edition 1993.

——. 'The writing of Australian history', in D. H. Borchardt and Victor Crittenden (eds), *Australians: A Guide to Australian History Sources*, Sydney, Fairfax, Syme & Weldon Associates, 1987, pp. 1-29.

——. *Knowing and Possessing: Ernest Scott's Circumnavigation of Australian History*, An inaugural lecture, Melbourne, University of Melbourne, 1991.

——. *History, the University and the Nation*, The Trevor Reese Memorial Lecture 1992, London, Sir Robert Menzies Centre for Australian Studies, 1992.

——. *A History for a Nation: Ernest Scott and the Making of Australian History*, Melbourne, Melbourne University Press, 1994.

MacKenzie, John M. *The Empire of Nature: Hunting, Conservation and British Imperialism*, Manchester and New York, Manchester University Press, 1988.

MacKenzie, Sir Colin. 'The Aborigines of South Gippsland', in H. J. Malone, *A Short History of Central South Gippsland*, Buffalo, State School, 1932.

McKernan, Michael and Margaret Browne (eds). *Australia: Two Centuries of War and Peace*, Canberra, Australian War Memorial in association with Allen & Unwin, 1988.

MacLeod, Roy (ed.). *The Commonwealth of Science: ANZAAS and the Scientific Enterprise in Australasia, 1888-1988*, Melbourne, Oxford University Press, 1988.

McNeill, Barry H. 'Richmond: A Progress Report on Town Conservation', in *Preservation of Urban Landscapes*, pp. 45-50, 79-83.

McNicoll, Ronald. 'Alfred Stephen Kenyon (1867-1943)', in B. Nairn and G. Serle (eds), *Australian Dictionary of Biography*, vol. 9, Carlton, Vic., Melbourne University Press, 1983, pp. 572-3.

McQueen, James. *The Franklin: Not Just a River*, Ringwood, Vic., Penguin, 1983.

Madigan, C. T. *Central Australia*, London, Oxford University Press, 1936.

Mahony, D. J. 'The Problem of Antiquity of Man in Australia', *Memoirs of the National Museum of Victoria*, no. 13, 1943, pp. 7-56.

Mair, Ian. 'The upsurge in Australian writing—Australian history and politics', *Age*, 9 December 1955, p. 18.

Maldon. *Descriptive Souvenir of Past and Present Picturesque Maldon*, Maldon, The Tarrangower Times, n.d.

Mandle, W. F. 'Games People Played: Cricket and Football in England and Victoria in the late Nineteenth Century', *Historical Studies*, vol. 15, 1973, pp. 511-35.

Mansfield, Peter. 'The Australian Historical Record Society 1896-1906', *Ballarat Historian*, vol. 1, no. 6, September 1982, pp. 23-31, and vol. 3, no. 2, September 1986.

Marcus, Julie. 'The Journey Out To The Centre: The Cultural Appropriation of Ayers Rock', in Anna Rutherford (ed.), *Aboriginal Culture Today*, Sydney, Dangaroo Press, 1988, pp. 254-74.

Marcus, Julie (ed.). *First in their Field: Women and Australian Anthropology*, Carlton, Vic., Melbourne University Press, 1993.

Markus, Andrew. 'William Cooper and the 1937 Petition to the King', *Aboriginal History*, vol. 7, part 1, 1983, pp. 46-60.

——. *Governing Savages*, Sydney, Allen & Unwin, 1990.

Martin, Calvin (ed.). *The American Indian and the Problem of History*, New York, Oxford University Press, 1987.

Martin, Calvin. *In the Spirit of the Earth: Rethinking History and Time*, Baltimore and London, The Johns Hopkins University Press, 1992.

Massola, Aldo. *Journey to Aboriginal Victoria*, Adelaide, 1969.

——. 'The Challicum Bun-Yip', *Victorian Naturalist*, no. 74, October 1957, pp. 80-2.

Matthews, Patricia. ' "Uplifting our Aboriginal People": The Victorian Aboriginal Group, 1930-1971', BA(Hons) thesis, Monash University, 1985.

Mayne, Alan. 'City as Artifact: Heritage Preservation in Comparative Perspective', *Journal of Policy History*, vol. 5, no. 1, 1993, pp. 153-88.

Melville, Henry. *The History of Van Diemen's land from the year 1824 to 1835 inclusive*, George Mackaness (ed.), Sydney, 1965 (first published 1835).

Merrillees, Robert S., with the collaboration of Colin A. Hope, Graeme L. Pretty and Piers Crocker. *Living with Egypt's Past in Australia*, Melbourne, Museum of Victoria, 1990.

Merwick, Donna (ed.). *Dangerous Liaisons: Essays in Honour of Greg Dening*, Melbourne, Melbourne University History Monograph Series, no. 19, 1994.

Meyrick, F. J. *Life in the Bush (1840-1847): A memoir of Henry Howard Meyrick*, London and Melbourne, Nelson, 1939.

Merchant, Carolyn. *Ecological Revolutions: nature, gender and science in New England*, Chapel Hill and London, The University of North Carolina Press, 1989.

Miller, James. *Koori: A Will To Win*, London, Angus & Robertson, 1985.

Mitchell, Ann. 'Dr Frederick Watson and *Historical Records of Australia*', *Historical Studies*, vol. 20, no. 79, October 1982, pp. 171-97.

Mitchell, Stanley Robert—Obituary, *Proceedings of the Royal Society of Victoria*, vol. 77, part 2, 1964, pp. 618-19.

Mitchell, Thomas. *Three Expeditions into the Interior of Eastern Australia With Descriptions of the Recently Explored Regions of Australia Felix, and the Present Colony of New South Wales*, London, T. & W. Boone, 1839.

Molony, John. *Eureka*, Ringwood, Vic., Viking, 1984.

Morgan, Hugh. Australia Day address, *Age*, 28 January 1985, p. 11.

Morgan, Marjorie. *The Old Melbourne Cemetery 1837-1932*, Oakleigh, Vic., Australian Institute of Genealogical Studies Inc., 1982.

Morgan, Patrick. 'Hal Porter's Bairnsdale', *Quadrant*, October 1977, pp. 76-9.

Morgan, Sally. *My Place*, Fremantle, Fremantle Arts Centre Press, 1987.

Morison, Margaret Pitt, and John White (eds). *Western Towns and Buildings*, Perth, University of Western Australia Press, 1979.

Morris, Meaghan. 'Panorama: The Live, The Dead and the Living', in Paul Foss (ed.), *Island in the Stream: Myths of Place in Australian Culture*, Leichhardt, Pluto Press, 1988, pp. 160-87.

Mortlake and District Historical Society Newsletter, 1980-84.

Mortlake History Committee. *Pastures of Peace: A Tapestry of Mortlake Shire*, Mortlake, 1985.

Morton, P. *The Vital Science: Biology and the Literary Imagination, 1860-1900*, London, George Allen & Unwin, 1984.

Moses, John A. (ed.). *Historical Disciplines and Culture in Australasia*, St Lucia, University of Queensland Press, 1979.

Mosley, J. G. (ed.). *Australia's Wilderness: Conservation Progress and Plans*, Melbourne, 1978.

Mosley, J. G. and J. Messer (eds). *Fighting for Wilderness*, Sydney and Melbourne, Fontana and the Australian Conservation Foundation, 1984.

Mountain and District Cattlemen's Association. *Voice of the Mountains* (journal).

Mountford, Charles P. *Brown Men and Red Sand: Journeyings in Wild Australia*, Sydney, Angus & Robertson, 1962 (first published 1950).

Mountford, Charles (with a foreword by R. H. Croll). *The Art of Albert Namatjira*, Melbourne, Bread and Cheese Club, 1944.

Moyal, Ann. *'a bright and savage land': Scientists in colonial Australia*, Sydney, William Collins, 1986.

Mulvaney, D. J. 'A New Time Machine', *Twentieth Century*, vol. viii, Spring 1952, pp. 16-23; also appears in his *Prehistory and Heritage: The Writings of John Mulvaney*, Canberra, Department of Prehistory, Australian National University, 1990, pp. 11-15.

——. 'The Australian Aborigines 1606-1929: Opinion and Fieldwork', *Historical Studies*, vol. 8, 1958, pp. 131-51, 297-314.

——. 'The Stone Age of Australia', *Proceedings of the Prehistoric Society*, no. 4, New Series, vol. xxvii, 1961, pp. 56-107.

——. 'Australian Archaeology 1929-1964: Problems and Policies', *Australian Journal of Science*, vol. 27, no. 2, August 1964, pp. 39-44.

——. 'Fact, Fancy and Aboriginal Australian Ethnic Origins', *Mankind*, vol. 6, no. 7, June 1966, pp. 299-305.

——. 'The Ascent of Aboriginal Man: Howitt as Anthropologist', in Mary Howitt Walker, *Come Wind, Come Weather*, Carlton, Vic., Melbourne University Press, 1971, pp. 285-312.

——. *Discovering Man's Place in Nature*, Sydney, Sydney University Press for the Australian Academy of the Humanities, 1971.

——. 'Prehistory from Antipodean Perspectives', *Proceedings of the Prehistoric Society*, vol. 37, 1971, pp. 228-52.

——. *The Prehistory of Australia*, Ringwood, Vic., Penguin, 1975.

——. 'Classification and typology in Australia: The first 340 Years', in R. V. S. Wright (ed.), *Stone Tools as Cultural Markers: change, evolution and complexity*, Canberra, Australian Institute of Aboriginal Studies, 1977, pp. 263-8.

——. 'Obituary: D. A. Casey, M.C., F.S.A.', *The Artefact*, vol. 2, no. 4, 1977, pp. 225-7.

——. 'Australia before the Europeans', *Bulletin No. 15*, Institute of Archaeology, London, 1978, pp. 35-48.

——. 'Blood from stones and bones: Aboriginal Australians and Australian Prehistory', *Search*, vol. 10, no. 6, June 1979, pp. 214-18.

——. 'The proposed Gallery of Aboriginal Australia', in Robert Edwards and Jenny Stewart (eds), *Preserving Indigenous Cultures: A New Role for Museums*, Canberra, Australian Government Publishing Service, 1980, pp. 72-8.

——. *Frederick David McCarthy and Norman Barnett Tindale: Citation for Honorary Degrees*, Canberra, Australian National University, 1980.

——. 'Gum Leaves on the Golden Bough: Australia's Palaeolithic Survivals Discovered', in J. D. Evans, B. Cunliffe and C. Renfrew (eds), *Antiquity and Man*, London, Thames & Hudson, 1981, pp. 52-64.

——. 'Archaeological Retrospect 9', *Antiquity*, vol. lx, 1986, pp. 96-107.

——. 'Australasian Anthropology and ANZAAS: 'Strictly Scientific and Critical'', in Roy MacLeod (ed.), *The Commonwealth of Science: ANZAAS and the Scientific Enterprise in Australasia, 1888-1988*, Melbourne, Oxford University Press, 1988, pp. 196-221.

——. 'Gudgenby: A cultural heritage asset', *NPA Bulletin*, vol. 25, no. 4, 1988, pp. 6-7.

——. Letter to the Federal Minister for the Environment (dated 20 May 1988). Published in *Wilderness News*, vol. 9, no. 5, July 1988, p. 18; see also *ANU Reporter*, vol. 19, no. 8, 10 June 1988.

——. *Encounters in Place: Outsiders and Aboriginal Australians, 1606-1985*, St Lucia, University of Queensland Press, 1989.

——. 'Reflections on the Murray Black Collection', *Australian Natural History*, vol. 23, no. 1, winter 1989, pp. 66-73.

——'Reflections on the future of Past Cultural Landscapes', *Historic Environment*, vol. 7, no. 2, 1989.

——. *Prehistory and Heritage: The Writings of John Mulvaney*, Canberra, Department of Prehistory, Australian National University, 1990.

——. 'Museums, Anthropologists and Indigenous Peoples', *Bulletin of the Conference of Museum Anthropologists '89*, no. 23, April 1990, pp. 1-11.

——. 'Past regained, future lost: the Kow Swamp Pleistocene burials', *Antiquity*, vol. 65, no. 246, March 1991, pp. 12-21.

——. 'Sesqui-centenary to Bicentenary: Reflections on a museologist', *Records of the Australian Museum*, Supplement 17, 1993, pp. 17-24.

Mulvaney, D. J. (ed.) *The Humanities and the Australian Environment* (proceedings of the 1990 Australian Academy of Humanities conference), Canberra, 1991.

Mulvaney, D. J. and J. H. Calaby *'So Much That Is New': Baldwin Spencer 1860-1929, A Biography*, Carlton, Vic., Melbourne University Press, 1985.

Mulvaney, John and Bernie Joyce. 'Archaeological and Geomorphological Investigations on Mt Moffat Station, Queensland, Australia', *Proceedings of the Prehistoric Society*, vol. 31, 1965, pp. 147-212.

Mulvaney, Richard. 'From Curio to Curation: The Morrison Collection of Aboriginal wooden artefacts', Bachelor of Letters thesis, Department of Prehistory and Anthropology, Australian National University, 1983.

Murray, Les. 'The Lore of High Places', in his *The Peasant Mandarin: Prose Pieces*, St Lucia, University of Queensland Press, 1978, pp. 45-50.

——. 'The Human-Hair Thread', *Meanjin*, 4/1977, pp. 550-71.

——. 'Eric Rolls and the Golden Disobedience', in his *Persistence in Folly*, London and Sydney, Angus & Robertson, 1984, pp. 149-67.

——. 'In a Working Forest', in Roger Macdonald (ed.), *Gone Bush*, Sydney, Bantam Books, 1990, pp. 29-47.

Murray, T. and J. P. White. 'Cambridge in the Bush?', *World Archaeology*, vol. 13, no. 2, 1981, pp. 255-63.

Murray, Tim. 'Aboriginal (Pre)History and Australian Archaeology: The Discourse of Australian Prehistoric Archaeology', in Bain Attwood and John Arnold (eds), *Power, Knowledge and Aborigines*, special edition of the *Journal of Australian Studies*, Bundoora, Vic., La Trobe University Press in association with the National Centre for Australian Studies, Monash University, pp. 1-19.

Museums in Australia. Report of the Committee of Inquiry on Museums and National Collections including the Report of the Planning Committee on the Gallery of Aboriginal Australia, Canberra, Australian Government Publishing Service, 1975.

Mutitjulu Community. *Sharing the Park: Anangu Initiatives in Ayers Rock Tourism*, Alice Springs, Institute for Aboriginal Development, 1991.

Nash, Roderick. *Wilderness and the American Mind*, 3rd edn, New Haven and London, Yale University Press, 1982 (first edition 1967).

——. *The Nervous Generation: American Thought, 1917-1930*, Chicago, Rand McNally College Publishing Company, 1970.

Nash, Roderick Frazier. *The Rights of Nature: A History of Environmental Ethics*, Leichhardt, NSW, Primavera Press, 1990 (first published Wisconsin, University of Wisconsin Press 1989).

National Trust. *Preservation of Urban Landscapes in Australia*, Canberra, Dept of Adult Education, ANU, and Sydney, Australian Council of National Trusts, 1968.

National Trust. *Urban Conservation at the Local Level*, National Trust of Australia (Victoria), Melbourne, 1981.

Neutze, Max. 'City, country, town: Australian peculiarities', *Australian Cultural History*, no. 4, 1985, pp. 7-23.

Newland, Elizabeth Dalton. 'Dr George Bennett: Sir Richard Owen's man in Australia?', Typescript of paper presented to the 'Nationalism and Internationalism in Science' Conference, Melbourne, 22-26 May 1988.

Norman, F. I. and A. D. Young. ' "Short-Sighted and Doubly Short-Sighted are They . . . " Game Laws of Victoria, 1858-1958', *Journal of Australian Studies*, no. 7, November 1980, pp. 2-24.

Noye, Robert J. *Clare: A District History*, Coromandel Valley, Lynton Publications Pty Ltd, 1975.

Oddie, James (ed.). *Peter Lalor and the History of the Stockade*, Ballarat, The author in association with the historical 50th anniversary of the Eureka Stockade, 1904.

O'Dowd, Bernard. 'Wood-Wind and Wattle Breath', *Socialist*, 11 January 1908.

Oelschlaeger, Max. *The Idea of Wilderness: From Prehistory to the Age of Ecology*, New Haven and London, Yale University Press, 1991.

O'Neill, Frances. *Picturesque Charity: The Old Colonists' Homes, North Fitzroy*, Clayton Vic., Monash Publications in History, no. 9, Department of History, Monash University, 1991.

Orwell, Sonia and Ian Angus (eds). *The Collected Essays, Journalism and Letters of George Orwell*, vol. 1, Harmondsworth, Penguin, 1970.

Owen, Richard. 'On the Discovery of the Remains of a Mastodontid Pachyderm in Australia', *Annual Magazine of Natural History*, no. 11, 1843, pp. 7-12.

Owens, Robert Dale. *The Debatable Land Between This World and the Next*, London, Trubner & Co., 1874.

Padley, A. H. *The Old Melbourne Cemetery*, Melbourne, n.d. [circa 1920].

Palmer, Yvonne. *Track of the Years*, Carlton, Vic., Melbourne University Press, 1955.

Pardoe, Colin. 'Sharing the Past: Aboriginal influence on archaeological practice, a case study from New South Wales', *Aboriginal History*, vol. 14, no. 2, 1990, pp. 208-23.

Parsons, Jonathan. 'Aboriginal motifs in design: Frances Derham and the Arts and Crafts Society of Victoria', in Tom Griffiths (ed.), *Koori History: Sources of Aboriginal Studies in the State Library of Victoria*, special issue of the *La Trobe Library Journal*, vol. 11, no. 43, Autumn 1989, pp. 41-2.

Pascoe, Rob. *The Manufacture of Australian History*, Melbourne, Oxford University Press, 1979.

Pennay, Bruce. 'Deciding on a heritage in Goulburn', *Historic Environment*, vol. 5 no. 4, 1986, pp. 15-23.

Penney, Jan. 'Queen Aggie: The Last of Her Tribe', in Marilyn Lake and Farley Kelly (eds), *Double Time: Women in Victoria—150 Years*, Ringwood, Vic., Penguin, 1984, pp. 97-103.

Perry, Charles. *Science and the Bible*, Melbourne, 1869.

Pescott, E. E. *James Bonwick, A Writer of School Books and Histories, with a bibliography of his writings*, Melbourne, H. A. Evans and Son, 1939.

Pick, Daniel. *Faces of Degeneration: A European Disorder, c. 1848–c. 1918*, Cambridge, Cambridge University Press, 1989.

Piggott, Stuart. *Ruins in a Landscape: Essays in Antiquarianism*, Edinburgh, Edinburgh University Press, 1976.

——. *Ancient Britons and the Antiquarian Imagination: Ideas from the Renaissance to the Regency*, London, Thames and Hudson, 1989.

Pike, Douglas *Australia: The Quiet Continent*, London, Cambridge University Press, 1970 (first edition 1962).

Pitt-Rivers, General. *An Address delivered at the opening of the Dorset County Museum, on Tuesday, January 7th, 1884*, Dorchester, James Foster, 1884 [republished by The Friary Press, Dorchester, 1984].

Plant, Margaret. 'Visual Victoria: Waterfalls, Tents and Meat Pies', in A. G. L. Shaw (ed.), *Victoria's Heritage: Lectures to Celebrate the 150th Anniversary of European Settlement in Victoria*, Sydney, Allen & Unwin, 1986, pp. 109–43.

Plant, Vikki. ' "The Garden City of a Garden State": Melbourne in the 1934 Centennial Celebrations', in Graeme Davison and Andrew May (eds), *Melbourne Centre Stage: The Corporation of Melbourne 1842–1992*, special issue of the *Victorian Historical Journal*, vol. 63, nos 2 and 3, October 1992, pp. 86–100.

Plumb, J. H. *The Death of the Past*, London, 1969.

Popular Memory Group. 'Popular memory: theory, politics, memory', in Richard Johnson *et al.* (eds), *Making Histories*, London, Hutchinson with the Centre for Contemporary Cultural Studies, University of Birmingham, 1982.

Porter, Hal. *The Watcher on the Cast-Iron Balcony*, London, Faber & Faber, 1963.

——. 'South Gippsland and its Towns', *Australian Letters*, vol. 6, nos 3 and 4, September 1964, pp. 22–50.

——. *Bairnsdale: Portrait of an Australian Country Town*, Sydney, John Ferguson, 1977.

Porter, Roy. 'Gentlemen and Geology: The emergence of a scientific career, 1660–1920', *The Historical Journal*, 21, 4, 1978, pp. 809–836.

Powell J. M. *An historical geography of modern Australia: The restive fringe*, Cambridge, Cambridge University Press, 1988.

——. *Griffith Taylor and 'Australia Unlimited'*, The John Murtagh Macrossan Memorial Lecture, University of Queensland, 13 May 1992, St Lucia, University of Queensland Press, 1993.

Pybus, Cassandra. *Community of Thieves*, Port Melbourne, William Heinemann, 1991.

Pyne, Stephen J. *Fire in America: A Cultural History of Wildland and Rural Fire*, Princeton, Princeton University Press, 1982.

——. *The Ice: A Journey to Antarctica*, Iowa City, University of Iowa Press, 1986.

——. *Burning Bush: A Fire History of Australia*, Sydney, Allen & Unwin, 1991.

Ramsay, Margery and Walter Struve (editors and translators), Hermann Beckler, 'A Visit to the Library in 1859', *La Trobe Library Journal*, vol. 7, no. 25, April 1980, pp. 8–11.

Ranger, Terence. 'Taking hold of the land: Holy places and pilgrimages in twentieth-century Zimbabwe', *Past and Present*, no. 117, November 1987, pp. 158-94.

——. 'Whose Heritage? The Case of the Matobo National Park', *Journal of Southern African Studies*, vol. 15, no. 2, January 1989, pp. 217-49.

Rapoport, Amos (ed.). *Australia as Human Setting*, Sydney, Angus & Robertson, 1972.

Read, Peter. *The Stolen Generations: The Removal of Aboriginal Children in New South Wales, 1883-1969*, Sydney, Government Printer, 1982.

——. ' "A rape of the soul so profound": some reflections on the dispersal policy in New South Wales', *Aboriginal History*, vol. 7, part 1, 1983, pp. 23-33.

——. ' "Breaking up these camps entirely": the dispersal policy in Wiradjuri country 1909-1929', *Aboriginal History*, vol. 8, part 1, 1984, pp. 45-55.

——. *A Hundred Years War: The Wiradjuri People and the State*, Canberra, Australian National University Press, 1988.

——. 'The look of the rocks and the grass and the hills: A rural life site on the south coast of New South Wales', *Voices*, Winter 1992, vol. II, no. 2, pp. 37-48.

——. 'Our lost drowned town in the valley: Perceptions of the inundation of Adaminaby 1956-1957', *Public History Review*, vol. 1, 1992, pp. 160-74.

Read, Peter (ed.). *Down There With Me on the Cowra Mission: An Oral History of Erambie Aboriginal Reserve, Cowra, New South Wales*, Sydney, Pergamon, 1984.

Read, Peter and Coral Edwards (eds). *The Lost Children: Thirteen Australians taken from their Aboriginal families tell of the struggle to find their natural parents*, Sydney, Doubleday, 1989.

Reece, R. H. W. 'The Aborigines in Australian Historiography', in John A. Moses (ed.), *Historical Disciplines and Culture in Australasia*, St Lucia, University of Queensland Press, 1979.

Reid, J. R. W., J. A. Kerle and S. R. Morton. *Uluru Fauna: The Distribution and Abundance of Vertebrate Fauna of Uluru (Ayers Rock-Mt Olga) National Park, Northern Territory*, Canberra, Australian National Parks and Wildlife Service, 1993.

Reingold, Nathan and Marc Rothenberg (eds). *Scientific Colonialism, 1800-1930: A Cross Cultural Comparison*, Washington, DC: Smithsonian Institution Press, 1987, pp. 79-100.

Reynolds, Henry. ' "That Hated Stain": The Aftermath of Transportation in Tasmania', *Historical Studies*, vol. 14, 1969, pp. 19-30.

——. 'Violence, the Aboriginals, and the Australian Historian', *Meanjin*, vol. XXXI, 1972.

——. 'Progress, Morality and the Dispossession of the Aborigines', *Meanjin*, vol. XXXIII, 1974.

——. *The Other Side of the Frontier*, Ringwood, Vic., Penguin, 1982.

——. *Frontier: Aborigines, Settlers and Land*, Sydney, Allen & Unwin, 1987.

——. *The Law of the Land*, Ringwood, Vic., Penguin, 1992.

Rickard, John. *Australia: A Cultural History*, Melbourne, Longman Cheshire, 1988.

Rickard, John and Peter Spearritt. *Packaging the Past? Public Histories*, A special issue of *Australian Historical Studies*, Carlton, Vic., Melbourne University Press, 1991.

Roberts, Alan. 'The Development of Australian Oral History, 1798-1984', *Oral History Association of Australia Journal*, no. 7, 1985, pp. 3-22.

Roberts, Alan (ed.). *Grass Roots History*, Canberra, Federation of Australian Historical Societies, 1991.

Roberts, S. H. 'An appreciation of Scott', *Australian Journal of Science*, vol. 2, no. 3, 21 December 1939.

Robin, Libby. 'Visions of Nature: *Wild Life* 1938-1954', *Victorian Naturalist*, vol. 102, 1985, pp. 153-61.

——. 'Of desert and watershed: The rise of ecological consciousness in Victoria, Australia', in Michael Shortland (ed.), *Science and Nature: Essays in the history of the environmental sciences*, Oxford, British Society for the History of Science, 1993, pp. 115-49.

——. 'The Rise of Ecological Consciousness in Victoria: The Little Desert Dispute, its Context and Consequences', PhD thesis, University of Melbourne, 1993.

Robson, L. L. *The Convict Settlers of Australia: An Enquiry into the Origin and Character of the Convicts Transported to New South Wales and Van Diemen's Land 1787-1852*, Carlton, Vic., Melbourne University Press, 1965.

Robson, Merryl K. *Keeping the Culture Alive: an exhibition of Aboriginal fibrecraft featuring Connie Hart, an Elder of the Gunditjmara people with significant items on loan from the Museum of Victoria*, Hamilton, Aboriginal Keeping Place and Hamilton City Council, 1986.

Roe, Jill. 'Historiography in Melbourne in the Eighteen Seventies and Eighties', *Australian Literary Studies*, 4, 1969-70, pp. 130-38.

Roe, Michael. *Nine Australian Progressives: Vitalism in Bourgeois Social Thought 1890-1960*, St Lucia, University of Queensland Press, 1984.

Rolls, Eric. *A Million Wild Acres*, Melbourne, Nelson, 1981.

——. *From Forest to Sea: Australia's Changing Environment*, St Lucia, University of Queensland Press, 1993.

Roper, Michael. 'Inventing Traditions in Goldfields Society: Public Rituals and Townbuilding in Sandhurst, 1867-1885', MA thesis, Monash University, 1986.

Rose, D.B. 'Hidden Histories', *Island*, no. 51, Winter 1992, pp. 14-19.

Rose, Deborah Bird. 'Exploring an Aboriginal Land Ethic', *Meanjin*, 3/1988, pp. 378-87.

——. 'Remembrance', *Aboriginal History*, vol. 13, part 2, 1989, pp. 135-48.

——. 'Breathing and seeing country', *The Olive Pink Society Bulletin*, vol. 4, no. 1, December 1992, pp. 22-7.

Ross, Dorothy. 'Historical Consciousness in Nineteenth-Century America', *American Historical Review*, no. 89, 1984, pp. 909-28.

Roth, H. Ling *et al.* *The Aborigines of Tasmania*, first edition, 1890, republished Hobart, Fullars Bookshop, 1968.

Rothenberg, Marc (ed.). *Scientific Colonialism, 1800-1930: A Cross Cultural Comparison*, Melbourne, 1986.

Rowse, Tim. *After Mabo: Interpreting Indigenous Traditions*, Carlton, Vic., Melbourne University Press, 1993.

Royal Geographical Society of Australasia. *Transactions of the Royal Geographical Society of Australasia*, Melbourne, vol. ix, 1891; vol. x, March 1893, p. 8; vol. xi, June 1894.

Runte, Alfred. *National Parks: The American Experience,* 2nd edn, Lincoln and London, University of Nebraska Press, 1979 republished 1987.

Russell, J. A. *Valuing Cultural Landscapes in the USA, Britain, and Australia*, Hobart, University of Tasmania, 1988.

——. 'The Genesis of Historic Landscape Conservation in Australia', *Landscape and Urban Planning*, vol. 17, 1989, pp. 305-12.

Russell, Jim. 'Challenging History: An Environmental Perspective', *Public History Review*, vol. 2, 1993, pp. 35-53.

Sahlins, Marshall. *Stone Age Economics*, London, Tavistock Publications, 1974.

Saunders, David. 'Man and the Past' in Amos Rapoport (ed.), *Australia as Human Setting*, Sydney, Angus & Robertson, 1972.

Scates, Bruce. 'A Monument to Murder: Celebrating the Conquest of Aboriginal Australia', in Lenore Layman and Tom Stannage (eds), *Celebrations in Western Australian History* (volume 10 of *Studies in Western Australian History*), Nedlands, University of Western Australia, 1989, pp. 21-31.

Scott, Ernest. *Terre Napoleon: A History of French Exploration and Projects in Australia*, London, Methuen, 1910.

——. *Life of Lapérouse*, Sydney, Angus & Robertson, 1912.

——. *The Life of Captain Matthew Flinders*, Sydney, Angus & Robertson, 1914.

——. *A Short History of Australia*, 4th edn, Melbourne, Oxford University Press, 1920.

Scougall, Babette (ed.). *Cultural Heritage of the Australian Alps: Proceedings of the 1991 Symposium*, Canberra, Australian Alps Liaison Committee, 1992.

Sculthorpe, Gaye. 'What has Aboriginalisation meant at the Museum of Victoria?', *Bulletin of the Conference of Museum Anthropologists*, no. 22, April 1989, pp. 17-24.

——. 'Aborigines and Anthropology in the Museum', Paper presented to the Australian Anthropological Society Conference, Melbourne, 29 September-1 October 1993.

Seddon, George. 'Eurocentrism and Australian Science: Some Examples', *Search*, vol. 12, no. 12, December 1981-January 1982.

——. 'Managing a Resources Boom or In Praise of Country Boys', in Stephen Murray-Smith (ed.), *Melbourne Studies in Education 1982*, Carlton, Vic., Melbourne University Press, 1983, pp. 42-8.

——. '*Cuddlepie* and other Surrogates', *Westerly*, no. 2, June 1988, pp. 143-55.

Seddon, George and Mari Davis (eds). *Man and Landscape in Australia: Towards an Ecological Vision*, Canberra, Australian UNESCO Committee for Man and the Biosphere, Publication No. 2, Australian Government Publishing Service, 1976.

Selby, Isaac. *The Old Pioneers' Memorial History of Melbourne*, Melbourne, The Old Pioneers' Memorial Fund, 1924.

Serle, Geoffrey. *The Golden Age*, Carlton, Melbourne University Press, 1968.

———. *From Deserts the Prophets Come: The Creative Spirit in Australia 1788-1972*, Melbourne, Heinemann, 1973.

———. 'Robert Henderson Croll, (1869-1947)', in Bede Nairn and Geoffrey Serle (eds), *Australian Dictionary of Biography*, vol. 8, Carlton, Vic., Melbourne University Press, 1981, pp. 154-5.

———. 'James Stuart MacDonald' (1878-1952)' in Bede Nairn and Geoffrey Serle (eds), *Australian Dictionary of Biography*, vol. 10, Carlton, Vic., Melbourne University Press, 1986, pp. 251-2.

Serventy, D. L. 'A Historical Background of Ornithology with special reference to Australia', *The Emu*, vol. 72, part 2, April 1972, pp. 41-50.

Serville, Paul de. *Port Phillip Gentlemen*, Melbourne, Oxford University Press, 1980.

Sharp, P. 'Fear, disbelief and urgency in Kakadu', *Wilderness News*, no. 112, May 1990, pp. 11-12.

Shaw, A. G. L. (ed.). *Victoria's Heritage: Lectures to Celebrate the 150th anniversary of European Settlement in Victoria*, Sydney, Allen & Unwin, 1986.

Sheehan, Margaret Mary. 'Duty and Self-Sacrifice in War: The Principles of "Good Citizenship" in the Victorian *School Paper* before 1914', BA(Hons) thesis, Monash University, 1987.

Sheets-Pyenson, S. 'Cathedrals of Science: The development of colonial natural history museums during the late nineteenth century', *History of Science*, vol. xxv, 1986, pp. 279-300.

Shellshear, Joseph. 'An Appeal for the Preservation of Prehistoric Remains in Australia', *Australian Museum Magazine*, 20 Feb. 1937, pp. 169-75.

Shepard, Paul. *Man in the landscape: A historic view of the esthetics of nature*, New York, Alfred A. Knopf, 1967.

Shoard, Marion. 'The lure of the moors', in John R. Gold and Jacquelin Burgess (eds), *Valued Environments*, London and Boston, George Allen & Unwin, 1982, pp. 55-73.

[Siggers, W. S. C.] 'Esegar' *The God and the Religion of Science and the Bible*, Melbourne, Melville, Mullen & Slade, 1890.

Slater, A. L.—Obituary, *The Ovens and Murray Advertiser*, 11 January 1870.

Slater, Peter. *Masterpieces of Australian Bird Photography*, Adelaide, Rigby, 1980.

Smith, Bernard. 'The Interpretation of Australian Nature during the Nineteenth Century', BA(Hons) thesis, University of Sydney, 1952.

———. *The Antipodean Manifesto*, Melbourne, Oxford University Press, 1975 (reprinted 1976).

———. *The Spectre of Truganini*, Sydney, Boyer Lectures, ABC, 1980.

———. *European Vision and the South Pacific*, 2nd edn, Sydney, Harper and Row, 1985 (first edition, Oxford, Clarendon Press, 1960).

——. 'Art Objects and Historical Usage', in Isabel McBryde (ed.), *Who Owns the Past?*, Melbourne, Oxford University Press, 1985, pp. 74-85.

——. 'History and the collector', in his *The Death of the Artist as Hero: Essays in History and Culture*, Melbourne, Oxford University Press, 1988, pp. 95-100.

——. 'On cultural convergence', in his *The Death of The Artist as Hero: Essays in History and Culture*, Melbourne, Oxford University Press, 1988, pp. 289-302.

——. Extract from his 1988 Boyer Lecture, *Australian Society*, December 1988/January 1989, pp. 43-4.

——. *Noel Counihan: Artist and Revolutionary*, Melbourne, Oxford University Press, 1993.

Smith, Bernard (ed.). *Documents in Art and Taste in Australia: The Colonial Period, 1770-1914*, Melbourne, Oxford University Press, 1975.

Smith, Diane and Boronia Halstead. *Lookin for your mob*, Canberra, Aboriginal Studies Press, 1990.

Smith, F. B. 'Stalwarts of the Garrison: Some Irish Academics in Australia', *Australian Cultural History*, no. 6, 1987, pp. 74-93.

Smith, L. M. (ed.). *The Making of Britain: The Age of Revolution*, Hampshire and London, Macmillan, 1987.

Smyth, R. Brough. *The Aborigines of Victoria*, 2 volumes, Melbourne and London, Government Printer, 1878.

Somerville, Margaret, Marie Dundas, May Head, Janet Robinson and Maureen Sulter. *The Sun Dancin': People and Place in Coonabarabran*, Canberra, Aboriginal Studies Press, 1994.

Sontag, Susan. *On Photography*, Middlesex, England, Penguin, 1979.

Spencer, B. and R. H. Walcott. 'The Origin of Cuts on Bones of Australian Extinct Marsupials', *Proceedings of the Royal Society of Victoria*, vol. 24, part 1, 1911, pp. 92-123.

Spencer, Sir Baldwin. *Wanderings in Wild Australia*, London, Macmillan, 1928, 2 volumes.

Spurway, John. 'The Growth of Family History in Australia', *Push*, no. 27, 1989.

Staal, Paul. *A Foreigner Looks at Australia*, London, 1936.

Stafford, Barbara Maria. *Voyage into Substance: Art, Science, Nature, and the Illustrated Travel Account, 1760-1840*, Cambridge, MA, and London, MIT Press, 1984.

Stanner, W. E. H. *After the Dreaming*, Sydney, Boyer Lectures, ABC, 1969.

——. ' "The history of indifference thus begins" ', *Aboriginal History*, vol. 1, 1977, pp. 3-26.

Stepan, Nancy. *The Idea of Race in Science: Great Britain 1800-1960*, London and Basingstoke, The Macmillan Press, 1982.

Stephen, Sarah. 'Marriage and the Family in Bohemian Melbourne 1890-1914', *Australia 1888 Bulletin*, no. 9, 1982, pp. 20-8.

Stewart, Susan. *On Longing: Narratives of the Miniature, the Gigantic, the Souvenir, the Collection*, Baltimore, The Johns Hopkins University Press, 1984.

Stocking, George. 'What's in a name? The Origins of the Royal Anthropological Institute (1837-71)', *Man*, vol. 6, no. 3, 1971, pp. 369-90.

——. *Victorian Anthropology*, New York, The Free Press, 1987.

Strangman, Denis. 'A Forgotten Victorian Gold Rush: Lamplough, via Avoca, 1859-1860', *Victorian Historical Journal*, vol. 60, no. 1, March 1989, pp. 3-26.

Suggate, R. P. and M. M. Cresswell (eds). *Quaternary Studies*, Wellington, Royal Society of New Zealand, Bulletin 13, 1975.

Sullivan, Sharon. 'The Custodianship of Aboriginal Sites in Southeastern Australia', in Isabel McBryde (ed.), *Who Owns the Past?*, Carlton, Vic., Melbourne University Press, 1985, pp. 139-56.

Sunderland, S. and L. J. Ray. 'A Note on the Murray Black Collection of Australian Aboriginal Skeletons' [paper read 12 September 1957], *Proceedings of the Royal Society of Victoria*, vol. 71, part 1, Melbourne, February 1959, pp. 45-8.

Sutherland, Alexander. *Victoria and its Metropolis*, Melbourne, Today's Heritage, vol. I, 1977 (first published 1888).

Sutton, Peter. 'Myth as history, history as myth', in Ian Keen (ed.), *Being Black: Aboriginal cultures in 'settled' Australia*, Canberra, Aboriginal Studies Press, 1988, pp. 251-68.

Symes, Shirley. 'Charters Towers', *Australia ICOMOS Newsletter*, vol. 1 no. 3, Spring 1978.

Symonds, Sally. *Healesville: History in the Hills*, Lilydale, Vic., Pioneer Design Studio Pty Ltd, 1982.

Tailings. Monthly newsletter published by the Goldfields Historical Society, Dunolly and district, no. 2, April 1963-1980.

Tate, Frank. 'Education in Australia', *Australia To-Day*, 1 November 1910, p. 103.

——. 'Introduction' to J. A. Leach, *An Australian Bird Book: A Pocket Book for Field Use*, Melbourne, Whitcombe & Tombs, 1911, pp. 1-6.

Tatnall, David. 'Dibbins Hut—heritage destroyed', *Parkwatch*, March 1988, p. 9.

Taylor, Ken. 'Rural landscape protection—the need for a broader conservation base', *Heritage Australia*, Summer 1984, pp. 3-8.

——. 'Rural cultural landscapes', *Landscape Australia*, 1/1989, pp. 28-34.

Taylor, R. M. 'Summoning the Wandering Tribes: Genealogy and Family Reunions in American History', *Journal of Social History*, vol. 16, no. 2, 1982, pp. 21-38.

Thelen David (ed.). *Memory and American History*, Bloomington and Indianapolis, Indiana University Press, 1989.

Thomas, Keith. *Man and the Natural World: Changing Attitudes in England 1500-1800*, London, Allen Lane, 1983.

Thomis, Malcolm I. 'Self-Perceptions of a Small Country Town: Blackall', *Australian Cultural History*, no. 4, 1985, pp. 24-33.

Thompson, E. P. *Folklore, Anthropology and Social History*, A Studies in Labour History Pamphlet, Brighton, John L. Noyce, 1979.

Thompson, Patrick. 'Myles Dunphy, The Father of Australian Wilderness', in J. G. Mosley and J. Messer (eds), *Fighting for Wilderness*, Sydney and Melbourne, Fontana and the Australian Conservation Foundation, 1984, pp. 125-32.

Thompson, P. *Bob Brown and the Franklin River*, Sydney, Allen & Unwin, 1984.

Thompson, Patrick (ed.). *Myles Dunphy: Selected Writings*, Sydney, Ballagirin, 1986.

Thorne, Alan and Phil Macumber. 'Discoveries of Late Pleistocene Man at Kow Swamp, Australia', *Nature*, no. 238, 1972.

Tindale, N. B. *Aboriginal Tribes of Australia*, Canberra, Australian National University Press, 1974.

Tokar, Brian. 'Social Ecology, Deep Ecology and the Future of Green Political Thought', *The Ecologist*, vol. 18, no. 4/5, 1988, pp. 132–41.

Tonkin, Ray. 'A Role for Local Government in Urban Conservation?', Master of Urban Planning Minor Thesis, University of Melbourne, 1983.

Toothman, S. S. and M. Webb. 'The National Park Service and Historic Preservation', *The Public Historian*, vol. 9, no. 2, Spring 1987.

Trigger, Bruce. 'Alternative Archaeologies: Nationalist, Colonialist, Imperialist', *Man*, vol. 19, 1984, pp. 355–70.

——. 'The Past as Power', in Isabel McBryde (ed.), *Who Owns the Past?*, Melbourne, Oxford University Press, 1985, pp. 11–40.

Turnbull, Paul. ' "Ramsay's Regime": The Australian Museum and the Procurement of Aboriginal Bodies, c. 1874–1900', *Aboriginal History*, vol. 15, no. 2, 1991, pp. 108–21.

Turner, Frederick. *Beyond geography: The western spirit against the wilderness*, Viking Press, New York, 1980.

Turner, Henry Gyles. *A history of the colony of Victoria*, Melbourne, Heritage Publications, 1973 (first published 1904).

Tylor, E. B. Preface to H. Ling Roth. *The Aborigines of Tasmania*, first edition, 1890, republished 1968.

Urry, James. ' "Savage Sportsmen" ', in Ian and Tamsin Donaldson (eds), *Seeing the First Australians*, Sydney, George Allen & Unwin, 1985, pp. 51–67.

Verran, Helen. 'Othered Voices', *Arena Magazine*, February/March 1994, pp. 45–47.

Vickers-Rich, P., J. M. Monaghan, R. F. Baird and T. H. Rich. *Vertebrate Palaeontology of Australasia*, Lilydale, Vic., Pioneer Design Studio, 1991.

Victoria, Ministry for Conservation *'No Future without the Past': Victoria Heritage Plan Conference Discussion Papers*, Melbourne, Ministry for Conservation, September 1981.

Victorian Aboriginal Group. *Annual Report*, Melbourne, 1935.

Victorian National Parks Association. *Parkwatch* (quarterly journal) (called *Parkwatch* since March 1978, 'Newsletter No. 112'. *Newsletters* have also continued to be issued).

Walker, Mary Howitt. *Come Wind, Come Weather*, Carlton, Vic., Melbourne University Press, 1971, pp. 285–312.

Wallace, P. J. C. 'The Genesis of Gippsland', *The Leader*, 6 March 1920.

Ward, Andrew, and Auty Wilson and Herriot Pty Ltd. *Warrnambool Urban Conservation Study*, Warrnambool, 1983.

Ward, Russel. *The Australian Legend*, Melbourne, Oxford University Press, 1966.

Warren, Louis Michael. 'Collectors and Collections', BA(Hons) thesis, Department of Archaeology, La Trobe University, 1985.

Watson, Don. 'The War on Australia's Frontier', *Meanjin*, XLI, 1982.

———. *Caledonia Australis: Scottish Highlanders on the Frontier of Australia*, Sydney, Collins, 1984.

Watson, Ian. *Fighting over the Forests*, Sydney, Allen & Unwin, 1990, pp. 104-9.

Webb, S. 'Reburying Australian Skeletons', *Antiquity*, no. 61, 1987, pp. 292-6.

Wettenhall, Gib. 'The Murray Black collection goes home', *Australian Society*, December 1988/January 1989, pp. 17-19.

West, A. L. 'Aboriginal Man at Kow Swamp, Northern Victoria: The Problem of Locating the Burial Site of the KS1 Skeleton', *The Artefact*, vol. 2, no. 1, March 1977, pp. 19-30.

West, Francis. 'Multi-cultural Wisdom for the Intellectual Trendies', *Age*, 27 September 1980.

West, John. *The History of Tasmania*, Launceston, 1852; facsimile edn, 1966.

Westgarth, William. *Personal Recollections of Early Melbourne and Victoria*, Melbourne and Sydney, George Robertson & Co., 1888.

Wheeler, A. A. 'Women's Clubs', in Frances Fraser and Nettie Palmer (eds), *Centenary Gift Book*, Melbourne, Robertson & Mullens for the Women's Centenary Council, 1934.

Wheelwright, H. W. *Bush Wanderings of a Naturalist, or Notes on the Field Sports and Fauna of Australia Felix*, London, Routledge, Warne & Routledge, 1861.

White, Gilbert. *The Natural History of Selborne*, London, J. M. Dent & Sons, 1906 (first published 1789).

White, Richard. *Inventing Australia: Images and Identity 1688-1980*, Sydney, George Allen & Unwin, 1981.

———. 'Sun, sand and syphilis: Australian soldiers and the Orient, Egypt 1914', *Australian Cultural History*, no. 9, 1990, pp. 49-64.

Whitelock, Derek (ed.). *Hahndorf: Past, Present and Future*, Papers given at a University of Adelaide Seminar at Hahndorf on 16 October 1976, Adelaide, University of Adelaide, 1976.

Wiener, Martin J. *English Culture and the Decline of the Industrial Spirit, 1850-1980*, Cambridge, Cambridge University Press, 1982.

Williams, Elizabeth. 'Complex hunter-gatherers: a view from Australia', *Antiquity*, no. 61, 1987, pp. 310-21.

Williams, Peter (ed.). *Social Process and the City*, Sydney, George Allen & Unwin, 1983.

Wilmott, Eric. *Australia: The Last Experiment*, 1986 ABC Boyer Lectures, Sydney, ABC, 1987.

Wilson, Lawrie and Associates. *Bendigo Urban Area Conservation Study*, Melbourne, 1977.

Wilson, William Hardy. *Old Colonial Architecture in New South Wales and Tasmania*, Sydney, published by the author at Union House, 1924.

Wolf, Eric R. *Europe and the People Without History*, Berkeley, University of California Press, 1982.

Wolfe, Patrick. 'On Being Woken Up: The Dreamtime in Anthropology and in Australian Settler Culture', *Comparative Studies of Society and History*, vol. 33, no. 2, 1991, pp. 197–224.

'The Woodlanders' [Charles Barrett]. 'Our Bush Hut on Olinda', Parts 1–5, *The New Idea: A Woman's Home Journal for Australasia*, October, November, December 1905, January, February 1906.

Worsnop, Thomas. *The Prehistoric Arts, Manufactures, Works, Weapons, etc., of the Aborigines of Australia*, Adelaide, C. E. Bristow Government Printer, 1897.

Worster, Donald. *Nature's Economy: A History of Ecological Ideas*, Cambridge, Cambridge University Press, 1985.

Worster, Donald (ed.). *The Ends of the Earth: Perspectives on Modern Environmental History*, Cambridge, Cambridge University Press 1988.

Wright, Judith. *Born of the Conquerors*, Canberra, Aboriginal Studies Press, 1991.

Wright, R. V. S. (ed.). *Stone Tools as Cultural Markers: change, evolution and complexity*, Canberra, Australian Institute of Aboriginal Studies, 1977.

Zonabend, Françoise. *The Enduring Memory: Time and History in a French Village*, translated by Anthony Forster, Manchester, Manchester University Press, 1984.

Index

Pfeiffer, J., 99
Aboriginal reserves, land rites, 151-2
Aboriginal skulls, collectors, 28-9
Aboriginal technology
  Johns, R.E., 40-2
  Mulvaney, J., 56
  stone implements, 56
  tool-making, 56
Aborigines Uplift Society, 83
Aborigines and wilderness, 263
  conservation, 264-5
  fire regimes, 263-4
  land-use strategies, 265
  Tasmania, 265
Agassiz, Louis, 44
Aire River excavation, Mulvaney, J., 90-1
Aiston, George, 181-2
Alderson, John, 222
Allen, David Elliston, 16-19, 132, 142-2
amateur history, 210-11
Anderson, David, 95
anthropological research
  Elkin, A.P., 80
  Kaberry, P., 80
  Kenyon, A.S., 80
  Radcliffe-Brown, A., 80
  Strehlow, E., 80
  Thomson, D., 80
  Warner, L., 80
Anthropological Society of Victoria, 82,
    84
  Mahony, D., 82
  Mitchell, S., 82
anthropology
  biblical tradition, 38-9
  racism and scientific thought, 39
  relationship with history, 25-7
antiquarianism, Davison, G., 2
antiquities, 144
  Ashmolean Museum, 21
  collecting and display, 21
antiquity, Smith, Bernard, 105
Arbor Day, 142
  Barrett, J., 142
  Tate, F., 142
archaeology, Mulvaney, J., 91-2
Archibald, Joseph Patrick, 40, 184
  curator Warrnambool Museum, 60-2
  police service, 60-1
  Warrnambool slab, 60, 62
Archibald, Jules François, 60
Archibald, Lucy, 60-1
archival research, Bonwick, J. 202
Arden, George, 107
Ashmolean Museum, antiquities, 21
Aston, Tilly, 199
Atkinson, Graham, 231

Atkinson, John (Sandy), 231
Attwood, Bain, 4
Australia as terra nova, 9
Australian environment, aridity, 186
  Taylor, G., 186
Australian Heritage Commission, 195
Australian Historical Records Society, 203
Australian Historical Society, 204-5
  Mitchell, D.S., 205
Australian Natives Association, 112, 204
Australian Natural History Medallion,
    Mitchell, S., 173
Australian nature writers, 122-3
Avoca district, Johns, R.E., 33, 52
Avoca Shire Council, R.E. Johns Museum,
    47-8

Babington, Churchill, 19
baby health movement, Barrett, J., 188
Bacon, Francis, 21
Baden-Powell, Robert Stephenson Smyth,
    19, 139, 166
Bairnsdale, conservation, 252-4
  town planning, 252-4
Balfour, H.R., 67, 68
Ballarat East Public Library
  Huyghue, S., 49
  R.E. Johns Museum, 48-9
Banks, Joseph, 121-2
Baragwanath, B., 66
Barker, Jimmy, 225
Barkly, Henry, 18
Barrett, Bernard, 114
Barrett, Charles
  Aboriginal antiquity, 145-6
  collaboration with A.S. Kenyon, 72
  fossil skulls, 63-4
  human dimensions of the land, 118
  influence of D. Macdonald, 128-9
  nature writer, 122, 127-33, 148-9
  Puralka flint, 60
Barrett, Helen, 140
Barrett, James (Sir)
  baby health movement, 188
  commemoration of pioneers, 150
  memorial movement, 158
  national monuments, 156
  nature writings, 142-4
  pioneer monuments, 165
  preservation of buildings, 144-5
  urban progressives, 142
  Victorian Historical Memorial
    Committee, 159-60
  vitalism, 142
Barwick, Diane, 228
Bate, Weston, 217
Batman, John, 165-6